JUSTICE AND EFFICIENCY

GENERAL REPORTS AND DISCUSSIONS

This book was published in co-operation with the T.M.C. Asser Instituut – Institute for International and European Law, The Hague, and with the Assistance of the Netherlands Institute for Social and Economic law Research (NISER), University of Utrecht.

Dutch Association for Procedural Law

Founded in 1979, the Dutch Association for Procedural Law has for its objects the study of both the theory and practice of procedural law issues. President for the time being is Dr. B.C. Punt; secretary is Mr. P.M. Strengers. The secretariat's address is: Spoorstraat 5, 3811 MN Amersfoort, Netherlands (Tel. (0)33-612940; Telefax (0)33-618630).

DUTCH ASSOCIATION FOR PROCEDURAL LAW

The Eighth World Conference
on Procedural Law

JUSTICE AND EFFICIENCY

GENERAL REPORTS AND DISCUSSIONS

edited by

Dr. W. Wedekind

Kluwer Law and Taxation Publishers
Deventer • Antwerp • Boston

T.M.C. Asser Instituut — Institute for International and European Law
20-22 Alexanderstraat, 2514 JM The Hague, The Netherlands — Tel. (0)70-630900 — Telex 34273 asser nl. — Telefax (0)70-638171
Director: C.C.A. Voskuil
The T.M.C. Asser Instituut was founded in 1965 by the Dutch universities offering courses in international law to promote education and research in the fields of law covered by the departments of the Institute: Private International Law, Public International Law, including the Law of International Organisations, Law of the European Communities and International Commercial Arbitration. The Institute discharges this task by the establishment and management of documentation and research projects, in some instances in co-operation with non-Dutch or international organisations, by the dissemination of information deriving therefrom and by publication of monographs and series. In addition, the Institute participates in the editing of the Yearbook Commercial Arbitration and in the editing and publishing of, *inter alia,* the Netherlands International Law Review and the Netherlands Yearbook of International Law.

NISER

Netherlands Institute for Social and Economic law Research
Boothstraat 6, 3512 BW Utrecht, The Netherlands, Tel. (0)30-393230
Telefax: (0)30-393242
Director: Prof.dr. G.J.H. van Hoof
Executive director: A. van Schalm
Senior Researchers: F.J.A. van der Velden, J.A.E. Vervaele, W.G.Ph.E. Wedekind, R.J.G.M. Widdershoven
The Netherlands Institute for Social and Economic law Research (NISER) is the research-institute of the Law Faculty of the University of Utrecht. NISER's main task consists of stimulating both fundamental and practice-oriented research in the field of social and economic law. For this purpose the Institute coordinates and itself conducts research in the field. In addition the Institute aims to support research by facilitating the publication of research results, the organization of conferences, symposia and seminars, as well as documentation.

Library of Congress Cataloging-in-Publication Data

World Conference on Procedural Law (8th : 1987 : Utrecht, Netherlands)
Justice and efficiency.

At head of title: Dutch Association for Procedural Law.
1. Procedure (Law)--Congresses. 2. Court congestion and delay--Congresses. 3. Justice, Administration of--Congresses. I. Wedekind, W. II. Nederlandse Vereniging voor Procesrecht. III. Title.
K2100.A55 1987 347'.05 88-13795
ISBN 90-6544-393-2 342.75

ISBN 90 6544 393 2
Kluwer Law and Taxation Publishers
Deventer, The Netherlands

D/1988/2664/97
ISBN 90 6321 374 3
Kluwer rechtswetenschappen
Antwerp, Belgium

PREFACE

It is with great pleasure that I, in my function of vice-president of the Dutch Association for Procedural Law, present in print the General Reports and Reports of Discussions of the Eighth World Conference on Procedural Law. With this publication the tradition established by the preceding conferences is continued.

The Eighth World Conference on Procedural Law, with the theme of Justice and Efficiency, was held in Utrecht, the Netherlands, from 24-28 August 1987. The Conference, which was organised by the Dutch Association for Procedural Law in collaboration with the International Association for Procedural Law and the University of Utrecht (Law Faculty), attracted a great deal of international attention.

The overall and current problem of an overloaded civil judiciary prompted the theme of Justice and Efficiency. The problem of overload was discussed in general and specifically with regard to the appellate courts. Other subjects of discussion centred on the possibility of alternative procedures to or within the civil jurisdiction, such as consumer complaints and the use of summary proceedings. In addition, it was queried whether there were lessons to be learned from arbitration and administrative procedures as well as whether improvements might be introduced into the law of evidence and into enforcement law. And, finally, the important issue of technology and informatics in court administration was discussed.

I wish to express my special gratitude to the authors of the various texts in this collection, to the T.M.C. Asser Instituut, the Netherlands Institute for Social and Economic law Research (NISER) and to Kluwer Law and Taxation Publishers, all of whom contributed to the making of this book. For lack of space it is impossible to extend personal thanks to all those involved in the publication of the volume. I should, however, like to mention the publishing departments of the Asser Institute and of NISER, to whose concerted efforts the book owes its final shape.

Utrecht, October 1988 *Dr. W. Wedekind*

TABLE OF CONTENTS

OPENING SPEECHES

INTRODUCTION TO THE OPENING OF THE WORLD CONFERENCE

J.F. Bellaart
President of the Dutch Association for Procedural Law

Your Royal Highness, Excellency, Highly Honored Guests, Ladies and Gentlemen,

It is an honour and a pleasure to bid you welcome on behalf of the Nederlandse Vereniging voor Procesrecht at the opening of the Eighth International Conference for Procedural Law.

The highly honored presence of Your Royal Highness is a sign of the interest that You and as we know Her Majesty the Queen take in the organization of the administration of justice as well as in the scholarly and actual practice of procedural law. It emphasizes the national and particularly the international importance of this conference.

We are very pleased that our Minister of Justice is prepared to open this conference. Without the active cooperation and support from the Department of Justice, it would have been impossible to organize this conference. While exercising your important duties, you were always taking a firm stand for the interests of a good administration of justice, and your legislative work give evidence of a sense of efficiency. During your term of office a plan for tearing down the courthouse of de Hoge Raad der Nederlanden, in order to extend the parliament buildings, has been carried out. The highest court obtains a new accommodation, where it will be possible to work more efficiently. It is unfortunate, however, that with that something irreplaceable will be demolished, namely a wall plate with a maxim in the courtroom. It is a maxim, that, even if work is being done now more efficiently, should remain for all of us an omen on the wall. Moreover, it is a maxim that applies here to the topics that come up in this conference. I am talking about: 'Ubi iudicia deficiunt, incipit bellum', which means as much as 'the absence of judicial decisions leads to war'.

It is this war, this chaos in society that comes into being, when problems are not being solved in time through a proper administration of justice, that we as lawyers attempt to avoid. If we are international in scope, we can see the actions for the International Association of Procedural Law, under the inspiring direction of Professor Cappelletti, who will speak at this occasion.

While meeting here, gathered from all over the world, to discuss the problems in procedural law, we should be wary of some overestimation of one-self. We will not be able, however much we would like to, to improve world. We can only make guesses as to the effect of our work. How can we make manifest, that after the Conference in Gent the Administration of Justice has acquired a more human look, and that after Würzburg the effectiveness of legal protection has increased?

On the other hand the value of meetings like this one should not underestimate, because we exchange ideas and thoughts of different social structure while discussing items in the fields of procedural law we are interested in. This way we can learn a lot from each other. Undoubtedly it will be of great influence on judicial thinking and consequently its effect in practice in many countries in the world, even though these effects cannot be measured.

Participation in the World Conference in Gent initiated the foundation of the Nederlandse Vereniging voor Procesrecht. We were very pleased and satisfied that the International Association for Procedural Law has assigned the organization of the World conference for the first time to a national association. This could perhaps be an inducement for other countries to found similar associations. In our opinion a network of such associations in which all people dealing with procedural law are represented, would facilitate future contacts and the organization of conferences. We experienced that it is not easy to successfully organize a congress. That is why we have even more admiration for the successful way in which Professor Habscheid organized a previous conference in Würzburg and Professor Storme in Gent.

We would not have been able to do so without the active help of the Faculty of Law of the University of Utrecht. We are very grateful that this Dutch university was willing to give us an enormous support. A fortunate result is that we are now able to enjoy, in the historically interesting environment of the cathedral, the hospitality of the beautiful town of Utrecht which is governed by a mayor who knows drawing the line.

It would lead to far afield to welcome personally all who contributed to the success of the organization, including the county board, the recommending committee and the sponsors who provided the necessary financial support. We owe them all many thanks.

Finally, I would like to wish all the participants a good and fruitful Conference in Utrecht under the motto of the university 'Sol Iustitiae illustra nos' - may the sun of justice bring light upon us!

OPENING SPEECH

M. Cappelletti
President of the International Association for Procedural Law

Altesse Royale,
M. le Ministre de la Justice,
M. le Président de l'Association Néerlandaise,
Autorités, Chers Collègues et Confrères,
Mesdames et Messieurs!

Au nom de l'Association Internationale de Droit Judiciaire, je souhaite remercier les autorités, les institutions, et les collègues qui ont rendu possible ce congrès. Je tiens à remercier spécialement l'Université d'Utrecht et sa Faculté de Droit, l'Association et la Fondation Hollandaises de Droit Judiciaire, ainsi que le Comité d'Organisation composé de Messieurs les Professeurs Hondius et Meijknecht, de Messieurs les Docteurs Punt et Wedekind, et du Secrétaire Général de notre Association, le Professeur Storme.

Notre Association exprime aussi sa gratitude à tous les rapporteurs pour la contribution précieuse qu'ils nous ont apporté ainsi qu'à tous les spécialistes du droit judiciaire venus de nombreux pays pour participer à cette manifestation. Nous sommes tous impatients d'entendre les comptes rendus des rapporteurs et de discuter des résultats de leurs recherches et de leurs conclusions avec cet esprit d'analyse critique et constructive qui caractérise notre Association - ou, comme je serais tenté de l'appeler: notre *famille* - de spécialistes en droit judiciaire venant du monde entier.

Ce congrès sera certainement une étape très importante dans la vie et les activités de cette 'famille' qui est la nôtre. Utrecht est, en effet, la huitième étape, venant à la suite de Florence en 1950, Vienne en 1953, Athènes en 1967, Mexico en 1972, Gand en 1977, et enfin Wurzbourg il y a quatre ans. Il est vrai que notre Association n'a été établie formellement qu'à l'occasion du cinquième congrès mondial, celui de Mexico; permettez-moi de vous rappeler cependant, que déjà lors du premier congrès, à Florence, la propostition avait été faite et mise en oeuvre 'd'établir un Comité de Relations Internationales' entre les spécialistes du droit judiciaire. Ce Comité, composé des Professeurs Enrico Redenti, Hans Schima, Adolf Schönke, Victor Fairén Guillen, Robert Wynes Millar, Niceto Alcalá Zamora, Oscar da Cunha et Eduardo Couture, était censé s'ouvrir à d'autres participants afin d'élargir son caractère international, et était expressément défini comme 'le premier pas vers la création d'un institut international de droit judiciaire'[1]. D'une certaine façon, donc, la naissance de notre Association, ou du moins sa conception, remonte à ce congrès mémorable qui a eu lieu il y a trente sept ans à Florence.

Les noms que je viens de citer nous rappellent certains des grands Maîtres dans l'histoire récente du droit judiciaire, noms désormais presque légendaires dans notre mémoire: Calamandrei, Schima, Carnelutti et Alcalá en particulier, ainsi que Rammos, ont été les principaux organisateurs des cinq premiers congrès internationaux.

Quant aux sixième et septième congrès tenus respectivement à Gand et à Wurzbourg, ils sont bien sûr très présents dans le souvenir de beaucoup d'entre nous. C'est peut-être pour cette raison que nous avons tendance à les considérer de façon pour ainsi dire moins 'mythique', et avec un esprit plus réaliste. Ceci non pas parce qu'ils ont été moins importants, car au contraire, ils sont et resteront des moments fondamentaux dans le dialogue international entre 'procéduralistes'. Combien de fois, dans notre travail quotidien, nous devons recourir à ces splendides séries de rapports des congrès de Gand et de Wurzbourg avec admiration et gratitude envers les participants et surtout envers nos collègues Storme et Habscheid, qui les ont organisés. Mais, du moins dans mon esprit, les rencontres de Gand et de Wurzbourg apparaissent comme les deux premiers actes d'un seul et même grand ouvrage, les deux premières parties d'une trilogie dont nous allons célébrer cette semaine la troisième partie. Tandis que les congrès antérieurs me semblent très distants - même si j'ai moi-même participé à certains d'entre eux - ceux de Gand et de Wurzbourg sont au contraire, pour ainsi dire, ici avec nous, quasiment les prémisses nécessaires de notre congrès de Utrecht. Je me demande si une des raisons de ce sentiment personnel ne tient pas au fait que, ces deux dernières rencontres, tout en ayant été un accomplissement admirable de nos deux éminents collègues et de leurs écoles, constituaient aussi, en même temps, l'accomplissement collectif de notre Association - une Association qui entre temps avait commencé à exister réellement, et qui a de nouveau prouvé son dynamisme récemment par une autre initiative, l'organisation de symposia à thème unique, tels que celui tenu à Lund en 1985 et celui qui se tiendra à Bologne en 1988.

Cette présence dynamique est apparue peut-être de façon encore plus évidente dans la conception et la mise en place de ce huitième congrès. Ce congrès, je tiens à le souligner encore une fois, doit énormément à de nombreuses personnalités et institutions, en particulier néerlandaises - mais 'le protagoniste' reste cette grande famille mondiale à laquelle nous appartenons et qui se retrouve dans notre Association.

Ainsi mes derniers remerciements s'adressent à tous les membres de l'Association, ceux qui ont pu venir à Utrecht et ceux qui en ont été empêchés - en

---

1 Voir **Atti del congresso Internazionale di Diritto Processuale Civile**, 30 septembre - 3 octobre 1950, Padova, Cedam, 1953, p.X. L'Organisation du deuxième congrès international qui a eu lieu à Vienne en 1953, est considérée comme le résultat d'une coopération entre ce 'Comité de Relations Internationales' et la Faculté de Droit (spécialement le Prof. Schima) de l'Université de Vienne; voir **T. Carnacini**, 'I lavori del secondo congresso internazionale di diritto processuale civile', in 7 **Rivista trimestrale di diritto e procedura civile** p. 1097 (1953). Ainsi, la décision prise à Florence a été confirmée à Vienne et l'organisation ainsi envisagée a été re-baptisée 'Association Internationale de Droit Judiciaire', voir **id.** p. 1099.

pleine confiance que ce même sens de solidarité entre les 'procéduralistes' qui fût la force motrice du premier congrès international ainsi que des suivants, continuera à inspirer notre Association et à nous aider à franchir les frontières et les divisions entre nations et continents.

L'Association internationale de droit judiciaire, née de ce sens de solidarité scientifique internationale, aura toujours pour mission de soutenir et promouvoir cet esprit: l'esprit d'une *communitas* unie dans la quête d'une justice à visage humain, ce qui est l'aspiration et le but ultime de tous les 'procéduralistes' dans le monde.

Permettez-moi de conclure cette brève intervention par un hommage aux Membres de notre Association disparus au cours des quatres années qui ont suivi notre dernière réunion à Wurzbourg. Il s'agit là de cinq personnalités qui sont spécialement chères à notre mémoire: Niceto Alcalá Zamora y Castillo, le premier Président et premier Président honoraire de l'Association, qui nous a quitté en 1985; Tito Carnacini, membre du Conseil de l'Association et pendant de nombreuses années le Président de l'Association italienne des 'procéduralistes', qui nous quitta quelques jours après le congrès de Wurzbourg auquel il avait participé activement; Luís Loreto et Georgios Rammos, les illustres 'doyens' des Ecoles de procédure civile venézuelienne et grecque, respectivement; et cet éminent savant, Enrico Tullio Liebman, qui nous quitta fin 1986 après une longue période pendant laquelle son corps, mais non son esprit, est resté cruellement paralysé. Le fait que Alcalá et Liebman, exilés d'Europe alors que ce continent était la proie d'un fanatisme insensé, de la tyrannie et de la guerre, ont trouvé un accueil honorable et ont pu créer de nouvelles et florissantes écoles dans le Nouveau Monde, est la meilleure preuve de cette solidarité et de cette *communitas* qui existe entre les scientifiques et qui est un de nos biens les plus précieux. Alcalá, Carnacini, Liebman, Loreto, Rammos, et tous ceux qui ont consacré leur vie à la science du droit judiciaire et au progrès de la justice, nous ont laissé un héritage gigantesque de savoir et d'humanité. Nous nous inclinons devant leur mémoire qui continuera à enrichir notre activité et notre vie.

JUSTICE AND EFFICIENCY

F. Korthals-Altes
Minister of Justice of the Netherlands

Dear Listeners,

It is a great honour and a special pleasure for me that I may open this eight World Conference on Procedural Law and on this occasion address so select a gathering of practicing lawyers and legal scholars from all over the world. I warmly welcome you to Utrecht. We are very happy that the organization of this conference has been entrusted to the Netherlands and also that it could be organized in this famous old town. In my capacity of Minister of Justice I promised my support of and co-operation to this conference at an early stage of the preparations, since I was convinced of the importance of this conference for the quality of the administration of justice for which I in particular am responsible. It is a source of satisfaction to me that the not inconsiderable task of organizing this conference in 1987 has been placed on the shoulders of the- not so ancient yet, but already renowned - Netherlands Association for Procedural Law, in collaboration with the faculty of law of the University of Utrecht - ancient indeed but also renowned. The apparent confidence of the International Association for Procedural Law is a compliment for these organizers and also for the other Dutch practitioners of procedural law. In the coming week, and also I hope for a long time afterwards, you will be able to reap the fruits of the results of this special collaboration.

Ladies and Gentlemen,

The main theme of your conference, Justice and Efficiency, fits our time well. Overload endangers the efficiency of judicial procedures and consequently the quality of the administration of justice as well. It is curious that in the eighties overload in the administration of justice has, more or less simultaneously, become a serious problem in a great number of countries, including the Netherlands. I call this curious because one might think that the main problem would be some organizational imperfections of a strongly local nature. But on the contrary it appears to be a very persistent and widespread problem, suddenly manifesting itself everywhere. In the field of civil litigation the important developments which call for a response are evidently largely 'internationalized' as well. The problem of overload is not the first sign of this fact. But the question arises why this is so. I at any rate find it a happy idea to let the discussions on efficiency in judicial procedures be preceded by an analysis of the causes of the overload. Undoubtedly the international dimension of this problem will be discussed as well. When the subject is a problem that is so widespread, its analysis at an international conference like the present one is not only warranted, but even essential. Even the practitioners of procedural law, which of old is a branch of law that is strongly bound to one country, can then no longer afford to find national solutions without knowing which way the wind blows, to use a Dutch expression. This, to use the literal translation of another Dutch expression, would be 'mopping up water with the tap running'. Even in this wet country that is not the way we like to solve problems.

When we are talking about coping with the problems of overload in the administration of justice, an international approach has, in my opinion, at least two quite tangible advantages. In the first place in the field of legislature. Measures that are intended to increase efficiency are often rather controversial. In the Netherlands, for instance, there have been extensive discussions in recent years about the question whether cases in first instance and also cases in higher instances might be heard by a smaller number of judges. Proposals which are directed purely at the saving of judges' time.

I think that an acquaintance with other legal systems will show that one should not be too hasty in concluding that such measures endanger the constitutional state. To take a recent example, we found it encouraging that in France the hearing of appeals in cassation by three judges instead of five had already been possible for several years, when in 1986 we also introduced this possibility. But we are not concerned exclusively, and probably not even in the first place, with changes in legislation. Improvement of efficiency is mainly a matter of management. This is also true for the business of jurisdiction. One of the consequences of this insight is my recent decision to decentralize the management within this business to a large degree. The power of decision in respect of the deployment of people and resources at the courts has been transferred to an officer at the regional level. I would not be surprised, for that matter, if such decentralized management already existed in many of your countries. But up to the present we have a tradition of centralized management in our country. The use of information technology in court administration is closely connected with this issue. This is an outstanding example of an area in which part of the technical and practical know-how in any country comes from abroad. It is a sign of a sensible and realistic approach that this topic has been included in your programme. I applaud the fact that scholars of the law of procedure are exchanging their ivory towers for the realism of automation and computers (whether ivory-coloured or not). I have been able to make only a small selection; there are many more issues that you will be dealing with. I can assure you that I am looking forward with great interest to the results of your deliberations. It would be very pleasant if you could come up with concrete recommendations. That will not be easy, with so many participants. I wish you all success, but also a lot of pleasure.

Ladies and Gentlemen,

Finally, I hope that you will also have some time left for non-legal things of interest in Utrecht or elsewhere in the Netherlands.

Fortunately the conference programma includes some suggestions in this respect. I hope that the wet and windy weather of this country may not hinder you in this respect, but will on the contrary make an authentic and essential contribution to a typical Dutch experience that you will remember with great pleasure.

I herewith declare the eight World Conference for Procedural Law open.

INTRODUCTORY ADDRESS

M. Storme
Secretary-General International Association for Procedural Law

Royal Highness,
Mister Minister of Justice,
Mister Chairman of this meeting and Mister President of the International Association for Procedural Law,
Esteemed Assembly,
Ladies and Gentlemen,
Good friends of our Association,

Today is a double high-day for me. In the first place, after years of sometimes difficult preparations with our friends of the Dutch Association for Procedural Law, there is the pleasure of seeing that this international meeting has been realized as a festival of scholarship and friendship in the spirit envisaged by us.

The fact that this meeting takes place in Utrecht has a special symbolic significance. It is the city in which my wife and I had the good fortune of enjoying hospitality in difficult years. Above all it is a city, situated in the heart of Holland, in which it is almost a natural thing to hold a conference on procedural law, since 'Procedure lies at the heart of the law' (Amos, M., A day in Court at home and abroad, (1926) 2 Cam. L.J., 340).

Royal Highness,

During the preparations for this conference we have continuously borne in mind the famous motto of our mutual prince William of Orange: 'Point n'est besoin d'espérer pour entreprendre, ni de réussir pour persévérer'.

But the privilege of being allowed to deliver the opening speech for this international conference - for a small part in my mother tongue, which the large number of participants speaking other languages will tolerate - is also a very exceptional occasion.

Our Association started with a small group of eminent specialists of procedural law, who laid the foundations for a subsequent worldwide association. Indeed, after five rather closed conferences I was able, thanks to the support of Mauro Cappelletti and Vittorio Denti, to break through this closed character and organize the first world conference in Ghent. These two colleagues and friends are both distinguished exponents of the famous Italian school for procedural law, to which colleague Habscheid, who is also secretary general of our Association, implicitly wished to pay tribute by publishing his Handbook on comparative procedural law in the Italian language.

In that way the International association was able to provide a platform, successively in Ghent (1977), in Würzburg (1983) and now in Utrecht (1987), to all those who all over the world and either from a scholarly point of view or from the point of view of legal practice, were and are concerned for the proper functioning of the courts, which is the fundamental pillar of the Constitutional State ('Rechtstaat').

A major concern of our Association in organizing these conferences has been to ensure that the best qualified 'scholars in procedural law' would participate, irrespective of the legal system, language, creed or ideology to which they belonged. For real scholars can nor may ever be identified with any (one) ideological or political system.

We have always taken great care that eminent specialists, coming from the widest possible range of political regimes and without any exclusion, would find a meeting place where they could exchange ideas and from which they could return to their countries to contribute there to the achievement of a 'justice with a human face'.

We wish to safeguard this concern for the future.

Mister Minister of Justice,

One of your esteemed predecessors, Mr Van Agt, in what has become a winged expression underlined the fact that 'het Recht geen rustig bezit meer is' (Justice is no longer an undisturbed possession). We find ourselves in a conflictory society, in which the efficient settlement of personal and social conflicts through judicial intervention is a sine qua non for a peaceful society.

It is not without reason that (over) the entrance of the building of the Supreme Court in The Hague one can read the inscription: 'Ubi iudicia deficiunt, incipit bellum'.

Maintaining social peace is indeed one of the fundamental tasks of a constitutional state.

It is true that the concept of the Constitutional State dates back to the law philosophers of the XVIIth century, but it is only in present times that all over the world we are facing the full extent of what this concept really means.

'Die vollkommene Majestät des Rechts' requires not only that social norms be established by the law, but also that the authorities, just like the citizens, subject themselves to the 'rule of law' and that the ultimate control over this be vested in the courts. The centurion, too, was subject to authority (Lucas, 7, 8).

The 'Kampf ums Recht' implies an invitation to the citizens, whose rights and freedoms are menaced, to let the full efficiency of the law come into play.

Well, we find that the fundamental human rights and freedoms are not being properly respected. Actually, in September 1988 our International Association will devote a colloquium to this subject, which will take place in Bologna as part of the festivities celebrating the 900th anniversary of the University of Bologna (September 1988).

The main fact found by us is, that Montesquieu's trias politica is gradually being replaced by the duopoly of judiciary and government. Not only has the 'Gesetzgebundsstaat' turned into a 'Richterstaat', but all over the world the executive has assumed an ever increasing range of powers. In exercising these powers governments sometimes tend to high-handedly ignore the rules of law, and even to shirk obligations arising under international treaties.

The result of all this is that more and more control tasks are passed on to the courts, so that we can speak of an 'Ueberfordering des Richters'.

Such a development - on which I do not wish to pass judgment here and now - makes it more than ever before appropriate to safeguard the independence of the judiciary. But independence also means responsibility. Isn't it characteristic, for instance, that one of the central issues in the political crisis of last May in Italy was the problem of judges' liability?

In this context it becomes understandable that today the law of procedure is receiving more than usual attention.

First and foremost the law of procedure has developed into a branch of law with a much greater significance than that of a merely technical set of instruments.

As late as 1921 Friedrich Stein could still write: 'Der Prozess ist für mich das 'technische Recht' in seiner allerschärfsten Ausprägung, von wechselnden Zweckmäszigkeiten beherrscht, der Ewigkeitswerte bar' (Grundrisz des Zivilprozessrechts und des Konkursrechts, Vorwort zur 1. Auflage, 1921). Fortunately, such a view has been completely superseded today.

But more than anything else litigation is transcending the conflict of the individualistic interests of the parties: it is becoming a social phenomenon. Even Franz Klein already opposed von Jhering's 'Kampfbild', when he stated clearly: 'Die Zivilrechtspflege ist Pflege aktuellen wirtschaftlichen und sozialen Lebens, nicht gelehrte Forschung, sondern angewandte Wissenschaft, wenn man das Wort im höheren Sinne nimmt, eine der Aufrechterhaltung der gegebenen sozialen und Wirtschaftsordnung dienende Verwaltungstätigkeit' (Vorlesungen über die Praxis des Zivilprozesses, Wien, 1900, 9 ff.).

Litigation has become a fundamental link in the history of human civilization. The milestones of this history are no longer exclusively the names of famous battles or of great discoveries, but also those of judicial decisions, which can be remembered as as many milestone-judgments.

I quote a few: Brown (U.S. Supreme Court: segregation), Van Gend en Loos (Luxembourg: direct effect), Marckx (Strasbourg: discrimination of legitimate and natural children), Sunday Times (Strasbourg: freedom of press),...

Isn't it remarkable, for that matter, that the media pay about the same amount of attention to court reporting as to political reporting? The micro-law of procedure which has significance only for the litigating parties has become a macro-law of procedure, concerning the entire society.

The law of procedure did not only acquire new dimensions, but also went through an explosive increase of applications. People talked of 'le délire de la procédure' (Crozier) and 'la judiciarisation de notre société' (Peyrefitte).

This means that gradually we shall have to abandon the traditional approach of the law of procedure and adopt options that are fundamentally different.

In the first place the law of procedure has finally torn itself completely loose from substantive law. Formerly it was still possible to say that subjective right and the court action merely formed one whole. At that time people talked about 'le droit casqué et armé en guerre' (sic) to which was added 'que l'action n'est autre chose que le droit lui-même' (Garsonnet et Cézar-Bru, I, nr. 351).

The law of procedure has become an autonomous branch of law with its own interpretative methods and its own rules. These own rules have been proclaimed general principles of proper litigation, which can best be summed up as the rule of 'fair trial'.

There has been another remarkable shift: the law of procedure is no longer a national nor even a nationalistic branch of law.

Bordeaux wrote that it would be vain to search history for an example of a people which has taken over the judicial procedures of another nation without losing its independence.

Today this is no longer true. The comparative law method has become the method eminently suited for finding appropriate structures, models and procedures in other countries which can improve and refine the own national law of procedure.

Two examples may illustrate this. Via the Benelux Convention we in Belgium have imported from Holland the institution of the special injunction of a penal sum ('dwangsom', 'astreinte'). Since 1980 this instrument, which is eminently suited to enforce performance of courts orders, has been functioning very satisfactorily in my country.

In England the 'Mareva-injunction' was imported from the European continent; in this way the conservatory attachment known in the civil-law countries was incorporated in the common-law system.

The law of procedure has become a 'terre d'élection for international and comparative law research. This development indeed also explains the success which characterizes the conferences of our International Association.

It has always been said, moreover, that the law of procedure is an outstanding example of a politico-ideological branch of law. In line with the theory of François Gény it could be said that the law of procedure clearly showed the marks of the historical, political and ideological backgrounds of each individual country. The classical example of this is the predilection of certain countries for an adversory system and of other countries for an inquisitorial system.

Yet here too a clear shift can be observed in the sense that today the law of procedure is less the product of a given socio-political system than a power which is able to influence the constitutional system. The law of procedure is no longer mainly the reflection of a given society, but rather a driving force of social change.

The most striking example of this is the development of the access-to-justice issue. Initially it was the access of the poor to the courts that was at issue, nowadays - as Cappelletti expressed it in his 'four waves-theory' - the issue has become the access to the legal system and to the welfare state.

In connection with this - and this will be my fourth and last observation- the lawsuit has become a mass product. In former days it could be said that litigation was a luxury for a small number of privileged people, for whom the conduct of legal proceedings could be considered to be a leisure activity covering several generations. We all know the story of the young lawyer, proudly telling his father - also a lawyer - that he has settled and closed the old file of X vs Y, to which the father furiously responds: 'That is the file we have been living on for generations'!

With our conferences we have kept a close track of these modern developments of the law of procedure and tried to provide answers to the most burning topical questions of the day. In this connection I may recall the conferences of Ghent (1977) and Würzburg (1983).

In Ghent the central theme was 'Towards a justice with a human face', a theme in which emphasis was put above all on the need to ensure that litigation, which essentially is an evil, is at any rate carried on in a more decent way.

At this Ghent conference attention was paid mainly to the humanization of legal proceedings in general, to the accessibility of the court and to the improvement of procedures for small claims; there were also extensive reports on the special role of the professional and paraprofessional legal advisers and of the judges in assisting the litigating parties.

Besides, the basic principles of the law of procedure were expounded extensively and, finally, attention was paid to classical themes which are on today's agenda as well: legal remedies (appellate proceedings), international law of procedure, speeding up of the proceedings and law of evidence.

In Würzburg the main emphasis was on the 'Effectiveness of judicial protection and constitutional order'. The intention was to examine how judicial protection could be made adequately effective, proceeding on the assumption that judicial protection is a basic civil right and must as such be safeguarded constitutionally.

While at the Ghent conference attention was focused mainly on the human care and support of the litigating parties before, during and after the proceedings, at Würzburg the emphasis lay on the duty of the Government to provide adequate judicial protection, because justice is the twin sister of freedom (von Jhering). Or in the words of Sir Jack Jacob: In Ghent we proceeded on the assumption that litigation is an evil, which should be avoided; in Würzburg on the contrary the assumption was 'that litigation is a healthy and proper exercise of citizenship' (Justice between man and man, Current legal problems, 1985, 211 ff., 229).

At the conference here in Utrecht we wish to lay emphasis on the efficient management of the courts. In all countries of the world the machinery of justice sensu latissimo has indeed become one large business, the efficiency and productivity of which are usually unsatisfactory.

In the United States there are, for a population of 220 million, 700,000 lawyers who together receive approximately 55 billion dollars per year in fees (Schneider, U.H., Zur Verantwortung der Rechtswissenschaft, J.Z., 1987, 696 ff., 699). For England and Wales it was estimated that every year 1/10 of the population is involved in the civil judicial process (Jacob, J., o.c., 219).

These are only two examples in figures which serve to illustrate to what extent the judicial industry has acquired a central place in our modern societies. Hence the question that is the central issue of the Utrecht conference: How can we improve the efficiency of this industry?

For all of us the overload of the judicial system constitutes a challenge in the style of what Charles Dickens wrote about the French Revolution: 'It was the winter of despair, it was the spring of hope'.

There is a final question which, though it does not form part of the theme of this conference, can perhaps form the background of all our debates: Isn't the law of procedure a suitable instrument for the unification of the law?

There are few international conferences, which like our conference are centred round one general theme, which aim at legal practice and which bring together so many specialists.

Its impact is enormous, if the frequency with which the conference reports of Ghent and Würzburg are cited in the international literature of procedural law is taken as a criterion. There is not a single important handbook which does not refer to these doctrinal contributions.

But we must go further and ask the question whether doctrinal comparative law should not result in a universal law of procedure, to be introduced in the legislation of all countries of the world: a 'ius commune' obtaining everywhere.

True, it can be said that the unification of the law of procedure, which used to have such an intensely national colour, is probably the most difficult form of unification. But on the other hand the fact must be stressed that the need for unification in this field is all the greater, now that with the internationalization of legal transactions we are so heavily confronted with differences in the laws of procedures when dealing with the judicial protection of these transactions.

This project is less Utopian than one would think, if our starting point is formed by regional unification projects, like the ones of which prospects are already being held out.

In fact, as early as in 1967 the Instituto Iberoamericano de Derecho Procesal decided to draw up a model codex for civil procedural law for the procedural law in the Ibero-American countries. At present a first text of 370 sections lies before us, based on the preparatory work done by our colleagues Vescovi, Gelsi and Torello and titled: 'Anteproyecto de Codigo tipo del Proceso civil para Iberoamerica'.

Within the framework of the E.E.C. a project has already been started, under the leadership of Professor Ole Lando, for the unification of the law of contract. I used this example to request the E.E.C.-Commission also to support a proposal to try and work out common basic principles for a general section of a European judiciary code for the twelve member-states of the European Community.

Today I may announce to you, and you are the first to hear about it, that this support has been promised by the Commission and that a small group of experts will soon start the work.

May the Ibero-American and European examples provide a stimulus to others to set up regional unification projects elsewhere too, on the way to a universal law of procedure.

It is no coincidence that the theme of 'Justice and Efficiency' is dealt with in the Netherlands, a country which for centuries has been known as a trading power. May the localization of our conference be a herald of excellent reports, fruitful discussions and practical conclusions.

To begin with there will be a general introduction dealing the historical, sociological and present-day causes of the overload of the courts. Professor Borucka-Arctova, Professor Gimeno-Sendra and Professor Julien will provide comments. The merit of the two last-mentioned rapporteurs is the greater in that they were entrusted with this task at a very late date.

It was an original idea to examine whether it would not be possible to derive lessons from arbitration procedures - which are characterized by flexibility and efficiency - and from administrative procedures - which are the youngest in line - for the purpose of improving civil litigation. For these subjects we have been able to call upon the assistance of Professor Habscheid, Professor Schlosser, Professor Garth and Professor Vescovi, respectively.

The question whether informal alternatives can be found within or outside the ordinary law of procedure will be dealt with by Professor Taniguchi and Professor Blankenburg.

Within the scope of court proceedings attention had of course to be paid to two important domains which tend to be a considerable burden to litigation, namely that of evidence and that of legal remedies.

The rapporteurs for these subjects are colleagues Denti and Taruffo, Jolowicz and Nemeth.

Because of the slow progress of the trial of cases, people are looking for special procedures which can be used for quick and efficient results. Summary proceedings provide an apt illustration of this, the more so since the Netherlands have an especially rich experience in this field. This is the reason why the report has been drawn up by our Utrecht colleagues Meyknecht and Verschuur.

In many cases the enforcement of judicial decisions proves to be efficient. Therefore the two reports of Professor Barbosa Moreira and Professor Kerameus deal with the enforcement of foreign judgments and arbitral awards.

Finally, technology and informatics have developed into instruments which can also be used in court administration. This is the subject matter of the report by Mr Koers and Mr Pelger.

We have gathered here in Utrecht with distinguished specialists of procedural law from 50 countries in order to consider the theme of 'Justice and Efficiency'. I am sure that we shall, in open discussions, formulate here the ideal principles for an adequately functioning law of procedure.

In the end we shall all return home with the firm resolution to do something about it in our home countries, thanks to the experience gained here.

In this way theory and practice, dream and deed, will not be torn apart. Or as Yntema, chief editor of 'The American Journal of Comparative Law' once expressed it: 'Don't send articles *about* comparative law; get busy and *do* some comparing!'.

But above all we must return home in the conviction that 'neither speed, nor cheapness, nor universality are the ultimate ends of litigation. The ultimate end is justice' (Mr. Quintin Hogg, later Lord Chancellor, House of Commons, 25 May 1949).

CAUSES AND ORIGINS OF THE ACTUAL PROBLEMS OF OVERLOAD

CAUSAS HISTORICAS DE LA INEFICACIA DE LA JUSTICIA

Gimeno Sendra
Catedratico de derecho procesal
Universidad Autónoma de Madrid (Espana)

1 LA EFICACIA DE LA JUSTICIA

Antes de abordar el tema de nuestra ponencia conviene, como cuestión previa, que determinemos lo que debe entenderse hoy por 'eficacia de la justicia', habida cuenta de que el término 'eficacia' no encierra un concepto juridico, sino un estandard que precisa ser integrado por una valoración social colectiva, la cual, como es evidente, no puede resultar la misma a través de todas las sociedades y tiempos.

En nuestra sociedad contemporánea, y con arreglo a la jurisprudencia establecida por nuestros más altos tribunales (Europeo de Derechos Humanos, Constitucionales o Supremos), puede afirmarse que una Administración de Justicia es eficaz cuando en ella concurren las siguientes garantías o notas esenciales: a) Libre ejercicio del derecho de acción y de defensa, b) Solución del conflicto en un plazo razonable (sin dilaciones indebidas) por un órgano independiente y mediante la aplicación del Derecho a la relación juridico-material debatida, y c) Existencia en los procesos de unas medidas cautelares y de ejecución que posibiliten la tutela efectiva de los derechos e intereses legitimos (cfr. arts. 14 del Pacto Internacional de Derechos Civiles y Politicos de Nueva York, 6 y 13 del Convenio de Roma para la protección de los Derechos Humanos).

La idea, pues, de la eficacia de la justicia se encuentra en la actualidad intimamente ligada a la de un modelo de proceso que, sin olvidar sus principios consustanciales (contradicción, igualdad de armas, dispositivo en las democracias occidentales), posibilite una rápida solución del conflicto, mediante el descubrimiento de la relación juridico-material debatida y la aplicación a ella del derecho objetivo, y con los minimos costes para las partes. Celeridad, economía y justicia material, conforman los nuevos postulados del modelo procesal del Estado Social de Derecho, que se han venido a superponer a los ya clásicos del liberalismo.

Tales nuevas exigencias de la sociedad contemporánea, como es sabido, no han surgido de la improvisación sino, antes al contrario, son fruto del propio curso de la Historia, en la que, en cada una de sus más importantes etapas se ha podido constatar la existencia de un modelo especifico de organización social y, con ella, de la justicia, de tal suerte que a la sociedad feudal corresponde un tipo de justicia, que podriamos denominar *estamental*, al Estado Moderno de los siglos XVIII y XIX una justicia *liberal* y al del Estado contemporáneo una justicia *social*.

2 LA JUSTICIA ESTAMENTAL

2.1 LA ORGANIZACION JUDICIAL

Desde un punto de vista orgánico, la administración de justicia en el Bajo Medioevo Europeo adolecia de todos los defectos del sistema feudal: al igual que la fragmentación politica del Estado coexiste la de la propia Jurisdicción, que es ejercida por una multiplicidad de *jurisdicciones especiales* (eclesiástica, real, corporativa o gremial, municipal etc...)[1], cuyo común denominador es la falta de 'independencia judicial', en un sistema judicial en el que, bien no aparencían diferenciadas la función legislativa de la judicial (vgr. la *Urteilsschelte* o sentencias de censura de las asambleas populares del derecho germánico)[2], bien el Monarca concentraba todos los poderes, siendo los tribunales una mera emanación o delegación suya.

Naturalmente, han sido pocas las instituciones judiciales que se han mantenido vigentes desde aquella primitiva organización social, por lo que nos limitaremos a señalar las que han adquirido un mayor arraigo o difusión en los Estados contemporáneos, debiéndose citar expresamente a los *tribunales de escabinos* y al nacimiento de los *Tribunales Supremos*.

2.1.1 Los tribunales de escabinos

Los *rachimburgi* de la Ley Sálica o 'scabini' del antiguo derecho franco eran representantes del pueblo que, presididos por un delegado del poder real (el *comes*), constituían un colegio único, a quien, en caso de conflicto, acudían las partes y a quien incumbia la función de emitir una propuesta de sentencia a la asamblea popular, que definitivamente fijaba su contenido[3].

En la actualidad, y en la esfera procesal civil, subsisten tribunales mixtos, constituidos por un juez técnico y diversos 'asesores' legos en determinados países nórdicos (Suecia, Noruega, Dinamarca, Finlandia, Holanda...) para el enjuiciamiento de determinados asuntos civiles de caracter rural, en materia de aguas etc...[4].

Pero en donde ha tenido una mayor implantación el *escabinado* ha sido en la esfera del proceso penal, en donde el jurado anglosajón ha sido, durante el S. XX, desplazado por esta forma de participación popular, tal y como examinaremos más adelante (infra, 4.1.2).

---

1 TARUFO, **Cause storiche del l'inefficienza della giustizia**, 'Ponencia nacional italiana', Utrecht 1987, p. 1.

2 BRUNNER, **Deutsche Rechtsgeschichte**, I, Leipzig 1906, pp. 208 y ss, cit. por CALAMANDREI, **Opere Giuridiche**, VI, 1976, pp. 91 y ss.

3 Sobre los orígenes del Escabinado, vide BENZ, **Zur Rolle der Laienrichter im Strafprozess**, Lubeck 1982, p. 16 y ss; BRUNNER, **Deutsche Rechtsgeschichte**, I, Berlin 1961, pp. 204 y ss; SCHMIDT, E., **Die Unabhängigkeit der Gerichte und der deutschen Strafrechtspflege**, Göttingen, p. 41 y ss.

4 FAIREN, **Los procesos europeos desde Finlandia hasta Grecia**, Valencia 1977, pp. 22 y ss; VILKKONEN, **Court Organization and Procedure**, 'The finnish legal system', Ed. by JAAKKO UOTILA, Mikkeli 1985; **'The Netherlands judicial system'**, Council of Europe, United Kingdom 1975.

2.1.2 Los tribunales supremos

Mucha mayor relevancia han adquirido los Tribunales Supremos que, en esta época histórica, aparecen en Europa, ligados al fortalecimiento del poder real con el advenimiento del Absolutismo y a la recepción del Derecho Romano y, con él, la implantación de la 'apellatio' y de la 'supplicatio' imperial, que, desde el punto de vista político, van a contribuir a la unificación del Estado feudal mediante la concentración del poder jurisdiccional en el Monarca.

Son, en efecto, los consejos politicos del Rey quienes, en un primer momento como meros apéndices de la 'justicia real de gabinete' y, a partir de los siglos XIV y XV como dotados ya de una mayor autonomía (la 'Curia Regis', el Reichskammergericht, el Consejo Real) se convierten en órganos, a los que el Rey les concede por delegación suya la facultad de revolver todos los conflictos en tercera y última instancia[5].

Lógicamente, en un sistema jurídico material en el que predominaba la dispersión normativa, ante la coexistencia del derecho real, junto con el romano, municipal y consuetudinario, la función de tales Tribunales Supremos no era la de unificar la jurisprudencia, sino la de aplicar el derecho a los casos concretos, utilizando amplias facultades cognoscitivas (apelación amplia).

Pero, en la medida en que el poder del Monarca se fue incrementando, precisamente para garantizar la supremacía de las Ordenanzas Regias dentro del derecho objetivo, surgirá la *casación* como instrumento del Poder Ejecutivo para asegurar la aplicación preferente del derecho real por parte de los 'parlamentos' o tribunales. A esta finalidad respondió en 1578 la segregación del 'Conseil des parties' del 'Conseil du Roi', quien, desde aquella fecha, y salvo las importantes modificaciones legislativas revolucionarias, ha venido conociendo hasta la actualidad de las 'demandes en cassation'[6].

2.2 EL SISTEMA PROCESAL

Si el derecho material de la Europa medieval presentaba un marcado carácter caótico, ante la multiplicidad de fuentes normativas, y la estructura judicial aparecía atomizada por la pluralidad de jurisdicciones especiales, no mejor fortuna tuvo el ordenamiento procesal que, hasta principios del siglo XIX, venía caracterizado por la coexistencia de solemnes procedimientos *ordinarios*, junto con múltiples procedimientos abreviados, tales como los *sumarios* y *plenarios rápidos*.

Con la recepción del derecho justinianeo y la influencia del canónico, se instaura en Europa un tipo procedimental ordinario (el 'solemnis ordo iudiciarium') que, conservando la *litis contestatio*, se caracterizaba por la vigencia de los principios despositivo, de aportación, escritura, mediación, prueba legal o tasada y dispersión de los actos procesales como consecuencia de la posibilidad de impugnación (devolutiva y suspensiva) de las resoluciones interlocutorias[7].

---

5 CALAMANDREI, **Opere** ..., cit., VI, pp. 211 y ss.

6 CALAMANDREI, op.cit., pp. 295 y ss.

7 CAPPELLETTI, **La oralidad y las pruebas en el proceso civil**, Buenos Aires 1972, pp. 34-42.

Si a la vigencia de tales principios se une una generosa concepción de la fase de alegaciones y del principio de igualdad de armas (demanda-contestación, réplica-dúplica, tríplica-cuadrúplica...[8], la coexistencia, hasta su fusión, de la 'apellatio', junto con la *querella nullitatis*[9] con unos plazos muy dilatados para el ejercicio de los recursos, el caracter amplísimo de la segunda instancia, el mantenimiento de medios extraordinarios de impugnación en el derecho intermedio, tales como la 'supplicatio' y la 'restitutio in integrum' o la existencia generalizada de tres instancias[10], no resulta aventurado afirmar que el proceso común romano-canónico era un procedimiento excesivamente lento, oneroso, rigurosamente formalista y poco propicio para el descubrimiento de la verdad material.

Debido a la circunstancia de que el referido procedimiento, tan sólo a lo sumo satisfacía las necesidades de una aristocratica rural, que podía perder su tiempo y dinero en largos y costosos litigios, pero que en modo alguno se manifestaba adecuado para dar una pronta respuesta a las exigencias del tráfico juridico surgido con la expansión del comercio en el Mediterráneo, el derecho estatutario italiano conoció, durante los siglos XIII y XIV el surgimiento de los procesos plenarios rápidos[11] que, inspirados en los principios de oralidad, concentración e investigación, trazados por la famosa *Saepe contingit* del Papa Clemente V (1306), pronto se expandieron por toda Europa[12].

Paralelamente a la aparición de estos simples y rápidos procedimientos ordinarios, en los que se encontraba ausente la 'litis contestatio', obtuvieron también los comerciantes los *procesos sumarios ejecutivos*, destinados a evitar la fase declarativa o a limitar las excepciones del deudor, que previamente se hubiese sometido a un *pactum executivum* o a determinados *instrumenta guarentigiata*.

La proliferación de los tales procedimientos sumarios, de los que hay que hacer una especial mención, por su eficacia y generalización, al procedimiento civil monitorio del derecho germánico (el *Mannverfahren*)[13] fue tal, que los autores del siglo XVIII solían sistematizarlos hasta en cuatro categorías ('ratione parva quantitatis', 'parvi perjudicii', 'urgentia necessitatis' y 'miserabilium personarum')[14].

La importancia que para la construcción de un ordenamiento procesal civil eficaz, han tenido los referidos procedimientos plenarios rápidos y sumarios es evidente, si se piensa que los nuevos principios procedimentales, que incorporaron, son los mismos que los que han presidido las grandes reformas del proceso civil ordinario de la edad contemporánea.

---

8 CHIOVENDA, **Principios de derecho procesal civil**, I, Madrid 1922, p. 10.

9 Cfr. MORENO - GIMENO - CORTES - ALMAGRO, **Derecho Procesal**, T. I, Vol. II, Valencia 1986, pp. 31 y ss.

10 CALAMANDREI, op. cit., VI, pp. 134, 140 y 174 y ss.

11 Conforme a la denominación de BRIEGLEB (**Einleitung in die Theorie der summarischen Prozesse**, Leipzig 1859, pp. 108 y ss), recogida por FAIREN (**Estudios de derecho procesal**, Madrid 1955, p. 28, **El juicio ordinario y los plenarios ràpidos**, Barcelona 1953).

12 FAIREN, **Temas de Ordenamiento Procesal**, I, Madrid 1969, pp. 443-444.

13 CHIOVENDA, op. cit., p. 6; CALAMANDREI, **El proceso monitorio**, Buenos Aires 1953, pp. 26-36.

14 VAÑEZ PARLADORIO, **Opera Juridica** (Colonia Allobrogum, sumptibus fratum de Tourmes, 1761, pp. 375 y ss), cit. por FAIREN, **Estudios**..., cit., p. 376.

Ello no obstante, determinados países entre los que hay que citar al mio, a España, permanecieron anclados en esta etapa histórica, y, en vez de incrementar los principios de oralidad, inmediación e investigación en el proceso civil ordinario, optaron por una via de signo inverso, consistente en extraer numerosos litigios de ámbito de aplicación del 'solemnis ordo iudiciarium' y crear nuevos tipos de procedimientos especiales y sumarios más acelerados[15]. El resultado de esta política legislativa es que España cuenta con 4 procedimientos ordinarios y màs de 60 especiales y sumarios, lo que ha obligado a mi Gobierno a anunciar una profunda reforma de los procedimientos ordinarios que ha de acabar con esta caótica y profunda selva de procedimientos especiales.

3 LA JUSTICIA LIBERAL

La justicia 'estamental', como es sabido, corrió la misma suerte que el Antiguo Régimen. Tras la Revolución Francesa, y a través de una serie de reformas, primero en lo orgánico y después en lo procesal, empezaron a sentarse las bases en los distintos Estados europeos de un nuevo modelo de justicia tendente a llevar a la práctica los valores de 'libertad' e 'igualdad' proclamados por el pensamiento liberal.

3.1 LA JURISDICCION

En el ámbito del derecho judicial orgánico, se asiste a la configuración de la función judicial como un auténtico *Poder* dentro del Estado y al robustecimiento de su legitimación democrática, mediante la participación de los *jueces legos*, la instauración de la independencia judicial y la proclamación del principio de *sumisión del juez a la ley* en tanto que aplicación de la voluntad general.

3.1.1 La jurisdicción como poder

Frente a la multiplicidad de 'jurisdicciones especiales', el nuevo Estado liberal se apresuró en abolirlas y en proclamar los principios de *unidad y exclusividad jurisdiccional*. En adelante, pues, y con la sola excepción de la jurisdicción castrense en determinados países (pero ceñida exclusivamente al ámbito militar) la potestad de juzgar y hacer ejecutar lo juzgado corresponderá en régimen de monopolio a los juzgados y tribunales ordinarios.

La consagración, por otra parte, del principio del juez legal y consiguiente prohibición de los 'tribunales de excepción' (*ad hoc o ad personam*), de los que tanto se abusó en el Antiguo Régimen, proscribió las injerencias del Poder Ejecutivo en la constitución y funcionamiento de los tribunales, a la vez que garantizó la vigencias del principio de igualdad en el ejercicio del derecho de acción por los justiciables[16].

---

15 MORENO CATENA, **Ponencia nacional española**, Utrecht, 1987, pp. 22-23.

16 KERN-WOLF, **Gerichtverfassungsrecht**, Munich 1975, pp. 36-48; BETTERMAN, **Die Unabhängigkeit der Gerichte und der gesetzliche Richter**, 'Die Grundrechte', III, Berlin 1959, p. 572; HENKEL, **Der gesetzliche Richter**, Göttingen 1968.

La instauración de todo este conjunto de principios, hoy constitucionales, junto con la creación de otro grupo de garantías, tales como la *casación* o el *recurso contencioso-administrativo*, que, dentro del marco de la 'división de poderes', otorgará a los tribunales la función de *control de la legalidad*, permitirá configurar a la Jurisdicción como el 'más alto Poder de decisión dentro del Estado'[17].

3.1.2 Los Jueces Legos

En cuanto a la legitimación de este 'Tercer Poder del Estado', era natural, en un primer momento y en el pensamiento liberal que, si la soberanía reside en el pueblo, la justificación del oficio judicial había que encontrarla en la propia participación del pueblo en la administración de justicia.

Esta idea, junto con la de MONTESQUIEU de evitar la venalidad por parte de los 'senados' permanentes, estimuló la instauración de la *justicia popular o electa* en determinados países, tales como U.S.A., distintos cantones de la Confederación helvética y más tarde, aunque con otro fundamento, en la U.R.S.S.[18].

Mucha mayor implantación tuvo, sin embargo, la importación del *Jurado* anglosajón a Francia y al resto de los países europeos. La instauración del Jurado en el proceso penal, no sólo contribuyó a incrementar los principios de oralidad, inmediación y publicidad, sino que, sobre todo, introdujo por vez primera, y ante el desconocimiento de los jueces legos de las complicadas reglas de la prueba tasada, el sistema de *libre valoración de la prueba*[19], que acabaría posteriormente instaurándose tambien en el proceso civil.

3.1.3 La Independencia Judicial

Si la justicia popular habia de otorgar un cierto grado de legitimidad en el inicio de la función judicial, la conquista que supuso la consagración de la independencia había de dotar de plena legitimación al oficio judicial en su continuidad.

A la independencia judicial se llegó fundamentalmente a través de la *inamovilidad* judicial, y esta se obtuvo, en sus primeros orígenes, mediante un procedimiento tan rudimentario como lo fue la 'compraventa de oficios' que, si bien tuvo como efecto positivo dotar de inviolabilidad a los Parlamentos franceses (obligando al Poder Legislativo a instaurar la 'Court de Cassation' como órgano de control *politico* para obtener la aplicación de la ley por los tribunales)[20] constituyó, al propio tiempo, la expresión del procedimiento de

---

17 BLOMEYER, **Zivilprozessrecht**, Göttingen 1963, p. 18.

18 La critica de este modelo puede verse en: KAISER, **Die Auswahl der Richter in der englischen und americanischen Rechtspraxis**, Berlin 1969, pp. 215 y ss; CASTELLA, **La independenza dei giudice in Svizzerra**, 'Magistrati o funzionari', Milano 1962, pp. 178 y ss; CHAMBRE, **Le pouvoir sovietique**, Paris 1959, p. 98.

19 CAPPELLETTI, **La oralidad....**, cit., p. 66.

20 CALAMANDREI, **Opera...**, cit., VI, pp. 382 ky ss.

acceso a la función judicial de la burguesia, clase social de la que se nutrió la Magistratura europea del siglo XIX[21].

Pero el sistema que acabó imperando fue, como es sabido, el de la relación funcionarial que, unido a un complejo cuadro de incapacidades, incompatiblidades y prohibiciones (entre las que destacaban las contenidas en estándares morales tales como la 'buena conducta' del juez o la 'dignidad de su caracter') habia de posibilitar la independencia del juez frente a la sociedad y a las partes.

No ocurrió lo mismo, sin embargo, con la independencia judicial frente a los demás Poderes del Estado y, de modo especial, frente al Ejecutivo pues, con la única salvedad de Inglaterra, las organizaciones judiciales europeas del XIX (y buena parte de las actuales) secundaron el modelo bonapartista, trazado por la Ley Orgánica francesa de 10 de abril de 1810, que residenciaba en última instancia en el 'grand juge M. le Ministre de la Justice'[22] toda la politica de nombramientos, ascensos y el régimen disciplinario de la judicatura, en una administración de justicia fuertemente jerarquizada[23].

3.1.4 La Función del Juez

Si el juez del Estado liberal, aunque a un nivel meramente individual, era *independiente*, el corolario de dicha independencia habia de ser su *sumisión a la ley*, de tal suerte que su única misión habia de estribar en aplicar el derecho legal al caso concreto con prohibición de ejercicio de cualesquiera otra función normativa o politica.

El papel del juez había de ser, según MONTESQUIEU, el de la 'boca que pronuncie las palabras de la ley'[24] en un ordenamiento que, por haber sido codificado, se consideraba perfecto (principio de *plenitud o hermenéutica*), por lo que el juez no podía rehusar a fallar 'bajo el pretexto de obscuridad, insuficiencia o silencio de la ley'.

Bajo la égida del positivismo legal cientifico, el juez se convirtió, pues, en un *Subsuntionsautomat*[25] cuya actividad habia de quedar ceñida a una labor meramente cognoscitiva en la que, fijados los hechos por las partes, habia de

21 Señalaba THIERS a este respecto que 'nous voulons des juges qui défendent la propiété privée et c'est pourquoi nous voulons ces juges propiétaires', CALDUS, Pour une réforme de la Justice, Paris 1969, p. 11. En los últimos decenios, sin embargo, la extracción social de la Magistratura ha provenido, fundamentalmente, de las clases media-baja; vide RICHTER, **Zur soziologischen Struktur der deutschen Richterschaft**, Stuttgart 1968; TOHARIA, **El juez español; un análisis sociológico**, Madrid 1975, pp. 64-73.

22 La frase es de PICARDI, **Problemi attuali della responsabilitá del giudize**, RTDPC, 1979, p. 1491.

23 Similar a 'une serie d'échelons ... quelque peu analogues á ceux que l'on rencontre dans l'armé, ROUSSELET **Histoire de la Magistrature française**, II, Paris 1957, p. 130.

24 **Oeuvres Complètes**, II, Paris 1958, p. 404. 'Su función - afirmaba FEUERBACH - no debe ser otra que comparar cada caso con este tenor literal y, sin preocuparse del sentido y espiritu de la ley, condenar si el sonido de la palabra condena y, si lo absuelve , absolver', **Kritik des Kleinschrodtschen Entwurfs zu einen Peinlichen Gesetzbuch für die Chuz-Pfalz-Bayerischen Staaten**, II, Giessen 1804, p. 20.

25 WIEACKER, **Privatrechtsgeschichte der Neuzeit unter besonder Berücksichtigung der deutschen Entwicklung**, Göttingen 1967, pp. 458 y ss.

proceder a la aplicación de la norma con exclusión de cualquier tarea interpretativa[26].

3.2 EL ORDENAMIENTO PROCESAL

A esta concepción mecánica y pasiva de la actividad judicial, contribuyó notablemente la legislación procesal de la época que, inspirada en el modelo del Estado 'vigilante', en una sociedad presidida por el valor de la 'libertad' y el principio de la 'autonomia privada', configuraría un modelo de juez que, para salvaguardar su imparcialidad, habia de permanecer impasible ante la noble contienda o 'duelo con igualdad de armas'[27] que las partes habian de representarle dentro del proceso.

3.2.1 El proceso Civil

El proceso civil, que inauguró el Code de Procédure Civile de 1806 y que fue secundado por la mayoria de los códigos europeos[28], de entre los que cabe señalar la Ordenanza de Hannover de 1850 y la C.P.O. alemana de 1877, aparece, pues, claramente informado por los principios *dispositivo* y de *aportación*, *oralidad* y *publicidad*, *eventualidad* y sistema mixto de apreciación de la prueba con predominio de la *libre valoración*.

Si al los ciudadanos el ordenamiento material les reconocia el absoluto dominio sobre sus derechos subjetivos, a nadie se le podía constreñir a reclamar su defensa ante los tribunales. El resultado de dicha concepción es el de que 'wo kein Klager, da kein Richter', 'ne procedat iudex ex officio': a las partes les incumbe plenamente el ejercicio de la acción y la fijación del objeto procesal, estando vinculado el juez, a través de su deber de congruencia, a respetar las pretensiones por ellas deducidas.

Pero, esta vigencia del principio despositivo, por lo demás consustancial al proceso civil de los Estados democráticos contemporáneos, no se limita, en el modelo liberal, exclusivamente al derecho de acción e interposición de la pretensión, sino que se extiende también a los actos procesales, a la introducción de los hechos en el proceso y a su actividad probatoria. De este modo, y aunque la determinación de los plazos permanece en manos del tribunal, las notificaciones y citaciones corresponden a las partes, quienes pueden ponerse de acuerdo sobre el señalamiento del juicio[29] y a quienes corresponde, en general, el impulso del procedimiento.

Todavia era más importante el dominio de las partes sobre la aportación y prueba de los hechos en el proceso. La vigencia del principio de aportación

---

26 WIEACKER, **Gesetz und Richterkunst**, Karlsruhe 1958, pp. 4-5.

27 BOTTICHER, **Die Gleichheit vor der Richter**, 'Hamburger Universität', XIV, Hambourg 1954, p. 7.

28 El Código napoleónico influyó decisivamente en la Ley Belga de 25 de marzo de 1876, holandesa de 19 de septiembre de 1896, rusa de 20 de noviembre 1864 y en diversos cantones suizos; vide: CHIOVENDA, **Principios**..., cit., pp. 14-15. En Italia tuvo una honda repercusión en el Estado Pontificio (motu proprio de 1817, 1824 y 1834), en Nápoles (Códice de 1819), Parma (Códice de 1820) y Piamonte (Códice de 1854-1859); vide: TARUFO, **Ponencia nacional**..., cit., p. 3.

29 STURNER, **Grunde und Ursachen des Problems der Ineffektivität von Gerichtsverfahren: ein historischen Ueberblick**, Ponencia nacional alemana, Utrecht 1987, pp. 2-3.

(*Verhandlungmaxime*) se resume en el más estricto cumplimiento de la máxima 'iudex iudicare debet secundum allegata et probata partium', para lo cual el procedimiento aparece claramente separado en dos fases: la primera, escrita, en la que las partes habían de formalizar sus alegaciones y, la segunda, oral, en la que las mismas partes habían de ejecutar la prueba por ellas propuesta[30].

Como consecuencia del absoluto predominio del principio de aportación y de la inexistencia de una obligación procesal de veracidad de las partes (*Warheitspflicht*), la función de la prueba y del proceso quedaba limitada a la obtención de una verdad formal[31] frente a la material o histórica, a la que el juez no podía acceder debido a la escasa entidad de sus poderes de 'investigación', fuera de los estrechos cauces del ejercicio de su derecho a formular preguntas (*Fragerecht*) a los intervinientes en la prueba, del cumplimiento de su obligación de formular observaciones (*Hinweispflicht*)[32] sobre la oscuridad de las alegaciones o de proponer de oficio la ejecución de determinados medios de prueba[33].

En cuanto a la forma en que debía ejecutarse la prueba, frente a la justicia secreta y 'de gabinete' del Antiguo Régimen, el movimiento liberal opuso los principios de oralidad y de publicidad, como garantía politica para evitar las presiones del Ejecutivo en la función judicial, y para acentuar la confianza del pueblo en los tribunales[34].

El principio de la escritura es, pues, sustituido por el de que 'quod non in ore non in mundo', consagrado por la Ordenanza de Hannover (parágrafo 101). En base al mismo, no sólo la demanda y contestación escritas, sino incluso la propia prueba documental, para ser tomadas en consideración por el órgano jurisdiccional, habían de ser leidas bajo su inmediación en el juício oral[35].

La introducción de los principios de oralidad e inmediación no produjo, sin embargo, la plenitud de sus efectos favorables en punto a la obtención del descubrimiento de la relación juridica-material en el proceso, por cuanto todavía sobrevivieron, en la C.P.O. de 1877, determinados institutos típicos de la prueba legal, tales como el *juramento decisorio* y, con él, el valor priviligiado de la confesión, cuyo objeto permanecía siendo considerado como 'asunto de las partes'[36].

---

30 STURNER, op. cit., p. 3; WASSERMANN, **Der soziale Zivilprozess**, Neuwied/Darmstadt 1978, p. 37.

31 WASSERMANN, op. cit., p. 36. SAUER, **Allgemeine Prozessrechtlehre**, Detmold 1951, p. 68.

32 Dicha obligación fue instituida por la Ordenanza procesal de Hannover de 1850 (parágrafo 111); STURNER, op.cit., p. 14.

33 La referida Ordenanza de 1850 expresamente consagraba la prueba de 'peritos', 'testigos' y la subsidiaria de 'confesión' (parágrafos 237, 280, 281, 300; STURNER, op. y loc. cit.). El art. 340 de la L.E.C. española de 1881 contemplaba la posibilidad de ejercicio 'ex officio', en el trámite de 'diligencias para mejor proveer', de todos los medios de prueba a excepción de la 'testifical'.

34 WASSERMANN, op. cit., p. 42; GRUNSKY, **Grundlagen des Verfahrenrechts**, Bielefeld 1974, p. 224; AUBY, **Le principe de la publicité de la Justice et le droit public**, en 'Le principe de la publicité de la Justice', Paris 1969, pp. 9 y ss.

35 STURNER, op. cit., pp. 8-9; CAPPELLETTI, op. cit., pp. 48-49; ROSEMBERG-SCHWAB, **Zivilprozessrecht**, Munich 1974, p. 339. En general, sobre la historia de la oralidad, vide KIP, **Das sogenannte Mundlichkeitsprinzip**, Koln/Berlin 1952, pp. 4 y ss.

36 CAPPELLETTI, op. cit., p. 49.

El resultado de todo ello fue, como se ha dicho, la configuración de un proceso civil similar a una 'formalista guerra procesal o lucha de las partes bajo la inspección arbitral del juez'[37].

3.2.2 El Proceso Penal

Mucho más profunda fue todavia la reforma que emprendió el movimiento liberal en el proceso penal. Dicha reforma puede sintetizarse en la instauración del principio *acusatorio* formal o sistema mixto.

Frente al procedimiento penal *inquisitivo*, secreto y, en general, inhumano del Antiguo Régimen, el proceso penal liberal aparece claramente dividido en dos fases, la de instrucción y la de juicio oral, en las que, para evitar el prejuzgamiento o falta de independencia del órgano decisor, habían de ser encomendadas a dos distintos órganos jurisdiccionales[38]: el juez instructor, cuya figura, secundando el modelo francés, acabará imponiendose en toda la Europa continental, y el Jurado anglosajón, en sus dos vertientes de jurado de acusación y de decisión, si bien la mayoria de los países pronto suprimirían el primero para conferir el conocimiento del juicio oral a un único jurado.

Para evitar, en segundo lugar, la confusión de 'roles' entre el órgano juzgador y el acusador, los países europeos, siguiendo también en este punto al modelo francés, confieren al Ministerio Público, en tanto que defensor de la legalidad, la función de ejercicio de la acción penal, que asume en régimen de monopolio, así como la de realizar una 'investigación preliminar' en determinados países (Francia, Italia, Portugal...). La intervención de las partes privadas queda, pues, a lo sumo, reducida al sostenimiento de la pretensión civil acumulada al proceso penal, con las solas excepciones de la StPO austriaca y el CPP portugués, que mantienen la acción penal 'adhesiva' del ofendido[39], y las del Reino Unido y España que conocen el fenómeno de la acusación popular y privada.

En cuanto a la intervención del abogado defensor, su régimen viene establecido desde bases esencialmente *privatísticas*. En la instrucción predomina la 'autodefensa' o defensa privada del imputado[40], estando sometida la defensa pública a la superación de diversas etapas procedimentales: la defensa 'prohibida' del abogado en la investigación preliminar de la policia o M.P., la defensa técnica 'permitida' a partir de la primera comparecencia ante el juez del imputado (quien desde ese momento puede designar abogado de confianza o reclamar uno del turno de oficio), y la defensa técnica 'obligatoria' que tendrá lugar con la apertura del juício oral.

Al contrario de la fase instructora, presidida por los principios de investigación, publicidad relativa o secreto y escritura, la del juicio oral se encuentra regida por los de aportación, contradicción e igualdad (con interrogatorio bajo 'cross examination' en la mayoria de los ordenamientos),

---

37 'Der Zivilprozess nach der Z.P.O. hat damit das Bild eines formalisierter Prozesskrieges oder Parteienzweikampfes unterschiedsrichterlichter Aufsicht', WASSERMANN, op. cit. p. 40.

38 BAUMANN, **Grundbegriffe und Verfahrensprincipien des Strafprozessrechts**, Stuttgart 1972, p. 29; GOSSEL, **Strafverfahrenrechts**, Stuttgart 1977, p. 33; ZIPF, **Strafprozessrecht**, Berlin 1972, pp. 66-67.

39 BERTEL, **Grundriss des össterreichischen Strafprozessrechts**, Wien 1975, pp. 53-55.

40 FOSCHINI, **L'imputato**, Milan 1956, pp. 25-43.

oralidad y publicidad absoluta y libre valoración de la prueba, con deber de congruencia del tribunal exclusivamente ceñida al hecho punible.

4 LA JUSTICIA 'SOCIAL': UNA REFORMA INACABADA

A diferencia de la justicia 'liberal', la cual surge con la propia Revolución Francesa como una clara ruptura y alternativa a la del Antiguo Régimen, la justicia social no nace en el seno de revolución alguna, ni pretende arrumbar con todas las conquistas del pensamiento liberal, sino, antes al contrario, su objetivo es el de incorporar a los clásicos principios del liberalismo determinadas exigencias del Estado Social de Derecho, cuales son la de garantizar el acceso *efectivo* de todos los ciudadanos ante los tribunales, quienes han de asumir la tutela *material* de sus derechos e intereses legitimos, mediante procedimientos *rápidos y poco costosos* para la sociedad y el Estado.

4.1 LA JURISDICCION

En materia de derecho judicial orgánico pocas han sido las innovaciones realizadas en estos últimos cien años puesto que, con la sola excepción de las democracias populares, la organización judicial contemporánea ha sido respetuosa con los postulados del liberalismo. Con todo, se hace obligado señalar el nacimiento, en esta época, de la justicia constitucional y supranacional, la crisis de los jueces legos, la potenciación de la independencia judicial 'colectiva' y la ampliación de la función del juez al derecho judicial.

4.1.1 La sobrecarga de trabajo de los Tribunales Supremos y la Justicia Constitucional

A lo largo de este último siglo, dos han sido los problemas que todavía ocupan a nuestros Tribunales Supremos: su sobrecarga de trabajo[41] y la incorporación de la justicia constitucional.

No nos corresponde a nosotros determinar las alternativas para evitar dicha sobrecarga, por lo que nos limitaremos a señalar distintas soluciones apuntadas en la historia, cuales son el establecimiento de una 'summa gravaminis' para la admisibilidad del recurso, instaurada por la Ley Prusiana de 1833[42], o las clásicas soluciones francesas consistentes en incrementar los poderes de la 'Chambre des Requetes' o sala de admisión, a fin de poder repeler los recursos manifiestamente mal fundados[43], así como la posibilidad de imposición de multas o pérdida de depósitos a los recurrentes temerarios[44]. Destaquemos finalmente que, para evitar la posibilidad de que la referida avalancha de recursos pudiera atentar a la uniformidad de la jurisprudencia entre las distintas Salas del T.S., la Ley Prusiana de 1 de agosto 1836 estableció la necesidad de que, cuando una sala se viera obligada a modificar su jurisprudencia, habia de plantear cuestión

---

41 SOBERANES, **Ponencia nacional mexicana**, Utrecht 1987, p. 9.

42 CALAMANDREI, **Opere...**, cit., p. 548.

43 Solución adoptada en la actualidad por la Comisón Europea de Derechos Humanos (art. 27.2 CEDH).

44 CALAMANDREI, op.cit., p. 586.

prejudicial al Pleno del Tribunal Supremo[45]. Dicho sistema ha sido perfeccionado en Austria mediante la ley de 19 de junio de 1968[46].

Pero, junto a este grave problema sociológico, ha surgido en este último siglo otro de caracter jurídico, derivado de la necesidad de obtener también una aplicación uniforme de las normas constitucionales, garantes de los derechos fundamentales. De este modo, junto a la casación ordinaria se ha superpuesto otra especial[47], cuya finalidad es obtener la aplicación inmediata y directa de las normas constitucionales por los poderes públicos, asegurando su aplicación uniforme.

Históricamente, esta función negativa de control de la constitucionalidad de las normas del ordenamiento y de restablecimiento de los derechos fundamentales vulnerados, se la irrogó el T.S. de los E.E.U.U. a través de la jurisprudencia de los jueces MARSHALL Y COCKE[48], habiendo secundado este modelo de control difuso de las normas constitucionales determinados países latinoamericanos[49] y europeos, tales como los nórdicos o Suiza. Por el contrario, otro grupo de países, entre los que cabe destacar a Austria, R.F.A., Italia, Francia o España, se inclinaron por el modelo de jurisdicción concentrada, diseñado por vez primera por KELSEN tras la Primera Guerra Mundial[50] y encomendando dicha función de control de constitucionalidad a un órgano especial, el *Tribunal Constitucional*, a quien determinados países (Austria, R.F.A. y España) le conceden también la función de protección de los derechos fundamentales a través del ejercicio por los ciudadanos de un recurso constitutional individual ('Berufverfassungsbeschwerde' o 'recurso de amparo').

Sin embargo, esta función de protección de los derechos fundamentales por los Tribunales Constitucionales o Supremos europeos no es definitiva e irrevocable, pues el ciudadano siempre tiene la posibilidad de acudir a la Comisión y Tribunal Europeo de Derechos Humanos, con sede en Estrasburgo que, junto con el Tribunal de las Comunidades Europeas de Luxemburgo, ostentan la última palabra en la protección de los derechos humanos y en la aplicación del derecho comunitario europeo[51].

4.1.2 La Crisis de los Jueces Legos

Otra de las instituciones de la justicia liberal que se ha visto sometida a una profunda revisión es el jurado anglosajón, el cual ha venido permaneciendo

---

45 CALAMANDREI, op. cit., p. 550.

46 En la actualidad de Sala ha de incrementarse con 6 miembros más; FASCHING, **Evolución de las tendencias en el proceso civil moderno**, p. 401. Similar sistema ha secundado el BVerfG alemán.

47 BURMEISTER, **Das Bundesverfassungsgericht als Revisioninstanz**, DVBI 1969, pp. 605 y ss; STERN, **Kommentar zur Bonner Grundgesetz**, Hambourg 1982, p. 168.

48 CORWIN, **Marbury v. Madison and the doctrine of judicial review**, en 'The doctrine of judicial review, its legal and historical basis and other essays', Peter Smith, Gloucester 1963, pp. 1 y ss; PLUNCKNETT, **Bonhan's case an judicial review**, en 'Harvard Law Review', vol. XL, n. 1/1926, pp. 35-48.

49 Cfr. FIX ZAMUDIO, **Tribunales Constitucionales y Derechos Fundamentales**, México 1985, passim; idem, **La protección de los derechos humanos ante las Jurisdicciones nacionales**, Madrid/México 1981.

50 KELSEN, **La garantie jurisdictionnelle de la Constitution**, RDPSP 1928, pp. 204-205.

51 STORME, **Perorazione per un Diritto Giudiziario Europeo**, Riv. D.P. 1986, pp. 293 y ss.

vigente hasta la Segunda Guerra Mundial en la práctica totalidad de los países europeos.

Las causas de su fracaso hay que situarlas en su funcionamiento práctico. La absoluta separación entre los jueces de hecho y de derecho provocaba no pocos veredictos absolutorios injustificados, motivados por una desconfianza de los jurados frente al tribunal de derecho, consistente en que, de pronunciar un veredicto de culpabilidad, aplicaran los magistrados una pena excesivamente rigurosa. Por esta razón, la ley francesa de 5 de marzo de 1932 amplió la competencia del jurado a la determinación de la pena, conjuntamente con los Magistrados[52]. Este sistema mixto, de soberania del jurado sobre el veredicto y posterior deliberación conjunta con los Magistrados para la determinación de la pena, se mantiene todavía vigente en países tales como Bélgica, Austria y el nuevo Código procesal penal noruego, entrado en vigor el 1 de enero de 1985.

Por el contrario, la mayoria de los países europeos, secundaron la reforma alemana EMMINGER de 1924 e instauraron el escabinado[53]. Esta solución se impuso, no sólo en Francia (ley de 25 de noviembre de 1941), sino también en países tales como Italia, cantones suizos, Suecia, Grecia, Portugal y la R.F.A., si bien este país tras la reforma de 1974 ha reducido drásticamente la participación popular en los 'Landgerichte' (3 Magistrados y 2 ciudadanos).

4.1.3 La Independencia Judicial colectiva: el Autogobierno

Si los sistemas de legitimación del oficio judicial a través de la designación popular han caido en franco retroceso[54], no podemos decir otro tanto con la independencia judicial como elemento mediante el cual la Jurisdicción misma se legitima, la cual se ha fortalecido en estos últimos tiempos con la instauración de los sistemas de *autogobierno* de la magistratura.

En efecto, como consecuencia de la implantación en Europa de los sistemas totalitarios, en los que la presión del Ejecutivo sobre la Magistratura alcanzó límites fuera de lo tolerable, a la salida de la Segunda Guerra Mundial se formó un fuerte movimiento asociativo en la Magistratura, tendente a reclamar, frente a la figura del juez 'individualmente' independiente del liberalismo, la independencia colectiva de la Magistratura[55], la cual habría de obtenerse a través de la derogación del sistema 'bonapartista' de nombramientos, ascensos y régimen disciplinario y su concesión al Consejo Superior de la Magistratura.

En cuanto a la composición de dicho órgano de autogobierno de la Magistratura, cuatro han sido los sistemas que se han sucedido o coexisten en la actualidad: a) el *administrativo* o francés, en el que, junto a los Magistrados que integran el 'Conseil Superieur de la Magistrature', aparecen importantes

---

52 La evolución del jurado francés hasta su plena transformación en 'escabinado' puede verse en IMBERT-LEVASSEUR, **Le pouvoir, les juges et les boureaux**, Paris 1972, pp. 232-233; MERLE-VITU, **Traité du Droit Criminel**, II, Paris 1973, pp. 493-495.

53 Sobre la reforma de 4 de enero de 1924, KERN, **Geschichte des Gerichtverfassungsrechts**, Munich 1954, pp. 140 y ss.

54 Porque, tal y como se ha afirmado, no es suficiente que el pueblo elija a sus tribunales para pensar que, sólo por esa circunstancia, la imparcialidad y el acierto van a estar presentes en sus resoluciones. Cfr. KERN-WOLF, **Gerichtsverfassungsrecht**, Munich 1975, p. 10.

55 MORIONDO, **L'ideologia della Magistratura italiana**, Bari 1967, p. 69.

miembros del Poder Ejecutivo (Ordenanza de 22 de diciembre de 1958); b) el sistema *mixto* o integrado por representantes del Poden Legislativo y del Judicial, que fue inaugurado por Italia con la ley de 24 de marzo de 1958, y secundado por España (ley de 10 de enoro de 1980) y Portugal (art. 223 de la Constitución); c) el sistema *judicialista* es, en la actualidad, el vigente en Italia tras la declaración de inconstitucionalidad de aquélla ley y sus sustitución por la vigente de 18 de diciembre de 1967, y d) el sistema *parlamentario* o de designación, bien del Tribunal Supremo Federal (art. 1 de la ley suiza de 16 de diciembre de 1943) o bien del Consejo General del Poder Judicial (ley española de 1 de julio de 1985) por el Poder Legislativo[56].

4.1.4 La Función del Juez

También el modelo de juez 'técnico de la subsunción' del liberalismo, ha sido puesto en cuestión en estos últimos cien años como consecuencia de la revolución técnico-científica surgida en el último tercio del siglo XIX y de la aparición de los Estados totalitarios.

Debido a los rápidos cambios económico-cientificos y al nacimiento de la clase obrera, el dogma de la 'hermenéutica del ordenamiento' y de la inmutabilidad de los valores contenidos en la codificación, sufrieron sus primeras grietas, las cuales tuvieron que ser integradas por la jurisprudencia de los tribunales[57]. Aparece así, junto al derecho legislado, un *derecho judicial*[58] el cual ya no viene concebido como resultado de una mera operación mecánica o silogística del juez, sino como resultado de su actividad *interpretativa* de las normas, en la que, con independencia de la *mens legislatoris* debe el juez extraer todo su sentido lógico actual.

Esta actividad interpretativa y hasta cierto punto normativa de la función judicial, se verá reforzada en los distintos países europeos a la salida de la Segunda Guerra Mundial, como reacción frente a la exacerbación del formalismo del positivismo legal, realizado, para sus propios fines, por el nacional-socialismo alemán que, en un primer momento y con anterioridad a que la Constitución alemana fuera sustituida por el programa del partido nacional-socialista[59], afirmaba la doctrina, conforme a la cual 'el juez no está fundamentalmente facultado a rechazar la aplicación de una ley debidamente promulgada a causa de su contenido'[60].

---

56 Cfr. PRIETO CASTRO, **El autogobierno de la Magistratura**, R.D.P. 1970, pp. 265-266.

57 KERN-WOLF, op. cit., pp. 22-23.

58 ESSER, **Richterrecht Gerichtsgebrauch und Gewohnheitsrecht**, en 'Festschrift für Fritz von Hippel', Tubinga 1967, p. 113; WIEACKER, **Gesetzrecht und richterliche Kunstregel**, Jz. 1957, p. 704.

59 'La Constitución alemana es el programa del partido nacional-socialista', FRANK, **Die Zeit des Rechts**, D.R. 1936, p. 3. 'El Führer da las grandes directrices. En el periodo de transición es también asunto de los jueces juzgar conforme a esas directrices (los "Führerprinzip") antes que las viejas leyes existentes'. SCHMIDT-KLEVENOW, **Das Maerchen von den dinglidren Kirchensteuer**, D.R., 1938, p. 62; FREISLER, **Gedanken zu einer überheblichen Kritik zu Gemeinschaftschädigenden Vor-schlagen**, D.J. 1941, p. 1000.

60 Vide la jurisprudencia del T.S. federal y la de los distintos T.S. regionales alemanes, a partir del año 1933, en ECHTERHALTER, **Die Deutsche Justiz und der Nationalsocialismus**, II, 1970, pp. 125-131.

El principio liberal, pues, de sumisión del juez a la ley, no cabe entenderlo hoy como el de mecánica aplicación de cualesquiera norma juridica sino como 'vinculación a la ley y al derecho' (art. 20.3 *Bonnergrundgesetz*) de conformidad con el principio de 'jerarquía normativa', de tal suerte que incumbe al juez, previa a la aplicación de la norma, un doble examen, juridico-formal y material[61] tendente a constatar su legitimidad con la Constitución y el resto del ordenamiento juridico.

4.2 EL ORDENAMIENTO PROCESAL

A diferencia del ordenamiento liberal, en el que el juez asume el papel de mero espectador de la contienda, y el proceso sirve exclusivamente para la protección de los derechos subjetivos, en el Estado Social se destacará la figura del juez como 'Socialingenieur'[62] y el proceso, sin olvidar aquella clásica función, se concebirá también como un instrumento de politica social[63] o de pacificación social[64].

4.2.1 El Proceso Civil

A este fenómeno, conocido por 'socialización del proceso civil[65] se ha llegado a través de toda una serie de reformas legislativas en Europa que, partiendo, como es sabido, de la célebre reforma de Franz KLEIN a la Z.P.O. austriaca de 1895 (entrada en vigor el 1 de enero de 1898) alcanza a nuestros días y que, sin merma alguna de los clásicos principios de contradicción y dispositivo, tiene por objeto la satisfacción[66] material y efectiva de las pretensiones de las partes con el menor coste económico y en el menor espacio de tiempo.

Para el logro de esta politica legislativa se ha hecho necesario incrementar los poderes del juez civil, mediante la consagración de las *obligaciones procesales* y el fortalecimiento de los principios de *investigación*, *oralidad*, *concentración* y *libre valoración* de la prueba.

A fin de que el juez pueda descubrir la relación juridica material dentro del proceso, se hace necesario, en primer lugar, sujetar a las partes a los fines del proceso, evitando actitudes maliciosas u obstrucionistas.

Esta vinculación la obtuvo KLEIN a través de la instauración de las obligaciones procesales, con respecto a las cuales, si bien no fue su creador (puesto que determinadas obligaciones, tales como la de 'veracidad' o la judicial de formular 'observaciones' ya fueron establecidas por la Ordenanza Prusiana de

---

61 KERN-WOLF, op. cit., pp. 114 y 115.

62 BAUR, **Sociales Ausgleich durch Richterspruch**, Jz. 1957, pp. 193-197.

63 DENTI, **Processo civile e giustizia soziale**, Milano 1971, pp. 70-75.

64 LUHMANN, **Legitimation durch Verfahren**, Neuwied 1969, pp. 116-119; GRUNSKY, op.cit., pp. 12-15; HAGEN, **Allgemeine Verfahrenslehre und Verfassungsgerichtliches Verfahren**, Munich/Salzburg 1971, p. 25.

65 DEVIS ECHANDIA, **Liberalización y socialización del proceso civil**, RDP 1972, pp. 325 y ss; SERRA, **Liberalización y socialización del proceso civil**, RDP 1972.

66 FAIREN, **El proceso como función de statisfacción jurídica**, en 'Temas de ordenamiento procesal', Madrid 1969, I, pp. 355 y ss.

1792 -AGO- y por la de Hannover de 1850 respectivamente)[67], sí que fue su decidido impulsor, situando a la obligación de veracidad (*Wahrheitspflicht*) de las partes en el centro del proceso. Otras obligaciones, tales como la de *comparecencia* personal a la llamada del juez (parágrafo 198 del Proyecto de Z.P.O. austriaca) la de exhibición de documentos (parágrafo 199.2) o el derecho judicial a interrogar a las partes o testigos y la obligación judicial de dirección procesal (*Prozessleitungspflicht*), también fueron consagradas en la Z.P.O. austriaca de 1895[68].

En la actualidad, algunos de los derechos u obligaciones procesales se han transformado, tras sucesivas reformas legislativas, dando lugar a nuevas obligaciones procesales. Ello es lo que ha sucedido, por ejemplo, con el derecho judicial a formular preguntas (*Fragerecht*) que, mediante la Novela de 1909 de reforma a la C.P.O. alemana, se ha convertido en una auténtica obligación del tribunal de discutir con las partes (*Erörterungspflicht*) la relación juridica material a fin de obtener su completa aportación y esclarecimiento (*Vollstandigkeitspflicht*) o en la obligación de comparecencia personal que, en el ámbito de los procedimientos de paternidad, se ha convertido en la obligación de soportar un análisis sanguineo (parágrafo 372 de la vigente Z.P.O. alemana)[69].

En segundo lugar, este incremento de facultades del juez civil se ha obtenido en Europa, tras la reforma de KLEIN, a traves de la via de revisar el principio liberal de aportación, cuya vigencia, al igual que el dispositivo, permanece absolutamente válido en cuanto a la introducción de los hechos al proceso, que sigue siendo un 'asunto de las partes', pero no en todo lo referente a la proposición y ejecución de la prueba, con respecto a las cuales hay que conceder al juez la facultad de disponer de oficio la práctica de todos los medios de prueba pertinentes, asi como participar activamente en ella, formulando preguntas a sus intervinientes[70].

La actividad probatoria ha de realizarse bajo la vigencia de los principios de *oralidad* e *inmediación*. Frente a la proclamación absoluta del principio de oralidad en el liberalismo, lo decisivo hoy para la calificación de un proceso civil oral es su fase probatoria, de tal suerte que el juez haya de fundar su sentencia exclusivamente con el material de hecho aportado oralmente al juicio[71]. Por el contrario, determinadas actuaciones (alegaciones, prueba documental, sentencias, recurso de casación...) han de permanecer escritas; es más, en determinados ordenamientos, como el alemán, tras la reforma de 1976,

---

67 WASSERMANN, op. cit., p. 56; STURNER, op. cit., p. 14.

68 FAIREN, **El proyecto de Ordenanza Procesal Civil austriaca visto por FRANS KLEIN**, en 'Estudios ...' cit., p. 313.

69 STEIN-JONAS, **Kommentar zur Zivilprozessordnung**, I, Tubingen 1972, p. 21; ROSEMBERG-SCHWAB, op. cit., p. 8; BAUMGARTEL-MES, **Einführung in das Zivilprozessrecht mit Examinatorium**, J.A. 1977-5, p. 11.

La legitimidad de dicha obligación procesal ha sido declarada por la propia Comisión Europea en su Decisión 8287/78 de 13 de diciembre de 1979 contra el Estado austriaco.

70 GRUNSKY, op. cit., p. 165; DEVIS ECHANDIA, **La iniciativa probatoria del juez civil en el proceso comtemporáneo**, RDP 1967, pp. 645-647.

71 ROSEMBERG-SCHWAB, op. cit., p. 398; SCHONKE-SCHRODER-NIESE, **Lehrbuch des Zivilprozessrechts**, Karlsruhe 1956, p. 54.

inspirada en el modelo de Stuttgart[72], la preparación del juicio oral puede realizarse a través de una fase previa (el 'Vorverfahren'), regida por el principio de la escritura.

Para obtener, pues, la concentración del material instructorio a fin de que el juicio oral transcurra, a ser posible, en una sola audiencia, se hace preciso concentrarlo a través de una fase previa, regida por el principio de eventualidad, y que en la concepción de KLEIN adoptó la forma de 'audiencia preliminar' (*erste Termin*). Dicha audiencia previa, que encuentra un claro paralelismo en Brasil con la institución del 'despacho saneador'[73] y que en España ha sido introducida por la reforma de 1984, o fase preparatoria del juicio oral, asume las siguientes funciones: a) Evitar juicios innecesarios mediante la realización de la *conciliación intraprocesal*, puesto que la realización de dicho acto con caracter previo a la demanda, tal y como era regulado en el ordenamiento liberal, se convertía en un trámite dilatorio e ineficaz en la práctica[74]; b) purgar el proceso de aquellos obstáculos procesales que, por no guardar una estrecha relación con el objeto procesal, permiten un tratamiento previo y separado, y c) introducir el material de hecho al proceso, recabando, si fuere necesario, el auxilio del juez en punto a ejercitar la obligación de exhibición de documentos[75].

El principio de eventualidad de esta fase previa se complementó en el Proyecto de Z.P.O. de KLEIN mediante una rigida *preclusión* en el juicio oral y, en general, en la realización de actos de postulación que contuvieran peticiones intempestivas o incidentes dilatorios, los cuales habían de ser repelidos de oficio por el juez[76]. Dicho principio de *preclusión* se encuentra también presente en la segunda instancia austriaca, que al igual que la de la L.E.C. española, consagra la regla de prohibición del 'ius novorum' limitacións de las alegaciones a los 'nova reperta'.

Finalmente, la obra 'socializadora' de KLEIN culminó con la derogación del juramento decisorio y, con él, del último resquicio del sistema de la prueba legal, la *confesión*[77], instaurándose también en el proceso civil el sistema de la *libre valoración*, (con la sola excepción de determinados documentos públicos),

---

72 Ideado por FRUTZ BAUR y ROLF BENDER. Vide STURNER, op. cit., pp. 5-6.

73 La Z.P.O. austriaca tuvo una clara influencia en el Código Procesal Civil húngaro de 1911, en la Z.P.O. polaca de 1930, en Yugoslavia (código de 1929), Checoslovaquia, Dinamarca (ley de 1916), Noruega (Z.P.O. de 1915) y Suecia (Ley de 1942). FAIREN, op. cit., p. 306. Sobre el 'despacho saneador' brasileño, vide BARBOSA MOREIRA, **Saneamiento del proceso y audiencia preliminar**, en RDP 1/1986, pp. 7-24 y 2/1986, pp. 239-268.

74 STURNER, op. cit., pp. 17-19.

75 KLEIN-ENGEL, **Das Zivilprozess Oesterreichs**, Manhein/Berlin/Leipzig 1927, pp. 265 y ss.

76 KLEIN-ENGEL, op. cit., pp. 269-273. También el principio de preclusión estuvo presente en el Código Procesal Civil italiano de 1940-42; desgraciadamente la ley de 1950 ha provocado una contrareforma en esta materia. Vide: TARUFFO, op. cit. p. 6.

77 Porque, como afirmaba KLEIN, 'la libre apreciación de la prueba y el juramente reglado se avienen como el fuego y el agua' ('Freie Beweiswurdiging und normierter Eid vertragen sich wie Feuer und Wasser'), KLEIN-ENGEL, op. cit., p. 364.

sistema que, mediante la Novela de 1933, acabo introduciéndose también en la Z.P.O. alemana[78].

A partir de la reforma de KLEIN a la Z.P.O. austriaca, una nueva época se ha abierto en la historia procesal civil, en la que, frente a la figura del juez 'vigilante' del liberalismo, se ha opuesto la del juez 'director' del procedimiento, especialmente comprometido en la rápida y eficaz composición del conflicto y en la satisfacción exclusiva de aquellas pretensiones que, dentro y fuera del proceso, se encuentren fundadas en el derecho objetivo.

4.2.2 El Proceso Penal

Todo al contrario que el proceso civil, las reformas habidas en el proceso penal en esta último siglo no han estado orientadas, en general, a incrementar los poderes del órgano jurisdiccional, sino a fortalecer el derecho de defensa y el acusatorio, asi como a agilizar el funcionamiento de la justicia penal.

En efecto, como consecuencia de las violaciones de los derechos humanos cometidas en Europa durante la Segunda Guerra Mundial, a la salida de dicha contienda se observa en los distintos Estados europeos una politica legislativa (que se inicia con la ratificación de los Pactos Internacionales de Derechos Humanos y que culmina con diversas reformas a los Códigos Procesales Penales - 1969 en Italia, 1964 y 1974 en la R.F.A., 1978 y 1983 en España-), tendente a adelantar la obligatoriedad del nombramiento del abogado defensor a la fase instructora y muy especialmente a la adopción de cualesquiera medida cautelar (detención y prisión provisional)[79], así como a establecer plazos máximos de duración de la prisión provisional (vgr. reforma italiana de 1970 y española de 1983 y 1985).

Pero la potenciación del fenómeno terrorista en Europa, a partir del año 1975, pronto va a ocasionar una politica de signo inverso que, bien provocará la consiguiente reforma parcial del C.C.P. (vgr. la *Kontaktsperregesetz* alemana de 1977), bien provocará una legislación especial (vgr. ley antiterrorista italiana de 1980, secundada por la ley española de 1984), cuyo objeto consistirá en limitar el ejercicio de dicho derecho de defensa o en suspender determinadas garantías constitucionales, llegando incluso Francia recientemente (diciembre de 1986) a sustraer del Jurado el conocimiento de los delitos de terrorismo.

Junto a esta cruenta modalidad de delincuencia, una preocupación más generalizada de los Estados europeos se ha manifestado en el tratamiento de las infracciones menores o 'delitos bagatela' que, como consecuencia de la industrialización y el consumismo, ponen en riesgo de paralización a los juzgados. De este modo, y con independencia de las medidas despenalizadoras, se ha puesto en evidencia la necesidad en ciertos países, de reforzar el número de jueces y fiscales, de revisar las demarcaciones judiciales decimonónicas[80], introducir la informática, medios modernos de comunicación en la oficina judicial

---

78 BOMSDORF, **Prozessmaximen** ...., cit., pp. 275 y ss; SCHNEIDER, **Beweis und Beweiswurdigung**, Munchen 1978, pp. 11 y ss.

79 Dentro de esta politica legislativa, una especial mención merece la reforma española de 1983 y 1985 en la que, junto a la instauración del Habeas Corpus, se ha establecido la intervención obligatoria del abogado defensor en la dentención policial.

80 Tal es el caso de mi país, vide: MORENO CATENA, op. cit., pp. 6 y ss, 14 y 17.

y medios audiovisuales para la protocolización de los juicios orales, así como, sobre todo, de crear nuevos tipos de procedimientos penales simplificados, tales como el *monitorio penal*[81] o los de flagrante delito.

Dentro de esta línea de simplificación del procedimiento penal, merece ser destacada la revisión del principio de legalidad y la importación de los sistemas anglosajones del de 'oportunidad', que en sus dos formas de 'sobreseimiento puro' o 'bajo condición' (reparación a la víctima, realización de trabajos sociales, bajo 'probation' etc...) está imponiéndose en la práctica totalidad de los Estados europeos, de los que cabría destacar al Reino Unido ('guilty plea'), Países Bajos y Noruega, sin olvidar recientes reformas, como la francesa de 1975, que ha instaurado un sobreseimiento bajo condición de rehabilitación voluntaria de drogadictos, o el 'patteggiamento' italiano (ley de 24 de noviembre de 1981), claramente inspirado en el 'plea bargain' americano[82].

CUESTIONARIO PARA LA PONENCIA 1A SOBRE LAS 'CAUSAS HISTORICAS DE LA INEFICACIA DE LA JUSTICIA'

1a. ¿Considera Vd. como una eficaz politica legislativa la inaugurada por el derecho estatutario italiano, durante los S. XIII y XVI, conforme a la cual debe mantenerse un procedimiento común solemne y escrito, con amplitud de alegaciones, instancias, posibilidad de impugnación suspensiva de resoluciones interlocutorias y prueba tasada para el conocimiento de los asuntos más importantes y la creación de varios procedimientos plenarios rápidos y multiples sumarios para el tratamiento de asuntos de escasa significación económica o que requieran una más rápida solución?

2a. ¿Qué juicio le merece, desde el punto de vista de la eficacia, el modelo *liberal* de la justicia, trazado por el Código francés de 1.806, la Ordenanza de Hannover de 1.850 o la CPO alemana de 1.977, que configuraban un juez pasivo o 'vigilante' y un proceso civil, que a modo de 'duelo con igualdad de armas', aparecía informado por la absoluta vigencia de los principios de aportación, oralidad, eventualidad e hipervaloración de la prueba de confesión?

3a. ¿Que juicio le merece, desde el punto de vista de la eficacia de la justicia, el modelo *social* de la justicia, inaugurado por reforma de KLEIN a la CPO austriaca de 1.898, que configuró un juez 'director' o interventor en el procedimiento y un proceso civil informado por los principios de aportación e investigación, oralidad relativa, concentración, preclusión y libre valoración de la prueba?

4a. ¿Cree Vd. que es conveniente, a fin de garantizar los fines del proceso, la instauración o potenciación de las obligaciones procesales, que inauguró la Ordenanza prusiana de 1.792 -AGO-, la de Hannover

---

81 Vigente en Austria, Dinamarca, Francia, R.F.A., Italia, Luxemburgo, Noruega, Suecia, Suiza y Turquia.

82 PISAPIA, **Compendio di Procedura Penale**, Padova 1982, p. 569.

de 1.850, ZPO austriaca de 1.895, Novela alemana de 1.909, etc.? En caso afirmativo, ¿qué tipo de sanciones debe preveer el ordenamiento frente a su incumplimiento?

5a. ¿Debe el acto de conciliación configurarse como un presupuesto de la interposición de la demanda, tal y como acontecía en el ordenamiento liberal o, por el contrario, revestir carácter *intraprocesal*, tal y como suele acontecer en los ordenamientos contemporáneos?

6a. ¿Considera Vd. que la fase de alegaciones, previa a la probatoria, debiera tener como única misión, tal y como sucedía en el modelo liberal, la de la introducción de los hechos por las partes o puede asumir además otras funciones, tales como la de evitar, mediante la conciliación, juicios innecesarios, purgar al proceso de eventuales obstáculos procesales, introducir, mediante auxilio del juez, documentos no incorporados al proceso, etc., preparar, en definitiva, la realización del juicio oral?

7a. ¿Qué sistema de valoración, el medieval de la prueba tasada, el mixto de la justicia liberal o el de libre valoración de la justicia social se adecua mejor al descubrimiento de la relación juridico material en el proceso civil? ¿Debe este último sistema mantener alguna limitación (confesión, documentos públicos, etc.)?

8a. ¿Qué sistema histórico de apelación le parece más rápido y económico, el *restringido* con limitación al 'ius novorum' y carácter excepcional de la prueba en segunda instancia, vigente desde siempre en Austria y España, o el *amplio* existente en la mayoria de los paises europeos?

9a. ¿Qué juicio le merece, a fin de agilizar la casación, la instauración de la 'summa gravaminis' que realizó la Ley Prusiana de 1.833 o la solución histórica francesa de poder repeler, en la fase de admisión, los recursos manifiestamente mal fundados?

lOa. ¿Cree Vd. conveniente, en el ámbito del proceso penal, incrememtar los poderes del Ministerio Público en la instrucción e instaurar o potenciar el principio de 'oportunidad'? En caso afirmativo, ¿bajo qué condiciones debiera establecerse el principio de oportunidad?.

CAUSES ET ORIGINES DES PROBLÈMES ACTUELS DE L'ARRIÉRÉ JUDICIAIRE: APERÇU PROCÉDURAL

P. Julien
Professeur à la Faculté de Droit
Doyen Honoraire, Directeur de l'Institut d'études judiciaires, Nice

RAPPORT GÉNÉRAL (notes brèves)

Toute d'abord, je tiens à présenter mes excuses aux organisateurs du 8ème congrès mondial de procédure (Utrecht, 1987) ainsi qu'aux éminentes personnalités participant aux travaux de cette rencontre scientifique. Préssenti en avril-mai 1987 seulement pour présenter ce rapport général, je n'ai pu respecter les délais initialement prévus par les organisateurs pour l'envoi de mon travail. En outre, je n'ai reçu aucun rapport national, à l'exception du rapport excellent du professeur Adolfo Gelsi Bidart, de Montevideo (Uruguay), qui ne m'est parvenu qu'au début du mois de juillet 1987, et qui n'est pas, à proprement parler, un rapport particulier, national, sur le thème que je dois traiter, mais plutôt une étude complète, exhaustive, de l'inefficacité du procès en Amérique latine.[1] C'est dire que mon rapport général a dû être rédigé - très vite- d'après les seules pratique et expérience françaises, avec, en outre, l'appui d'informations personnelles que j'ai pu recueillir, de-ci, de-là, au sujet des pratiques et expériences non françaises.

Une question de terminologie, tout d'abord: le sujet sera envisagé sous l'angle, non de la seule procédure (au sens technique et étroit du mot), mais sous celui, plus ample, du droit judiciaire privé qui englobe, entre autres, les problèmes d'organisation judiciaire, de compétence et de procédure proprement dite.

Je laisserai de côté l'accroissement du contentieux en droit administratif, qui est certain, et qui dérive du développement de l'activité de l'Administration.

Je ne m'étendrai pas davantage sur l'accroissement du contentieux pénal qui a deux causes évidentes: l'accroissement du nombre des délinquants et l'accroissement des incriminations, notamment en matière économique (criminalité en 'col blanc'). En France, on est passé, de 1977 à 1985, de 2 millions à 4 millions de crimes et délits; de 40 crimes et délits pour 1000 habitants à 70 pour 1000.

J'axerai donc mes développements essentiellement autour de l'arriéré judiciaire dans le contentieux de droit privé, étant précisé, d'ailleurs, qu'un grand nombre

---

1 Le rapport national, substantiel et riche rédige par Dr. Paul A.J.Th. van Teeffelen, Vice-President de la District-Court de Breda, m'a été le 10 septembre 1987, soit 15 jours environ après la fin du congrès.

de causes de l'arriéré actuel du contentieux privé sont les mêmes pour l'arriéré du contentieux administratif et du contentieux pénal.

L'arriéré judiciaire, c'est-à-dire l'accroissement du rôle, des affaires restant à juger, est un phénomène que l'on étudie, en général, beaucoup plus sous l'angle de son importance, et des remèdes à y apporter, que sous celui de ses causes. En France, on observe, depuis 10 ans, un doublement des affaires soumises aux diverses juridictions. On parle de 'Justice submergée par la marée des contentieux', d''explosion judiciaire'.

Exemples:

- Nombre d'affaires civiles nouvelles:

Juridictions du 1er degré:	1971:	633.000
	1982:	1.136.000
Cours d'appel:	1971:	56.000
	1982:	135.000

- Durée moyenne des procédures:

Tribunal de grande instance (juridiction de droit commun du 1er degré):

	1971:	10 mois
	1981:	13 mois
Cour d'appel:	1971:	10 mois
	1981:	18 mois

1 CAUSES GÉNÉRALES DE L'ARRIÉRÉ JUDICIAIRE

1.1 Causes tenant à la règle de droit applicable

On observe, notamment en France, un phénomène d'inflation législative qui multiplie les règles de droit, les incriminations pénales, les modalités de l'exécution des peines. Le juriste est confronté à de nombreuses nouveautés et à de fréquentes modifications (en 1986: 1350 lois out été procural agrées et 1430 décrets).[2] On peut déplorer souvent la mauvaise qualité des textes nouveaux, soit qu'ils souffrent d'une rédaction hâtive ou trop complexe, soit que se manifestent des divergences entre la loi et son décret d'application. Cette instabilité législative et réglementaire et la qualité parfois médiocre des textes nouveaux augmentent les difficultés d'interprétation et, portant, le nombre des procès. Les magistrats et les auxiliaires de justice (avocats notamment) ne peuvent plus maîtriser l'ensemble d'une matière juridique devenue trop abondante et en constante mouvance; ils la connaissent souvent mal ou insuffisamment.

Il en résulte une incertitude juridique qui se traduit par des divergences de jurisprudence d'une juridiction à une autre, parfois au sein d'une même juridiction, parfois même au sein de la cour régulatrice. Il en résulte également une insécurité juridique qui nuit aux plaideurs honnêtes mais profite aux plaideurs peu scrupuleux.

---

2 En 1987, il en a été sensiblement de même, quoique à un degré mointre: 1160 lois et 1170 décrets environ.

1.2 Causes tenant aux magistrats

Leur nombre est-il insuffisant? Il y a en France, 5700 magistrats professionnels environ, c'est-à-dire guère plus qu'il y a 60 ou 70 ans; soit un magistrat pour 10.000 habitants environ.

Problème du maintien (trop fréquent?) de la formation collégiale, alors qu'un juge unique ferait aussi bien (mieux?) l'affaire. Des progrès en faveur d'un juge unique plus fréquent ont cependant été faits, notamment depuis la loi française du 10 juillet 1970 (art. 311.10 et s. code de l'organisation judiciaire).

Se pose aussi le problème de la médiocrité des conditions de travail des magistrats. Le manque de locaux a pour conséquence que les magistrats ne disposent pas tous d'un bureau au Palais de Justice; la plupart d'entre eux doivent donc emporter les dossiers chez eux où ils ne disposent pas nécessairement d'une documentation suffisante (livres,...) quand ils en ont besoin.

Se pose également le problème de l'inadaptation de leurs méthodes de travail aux besoins d'une justice moderne et aux possibilités offertes par la science (usage encore insuffisant de l'informatique; absence fréquente de collaborateurs qui, lorsqu'ils existent, sont utilisés à d'autres fins que celles pour lesquelles le législateur les a institués, à savoir aide et recherches). Les magistrats travaillent souvent de manière 'artisanale'. Se pose enfin le problème de la spécialisation des magistrats, lié à celui de l'inflation législative. Il s'agit d'un problème très controversé. Si on observe, en fait, une tendance à une certaine spécialisation (disparition du roulement; apparition de magistrats spécialisés: juge de l'application des peines, juge aux affaires matrimoniales...), cette spécialisation prend fin en cas de mutation (avancement) en raison des nécessités de service. Une spécialisation poussée à l'extrême serait-elle une bonne chose? L'idéal, sans doute, serait que, comme en médecine, les spécialistes soient, avant tout, de très bons généralistes!

1.3 Causes tenant aux justiciables

- Augmentation, en période de crise économique, des conflits de nature commerciale et sociale.
- 'Jusqu'au boutisme' des plaideurs qui, de plus en plus, refusent de s'incliner devant les décisions des juridictions du premier et du second degré qui leur sont défavorables, et cherchent, par tous les moyens, à faire juger une nouvelle fois leur affaire en utilisant, jusqu'à la dernière, toutes les voies de recours qui leur sont ouvertes, y compris le pourvoi en cassation (d'où, l'encombrement de la Cour de cassation), en oubliant que la Cour de cassation n'est pas-théoriquement - un troisième degré de juridiction. Ce comportement assez généralisé révèle une mentalité nouvelle de la part des plaideurs modernes (c'est là un problème de sociologie judiciaire); il n'est pas sans lien, de même, avec la gratuité (plus ou moins complète) de la justice, qui, en France du moins, prend de l'extension (développement de l'aide judiciaire qui, depuis 1972, est plus modulée et plus souple qu'auparavant; loi du 30 décembre 1977 instaurant (sic) la gratuité des actes de justice devant les juridictions civiles et administratives; remboursement possible à l'un des plaideurs - généralement, mais pas nécessairement, le gagnant - de ses dépens et d'une somme correspondant à tout ou partie des frais autres que les dépens: article 700 nouv. c. pr. civ.; possibilité pour un plaideur de se faire assister fréquemment par une

personne autre qu'un avocat: membre de sa famille, d'une organisation syndicale, ou autre...). Ainsi, les tribunaux sont amenés à connaître d'un contentieux abondant mais souvent 'médiocre' (économiquement), les importants litiges économiques étant, le plus souvent, soumis à l'arbitrage.

1.4 Causes tenant aux auxiliaires de justice

La multiplication des cabinets de groupe chez les avocats (développement des sociétés civiles professionnelles) explique et justifie le désir de chacun des associés de développer l'activité du groupe et de valoriser le cabinet. Il s'ensuit que, parfois, les avocats ne jouent plus le rôle de filtre qu'ils devraient tenir. La même remarque peut être faite pour les auxiliaires de justice titulaires de charges d'officier ministeriel, cessibles donc patrimoniales (avoués à la cour; avocats au Conseil d'Etat et à la Cour de cassation; huissiers de Justice).

2 CAUSES TECHNIQUES DE L'ARRIÉRÉ JUDICIAIRE

On regroupe sous cette rubrique un certain nombre d'éléments de discussion, techniques, de nature à ralentir le cours de la justice ou de nuire à la célérité de celle-ci.

a) Multiplication des juridictions d'exception, en soi critiquable, génératrice de conflits de compétence.

b) Pratique insuffisante de la conciliation, alors pourtant que législateur l'encourage.

c) Abondance des incidents de procédure, notamment des incidents rélatifs à l'instruction, et en particulier de l'expertise, qui ralentissent le cours de la justice. Le recours fréquent à l'expertise peut s'expliquer par la complexité des procès et les problèmes techniques qu'ils soulèvent. Ne révèle-t-il pas aussi, parfois, une certaine démission de la part des magistrats?

d) On ne peut manquer d'évoquer le problème du formalisme procédural. En soi, toute règle de procédure prescrivant l'accomplissement d'une formalité ou le respect d'un delai est génératrice de retard. Bien que le problème de la suppression de toute règle de procédure (ou presque) soit parfois discuté (on ne maintiendrait, dans cette perspective, que le principe de la contradiction), il semble impossible qu'on puisse un jour en arriver là, car la procédure représente une garantie d'ordre et de sécurité; elle évite l'anarchie et le chaos; portant, elle apparaît comme un facteur de paix, donc de liberté. Il reste que l'inobservation d'une règle de forme ou d'un délai peut aboutir à la nullité ou à l'irrecevabilité d'un acte de procédure. En France, on observe un volumineux contentieux en ce domaine, qui s'explique, pour une bonne part, par la jeunesse de la procédure civile applicable (le nouveau code de procédure civile date du 1er janvier 1976; le texte le plus ancien qui y est integré est un décret du 9 septembre 1971 qui était entré en vigueur le 16 septembre 1972). Cette procédure n'est pas toujours parfaitement connue des praticiens, lesquels peuvent, il est vrai, invoquer en leur faveur une excuse valable: depuis le 1er janvier 1976, le nouveau code de procédure civile a été modifié 22 fois (la dernière modification remonte au 29 juin 1987), plus ou moins profondement, soit 2 fois par an en moyenne.[3]

e) Effet suspensif des voies de recours ordinaires et, souvent en pratique, effet dissuasif des recours juridiquement non suspensifs. L'usage, beaucoup plus fréquent aujourd'hui qu'hier, des deux voies de recours les plus importantes (appel et pourvoi en cassation) est lié, d'une part au 'jusqu'au boutisme' des plaideurs (cf. supra 1.3), d'autre part à l'incertitude juridique qui découle de l'inflation législative et réglementaire (cf. supra 1.1). Dès lors, se pose, de nos jours, le problème suivant: ne faudrait-il pas supprimer l'effet suspensif des recours ordinaires? En d'autres termes, ne faudrait-il pas que toutes les décisions rendues par les juridictions du fond, au premier comme au second degré, soient automatiquement assorties de l'exécution provisoire (sauf à ce que celle-ci puisse, dans certains cas, être ultérieurement arrêtée)? Il serait très regrettable et dangereux qui on doive un jour en arriver là. A noter qu'en France, si l'opposition subsiste en procédure pénale, elle a disparu, en fait, de manière quasi-totale, en droit privé.

CONCLUSION

Le retard entretient, et accroît, le retard (pratique fréquente des recours dilatoires). Il s'agit là d'une situation grave et préoccupante à laquelle il est nécessaire que des remèdes soient rapidement portés.

POINTS DE DISCUSSION

CONSTATATION: DOUBLEMENT, DEPUIS DIX ANS, DU NOMBRE DES AFFAIRES SOUMISES AUX DIVERSES JURIDICTIONS

I) Causes générales

A) - Nombre insuffisant des magistrats.
Médiocrité de leurs conditions de travail.
Inadaptation de leurs méthodes de travail.

- Défaut de spécialisation des magistrats

B) Instabilité et inflation législative et réglementaire, qui multiplient les difficultés d'interprétation des textes et, partant, les procès.

- les magistrats et les auxiliaires de justice (avocats notamment) ne peuvent plus maîtriser l'ensemble d'une matière juridique devenue trop

---

3 Depuis lors, et à ce jour (septembre 1988), le nouveau code de procédure civile françois a été modifié encore 3 fois.

abondante et en constante mouvance; ils la connaissent souvent mal, insuffisament.

- incertitude juridique: divergences de jurisprudence d'une juridiction à une autre, parfois même au sein d'une même juridiction, parfois même au sein de la cour régulatrice (cour de cassation française par ex.).

- insécurité juridique, qui nuit aux plaideurs honnêtes, mais profite aux plaideurs peu scrupuleux.

C) Augmentation, en période de crise économique, des conflits de nature commerciale et sociale.

D) 'Jusqu'au boutisme' des plaideurs, qui, de plus en plus, refusent de s'incliner devant les décisions du premier ou du second degré qui leur sont défavorables et cherchent, par tous les moyens, à faire juger une nouvelle fois leur affaire en utilisant, jusqu'à la dernière, toutes les voies de recours qui leurs sont ouvertes, y compris le pourvoi en cassation (en oubliant que la Cour de cassation n'est - théoriquement - pas un troisième degré de juridiction).

E) Multiplication des cabinets de groupe chez les auxilioires de Justice (développement des sociétés civiles professionnelles). Désir de chacun des membres de développer l'activité du groupe et de valoriser le cabinet.

Parfois, les auxilioires de Justice (avocats par exemple) ne jouent plus le rôle de filtre qu'il devraient tenir.

II) Causes plus techniques

- Multiplication des juridictions d'exception, qui crée des conflits de compétence.
- Multiplication des incidents de procédure (expertise par exemple) qui ralentissent le cours de la justice.
- Pratique insuffisante de la conciliation.
- Gratuité (plus ou moins complète) de la justice et développement de l'aide judiciaire.
- Survivance d'un formalisme procédural, certes indispensable, mais générateur parfois de nullité ou d'irrecevabilité des actes de procédure développement du contentieux relatif à l'une et à l'autre.
- Effet suspensif de certains recours et, souvent, en pratique, effet dissuasif des recours qui, juridiquement, ne sont pas suspensifs.

CONCLUSION:

Le retard entretient (et accroît) le retard. Pratique fréquente des recours dilatoires.

CAUSES ET ORIGINES DES PROBLÈMES ACTUELS DE SURCHARGE: APERÇU SOCIOLOGIQUE

M. Borucka-Arctowa
Université de Cracovie, Pologne

Table des matières

Le présent rapport général est établi à partir des rapports nationaux provenant des pays suivants:
Allemagne Fédérale - Klaus F. Röhl
Argentine - Roberto 0. Berinzonce et Carlos A. Negueira
Belgique - Jean Van Houtte
Finlande - Gustaf Möller et Lea Turtiainen
Italie - Vincenzo Ferrari
Japon - Takeshi Kojima
Norvège - Hans M. Michelsen
Pays-Bas - Jan R.A. Verwoerd
Pologne - Maria Borucka-Arctowa et Krystyna Daniel
République Démocratique Allemande - Gerhard Haney

A part les rapports nationaux, nous nous sommes également basée sur les articles et les communiqués (titres dans les Notes), précieux pour notre rapport général, qui nous ont été transmis par: Erhard Blankenburg - Pays-Bas, Stephen Goldstein Israel, Francisco Ramos Mendez - Espagne ainsi que sur un communiqué envoyé en guise de complément du rapport national par Takeshi Kojima (à notre très grand regret, nous n'avons pas pu prendre en considération une nouvelle version de son rapport national qui nous est parvenue trop tard).

1 INTRODUCTION

Des problèmes de surcharge des tribunaux sont connus dans tous les pays modernes; ils éveillent l'intérêt des représentants de la pratique du droit et de l'administration judiciaire ainsi que de la science du droit. On est conduit à se demander si ce sont des problèmes nouveaux, caractéristiques et propres à la juridiction de notre époque. Les opinions ne sont pas unanimes. Certains prétendent que les discussions sur la surcharge à des tribunaux durent depuis bien longtemps et qu'elles sont étroitement liées aux activités des tribunaux. Le rapport de l'Allemagne Fédérale, se référant aux résultats des recherches de D. Strempl mentionne que le problème de la surcharge des tribunaux apparaissait, à partir de l'année 1877 (Reichjustizgesetze) dans chaque discussion qui précédait de grandes réformes judiciaires[1]. Donc les dimensions de cette surcharge, ses causes et ses origines caractéristiques pour les dernières décennies constituent aujourd'hui un problème intéressant. D'autres démontrent que le centre d'intérêt des discussions juridiques, qui, jusqu'à un certain moment se concentraient sur les problèmes du droit dogmatique s'est déplacé; le problème de la surcharge des tribunaux avec toutes les conséquences apparaît au moment où l'intérêt des chercheurs s'est orienté sur le fonctionnement réel du droit et des tribunaux dans un système judiciaire et social donné. Les deux opinions mettent l'accent sur les 'problèmes actuels' de la surcharge des tribunaux, ce qui se reflète dans le titre du rapport.

Le sujet est présenté sous trois aspects et dans trois rapports à part: aperçu procédural, aperçu historique et aperçu sociologique. Notre rapport général se concentre sur ce troisième aspect, il n'est pourtant pas possible de ne pas se référer aux deux premiers si l'on prend en considération la nécessité de tenir compte des conditions culturelles et des rélations entre les principes de l'organisation du système judiciaire ainsi que les règles procédurales et le fonctionnement réel de la juridiction.

La différence consiste dans la façon d'approcher l'objet de recherche et à chercher les réponses à des questions différemment formulées. Ces questions nécessitent une réflexion socio-juridique approfondie, appuyée par des données statistiques judiciaires, interprétées consciencieusement; l'observation de la pratique du droit et - là où cela est possible - les résultats des recherches empiriques consacrées à ces problèmes.

La façon la plus courante et en même temps assez simplifiée de présenter des problèmes de surcharge des tribunaux suit le schéma suivant: la surcharge des tribunaux est liée à l'affluence d'affaires (très souvent qualifiée 'd'excessive') ce qui entraîne par la suite un délai, des retards et exerce une influence néfaste sur l'efficacité des tribunaux. L'opinion stéréotypée sur les mesures à prendre s'exprime dans des postulats suggérant de faire diminuer le nombre d'affaires dont sont saisis les tribunaux et de faire accélérer la procédure.

Le schéma présenté ci-dessus exige pourtant une analyse socio-juridique plus approfondie. Dans la recherche des mesures à prendre nous devons tenir compte des possibilités réelles et en même temps nous ne pouvons pas perdre de

---

1 Rapport de l'Allemagne Fédérale, p. 3, D. Strempel, Rechtspflege in der Bundesrepublik Deutschland-Dokumentation und Bezugpunkte einer Strukturanalyse. Kritische Vierteljahresschrift für Gesetzgebung und Rechtswissenschaft 1986, pp. 242-262.

vue le problème principal et la question: à quoi sert le procès judiciaire et de quoi dépend la possibilité de réaliser ces buts.

Il faut souligner, dès le début, que les notions de 'surcharge', 'd'inefficacité' et 'de délai' sont ressenties de manière négative. Mais en même temps, plusieurs rapports insistent sur la relativité de ces notions, un manque de critères précis (à partir de quand nous pouvons parler d''un délai'?)[2]. En plus, le temps qui s'écoule du moment où le tribunal est saisi d'une affaire jusqu'au moment où cette affaire est terminée est jugée subjectivement et cette évaluation dépend non seulement de la culture juridique donnée, mais aussi de l'intéressé. L'opinion de la partie dépend de l'intérêt qu'elle prend à ce que le procès soit terminé ou, au contraire, de son souhait qu'il se prolonge le plus longtemps possible. Les organes de l'administration judiciaire contrôlant l'efficacité des tribunaux appliquent d'autres critères que la science du droit. Les appréciations des citoyens - l'opinion publique - sur la durée du procès dépend non seulement de la culture juridique, du genre d'affaires dont sont saisis les tribunaux, du degré d'efficacité d'autres institutions d'état, mais aussi des discussions que ce problème éveille et surtout de son écho dans les médias.

Les critères qui définissent 'l'efficacité' de la procédure sont aussi relatifs; d'habitude, l'efficacité est liée à la rapidité du procès. La rapidité du procès est un critère, mais pas le seul, servant à porter jugement sur l'application de la loi. Avoir tendance à accélérer au maximum le procès peut amener à porter atteinte aux buts de celui-ci ainsi qu'aux moyens normatifs qui servent ces buts. Donc, l'appréciation instrumentale de l'application de la loi du point de vue de sa rapidité peut être en conflit avec d'autres valeurs[3].

Ce point de vue ne met pas en doute la valeur de la rapidité du procès, par contre, attire l'attention sur les dangers de considérer la rapidité comme une valeur dont il faut viser la réalisation coûte que coûte. Réaliser le principe économique du minimax et garder les proportions nécessaires entre la rapidité et d'autres valeurs et buts du procès n'est pas toujours facile, mais cela ne veut pas dire que ce soit impossible.

Les indices que nous appliquons aux notions telles que: 'surcharge', 'rapidité du procès' doivent être considérés avec une grande précaution. Le nombre d'affaires traitées par un juge ou bien par un tribunal peut s'avérer, comme indice, bien trompeur, si nous ne prenons pas en considération la nature de ces affaires, si ce sont des affaires de routine ou bien des affaires difficiles et compliquées. Le temps qu'elles exigent peut dépendre aussi d'ambiguités et de changements des dispositions en vigueur dans une branche de droit donnée ainsi que d'une pluralité et d'une dispersion des sources de la loi dans ce domaine.

La même objection concerne également la notion de 'durée moyenne' du procès dont on se sert souvent dans différentes comparaisons. Elle devrait être

---

2 Rapport du Belgique, p. 5; rapport de l'Allemagne Fédérale, p. 3, 33 et suivantes; rapport de l'Italie, p. 1.

3 J. Wróblewski, Wartosci a decyzja sadowa /Valeurs et la décision judiciaire/ Wroclaw 1973, p. 181; S. Goldstein, 'The possibilities and problems of the acceleration of the civil litigation process', rapport présenté au colloque 'The Role of Courts in Society', Jérusalem 1986, p. 27. Le problème de la rapidité et de la qualité du procès est également soulevé dans les rapports de l'Allemagne Fédérale, Hollande, Japon, Italie, Argentine, Pologne.

complétée par une analyse des durées des différentes affaires qui, en conséquence, contribuent à cette 'durée moyenne'.

Dans le cas des indices concernant le nombre d'habitants par juge dans un pays donné, il faut prendre en considération le nombre inégal de juges dans les tribunaux de différentes régions et la densité de la population dans ces régions. Les conditions culturelles, le degré auquel des rélations reglées par différentes branches du droit peuvent engendrer des conflits, la volonté de choisir la voie judiciaire ainsi que la possibilité d'avoir recours à d'autres institutions en dehors des tribunaux sont aussi des données importantes.

Plusieurs rapports mettent l'accent sur le danger d'une exploitation erronnée des données statistiques sans faire référence à un point de répère. Le rapport hollandais de J. Verwoerd insiste sur le fait qu'uniquement la fusion d'une interprétation approfondie des données statistiques et des résultats de recherches empiriques peuvent permettre de formuler des questions d'une façon plus claire et de fournir des réponses plus complète dans le domaine traité. Dans un cas contraire les données déformées par une interprétation simplifiée peuvent être mises à profit pour des buts politiques ou bien pour servir une politique des cadres de l'administration de la justice et non les buts de la science du droit. Expliquer les origines des défaillances du fonctionnement de la juridiction par la science peut devenir un point de départ pour entreprendre des démarches pratiques afin d'éliminer ces défauts[4].

La comparaison des indices contenus dans les rapports nationaux pose de grandes difficultés. Ces données se rapportent aux différentes périodes choisies pour comparer le nombre et la durée des affaires dont sont saisis les tribunaux. Dans certains rapports la durée du procès est présentée comme taux sous forme de 'moyenne'; dans d'autres, on a procédé à une distinction (en taux) entre les affaires dont la durée ne dépasse pas 6 mois, un an, deux ans et plus (les périodes prises en considération ne sont pas les mêmes). La sélection des données présentées dépend souvent de la possibilité de les obtenir. Les difficultés dont nous parlons ici résultent d'un manque de données recueillies systématiquement, qui répondraient aux exigences 'd'une banque de données' pour les besoins de la science et de la pratique. J. Van Houtte qui dirige Le Centre des Recherches à Anvers insiste sur ce fait dans son rapport; il a déjà auparavant entre pris des démarches dans ce sens[5].

Les informations et les données de certains rapports ont été à empruntées aux statistiques générales et seulement pour une partie elles se réfèrent aux statistiques juridiques (qui ne sont pas faites de la même façon dans différents pays); d'autres rapports font également référence aux recherches effectuées (en Belgique, Hollande, Pologne et Allemagne Fédérale) qui mettent en évidence la nécessité d'une interprétation détaillée et approfondie ainsi que plus reservée de toutes ces données statistiques en démontrant d'autres facteurs intervenants qui n'ont pas été auparavant pris en considération.

Tout en tenant compte des objections formulées ci-dessus, il est difficile, dans des cas extrêmes de résister à l'envie de comparer des données statistiques qui peuvent servir d'indices caractérisant une situation générale de la juridiction dans chaque pays. Nous pouvons prendre comme exemple le nombre d'habitants

---

4 Rapport de la Hollande, pp. 3-4.

5 Rapport du Belgique, p. 9.

par juge. En Allemagne Fédérale - pays où le nombre de juges est très élevé-on compte, en moyenne, 3.600 habitants par juge[6] et en Argentine - pays où l'on constate un nombre insuffisant de juges et surtout leur placement terrétorial inégal, qui ne favorise pas l'accès à la justice - on compte, en moyenne, 27.000 habitants par juge; dans la capitale - Buenos Aires, cette proportion est de 1 : 14.000, mais dans la région de Buenos Aires déjà de 1 : 54.000 et dans le département de Moran de 1 : 88.OOO habitants[7].

Il faut souligner que l'analyse de la situation actuelle de la juridiction effectuée dans les rapports nationaux ne conduit pas toujours à affirmer que les tribunaux de ces pays sont surchargés. Le rapporteur de la République Démocratique Allemande constate que cette situation n'a pas lieu dans son pays; le rapporteur norvègien trouve, qu'en général, il serait difficile de parler d'une surcharge des tribunaux à une grande échelle et que ce problème concerne plutôt les affaires civiles que les affaires pénales. Une analyse approfondie et très détaillée de la situation actuelle de la juridiction en Allemagne Fédérale conduit K. Röhl à formuler l'opinion que malgré un accroissement considérable du nombre d'affaires, la juridiction a réussi à se conformer aux nouveaux besoins; une prolongation minimale de la durée du proces, pourtant sans diminution de sa qualité, en témoigne le mieux[8].

A la lumière d'autres rapports le problème de surcharge des tribunaux apparaît d'une façon claire et nette bien qu'il soit de différentes dimensions dans chaque pays. Une certaine différence entre les critères appliqués ainsi que le genre de matériaux sur lesquels le diagnostic est basé n'y est pas sans importance et sans signification. Le contenu de l'évaluation mis à part, nous trouvons dans tous les rapports une caractéristique des éléments déterminant l'affluence des affaires portées devant les tribunaux ainsi que l'efficacité de la juridiction contemporaine.

2 L'ANALYSE DES ELEMENTS DETERMINANT LE NOMBRE ET LE GENRE D'AFFAIRES

2.1 LES DÉTERMINANTS SOCIO-ÉCONOMIQUES

Le nombre d'affaires dont sont saisis les tribunaux présente, au cours de deux dernières décennies une tendance croissante[9]; la croissance est d'ordre de 40-50% et diffère fort en raison des branches du droit ou même de la nature des affaires dans le cadre d'une branche donnée du droit.

---

6 Rapport de l'Allemagne Fédérale, p. 6.

7 Rapport de l'Argentine, p. 9.

8 Rapport de la République Démocratique Allemande, p. 1; rapport du Norvège, pp. 1-2; rapport de l'Allemagne Fédérale, p.38.

9 Tous les rapports constatent ce fait, mais uniquement certains contiennent les données concernant l'accroissement du nombre à d'affaires; différentes périodes sont prises en considération. Ainsi, l'accroissement du nombre d'affaires en Allemagne Fédérale, à partir de l'année 1970 est d'ordre de 50% (Cf. rapport p. 8), en Pologne de 42% (Cf. rapport, p. 3), en Hollande dans la période de 1970-1982 de 52% (Cf. rapport, p. 22), au Japon dans les années 1955-1980 de 40% (Cf. rapport 'Le procès civil et l'administration dans le Japon moderne', p. 1.)

Plusieurs rapports insistent sur l'influence de la situation économique, de la crise, du chômage, de l'inflation sur la croissance du nombre d'affaires portées en justice. L'influence de la conjoncture économique se laisse observer surtout dans le domaine des affaires civiles; la période de prospérité se caractérise par un nombre inférieur d'affaires litigieuses; l'affluence des affaires aux tribunaux est propre à la période de crise. Le rapport de l'Allemagne Fédérale comporte une analyse intéressante de ces dépendances[10]. Les recherches à long terme effectuées dans ce pays (par H. Rottleuthner[11] et Ch. Wollschläger[12]) permettent d'estimer d'une façon plus modérée l'affluence des affaires portées devant les tribunaux, qualifiée souvent d''alarmante'. Dans les années 1822-1913 le nombre d'affaires civiles a augmenté cinq fois. Dans les années 30, donc la période où la crise bat son plein, on a noté que le nombre d'affaires avait triplé par rapport à la situation actuelle en Allemagne Fédérale. Ce phénomène s'explique par la gravité de la crise des années trente par rapport à la baisse de la conjoncture économique à notre époque qui, en comparaison des années 1964-1970, se caractérise également par un accroissement du nombre d'affaires (le nombre a doublé). Dans la situation actuelle, une brusque affluence d'affaires, d'après H. Rottleuthner, doit être considérée plutôt comme 'une vague' et non pas 'une inondation' (Verfahrensflut) d'un caractère durable.

K. Röhl tente de s'appuyer sur des données plus précises et de présenter les dépendances entre le nombre d'affaires civiles (les affaires familiales exclues) et le nombre d'entreprises s'étant déclarées insolvables ainsi que le nombre de sommations de payer (Mahnverfahren) prononcées par les tribunaux au cours de deux dernières décennies[13]. Il faut souligner, qu'en général, ce sont des affaires simples, où les deux parties, vu les sommes d'argent limitées dont elles disposent, tiennent compte des frais de justice; ces affaires ne durent pas longtemps et elles ne sont pas une cause de surcharge des tribunaux[14].

Le rapport polonais souligne qu'une inflation immuable est également à l'origine d'un accroissement considérable du nombre à de procès[15]. Les tribunaux de la famille sont saisis des affaires concernant l'augmentation des pensions alimentaires attribuées auparavant. Ces affaires ne sont pas compliquées, par contre, elles sont un exemple d'affaires que l'on pourrait éliminer si les pensions alimentaires à verser étaient calculées sous forme d'un pourcentage des revenus de la personne obligée de les verser et non pas sous forme d'une somme fixée, comme cela se pratique de nos jours (en 1985 uniquement 2% des pensions alimentaires ont été calculées sous cette forme).

On observe également un accroissement du nombre d'affaires portées devant les tribunaux du travail et des assurances sociales, affaires concernant l'augmentation ou les modalité de paiement des pensions; les modalités compliquées et changeantes. Durant les cinq dernières années le nombre de ces affaires a doublé.

---

10 Rapport de l'Allemagne Fédérale, p. 37.

11 H.Rottleuthner, Verfahrensflut und Verfahrensebbe, ZRP 1985, p. 117 et suivantes.

12 Ch. Wollschläger, Zivilprozessentwicklung und Wirtschaftsentwicklung in Preussen im 18. und 19. Jahrhundert, Zeitschrift für neuere Rechtsgeschichte 1981, p. 16 et suivantes.

13 Rapport de l'Allemagne Fédérale, p. 22 et suivantes.

14 Rapport de l'Allemagne Fédérale p. 21.

15 Rapport de la Pologne, p. 4-6.

Comme exemple d'une affaire qui se complique suite à l'inflation, donc en conséquence, qui exige beaucoup de temps, nous pouvons citer les affaires civiles en matière de succession où il est question de partager une ferme individuelle. Dans le cas de ces affaires il faut procéder à une procédure probatoire compliquée afin d'évaluer la valeur marchande de cette propriété. Durant le procès on se heurte à une complication supplémentaire: les deux parties tendant à obtenir leur part en nature et non pas sous forme d'équivalents en argent de la part successorale; ce phénomène s'explique justement par une inflation immuable[16].

Le rapport du Japon démontre que le genre d'affaires qui se situent au premier plan est variable et qu'il reste étroitement lié aux déterminants socio-économiques caractéristiques à une période donnée[17]. Ainsi dans les années d'après la guerre, une énorme pénurie de logements engendrée par une démolition des vieux bâtiments dans les grandes villes a été à l'origine d'une affluence des affaires contentieuses en matière d'expultions, donc des litiges entre le preneur et le bailleur. Un grand problème à l'époque était de chercher des mesures de protection de la partie la plus faible: le preneur; il était dans son intérêt de faire prolonger au maximum la durée du procès. La crise économique de la période d'après la guerre a également entraîné un accroissement des affaires en matière de licenciements.

Dans les années 1955-1965 on observe une vraie 'explosion' des affaires suite aux accidents de la circulation. Cette situation a obligé le tribunal de Tokyo à créer une nouvelle chambre pour juger ces affaires; celle-ci ayant appliqué une tactique spéciale des critères très détaillés et bien définis durant les procès et les ayant portés à la connaissance publique a contribué à faire diminuer trois fois le nombre d'affaires en matière des accidents de la circulation portées en justice. Le rapporteur s'appuyant sur cet exemple est conduit à formuler une thèse qu'un accroissement des affaires nouvelles conduit les tribunaux aux 'procès standarisés'. Ils servent de 'modèles' non seulement aux juges, mais aussi aux citoyens qui, en prévoyant la sentence du tribunal basée sur des critères clairs et précis, cherchent une solution à l'amiable en dehors des tribunaux. L'auteur y voit une mesure importante afin de limiter l'affluence d'un type donné d'affaires[18].

Les années suivantes, période d'une industrialisation accélérée, ont vu s'accroître les litiges concernant les brevets d'invention et les droits d'auteur surtout dans le domaine de l'audio-visuel. Suite à la pollution, toujours croissante, de l'environnement, on voit se multiplier les affaires portées en justice par les personnes atteintes de graves maladies. On a également observé s'accroître le nombre de plaintes portées par les consommateurs en matières des produits défectueux et surtout de procès concernant les effets secondaires des médicaments ainsi que de procès pour fautes médicales. Ce genre d'affaires a mis en relief le problème de la rapidité du procès comme étant essentielle pour celles-ci.

---

16 Rapport de la Pologne, p. 5.

17 Le procès civil; et l'administration ..., pp. 1-3.

18 Le procès civil et l'administration ..., p. 8.

2.2 LES CHANGEMENTS DANS LA STRUCTURE SOCIALE ET DANS LA CONSCIENCE JURIDIQUE

En analysant les changements qui sont survenus dans les structures sociales, nous devons prendre en considération non seulement l'accroissement de la population, mais aussi le nombre de personnes en l'âge de passer devant les tribunaux. Plusieurs rapports mettent en relief les changements qui se sont opérés à la suite de l'industrialisation et de l'urbanisation, donc, à la suite des migrations de populations qui interrompent les liens sociaux existants et demandent de s'adapter aux nouvelles conditions. Cela entraîne des infractions aux normes du droit pénal et fait augmenter le nombre de divorces ainsi que le nombre d'affaires du domaine du droit du travail (licenciements, abandon du poste, dommages causés à l'entreprise). Un grand afflux d'immigrants peut en être aussi un facteur important. Il peut être lié à certaines difficultés d'adaptation aux nouvelles conditions, mais peut être aussi à l'origine, comme p.ex. en Allemagne Fédérale, d'une flambée des affaires jugées par les tribunaux administratifs concernant les demandes d'asile, les demandes de nationalité, et après, les mesures prises par le législateur afin de limiter l'immigration en croissance[19].

Le rapport entre l'accroissement du nombre d'affaires dont sont saisis les tribunaux et l'éducation de la population, donc l'évolution de la conscience juridique, une meilleure connaissance du droit et de ses droits, et surtout des demandes formulées vis-à-vis de l'état, constitue un problème à part[20]. Les recherches empiriques démontrent que l'éducation est un facteur important et qu'il agit dans deux sens: d'une part il y a un accroissement de demandes, une approche critique des tribunaux et d'autres institutions judiciaires; d'autre part les gens avec des études supérieures sont plus réticents à l'égard des tribunaux et déclarent, plus rarement que les autres, la volonté de porter des affaires litigieuses devant les tribunaux[21].

Le degré auquel les membres de la société sont préparés à profiter de la voie juridique dans différentes branches du droit ainsi que leur conviction de l'efficacité des tribunaux est aussi un facteur important[22].

Un autre déterminant d'une importance considérable, qui ne reste pas sans liens avec les problèmes de la conscience juridique est la juridisation de la vie sociale, ce qui signifie que la régulation juridique gagne de plus en plus de terrain et qu'elle entre dans de nouveaux domaines qui, jusqu'alors, restaient en dehors de toute régulation juridique. Ces processus appelés 'juridisation', 'legalization', 'Verrechtlichung' sont souvent liés à 'welfare state' et surtout à l'interventionnisme d'état ainsi qu'au droit social[23]; des problèmes identiques

---

19 Rapport de l'Allemagne Fédérale, pp. 9, 18, 19.

20 Presque tous les rapports le soulignent.

21 Rapport de la Pologne, p. 4; rapport de l'Allemagne Fédérale, p. 20.

22 Rapport de la Hollande, pp. 4-5. Les origines et les effets de ce manque de préparation des personnes prenant part, de nos jours, aux transactions de droit civil, sont analysées par E. Letowska: 'Funkcjonowanie prawa cywilnego' ('Fonctionnement du droit civil'), Etat et Droit 1984/8, p. 7 et suivantes.

23 Rapport de l'Allemagne Fédérale, p. 19. Ces problèmes sont plus largement analysés dans les travaux suivants: R. Voigt (Hrsg.), Verrechtlichung. Analysen, zur Funktion und Wirkung von Parlamentarisierung, Burokratisierung und Justizialisierung sozialer, politischer und ekonomischer Prozesse.

apparaissent également dans les pays socialistes. Cela accroît le nombre de conflit entre l'individu et l'état; dans les pays socialistes cela concerne également les unités de l'économie socialisée (entreprises d'état, coopératives et organisations sociales qui mènent une activité économique).

Plus les rélations sociales deviennent impersonnelles et formelles, plus les conflits se prêtent à être considérés en termes juridiques avec le recours à la loi. La vie quotidienne de nos jours se caractérise justement par un accroissement de ce type de rélations à caractère anonyme (accidents de circulation, plaintes des consommateurs, rélations résultant du droit administratif). Cela entraîne - comme le souligne le rapport hollandais[24] un changement des rélations horizontales entre les individus en rélations verticales, donc des rélations entre l'individu et l'état. La communication entre l'individu et les pouvoir est fort formalisée. Dans les rélations verticales entre les individus des négociations ('bargaining') sont fréquentes; par contre, dans les rélations horizontales, les autorités ne veulent pas ou ne peuvent pas s'engager dans ce type de pourparlers. La plainte formulée en termes juridiques conduit vite devant le Tribunal. Dans plusieurs pays l'accès facile ou la facilité de la procédure dans les tribunaux administratifs favorisent cette démarche[25].

Dans des rélations à caractère personnel, la loi intervient, le plus souvent, 'en cas d'avarie', donc, elle est prise en considération là où d'autres normes s'avèrent inefficaces (cela concerne surtout le code de la famille); porter l'affaire devant le tribunal est le plus souvent lié à la décision de rompre tous les liens (divorce, licenciement, expulsion)[26]. 'Une mobilisation du droit'[27], donc une situation où la personne lesée commence à penser en catégories juridiques et à entreprendre des démarches en faisant référence à des normes juridiques données, peut amener à résoudre un conflit par un arrangement à l'amiable. Un échec peut amener à chercher l'aide d'un 'tiers'; celui-ci peut représenter une institution en dehors des tribunaux, plus ou moins à formalisée ou un tribunal; ou bien une partie peut renoncer à poursuivre ses prétentions et sa décision peut être liée et dictée par différentes motivations. Parmi ces motivations, la plus nuisible serait celle dictée par un manque de confiance vis-à-vis de la machine judiciaire dans la recherche de la justice et par une conviction que les 'dépenses', non seulement compris en tant que coût du procès, mais le temps perdu et la tension nerveuse sont disproportionnés par rapport au résultat. La

---

Koningstein 1980; F. Kubler (Hrsg.) Verrechtlichung von Wirtschaft, Arbeit und Solidarität, Baden-Baden 1984.

24 Rapport de la Hollande, p. 28.

25 Pour comparer: le nombre d'affaires aux tribunaux administratifs, dans les années 1970-1982 a augmenté de 100%, en Allemagne Fédérale de 200%, tandis que le nombre d'affaires civiles en Hollande a augmenté de 63% et en Allemagne Fédérale de 71% - rapport de la Hollande, p. 29, rapport de l'Allemagne Fédérale, pp. 9-10.

26 Rapport de la Hollande, p. 27.

27 Rapport de la Hollande, p. 29. E. Blankenburg, 'Mobilisierung von Recht', Zeitschrift für Rechtssoziologie 1980/1, pp. 4 et suivantes. N. Luhmann emploie la notion de 'thématisation' du droit et insiste sur différents éléments qui décident si les aspects juridiques d'une situation donnée deviennent l'objet d'un arrangement à l'amiable entre les parties ou l'objet d'une controverse. - N. Luhmann, Communication about law in interaction systems, dans: K. Knorr-Cetine et A.V. Cicourel (eds.), Advances in Social Theory and Methodology, London 1981, pp. 234 et suivantes.

renonciation peut être également dictée par une reticence à l'égard de la voie juridique, conditionnée par la culture, surtout en ce qui concerne un certain type d'affaires; elle peut être même dictée par une appréhension d''être stigmatisé' par le milieu.

Dans la procédure en matière des affaires pénales introduites sur l'accusation publique, l'accroissement de la délinquence, la découverte des délits ainsi que d'éventuels changements de dispositions du droit pénal influencent le nombre de ces affaires. Dans la procédure civile (comme dans la procédure pénale introduite sur l'accusation privée), les deux parties décident si l'affaire doit être portée devant le tribunal; l'accroissement des conflits en matière de rapports reglés par les prescriptions juridiques peut, mais pas toujours, être lié à l'accroissement des litiges portés devant le tribunal. (Cela est valable surtout pour des affaires qui ne peuvent pas être reglées sans intervention du tribunal comme le divorce ou l'établissement de la paternité.)

Les sociologues du droit comparent les affaires contentieuses portées devant les tribunaux à la partie d'un iceberg qui émerge de l'eau, tandis que la partie qui reste dans l'eau illustre tous les litiges. Cette comparaison indique qu'uniquement un petit nombre d'affaires est porté en justice.

Une question se pose: est-ce que le problème traité ici, concernant l'accroissement du nombre d'affaires portées devant les tribunaux signifie que l'iceberg émerge de plus en plus, ou bien que cet iceberg ainsi que sa partie émergée grandissent. Les déterminants socio-économiques présentés ci-dessus démontrent les causes d'un accroissement du nombre de conflits et de litiges dans le domaine des rapports reglés par les prescriptions juridiques. Les facteurs d'ordre culturel et l'évolution de la conscience juridique contribuent plutôt à la mobilisation du droit et à la décision de porter ou ne pas porter les affaires contentieuses en justice.

La prolongation du procès provoque des appréciations négatives et devient un facteur freinant l'affluence des affaires aux tribunaux, tandis que l'amélioration de l'efficacité des tribunaux peut contribuer au changement de l'attitude vis-à-vis de ces derniers et entraîne un accroissement du nombre d'affaires.

2.3 ALTERNATIVES DE JUSTICE ET L'ACCES A LA JUSTICE

L'opinion qu'une demande croissante vis-à-vis de la juridiction crée des difficultés pour satisfaire ces exigences (le même principe que la relation entre 'demand and supply') conduit à formuler des postulats (ainsi qu'à les réaliser) concernant les voies, alternatives en dehors des tribunaux[28]. Il s'agit donc de transmettre des affaires simples, traitées par les tribunaux comme des affaires de routine, aux institutions à caractère administratif ou social (quasi-juridique). Un moidre degré de formalisation, une procédure simplifiée, la rapidité du procès - voilà des qualités garantissant l'efficacité de ces institutions et, en même temps, en facilitant l'accès à plupart de la population. Les solutions de ce genre sont liées à un problème plus vaste, éveillant des controverses et de vives discussions, celui de la 'justice informelle'. Ce problème est abordé dans un autre rapport général, nous nous limiterons donc à mettre en relief des différences primordiales, qui, à la lumière des rapports nationaux, se laissent

28 Rapport de la Hollande, p. 18.

observer dans le fonctionnement des institutions de ce type dans différents pays ainsi qu'à procéder à leur évaluation du point de vue des sociologues du droit.

Les institutions de ce type se caractérisent par une grande hétérogénéité aussi bien du point de vue de la manière dont elles sont créées que de leur composition (qui assume les fonctions d'un 'tiers'), de leur caractère (administratif ou social) ainsi que de la pleine liberté d'y avoir recours ou l'obligation de les saisir dans certains cas.

Un système non judiciaire (à caractère administratif et seulement en partie social) très large et accepté par la population, fonctionne en Hollande et d'après le rapporteur national constitue un filtre qui allège les activités de la magistrature de la majorité des affaires[29]. Les recherches comparées, effectuées en Hollande et en Allemagne Fédérale (Nord-Westphalie) démontrent que ces institutions ont une portée très restreinte en Allemagne Fédérale, donc un nombre plus grand d'affaires qu'en Hollande est porté devant les tribunaux[30].

Les chiffres ci-dessous illustrent la situation dans les tribunaux sociaux en République Démocratique Allemande. A peu près 1.000 juges travaillent dans 230 tribunaux du premier degré (Kreisgerichte) tandis que dans les travaux de 32.000 tribunaux sociaux 230.OOO membres prennent part. Ils règlent tous les différends du travail (il est obligatoire de les saisir au cas d'un conflit; seulement 1/5 des affaires aboutissent devant les tribunaux à la suite d'un recours), des affaires civiles d'une moindre portée comme des conflits entre des voisins, conflits liés au paiement des loyers, menues dettes et autres affaires de même nature[31].

En Pologne la situation de ces tribunaux est complètement à l'opposée; tous les essais de transformer ces tribunaux en institutions fonctionnant réellement ont échoué. Conformément à la loi de 1985, dans le cas d'un conflit, le travailleur peut s'adresser à la commission de conciliation ou bien saisir directement le tribunal du travail récemment créé; la pratique démontre que le recours à la commission est très rare. Les commissions de conciliation fonctionnant dans les quartiers de grandes villes ne développent pas une activité d'une grande portée. La situation de ces commissions est meilleure à la campagne ou dans de petites villes où l'autorité et le prestige des personnages connus, membres de ces commissions invitent à avoir recours à leur aide pour résoudre des conflits. Les résultats des recherches effectuées en Pologne démontrent que la conciliation directement conclue entre deux parties (sans participation d'un 'tiers') est la voie privilegiée pour l'arrangement des conflits; si cette tentative échoue et les parties ne veulent pas rénoncer à leurs prétentions, elles portent leur affaire devant le tribunal. Ce n'est pas une voie qu'elles suivent sans réticence, mais elles la préfèrent aux autres institutions réglant les différends en dehors des tribunaux[32].

Ces exemples démontrent que le problème des moyens alternatifs par rapport à la justice est très complexe et nécessite des recherches approfondies en ce qui

---

29 Rapport de la Hollande, p. 21 et suivantes.

30 Rapport de l'Allemagne Fédérale, pp. 36-37; E. Blankenburg, 'Indikatorenvergleich der Rechtskulturen in der Bundesrepublik und den Niederlanden', Zeitschrift für Rechtssoziologie 1985/2, pp. 255 et suivantes.

31 Rapport de la République Démocratique Allemande, p. 4.

32 Rapport de la Pologne, pp. 8-9.

concerne les conditions culturelles et politiques ainsi que les expériences antérieures des citoyens dans ce domaine; ceci influençant l'attitude de la population.

Il serait utile de mentionner une discussion et des opinions controversées des sociologues du droit. Un fort courant propageant la nécessité d'élargir la portée de la justice informelle à entraîne une critique à l'égard de l'efficacité des tribunaux et de leurs possibilités restreintes (considérées non seulement sous son aspect juridique mais aussi social) de régler les conflits. Pour d'autres, la justice informelle se présente sous des aspects ambivalents ou éveille même des opinions critiques. On y voit une certaine idéalisation de vieilles formes traditionnelles qui ne sont pas capables d'assumer les rôles et les devoirs des tribunaux dans les sociétés post-industrielles qui diffèrent beaucoup des sociétés primitives homogènes et fort intégrées. La critique met l'accent sur les dangers entrainés par un manque de protection de la partie la plus faible au conflit, par la partialité d'un 'tiers' ainsi que par un contrôle insuffisant de ces activités[33].

Le problème de l'accès à la justice est inhérent à l'étendue et aux formes de l'aide judiciaire pratiquées dans différents pays. L'activité des institutions s'occupant de l'aide judiciaire peut jouer le rôle de filtre qui, en réglant beaucoup d'affaires à ce stade ou bien en les dirigeant aux organes non judiciares, élimine l'affluence des affaires aux tribunaux. D'autre part, pourtant, plusieurs rapports le soulignent, la popularisation du droit, la connaissance des droits et des possibilités de les revendiquer, et surtout la diminution ou bien la suppression des dépenses judiciaires favorisent l'accroissement du nombre d'affaires portées en justice. Dans les discussions sur la surcharge des tribunaux se font entendre également les voix soulignant l'accès trop facile à la justice. Les restrictions des dépenses budgétaires, opérées suite aux restrictions financières générales, peuvent aboutir ou bien amener à diminuer le budget de l'aide judiciaire.

Le problème de l'accès trop facile à la justice est étroitement lié aux formes d'assurances qui, dans certains pays, embrassent l'honoraire de l'avocat et le coût du procès, même du procès perdu (Rechtsschutzversicherung). Le rapport de la Finlande[34], met l'accent sur ce point, vu que cette forme d'assurance y a été créée récemment - dans les années soixante-dix - mais très vite elle s'est répandue et a concerné un grand nombre d'affaires (les affaires liées à l'activité professionnelle, aux différends du travail ainsi que certaines affaires de la famille en sont exclues). Les juristes sont convaincus qu'un moindre risque d'assumer le coût du procès entamé a contribué à l'accroissement du nombre d'affaires, surtout futiles dans lesquelles le coût du procès (où l'assistance de l'avocat est obligatoire) est disproportionné à l'objet du litige; d'autre part cela a favorisé des décisions hatives de porter une affaire en justice. Il s'agirait donc d'éliminer les affaires, qui dans le rapport sont qualifiées d''affaires inutiles' et auxquelles il faudrait renoncer.

Le rapport de l'Allemagne Fédérale informe d'opinions similaires de la part des juristes (surtout des juges) en ce qui concerne l'influence de 'Rechtsschutz-

---

33 R.Abel, 'A comparative theory of dispute institutions', Law and Society Review 1974, vol. 8 nr. 2, pp. 217 et suivantes; The contradictions of informal justice, R. Abel (editor), New York 1982.

34 Rapport de la Finlande, p. 6-7.

versicherung' sur l'accroissement du nombre d'affaires portées en justice. Les recherches entreprises en Finlande et effectuées également en Allemagne Fédérale relativisent l'importance de cette influence. Elles attirent l'attention sur certaines dépendances (surtout dans le domaine des assurances contre les accidents de circulation), les conclusions ne sont pas toujours identiques, donc ce problème nécessite par là même des recherches approfondies[35].

Les problèmes présentés ci-dessus mettent en évidence des opinions selon lesquelles l'accès à la justice est trop facile et qu'il faut le limiter. La notion d''accès trop facile aux tribunaux' n'est pas assez nette et provoque des discussions; ces opinions, par la suite, éveillent l'appréhension de créer des obstacles rendant difficile l'accès à la justice et de compromettre les succès dans le domaine de l'aide judiciaire.

Le postulat d'éliminer 'les affaires inutiles' relève d'un certain compromis et d'une volonté de trouver une solution rationelle à ce problème. Cette évaluation des affaires peut être liée à une selection erronnée des affaires portées devant les tribunaux par les particuliers et par les institutions qui n'ont pas eu recours aux démarches pouvant aboutir à régler l'affaire en dehors des tribunaux. Il se peut que l'on porte devant les tribunaux des affaires futiles, des affaires perdues d'avance ainsi que des affaires résultant des dispositions de la loi insuffisament claires, de la pluralité et de la dispersion des dispositions juridiques, donc, de certaines imperfections du droit matériel et du droit procédural; enfin, des affaires qui sont provoquées par la juriprudence elle-même (comme l'exemple cité des pensions alimentaires attribuées sous forme d'une somme fixée et non pas sous forme d'un pourcentage calculé sur les revenus de la personne obligée à les verser, ce qui entraîne, à la suite d'une inflation immuable, une affluence des affaires aux tribunaux de la famille).

2.4 LES CHANGEMENTS DE LA LOI

L'accroissement ou la diminution du nombre d'affaires portées devant un tribunal d'un certain ordre peut résulter des changement de la loi. Ainsi, en Italie, une procédure simplifiée une fois entrée en vigueur en matière du droit du travail, a entraîné une affluence de ces affaires aux tribunaux. La loi concernant le contrôle des loyers, promulguée dans ce pays en 1978 a également entraîné un nombre accru d'affaires portées en justice[36]. En Pologne, en 1985 ont été créés les tribunaux du travail. Tous les conflits de travail, aussi bien que les affaires concernant la responsabilité matérielle des travailleurs, jusqu'alors jugées par les tribunaux civils, ainsi que les conflits engendrés par les rapports du travail jusqu'alors résolus en première instance par les organes non judiciaires - les commissions de conciliation dans les entreprises - ont été transmis pour attribution aux tribunaux du travail. Ces tribunaux se sont chargés de tous les litiges en délai[37].

La loi promulguée en 1985 en Pologne a visiblement freiné l'affluence des affaires portées devant les tribunaux pénaux; cette loi transmet certaines affaires jugées jusqu'alors par les tribunaux aux organes collégiaux à caractère

35 Rapport de l'Allemagne Fédérale, p. 14 et rapport de la Finlande, p. 7.

36 Rapport de l'Italie, p. 7.

37 Rapport de la Pologne, p. 8.

administratifs les infractions (dans la majorité des cas, il existe la possibilité de pourvoi en appel au tribunal)[38].

Pour freiner 'une inondation' des tribunaux administratifs en Allemagne Fédérale par les demandes d'asile, une loi limitant les droits d'asile a été promulguée; par conséquent, le nombre à d'affaires portées devant ces tribunaux a diminué[39].

Ces exemples démontrent la nécessité de prendre en considération les changements de la loi comme facteur déterminant la nature et le nombre d'affaires portées en justice.

3 LES ELEMENTS DETERMINANT LA DUREE DU PROCES

3.1 L'ORGANISATION DE LA JURIDICTION ET DU TRAVAIL DU JUGE

L'accroissement du nombre d'affaires influençant la prolongation de la durée du procès nous servira de point de départ. Les données des rapports nationaux démontrent que dans certains tribunaux le procès se prolonge, dans d'autres sa durée ne change pas ou, parfois, elle diminue. Pour expliquer ces différences, il faut prendre en considération non seulement le genre d'affaires à traiter et le temps qu'elles exigent, mais aussi beaucoup d'autres éléments qui exercent une grande influence sur la durée du procès.

D'habitude, les affaires criminelles sont jugées plus rapidement; les affaires civiles durent plus longtemps et parmi elles, les affaires familiales exigent le plus de temps. La surcharge des tribunaux du travail ainsi que le temps nécessaire pour juger ces affaires présentent des différences. Cela depend, à un degré considérable, des déterminants socio-économiques caractérisés ci-dessus ainsi que du marché du travail, du chômage, de l'affluence des affaires en matières de licenciements ainsi que du fonctionnement des organes réglant les différends du travail en dehors des tribunaux.

La majorité des affaires sont jugées par les juridictions du premier degré qui, pour la plupart des litiges, relèvent des tribunaux de première instance. Le nombre d'affaires démontre la surcharge réelle de ces tribunaux uniquement au moment où nous disposons des données statistiques illustrant combien on trouve de jugements par défaut, arrêts d'acquiescement, ordannances de non-lieu, sommations de payer ainsi que de transactions conclues qui, d'habitude, contribuent à raccourcir la durée du procès. A la lumière des données présentées dans les rapports, en 70-80%, la durée du procès au tribunal de premier degré ne dépasse pas 6 mois (dans certains pays un an).

Le nombre d'affaires jugées par une juridiction supérieure est inférieur; cela dépend de la nature des affaires, d'habitude beaucoup plus importantes, qui relèvent de sa compétence ainsi que du nombre de pourvois en appel faits d'un jugement prononcé en premier degré. Le nombre d'affaires renvoyées devant les tribunaux de premier degré peut servir d'indice de l'efficacité des ceux derniers.

---

38 Rapport de la Pologne, p. 11.

39 Rapport de l'Allemagne Fédérale, p. 14.

La juridiction supérieure a moins d'affaires à juger, par contre, ce sont des affaires plus difficiles et plus compliquées ce qui prolonge la durée du procès. Les affaires portées devant la Cour Suprême demandent le plus de temps; la durée du procès (comptée du moment où l'affaire a été portée devant le tribunal de premier degré) varie, en général, d'un an et demi à deux ans, parfois cette durée se prolonge considérablement. La surcharge de ces tribunaux diffère d'un pays à l'autre.

L'organisation de la juridiction et surtout le placement des juges du point de vue territorial est un autre déterminant très important. Le nombre inégal de juges dans les tribunaux ou les régions est à l'origine des surcharges de ces tribunaux et des délais. Dans les cas extrêmes la situation devient alarmante comme c'était le cas de l'Argentine où les juges sont concentrés dans de grandes aglomérations urbaines et la province est souvent presque démunie de juges ce qui oblige la population à s'adresser à des tribunaux très éloignés (ou bien oblige à renoncer à la voie judiciaire). On observe également des difficultés en ce qui concerne les spécialisations dans les cadres des juridictions pénale et civile[40]. Le problème de la répartition des juges dans les différentes régions du pays - bien qu'à un moindre degré - est souligné également par d'autres rapporteurs (Italie, Pologne)[41].

Le rapporteur de la République Démocratique Allemande constate que les tribunaux dans son pays ne sont pas surchargés; il décrit les tribunaux dont la compétence territoriale répond à l'organisation administrative du pays; le nombre des tribunaux est adapté à la densité de la population d'un département et le nombre de juges est suffisant[42].

Dans le cas d'une affluence d'affaires, d'habitude, (mais pas toujours) on désigne de nouveaux juges; cela fait venir des personnes jeunes, dans la force de l'âge. Le rapport de l'Allemagne Fédérale met l'accent sur le fait que malgré un accroissement disproportionné des affaires par rapport à l'accroissement du nombre de juges ni la prolongation de la durée, ni la dévaluation de la qualité du procès n'ont été observées (si nous prenons en considération le nombre de retractations des décisions judiciaires dans la procédure de recours)[43].

La situation en Pologne est bien différente. Les dernières années ont été marquées par une retraite des juges dans la force de l'âge qui, tentés par des salaires plus élevés, se sont décidés d'exercer comme avocats ou conseillers juridiques. Leur décision a été dictée également par une surcharge de travail qui, en majorité était causée par un nombre insuffisant de personnel auxiliaire ainsi que le manque de compétence chez ce dernier[44].

Le problème du personnel est important; il faudrait qu'il soit proportionné à la charge de différentes juridictions - pénale et civile, et surtout des organismes créés récemment comme les tribunaux de la famille et les tribunaux du travail.

Comment donc se présente le travail du juge et qu'est-ce qui prolonge le temps qu'il consacre à ses obligations? Il y a une autre question primordiale qui

---

40 Rapport de l'Argentine, p. 9.

41 Rapport de l'Italie, p. 3; rapport de la Pologne, p. 18.

42 Rapport de la République Démocratique Allemande, p. 1

43 Rapport de l'Allemagne Fédérale, pp. 31, 27.

44 Rapport de la Pologne, p. 18 (proportion: 1,8 à 1 juge).

apparaît presque dans tous les rapports: à quel degré le juge est chargé des activités qui, effectivement sont liées à sa fonction et dont lui seul peut s'acquitter et à quel degré il est chargé des activités qui résultent d'une mauvaise organisation du travail, de la bureaucratie et sur tout d'un manque de personnel auxiliaire et de secrétariat efficace? Le rapport hollandais fait une distiction entre 'case-load' et 'workload'[45] donc, entre 'surcharge des affaires' et 'surcharge de travail', soulignant qu'il est nécessaire d'alleger le travail des juges en les soulageant d'une partie des travaux qui doivent être effectués par d'autres personnes. Le fait de charger le juge de travaux de ce type peut résulter d'un nombre insuffisant de personnel auxiliaire, des réductions des dépenses et du budget insuffisant prévu par l'Etat pour les dépenses du Ministère de la Justice; le poste du personnel auxiliaire au tribunal présente peu d'attraits, non seulement du point de vue financier - des salaires bas - qui ne sont même pas compensés par un prestige quelconque de ce type de travail (surtout dans de grandes villes; dans la province ce prestige est plus élevé, le poste présente donc plus d'attraits). Ceci est à l'origine des difficultés que pose le recrutement du personnel qualifié; par la suite on est confronté à la difficulté de le garder aux secrétariat des tribunaux afin qu'il acquière l'expérience et la routine[46]. Cela est également lié à l'organisation du travail, degré de modernisation, possibilité de se servir des photocopieuses, ordinateurs et d'autres appareils de ce type. Comme le démontre le rapport italien, dans certains tribunaux, photocopie un document pose déjà des problèmes[47]. En Allemagne Fédérale malgré un accroissement considérable du nombre d'affaires on n'observe pas de prolongation de la durée de la procédure; recrutement du personnel auxiliaire était moins élevé - 20% que l'accroissement du nombre de juges - 39%[48].

L'accent est donc mis non seulement sur le personnel auxiliaire mis à la disposition du juge mais surtout sur l'organisation du à travail et l'accès à l'équipement moderne.

L'autoestimation du travail et des conditions de travail faite par les juges eux-mêmes a une grande importance du point de vue psychologique; surtout quand de jeunes juges comparent leurs conditions de travail à l'équipement moderne, les locaux et le personnel auxiliaire qualifié mis à la disposition des juristes dans des entreprises ou dans de grands cabinets privés[49]. Il est intéressant de comparer les résultats des recherches effectuées en 1981 auprès des trois tribunaux en Hollande où les juges eux-mêmes évaluaient leur surcharge de travail. Le nombre d'heures effectives de travail (d'ailleurs dépassant un peu 40 heures par semaine et se situant entre 42-48 heures) n'est pas conforme à leur évaluation du temps de travail et du certain stress dû à la surcharge de travail[50].

Cela met en valeur le rôle que jouent les conditions et l'organisation du travail ainsi que la réalisation des attentes en ce qui concerne les buts que le

---

45 Rapport de la Hollande, p. 6 et suivantes.

46 Rapport de la Pologne, pp. 17-178.

47 Rapport de l'Italie, p. 3.

48 Rapport de l'Allemagne Fédérale, p. 8.

49 Rapport de la Hollande, p. 16.

50 Rapport de la Hollande, pp. 14-15.

travail du juge doit servir. A part les activités juridictionnelles proprement dites (qui parfois ne sont que des affaires de routine), le temps que le juge peut consacrer aux contacts professionnels ainsi qu'à l'aide qu'il porte à ses jeunes colègues et à la lecture de la littérature juridique n'est pas à négliger.

Certains rapports soulignent également l'importance de la préparation du juge à exercer sa fonction; cela est lié à l'évaluation des études du droit, aux exigences et aux études supplémentaires nécessaires avant son entrée en fonction du juge ainsi qu'à la possibilité de porter à la connaissance des juges de problèmes actuels du droit et de la juridiction au lieu de les laisser se borner aux connaissances acquises.

La pluralité et la dispersion des sources de la loi (surtout en dehors du code), manque de précision dans les lois promulguées qui entraîne des difficultés d'interprétation ainsi que des changements de lois sont aussi des facteurs rendant difficile le travail du juge. L'expérience et la préparation à l'exercice de la fonction dont nous avons parlé plus haut n'y est pas insignifiante. D'après le rapporteur du Japon le travail du juge dans le domaine des affaires nouvelles qui affluent aux tribunaux peut être facilité par les 'procès standarisés' qui, non seulement contribuent à la diminution du nombre d'affaires d'un certain type mais aussi peuvent servir de 'cas modèles' (model cases) aux juges[51].

Du point de vue de l'approche sociologique, la situation profesionnelle des juges ainsi que leur statut social, prestige de leur fonction, indépendance et salaire sont importants. Le contrôle de l'efficacité de leurs activités, effectué par les organes de l'administration judiciaire se présente de différentes manières. Il est discutable d'établir un nombres d'affaires à juge comme critère d'évaluation du travail du juge; d'une part cela éveille beaucoup de réticences comme critère qui peut entraîner à des résultats négatifs dont nous parlerons plus loin dans notre rapport; d'autre part un manque de tout mécanisme de contrôle que l'on observe dans certains systèmes judiciaires (ce contrôle à étant considéré comme un régulateur de ce système et non pas comme un moyen de pression ou de repression) est ressenti comme élément déterminant l'inefficacité croissante des tribunaux[52].

La 'vie quotidienne', la situation sociale du juge ne peuvent pas être approchées en dehors des changements généraux de 'mode à de vie' qui s'opèrent dans des sociétés modernes. Il faut prendre en considération le modèle de la famille 'partnership' et la situation où les deux conjoints travaillent et chacun assume une part d'obligations et de devoirs familiaux; à cela, sans égard à la distinction entre les sexes, s'ajoutent encore des obligations professionnelles[53]. La féminisation de la profession de juge est un problème à part, soulevé et traité d'une façon plus large dans le rapport polonais[54]. En Pologne les femmes constituent 55% des juges; dans les tribunaux régionaux ce chiffre atteint 60%. La majorité d'entre elles sont jeunes, à l'âge de 30-40 ans. Les juges-femmes sont plus souvent absentes au travail que les jugeshommes; elles sont en congé de maternité, en congé pour élever les enfants ou en congé pour garder les enfants malades (à la lumière de la loi en viguer en Pologne

51 Comparer: note n° 18.

52 Rapport de l'Italie, p. 5; rapport de l'Argentine, p. 19.

53 Rapport de l'Allemagne Fédérale, p. 31; rapport de la Pologne, p. 19.

54 Rapport de la Pologne, pp. 18-19.

seulement la mère a droit à ce dernier type de congé; dans des cas exceptionnels ce droit est accordé au père). Si l'absence de la femme-juge se prolonge, les affaires qu'elle traite sont transmises à d'autres juges. D'habitude ces affaires sont repoussées et, étant donné que le nombre d'affaire par juge augmente, elles sont reglées avec des délais. Ce problème n'apparaît pas uniquement en ce qui concerne les juges; les remplacements en cas d'absences prolongées et de congés des femmes nécessite une solution globale.

Il faut aussi mentionner que les juges, surtout les juges de la jeune génération, ne sont pas prêts à prolonger les heures de travail; non seulement cela est lié à leurs obligations familiales mais aussi à l'envie de profiter du temps libre et des weekend et de les consacrer aux loisirs, recréations, sports, donc, d'adopter un mode de vie semblable à celui des gens exerçant d'autres professions.

3.2 L'INFLUENCE DE LA TACTIQUE DES PARTIES, DES AVOCATS ET DES JUGES SUR LA DUREE DU PROCES

Nous avons mentionné au début de notre rapport que les deux parties peuvent prendre un intérêt différent à prolonger ou à accélerer le procès. Les parties en conflit tendent à obtenir une solution favorable au maximum pour elles. D'habitude, la partie demanderesse prend intérêt à obtenir la décision le plus vite possible. Pourtant une décision favorable peut avoir pour elle plus d'importance qu'une décision rapide ('speedy justice'). Une question se pose- comme l'écrit J. Van Houtte[55] - à quel degré les parties essaient de manipuler la durée du procès afin d'obtenir une décision favorable pour elles? Les avocats et les parties qu'ils représentent n'ont pas toujours des intérêts identiques en ce qui concerne la rapidité du procès. Les avocats surchargés d'affaires cherchent à se donner un délai pour certains affaires afin de consacrer plus de temps et d'énergie aux autres. Mais pour eux, également, la possibilité de terminer une affaire dans les délais 'contrôlables' est importante et leur permet de prendre de nouveaux clients. La durée du procès, qui d'habitude relève de l'intérêt de la partie défenderesse (expulsion, prêt) peut être prolongée par une production de nouvelles preuves ou bien par la présentation de nouveaux témoins. Cela, sans doute, compromet le principe de la concentration du matériel du procès. Donc c'est un problème lié à l'aspect procédural, au délai et à la prolongation du procès. Les résultats des recherches concernant le fonctionnement des dispositions en matière de la procédure démontrent que, même là où le juge, par son rôle dirigeant au procès peut limiter l'étendue de ces pratiques, il prend rarement une telle attitude. Tous les rapports postulent donc une réalisation plus rigoureuse du principe de la concentration du procès ou bien demandent de l'introduire.

Une telle attitude des juges n'est pas rare dans la pratique et résulte également d'un manque de temps nécessaire pour préparer l'affaire. (La date de la première audience fixée trop hativement peut être causée par le système d'évaluation de la qualité du travail des juges par les organes de la surveillance

---

55 Rapport du Belgique, pp. 5-6. F.R. Mendez dans: 'Problemi attuali del processo civile in Spagna', Rivista de Diritto Procesuale, 1984 N° 3 attire l'attention sur les conséquences nuisible de ces activités à l'intérêt de la partie.

judiciaire.) Dans ce cas la tactique des parties est volontairement mise à profit par les juges pour fixer une date ultérieure de l'audience suivante. L'attitude du juge peut dépendre des buts principaux du procès, donc, p.ex. du principe de la vérité objective; ce principe est en vigueur dans les pays socialistes. Le juge ne peut limiter le droit à la preuve et souvent, il entreprend lui-même la recherche des preuves si les parties ne sont pas assez actives[56]. Cette attitude, sans doute, prolonge la durée du procès.

Les avocats agissent parfois selon certaines 'règles du jeu' consacrées par la pratique; comme le mentionne S. Goldstein[57], en Israel, les avocats n'aiment pas gagner les affaires en l'absence de l'avocat de l'autre partie: comme s'il y était en vigueur 'un tarif de réciprocité' - aujourd'hui c'est moi, demain c'est toi dans une situation analogique - le temps et d'autres affaires en cours ne te permettront pas d'assister à l'audience. Le prolongement de la durée du procès concerne aussi bien les affaires civiles que les affaires pénales où les avocats, durant l'audience, mettent en question l'opinion des experts, les résultats des expériences judiciaires où demandent d'interroger d'autres témoins; ceci devant être fait lors de la procédure préparatoire. Cela ne relève pas toujours de la tactique des avocats, mais résulte de la tactique des organes de poursuite et de la situation où l'avocat n'a pas d'accès au matériel dont ils disposent.

La surcharge des avocats mène à la situation où les affaires ne sont pas convénablement préparées (priorité étant accordée aux affaires plus compliquées ou plus urgentes), et en conséquence, les avocats ne possèdent pas de conception élaborée de la procédure probatoire.

Les résultats des recherches sur l'arrangement des conflits dans la procédure civile par un jugement ou une transaction, démontrent que l'assistance de l'avocat ne favorise pas l'augmentation du nombre de transactions conclues et prolonge la durée du procès; le rôle médiateur de l'avocat, avant que le tribunal ne soit saisi d'une affaire est un problème à part.

Dans plusieurs pays le nombre d'avocats s'est accru; leurs démarches pour gagner une clientèle sont également considérées comme un facteur important contribuant à une augmentation de nombre d'affaires. Une certaine rivalité peut s'avérer propice à une meilleure préparation des affaires. D'habitude, cela ne change rien en ce qui concerne la charge inégale des avocats; certains avocats ont beaucoup d'affaires, d'autres en ont moins ou très peu. Certaines formes d'organisation de travail des avocats dans différents pays ont aussi leur importance; certains avocats exercent une profession libérale et possède leurs cabinets, d'autres peuvent exercer au sein d'une association, d'une à coopérative d'avocats ou prendre part aux travaux des bureaux de l'aide judiciaire; dans certains pays la loi prévoit l'assistance d'office d'un avocat dans certaines affaires ou donne la possibilité d'apparaître en tant que défenseur devant les tribunaux non seulement aux avocats mais aussi à d'autres personnes ayant une formation juridique.

La tactique choisie pour le procès, le principe de la concentration du procès et son application réelle sont des problèmes à étroitement liés à l'influence des dispositions procédurales sur la durée du procès. Une approche plus générale laissent apercevoir différents avis. E. Blankenburg insiste sur la tendence

---

56 Rapport de la Pologne, pp. 15 et suivantes.

57 S. Goldstein, 'Possibilities and problems of the acceleration of the civil litigation process', p. 9.

croissante à formaliser les dispositions procédurales comme facteur très important de la prolongation de la durée du procès. K. Röhl trouve[58], en s'appuyant sur l'exemple de l'Allemagne Fédérale, que les dispositions procédurales ne freinent pas la rapidité du procès; dans son pays, malgré une affluence d'affaires aux tribunaux, une nette prolongation de la durée du procès ni une diminution de sa qualité n'ont été notées. A. Abel avertit des dangers que peut engendrer une procédure fort déformalisée. Un certain degré de formalisation des procédures garantit la réalisation du principe de la légalité, permet de régler les conflits d'une façon rationnelle et objective et devient ainsi un déterminant légitimant la juridiction[59].

4 CONCLUSIONS ET QUESTIONS SOUMISES A LA DISCUSSION

Les problèmes principaux qui apparaissent à la lumière du rapport général peuvent être présentés sous formes de questions qui serviront de point de depart à la discussion.

1. Quand pouvons-nous parler de la surcharge des tribunaux, des délais et d'une prolongation excessive du procès? Est-ce que nous pouvons nous référer à des critères objectifs, et dans l'affirmative, est-ce que ces critères sont les mêmes dans différents pays et différentes cultures juridiques?
2. Si, malgré un accroissement considérable du nombre d'affaires d'un certain type (disproportionné par rapport au nombre de juges) la durée du procès ne se prolonge pas, cela ne se fait-il pas aux dépens de la qualité du procès? Est-ce que nous pouvons appliquer ici des indices objectifs, p.ex. le nombre d'affaires renvoyées aux tribunaux de premier degré ou bien d'autres indices et lesquels?
3. A quel degré l'affluence des affaires aux tribunaux est inhérente au changement des rapports sociaux (de leur caractère): migrations, cycles économiques et à la juridisation de la vie sociale, et à quel degré peut-elle être attribuée aux changements de la structure sociale et au changement de la conscience à juridique, aux attitudes revendicatives plus fréquentes tendant à la réalisation des droits par voie judiciaire?
4. Est-ce que l'on peut réaliser le postulat de limiter un accès trop facile à la justice sans compromettre l'accès au droit et à l'aide juridique? A quel degré pouvons-nous avoir recours à: a) élimination des 'affaires inutiles', b) restrictions en matière des assurances du type 'Rechtsschutzversicherung', c) augmentation des coûts du procès, d) des 'procès standarisés?
5. Faut-il alléger les tribunaux des affaires futiles, jugées comme affaires de routine ou des affaires liées aux rapports du travail et aux contracts collectifs en les transmettant pour attribution aux institutions à caractère social ou administratif (conformément à la nature de l'affaire) et, dans ce cas, simplifier au maximum la procédure? Faut-il donc laisser aux tribunaux uniquement les

58 K. Röhl (Hrsg.), Der Vergleich im Zivilprozess, Opladen 1983, p. 196. 'Skutecznosc rozstrzygania sporów w postepowaniu cywilnym w praktyce i opinii stron' ('Efficacité du procès civil en matière d'arrangement des litiges à la lumière de la pratique et des opinions des parties') sous la direction de M. Borucka-Arctowa (ouvrage sous presse).

59 R. Abel, 'Delegalization: A critical review of its ideology, manifestations and social consequences', dans: Alternativen Rechtsformen und Alternativen zum Recht 1980, Opladen, pp. 39 et suivantes.

affaires importantes, compliquées, qui exigent une approche individualisée et auxquelles il faut consacrer plus de temps? Est-ce que, au contraire, les devoirs de la justice ne peuvent pas être transmis de plus en plus souvent à d'autres institutions compte tenu du fait qu'ils ne donnent pas toutes les garanties en matière du procès et que la fonction des tribunaux ne consiste pas uniquement à trancher les conflits, mais aussi à confirmer certaines valeurs et normes, 'ce qui est à juste' donc à la légitimation du droit?

6. Est-il juste de tendre à diminuer la formalisation des prescriptions procédurales ce qui contribuera à raccourcissement du procès? Ou bien l'opinion que surtout d'autres facteurs influencent la durée du procès et qu'une déformalisation du procès met en danger les valeurs telles que: légalité, objectivité et sûreté du droit, est-elle plus convaincante?

7. A quel degré le principe de concentration du procès peut-il attribuer à raccourcir sa durée, compte tenu du fait que la tactique (sous différentes formes) de faire prolonger la durée du procès est enracinée et acceptée dans la pratique pour différentes raisons présentées dans le présent rapport?

8. Est-ce que la thèse selon laquelle la surcharge des tribunaux dépend de l'organisation du système judiciaire ainsi que de la surcharge des juges du travail relevant de la compétence du personnel est juste? Est-ce que cela ne se présente pas comme un élément déterminant l'estimation de leur travail par les juges eux-mêmes et la satisfaction de leur profession?

CONCLUSIONS ET QUESTIONS SOUMISES DE LA DISCUSSION

Les problèmes principaux qui apparaissent à la lumière du rapport général peuvent être présentés sous formes de questions qui serviront de point de départ à la discussion.

1. Quand pouvons-nous parler de la surcharge des tribunaux, des délais et d'une prolongation excessive du procès? Est-ce que nous pouvons nous référer à des critères objectifs, et dans l'affirmative, est-ce que ces critères sont les mêmes dans différents pays et différentes cultures juridiques?

2. Si, malgré un accroissement considérable du nombre d'affaire d'un certain type (disproportionné par rapport au nombre de juges) la durée du procès ne se prolonge pas, cela ne se fait-il pas aux dépens de la qualité du procès? Est-ce que nous pouvons appliquer ici des indices objectifs, p.ex. le nombre d'affaires renvoyées aux tribunaux de premier degré ou bien d'autres indices et lesquels?

3. A quel degré l'affluence des affaires aux tribunaux est inhérente au changement des rapports sociaux (de leur caractère): migrations, cycles économiques et à la juridisation de la vie sociale, et à quel degré peut-elle être attribuée aux changements de la structure sociale et au changement de la conscience juridique, aux attitudes revendicatives plus fréquentes tendant à la réalisation des droits par voie judiciaire?

4. Est-ce que l'on peut réaliser le postulat de limiter un accès trop facile à la justice sans compromettre l'accès au droit et à l'aide juridique? A quel degré pouvons-nous avoir recours à: a) élimination des 'affaires inutiles', b) restrictions en matière des assurances du type 'Rechtsschutzversicherung', c) augmentation des coûts du procès, d) popularisation des 'procès standarisés?

5. Faut-il alleger les tribunaux des affaires futiles, jugées comme affaires de routine ou des affaires liées aux rapports du travail et aux contracts collectifs en les transmettant pour attribution aux institutions à caractère social ou administratif (conformément à la nature de l'affaire) et, dans ce cas, simplifier au maximum la procédure? Faut-il donc laisser aux tribunaux uniquement les affaires importantes, compliquées, qui exigent une approche individualisée et auxquelles il faut consacrer plus de temps? Est-ce que, au contraire, les devoirs de la justice ne peuvent pas être transmis de plus en plus souvent à d'autres institutions compte tenu du fait qu'ils de donnent pas toutes les garanties en matiere du procès et que la fonction des tribunaux ne consiste pas uniquement à trancher les conflits, mais aussi à confirmer certaines valeurs et normes, 'ce qui est juste' donc à la légitimation du droit?

6. Est-il juste de tendre à diminuer la formalisation des prescriptions procédurales ce qui contribuera à un raccourcissement du procès? Ou bien l'opinion que surtout d'autres facteurs influencent la durée du procès et qu'une déformalisation du procès met en danger les valeurs telles que: légalité, objectivité et sûreté du droit, est-elle plus convaincante?

7. A quel degré le principe de concentration du procès peut-il attribuer à raccourcir sa durée, compte tenu du fait que la tactique (sous différentes formes) de faire prolonger la durée du procès est enracinée et acceptée dans la pratique pour différentes raisons présentées dans le présent rapport?

8. Est-ce que la thèse selon laquelle la surcharge des tribunaux dépend de l'organisation du système judiciaire ainsi que de la surcharge des juges du travail relevant de la compétence du personnel est juste? Est-ce que cela ne se présente pas comme un élément déterminant l'estimation de leur travail par les juges eux-mêmes et la satisfaction de leur profession?

REPORT OF THE DISCUSSION

Chairman: *E. Vescovi (Uruguay)*
Vice-chairman: *R.O. Berinzonce (Argentina)*
Secretary: *S.E. Römer (Netherlands Antilles)*

The discussionpoints are to be found at the pages 37, 43 and 65.

Mr. Römer's report of the discussion did not reach us in time, due to illness.

MANAGING OVERLOAD IN APPELLATE COURTS (INCLUDING SUPREME JURISDICTION)

MANAGING OVERLOAD IN APPELLATE COURTS: 'WESTERN' COUNTRIES

J.A. Jolowicz[1]
Professor of Comparative Law in the University of Cambridge

National reports from eighteen countries have been received for this part of the general report[2]. Though all deal with countries of the 'West'[3], they reveal so great a variety of appellate systems that it is difficult to find common ground on which to base a comparative account of the problem of overload and its management, and the difficulty is compounded by the fact that, naturally and correctly, the national reporters tend to take more or less for granted the

---

1 To some extent this report is a sequel to the author's general report to the International Congress on the Law of Civil Procedure held in Ghent in 1977. That report is published under the title 'Appellate Proceedings' in Storme and Casman (ed.), **Towards a Justice with a Human Face**, 1978, pp. 127-165, and is hereafter cited as 'Jolowicz'.

2 The general reporter expresses his most sincere gratitude to the national reporters whose names are set out below. Many of the reports contain a wealth of information much of which it has been impossible to mention here. The shape of the general report and the matters with which it deals is the choice of the general reporter alone, and he apologises to those national reporters whose views he may have misrepresented or of whose reports he has taken inadequate account. The following reports have been received:
Australia: Mr. E W. Wright
Austria: Dr. Ena-Marlis Bajons
Belgium: Prof. J. van Compernolle and Mme. G. Closset-Marchal
Canada: Prof. G.D. Watson
Chile: Profs. Carlos Pecchi Croce and Eleodoro Ortiz Sepulveda
England: Mr. Registrar J.D.R. Adams
France: Mlle. Françoise Grivart de Kerstrat
Federal Republic of Germany: Prof. Peter Gottwald
Greece: Prof. P. Kargados
Israel: Prof. Shimon Shetreet
Italy: Prof. Romano Vaccarella
Japan: Prof. A. Ishikawa
Netherlands: Prof. H.J. Snijders
South Africa: Prof. J. Taitz
Spain: Prof. Victor Fairen-Guillen
Sweden: Judge Anders Bruzelius
Uruguay: Profs. Martha Jardi Abella and Graciela Barcelona
United States of America: Prof. Robert S. Thompson
A report for India by Prof. K.B. Agrawal was also received but, unfortunately, too late for it to be taken into acount in the preparation of this report.

3 For the position in the socialist countries of Europe see the separate report by Dr. Janos Németh.

fundamentals of their own systems even though those fundamentals are by no means the same for all. Again, most of the national reports enter into considerable detail and between them provide not only a most valuable collection of material on different legal systems but a vivid illustration of the dissimilarities that are to be found even amongst systems which share a common history and tradition. There are systems which distinguish sharply between 'appeal', strictly so called, and 'cassation'; there are federal systems in which the federal supreme court acts as the final court of appeal for the whole country and others in which it acts only in federal cases; there are systems which, though unitary, have separate jurisdictions for 'private' and 'public' law cases and others with a unified hierarchy of courts: there are systems with one tier only after first instance and others with two or even more; there are systems in which the appeal has a suspensive effect and others in which first instance judgments are enforceable as soon as given. Even more striking than these differences, however, is the difference in the volume of appellate work in countries of roughly comparable size, and in their attitudes to the 'right of appeal' and to possible limitations of it. So, to take a dramatic example, in England the 'supreme court' - the House of Lords - has jurisdiction in 'public' as well as 'private' law, has a mere ten full time judges, is not divided into several chambers, is a court of appeal not cassation, and delivers judgment in about 50 cases a year. In Italy, by contrast, the supreme court has only limited 'public' law jurisdiction, is divided into several chambers which sit simultaneously, is a court of cassation not of appeal, and delivers judgment in several thousand cases every year. In England appeal to the House of Lords is possible only with the prior leave of the court *a quo* or the House itself, while in Italy the right of recourse to the court of cassation is constitutionally protected and, though this alone is not sufficient to explain such different caseloads, it does illustrate a difference of attitude: in Italy recourse to the supreme court is a matter of right; in England it is exceptional.

Faced with such extremes, faced also with differences in the character of the proceedings at first instance[4], the general reporter must limit the scope of his report and must proceed on the basis of a number of assumptions. It is necessary to ride rough shod over some of the distinctions which are built in to some systems but unknown in others such as, for example, the distinction between 'appeal' and 'cassation'. To change the metaphor, a broad brush tends admittedly to conceal nice points of detail but is essential to a comparative report which crosses the dividing line between legal 'families', and if one were not used here this report would not only be of inordinate length but would be incoherent and incomprehensible.

For the purposes of this report, save where the context otherwise indicates, it is necessary to adopt the following conventions:

1. The word 'appeal' is used in relation to any proceedings subsequent to the decision at first instance[5] which come before a court higher than the court of

---

4 See Jolowicz, 137-141.

5 Including decisions which are interlocutory or 'avant dire droit'.

first instance[6], whether classified internally as 'appeal', 'cassation', or 'revision', and whether that higher court can give its own decision on the substance of the case or is limited to the affirmation or annulment of the decision *a quo*. 'Appeal' does not, however, extend to procedures which come before the court of first instance itself such as the *opposition* or the American application to the trial judge himself for a new trial.

2. Although, of course, where an appellate court has criminal as well as civil jurisdiction criminal appeals form part of its caseload[7], only civil appeals will be directly considered. On the other hand, save by necessary implication, the distinction between appeals in 'civil' and in 'administrative' cases, which exists where there are separate jurisdictions but not elsewhere, will be ignored.

3. Account will be taken only of appeals from first instance decisions made within the regular judicial hierarchy. This includes appeals from judicial determinations of the validity or otherwise of decisions originally made outside that hierarchy such as the decisions of 'administrative tribunals' as known in England, but it does not include procedures such as the English 'application for judicial review'[8] whereby those decisions can be challenged in the courts of first instance.

4. It will be assumed that appeals are instituted by a party to the original litigation or, at least, by a person who has a direct interest in the outcome of the litigation. As will appear, the right of recourse to the supreme court which is accorded in some countries to a representative of the public to be used 'in the interest of the law' has important theoretical implications, but it is little used in practice.

5. Finally, and most importantly, it will be taken for granted that every appellate system has a purpose or purposes, however concealed, against which the existence of overload can be determined - a court is overloaded not only if it has a growing backlog of pending cases but also if it cannot adequately fulfil the purpose or purposes for which it exists - and against which measures taken or to be taken for the 'management' of overload can be assessed. As used here, therefore, 'purpose' does not refer to the purpose of the individual litigant who exercises a right of appeal but to the purpose for which the right is granted. It follows, since no procedural right is granted in order that it may be abused, that measures intended to minimise abuse of the right of appeal are intrinsically justifiable provided only that they do not jeopardise fulfillment of the purposes for which the right itself exists. This aspect of the management of overload is mentioned later in this report, but otherwise it will be assumed that where a right of appeal is exercised it is exercised in good faith.

---

6 A 'Full Court' such as the Full Court of the Australian State Supreme Courts, though a manifestation of the same court as the court of first instance, is here treated as a 'higher' court. See, however post, p. 13.

7 See U.S.A., pp. 3-5.

8 R.S.C. 0. 53.

1 PURPOSE OF APPEAL

It is a wide spread phenomenon of the contemporary world that, by comparison with the past, there has been a great increase in litigation generally. The reasons for this are beyond the scope of this report, but obviously it has led to increased demands on the appellate system. To some extent this increase in demand can be and has been met by an increase in the total number of appellate judges and by a reduction in the quorum of judges required to constitute a court or chamber for the decision of a given case. There are, however, limits to what can be done in this way, and the limits are not only economic: if the number of judges is increased by too many it may be difficult to find sufficient people of the right calibre for appointment[9]; if too many courts or chambers are in session simultaneously the danger that even supreme courts will produce decisions which conflict with one another and thus endanger both the coherence and the comprehensibility of the law will be increased[10]. Almost everywhere, therefore, a variety of procedural techniques has been adopted or is under active consideration with a view to keeping the case loads of appellate courts within bounds.

By and large, these techniques fall into two main groups. In the first place there are techniques which are intended to control the number of cases in which an appeal is instituted, of which an obvious, widely adopted, and rather crude, example is the simple denial of all right of appeal in certain kinds of case. In the second place there are techniques which are intended to enable appellate courts to dispose more expeditiously of the cases that actually come before them. It is the principal purpose of this report to consider some of these techniques, but if it is manifest that an appellate court is overloaded if its backlog of pending cases increases from year to year, it is also manifest that overload can prejudice its ability to fulfil the purposes for which it exists. Unfortunately, devices or techniques adopted to reduce or 'manage' overload may also affect adversely the capacity of an appellate court to fulfil those purposes. It is necessary, therefore, to set out briefly, and perhaps somewhat superficially, the purposes for which appellate systems exist. These purposes can be divided into two broad categories which, for convenience, are here called the 'private' and the 'public', but, although each is separately outlined below, it should not be supposed that they are or can be kept rigidly apart in practice.

1.1 THE 'PRIVATE' PURPOSE

The 'private' purpose behind the grant of a right of appeal is two-fold, but its two parts coalesce. On the one hand it is to respond to the natural desire that failure at first instance may inspire in a litigant to have his case reconsidered at a higher level, and on the other it is to ensure so far as possible that justice is done to the parties. To fulfil the private purpose to the maximum possible extent, therefore, an appellate court needs jurisdiction to entertain

9 See Chile, p. 11; Israel, pp. 23, 27; Uruguay, p. 17.

10 U.S.A., p. 18.

questions of fact as well as of law, it needs the right to substitute its own decision for that of the court *a quo* not merely to declare that decision right or wrong, and it needs the right to receive evidence that was not available and arguments that were not submitted to that court; *nova* should not, in principle, be excluded.

The extent to which appellate courts satisfy these requirements in practice varies greatly, not only from one legal system to another but between different levels within a single legal system, especially when one level is of 'appeal', the other of 'cassation.' The further a particular appellate procedure departs from the theoretical concept of a complete *novum judicium* the less able it is to fulfil the private purpose in those cases that come before the courts, but 'justice delayed is justice denied' and so, if the private purpose is to be adequately met whenever the right of appeal is invoked, some such departure is almost inevitable; in few, if any, appellate courts today is a complete *novum judicium* available. On the other hand, bearing in mind that except when the appeal is brought by a public authority 'in the interest of the law'[11], no court is seized of an appeal except on the initiative of a party, it is almost inevitable that the judges will pay some regard to the interests of the parties before them whatever the nature of the procedure. To a greater or lesser extent, the private purpose is always there.

1.2 THE 'PUBLIC' PURPOSE

To some extent, in theory as well as practice, there is overlap between the public and the private purposes if only because a legal system which fails adequately to meet the latter will forfeit public confidence, and it is essential in the public interest that confidence in the administration of justice be maintained. More specifically, however, appellate courts serve a public purpose in at least two different ways. First, and most obviously, when an appeal is brought on the ground of an alleged procedural error in the court below, they act in a supervisory capacity to ensure that courts of first instance themselves act in accordance with the law. Secondly, the decisions of appellate courts- especially but by no means exclusively those of supreme courts - make essential contributions to the development and clarification of the law itself. In common law countries which formally recognise the rule *stare decisis* this is obviously the case, but it is unnecessary to discuss the place of judicial decisions as a 'source of law' in other countries for there are few if any of the countries whose law is codified which still deny that judicial decisions as such contribute to the content of the law. It is sufficient here simply to cite the Italian law which states, in regard to the court of cassation of that country, that its task is to ensure 'the exact observance and the uniform interpretation of the law, the unity of national law'[12]. It is obvious that overload of an appellate court can have serious adverse effects on its ability to fulfil at least this aspect of the public purpose for the simple reason that its judges will not be able to devote the time necessary to the full consideration and discussion of those

---

11 Typically, the outcome of such appeals does not affect the parties to the litigation.

12 Law on Court Organization, art. 65, transl., Cappelletti and others, **The Italian Legal System**, p. 150.

cases which raise difficult and important questions of law if their case load is too great. Paradoxically, it appears that this problem is most serious in courts of cassation where, theoretically, questions of fact are not open and the public purpose, theoretically, predominates, than it is in common law supreme courts whose procedures differ little from those of the intermediate courts of appeal and whose role as 'guardian' of the law is not legislatively spelled out.

2 RESTRICTION ON RIGHT OF APPEAL

It is the intention of this section to examine some of the techniques which are used to keep cases out of the appellate courts by restricting the right of appeal or by qualifying it in some way. It must not be overlooked, however, that the initiation of an appeal is a voluntary act, and if an unsuccessful litigant is content to allow the judgment against him to stand he will not appeal. The risk of incurring an additional liability for costs is, no doubt, a factor of importance[13] and may explain, at least historically, the extremely low case load of some courts such as the House of Lords in England but, while an element of disincentive through the costs sanction may be justifiable, as a matter of principle it must not be carried too far. On the other hand, if even the defeated litigant at first instance normally accepts the decision as final, recognising that justice has been done, there will be relatively few appeals. Conversely, if the appeal is regarded as little more than a continuation of the proceedings at first instance, if it comes to be the general opinion that a 'real' decision is given only in the appellate court, then the burden on that court is obviously increased. The national reports reveal a cleavage of attitudes to the place of the (first) appeal which must be mentioned before turning to more detailed matters.

2.1 THE 'FINALITY' OF THE FIRST INSTANCE

It was not until the nineteenth Century that the English common law came to have a true appeal - the 'writ of error' was both technical and limited in scope - and in any event most cases were tried at first instance before a jury. Even today, although an extensive right of appeal exists and is recognised as essential to the due administration of justice[14], it continues to be insisted that all rights of appeal are 'statutory', the significance of which is that if specific provision for appeal is not made no right of appeal exists. It follows that, both in the past and at the present time, the decision at first instance is usually taken as final, and the same is true by and large in other common law countries. So, for example, a first instance judgment is enforceable as soon as given - the appeal has no 'suspensive' effect unless a stay of execution is granted by the court - and even where the appeal is described as a 'rehearing', as it is in most common law countries other than the United States, it falls well short of a complete *novum judicium*. Most common lawyers, it is believed,

13 See e.g. Germany, p. 3; Israel, p. 18; Netherlands, pp. 17-18; Spain, p. 4.

14 See, e.g. **Final Report of the Committee on Supreme Court Practice and Procedure**, Cmd. 8878 (1953), para. 473.

would agree with the view recently expressed by an Australian judge that, 'It is fundamental to the due administration of justice that the substantial issues between the parties are ordinarily settled at the trial. If it were not so the main arena for the settlement of disputes would move from the court of first instance to the appellate court, tending to reduce proceedings in the former to little more than a preliminary skirmish'[15].

A similar attitude prevails in Austria, in accordance with the opinion of the architect of its code, Franz Klein[16], but in most of the other countries covered by this report, the principle of the double instance is held to be an essential guarantee of justice, and, unless 'provisional execution' is ordered, and subject to a few exceptions[17], no judgment is enforceable until the time for appealing has expired or the appeal has been determined[18]. In these countries there must be at least a risk that the degradation of the first instance mentioned above may become a reality as, apparently, occurred in Germany[19]. In that country reforms introduced in 1976 were intended, amongst other things, to improve the status of first instance decisions, and it appears that the measures taken succeeded for a time. Now, however, the national reporter indicates that the number of appeals entered is rising once more[20].

2.2 EXCLUSION FROM APPEAL

(a) Small cases. In many countries no right of appeal exists from decisions in cases of less than a certain value[21]. Most of these, however, are countries in which the 'appeal' is sharply distinguished from cassation, and, generally, the

---

15 **Coulton** v. **Holcombe** (1986) 60 A.L.J.R. 470, 473, **per** Gibbs C.J. , cited Australia, 13. See also, the opinion of Professor Denti, cited Italy, p. 7.

16 Austria, p. 2.

17 E.g., Uruguay, p. 12 (maintenance of children).

18 Belgium, p. 3, Chile, para. 2.1.1, France, p. 3, Germany, pp. 5, 24, Greece, pp. 3, 5, 8, Italy, pp. 6-7, Japan, pp. 12, 13, Netherlands, pp. 4, 6, Spain, p. 3, Sweden, p. B 18, Uruguay, p. 3. See Jolowicz, pp. 160-162. Usually commencement of cassation proceedings has no similar 'suspensive' effect, but this is not the case in Uruguay, where a procedure in the nature of cassation was introduced in replacement of a third instance only in 1979: Uruguay, pp. 3, 13. In Italy, a change in the law to remove the automatic 'suspensive' effect is under consideration notwithstanding its reaffirmation as recently as 198[illegible], but as the Italian reporter observes, the new proposal coincides in time with an extension in the use of single-judge courts of first instance and therefore risks giving too much power to a single judge: Italy, pp. 8-9.

19 See Gilles, 'Die Berufung in Zivilsachen und die zivilgerichtliche Instanzordnung', a report originally prepared for the 1977 Congress of the Association, in **Humane Justiz** (ed. Gilles, 1977), pp. 150, 154. Germany, p. 24; Greece, p. 3. See Jolowicz, p. 145.

20 Germany, pp. 21, 22.

21 Belgium, p. 9 (appeal is, however, available against all decisions of industrial tribunals); Chile, p. 5; France, p. 3; Germany, p. 2; Greece, pp. 3-4, 21 where, however, the exclusion of appeals is relatively easily overcome; Italy, Liebman, **Manuale di diritto processuale civile.** ed. 4, II, no. 315; Netherlands, p. 4; Uruguay, p. 5. A similar exclusion of appeal for cases of low value exists in some Provinces of Canada (Canada, p. 16) and some states of the U.S.A. (U.S.A., p. 8). For the difficulties that may be experienced in determining the value of a case, see Belgium, pp. 10-11.

exclusion of the 'appeal' does not involve also the exclusion of cassation[22], but this is not the case in Chile[23], while in the Netherlands cassation in small cases is available only on the ground of violation by the court below of procedural requirements[24]. A similar emphasis on procedural requirements is found in Austria where, although in principle all first instance judgments are appealable, in small cases the admissible grounds of appeal are restricted[25].

No doubt, the removal of small cases from the appellate system provides a measure of relief, and the Spanish reporter refers specifically to the absence of a relevant rule of exclusion in his country as one of the causes of congestion[26]. This does not, however, lead him to the conclusion that such a rule should be introduced since to do so would reduce the guarantee of justice, especially for the less well-endowed litigants[27], and the Austrian reporter makes a similar criticism of the parallel rule in that country[28]. The Dutch reporter, by contrast, considers that even the limited right of recourse to the court of cassation allowed in the Netherlands in small cases should be removed on account of the disproportionate cost that is involved[29].

The conflict of policy that arises when the exclusion of small cases from the appellate system is achieved by direct rule is clear, and it can be avoided, though not without the introduction of other difficulties, if the right of appeal is subjected to the prior grant of leave, and this is the preferred method of control in some common law countries[30] and also in Sweden[31]. So, to take the example of English law as it has been since 1981, no appeal lies from a decision of a County Court in any case in which the amount at stake is equal to less than one half of the jurisdictional limit of that court unless leave to appeal is granted by either the judge of the County Court or the Court of Appeal itself[32].

---

22 Belgium, II, p. 5; France, p. 5; Italy, Liebman, **op. cit.**, no. 332.

23 Chile, p. 5.

24 Netherlands, p. 6.

25 Austria, p. 13.

26 Spain, p. 3.

27 **Ibid.**, p. 4.

28 Austria, p. 19.

29 Netherlands, pp. 6-7. In the Netherlands cassation is only open in small case on the ground of violation of procedural rules. In Japan, the **Jokuku** appeal, which is similar to cassation, comes before the High Court, not the Supreme Court, in small cases, with a possibility that the case may still reach the supreme court: Japan, pp. 14-15.

30 Australia, pp. 31-32; England, p. 2.

31 Sweden, p. B9, where the criteria for the grant of leave are set out.

32 County Courts Act 1959, s. 108, as amended in 1981; County Courts Appeals Order, 1981. If leave is refused by the County Court Judge the application for leave is ordinarily dealt with by a single judge of the Court of Appeal. The new rule has the advantage that, unlike its predecessor, it makes no use of the elusive distinction between questions of law and questions of fact. See Jolowicz, pp. 134-137.

(b) Interlocutory decisions. In countries in which the principle of double instance is held to be an essential guarantee of justice, any exclusion of a right of appeal, even against a relatively insignificant interlocutory decision, requires special legislation, and though such legislation exists it tends to receive a restrictive interpretation[33]. Nevertheless, as is pointed out most forcibly by the Chilean reporters[34], interlocutory appeals hold up the progress of the litigation and may be introduced purely for the purpose of causing delay. It is not uncommon, therefore, that specific legislation excludes altogether appeals from certain interlocutory decisions - those which can affect the final outcome only indirectly if at all[35]. A rule of more general application is, however, adopted in a number of countries in accordance with which the appeal against an interlocutory decision is available only in conjunction with the appeal against the final decision of the case at first instance[36]. This has the advantage of preserving the right of appeal while preventing its exercise from delaying a decision, but conversely it gives rise to a need to define more or less precisely what is truly an 'interlocutory' decision and that in itself can cause difficulty[37].

The postponement of interlocutory appeals as just described is not possible in the common law systems; any such appeal must be disposed of before the trial of the action for the simple reason that the main purpose of interlocutory proceedings is to prepare the case for trial. Nowhere, however, is there any longer an absolute right of appeal against interlocutory decisions[38]. An appeal lies only with leave[39]. Here too, difficulty sometimes arises in determining whether a particular decision is 'interlocutory' for the purposes of the rule requiring leave[40], and, of course, decision of the question whether leave should be granted itself involves the use of judicial time[41]. Unless interlocutory appeals were to be forbidden altogether, however, and that seems nowhere to be in contemplation, the requirement of leave seems to be the only control that is possible.

---

33 E.g. Belgium, pp. 6-7.

34 Chile, no. 3.7.a); Italy, pp. 11-12.

35 Austria, p. 15; Belgium, p. 7; Chile, no. 1.3.b); Germany, p. 3; Uruguay, p. 6. In France certain decisions such as those ordering an expertise or to delay judgment can be appealed as soon as given only with the prior authorization of the Premier Président of the Court of Appeal: n.c.p.c., arts. 272, 377.

36 Austria, p. 15; France, p. 3; Germany, p. 3; Greece, p. 4; Spain, but only in specified categories of litigation, p. 4; Uruguay, pp. 5-6. The reports for the Netherlands (see p. 5) and for Sweden (see p. B.14) deal only with appeals from final judgments.

37 See e.g. France, p. 4.

38 It is true that in England, where interlocutory decisions are usually made in the first instance by a 'Master', the Masters' decisions can always be reconsidered **de novo** by a judge, but this does not involve the appellate courts and, it seems, does not create a serious problem of delay.

39 Australia, p. 14; Canada, p. 15, where it is stated that in Ontario, at least, that leave may be granted only for specified reasons; England, p. 2; Israel, p. 2; U.S.A., p. 9.

40 E.g. Canada, p. 15 and the English **Supreme Court Practice 1985**. paras. 59/1/15 - 59/1/17.

41 See e.g. U.S.A., p. 9. The requirement of a grant of leave to appeal is widely used in common law jurisdictions and in some other countries including Austria and Sweden.

(c) Appeal subject to leave (Supreme Courts). Interlocutory appeals apart, the requirement that an appellant first obtain leave to appeal is now widely used to control the case load of the supreme court. In the common law countries covered by this report it is only where there is no 'intermediate' court of appeal, so that the only appeal is to the supreme court, that no prior grant of leave is required[42]. In South Africa, since 1983, leave is required for an appeal to the supreme court - the Appellate Division - even though there is no intermediate appeal[43]. Leave to appeal to the supreme court is now also required in Sweden[44], in Germany[45] and, where there is less than a certain sum at stake, in Austria[46]. No such requirement exists, on the other hand, in countries whose legal systems follow the French model[47]. There, in principle, appeal to the supreme court is limited to questions of law, and this limitation is considered in the next section. The attempt will then be made to give a brief comparative account of the way in which each method of control operates to enable supreme courts to fulfil the purposes for which they exist.

Obviously, the interposition of a requirement that leave to appeal be obtained involves the use of judicial time in the hearing of applications for such leave[48], and there is considerable variation in the procedures adopted. In some countries, such as England[49], application for leave to appeal to the House of Lords is made, first, to the Court of Appeal and if rejected a further application may be made to a committee of the House of Lords; in Australia[50], Canada[51], and the United States[52], the supreme court alone controls the cases that come before it, and the same is true for Sweden[53]. In Germany the task is divided between the courts of appeal and the Supreme Court according to the value of

42 I.e., a few of the American states (U.S.A., p. 2); Israel, except when the case was decided at first instance in a Magistrates Courts, in which case appeal lies to the District Court and a further appeal is then possible, but only with leave, to the Supreme Court: Israel, p. 2.

43 South Africa, p. 6.

44 Sweden, p. B9.

45 Germany, pp. 2-3, 17. Until 1975 no leave was necessary in cases involving more than DM 40,000 (c. £14,000).

46 At present AS 300,000 (c. £12,500). The position is actually very complex since in some circumstances a distinction falls to be taken between appeals from appellate decisions which affirm the decision at first instance and from those which modify it or set it aside: Austria, pp. 13-14.

47 See, e.g., Netherlands, p. 20. The old Chambre des Requêtes of the French Cour de cassation, which was abolished in 1947, might be regarded as a body which, in effect, granted or withheld 'leave to appeal' since it could reject but could not allow an appeal, and the same might be said of the 'formations restreintes' as originally created in 1979. Since 1981, however, the formations restreintes have had power in appropriate cases to allow as well as to dismiss the appeal: see **post** p. 13.

48 See e.g. U.S.A., p. 18 and the discussion in Netherlands, p. 20.

49 Administration of Justice (Appeals) Act 1934. The position since 1983 is similar in South Africa: South Africa, p. 6. In Austria also, both levels of jurisdiction may be involved: Austria, p. 14.

50 Australia, p. 10.

51 Canada, p. 5. Prior to 1975, leave to appeal to the Supreme Court was not required if the amount at stake was more than $10,000 (c. £6,500).

52 U.S.A., p. 18.

53 Sweden, p. B9.

the case[54]. There is also a good deal of variation in the procedure for dealing with applications for leave to appeal. Where these are dealt with by the court *a quo*, the matter can be quickly and informally disposed of since the court already has full knowledge of the case, but where they come before the supreme court something more elaborate is required. To take just two examples, in England applications come before a committee of three judges of the House of Lords and the procedure is initially written: a petition may be dismissed, but not granted, without an oral hearing[55]. In Canada there is an oral hearing before three Supreme Court judges with argument limited to 15 minutes on each side, but legislation is pending to allow a decision to be made on a written procedure unless an oral hearing is specifically ordered[56]. Similar proposals have, however, been rejected in Australia on the ground that it is an important part of the court's business to decide what cases it will hear[57].

One final variation must be mentioned, namely the extent to which, if at all, the grounds upon which leave to appeal may be granted is specified by law. In Germany only questions of law may be entertained[58], in Canada the legislation makes it clear that leave will not be granted if the case is of interest only to the parties; there must be an important issue of law or at least a question of public importance[59]. In most common law countries, however, there is little legislative control and the grant of leave is left to judicial discretion. In the United States, for example, the Supreme Court will hear an appeal only if there are 'special reasons'[60] and in England no criteria are stated. Whatever the legislation, however, and exceptional cases only apart, appeals to supreme courts are admitted only if there is a point of importance calling for decision at that level; the number of cases admitted for full consideration is kept low enough to enable the judges to give to each the attention necessary for its fully motivated decision. This is not to say that some supreme courts are not under pressure but, at least by comparison with courts of cassation, their case loads are very low indeed. In England the House of Lords decides only about 50 civil cases per year[61]; in Australia, Canada and Sweden the number is similar[62], while in the United States it is under 200[63]. Of the countries so far mentioned, only the

---

54 Germany, p. 2.

55 Directions as to Procedure, **Supreme Court Practice**, 1985, paras. 6-8.

56 Canada, p. 6.

57 Australia, p. 42.

58 Germany, pp. 2-4 See also Austria, pp. 13-14; Sweden, pp. B9-10, cf. p. B20.

59 Canada, p. 5. A remarkable feature of the Canadian position is that the Supreme Court has itself established administrative guidelines for the number of cases in which leave will be granted in each year.

60 Supreme Court Rules, Rule 19(1).

61 In 1985 it disposed of 66 cases in all, of which 10 were from Scotland and 14 were in criminal cases. In the same year it dealt with 125 civil applications for leave to appeal and the appeals committee sat on 15 days.

62 Australia, p. 9; Canada, p. 5 (but there are 400-500 applications for leave); Sweden, p. C.3.6.

63 U.S., p. 14 (but there are some thousands of applications for **certiorari**); **ibid.** p. 18, where the reporter expresses the view that 150 cases a year is about the maximum that the court could manage consistently with fulfillment of its purpose.

supreme courts of Austria and Germany have case loads greatly in excess of that[64], and in those countries, unlike the others so far mentioned, the supreme court sits in more than one chamber.

(c) Appeal limited to questions of law (Supreme Courts). A rule that an appellate court shall not entertain questions of fact is not inconsistent with a requirement that leave to appeal be obtained; this is the case, for example, in Germany[65]. In courts that are recognised as courts of cassation rather than courts of appeal or revision, however, the litigant's right of access is jealously and sometimes even constitutionally protected[66]: even small cases in which no regular appeal is available may still come before the supreme court[67].

Courts of cassation and, for that matter, courts of *revision*, do not receive evidence or proofs but must, in principle, accept the facts as found below. Traditionally, courts of cassation have no power to give their own decisions on the merits of their cases; if they cannot affirm the decision below they must remit the case elsewhere for a fresh decision. In theory these principles should suffice to limit caseloads and to ensure that the courts have to deal only with questions of law of some importance. In practice, in most countries, they have failed to do so, and courts of cassation have become grossly overloaded. In France[68] and Italy[69], to mention the most dramatic cases for which figures are available to the general reporter, the number of decisions runs into many thousands per year.

Part of the explanation for this probably lies in the extreme fluidity of the distinction between questions of fact and questions of law[70]; questions such as the qualification of the facts or the sufficiency of the factual motivation of the decision of the court below are commonly open in courts of cassation. The judges of these courts seem to have taken advantage of this fluidity out of a 'humane' desire to do the best justice possible to the parties[71], and, or so it seems to an outsider, as courts of cassation have come to concern themselves more and more with the rights and obligations of the parties before them as distinct from the purely legal aspects of their cases, so some legislatures have tended to make it easier for them to do so. In Spain, for example, legislation of

---

64 In both countries the load is over 2,000 cases; Austria, p. 24; Germany, p. 14.

65 Germany, pp. 2-4. See also Austria, pp. 13-14; Sweden, pp. B9-10, cf. p. B20.

66 Italian Constitution, art. 111.

67 **Ante** para. 2 (a).

68 The total number has been stated by Professor Tunc to be some 16,000: 'La Cour de cassation en crise' in **Archives de la Philosophie de Droit**, Vol. 30 (1985), 157, 162.

69 A little under 9,000 cases per year but with a growing backlog which, at the beginning of the year 1985-1986 had grown to more than 30,000: Italy, Table 2. Of the countries for which figures are available to the general reporter, only the courts of Chile, The Netherlands and Urugyay decide less than 1,000 cases per year. The reporter for the Netherlands considers that the caseload of the Dutch supreme court is not such as to impair the quality of its decisions but admits to a growing backlog in that court: Netherlands, p. 15.

70 See Jolowicz, pp. 134-137.

71 Mazeaud, Mazeaud et Chabres, **Traité théorique et pratique de la responsabilité civile**, III, ed. 6, 473.

1984 introduced, as an additional ground of cassation, 'error in the appreciation of proofs'[72] while in Italy it is now a legal ground for cassation that the findings of fact of the court below are insufficiently motivated[73]. Again, and probably with an eye to procedural economy, some courts of cassation have acquired the power to dispose finally of a case rather than remit it elsewhere for decision after the original judgment has been annulled. This is not possible everywhere - it is apparently prevented in Belgium by the Constitution itself[74] - but it has long been the case in Spain[75] and is now so even in France provided that the new decision can be reached without further investigation of the facts[76]. In Greece the supreme court, having annulled the decision *a quo*, may actually admit additional proofs and decide the case afresh for itself[77].

A Comparative Excursus

A broadly based comparison between the situation of the supreme courts of the common law countries, together with Sweden, on the one hand and those which are 'courts of cassation', on the other[78], reveals a paradoxical situation: the ostensible and the actual purposes principally fulfilled by each have become reversed.

Courts of Cassation. Where the supreme court is a court of cassation, 'cassation' is sharply distinguished from 'appeal', and the 'public' purpose of cassation is stressed. In Italy, as has been mentioned, the law specifies that the business of the court of cassation is to ensure 'the exact observance and the uniform interpretation of the law, the unity of national law'[79], and recourse by a public authority 'in the interest of the law'[80] is available in many countries even if little used, and special chambers of the court are constituted for cases of special legal difficulty. Ordinarily, no doubt, a case will only reach the court of cassation on the initiative of a party, but this is explained by Calamandrei's well known statement that the state makes use of the private self-interested initiative of the disappointed party by putting it to the wider interests of society[81], and notwithstanding the absence of formal recognition of the rule *stare decisis* in the countries concerned, it is now widely accepted that the

72 Ley de Reforma Urgente de la Ley de Enjuiciaminto, of 6 August 1984. The Spanish reporter states that this is an enormous extension of the traditional limits of cassation: Spain, p. 2.

73 C.p.c. art. 360 5). A similar result has been achieved in France without the aid of legislation. See, e.g., Motulsky, 'Le 'manque de base légale', pierre de touche de la technique juridique'. J.C.P. 1949, I, 775.

74 Art. 95. See Belgium, II, pp. 2-3. The position is apparently the same in Italy: c.p.c. art. 383.

75 L.E.C., art. 1748.

76 Loi no. 79-9 of 3rd January 1979; C. org. jud., art. L. 131-5; n.c.p.c., art. 675.

77 Greece, p. 16.

78 Austria and Germany occupy a position midway between these two extremes.

79 French law states that the 'pourvoi en cassation' leads to censure of the non-conformity of the judgment with the rules of law. N.c.p.c., art. 604. See also Belgium, p. 2.

80 France, n.c.p.c., art. 618-1; Belgium, CJ, arts. 1089, 1090; Italy, c.p.c., art. 363; Netherlands, p. 9. In Germany (p. 11) and Chile (no. 2.2) the situation is not quite the same, but a similar idea exists.

81 **La Cassazione Civile**, II, Cap. 6, no. 64, in Piero Calamandrei, **Opere Giuridiche**, a cura di Mauro Cappelletti, VII, 133. See too Jolowicz, 127, 154.

decisions of courts of cassation are important to the development and clarification of the law[82]. As things have developed, however. the case load of courts of cassation has almost everywhere become so great that adequate performance of the public purpose is extremely difficult if not actually impossible. Thus, the Italian reporter cites a statement that the 'funzione nomofilattica' has become 'utopistico retaggi di ordinamenti superati'[83], and Professor Tunc has written of France that 'la Cour de cassation doit désormais statuer sur plus de 16,000 affaires par an. Quelle que soit la conscience de ses membres, il est vain de prétendre qu'elle puisse faire un travail de la qualité désirable'[84]. Indeed, it has been estimated for France that of all the cases decided by the court of cassation of that country only 1.5% merited the court's attention as raising significant points of law[85]. The original, predominantly public, purpose of these courts has become submerged in the 'humane' desire to do the best justice possible to the parties[86].

Supreme courts of 'third instance'. So far as the cases which actually come before supreme courts which are not courts of cassation are concerned, the powers of those courts are, typically, much the same as those of the (intermediate) appellate court[87] and, at least in primary legislation, no statement equivalent to the Italian provision quoted above is to be found. On the other hand, by secondary legislation or by simple practice, only cases involving points of law of some importance are likely to reach these courts and care is taken to see that their judges have adequate time to consider each case fully and to formulate with considerable attention to detail the reasons for their decisions. This may be and is ultimately achieved by strict application of the requirement of leave to appeal[88], but other factors such as cost, delay, the advice of experienced advocates and widespread recognition that save in exceptional cases

82 Belgium, p. 5; Italy, pp. 15-16. For France, Professor Tunc, citing Portalis, has described as the highest function of the court that of clarifying the application of the codes to differing circumstances ('le juge est législateur des cas particuliers'), of filling actual gaps in the law and also future gaps, that is, adapting the law to the needs of contemporary society: Tunc, 'La Cour de cassation en crise' in **Archives de la Philosophie de Droit**. Vol. 30 (1985), 157, 162. See also Touffait et Tunc, 'Pour une motivation plus explicite des décisions de justice notamment celles de la Cour de cassation': 1974. Rev. trim. dr. civ. 487, 505-506.

83 Giuseppe Mirabelli, as President of a ministerial commission reporting in 1986: Italy, p. 15. See too, Greece, p. 23: 'The Areopag is (in certain not uncommon circumstances) side tracked from considering the unified application of the law and has to concern itself with the rights and wrongs of individual cases, which is not its primary function'.

84 **Loc. cit.**

85 Report of the Garde des Sceaux for 1970-71, cited Tunc, **loc. cit.**

86 Comparison of two successive editions of a well known French treatise reveals the shift in emphasis. The 19th edition (1978) of Vincent, **Procédure Civile** gives the traditional account of the court of cassation and its role in assuring unification in the interpretation of the law. The 20th edition of 1981, by Vincent and Guinchard, states that the court does not have as its sole objective the interests of the parties but is concerned also with the general interests of society.

87 Jolowicz, 146-151.

88 See e.g. Canada, notes 39 and 42, **supra** and p. 7, where it is stated that 'the Supreme Court no longer performs the appellate function of correcting error'; U.S.A., note 63, **supra**.

the intermediate is also the final court of appeal all operate to keep down the number of appeals. It may even be the case that the case load of, for example, the English House of Lords could usefully be increased[89], and in Sweden consideration is actually being given to methods whereby the supreme court's contributions to the law might be enlarged[90].

It can, no doubt, be argued that the paradox derives from the fact that in common law countries the decisions of the courts, and most especially the supreme courts, are recognized as sources of law while this is not the case in countries whose law is codified, That, however, would be to ignore not only the present importance of *jurisprudence* in those countries but also the traditional and still commonly stated role of supreme courts of cassation as guardians of the law. For better or for worse, those courts have come more and more to concern themselves with the rights and obligations of the parties and, because of their huge case loads, have great difficulty in fulfilling their 'public' purpose. Supreme courts which are ostensibly courts of appeal, which are ostensibly no more concerned with the 'public' purpose than are the courts below them in the judicial hierarchy, have become almost exclusively devoted to the development and clarification of the law.

2 RESTRICTION ON CONTENT OF APPEAL

The fullest possible appeal and also the most costly and time consuming involves a complete rehearing of the case - a 'second first instance.' The extent to which different systems of appeal (not cassation) approximate to this, the importance to the enquiry of the character of the procedure used at first instance and the extent to which new matter may be introduced on appeal have been discussed in an earlier report[91]. One matter only is considered under this head, namely the unwillingness or outright refusal of appellate courts to reconsider certain types of question decided at first instance. The topic is important for present purposes because, clearly, if the legal profession is aware that certain types of question will not be reopened on appeal then appeals will not be brought against decisions of such questions.

In those countries which adhere as a matter of principle to the rule of 'double instance', and especially where it is held that a principal function of the appeal is to ensure so far as possible that the facts are correctly found[92], it is unlikely that any question will be regarded as falling outside the purview of the appellate court. Things are different, however, in common law countries, and two types of question in which appellate courts act with particular restraint must be mentioned.

---

89 Jolowicz, 155.

90 Report of the Judicial Procedure Commission, 1986, summarised in Sweden, Appendix D.

91 Jolowicz, 137-146. Some of the national reports contain additional information on these subjects, but space precludes their examination in this report.

92 E.g. Belgium, p. 4, Chile, pp. 2-3, France, pp. 5, 9, Germany, p. 4, Greece, p. 8, Italy, p. 10, Japan, p. 23, Netherlands, p. 18, Spain, p. 3, Uruguay, p. 3.

(a) Questions of fact. In the United States the procedure of appeal is 'a review concerning whether prejudicial error occurred'[93]. Elsewhere it is a procedure of 'rehearing'[94]. Under neither form of procedure are questions of fact entirely precluded from appeal, but witnesses are not heard over again and the appellate court proceeds on the basis of a written transcript of the proceedings, including, where necessary, the evidence, given below. It follows that in so far as decisions of fact were based on the trial court's assessment of the relative credibility of witnesses. the appellate court will not, save in most exceptional circumstances, intervene[95]. Beyond that, the willingness of appellate courts to reconsider questions of fact varies from one country to another and within one country from one period to another[96]. It is a matter for speculation whether this reflects a reaction to awareness of overload. In Australia and England, at the present time, appellate courts are relatively willing to come to their own decisions on questions such as the qualification of conduct. In Canada, on the other hand, practice has changed, and it is now the rule that the appellate court will intervene only if it is shown that the decision in question was 'clearly wrong.' As the Canadian reporter observes, this has the practical effect of limiting the number of appeals[97].

(b) Questions of 'discretion.' Some judicial decisions, mainly but not exclusively those relating to the actual conduct of the proceedings, are said to depend on the judge's 'discretion'; others, such as, for example, the assessment of the relative culpability of the parties in an accident case, the assessment of non-pecuniary damages in a case of personal injury, or even the determination of what would best promote the welfare of a child in a guardianship case cannot be the subject of precise rules. Such decisions may not be 'of fact', nor do they normally depend on the credibility of witnesses, but on such questions an appellate court is likely to act with restraint, giving very great weight, at least, to the view of the judge of first instance. As the point was stated in the House of Lords for English law, 'an appellate court ought not to substitute its own "discretion" for that of the judge merely because its members would themselves have regarded the balance as tipped against the way in which he decided the matter. They should regard their function as primarily a reviewing function and should reverse his decision only in cases either (1) where they are satisfied that the judge has erred in principle ...; or (2)...in order to promote consistency in the exercise of their discretion by judges as a whole where there appear, in closely comparable circumstances, to be two conflicting schools of judicial opinion as to the relative weight to be given to particular circumstances'[98].

---

93 James & Hazard, **Civil Procedure**, ed. 2, no. 13.8. See U.S., p. 10.

94 E.g., for England, R.S.C., 0. 59, r. 3.

95 Where the trial has been by jury, findings of fact are almost sacrosanct and if, for some reason, an appeal on fact succeeds it will almost certainly require a new trial.

96 Australia, p. 21, Canada, pp. 17-18, Jolowicz, p. 137.

97 Canada, pp. 17-18.

98 **Birkett** v. **James** [1978] A.C. 297, 317, **per** Lord Diplock. See also Australia, pp. 21-27.

It is likely that other examples of appellate 'self-restraint' can be found, but it is hoped that the point is sufficiently made. There is nothing here of strict legal rule, and when the need arises in the interests of legal development to open more widely a particular door to the appellate court this can be done. But knowledge that questions of a particular character will not be reconsidered on appeal, exceptional cases apart, has an important and valuable effect on those who advise whether an appeal should be launched.

4 EFFICIENCY DEVICES

The previous section has been mainly concerned with methods for controlling the number of appeals actually launched. This section is intended to mention briefly a different aspect of the problem, namely the adoption of means intended to dispose as rapidly and efficiently as possible of the cases that actually do reach the appellate courts. Two topics will be considered, first the use of 'special' appellate courts, that is, either courts which are not part of the normal appellate hierarchy or which are composed of fewer judges than the normal, and, secondly, devices directed specifically to the actual handling of the cases.

4.1 'SPECIAL' APPELLATE JURISDICTIONS

The case loads of the regular appellate courts, that is courts created specifically as courts of appeal can be lightened or disposed of with more economical use of judge time if either use is made of courts normally of first instance as courts of appeal for certain cases or if the regular courts of appeal can sit for some cases with less than the usual number of judges. Examples of both are to be found in the national reports.

(a) First instance court as court of appeal. Where courts of first instance exist at two levels, the lower level of court dealing with 'small' cases, it is common that appeal from that court lies to the court of first instance of general jurisdiction[99]. In Japan this system is carried a step further so that in small cases the second appeal, the *Jokoku* appeal which is in the nature of cassation, comes before the High Court which is normally a court of first appeal and reaches the Supreme Court only in rare cases; if the High Court considers that there is a point of law on which a Supreme Court decision is required it can transfer the case to the Supreme Court and if there is a point of constitutional law a further, Special *Jokoku*, appeal to the Supreme Court is possible[100].

It is not only in small cases, however, that courts of first instance may serve also as courts of appeal. In the Australian States, for example, with the exception of New South Wales, the State Supreme Court serves as both court of first instance and court of appeal, in the latter capacity sitting as a Full

---

99 Austria, pp. 7-8; Belgium, p. 4; Chile, p. 2; Germany, p. 1; Israel, pp. 2-3; Italy, p. 2; Netherlands, p. 2; South Africa, p. 1; Uruguay, p. 7; U.S.A., p. 6.

100 Japan, pp. 14-15.

Court[101]. In South Africa a similar solution is adopted for those appeals not regarded as of sufficient legal importance to warrant the attention of the Supreme Court as preferable to the creation of an intermediate court of appeal[102], and in the Canadian Province of Ontario, since 1985, a 'Divisional Court' consisting of three ordinary judges of the Provincial Supreme Court on a rotating basis hears appeals involving claims for not more than $25,000. There, however, the solution is regarded as a prelude to the creation of a Provincial intermediate court of appeal[103].

(b) Reduction in size of appellate court. The number of judges required to constitute a chamber or session of an appellate court varies from one country to another, and in some that number has been reduced as a means of making more economical use of judges' time. Of greater interest here, however, is the use of reduced size courts for certain categories of case. In England, for example, the Court of Appeal sits normally as a court of three judges, but two judges only usually sit to hear interlocutory appeals and, now, the same is true for appeals from the County Court, which has jurisdiction up to £5,000, unless the contrary is ordered because of the importance or difficulty of the appeal[104]. Again, in France, the Court of cassation can now sit in a '*formation restreinte*' of three judges instead of the usual five where it appears that the solution of the case is clear. If any member of a *formation restreinte* considers that the case should be heard by a full chamber it will be transferred[105].

4.2 EFFICIENCY

In the conduct of an appeal the parties will look primarily to their own interests individually and, occasionally, to their joint interests. They are unlikely to take into account the interests of other litigants whose appeals are pending or the delays caused by appellate overload. The 'penalty' of costs may, no doubt, discourage inefficient handling of an appeal by the parties, but in

---

101 Australia, pp. 28-31. The Australian reporter makes an interesting comparison between the position in Victoria, where the same judges sit as judges of first instance and, in the Full Court, as judges of appeal, and that in New South Wales where there is a full-time court of appeal. 'A Full Court judge may identify more closely with the trial judge; he may attach more importance to and have greater respect for the work the trial judge has done. And, perhaps, a Full Court judge feels a fuller measure of the restraint imposed by 'the lack of overweening certainty in one's own opinions' - they are equals in a way their counterparts in New South Wales are not, and their places will frequently be reversed. The pressures on a specialist Court of Appeal judge are the other way -it is not wholly waggish to observe that appellate judges do not make their mark in the legal community by affirming'.

102 South Africa, p. 18.

103 Canada, p. 11.

104 The use of two-judge courts has greatly increased since 1982. In 1985, of the 1545 civil appeals instituted, 947 (61%) came before two-judge courts. The problem of disagreement is not serious; in four years there have been only twelve cases of disagreement in a two-judge court: England, p. 2. There have, however, been occasional protests that cases put to a two-judge court should have gone before a three judge court in view of the legal difficulty of the case.

105 France, p. 1; Code de l'organisation judiciaire, art. L. 131-6.

some countries there is a tradition of court control of the procedure[106], and that control can be exercised either to prevent one party from behaving inappropriately or to improve the efficiency with which appeals are disposed of. In the common law countries, however, the parties have traditionally been allowed complete freedom subject only to Rules of Court, and it is therefore of interest that there is today an increasing degree of court involvement in the preparation of cases which comes as a response to overload. One aspect of this is the development, for example in Australia and in England, of strict enforcement of time limits[107]. The English reporter, himself Registrar of the Court of Appeal, states that since 1982, when a new regime was introduced, the policy has been that of an 'interventionist' court; if, for example, an appellant fails to observe certain time limits he will be required to show cause why his appeal should not be dismissed out of hand[108]. The prevailing view is shown by the words of a judge of the Court of Appeal when he took the opportunity 'now to warn the profession that the attitude of the court to the previous lax practices is hardening in order to ensure for the benefit of all litigants that the business of the Court of Appeal is conducted in an expeditious and orderly manner'[109].

In addition to such enforcement of procedural discipline on the parties, various attempts are being made to improve the efficiency of the actual determination of the appeal by reduction of the common law emphasis on oral argument. Reliance on documentation and the use of written briefs together with strictly limited time for oral argument has long been a feature of American appellate procedure, especially in the Supreme Court of the United States, but increasing use of written procedures is now becoming common elsewhere. In a number of countries the parties must now produce 'skeleton arguments' which the judges will read in advance of the oral hearing[110]. In Israel a flexible system has been introduced whereby the court may order the parties to present their arguments in writing on either the whole of their cases or on specific aspects and it may dispense with oral argument altogether or order such argument only by way of supplement to the written submissions. Even where oral argument is to be used, written summaries must be presented to the court at least seven days before the hearing and no argument not there mentioned can be raised at the hearing[111].

'Efficiency' in the use of judge time may also be improved by the delegation to officials or others who do not hold judicial appointments of tasks in addition to the purely administrative. In England, for example, there is now a Registrar of the Court of Appeal who may himself settle certain questions or hold a pre-

---

106 E.g. Germany, pp. 5-6. In France cases come under the control of the 'conseiller de la mise en état': France, p. 6.

107 Australia, p. 44; England, p. 1.

108 See also Canada, p. 16.

109 **Van Stillevoldt BV** v. **E.L. Carriers** [1983] 1 All E.R. 699, 703, **per** Griffiths L.J. See also **Practice Note** [1986] 3 All E.R. 630 and the warning give by the Master of the Rolls.

110 Australia, p. 44; Canada, p. 10 (a written 'factum' is required from each party); England, p. 4.

111 Israel, p. 20.

appeal review[112], but as appears clearly from the American report[113], it is in the United States that the search for efficiency has been carried the furthest. In a most interesting account, the American reporter describes a variety of devices for the saving of judicial time by the use of assistance not only during the preparatory stages of an appeal but in the formation of decisions. The report cannot be summarised here, but attention may be drawn to the practice, now apparently wide spread, of leaving to lawyers on the staff of the court the preparation of the initial drafts of judgments to be delivered[114]. As the reporter states, there is in his view 'no inherent incompatibility between justice...and the employment of mechanisms which increase judicial capacity to decide appeals and hence to cope with increasing work loads,' but they must be used with caution. One danger to which the reporter draws attention is the emergence of 'courtwide' norms for decision which are not articulated and may even come to be substituted for the articulated norms. Safeguards must be evolved. 'The accepted standard of decision is that judges determine the result on appeal by reasoned analysis of a universe of information consisting of the record from the trial court, constitutional principle, statute, precedent, secondary authority, and underlying policy. So long as information obtained by staff is complete and accurate judicial capacity to decide is enhanced and the decision is that of the judge. If staff supplied information is incomplete or inaccurate the standard is not met; staff analysis then so influences the decision that it is a staff and not judicial product. Here again the potential of departure from an expected standard is no reason to forgo the contribution to appellate efficiency of the use of supporting personnel. It is a warning that safeguards to ensure the completeness and accuracy of information reaching the judges should be employed.' Is this the way ahead for other systems, or is the provision of extensive assistance to appellate judges something peculiar to the United States? Can other systems learn from the United States how to increase the efficiency - perhaps 'productivity' is the right word - of appellate judges without thereby sacrificing justice in any of the manifold senses of that word?

5 ABUSE OF THE RIGHT OF APPEAL

Finally, before turning to a conclusion of this report, brief mention must be made of the possible abuse of the right of appeal[115]. Although this is mentioned specifically only by the reporters for Chile and for Italy, the danger that a right of appeal, like any other procedural right, may be abused, is ever present: the entry of an interlocutory appeal before final judgment at first instance may delay that judgment to the advantage of the defendant; the entry of an appeal against the final judgment itself may delay its execution.

---

112 England, pp. 3, 4. Further, although the Court of Appeal is normally collegiate, a variety of incidental questions may now be decided by a single judge.

113 See also, by the same author with John B. Oakley, 'From Information to Opinion in Appellate Courts; How Funny Things Happen on the Way Through the Forum' (1986) Arizona State Law Journal, 1.

114 U.S.A., p. 30.

115 See Jolowicz, pp. 160-162.

a) Interlocutory decisions. In the common law procedure it is inevitable that an interlocutory appeal be disposed of before the trial for the simple reason that the purpose of the interlocutory proceedings is to prepare the case for trial. Nowhere, however, is there any longer an absolute right of appeal against an interlocutory decision. An appeal lies only with leave. In a number of civilian countries, on the other hand, it has now been enacted for most kinds of interlocutory appeal that, if appeal is possible at all, it can be taken only with an appeal against the final decision itself. This, however, is not the case everywhere, and the Chilean reporters place high in their list of causes of overload the fact that 'every appeal paralyses the progress of the action at first instance which has the result that the lawyers, mainly those acting for the defendant, enter an appeal for the sole purpose of causing delay'[116]. They propose, therefore, for their country that the 'suspensive' effect of the appeal should be removed except where the judgment appealed from is final or otherwise disposes finally of the litigation.

b) Final decisions. The Italian reporter is, on balance, prepared to go further, for a recent law reform proposal[117] would remove the suspensive effect of the appeal even against final judgments unless the judge otherwise orders. If brought into operation, this would be in effect to adopt the solution of the common law and would surely help to cut down abusive appeals. As the Italian reporter points out, however, if the change is accompanied not only by the increasing use of single-judge courts of first instance but also with restrictions on the use of *nova* in appellate courts, the result may be to remove much of the value of the appeal in genuine cases: this, apparently, is the general opinion concerning the position now reached in labour cases[118]; it may also explain the unwillingness of the Chilean reporters to take this step.

It is not for a general reporter to enter directly into the question. It is, however, legitimate for him to stress that if overload is a problem then it is even more necessary than it would otherwise be to take steps to eliminate abusive appeals and this, it is suggested, means that whatever can be done to remove the advantages that a party may obtain from delay should be done; perhaps it is also legitimate for him to point out to his friends in countries which distinguish between 'appeal' and 'cassation' that the entry of an application to the court of cassation has no suspensive effect. Would it be so drastic a change for the automatic suspensive effect of the appeal to be removed, leaving it to the discretion of the court to apply the suspensive effect where appropriate?[119]

---

116 Chile, no. 3.7.a).

117 A proposal by the Minister of Justice submitted to the Council of Ministers on 6 February 1987: Italy, pp. 4, 9.

118 **Ibid.**, p. 8.

119 This is already the position in some countries in certain categories of case: Uruguay, p. 12.

6 CONCLUSION

This is not the first occasion on which the general reporter has been grateful for the understanding that it is no part of a comparative lawyer's function to propose concrete solutions for adoption by any legal system save perhaps his own, but his gratitude has never been more sincere. The problem of overload in appellate courts is of the most intractable. There are several reasons for this, foremost amongst which, it is suggested, is that the measures that have been or might be adopted to relieve the pressure on appellate courts have disadvantages that may outweigh the advantages they can produce. A few examples will suffice to make the point.

1. Techniques such as the requirement of leave to appeal which are used in common law supreme courts and some others, which are intended to allow the judges of those courts the time they need to fulfil adequately the 'public' purpose, effectively deny access to the majority of litigants and so tend to prevent those courts from fulfilling adequately or at all the 'private' purpose. They tend also to cast upon the intermediate court of appeal a major role in the development and clarification of the law, and thus generate a need that those courts also should not receive an excessive number of appeals[120]. Conversely where, as in many countries whose supreme court is a court of cassation, there is no similar barrier to access, the number of cases that reach the court is so great that its capacity to fulfil adequately the 'public' purpose is, at least, seriously compromised.

2. At the opposite end of the spectrum, the absolute denial of a right of appeal in some cases can be advantageous only in easing the passage of others while the introduction of a requirement of leave to appeal for 'small' cases makes increased demands on judicial time and in any case tends to defeat the 'private' purpose where leave is denied, while it increases both the cost and the time involved where leave is granted.

3. Increases in the number of appellate judges or reductions in the size of collegiate courts risks diluting the quality of decision making and, which is potentially even more serious, risks encouraging the demand for yet more instances as public confidence in the intermediate courts declines.

4. 'Efficiency' devices designed to reduce the time taken by individual cases such as rigid adherence to time limits sanctioned by dismissal of an appeal unheard or the refusal to have regard to arguments not stated in a written notice of appeal may affect adversely the quality of decision and, even more serious, may give rise to the idea that litigants are denied justice because of

---

120 The Canadian reporter cites an Ontario appellate judge as saying that 'the appellate function of correcting error ends with our court and to some extent, so does the function of clarifying and developing the law so far as Ontario is concerned': Canada, p. 8. In common law countries generally the intermediate court of appeal, where there is one, contributes far more, quantitatively, to the law than does the supreme court. In England, for example, 96% of the cases that reach the Court of Appeal go no further: England, p. 1.

the shortcomings of their lawyers. Efficiency devices such as those described by the American reporter no doubt carry the greatest risk, especially because they seem partially to prevent litigants from making their cases directly to the judges, but no 'efficiency' device can work except by making the appellate judges' personal consideration of their cases less than complete.

If this is right, if it is correct that the problem of overload cannot be alleviated let alone resolved without compromise and the sacrifice of some of the traditional values of a legal system[121], it is not to be expected that any universally acceptable panacea can be found[122]. Each legal system must find its own compromises, and it is at least likely that its choices will be largely controlled by what is regarded, or what is silently assumed, to be fundamental to it. It is, for example, easier for common law countries than for others to restrict the right even of a first appeal simply because those countries have never accepted the principle of double instance as fundamental. Conversely, given the strength of the 'adversary' tradition of their procedure, it is more difficult for common law countries than for others to strengthen the hands of the court itself in controlling the parties during the preparatory stages of appellate procedure and in the presentation of their cases. Nevertheless, three ideas or suggestions may be offered by way of conclusion to this report and as possible subjects of discussion.

1. While it is not suggested that cases should be 'positively' selected for hearing by supreme courts for their particular legal interest,[123] there does seem to be room in many countries for greater emphasis to be placed on the 'public' purpose which those courts fulfil and for the development of techniques whereby the time of supreme court judges is not unduly diverted from it. If, as seems to be the case, the introduction of a requirement of leave to appeal is out of the question where the supreme court is a court of cassation, other techniques such as, perhaps, the French use of 'formations restreintes' are necessary; only those cases which merit the attention of the fully constituted supreme court should receive it. Supreme courts whose case loads run into thousands should be 'de-humanised'[124].

2. Even where the principle of double instance is not accepted as a fundamental, there is general agreement that a litigant dissatisfied at first instance should be entitled to an appeal of some kind not limited to questions of law alone, and the exclusion of small cases from appeal, where it exists, is generally regarded as unsatisfactory for reasons which are obvious. Save for appeals from interlocutory decisions, legal rules restricting a right of first appeal are

---

121 As the American reporter to the 1977 Congress observed in his report, 'A trial, a meaningful appeal, and an opportunity to present a novel point of law to the highest court, taken together, may be regarded as the fullest form of adjudicative justice. If so, most litigants will have to be given less than that': cited, Jolowicz, p. 159.

122 It may, however, be possible to say that some solutions such as the raising of costs so as to put appeal out of the reach of all but a few litigants would be universally unacceptable.

123 See Jolowicz, p. 157.

124 Jolowicz, p. 153.

justified only as a crude response to a critical situation; for the sake of individual justice and of the reputation of the legal system as a whole, such restrictions must be kept to a minimum. This does not mean, however, that any and every question that was or might have been raised at first instance must be open on appeal, a point which goes beyond simple exclusion of 'new demands' and strict control on the admissibility of new evidence or proof. On many matters decided at first instance - whether classified as 'fact' or 'discretion' or otherwise - the decision of appellate judges is little more than 'another view', and it is permissible to ask why a litigant should be entitled to that[125]. Is there a better way of discouraging a would-be appellant whose only complaint is that the decision went against him than for his lawyer to advise him that although he has a right to appeal it is most unlikely that his appeal will succeed?

3. The present era has everywhere seen a great increase in litigation and, obviously, the more decisions there are at first instance the greater will be the pressure on appellate courts. Many of these decisions concern directly the rights and obligations of individuals as consumers, as employees and as subjects of the Welfare State. The general reporter has already suggested[126] that, from the 'human' point of view, the best appellate system is one which neither party to litigation feels it necessary to invoke. There will, no doubt, always be litigants who seek to use their right of appeal for ulterior purposes, and in some countries it appears that there is an actual enthusiasm for litigation and for appeal[127]. Such enthusiasm will, no doubt, prove difficult to contain, at least in the short term, but ultimately, and however difficult it may be, especially in those countries whose judges enter on the judicial career at an early age, it is only by strengthening the courts of first instance and ensuring their high repute in public consciousness that the problem of appellate overload can be met. Only 'demand side' control can provide a satisfactory solution; 'supply side' control can be nothing but a palliative.

---

125 This point is, probably, of greater weight where the judges, including those of first instance, are appointed from experienced practitioners than where there is a judicial career such that some judges of first instance are likely to be young and with little experience.

126 Jolowicz, p. 154.

127 E.g. Germany, pp. 19, 21; Greece, p. 4; Israel, pp. 9-12.

ZUR BEWÄLTIGUNG DER ÜBERLASTUNG DER RECHTSMITTELGERICHTE IN DEN EUROPÄISCHEN SOZIALISTISCHEN LÄNDERN

J. Németh
University of Budapest[1]

---

1 Leiter des Lehrstuhls für Zivilverfahrensrecht an der Eötvös Loránd Universität in Budapest, Rechtsanwalt.

EINLEITUNG

1. Individuelles Ziel des Zivilprozesses ist die Sicherung der Rechte und gesetzlichen Interessen der Prozessparteien. Gleichzeitig ist es zweifellos Tatsache, dass der Zivilprozess auch über eine allgemeine oder gesellschaftliche Zielsetzung verfügt: die Gewährleistung der einheitlichen und wirklichen Gesetzlichkeit. Im Interesse der Durchführung dieser Zielsetzungen ist es einerseits Pflicht des Gerichtes, die materiell - und verfahrensrechtlichen Bestimmungen, die sich auf die unter Beurteilung gezogene Zivilangelegenheit beziehen, streng einzuhalten, andererseits den der objektiven Wahrheit entsprechenden Tatbestand aufzudecken und eine mit den Rechtsregeln im Einklang stehende Entscheidung zu treffen.

Die vom Gericht getroffene Entscheidung entspricht jedoch - aus unterschiedlichen Gründen - nicht immer der Forderung nach Gesetzlichkeit und verletzt dadurch sowohl individuelle als auch gemeinschaftliche Interessen.

Die Möglichkeit, dass die Gerichte gesetzesverletzende Entscheidungen treffen, erfordert wiederum die Ausgestaltung solcher Rechtsinstitutionen, unter Anwendung derer es zur Anfechtung und Änderung (Aufhebung) der gesetzesverletzenden Gerichtsentscheidungen kommen kann. Diese Rechtsinstitutionen sind die Rechtsbehelfe[2].

Vom Gesichtspunkt des untersuchten Themas - die Überlastung der Rechtsmittelgerichte - aus können jedoch unter den Rechtsbehelfen nur diejenigen in Betracht gezogen werden, deren Beurteilung vor einem übergeordneten Gericht erfolgt. Solche sind vor allem die über den Devolutiveffekt und den Suspensiveffekt verfügenden Rechtsmittel. Neben den Rechtsmitteln sind im Zivilverfahrensrecht der einzelnen europäischen sozialistischen Länder auch solche Rechtsbehelfe anzutreffen, die zwar über keinen Suspensiveffekt verfügen, da sie gegen rechtskräftige Gerichtsentscheidungen gerichtet sind, doch schon über einen Devolutiveffekt, da zu ihrer Beurteilung ein übergeordnetes Gericht (zumeist das oberste Gericht) berechtigt ist. Diese sogenannten ausserordentlichen Rechtsbehelfe verursachen aber oft den Rechtsmittelgerichten eine grössere Überlastung, als gleich welches Rechtsmittel, deshalb kann ihre Behandlung im folgenden nicht umgangen werden.

---

2 Unter dem Begriff Rechtsbehelfe werden von mehreren Autoren in den deutschsprachigen Rechtsgebieten - in Übereinstimmung mit der Meinung des Referenten - all diejenigen Rechtsinstitutionen verstanden, die gegen die Gerichtsentscheidungen in Anspruch genommen werden können. So zum Beispiel: R. **Sprung**, Konkurrenz von Rechtsbehelfen in zivilgerichtlichen Verfahren, Wien - New York, 1966, S. 21 ff.; A. **Schöncke**/K. Kuchinke, Zivilprozessrecht, Karlsruhe, 1969, S. 376 f.; R. **Holzhammer**, Österreichisches Zivilprozessrecht, Wien - New York, 1976, S. 314; P. **Gilles**, Die Berufung in Zivilsachen und die zivilgerichtliche Instanzordnung. In: P. **Gilles**, (Hrsg.), Humane Justiz, Kronberg/Ts., 1977, S. 148 ff.; R. **Bruns**, Zivilprozessrecht, München, 1979, S. 405; M. **Guldener**, Schweizerisches Zivilprozessrecht, Zürich, 1979, S. 474 f.; H. **Kellner**, Zivilprozessrecht, Berlin, 1980, S. 393 f.; P. von **Salis**, Probleme des Suspensiveffektes von Rechtsmitteln im Zivilprozess- und Schuldbetreibungs- und Konkursrecht, Zürich, 1980, S. 14 ff.; G. **Baumgärtel**/P. **Mes**, Einführung in das Zivilprozessrecht mit Examinatorium, Bielefeld, 1982, S. 67.

2. Dieser Teil des Generalberichtes stützt sich auf folgende sieben Nationalberichte:
Bulgarien: Stefan Braikow (Sofia);
Deutsche Demokratische Republik: Dr. Horst Kellner (Berlin);
Jugoslawien: Dr. Vesna Rakic-Vodinelic (Belgrad);
Rumänien: Dr. Savelly Zilberstein - Dr. Viorel Ciobanu (Bukarest);
Sowjetunion: Anatoli Alexandrowitsch Melnikow ( ) (Moskau);
Tschechoslowakei: Dr. Alena Winterová (Prag);
Ungarn: Dr. László Gáspárdy (Miskolc).

Der Verfasser dieses Berichtes bedankt sich auch an dieser Stelle bei den Nationalberichterstattern ganz herzlich für ihre wertvolle Mitarbeit und gedenkt mit voller Ehre dem Andenken des namhaften sowjetischen Zivilverfahrensrechtlers A.A. Melnikow, der nicht lange nach der Verfertigung des Nationalberichtes unerwartet verschieden ist.

Ebenfalls bedankt sich der Autor bei den Professoren Dr. Peter Gottwald (Bundesrepublik Deutschland) und H.J. Snijders (Niederlande), die zur herzlichen Information ihm ihre wertvollen Nationalberichte übersandt haben, die sie zum Generalbericht von Professor J.A. Jolowicz unter dem Titel 'Managing Overload in Appellate Courts of "Western" Countries' gefertigt haben.

Es ist zu bedauern, dass hier nicht alle europäischen sozialistischen Länder mit einem Nationalbericht vertreten sind, doch ist dies im Falle von Polen nur auf ein kollegiales Missverständnis administrativen Charakters, im Falle von Albanien jedoch auf den fast völligen Mangel der wissenschaftlich-kulturellen Beziehungen zurückzuführen.

Der Referent zieht jedoch trotz des zweifellosen Mangels dieser Nationalberichte - den Möglichkeiten angerechnet - die Eigentümlichkeiten der albanischen und polnischen rechtlichen Regelung in Verbindung mit dem untersuchten Thema in Betracht, ja er versucht das gleiche auch in Hinsicht einiger aussereuropäischer sozialistischer Staaten.

3. Die Überlastung der Rechtsmittelgerichte kann sowohl auf dem Gebiet der Straf- als auch der Zivilrechtspflege untersucht werden. Dieser Bericht beschäftigt sich allerdings - nach vorheriger Abstimmung mit dem Partnerberichterstatter, Kollegen Professor J.A. Jolowicz - nur mit dem Problem der in der Zivilrechtspflege vorgehenden Rechtsmittelgerichte. Zum Kreis der Zivilrechtspflege gehörend betrachtet der Referent dagegen nicht nur die sich aus dem eng verstandenen Zivilrecht, sondern auch die sich aus dem Arbeitsrecht, dem Familienrecht, dem Wirtschaftsrecht, dem Verwaltungsrecht usw. ergebenden Prozesse, unabhängig davon, dass diese nicht von den ordentlichen Gerichten, sondern den zu diesem Zweck geschaffenen Sondergerichten beurteilt werden.

1 GRUNDLINIEN VON INSTANZENZUG UND ORGANISATION DER ZIVILGERICHTSBARKEIT

1.1 AUFBAU DER GERICHTE

In der Mehrzahl der europäischen sozialistischen Länder sind die *ordentlichen*

Gerichte dreistufig gegliedert[3]. In Jugoslawien, der Sowjetunion und der Tschechoslowakei dagegen ist der Aufbau der ordentlichen Gerichte - entsprechend dem föderativen Staatssystem dieser Länder - vierstufig[4].

Sondergerichte, die vom Gesichtspunkt der Zivilrechtspflege aus in Betracht kommen könnten, sind nur in Jugoslawien, in Polen und in Ungarn anzutreffen. In einzelnen föderativen Republiken von Jugoslawien gehen in *Wirtschaftsprozessen* in erster Instanz als Sondergerichte die *Kreiswirtschaftsgerichte* vor, während in zweiter Instanz das *Rechtsmittelwirtschaftsgericht* urteilt, dessen Zuständigkeit sich auf das gesamte Gebiet der föderativen Republik erstreckt[5]. In Polen ist das *Verwaltungshauptgericht* zur gerichtlichen Überprüfung von Verwaltungsakten berechtigt[6]. Dieses Sondergericht[7] - welches vom Sejm der Polnischen Volksrepublik durch das am 31. Januar 1980 verabschiedete Gesetz

---

3 So in Albanien, Bulgarien, der DDR, Polen, Rumänien, Ungarn. Die gleiche ist die Lage auch in Kuba und in der Mongolei.

4 Der sowjetische Nationalreferent verweist in seinem Bericht darauf, dass in der Sowjetunion die Verwaltungs- und territoriale Aufteilung der einzelnen föderativen Republiken nicht identisch ist. Daraus ergibt sich, dass auch ihr Gerichtssystem voneinander abweicht. Am komplexesten - und daher vielleicht am interessantesten - ist die Verwaltungs- und territoriale Aufteilung der Russischen Sozialistischen Föderativen Sowjetrepublik (im weiteren kurz: RSFSR). Zum Gerichtssystem dieser Republik gehören: das Oberste Gericht der RSFSR, die obersten Gerichte der autonomen Republiken (in der RSFSR gibt es 16 oberste Gerichte von autonomen Republiken), die regionalen Gerichte, die territorialen Gerichte und die diesem Niveau entsprechenden Gerichte (die Gerichte der Städte Moskau und Leningrad, die Gerichte der autonomen Territorien und Bezirke), Kreis- (Stadt-) Volksgerichte. Die Aufsicht über die aufgezählten Republikgerichte wird - in einem vom Gesetz festgelegten Masse - von dem Obersten Gericht der Sowjetunion als dem obersten Gerich-tsorgan der Sowjetunion ausgeübt (vgl. **Melnikow**, Nationalbericht, S. 2 f.).

5 Vgl. **Rakic-Vodinelic**, Nationalbericht, S. 2 f.

6 Vgl. M. **Wyrzykowski**, Pozycja ustrojowa Naczelnego Sadu Administracyjnego, Panstwo i Prawo, 1980/10, S. 51 ff.: A. **Zielinski**, U zrodel koncepcji ustrojowej Naczelnego Sadu Administracyjnego, Panstwo i Prawo, 1983/6, S. 5 ff.

7 Ebenfalls getrennt von den ordentlichen Gerichten wurden in Polen das **Staatsgericht** und das **Verfassungsgericht** geschaffen. Das Staatsgericht hat - da seine Aufgabe in der Feststellung der politischen bzw. eventuellen strafrechtlichen Verantwortung einzelner hoher staatlicher Leiter besteht - keine Wirkung auf die Zivilgerichtsbarkeit. Ganz anders dagegen verhält es sich mit dem Verfassungsgericht, welches von der in der polnischen Rechtswissenschaft herrschenden Auffassung als **Sondergericht** betrachtet wird (vgl. F. **Siemenski**, Pozycja ustrojowa i wlasciwosc Trybunalu Konstytucyjnego, Ruch Prawniczy, Ekonomiczny i Socjologiczny, 1985/4, S. 90 ff.; S. **Pawela**, Trybunal Konstytucyjny PRL, Manuskript, 1987, S. 2; M. **Wyrzykowski**, Der Verfassungsgerichtshof der Volksrepublik Polen, Archiv des öffentlichen Rechts, 1987/1, S. 93 ff.). Das Verfahren und die Entscheidungen des Verfassungsgerichtes haben nämlich Folgen in der Zivilgerichtsbarkeit, bzw. können sie sie haben, vollkommen unabhängig davon, dass sich das Verfahren des Verfassungsgerichtes hinsichtlich seines Modells grundlegend vom Zivilund Strafverfahren, als auch vom Verwaltungsverfahren unterscheidet (vgl. A. **Kabat**/S. **Pawela**, Zasady postepowania i formy orzekania Trybunalu Konstytucyjnego, Nowe Prawo, 1986/10, S. 3 ff.; A. **Kabat**/S. **Pawela**, Przebieg postepowania przed Trybunalem Konstytucyjnym, Panstwo i Prawo, 1986/10, S. 43 ff.) Unter Hinsicht jedoch auf die Tatsache, dass das Verfassungsgericht erst seit dem 1. Januar 1986 tätig ist und im ersten Jahr seines Wirkens insgesamt acht Entscheidungen getroffen hat, können seine Tätigkeit und sein Wirken im weiteren ausser Acht gelassen werden.

geschaffen wurde - sowie dessen im Land verteilte Zentralen erfüllen laut bisherigen Erfahrungen im Interesse des Schutzes der staatsbürgerlichen Rechte eine wichtige Rolle[8]. Die *Arbeitsgerichte* in Ungarn, die in den mit dem Arbeitsverhältnis und dem genossenschaftlichen Mitgliedsverhältnis verbundenen Prozessen urteilen, sind formell Sondergerichte, 'in Wirklichkeit aber erstinstanzliche Gerichte von sachlicher Zuständigkeit'[9]. Die Berufungen gegen die Entscheidungen der Arbeitsgerichte wiederum - die nur in den vom Gesetz festgelegten Fällen eingelegt werden können - werden nicht von einem neueren Sondergericht, sondern von den sich inmitten der ordentlichen Gerichtsorganisation befindlichen Komitatsgerichten beurteilt.

1.2 ZUSTÄNDIGKEIT DER GERICHTE

In jedem der europäischen sozialistischen Länder - sowie auch in China und in der Mongolei - kommt *das einstufige Rechtsmittelsystem* und der dementsprechende *Zweiinstanzenzug* zur Geltung. Die Zivilgerichtsbarkeit dieser Länder kennt das sog. 'Sprungsrechtsmittel' nicht, daraus folgt, dass das Rechtsmittelverfahren fast immer vor dem unmittelbar vorgesetzten Gericht[10] des in erster Instanz vorgegangenen Gerichtes erfolgt. In Wirklichkeit hängt also die zweitinstanzliche Verfahrensberechtigung der Rechtsmittelgerichte in voller Gänze davon ab, wie sich die sachliche Zuständigkeit zwischen den Gerichten erster Instanz verteilt.

Zwischen den unterschiedlichen ordentlichen Gerichten verteilt sich die erstinstanzliche sachliche Zuständigkeit - unabhängig davon, über wieviele Instanzen der Aufbau der Gerichte in dem gegebenen Land verfügt - in der Regel so, dass zur Beurteilung der grossen Mehrzahl der Rechtsstreite die unteren Gerichte berechtigt sind (allgemeine sachliche Zuständigkeit), die unmittelbar darüber organisierten Gerichte dagegen gehen nur in einzelnen, besonders festgelegten Fällen vor (besondere sachliche Zuständigkeit).

Abweichungen von dieser Lösung ergeben sich in beiden Richtungen.

In Jugoslawien z.B. geht das *Föderative Gericht* - welches das Gericht höchster Ebene mit einer sich auf das gesamte Gebiet des Staatenbundes erstreckenden Zuständigkeit darstellt - ausnahmsweise *in erster Instanz* in vermögensrechtlichen Prozessen zwischen dem Staatenbund und den föderativen Republiken sowie zwischen den einzelnen föderativen Republiken vor[11]. Eine ähnliche Regelung kommt auch in zwei anderen asiatischen sozialistischen Ländern zur

---

8 Vgl. A. **Domány**, Uj vonások a Szejm müködésében és a birósági rendszerben Lengyelországban, Jogtudományi Közlöny, 1984/1, S. 54 f.; M. **Rybiczki**, Alkotmányi változások a népi Lengyelországban, Jogtudományi Közlöny, 1985/12, S. 702.

9 So **Gáspárdy**, Nationalbericht II, S. 2.

10 In einzelnen sozialistischen Ländern ist das Oberste Gericht berechtigt, die Angelegenheit zur zweitinstanzlichen Beurteilung von dem ansonsten über die dazu berufenen Zuständigkeit verfügenden Gericht zweiter Instanz heranzuziehen (vgl. den Artikel 391 § 1 des am 17. November 1964 verabschiedeten Gesetzes Nr. 296 uber das polnische Zivilverfahren - im weiteren: polnisches ZVG -den § 23/A des Gesetzes III des Jahres 1952 über die ungarische Zivilprozessordnung - im weiteren: ungarische ZPO -).

11 Vgl. **Rakic-Vodinelic**, Nationalbericht, S. 3.

Geltung. Das *Oberste Volksgericht* der Volksrepublik China geht nämlich in erster Instanz in denjenigen Angelegenheiten vor, die auf das ganze Land grosse Auswirkungen haben, beziehungsweise bei denen es der Ansicht ist, dass sie von ihm selbst behandelt und entschieden werden müssen[12]. Ebenfalls in erster Instanz urteilt auch das *Oberste Gericht* der Mongolischen Volksrepublik in Prozessen, in denen die eine Partei das sich in der Mitte der Gerichtshierarchie befindliche 'Ajmak'- oder Stadtgericht ist[13].

Demgegenüber gehen in der Sowjetunion 'in jeder zur sachlichen Zuständigkeit des Gerichtes gehörenden Zivilangelegenheit die Kreis- (Stadt-) Volksgerichte in erster Instanz vor'[14]. Zur Wahrheit gehört aber auch, dass die Regeln des sowjetischen Zivilverfahrensrechtes - die zum grössten Teil in den Grundlagen der Zivilrechtsprechung der Union der Sozialistischen Sowjetrepubliken und der föderativen Republiken[15] sowie den sich darauf aufbauenden Zivilverfahrensrechtskodexen der föderativen Republiken[16] enthalten sind - den übergeordneten Gerichten ermöglichen, die *zur erstinstanzlichen sachlichen Zuständigkeit der unteren Gerichte gehörenden Verfahren an sich heranzuziehen*. Das bedeutet zum Beispiel, dass in der RSFSR die obersten Gerichte der autonomen Republiken sowie die regionalen und territorialen Gerichte berechtigt sind, *gleich welche Angelegenheit vom Kreis- (Stadt-) Volksgericht* und das Oberste Gericht der RSFSR *von gleich welchem Gericht der Republik*[17] an sich heranzuziehen. Die Plenarsitzung des Obersten Gerichtes der Sowjetunion hat in mehreren prinzipiellen Entscheidungen den regionalen, territorialen sowie den obersten Gerichten der autonomen und föderativen Republiken vorgeschlagen, dass

- 'sie die bedeutendsten und kompliziertesten Zivilangelegenheiten (Arbeitsrechts-, Wohnungs- und Neuerungsangelegenheiten usw.) zum erstinstanzlichen Verfahren heranziehen, unter Hinsicht darauf, dass die Beurteilung dieser Angelegenheiten von grosser Bedeutung vom Gesichtspunkt der Praxis der Gerichte unterer Ebene ist', bzw.
- 'sie im Falle der mehrfachen Ausserkraftsetzung der Gerichtsentscheidung die Frage in Betracht ziehen sollen, ob sie die Angelegenheit nicht in eigene sachliche Zuständigkeit heranziehen sollten.'[18]

Die auf unterschiedliche Weise erfolgende *Heranziehung der erstinstanzlichen sachlichen Zuständigkeit* der unteren Gerichte oder die *freiwillige überlassung*

---

12 Vgl. den § 19 des am 8. März 1982 zur versuchsweisen Anwendung verabschiedeten Gesetzes über die chinesische Zivilprozessordnung im weiteren: chinesische ZPO/.

13 Vgl. den § 26 des am 29. Juni 1967 verabschiedeten Gesetzes über das mongolische Zivilverfahren (im weiteren: mongolisches ZVG).

14 So **Melnikow**, Nationalbericht, S. 5.

15 In: Wedomosti Werchownogo Sowjeta SSSR Nr. 50, 1961, S. 526 ff. oder Nr. 42, 1979, S. 697 ff.

16 Unter den unterschiedlichen föderativen Republiken in der Sowjetunion ist die grösste und politisch die bedeutendste die RSFSR. Deshalb behandelt der Referent - im Interesse der Überschaubarkeit- die mit dem untersuchten Thema zusammenhängenden Eigentümlichkeiten des sowjetischen Zivilverfahrensrechtes aufgrund des am 11. Juni 1964 verabschiedeten Gesetzes über das Zivilverfahren der RSFSR (im weiteren: ZVG der RSFSR).

17 Im wesentlichen die gleiche Lösung kommt auch in der Mongolei zur Geltung. Vgl. die §§ 25-26 des mongolischen ZVG.

18 Sbornik postanowleni Plenuma Werchownogo Suda SSSR, 1924-1977, Moskau, 1978, S. 114, 323, 328.

dieser dem übergeordneten Gericht wird auch in anderen sozialistischen Ländern geregelt[19].

So können in Bulgarien und Ungarn das Oberste Gericht[20], bzw. dessen Präsident[21] in Ausnahmefällen *gleich welche Angelegenheit gleich welchen Gerichtes* sowohl in erster als auch in zweiter Instanz gleichermassen in die sachliche Zuständigkeit des Obersten Gerichtes heranziehen. In der DDR tritt eine solche Heranziehung der sachlichen Zuständigkeit dann ein, wenn der Staatsanwalt des Bezirkes - 'wegen der Bedeutung, Folgen oder Zusammenhänge'[22] - die Verhandlung der Sache vor dem Bezirksgericht beantragt oder der Direktor des Bezirksgerichtes das Verfahren an das Bezirksgericht herangezogen hat, in diesem Fall nämlich gibt das Kreisgericht die Sache an das Bezirksgericht ab[23]. Eine spezielle und von der bisher behandelten völlig abweichende Regelung dagegen kommt in Polen zur Geltung. Dort hat nämlich der Gesetzgeber nicht den übergeordneten Gerichten ermöglicht, in bestimmten Fällen von den unteren Gerichten die erstinstanzliche sachliche Zuständigkeit heranzuziehen, sondern umgekehrt, er hat die freiwillige übertragung der sachlichen Zuständigkeit gewährt. Diese übertragung ist dann gestattet, wenn im Laufe der Verhandlung der Sache vor dem Kreisgericht eine ernste Zweifel weckende rechtliche Frage auftaucht. In diesem Fall kann das *Kreisgericht* - mit einem begründeten Beschluss - die Sache zur Beurteilung *an das übergeordnete Woiwodschaftsgericht verlegen*[24].

Aus dem oben Dargelegten ist ersichtlich, dass in den europäischen sozialistischen Staaten die Regelung der erstinstanzlichen sachlichen Zuständigkeit der Gerichte ziemlich 'unterschiedlich' ist. Vom Gesichtspunkt des untersuchten Themas aus regen vor allem diejenigen Lösungen zum Nachdenken an, welche:

- den obersten Gerichten die Möglichkeit zum Vorgehen in erster Instanz gewähren oder
- ausser dem obersten Gericht anderen Rechtsmittelgerichten die Ermächtigung zur Heranziehung der erstinstanzlichen sachlichen Zuständigkeit von irgendeinem unteren Gericht gewähren beziehungsweise
- den Gerichten gestatten, eine in ihre erstinstanzliche sachliche Zuständigkeit gehörende Sache zur Beurteilung an das Rechtsmittelgericht zu überlassen.

In diesen Fällen *versehen die Rechtsmittelgerichte* - zumindest nach der Meinung des Referenten - *nur zum Teil* diejenigen *Aufgaben von allgemeinem Interesse*, zu deren Realisierung sie geschaffen wurden. Es ist nämlich die *ausserordentlich wichtige Aufgabe* der Rechtsmittelgerichte - über die den Prozessparteien zustehende gewährung des Rechtsschutzes hinausgehend -, *das Verfahren der erstinstanzlichen Gerichte zu kontrollieren und zugleich* auch

---

19 Eine Ausnahme in dieser Hinsicht stellt unter anderem die Tschechoslowakei dar, wo - wie darauf auch vom nationalen Referenten verwiesen wird - keine solche Regelung existiert. Vgl. **Winterová**, Nationalbericht, S. 1.

20 Vgl. **Braikow**, Nationalbericht I, S. 1.

21 Vgl. den § 23/A der ungarischen ZPO.

22 So **Kellner**, Nationalbericht, S. 4.

23 Vgl. den § 26 Abs. des am 19. Juni 1975 verabschiedeten Gesetzes er r die Zivilprozessordnung der DDR (im weiteren: ZPO der DDR).

24 Vgl. den Art. 18 § 1 des polnischen ZVG.

diese Gerichte anzuleiten, vornehmlich durch das Beispiel ihrer eigenen Verfahrensweise und durch die von ihnen erlassenen Entscheidungen.

Die letztere Aufgabe - die *Anleitung der unteren Gerichte* ist zweifellos auch dann verwirklicht, wenn das Rechtsmittelgericht in der herangezogenen Sache oder in dem zu ihm verwiesenen Prozess in erster Instanz eine Entscheidung trifft. Das Rechtsmittelgericht ist nämlich durch die Art des Verfahrens in erster Instanz und die dabei getroffene Entscheidung bzw. durch die dabei zum Ausdruck kommende Rechtsauffassung auch in der Lage, eine Richtung in der Hinsicht zu weisen, dass in der gegebenen Sache bzw. den gegebenen Sachengruppen welche Rechtsregeln auf welche Weise angewandt werden müssen. Eine derartige Tätigkeit kann - gerade wegen ihrer Ausnahme - zumindest genauso vereinheitlichend auf die Praxis der unteren Gerichte wirken, als wenn es als Berufungsgericht die gleiche Entscheidung in zweiter Instanz fällen würde. Das ist besonders dann so, wenn das Oberste Gericht irgendeines Staates in erster Instanz vorgeht[25].

Es ist eine andere Frage, dass in solchen Fällen wiederum *das Oberste Gericht als erste und einzige* Instanz vorgeht, denn gegen seine Entscheidung kann keine Berufung eingelegt werden, da es kein über es geordnetes Gericht gibt. Das erstinstanzliche Verfahren des Obersten Gerichtes - geht es nun in einer für es im Gesetz festgelegten sachlichen Zuständigkeit oder in Heranziehung der sachlichen Zuständigkeit vor - hat also immer zum Ergebnis, dass einerseits *die Berechtigten das ihnen ansonsten zustehende Berufungsrecht nicht in Anspruch nehmen können*, andererseits wird das der allgemeinen Regel gemässe *zweiinstanzliche Verfahren zu einem eininstanzlichen*[26].

Vom Gesichtspunkt der Anleitung der unteren Gerichte aus bedeutet oder kann also die Art des erstinstanzlichen Verfahrens des Rechtsmittelgerichtes sowie seine im Laufe des Verfahrens geholte Entscheidung eine entsprechende Lösung bedeuten. Zweifellose Tatsache ist es allerdings, dass *in einem solchen Fall das Rechtsmittelgericht seine Kontrollaufgabe* über die Tätigkeit und das Verfahren der zu ihm gehörenden erstinstanzlichen Gerichte *nicht erfüllt* - und sie sinngemäss auch nicht erfüllen kann. Daneben kann als Folge der Heranziehung oder überlassung der erstinstanzlichen sachlichen Zuständigkeit auch noch *mit weiteren Nachteilen* gerechnet werden. Solche sind unter anderem:

- *Die Arbeitslast der Berufungsgerichte nimmt zu*, weil die Beurteilung eines Prozesses in erster Instanz im allgemeinen mehr Zeit in Anspruch nimmt, als in zweiter Instanz.

---

25 In Ungarn stellt es einen ausserordentlich seltenen Fall dar, dass der Vorsitzende des Obersten Gerichtes irgendeine vom Gesichtspunkt der prinzipiellen Anleitung der Gerichte aus wichtige oder in sonstiger Hinsicht über herausragende Bedeutung verfügende Sache in erster Instanz an die sachliche Zuständigkeit des Obersten Gerichtes heranzieht. In der Praxis kommt es in der Regel eher in der zweiten Instanz dazu (vgl. J. **Szilbereky**, Joghatóság, hatáskör, illetékesség, in: J. **Farkas**/J. **Németh**/L. **Névai**/J. **Szilbereky**/Gy. **Varga**/L. **Vida**, Polgári eljárásjog I, Budapest, 1980, S. 95).

26 In gewissen ausserordentlichen Fällen muss freilich der Gesetzgeber auch diese nachteiligen Folgen auf sich nehmen - so z.B. bei der Festsetzung der erstinstanzlichen sachlichen Zuständigkeit des Jugoslawischen Föderativen Gerichtes -, da es ja vorkommen kann, dass es zur Beurteilung gegebener Rechtsstreitigkeiten innerhalb der ordentlichen Gerichtsorganisation keine andere reale Möglichkeit gibt.

- *Der Sachverkehr der Berufungsgerichte erhöht sich*, denn es kann sein, dass sie in der Sache, in der sie in erster Instanz vorgehen, infolge Mangel der Berufung zweitinstanzlich überhaupt nicht hätten vorgehen müssen, wenn die Sache bei dem ursprünglich über die erstinstanzliche sachliche Zuständigkeit verfügenden unteren Gericht verbleibt.
- *Auch die zweitinstanzliche sachliche Zuständigkeit 'rutscht' weiter nach oben* - vorausgesetzt, dass nicht das Oberste Gericht die Angelegenheit in erster Instanz in seine sachliche Zuständigkeit heranzieht -, infolge dessen im Falle einer Berufung ein solches Gericht in dem gegebenen Prozess vorgeht, welches in diesem ansonsten nicht vorgegangen wäre[27]. So kann es auch vorkommen, dass das Oberste Gericht als 'Plusaufgabe' in zweiter Instanz in einer konkreten Sache verhandeln und urteilen muss, und dadurch eventuell von wichtigeren Leitungs- und Kontrollaufgaben prinzipiellen Charakters abgelenkt wird.

Diese skizzenhaft dargelegten nachteiligen *Folgen* wiederum tragen oder können *zur Überlastung der Rechtsmittelgerichte beitragen*[28]. Deshalb - sowie aus dem Grunde, dass die Berufungsgerichte ihre Aufgaben von öffentlichem Interesse in voller Gänze erfüllen können - wäre es angezeigt, in den betroffenen Ländern das erstinstanzliche Verfahren der obersten Gerichte bzw. die sich auf die Heranziehung oder überlassung der erstinstanzlichen sachlichen Zuständigkeit beziehende gegenwärtige Regelung zu überprüfen. Als Ergebnis der überprüfung könnte es eventuell ermöglicht werden, eine den theoretischen und praktischen Forderungen besser als heute entsprechende Lösung auszugestalten, die eine weitere Zunahme der sich den Berufungsgerichten auferlegenden Arbeitslast - wenigstens auf diesem Gebiet - verhindern würde[29].

1.3 SPRUCHKÖRPER UND PERSONALBESTAND

Die Besetzung der Gerichte wird in der Zivilrechtspflege der sozialistischen Staaten von *zwei Grundprinzipien bestimmt*, die nicht nur für das Zivilprozess-

---

27 Es ist möglich, dass die Heranziehung der erstinstanzlichen sachlichen Zuständigkeit an das Rechtsmittelgericht gerade dies zum Ziel hat. In der DDR muss zum Beispiel vor der Heranziehung einer Sache vom Kreisgericht an das Bezirksgericht sorgfältig untersucht werden, 'ob es nicht zweckmässig ist, sie durch Begründung der Zuständigkeit des Bezirksgerichtes in erster Instanz eventuell auch dem Obersten Gericht im Wege eines Rechtsmittelverfahrens zugänglich zu machen'. So **Kellner**, Zivilprozessrecht, S. 133. Vgl. H. **Reinwarth**, Zur Heranziehung von Zivil-, Familien- und Arbeitsrechtssachen, Neue Justiz, 1966/11. S. 323 f.

28 Die Entziehung der erstinstanzlichen sachlichen Zuständigkeit durch die Berufungsgerichte ist entsprechend den dem Referenten zur Verfügung stehenden Informationen nicht allzu häufig. In der DDR betrifft dies erfahrungsgemäss nur wenige Fälle pro Jahr (vgl. **Kellner**, Nationalbericht, S. 4). Auch in der Sowjetunion ist die Praxis, dass ein Gericht höherer.Instanz Zivilsachen von den Kreis- (Stadt-) Volksgerichten heranzieht und als Rechtsmittelgericht in erster Instanz vorgeht, nicht bedeutend (vgl. **Melnikow**, Nationalbericht, S. 6).

29 Als eine solche Lösung erscheint in Ungarn - wo bereits seit vier Jahren die Kodifikationsarbeit zur Schaffung der neuen Zivilprozessordnung im Gange ist - die Vorstellung des Gesetzgebers, derzufolge das heute noch bestehende Recht des Vorsitzenden des Obersten Gerichtes gleich welche Sache von gleich welchem Gericht zur Beurteilung in erster Instanz ausnahmsweise in die sachliche Zuständigkeit des Obersten Gerichtes heranzuziehen abgeschafft wird. Seine Berechtigung würde also nur ausschliesslich bezüglich der Beurteilung in zweiter Instanz bestehen bleiben.

recht, sondern auch für das Gerichtsverfassungs- und Strafprozessrecht charakteristisch sind.

Diese Grundprinzipien sind:
- das Prinzip der Kollegialität des Gerichtes,
- das Prinzip der Teilnahme der Werktätigen an der Rechtsprechung.

Im Sinne des zuerst erwähnten Grundprinzipes werden die Rechtsstreitigkeiten gewöhnlich von *Kollegien* entschieden.

Die Mehrzahl der Länder jedoch gewährt unter Berufung auf unterschiedliche Gründe - so zum Beispiel die Steigerung der Operativität und Besserung der Qualität der Rechtspflege[30] auch die Möglichkeit dazu, dass *in Verfahren erster Instanz* in bestimmten Sachen oder beim Vorliegen bestimmter Umstände *ein Einzelrichter*[31] vorgeht. Eine Ausnahme in dieser Hinsicht bilden die Mongolei und die Sowjetunion, wo die Gerichte immer in Kollegien vorgehen[32]. *Im ersten Rechtszuge sind die Kollegien* meistens *mit drei Richtern besetzt*. Eine davon abweichende Lösung kommt in Rumänien zur Geltung, wo die Kollegien in erster Instanz *mit zwei Richtern* besetzt sind, und nur im Falle von Meinungsunterschieden wird das Kollegium durch den Vorsitzenden oder den stellvertretenden Vorsitzenden des Gerichtes bzw. durch den vom Vorsitzenden bestimmten Richter ergänzt[33].

In zweiter Instanz jedoch kann in keinem der sozialistischen Länder ein Einzelrichter vorgehen, *nur Kollegien*, die im allgemeinen ebenfalls *aus drei Richtern* bestehen[34]. In speziellen Fällen gibt es freilich auch hier Ausnahmen, so z.B.: das Kollegium des Rechtsmittelgerichtes für Arbeitsrechtssachen beim Obersten Gericht der DDR besteht aus *fünf Mitgliedern*[35], bzw. in Jugoslawien dann, wenn das Rechtsmittelgericht bei der mündlichen Verhandlung ein Urteil füllt[36]. In einem *aus zwei Richtern* bestehenden Kollegium geht in Rumänien das Berufungsgericht vor, wenn die Berufung gegen ein solches Urteil gerichtet ist, welches von einem Einzelrichter getroffen wurde[37].

Was das zweite Grundprinzip, das Prinzip der Teilnahme der Werktätigen an der Rechtsprechung betrifft, so wird dies in der Praxis so verwirklicht, dass im vorgehenden Gerichtskollegium neben dem Berufsrichter oder den Berufsrichtern

---

30 So **Zilberstein/Ciobanu**, Nationalbericht, S. 30.

31 Nach einer einjährigen tatsächlichen Gerichtspraxis - jedoch noch vor Ablegung der Eignungsprüfung - können in Rumänien **auch die Referendare** in denjenigen Angelegenheiten verhandeln, in denen ein Einzelrichter berechtigt ist, vorzugehen (vgl. **Zilberstein/Ciobanu**, Nationalbericht, S. 30).

32 Vgl. den § 13 des mongolischen ZVG und **Melnikow**, Nationalbericht, S. 5, 18.

33 Vgl. **Zilberstein/Ciobanu**, Nationalbericht, S. 29.

34 Zahlenmässig ist die Mitgliederzahl der in erster sowie in zweiter Instanz vorgehenden Kollegien in China nicht festgelegt. Vom Gesetzgeber wurde nur vorgeschrieben, dass 'ein Kollegium eine ungerade Zahl von Mitgliedern zu haben hat' (vgl. die §§ 35-36 der chinesischen ZPO).

35 Vgl. **Kellner**, Zivilprozessrecht, S. 105.

36 Vgl. **Rakic-Vodinelic**, Nationalbericht, S. 28.

37 Vgl. **Zilberstein/Ciobanu**, Nationalbericht, S. 31.

von der Bevölkerung direkt[38], bzw. zumeist durch die Organe der Volksvertretung gewählte und im allgemeinen juristisch nicht vorgebildete[39] Schöffen- einer anderen Bezeichnung gemäss Volksbeisitzer - vorgehen und urteilen.

Die Schöffen nehmen im allgemeinen *beim erstinstanzlichen Verfahren* an der Rechtsprechung in der Weise teil, dass *zwei Schöffen zusammen mit einem Berufsrichter* ein Kollegium bilden, dessen Vorsitzender der Berufsrichter ist. Natürlich geht kein Schöffe im erstinstanzlichen Verfahren dann vor, wenn ein Einzelrichter urteilt[40], oder wenn der Bestimmung des Gesetzes zufolge zur Beurteilung bestimmter Sachen das vorgehende Kollegium aus drei Berufsrichtern gebildet werden muss[41]. In Wirklichkeit können auch heute schon unter den sozialistischen Ländern nur wenig solche angetroffen werden, bei denen im erstinstanzlichen Verfahren ausnahmslos immer Schöffen teilnehmen[42].

Einer allgemeinen Regel zufolge urteilt *im zweitinstanzlichen Verfahren ein aus Berufsrichtern bestehendes Kollegium ohne die Teilnahme von Schöffen*. Es kommt nur in ganz ausnahmsweisen Fällen vor - dann, wenn in der DDR bzw. in Jugoslawien das Berufungsgericht in einem aus fünf Mitgliedern bestehenden Kollegium vorgeht[43] -, dass die Zusammensetzung des Kollegiums folgendermassen aussieht: zwei Berufsrichter und drei Schöffen. Ebenfalls in der DDR kommt die Regel zur Geltung, dass in zweiter Instanz in Arbeitsrechtssachen bei den Bezirksgerichten an dem aus drei Mitgliedern bestehenden Kollegium zwei Schöffen beteiligt sind[44].

1.4 BELASTUNG DER GERICHTE IN ERSTER UND ZWEITER INSTANZ

Aus der oben skizzierten praktischen Verwirklichung der zwei Grundprinzipien, welche die Zusammensetzung der Gerichte festlegen, kann eindeutig festgestellt werden, dass *die Durchführung der Sachaufgaben der Berufungsgerichte*- verständlicherweise - *den Berufsrichtern zufällt*. Innerhalb eines gegebenen Landes also macht die Kenntnis der Zahl der Berufsrichter in Zivilsachen an den Berufungsgerichten und der Zahl der angefochtenen erstinstanzlichen zivil-

---

38 In der Sowjetunion werden zum Beispiel die Volksbeisitzer der als Grundeinheiten des Gerichtssystems geltenden Volksgerichte von den Staatsbürgern unmittelbar gewählt. Zuletzt wurden am 20. Juni 1982 die Volksbeisitzer dieser Gerichte - auf Versammlungen nach Arbeits- oder Wohnort, durch offene Abstimmung gewählt, und zwar zahlenmässig insgesamt 738 751 (vgl. **Melnikow**, Nationalbericht, S. 3, 5).

39 Die juristische Vorbildung ist im allgemeinen keine ausschliessende Bedingung bei der Wahl zum Volksbeisitzer, ja vielmehr noch - in einzelnen Ländern, so z.B. in Ungarn sind die überwiegende Mehrzahl der für das Oberste Gericht gewählten Volksbeisitzer Juristen, die über eine hohe theoretische Ausbildung verfügen und als Lehrer an den Universitäten tätig sind.

40 Der Einzelrichter ist nämlich immer ein Berufsrichter.

41 Eine solche Vorschrift ist z.B. in Polen anzutreffen (vgl. den Art. 47 § 3 des polnischen TVG) und in Ungarn (vgl. den § 66 Abs. 2 des Gesetzes II des Jahres 1969 über den Patentschutz der Erfindungen sowie den § 46 Abs. 2 des Gesetzes IX des Jahres 1969 er r die Warenzeichen).

42 So zum Beispiel die Mongolei und die Sowjetunion (vgl. den § 13 des mongolischen ZVG und **Melnikow**, Nationalbericht, S. 5).

43 Vgl. Fussnoten 35 und 36.

44 Vgl. **Kellner**, Zivilprozessrecht, S. 105.

gerichtlichen Entscheidungen bereits möglich, gewisse grobe Schlussfolgerungen bezüglich einer eventuellen überlastung der Rechtsmittelgerichte zu ziehen. Daneben ermöglichen natürlich weitere Daten und charakteristische Kennzeichen detailliertere und begründetere Schlussfolgerungen so z.B.: die Zahl der Bevölkerung des Landes sowie die Zahl der innerhalb eines Jahres angestrengten bzw. erstinstanzlich entschiedenen Prozesse, die Verteilung der Richter nach Geschlecht, Lebensalter, Niveau ihrer fachlichen Bildung usw. Leider hat der Referent - trotz seiner nachdrücklichen Bitte von den Nationalreferenten, ausgenommen den jugoslawischen und den ungarischen nationalen Referenten, Daten entweder nur auf Details beschränkt oder überhaupt nicht erhalten. Einige Nationalreferenten weisen in ihrem Bericht ohne jegliche Umschweife auch sehr aufrichtig darauf hin, dass gewisse Angaben in ihren Ländern nicht an die öffentlichkeit gebracht werden[45], bzw. diese ihnen auch nicht zur Verfügung stehen[46].

Unter solchen Umständen ist der Referent gezwungen, von einem sich auf die Gerichte - und innerhalb derer sich auf die Rechtsmittelgerichte - beziehenden und auf die europäischen sozialistischen Länder erstreckenden zahlenmässigen Vergleich abzusehen. Gleichzeitig aber geben die zur Verfügung stehenden Angaben die Möglichkeit zu einigen solchen, auch vom Gesichtspunkt des untersuchten Themas aus bedeutenden Vergleichen, welche beweisen, dass in den verschiedenen sozialistischen Ländern die Zivilgerichtsbarkeit manchmal unter sehr stark voneinander abweichenden Bedingungen funktioniert.

So kann unter anderem festgestellt werden, dass bezüglich der *Zahl der Richter*[47], bzw. der *Einwohnerzahl des Landes* die Lage am günstigsten in Jugoslawien ist[48], wo das Verhältnis von Richtern und Einwohnerzahl 1 : 4335 ist. Wesentlich schlechter ist die Lage in Ungarn[49] und in der Tschechischen Sozialistischen Republik[50], in diesen Ländern beträgt das Verhältnis schon 1 : 7087 beziehungsweise 1 : 7370. Entsprechend der zur Verfügung stehenden Angaben sind bezüglich der 'Versorgung mit Richtern' die Umstände in der

---

45 Vgl. **Kellner**, Nationalbericht, S. 3; **Zilberststein/Ciobanu**, Nationalbericht, S. 16.

46 Vgl. **Braikow**, Nationalbericht II, S. 2.

47 Die Richter in Strafsachen und in Zivilsachen wurden zahlenmässig nur vom ungarischen Nationalreferenten unterschieden, der damit kennzeichnen wollte, dass zwei Drittel davon Richter in Zivilsachen sind (vgl. **Gáspárdy**, Nationalbericht I, S. 10). Bei anderen nationalen Referenten - unter denjenigen, die überhaupt Angaben hinsichtlich der Zahl der Richter mitteilten gibt es keine solche Unterscheidung, die ja im gegebenen Falle auch nicht getroffen werden kann, weil z.B. in der Sowjetunion die 'Volksrichter' der Kreis-, (Stadt-) Volksgerichte nicht spezialisiert sind, d.h. in Straf- und Zivilprozessen gleichermassen urteilen. Deshalb beinhaltet die bei einzelnen Ländern angegebene Anzahl der Richter nicht nur die Richter in Zivil-, sondern auch diejenigen in Strafsachen.

48 Die Bevölkerung von Jugoslawien: 22 424 711, die Zahl der Richter: 5 172 (vgl. **Rakic-Vodinelic**, Nationalbericht, S. 10 f.).

49 Die Bevölkerung von Ungarn: 10 630 000, die Zahl der Richter: 1 500, die Zahl der den Richtern beistehenden und zu 88 % aus Frauen bestehenden sonstigen Bediensteten beträgt 2 706 (vgl. **Gáspárdy**, Nationalbericht I, S. 10).

50 Die Bevölkerung der Tschechischen Sozialistischen Republik: 10 200 000, die Zahl ihrer Richter: 1 384 (vgl. **Winterová**, Nationalbericht, S. 5). Bezüglich des anderen Mitgliedes des Föderativstaates, der Slowakischen Sozialistischen Republik, teilte der tschechoslowakische Nationalreferent keine Angaben mit.

Sowjetunion am schlechtesten[51], dort beträgt nämlich das Verhältnis von Richtern und Bevölkerungszahl 1 : 25475[52].

Ein interessantes Bild zeigt auch der Vergleich *der erstinstanzlichen Zivilprozesse* mit der *Zahl der Bevölkerung*. Die 'Prozesslust' ist in der DDR am geringsten[53], dort weist nämlich die Zahl der erstinstanzlichen Zivilprozesse im Vergleich zur Zahl der Bevölkerung ein Verhältnis von 1 : 106 auf. Viel höher ist die Zahl der vor dem erstinstanzlichen Gericht angestrengten Prozesse im Vergleich zur Zahl der Bevölkerung in der Tschechischen Sozialistischen Republik[54], in Ungarn[55] und in Jugoslawien[56], wo die Verhältniszahlen 1 : 54, 1 : 51 und 1 : 49 betragen.

Die sich den Gerichten auferlegende Arbeitslast bzw. deren landesweise Abweichung wird vielleicht durch den Vergleich der dem Referenten zur Verfügung stehenden geringen Angaben am besten nachgewiesen, welche sich auf die *Zahl der Richter* und der *erstinstanzlichen Zivilprozesse* beziehen. Die Zahl der Richter und der erstinstanzlichen Zivilprozesse verglichen stellt sich nämlich heraus, dass auf einen Richter in Jugoslawien 89, in der Tschechischen Sozialistischen Republik 135, in Ungarn dagegen 140 erstinstanzliche Zivilprozesse entfallen. Doch können diese Verhältniszahlen nur als Ausgangsgrundlage zu einer späteren annähernden Schätzung dienen. In der Gesamtzahl der Richter sind nämlich sowohl die Richter in Strafsachen als auch die Richter in Zivilsachen in zweiter Instanz[57] enthalten, wobei sie doch keine erstinstanzlichen Zivilprozesse verhandeln. Es ist auch allgemein bekannt, dass die Zahl der

---

51 Die Bevölkerung der Sowjetunion: 280 230 000, die Zahl ihrer Richter: ca. 11 000 (vgl. **Melnikow**, Nationalbericht, S. 5).

52 In Kenntnis dieses Verhältnisses ist es vollkommen verständlich - auch dann, wenn der sowjetische Nationalreferent über die Zahl der Prozesse keine Angaben mitteilt -, dass einzelne sowjetische Autoren in der letzten Zeit in ihren Artikeln und Studien die Aufmerksamkeit auf die Zunahme der den Richtern auferlegten Belastung bzw. das ausserordentliche Wesen dieser Belastung richten (vgl. z.B. N. Ja. **Sokolow**, Sowjetskie juristy kak sozialno-professionalnaja gruppa, Sowjetskoe gosudarstwo i prawo, 1986/2, S. 57; D. M. **Tschetschot**: A szovjet polgári eljárásjog időszerű problémái, Magyar Jog, 1987/3, S. 274). Der sowjetische Referent informiert übrigens darüber, dass **aufgrund einer** vom Justizministerium der Sowjetunion festgelegten **Norm** 'ein Volksrichter pro Monat 6 Strafsachen und 10 Zivilsachen sowie 20 Verwaltungsangelegenheiten verhandelt bzw. untersucht' (vgl. **Melnikow**, Nationalbericht S. 4). An dem gegebenen Gericht muss nur dann ein neuer Volksrichterstatus geschaffen werden, wenn Strafsachen zu einem die monatliche Norm um 75 % überschreitenden Masse beim Gericht ankommen (Nautschnaja organisazija truda w apparate sudow i utschreschdeni justizii, Moskau, 1984, S. 80).

53 Die Bevölkerung der DDR: 16 620 000, die Zahl der erstinstanzlichen Zivilprozesse im Jahre 1984: 156 780 (vgl. **Kellner**, Nationalbericht, S. 3).

54 In der Tschechischen Sozialistischen Republik betrug die Zahl der erstinstanzlichen Zivilprozesse im Jahre 1986: 187 230 (vgl. **Winterová**, Nationalbericht, S. 5).

55 Die Zahl der erstinstanzlichen Zivilprozesse in Ungarn im Jahre 1986: 209 508 (vgl. **Gáspárdy**, Nationalbericht I, S. 10).

56 In Jugoslawien betrug die Zahl der erstinstanzlichen Zivilprozesse im Jahre 1985: 461 000 (vgl. **Rakic-Vodinelic**, Nationalbericht, S. 11).

57 In Jugoslawien und Ungarn verhandelt und urteilt annähernd ein Viertel bzw. ein Drittel der Richter in Zivilsachen in zweiter Instanz (vgl. **Rakic-Vodinelic**, Nationalbericht, S. 11; **Gáspárdy**, Nationalbericht I, S. 10).

tatsächlich tätigen Richter - infolge von Krankheit, Geburt, Kinderpflege usw.[58] immer niedriger als die Zahl der Richter in Stellung ist. Daher ist es gar nicht überraschend, dass z.B. in Ungarn ein am erstinstanzlichen Gericht tätiger Richter in Wirklichkeit pro Jahr mehr als 300 Prozesse abschliesst und daneben noch in einer beträchtlichen Zahl unterschiedliche Sachen der freiwilligen Gerichtsbarkeit erledigt. Gleichzeitig muss in der Sowjetunion ein am Kreis-(Stadt-) Volksgericht urteilender erstinstanzlicher Richter - der vom Justizministerium festgelegten Norm[59] folgend - jährlich insgesamt etwas mehr als 400 Angelegenheiten abschliessen.

Annähernd ähnlich ist die Arbeitslast der Richter auch an den Berufungsgerichten einiger Länder. So mussten zum Beispiel 1985 in Jugoslawien die annähernd 430, zumeist aus drei Richtern bestehenden zweitinstanzlichen Kollegien 111 870 Berufungen beurteilen, in Ungarn dagegen die ca. 100, immer aus drei Richtern bestehenden zweitinstanzlichen Kollegien 28 727 Berufungen; das ist eine Anfechtungsquote von 14 % der erstinstanzlichen streitigen Entscheidungen[60]. Das bedeutet, dass in beiden Ländern die an den Berufungsgerichten tätigen Richter durchschnittlich jährlich in 260 bzw. in 187 Zivilprozessen in zweiter Instanz vorgehen mussten. Der Durchschnitt deckt allerdings oft eine sehr abweichende Arbeitsbelastung, denn die obersten Gerichte - die sich ausser der prinzipiellen anleitenden Arbeit in der Regel auch mit einer grossen Zahl, in weiterem Sinne verstandener ausserordentlicher Rechtsbehelfe beschäftigen müssen - beurteilen im allgemeinen weit weniger Berufungen als die mittleren Berufungsgerichte[61].

Die sich den Berufungsgerichten auferlegende Arbeitslast weicht jedoch auch landesweise sehr wesentlich voneinander ab. Sehr gut ist das zum Beispiel im Verhältnis von der DDR und Ungarn nachzuweisen. während nämlich in der DDR nach der Meinung des Nationalreferenten: 'verglichen mit der Situation in anderen Ländern, von einer überlastung der Berufungsgerichte ... nicht die Rede sein kann'[62], wird in Ungarn die sich den Gerichten - und innerhalb derer natürlich auch den Berufungsgerichten auferlegende Arbeitslast vom Justizminister bereits als von solchem Ausmasse qualifiziert, welche Qualität und Zeitgemässheit des Urteilens gleichermassen gefährdet[63].

---

58 In den sozialistischen Ländern gibt es ziemlich viele Richterinnen, hauptsächlich an den Gerichten erster Instanz. So beträgt zum Beispiel in der DDR bei den Kreisgerichten der Anteil der Richterinnen 55,1 %, in der Sowjetunion bei den Kreis(Stadt-) Volksgerichten 36,5 % und in Ungarn bei den örtlichen Gerichten annähernd 60 % (vgl. **Kellner**, Nationalbericht, S. 5; **Melnikow**, Nationalbericht, S. 5; **Gáspárdy**, Nationalbericht I, S. 10).

59 Vgl. Fussnote 52.

60 Vgl. **Rakic-Vodinelic**, Nationalbericht, S. 12; **Gáspárdy**, Nationalbericht I, S. 7, 10.

61 Entsprechend der Information des ungarischen Nationalreferenten bedeuten die in Ungarn im jährlichen Durchschnitt pro Senat verhandelten 287 zweitinstanzlichen Prozesse bei den Komitatsgerichten ca. 300 Sachen pro Senat jährlich, beim Obersten Gericht dagegen ca. 131 Sachen pro Senat und Jahr (vgl. **Gáspárdy**, Nationalbericht I, S. 11).

62 So **Kellner**, Nationalbericht, S. 4.

63 Vgl. I. **Markója**, A XIII. Kongresszus határozataiból az igazságügyi szervekre háruló feladatok, Magyar Jog, 1986/7-8, S. 583 ff.

2 DIE RECHTSMITTEL

2.1 RECHT AUF DAS RECHTSMITTEL

In der Zivilrechtspflege der europäischen sozialistischen Länder ist es ein allgemein zur Geltung kommender Grundsatz, dass die Prozessparteien und die anderen, im Gesetz genannten Rechtssubjekte ein *Recht auf Rechtsmittel gegenüber* den von ihnen als unrichtig gehaltenen *Entscheidungen der erstinstanzlichen Gerichte* haben. Dieses Recht des Berechtigten wird in einigen Ländern - wie z.B. in Jugoslawien[64] - von der Verfassung selbst festgesetzt, in anderen Ländern dagegen vom Gerichtsverfassungsgesetz bzw. von der Zivilprozessordnung gewährleistet[65].

Dieses Recht kommt - unter Hinsicht darauf, dass es von den Berechtigten immer nur gegen die Entscheidung des erstinstanzlichen Gerichtes in Anspruch genommen werden kann - innerhalb des Rahmens des einstufigen Rechtsmittelsystems zur Geltung. Früher, vor dem übergang zur sozialistischen Gesellschaftsordnung oder noch eine Zeitlang danach stand in einigen Ländern[66] den Berechtigten das Recht auf Rechtsmittel auch gegen die Entscheidung des Gerichtes zweiter Instanz zu. Infolgedessen war also in den betreffenden Ländern das Rechtsmittelsystem zweistufig. Die *wesentlichen* Vorteile *des einstufigen Rechtsmittelsystems* gegenüber dem zweistufigen werden von mehreren Nationalreferenten darin gesehen, dass es

- das Verfahren konzentriert und beschleunigt,
- die Verschleppung des Prozesses erschwert,
- den alsbaldigen endgültigen Abschluss des Prozesses fördert,
- die im Zusammenhang mit dem Prozess auftauchenden Kosten verringert und dadurch
- die Lage der Prozessparteien erleichtert[67].

---

64 Vgl. **Rakic-Vodinelic**, Nationalbericht, S. 4, 28.

65 Vgl. den § 11 des am 17. März 1958 verabschiedeten Gesetzes Nr. 2625 über das albanische Zivilverfahren (im weiteren: albanisches ZVG); den Art. 196 der am 2. Februar 1952 erlassenen Verordnung mit Gesetzeskraft Nr. 56 über das bulgarische Zivilverfahren (im weiteren: bulgarisches ZVG); den § 147 der ZPO der DDR; den Art. 348 des am 24. Dezember 1976 verabschiedeten Gesetzes über das jugoslawische Zivilverfahren (im weiteren: jugoslawisches ZVG); den Art. 367 des polnischen ZVG; den Art. 299 des am 12. Februar 1948 verabschiedeten Gesetzes Nr. 18 über die Modifizierung und Neuherausgabe des rumänischen Zivilverfahrensgesetzbuches (im weiteren: rumänisches ZVG); den § 282 des ZVG der RSFSR; den § 201 des Gesetzes über das tschechoslowakische Zivilgerichtsverfahren Nr. 99/1963, welches am 4. Dezember 1963 verabschiedet wurde (im weiteren: tschechoslowakisches ZVG); den § 233 Abs. 1 der ungarischen ZPO. Auch in einigen aussereuropäischen sozialistischen Ländern verfügen die Verfahrensgesetze über das Recht auf ein Rechtsmittel. Vgl. z.B. den § 144 der chinesischen ZPO; den § 618 des am 19. August 1977 verabschiedeten Gesetzes Nr. 7 über das kubanische Zivil-, Verwaltungs- und Arbeitsrechtsverfahren (im weiteren: kubanisches ZVG) und den § 205 des mongolischen ZVG.

66 So zum Beispiel in der DDR, in Rumänien und in Ungarn.

67 Vgl. **Braikow**, Nationalbericht I, S. 1; **Gáspárdy**, Nationalbericht I, S. 1; **Kellner**, Nationalbericht, S. 1; **Zilberstein/Ciobanu**, Nationalbericht, S. 3.

Neben den aufgezählten Vorteilen hält der Referent auch die Tatsache für wesentlich, dass im einstufigen Rechtsmittelsystem - in dem das Recht auf Rechtsmittel prinzipiell in voller Gänze zur Geltung kommt -, infolge des Ausbleibens eines weiteren Rechtsmittels der Sachverkehr und die Arbeitslast der Rechtsmittelgerichte und innerhalb derer auch in erster Linie der obersten Gerichte geringer sind, als im zweistufigen Rechtsmittelsystem.

2.2 ARTEN DER RECHTSMITTEL

Die sozialistischen Zivilprozessrechte kennen als Rechtsmittel *die Berufung, den Protest* und *die Beschwerde*.

Die Berufung ist - der bulgarischen, der polnischen und der Regelung in der DDR gemäss[68] - gegen in erster Instanz ergangene Urteile zulässig. Davon abweichend dagegen wird vom albanischen, jugoslawischen, rumänischen, sowjetischen, tschechoslowakischen, ungarischen sowie dem chinesischen, kubanischen und mongolischen Zivilverfahrensrecht[69] die Berufung als ein solches Rechtsmittel geregelt, welches sowohl gegen Urteile als auch Beschlüsse und Verfügungen innerhalb gleicher Frist[70] in Anspruch genommen werden kann.

Der Protest ist ein solches, dem Staatsanwalt zur Verfügung stehendes Rechtsmittel, welches in einigen Ländern vom Gesetzgeber durch eine von der Berufung etwas abweichende Regelung und unter anderem Namen ausgestaltet wurde. Den Regeln des albanischen, des bulgarischen, des sowjetischen, des DDR- und des mongolischen Zivilverfahrensrechtes gemäss kann der Staatsanwalt - mit gewissen Ausnahmen - gegen die erstinstanzlichen Urteile und Beschlüsse Protest einlegen[71]. Der Staatsanwalt ist zur Einlegung des Protestes auch dann berechtigt, wenn er am erstinstanzlichen Verfahren nicht teilgenommen hat[72].

Die Beschwerde als Rechtsmittel, das gegen erstinstanzliche Beschlüsse und Verfügungen in Anspruch genommen werden kann, wird nur in Bulgarien, der DDR und Polen vom Zivilverfahrensrecht gekannt[73].

---

68 Vgl. den Art. 196 des bulgarischen ZVG; den § 147 Abs. 1 der ZPO der DDR; den Art. 367 des polnischen ZVG.

69 Vgl. die §§ 249 und 282 des albanischen ZVG; die Art. 348 und 378 des jugoslawischen ZVG; den Art. 299 des rumänischen ZVG; die §§ 282 und 315 des ZVG der RSFSR; den § 201 des tschechoslowakischen ZVG; den § 233 Abs. 1 der ungarischen ZPO; den § 144 der chinesischen ZPO; den § 618 des kubanischen ZVG; die §§ 205 und 233 des mongolischen ZVG.

70 Das Adjektiv 'gleich' bedeutet hier nur, dass die Zivilverfahrenskodexe der aufgezählten Länder **zur Anfechtung eines Urteils oder eines Beschlusses innerhalb ihres eigenen Rechtssystems eine gleiche Frist** gewähren, und nicht, dass diese Fristen in den einzelnen Ländern auch gleich sind, denn zum Beispiel nach dem § 619 des kubanischen ZVG beträgt die Berufungsfrist lediglich 5 Tage, während sie anderswo überall länger ist.

71 Vgl. die §§ 11 und 71 des albanischen ZVG; den Art. 30 des bulgarischen ZVG; den § 149 Abs. 1 und den § 7 bzw. den § 159 Abs. 3 der ZPO der DDR; die §§ 282 und 315 des ZVG der RSFSR; die §§ 205 und 233 des mongolischen ZVG.

72 Vgl. Fussnote 71 sowie **Braikow**, Nationalbericht I, S. 2; 0. **Stamboliew**, Prokurorat w iskowija graschdanski prozes, Sofia, 1983, S. 84 ff.; **Kellner**, Nationalbericht, S. 2; **Melnikow**, Nationalbericht, S. 8 ff.

73 Vgl. die Art. 213 und 218 des bulgarischen ZVG; den § 158 Abs. 1 der ZPO der DDR; den Art. 394 § 1 und den Art. 398 des polnischen ZVG.

Diese drei Arten der Rechtsmittel werden vom Referenten im weiteren der Einfachheit halber gemeinsam, im Kreise der mit der Berufung verbundenen Fragen untersucht. Die Möglichkeit einer solchen gemeinsamen Untersuchung ergibt sich übrigens auch aus den geltenden Regeln der betroffenen Länder, denen zufolge auf den Protest und die Beschwerde die Bestimmungen über die Berufung entsprechend anzuwenden sind[74].

2.3 BERUFUNGSBERECHTIGTE

Auch unter Hinsicht auf die Grundwahrheit von *volenti non fit iniuria* ist in den sozialistischen Zivilverfahrensrechten das *ex officio* beginnende Berufungsverfahren unbekannt. Das Berufungsverfahren wird nur und ausschliesslich *auf Verlangen der Berechtigten* eingeleitet[75].

Zur Einlegung der Berufung sind in erster Linie *die Prozessparteien* berechtigt. Die Parteien können ihre Berufung entweder persönlich oder durch *ihren Vertreter* einlegen und können sich so auch am Berufungsverfahren beteiligen. Das bedeutet, dass in den im Referat untersuchten Ländern es nicht nur in erster Instanz, sondern auch in zweiter Instanz keinen *Anwaltszwang* gibt, die Prozessparteien können - ihrer Entscheidung folgend - sogar auch vor dem höchsten richterlichen Forum persönlich vorgehen.

Die Realität des persönlichen Vorgehens der Parteien wird übrigens durch den Umstand gewährleistet, dass die sozialistischen Gerichte eine Beratungs-, Hinweis- und Unterstützungspflicht gegenüber den Prozessparteien haben, die- wie das auch vom DDR-Referenten betont wird - 'in aller Regel verantwortungsbewusst ausgeübt wird'[76], und daher bedürfen die Prozessparteien in den meisten Fällen keiner besonderen anwaltlichen Unterstützung. Es ist eine andere Frage, dass die Prozessparteien in allen solchen Fällen, wenn sie das- auch aufgrund der Empfehlung des Gerichtes - für erforderlich halten, frei die Hilfe eines Anwaltes oder sonstiger, die rechtliche Vertretung berufsmässig versehender Organe in Anspruch nehmen können[77]. Diese Hilfe kann bei gewissen Prozessarten unter einem bestimmten Einkommensniveau der Prozesspartei z.B. unentgeltlich sein - sie wird also in voller Gänze vom Staat, den Gewerkschaften oder den Genossenschaften bzw. den Rechtsanwaltskammern[78]

---

74 Vgl. den § 11 des albanischen ZVG; die Art. 29 und 217 des bulgarischen ZVG; den § 149 Abs. 3 und den § 159 Abs. 3 der ZPO der DDR; den Art. 397 § 2 des polnischen ZVG; die §§ 282 und 316 des ZVG der RSFSR; die §§ 205 und 234 des mongolischen ZVG.

75 Vgl. **Braikow**, Nationalbericht I, S. 2; **Kellner**, Nationalbericht, S. 2; **Zilberstein/Ciobanu**, Nationalbericht, S. 8; **Winterová**, Nationalbericht, S. 1; **Gáspárdy**, Nationalbericht I, S. 5.

76 So **Kellner**, Nationalbericht, S. 3.

77 In Ungarn zum Beispiel versehen neben den in Arbeitsgemeinschaften tätigen Rechtsanwälten auch die Arbeitsgemeinschaften zur Rechtsvertretung der Lehrer an den Universitäten, die Arbeitsgemeinschaften der Rechtsberater sowie die Rechtshilfedienste der Gewerkschaften und der Genossenschaften berufsmässig die Rechtsvertretung.

78 In der Sowjetunion trägt z.B. der Staat die Rechtsanwaltkosten, wenn das Gericht den Staatsbürger von deren Zahlung befreit, in dem Fall jedoch, wenn der Staatsbürger diese Befreiung vom Leiter der Arbeitsgemeinschaft der Rechtsanwälte oder vom Vorstand der Rechtsanwaltskammer erhalten hat, dann wird das Honorar des Rechtsanwaltes von der Arbeitsgemeinschaft finanziert /vgl. **Melnikow**, Nationalbericht, S. 11/.

gezahlt - oder die Prozesspartei bekommt in solchem Falle einen Gebührennachlass.

Es ist eine unzweifelhafte Tatsache, dass das persönliche Vorgehen der Parteien im Prozess die Berührung zwischen dem Gericht und den Parteien unmittelbarer gestaltet, von gewissem Gesichtspunkt aus das Verfahren vereinfacht usw., der Anwaltszwang dagegen ein in den Hintergrunddrängen des Grundsatzes der Unmittelbarkeit zur Folge hat und fallweise unnötig den Prozess verteuert. Der Referent hält es dennoch für wert zu überlegen, ob es im Interesse der fachgemässeren Vorbereitung der Verhandlung und ihres Ablaufes sowie der sich daraus ergebenden Verkürzung der Prozessdauer nicht zweckmässig wäre, im Verfahren vor bestimmten Gerichten oder in einzelnen Angelegenheiten die rechtliche Vertretung obligatorisch zu gestalten. Solche Vorschläge - deren Wesen darin besteht, dass bei Prozessen, die zur erstinstanzlichen sachlichen Zuständigkeit der sich auf der mittleren Ebene der Gerichtshierarchie befindenden Komitatsgerichte gehören, und bei Verfahren vor dem Obersten Gericht sowie bei prozesslicher Vertretung von Rechtspersonen die Rechtsvertretung obligatorisch sein soll - werden in letzter Zeit in Ungarn häufiger aufgeworfen[79]. Ziel dieser Vorschläge ist die Minderung der Arbeitslast der Gerichte und innerhalb dieser natürlich der Rechtsmittelgerichte, die Förderung des schnelleren Abschlusses der Prozesse sowie die Mässigung der mit der Hinweispflicht der Gerichte einhergehenden und oft ernste Probleme verursachenden Aufgabe, wonach sie verpflichtet sind, Kläger und Beklagten gleichermassen über die Geltendmachung ihrer Rechte zu informieren.

Der Unterstützer irgendeiner der Prozessparteien ist der *Nebenintervenient*, der zwar mit gewisser Einschränkung, aber dennoch über die Rechtsstellung der von ihm unterstützten Partei verfügt. Deshalb ist zur Einlegung der Berufung- wie das von einigen Nationalreferenten gesondert hervorgehoben wird - auch der Nebenintervenient berechtigt, mit der Bedingung, dass seine Berufung nicht im Gegensatz zur Handlung oder zum Willen der von ihm unterstützten Partei steht[80], beziehungsweise die Partei, zu deren Gunsten der Nebenintervenient interveniert hatte, auch Berufung einlegte[81].

Ausser der Parteien und ihren Vertretern ist es *der Staatsanwalt*, der berechtigt ist, gegen fast jede erstinstanzliche Gerichtsentscheidung Berufung (beziehungsweise in einzelnen Ländern Protest) einzulegen, ohne Hinsicht darauf, ob er vorangehend am Prozess teilgenommen hat oder nicht. Die einzige Ausnahme in dieser Hinsicht bildet unter den europäischen sozialistischen Ländern Jugoslawien, wo der Staatsanwalt nur dann Berufung einlegen kann, wenn er vorangehend am Prozess teilgenommen hat[82].

Diese Berechtigung des Staatsanwaltes wird von den meisten Staaten - zwar in unterschiedlichen gesetzlichen Formulierungen im wesentlichen im Interesse der Wahrung der Gesetzlichkeit, des Schutzes des staatlichen oder gesellschaftlichen Interesses bzw. des Schutzes der Rechte und gesetzlichen Interessen der

---

79 Vgl. **Gáspárdy**, Nationalbericht I, S. 6; J. **Németh**, A polgári eljárásjog reformja, Magyar Jog, 1986/3, S. 202.

80 Vgl. **Rakic-Vodinelic**, Nationalbericht, S. 4; **Gáspárdy**, Nationalbericht, S. 4.

81 Vgl. **Zilberstein/Ciobanu**, Nationalbericht, S. 13.

82 Vgl. **Rakic-Vodinelic**, Nationalbericht, S. 6.

Staatsbürger gewährleistet[83]. Der Staatsanwalt wird also in diesen Ländern vom Gesetzgeber im Grunde genommen *als Vertreter des öffentlichen Interesses* betrachtet, der - der Formulierung des tschechoslowakischen ZVG zufolge - 'im Zivilprozess als Wächter der sozialistischen Gesetzlichkeit auftritt'[84]. Der Staatsanwalt nimmt seine Berufungsberechtigung in den verschiedenen Ländern in einem voneinander beträchtlich abweichenden Masse in Anspruch. In der DDR zum Beispiel nimmt der 'Staatsanwalt das ihm eingeräumte Rechtsmittel nur ganz ausnahmsweise' wahr[85]. Demgegenüber bildeten z.B. in Ungarn die vom Staatsanwalt eingelegten Berufungen - trotz der in den letzten Jahren feststellbaren ständig und gleichmässig sinkenden Tendenz ihrer Anzahl - noch 1985 fast 6 % sämtlicher Berufungen[86].

Neben dem Staatsanwalt wird in der Tschechoslowakei in den Zivilprozessen-wie das der Nationalreferent zum Ausdruck bringt - 'im grossen Umfang die Mitwirkung ... *der Nationalausschüsse* (wie in der CSSR die Stadt-, Kreis- und Bezirksräte genannt werden) sowie *verschiedener gesellschaftlicher Organisationen* (z.B. Gewerkschaften) zugelassen. Deshalb können auch diese Subjekte-neben den Beteiligten am Verfahren - Berufungsanträge stellen'[87]. Eine ähnliche Regelung im Interesse des Schutzes des öffentlichen Interesses oder bestimmter Gruppeninteressen bzw. der staatsbürgerlichen Rechte ist auch in anderen Ländern zu finden. So hat zum Beispiel in der DDR in einigen bestimmten familienrechtlichen Angelegenheiten *das Organ der Jugendhilfe* das Recht, Berufung einzulegen, ohne in erster Instanz Prozesspartei gewesen zu sein[88]. In Jugoslawien kann *der gesellschaftliche Rechtsschützer der Selbstverwaltung* Berufung gegen den Prozess einlegen, der zwischen anderen Personen im Gange befindlich ist, wenn er an diesem Prozess - aufgrund einer gesetzlichen Ermächtigung - teilnimmt[89]. In der Sowjetunion sind ausser den Parteien und dem Staatsanwalt auch *die am Prozess beteiligten anderen Personen* zur Berufung gegen die erstinstanzlichen Gerichtsentscheidungen berechtigt[90]. Solche andere Personen sind - neben dem Haupt- und dem Nebenintervenient-einerseits diejenigen Staatsverwaltungsorgane, Gewerkschaften, staatlichen Institutionen, Unternehmen, Kolchosen und sonstigen genossenschaftlichen bzw. gesellschaftlichen Organisationen oder einzelnen aussenstehenden Staatsbürger, die sich in vom Gesetz bestimmten Fällen im Interesse des Schutzes der Rechte und Interessen von anderen Personen an das Gericht wenden können, andererseits die Anzeigeerstattenden sowie die an einer aus Verwaltungsrechtsverhältnissen entstandenen Sache bzw. an einem besonderen Verfahren interessierten Personen[91].

---

83 Vgl. den Art. 27 des bulgarischen ZVG; den § 7 der ZPO der DDR; den Art. 7 des polnischen ZVG; den Art. 45 des rumänischen ZVG; den § 41 des ZVG der RSFSR; den § 35 Abs. 1 des tschechoslowakischen ZVG; den § 2/A der ungarischen ZPO; den § 45 des mongolischen ZVG.

84 Vgl. den § 35 Abs. 3 des tschechoslowakischen ZVG.

85 So **Kellner**, Nationalbericht, S. 2.

86 Unter den 28 727 Berufungen wurden 1 694 vom Staatsanwalt eingelegt.

87 So **Winterová**, Nationalbericht, S. 2.

88 Vgl. **Kellner**, Nationalbericht, S. 2; **Kellner**, Zivilprozessrecht, S. 397.

89 Vgl. den Art. 204 des jugoslawischen ZVG.

90 Vgl. die §§ 282 und 315 des ZVG der RSFSR.

91 Vgl. **Melnikow**, Nationalbericht, S. 8 sowie die §§ 4 und 42 des ZVG der RSFSR.

All diese Beispiele - und die dem Staatsanwalt gewährte Berufungsberechtigung - beweisen eindeutig, dass die sozialistischen Zivilverfahrensrechte ausser den im materiellen Sinne verstandenen Parteien (Kläger - Beklagter) in breitem Kreise auch andere Organe und Personen zur Einlegung der Berufung berechtigen, unabhängig oder abhängig von ihrer Teilnahme am Grundprozess. Diese Tatsache aber bedeutet unter anderem auch, dass:

a) Das Gericht zwar ex officio tatsächlich kein Berufungsverfahren inleiten kann, dem Staat aber zumeist die Möglichkeit dazu besteht, in den Zivilprozessen, in denen seiner Meinung nach die erstinstanzliche Gerichtsentscheidung unter Hinsicht auf das öffentliche Interesse usw. nicht entsprechend ist, sogar auch gegen den ausdrücklichen Willen der Prozessparteien durch bestimmte staatliche Organe Berufung einlegen zu lassen und dadurch das Berufungsverfahren einzuleitet.

b) Die Zahl der Berufungen und damit *die Arbeitslast der Rechtsmittelgerichte nicht nur und ausschliesslich aus dem Willen der Prozessparteien* oder aufgrund ihrer Entscheidung *zunehmen kann*. Daraus ergibt sich, dass ein Staat, in dem die überlastung der Berufungsgerichte tatsächlich besteht, durch eine rationelle Verringerung des Masses der staatlichen Einmischung im Interesse des öffentlichen Wohles in der Lage ist, die Arbeitsbelastung der Rechtsmittelgerichte vorteilhaft zu ändern.

2.4 BESCHRÄNKUNG DES GEGENSTANDES DER BERUFUNG

Aus dem Recht auf das Rechtsmittel folgt, dass prinzipiell jede erstinstanzliche Gerichtsentscheidung durch Berufung angefochten werden kann. Die Situation ist jedoch in der Praxis nicht so eindeutig und einfach.

Der Referent hat nämlich bereits oben (Punkt 1.2) darauf verwiesen, dass in Fällen, in denen das Oberste Gericht des gegebenen Staates oder innerhalb des föderativen Staatssystems die obersten Gerichte der föderativen Republiken in erster Instanz eine Entscheidung treffen - unabhängig davon, ob das gegebene Gericht in der für es durch Gesetz festgelegten oder lediglich in herangezogener Zuständigkeit vorgeht -, gegen die von ihnen getroffenen Entscheidungen mangels eines übergeordneten Gerichtes *die Berufung ausgeschlossen ist*[92].

Abgesehen jedoch von den von den obersten Gerichten getroffenen erstinstanzlichen Entscheidungen können die erstinstanzlichen Gerichts*urteile* - ohne Hinsicht auf die Berufungssumme - fast überall ohne Einschränkung durch Berufung angefochten werden. Eine Ausnahme in dieser Hinsicht kommt nur in Rumänien und in Ungarn dann zur Geltung, wenn die Gerichte im Prozess die überprüfung der Entscheidungen verschiedener, nicht zum Gerichtssystem gehörender Rechtsanwendungsorgane, so zum Beispiel der Konfliktkommissionen durchführen. In solchen Fällen nämlich schliesst der Gesetzgeber - davon ausgehend, dass das Verfahren der nicht zum Gerichtssystem gehörenden

92 Vgl. **Braikow**, Nationalbericht I, S. 1; **Rakic-Vodinelic**, Nationalbericht, S. 4; **Zilberstein/Ciobanu**, Nationalbericht, S. 10; **Melnikow**, Nationalbericht, S. 7; **Németh**, A fellebbezés, in: J. **Farkas**/J. **Németh**/L. **Névai**/J. **Szilbereky**/Gy. **Varga**/I. **Vida**, Polgári eljárásjog II, Budapest, 1981, S. 30 f. sowie den § 144 der chinesischen ZPO; den § 205 des mongolischen ZVG.

Rechtsanwendungsorgane als erste Stufe der Rechtspflege angenommen werden kann - die Berufung gegen die Urteile der erstinstanzlichen Gerichte aus[93]. Es besteht kein Zweifel, dass diese Lösung die Entlastung der Rechtsmittelgerichte sowie die Verringerung ihrer Arbeitslast zum Ziele hat. In Ungarn wird allerdings die Richtigkeit dieser gesetzgeberischen Konzeption von vielen bestritten, und man drängt auf die gewährung des Rechtes auf das Rechtsmittel auch in derartigen Prozessen[94]. Unter den erstinstanzlichen Gerichtsurteilen kann in Rumänien das den Vergleich billigende sowie das auf der einseitigen Willenserklärung irgendeiner Partei beruhende Urteil durch Berufung eben-falls nicht angefochten werden[95].

Ein *gesetzlicher Ausschluss* der Anfechtbarkeit erstinstanzlicher gerichtlicher Beschlüsse und Verfügungen kommt zumeist nur ausnahmsweise, bei im Laufe des Verfahrens - und nicht beim Abschluss des Verfahrens - getroffenen sog. *prozessleitenden Entscheidungen* vor[96]. Die Begründung für den Ausschluss der Anfechtbarkeit dieser prozessleitenden Entscheidungen liegt in dem zustimmbaren gesetzgeberischen Ziel, dass das Verfahren der Möglichkeit nach konzentriert und zügig erfolgen soll. Der Ausschluss der Anfechtbarkeit ist übrigens bei dem bedeutenden Teil dieser Entscheidungen *relativ*, weil er sich nur *auf die gesonderte Berufung* bezieht. In mehreren Ländern nämlich können die dazu Berechtigten auch die während des Verfahrens getroffenen, als nachteilig gehaltenen Entscheidungen in der Berufung des erstinstanzlichen Gerichtsurteiles anfechten[97], und dann überprüft das Berufungsgericht zusammen mit dem Urteil auch die übrigen angefochtenen Entscheidungen. Diese Lösung ist deshalb vorteilhaft, weil sie den Berechtigten zwar indirekt, aber dennoch das Recht auf das Rechtsmittel gewährleistet, und gleichzeitig nicht überflüssigerweise das Verfahren unterbricht, die Urteilsfällung nicht verzögert und zugleich mit dem Ausschluss der Einlegung der gesonderten Berufung wesentlich die Arbeitslast der Rechtsmittelgerichte verringert. Ausgehend von einer solchen überlegung ist es im rumänischen Zivilverfahrensrecht - abweichend von der Regelung der übrigen europäischen sozialistischen Länder - allgemeine Regel, dass 'die nicht sachentscheidenden Entscheidungen nur in der das Sa-cnurteil anfechtenden Berufung angefochten werden können'[98].

93 Vgl. **Zilberstein/Ciobanu**, Nationalbericht, S. 9 f.; **Gáspárdy**, Nationalbericht II, S. 3.

94 Vgl. z.B. I. **Zsembery**, A polgári eljárás ujraszabályozásáról, Magyar Jog, 1983/5, S. 540; Gy. **Gátos**, A polgári eljárásjog ujraszabályozása, Magyar Jog, 1983/11, S. 1017; J. **Németh**, Polgári perjogunk fejlödése a felszabadulás óta, Magyar Jog, 1985/3-4, S. 297; Gáspárdy, Nationalbericht I, S. 3.

95 Vgl. **Zilberstein/Ciobanu**, Nationalbericht, S. 10.

96 Vgl. die Art. 213 und 218 des bulgarischen ZVG; **Kellner**, Nationalbericht, S. 1 f.; den Art. 378 des jugoslawischen ZVG; den Art. 394 § 1 des polnischen ZVG; **Zilberstein/Ciobanu**, Nationalbericht, S. 10 f.; den § 315 des ZVG der RSFSR; den § 202 des tschechoslowakischen ZVG; den § 233 Abs. 3 der ungarischen ZPO; den § 233 des mongolischen ZVG.

97 Vgl. z.B. den Art. 378 des jugoslawischen ZVG; den § 315 des ZVG der RSFSR; den § 233 des mongolischen ZVG.

98 So **Zilberstein/Ciobanu**, Nationalbericht, S. 11.

2.5 DAS KOSTENRISIKO ALS BERUFUNGSSPERRE

Das Risiko, dass die ergebnislos Berufung einlegende Partei die in Verbindung mit dem Berufungsverfahren auftretenden Kosten tragen muss, bedeutet theoretisch im Prozess eine ernste Berufungssperre. Diese Sperre ist jedoch nur dann eine faktische, wenn sich die Kosten des Berufungsverfahrens - die Gerichts- und Anwaltsgebühren und sonstige Verfahrenskosten - in einer solchen Grössenordnung bewegen, dass sie vor allem diejenigen potentiellen Personen zur Überlegung anregen, die unbegründete und lediglich auf die Verschleppung des Prozesses gerichtete Berufungen einlegen wollen. Da unter den Berufungsgerichten der sozialistischen Länder einige nicht zur Durchführung des Beweisverfahrens berechtigt sind, und andere - wenn sie auch dazu berechtigt sind - im allgemeinen keine breite und mit grossen Kosten einhergehende Beweisaufnahme durchführen, muss man zu der Schlussfolgerung gelangen, dass es nur die Gerichts- und Anwaltskosten vom Gesichtspunkt dieser Sperre aus der Untersuchung wert sind und die sonstigen Verfahrenskosten ausser Acht gelassen werden können.

Der bulgarische Nationalreferent hat bei Darlegung der derartigen Regelung in seinem Lande die Meinung geäussert, dass 'die Gerichts- und Anwaltsgebühr gemässigt ist und kein Hindernis dafür bildet, dass Rechtsschutz - in dessen Gebiet auch die Berufung gehört - gesucht wird, aber auch nicht so sehr gering, dass sie zur Einlegung unbegründeter Klagen oder grundloser Berufungen anregt'[99]. Der erste Teil dieser Meinung, dass nämlich die gemässigte Gerichts- und Anwaltsgebühr kein Hindernis für die Berufung darstellt, ist ausser Bulgarien auch für andere sozialistische Länder zweifellos zutreffend, weil:

- *die von der Zahlung der Gebühr befreiende* persönliche oder sachliche Gerichtskostenfreiheit sowie Gerichtsgebührenfreiheit ausnahmslos überall bekannt sind und unter Berücksichtigung der wirtschaftlichen Verhältnisse der Prozessparteien bzw. des Gegenstandes des Verfahrens in breitem Kreise gewährleistet werden[100];

- *die Anwaltskosten nur eventuelle sind*, da es keinen Anwaltszwang gibt.

Auch der Umstand, dass in einigen Ländern die Gerichtsgebühr ziemlich niedrig ist, gewährleistet ebenfalls eher den Rechtsschutz, als dass er die unbegründete Berufung verhindert. Aufgrund der dem Referenten zur Verfügung stehenden Angaben kann nämlich festgestellt werden, dass *die Berufungsgebühr gegen das Urteil im allgemeinen*[101] nur die Hälfte[102] der Gebühr des erst*instanzlichen*

---

99 So **Braikow**, Nationalbericht II, S. 2.

100 Vgl. **Braikow**, Nationalbericht II, S. 1 f.; **Kellner**, Nationalbericht, S. 10 f.; den Art. 172 des jugoslawischen ZVG; den Art. 111 § 1 und den Art. 113 §§ 1-2 des polnischen ZVG; **Zilberstein/ /Ciobanu**, Nationalbericht, S. 25 f.; **Melnikow**, Nationalbericht, S. 14 f.; den § 138 Abs. 1 des tschechoslowakischen ZVG; den § 84 der ungarischen ZPO; den § 75 des mongolischen ZVG.

101 Eine Ausnahme kommt z.B. in der DDR zur Geltung, wo für das Berufungsverfahren - ebenso wie für das erstinstanzliche Verfahren eine volle Gebühr erhoben wird /vgl. **Kellner**, Nationalbericht, S. 10/. Die volle Gerichtsgebühr beträgt 5 % des Wertes des geltend gemachten Anspruchs /vgl. den § 165 Abs. 1 der ZPO der DDR/.

Verfahrens beträgt[103], im Falle einer Berufung gegen einen Beschluss noch weniger[104] oder in einzelnen Ländern - wie z.B. der Sowjetunion oder der Mongolei - existiert die letztere überhaupt nicht[105].

Was die im Berufungsverfahren eventuell auftauchende Anwaltsgebühr betrifft, so ist diese - wie dies vom sowjetischen Referenten gesondert hervorgehoben wird - nicht zu beträchtlich und stellt kein Hindernis für die Partei bei Inanspruchnahme fachgebildeter juristischer Hilfe dar[106]. In den verschiedenen Ländern sind ziemlich abweichenden Berechnungsarten und Masse der Anwaltsgebühr bekannt, sie wird jedoch mehrerenorts insofern auf ähnliche Weise geregelt, dass ihre Summe im Berufungsverfahren niedriger ist, als im erstinstanzlichen Verfahren[107]. Die Anwaltsgebühr ist übrigens im erstinstanzlichen Verfahren zum Beispiel in der DDR und auch in der Sowjetunion abhängig vom Streitwert stark degressiv[108], in Ungarn dagegen auf der gleichen Höhe[109].

Aus den oben skizzenhaft dargelegten Tatsachen kann nach Ansicht des Referenten die Schlussfolgerung gezogen werden, dass nicht in jedem Land die Gerichts- und Anwaltsgebühren in den Zivilprozessen eine faktische Berufungssperre darstellen. Daraus ergibt sich, dass *im Interesse* der Verringerung der Zahl der unbegründeten, die Beurteilung des Prozesses wesentlich verschleppenden und ergebnislosen Berufungen und damit einhergehend *der Minderung der*

---

102 Vgl. **Braikow**, Nationalbericht II, S. 1; **Zilberstein/Ciobanu**, Nationalbericht, S. 25; **Melnikow**, Nationalbericht, S. 14; **Gáspárdy**, Nationalbericht I, S. 13; den § 72 des mongolischen ZVG.

103 Die Gebühr des erstinstanzlichen Verfahrens beträgt in Bulgarien im allgemeinen 4 % des Streitwertes (vgl. **Braikow**, Nationalbericht II, S. 1). In der Sowjetunion beträgt bei Klagen von Vermögenscharakter bis zu einem Streitwert von 500 Rubel die im erstinstanzlichen Verfahren zu entrichtende Gebühr 1,5 - 2 %, über 500 Rubel Streitwert 6 %, während sie bei Klagen nicht von Vermögenscharakter und im Falle nicht zu schätzender Klagen einheitlich **0,3 Rubel** beträgt (vgl. den § 82 des ZVG der RSFSR). In Ungarn beträgt die Gebühr des erstinstanzlichen Verfahrens 6 % des Streitwertes (vgl. **Gáspárdy**, Nationalbericht I, S. 13), in der Mongolei dagegen müssen bis zu einem Streitwert von 3000 Tugrik 1,5 - 2 %, über 3000 Tugrik 5 % und im Falle von Klagen nicht von Vermögenscharakter usw. **3 oder 5 Tugrik** Gebühr im erstinstanzlichen Verfahren entrichtet werden (vgl. den § 72 des mongolischen ZVG).

104 In Ungarn z.B. beträgt die Gebühr der gegen den Beschluss eingelegten Berufung 1,5 % der strittigen Forderung (vgl. **Gáspárdy**, Nationalbericht I, S. 13).

105 Vgl. den § 82 des ZVG der RSFSR; den § 72 des mongolischen ZVG.

106 Vgl. **Melnikow**, Nationalbericht, S. 11.

107 In der Sowjetunion und in Ungarn z.B. kann sich diese Summe bis zu 50 bzw. 40 % der im erstinstanzlichen Verfahren zu vereinbarenden Anwaltsgebühren erstrecken, wenn die Partei im zweitinstanzlichen Verfahren von derselben Rechtsanwaltsarbeitsgemeinschaft vertreten wird. Wenn die Partei im erstinstanzlichen Verfahren keinen Vertreter hatte oder eine andere Rechtsanwaltsarbeitsgemeinschaft vorgegangen ist, dann können 80 % der für das erstinstanzliche Verfahren bemessenen Anwaltsgebühr berechnet werden (vgl. **Melnikow**, Nationalbericht, S. 11 und **Gáspárdy**, Nationalbericht I, S. 13 f.).

108 Die Anwaltsgebühr verringert sich in Abhängigkeit vom Streitwert in der DDR von 7 % auf 0,5 %, in der Sowjetunion dagegen von 5 % auf 3 % (vgl. **Kellner**, Nationalbericht, S. 7; **Melnikow**, Nationalbericht, S. 11).

109 In Ungarn beträgt die Anwaltsgebühr 4 % des Streitwertes, die in besonders komplizierten Angelegenheiten um höchstens 50 %, d.h. auf 6 % des Streitwertes erhöht werden kann (vgl. **Gáspárdy**, Nationalbericht I, S. 13 f.).

Arbeitslast der Berufungsgerichte in einigen Ländern - neben der Reduzierung der durch Gerichtskostenfreiheit und Gerichtsgebührenfreiheit gewährten Vergünstigungen - *die Erhöhung der Berufungsgebühr*, aber eventuell auch der Anwaltsgebühr begründet sein kann. Von einem solchen Aspekt aus sind diejenigen Vorschläge vollkommen verständlich, die sich in Ungarn - wo die Gerichte überlastet sind - auf die überprüfung der durch Gerichtsgebührenfreiheit gewährleisteten Begünstigungen und als Ergebnis dieser überprüfung auf die 'Beschränkung'[110] dieser bzw. die Erhöhung der Gerichtsgebühr bezogen haben[111].

2.6 ARTEN DER BEURTEILUNG DER BERUFUNG

Die Berufung wird in der Regel von dem unmittelbar übergeordneten Gericht des die angefochtene erstinstanzliche Entscheidung treffenden Gerichtes, vom Gericht zweiter Instanz beurteilt.

Von dieser allgemeinen Regel abweichend sind allerdings in einigen Ländern auch solche Lösungen bekannt, welche - im Interesse der Vereinfachung und Beschleunigung des Verfahrens und dadurch der zweifellosen Entlastung der Berufungsgerichte - ermöglichen, dass die *Berufung* auch vom *Gericht erster Instanz*, das die angegriffene Entscheidung getroffen hat, *selbst* verhandelt werden kann. Diese Möglichkeit bezieht sich immer *nur* auf die Beurteilung der Berufungen gegen *Beschlüsse und Verfügungen*, nicht aber der Berufungen gegen Urteile. In der DDR und in Polen ist das erstinstanzliche Gericht praktisch zur Beurteilung der Berufung *jedes von ihm getroffenen Beschlusses oder jeder von ihm erlassenen Verfügung* berechtigt, wenn es die Berufung in vollem Umfang für begründet hält[112]. In der Tschechoslowakei und in Ungarn dagegen kann das erstinstanzliche Gericht nur einige Berufungen beurteilen, so zum Beispiel diejenigen, die gegen einen sich auf die Prozessführung beziehenden oder einen einseitigen Antrag abweisenden Beschluss eingelegt worden waren[113].

Abgesehen von den obigen Ausnahmen ist es immer das Gericht zweiter Instanz, das in der Sache über die Berufung - und zwar entweder *in einer mündlichen Verhandlung* oder *ohne mündliche Verhandlung* - entscheidet.

In der überwiegenden Mehrzahl der sozialistischen Länder *wird der Beschluss über die Sache der Berufung von den Gerichten im allgemeinen in einer mündlichen Verhandlung getroffen*. Jugoslawien bildet von diesem Gesichtspunkt aus eine Ausnahme, dort entscheidet nämlich das Gericht im Falle einer Berufung gegen einen Beschluss immer, im Falle einer Berufung gegen ein Urteil im allgemeinen ohne mündliche Verhandlung. Der jugoslawische Nationalreferent hebt auch besonders hervor, dass das zweitinstanzliche Gericht im Gegenstand der Berufung nur ausnahmsweise - in der Praxis ausserordentlich selten - das Urteil in einer mündlichen Verhandlung trifft[114].

---

110 Vgl. I. **Zsembery**, A polgári eljárás ujraszabályozásáról, Magyar Jog, 1983/5, S. 541.

111 Vgl. Gy. **Gátos**, Olcsó-e a pereskedés? Jogpolitika, 1983/3, S. 6; K. **Berndt**, A Pp. tervezett reformja elé, Magyar Jog, 1984/2, S. 148.

112 Vgl. den § 159 Abs. 1 der ZPO der DDR; den Art. 395 § 1 und den Art. 398 des polnischen ZVG.

113 Vgl. **Winterová**, Nationalbericht, S. 2; den § 257 der ungarischen ZPO.

114 Vgl. **Rakic-Vodinelic**, Nationalbericht, S. 5

Die Beurteilung der Berufung ohne mündliche Verhandlung - in einer geschlossenen Sitzung des Kollegiums - ist ausser in Jugoslawien auch in anderen sozialistischen Ländern, so in der DDR, in Polen, der Tschechoslowakei, Ungarn und China eine bekannte Verfahrensform. In einer solchen Verfahrensform entscheiden die Gerichte *in der DDR* nur und ausschliesslich über Berufungen *gegen Beschlüsse*[115], während sie in den übrigen erwähnten Ländern neben den Beschlüssen auch über Berufungen gegen einige Urteile[116] entscheiden können. *Die Erledigung der Berufung ohne mündliche Verhandlung* vereinfacht und beschleunigt das Verfahren zweiter Instanz und vermindert dadurch *zweifellos die Arbeitslast* der Rechtsmittelgerichte[117]. Gleichzeitig aber kann diese, die Grundprinzipien der öffentlichkeit, der Mündlichkeit und der Unmittelbarkeit der Verhandlung verletzende Verfahrensform - wie darauf in der ungarischen Rechtsliteratur in letzter Zeit von mehreren Autoren verwiesen wurde[118] - im Widerspruch zu dem auf der XXI. Sitzungsperiode der Vollversammlung der Vereinten Nationen am 16. Dezember 1966 angenommenen Internationalen Abkommensdokument über die Zivilen und Politischen Rechte stehen. Dem Punkt 1 von Absatz 14 des Abkommensdokumentes gemäss hat nämlich 'jeder das Recht, dass ... über seine Rechte und Pflichten in irgendeinem Prozess durch ein vom Gesetz aufgestelltes unabhängiges und unparteiisches Gericht in einer gerechten und öffentlichen Verhandlung geurteilt wird.' Aus der zitierten Verfügung des Abkommensdokumentes folgt, dass in der Tat in jedem solchen Fall, in dem sich unter den Prozessparteien auch eine natürliche Person befindet, nur dann die Entscheidung der Berufung hinsichtlich der strittigen Rechte und Pflichten der Parteien ohne mündliche Verhandlung gestattet werden kann, wenn dazu die im Prozess als Partei auftretende natürliche Person - wenn auch stillschweigend - ihre Zustimmung gibt. Dieser Umstand müsste nach dem Standpunkt des Referenten auch von den zivilverfahrensrechtlichen Regelungen der einzelnen Länder in Betracht gezogen werden, und dies auch dann, wenn sich als Ergebnis dessen die Arbeitslast der Berufungsgerichte nicht verringert, sondern mit aller Sicherheit zunimmt.

Bei der Beurteilung der Berufung - geschieht dies nun entweder in der mündlichen Verhandlung[119] oder ohne mündliche Verhandlung - sind die Beru-

---

115 Vgl. den § 159 Abs. 1 der ZPO der DDR; **Kellner**, Zivilprozessrecht, S. 411.

116 Vgl. den Art. 375 und den Art. 376 § 1 des polnischen ZVG; den § 214 Abs. 2 des tschechoslowakischen ZVG; die §§ 256/A Abs. 1 und 257 der ungarischen ZPO; den § 150 der chinesischen ZPO.

117 So sind z.B. in Ungarn im Jahre 1985 die Berufungsgerichte bei 35 % der zweitinstanzlichen beurteilten Sachen ohne mündliche Verhandlung vorgegangen (vgl. **Gáspárdy**, Nationalbericht I, S. 19).

118 Vgl. z.B. L. **Gáspárdy**, Perjogi kodifikációnk - nemzetközi összefüggésben, Jogpolitika, 1982/3, S. 10; L. **Gáspárdy**, Gondolatok az uj Pp koncepciójához, Magyar Jog, 1983/6, S. 542; T. **Lábady**, Fellebbezés, Manuskript, Pécs, 1984, S. 53; E. **Horváth**, Fellebbezés, Manuskript, Zalaegerszeg, 1984, S. 68; J. **Németh**, A polgári perjogunk fejlődése a felszabadulás óta, Magyar Jog, 1985/3-4, S. 296 f.; J. **Németh**, Theoretische und praktische Grundprobleme des Rechtsmittelsystems in Ungarn, Annales Universitatis Scientiarum Budapestinehsis de Rolando Eötvös nominatae, Sectio iuridica, Tomus XXVII, Budapest, 1986, S. 171.

119 Es ist eine Eigentümlichkeit der Berufungsverhandlung in der Sowjetunion, dass nach den Vorträgen der am Prozess beteiligten Personen **der Staatsanwalt seine Meinung zur Gesetzlichkeit und Begründetheit des angegriffenen Urteils vorbringt** (vgl. **Melnikow**, Nationalbericht, S. 19). Eine einigermassen ähnliche Lösung kommt auch in der Mongolei zur Geltung (vgl. den § 223 des mongolischen ZVG).

fungsgerichte befugt, kassatorisch oder reformatorisch zu entscheiden. Die kassatorische Entscheidungsbefugnis und das kassatorische Verfahren bedeuten, dass das Berufungsgericht das Verfahren und die Entscheidung des Vordergerichtes auf Mängel überprüft, Beweise grundsätzlich nur in dem Masse erhebt, wie das zur Mängelfeststellung notwendig ist, fehlerhafte Entscheidungen in gegebenem Falle aufhebt und die Sache zur erneuten Verhandlung und Entscheidung an das Gericht erster Instanz zurückverweist. Demgegenüber sind unter der reformatorischen Entscheidungsbefugnis und dem reformatorischen Verfahren zu verstehen, dass das Berufungsgericht das Verfahren erster Instanz und die dort getroffene Entscheidung in der Weise überprüft, dass es das Verfahren - soweit nötig - wiederholt, also gewöhnlich eine mündliche Verhandlung durchführt und in diesem Rahmen selbst Beweise erhebt, das Verfahren im erforderlichen Umfang fortsetzt und grundsätzlich mit einer eigenen Entscheidung abschliesst.

Der kassatorische oder reformatorische Charakter der Entscheidungsbefugnis der Berufungsgerichte und das dementsprechende Verfahren kommen nicht immer in vollkommen reiner Form zur Geltung. Es können nämlich einzelne Elemente des kassatorischen und des reformatorischen Rechtsmittelsystems miteinander variiert werden, was auch oft geschieht. In der Mehrzahl der sozialistischen Länder - so in Albanien, Jugoslawien, Polen, Rumänien, der Sowjetunion, China und der Mongolei[120] - ist das Rechtsmittelsystem von kassatorischem Charakter. In Bulgarien[121], der DDR, der Tschechoslowakei und Ungarn[122] dagegen ist der Charakter des Rechtsmittelsystems reformatorisch.

Für die Berufungsgerichte bedeutet das kassatorische Rechtsmittelsystem eine weit geringere Arbeitslast als das reformatorische. Dies ergibt sich vor allem daraus, dass sich im kassatorischen Rechtsmittelsystem das zweitinstanzliche Gericht - zwar sehr vereinfacht, aber praktisch dennoch - nur mit der Rechtsfrage, nicht aber mit der Tatsachenfrage beschäftigen muss. Es stellt bereits ein anderes Problem dar, dass es manchmal nicht so sehr einfach ist, ja in einzelnen Fällen ausserordentlich schwierig und umstritten[123], die Tatsachen- und die Rechtsfrage voneinander zu trennen. Im kassatorischen Rechtsmittelsystem führt das zweitinstanzliche Gericht eine Beweisaufnahme - wenn überhaupt erforderlich - nur in sehr beschränktem Umfange oder überhaupt nicht[124] durch. Zu gleicher Zeit jedoch wird in dem mit völliger Konsequenz verwirklichten reformatorischen Rechtsmittelsystem das erstinstanzliche Verfahren in grossem Masse abgewertet und 'das *Berufungsverfahren* ist nicht

---

120 Vgl. den § 266 des albanischen ZVG; **Rakic-Vodinelic**, Nationalbericht, S. 13 f.; den Art. 385 §§ 1-4 und den Art. 390 § 1 des polnischen ZVG; **Zilberstein/Ciobanu**, Nationalbericht S. 4 f.; **Melnikow**, Nationalbericht, S. 20 ff.; den § 151 der chinesischen ZPO; die §§ 225-226 des mongolischen ZVG.

121 In Bulgarien war das zweitinstanzliche Verfahren bei Schaffung des bulgarischen ZVG von betont kassatorischem Charakter. Seit der 1983 erfolgten Reform des ZVG jedoch ist der reformatorische Charakter bestimmend geworden (vgl. **Braikow**, Nationalbericht II, S. 1; Sch. **Stalew**, Reformata na wtoroinstanzionnoto proiswodstwo po graschdanski dela, Sozialistitschesko prawo, 1983/6, S. 3 ff.; B. **Janowski**, Prodalschawa li nascheto obschalwane po GPK da bade kontrolnootmenitelno (Po obschtata postanowka na waprosa), Sozialistitschesko prawo, 1985/3, S. 21 ff.).

122 Vgl. den § 156 Abs. 1 der ZPO der DDR; **Winterová**, Nationalbericht, S. 2; **Gáspárdy**, Nationalbericht II, S. 5 ff.

123 Vgl. z.B. **Rakic-Vodinelic**, Nationalbericht, S. 18 ff.

124 Vgl. **Melnikow**, Nationalbericht, S. 21 f.; den § 225 des mongolischen ZVG.

viel mehr als eine weiterbetriebene ‚erneute, oder 'zweite Erstinstanz"[125]. Eine solche konsequente oder vielleicht eher extreme Lösung - die im übrigen auch für die sozialistischen Länder, wo das reformatorische Rechtsmittelsystem zur Geltung kommt, nicht charakteristisch ist, da ja in diesen Rechtsmittelsystemen auch kassatorische Elemente anzutreffen sind[126] - hat zum Ergebnis, dass das Berufungsgericht neben der Rechtsfrage auch die Tatsachenfrage in voller Gänze untersucht und im Zusammenhang mit letzterer auch eine neue, detaillierte Beweisaufnahme durchführt. Es ist also unumstritten, dass das reformatorische Rechtsmittelsystem vom Gesichtspunkt der Berufungsgerichte aus viel arbeits-, zeit-, kosten- usw. aufwendiger ist, als das kassatorische Rechtsmittelsystem.

Deshalb ist es verständlich, dass in einigen sozialistischen Ländern, die über ein Rechtsmittelsystem von reformatorischem Charakter verfügen, solche Bestrebungen anzutreffen sind, *die auf die Senkung der Belastung der Berufungsgerichte zielen*, und im wesentlichen *die Annäherung an das kassatorische Rechtsmittelsystem bezwecken*. So bringt zum Beispiel der bulgarische Nationalreferent zum Ausdruck, dass seit 1983 - d.h. seit in Bulgarien vom Rechtsmittelsystem kassatorischen Charakters auf das reformatorischen Charakters gewechselt wurde - die Arbeit der Berufungsgerichte und innerhalb derer besonders die des Obersten Gerichtes zugenommen hat, sich die Beurteilung der Berufungen beträchtlich verzögert und in Verbindung damit auch sonstige übrige ernste Probleme auftauchen. Als Lösungsvorschlag 'wurde im Interesse der Minderung der überlastung des Obersten Gerichtes eine solche überlegung vorgebracht, dass auf Kodifikationswege dem Obersten Gericht in breiterem Kreise ermöglicht werden müsse, nach der Ausserkraftsetzung der unrichtigen Entscheidung die Sache zur neuen Beurteilung an das erstinstanzliche Gericht zurückzuverweisen'[127]. Auch vom ungarischen Nationalreferenten wird beanstandet, dass eine einfachere Beurteilung der Berufungen von der ZPO selbst behindert wird, und zwar dadurch, dass sie eine Möglichkeit zur teilweisen Änderung der Klage bzw. der Widerklage im zweitinstanzlichen Verfahren gewährt, das Recht des beneficium novorum anerkennt und das zweitinstanzliche Gericht zur Beweisaufnahme verpflichtet. In Kenntnis dieser Möglichkeiten und Rechte wird nämlich ein Teil der Parteien bzw. ihrer Vertreter gleichsam dazu 'ermutigt', auch solche Erklärungen erst im Berufungsverfahren abzugeben, welche sie bereits im erstinstanzlichen Verfahren hätten abgeben können[128]. Infolge solcher, im Berufungsverfahren abgegebener Erklärungen kommt es auch vor, dass das zweitinstanzliche Gericht über einige Ansprüche in erster und letzter Instanz entscheidet. Deshalb wird auch von vielen in Frage gestellt- hebt der ungarische Nationalreferent hervor -, ob eine derartige Zulässigkeit des beneficium novorum und die Tatsache, dass das zweitinstanzliche Gericht zur Tatsacheninstanz wird, richtig sei[129].

---

125 So P. **Gilles**, Rechtsmittel im Zivilprozess aus juristischer Sicht, in: Rechtsmittel im Zivilprozess-unter besonderer Berücksichtigung der Berufung (hrsg. von Peter **Gilles**/Klaus F. **Röhl**/Paul **Schuster**/Dieter **Strempel**), Köln, Bundesanzeiger, 1985, (Rechtstatsachenforschung) S. 13.

126 Vgl. die Art. 208 und 209 des bulgarischen ZVG; den § 156 Abs. 1 der ZPO der DDR; den § 221 Abs. 1 des tschechoslowakischen ZVG; den § 252 der ungarischen ZPO.

127 So **Braikow**, Nationalbericht II, S. 2.

128 Vgl. **Gáspárdy**, Nationalbericht I, S. 16.

129 Vgl. **Gáspárdy**, Nationalbericht II, S. 6 f.

2.7 DAS VERBOT DER REFORMATIO IN PEIUS

Das Verbot der reformatio in peius bedeutet im wesentlichen - wie allgemein bekannt -, dass die Berufungspartei durch ihre eigene Berufung ihre prozessuale Lage nicht verschlechtern kann. Diese Rechtsinstitution ist auch in den Berufungsverfahren einiger sozialistischer Länder bekannt.

Das jugoslawische ZVG zum Beispiel verfügt in einem gesonderten Artikel darüber, dass das zweitinstanzliche Gericht das Urteil nicht zum Schaden der Berufungspartei verändern kann, wenn nur diese Berufung eingelegt hat[130]. Im wesentlichen das gleiche besagt ebenfalls ein gesonderter Artikel des polnischen ZVG[131].

Abweichend davon enthalten in einigen Ländern die Verfahrenskodexe kein ausgesprochenes Verbot der reformatio in peius, es kommt aber dennoch zur Geltung. So wird zum Beispiel in Bulgarien die Existenz dieser Rechtsinstitution von der Praxis des Obersten Gerichtes anerkannt[132] und dies folgt - gewissen theoretischen Standpunkten gemäss - auch aus der Funktion und dem Sinn der Berufung[133]. Ähnlich ist die Lage in Rumänien, wo Theorie und Praxis einheitlich sind dahingehend, dass 'das Prinzip der non reformatio in peius auch im Rahmen des Zivilverfahrens als ein logisches und Billigkeitselement der Rechtspflege angewandt werden muss'[134]. Als Begründung berufen sie sich darauf, dass im entgegengesetzten Fall die Prozesspartei - in Furcht davor, mit der Berufung ihre Lage eventuell weiter verschlechtern zu können - fallweise nicht das Risiko eingeht und lediglich aus diesem Grunde das Urteil auch dann nicht beanstandet, wenn dies gesetzesverletzend oder unhegründet ist und ihre subjektiven Rechte verletzt[135]. Der tschechoslowakische und der ungarische Nationalreferent informieren ebenfalls darüber, dass in ihren Ländern die zweitinstanzlichen Gerichte das Verbot der reformatio in peius - mit einigen Ausnahmen zwar, aber dennoch - beim Berufungsverfahren in Betracht ziehen[136].

Diese Rechtsinstitution kommt dagegen in Albanien, in der DDR, der Sowjetunion, China und der Mongolei überhaupt nicht zur Geltung[137]. In den aufgezählten Ländern wird - aus unterschiedlichen Gründen - dieses Verbot in den Zivilorozessen nicht für anerkennenswert befunden. In der DDR z.B. ging der Gesetzgeber bei der geltenden Regelung unter anderem davon aus, dass es den

---

130 Vgl. den Art. 374.

131 Vgl. den Art. 382.

132 Vgl. **Braikow**, Nationalbericht I, S. 2.

133 Vgl. Sch. **Stalew**, Balgarsko graschdansko prozesualno prawo, Sofia, 1979, S. 459; **Braikow**, Nationalbericht I, S. 2. Hinsichtlich einer entgegengesetzten Meinung siehe 0. **Stamboliew**, Sabranata so reformatio in peius i sawremennijat balgarski graschdanski proces, Sozialistitschesko prawo, 1982/1, S. 27 ff.

134 So **Zilberstein/Ciobanu**, Nationalbericht, S. 22. Vgl. I. **Stoenescu**/ S. **Zilberstein**, Traîté de Procédure civile, vol. 2, Bukarest, 1981, S. 65.

135 Vgl. **Zilberstein/Ciobanu**, Nationalbericht, S. 22; M. **Enescu**, Aplicarea principiului 'non reformatio in pejus' in procesul civil, Studii si Cercetari Juridice, 1965/3, S. 459.

136 Vgl. **Winterová**, Nationalbericht S. 2; **Gáspárdy**, Nationalbericht I, S. 12.

137 Vgl. den § 265 des albanischen ZVG; den § 154 Abs. 1 der ZPO der DDR; den § 294 des ZVG der RSFSR; den § 149 der chinesischen ZPO; den § 214 des mongolischen ZVG.

Berufungsgerichten im Hinblick auf die sozialistischen Prozessprinzipien nicht zugemutet werden kann, entgegen richtiger Erkenntnis unzulängliche Urteile zu erlassen und erforderlichenfalls gleichzeitig die dazu Berechtigten zur Einlegung eines Kassationsantrages anzuregen, um eine Wiederherstellung der Gesetzlichkeit zu veranlassen[138].

Im Zusammenhang mit dem Thema des Referates sind jedoch *nicht diejenigen Gründe wichtig*, welche die Nichtanwendung des Prinzips des Verbotes der reformatio in peius zum Ergebnis hatten, *sondern die Folge der Nichtanwendung des Prinzips*. Sie hat nämlich eine Befreiung *der Berufungsgerichte* von gewissen Gebundenheiten, *eine teilweise Vereinfachung ihrer Arbeit* zur Folge. Wie der Nationalreferent der DDR darauf verweist, wurde durch die das Verbot ignorierende und sich in seinem Land in der Praxis bewährte Regelung 'eine wesentliche Vereinfachung des Berufungsverfahrens erreicht. Es erübrigte sich nämlich die Normierung der bis 1975 geltenden selbständigen und unselbständigen Anschlussberufung und es entfielen die unter Umständen mit der sogenannten unselbständigen Anschlussberufung verbundenen unerwünschten Folgen'[139].

3 DIE AUSSERORDENTLICHEN RECHTSBEHELFE

3.1 ARTEN DER AUSSERORDENTLICHEN RECHTSBEHELFE

Die ausserordentlichen Rechtsbehelfe - die sich gegen bereits rechtskräftige Entscheidungen richten - können nach verschiedenen Kriterien klassifiziert werden. So können sie z.B. auf Grund der Tatsache unterschieden werden, ob im Falle ihrer Inanspruchnahme die überprüfung der angefochtenen Entscheidungen durch ein übergeordnetes Gericht erfolgt oder nicht. Wie darauf schon hingewiesen wurde, können vom Gesichtspunkt des untersuchten Themas aus - der Überlassung der Rechtsmittelgerichte - jedoch unter den ausserordentlichen Rechtsbehelfen nur diejenigen in Betracht gezogen werden, deren Beurteilung vor einem übergeordneten Gericht erfolgt. Solche, über vollen oder partiellen Devolutiveffekt verfügende ausserordentliche Rechtsbehelfe in den europäischen sozialistischen Ländern bzw. in einigen von ihnen sind folgende: *die Revision, der Antrag auf die ausserordentliche Revision einer rechtskräftigen Entscheidung, die Wiederaufnahme* und *die* sog. *Aufsichtsrevision*.

Unter diesen Rechtsinstitutionen ist aber die detailliertere Analyse nur der letzterwähnten Aufsichtsrevision begründet, in Hinsicht darauf, dass:

- die Revision und der Antrag auf die ausserordentliche Revision einer rechtskräftigen Entscheidung als ausserordentliche Rechtsbehelfe in der Rechtsfrage nur und ausschliesslich in Jugoslawien bekannt sind[140];
- die Wiederaufnahme nur in Albanien und in Bulgarien einen Devolutiveffekt hat[141], der Gesetzgeber erlaubt nämlich in diesen zwei Ländern die Aufhebung

---

138 Vgl. **Kellner**, Nationalbericht, S. 6.

139 So **Kellner**, Nationalbericht, S. 6.

140 Vgl. **Rakic-Vodinelic**, Nationalbericht, S. 6 ff.

141 Von einer ähnlichen devolutiven Wirkung ist die Wiederaufnahme in Kuba bzw. kann sie es fallweise in China sein (vgl. den § 645 des kubanischen ZVG; den § 158 der chinesischen ZPO).

eines rechtskräftigen Urteils infolge einer Wiederaufnahme nur dem Obersten Gericht[142].

In Anbetracht des obenangeführten beschäftigt sich der Referent im folgenden nur noch mit der Aufsichtsrevision als einem, gewöhnlich über Devolutiveffekt verfügenden ausserordentlichen Rechtsbehelf, die zwar unter unterschiedlicher Benennung[143], aber ausnahmslos in der Zivilrechtspflege jedes europäischen sozialistischen Landes nach ähnlichen Regeln[144] von den dazu Berechtigten in Anspruch genommen werden kann.

3.2 WESEN UND AUFGABEN DER AUFSICHTSREVISION

Die Aufsichtsrevision ist ihrem Wesen nach *eine solche Rechtsinstitution* des sozialistischen Zivilverfahrenrechtes, *die unabhängig vom Willen der Prozessparteien die Revision der rechtskräftigen Gerichtsentscheidungen ermöglicht* und den Rahmen bietet dafür, dass diese Entscheidungen *in einem staatlich initiierten Aufsichtsverfahren* auf ihre Gesetzlichkeit hin überprüft, erforderlichenfalls aufgehoben, durch anderweitige Entscheidungen ersetzt oder zur Neuverhandlung und Entscheidung an ein unteres Gericht zurückverwiesen werden[145].

Die primäre Aufgabe dieser Rechtsinstitution *ist die Sicherung der* konsequenten und einheitlichen *Gesetzlichkeit der Rechtsprechung.* Ihre weitere Aufgabe ist der *Schutz der Rechte der Prozessparteien*, um so eher, weil die Aufsichtsrevision - wie das der bulgarische Nationalreferent hervorhob - fallweise 'eine Korrektur des Fehlens des zweistufigen Rechtsmittelsystems darstellt'[146]. Im Zusammenhang mit diesem Korrekturcharakter der Aufsichtsrevision ist davon auszugehen, dass das einstufige Rechtsmittelsystem zweifellos Vorteile gegenüber dem zweistufigen Rechtsmittelsystem hat. Der Gesetzgeber hat im Interesse der Realisierung dieser Vorteile und des wirksamen Funktionierens des einstufigen Rechtsmittelsystems - damit nämlich die schnellere Beendigung des Prozesses dessen gesetzmässige und begründete Entscheidung nicht gefährdet - in das Grundverfahren auch verschiedene Garantien eingebaut. Solche Garantien sind

142 Vgl. den § 302 des albanischen ZVG; den Art. 234 des bulgarischen ZVG.

143 Die behandelte Rechtsinstitution wird in Albanien, Bulgarien und Rumänien Aufsichtsrevision genannt, in Jugoslawien und Ungarn Gesetzlichkeitsprotest, in Polen ausserordentliche Revision, in der Sowjetunion Aufsichtsprotest, in der Tschechoslowakei Beschwerde gegen eine Gesetzesverletzung, während sie in der DDR Kassationantrag heisst. Im Interesse der Umgehung eventueller Missverständnisse sowie der Gewährleistung der Überschaubarkeit **wird dieser Teil des Referates im weiteren überall die Bezeichnung Aufsichtsrevision** verwenden, ohne Hinsicht darauf, ob im gegebenen Land die Bezeichnung dieses ausserordentlichen Rechtsbehelfes eventuell anders lautet.

144 Diese ähnlichkeit wird sehr anschaulich in der Studiensammlung präsentiert, die von den vor kurzem verstorbenen Professoren A. **Dobrovolski** und L. **Névai** herausgegeben wurde. Vgl. A. **Dobrovolski/L. Névai** /Hrsg./, Graschdanski prozess v sozialistitscheskih stranach-tschlenach SEV, Moskau, Band I, 1977 bzw. Band II, 1978.

145 Vgl. **Kellner**, Zivilprozessrecht, S. 414.

146 So **Braikow**, Nationalbericht I, S. 1. Einen im wesentlichen ähnlichen Standpunkt vertreten auch der rumänische sowie der ungarische Nationalreferent (vgl. **Zilberstein/Ciobanu**, Nationalbericht, S. 5; **Gáspárdy**, Nationalbericht I, S. 1/).

z.B. 'die Aktivität und Initiative des Gerichts'[147], das heisst 'die Veroflichtung des Gerichts, an der allseitigen Aufklärung der tatsächlichen Rechte und Verhältnisse der Parteien aktiv teilzunehmen'[148] sowie 'die Mitwirkung und Dispositionsbefugnis der Prozessparteien'[149] und viele andere mehr. Trotz der Garantien kann es aber vorkommen und kommt es auch vor, dass eine rechtskräftige Entscheidung entweder des erst- oder des zweitinstanzlichen Gerichtes wesentliche Bestimmungen des Rechtes verletzt. In diesen Fällen kann die gegen die rechtskräftige Entscheidung des zweitinstanzlichen Gerichtes eingelegte Aufsichtsrevision tatsächlich auch als Korrektur des Fehlens des zweistufigen Rechtsmittelsystems aufgefasst werden.

3.3 GEGENSTAND UND GRUND DER AUFSICHTSREVISION

Nach allgemeiner Regel kann *jede rechtskräftige Gerichtsentscheidung Gegenstand* der Aufsichtsrevision sein, d.h. Urteil und Beschluss gleichermassen - als der Rechtskraft fähige Entscheidungen. Von dieser in der überwiegenden Mehrheit der untersuchten Länder geltenden Regel sind in beiden Richtungen gewisse Abweichungen zu finden. Negativen Charakters ist die Abweichung im polnischen Zivilverfahrensrecht, das die Inanspruchnahme der Aufsichtsrevision nur gegen *das Verfahren abschliessende*, rechtskräftige Gerichtsentscheidungen gestattet[150]. Über eine Abweichung positivem Charakters verfügen dagegen die ZPO der DDR und das tschechoslowakische ZVG. Diesen zwei Kodexen zufolge sind durch Aufsichtsrevision auch *die verbindliche gerichtliche Einigung* und selbständig *die Begründung einer rechtskräftigen Entscheiduno*[151] bzw. *die rechtskräftige Entscheidung des Staatlichen Notariats* anfechtbar[152].

Die Aufsichtsrevision kann von den dazu Berechtigten dann in Anspruch genommen werden, wenn die rechtskräftige Gerichtsentscheidung - mindestens ihrer Ansicht nach - eine materiellrechtliche oder verfahrensrechtliche Norm verletzt. Der *alleinige Grund* dieses ausserordentlichen Rechtsbehelfes ist also *in der Tat* in allen europäischen sozialistischen Ländern die *Gesetzesverletzung*[153]. Die Tatsache, dass die verfahrensrechtlichen Bestimmungen der einzelnen Länder als Grundlage der Aufsichtsrevision neben der Gesetzesverletzung auch noch sonstige Gründe angeben, ändert nichts an der Stichhaltigkeit dieser Feststellung. Solche sonstigen Gründe sind, wenn die Entscheidung

- unbegründet[154] bzw. offensichtlich unbegründet[155] ist,

---

147 So **Kellner**, Nationalbericht, S. 1.

148 So **Braikow**, Nationalbericht I, S. 1. Vgl. **Zilberstein/Ciobanu**, Nationalbericht, S. 4 f.

149 So **Kellner**, Nationalbericht, S. 1. Vgl. **Braikow**, Nationalbericht I, S. 1.

150 Vgl. den Art. 417 § 1 des polnischen ZVG.

151 Vgl. den § 160 Abs. 1 der ZPO der DDR. Die Möglichkeit einer Aufsichtsrevision gegen die Begründung einer rechtskräftigen Entscheidung wird auch vom polnischen ZVG gewährleistet /vgl. den Art. 417 § 1/.

152 Vgl. den § 236 Abs. 1 des tschechoslowakischen ZVG.

153 In einzelnen Ländern, so in Polen, in Rumänien und in der Sowjetunion die **grobe** bzw. **wesentliche** Gesetzesverletzung.

154 Vgl. den § 330 des ZVG der RSFSR; den § 270 Abs. 1 der ungarischen ZPO.

155 Vgl. **Zilberstein/Ciobanu**, Nationalbericht, S. 7.

- ein internationales Abkommen verletzt[156],
- schwer die Interessen der Volksrepublik verletzt[157].

Ebenfalls sonstige Gründe sind es, wenn die Begründung der Entscheidung
- gröblich unrichtig ist[158] oder
- entweder die Interessen der Volksrepublik oder die Rechte einer Partei verletzt bzw. die Ehre einer Partei grob verletzt[159].

Die aufgezählten Gründe gehören aber - nach Meinung des Referenten- ausnahmslos ins begriffliche Gebiet der Gesetzesverletzung, und es geht hier lediglich darum, dass der Gesetzgeber in gegebenem Falle auch die konkreten Erscheinungsformen der Gesetzesverletzung wegen der ihnen beigemessenen herausragenden Bedeutung ausdrücklich festgesetzt hat.

3.4 SUBJEKTE DES AUFSICHTSREVISIONSVERFAHRENS

Der Kreis der *zur Aufsichtsrevision Berechtigten* ist in den verschiedenen Ländern zum Teil gleich, zum Teil unterschiedlich begrenzt. Eine völlige Gleichheit hesteht darin, dass *der Generalstaatsanwalt des gegebenen Landes* bzw. in Jugoslawien *der Staatsanwalt der Föderation* berechtigt ist, Aufsichtsrevision gegen rechtskräftige Entscheidungen der Gerichte einzulegen[160]. Das gleiche Recht steht - auf ihr Zuständigkeitsgebiet begrenzt in der Sowjetunion und der Tschechoslowakei den Generalstaatsanwälten und in Jugoslawien den Staatsanwälten der föderativen Republiken zu[161]. Mit Ausnahme von Jugoslawien, Rumänien und der Tschechoslowakei kann in jedem der untersuchten Länder auch *der Vorsitzende des Obersten Gerichtes*[162] Aufsichtsrevision gegen die Gerichtsentscheidungen[163] einlegen. Wesentlich abweichend ist dagegen die Regelung bezüglich anderer Berechtigter. So kann z.B. in Polen auch *der Justizminister* diese Rechtsinstitution ohne Beschränkung gegen die Entscheidungen der Gerichte in Anspruch nehmen[164]. In der Tschechoslowakei verfügen dagegen nur noch *die Justizminister der föderativen Republiken* über eine solche

---

156 Vgl. **Rakic-Vodinelic**, Nationalbericht, S. 9.

157 Vgl. den Art. 417 § 1 des polnischen ZVG.

158 Vgl. den § 160 Abs. 1 der ZPO der DDR.

159 Vgl. den Art. 417 § 1 des polnischen ZVG.

160 Vgl. den § 291 des albanischen ZVG; den Art. 225 des bulgarischen ZVG; den § 160 Abs. 1 der ZPO der DDR; den Art. 409 des jugoslawischen ZVG; den Art. 417 § 1 des polnischen ZVG; den Art. 329 des rumänischen ZVG; den § 320 des ZVG der RSFSR; den § 237 Abs. 1 des tschechoslowakischen ZVG; den § 270 Abs. 1 der ungarischen ZPO.

161 Vgl. den § 320 des ZVG der RSFSR; den § 237 Abs. 1 des tschechoslowakischen ZVG; den Art. 403 des jugoslawischen ZVG.

162 Vgl. den § 291 des albanischen ZVG; den Art. 225 des bulgarischen ZVG; den § 160 Abs. 1 der ZPO der DDR; den Art. 417 § 1 des polnischen ZVG; den § 270 Abs. 1 der ungarischen ZPO.

163 Der Vorsitzende des Obersten Gerichtes der Sowjetunion kann nur gegen die Entscheidungen des Präsidialsenates sowie gegen die Entscheidungen der zivilen Kollegien der Obersten Gerichte der föderativen Republiken, die als erstinstanzliche Gerichte vorgehen, eine Aufsichtsrevision benutzen (vgl. den § 320 des ZVG der RSFSR).

164 Vgl. den Art. 417 § 1 des polnischen ZVG.

Befugnis, begrenzt auf die rechtskräftigen Entscheidungen eines Bezirks- oder Kreisgerichtes auf dem Gebiet der föderativen Republik[165]. In der DDR sind auch *die Staatsanwälte der Bezirke* und *die Direktoren der Bezirksgerichte* berechtigt, die Entscheidungen eines Kreisgerichtes oder die vor einem Kreisgericht abgeschlossene Einigung durch Aufsichtsrevision anzufechten[166]. Ausserdem können sich in der Sowjetunion auch *die Stellvertreter des Generalstaatsanwaltes* sowie *des Vorsitzenden des Obersten Gerichtes der Union, die Vorsitzenden der obersten Gerichte der föderativen Republiken* und *deren Stellvertreter, die Vorsitzenden territorialen* und *städtischen Gerichte, der autonomen territorialen* und *Bezirksgerichte, die Staatsanwälte der autonomen Republiken, der Regionen, der Territorien, der autonomen Territorien* und *der Bezirke* noch der Aufsichtsrevision gegen die im Gesetz bestimmten Gerichtsentscheidungen bedienen[167].

Aus dem Wesen der untersuchten Rechtsinstitution folgt, dass sie nicht von den Parteien in Anspruch genommen werden kann. Dieser Umstand heisst aber nicht, dass die betroffenen Parteien selbst oder andere Personen bzw. Organen durch ihren Antrag die Einlegung der Aufsichtsrevision nicht anregen dürfen; über diese Anträge entscheiden jedoch die Adressaten in diskretionärer Weise. In Bulgarien ist ein solcher von der Partei unterbreiteter Antrag - zweifellos, um unbegründete Anträge zu verhindern - gebührenoflichtig. Für den ersten Antrag sind 10 Lewa, für den zweiten 20 und für die weiteren 50 Lewa Gebühr zu entrichten. Diese Gebühr ist aber eine sog. 'Depositengebühr', welche die Partei in dem Fall zurückerhält, wenn der zum Einlegen der Aufsichtsrevision Berechtigte den entsprechend begründeten Antrag zum Teil oder gänzlich annimmt[168]. Aus dem Bericht des bulgarischen Nationalreferenten geht hervor, dass trotz dieser Gebühr von den Parteien ziemlich viele solche Anträge eingereicht werden, denn diese 'haben eine beträchtliche Belastung des Obersten Gerichtes zum Ergebnis'[169]. Ebenfalls hauptsächlich 'mit der Beurteilung dieser Anträge, der Zusammenstellung von Aufsichtsrevisionen und deren Beurteilung sowie mit der Ausarbeitung von prinzipiellen Richtlinien zur allgemeinen Anleitung der Gerichtspraxis beschäftigen sich die Richter'[170] auch in Ungarn. Aus dieser Feststellung - deren Stichhaltigkeit durch die Tatsache unterstützt wird, dass zwei Drittel der jährlich insgesamt 10 000, also etwa 5 % aller Rechtsstreiten entsprechenden Anträge, zum Vorsitzenden des Obersten Gerichtes ankommen[171], und dass sich mit diesen die zu dieser Aufgabe bestimmten Richter des Obersten Gerichtes beschäftigen müssen stellt sich eindeutig heraus, dass sich die prinzipiell-anleitende Aufgabe des Obersten Gerichtes leider auch im besten Falle nur in einem nebengeordneten Verhältnis zu der Beurteilung der Anträge auf Aufsichtsrevision befindet. In Ungarn sind übrigens

165 Vgl. den § 237 Abs. 1 des tschechoslowakischen ZVG.

166 Vgl. den § 160 Abs. 2 der ZPO der DDR.

167 Vgl. den § 320 des ZVG der RSFSR.

168 Vgl. **Braikow**, Nationalbericht II, S. 1.

169 So **Braikow**, Nationalbericht II, S. 2.

170 So **Gáspárdy**, Nationalbericht I, S. 16. Vgl. K. **Benedek**, Gondolatok a polgári eljárás reformjáról, Magyar Jog, 1984/6. S. 508.

171 Vgl. J. **Szilbereky**, Megjegyzések egy készülő törvénytervezet előkészitéséhez (A polgári eljárás ujraszabályozása), Magyar Jog, 1984/4, S. 299.

diese von den Parteien eingereichten Anträge in etwa zehn Prozent der Fälle erfolgreich[172]. Nicht viel besser kann dieses Verhältnis in der Sowjetunion sein, vielleicht ist es auch noch schlechter, wo es - wie darauf in der Rechtsliteratur verwiesen wurde - trotz der Anträge 'in den meisten Fällen nicht zur Einlegung der Aufsichtsrevision kommt'[173].

In Polen kommt eine interessante Lösung bei der Untersuchung der von den Parteien vorgebrachten Anträge auf Einlegung von Aufsichtsrevision zur Geltung, welche das Oberste Gericht entlastet. Das Wesen der Lösung besteht darin, dass - obwohl der Justizminister, der Vorsitzende des Obersten Gerichtes und der Generalstaatsanwalt gleichermassen berechtigt sind, Aufsichtsrevision einzulegen - die Parteien ihren derartigen Antrag nur ein einziges Mal, entweder dem Justizminister oder dem Generalstaatsanwalt unterbreiten können[174].

Die Anträge der Parteien in Verbindung mit dem behandelten ausserordentlichen Rechtsbehelf dürfen jedoch nicht lediglich als einen, Arbeitsbelastung verursachenden Faktor betrachtet werden. Diese Anträge sind nämlich sehr bedeutend - wie das auch von den rumänischen Nationalreferenten betont wird- vom Gesichtspunkt der Stärkung der Beziehung zwischen den Gerichten und den rechtsuchenden Staatsbürgern, d.h. vom Gesichtspunkt der Erweiterung der gesellschaftlichen Basis der Rechtsprechung aus[175].

Im wesentlichen geht es darum, dass das Aufsichtsrevisionsverfahren zumeist infolge der von den Parteien der vermeinten oder wirklichen Rechtsverletzungen wegen eingereichten Anträge eingeleitet wird. Das vorgehende Gericht hat also so die Möglichkeit, das gesetzesverletzende Wesen der angefochtenen Entscheidung festzustellen, und dient damit über die individuellen Interessen der Partei hinaus auch dem öffentlichen Interesse. Unter Inbetrachtziehung dieser das öffentliche Interesse fördernden Wirkung des Antrages der Partei sind in der Theorie des rumänischen Zivilverfahrensrechtes solche Standpunkte aufgetaucht, denen zufolge in dem Fall, wenn aufgrund des Antrages irgendeiner Prozesspartei der Generalstaatsanwalt Aufsichtsrevision einlegt, das Prinzip der 'non reformatio in peius' zur Geltung kommen soll[176]. Im entgegengesetzten Fall würde nämlich das sich der Partei auferlegende Risiko - dass das die Aufsichtsrevision beurteilende Gericht ihre Situation eventuell verschlechtert sie vor dem Einreichen des Antrages zurückhalten. Dieser theoretische Standpunkt wurde - für den Fall der Aufsichtsrevision gegen einen bestimmten Kreis der Urteile - auch vom rumänischen Obersten Gericht als richtig anerkannt und als zu befolgende Praxis festgelegt[177].

Die *Beurteilung der Aufsichtsrevision* ist in den meisten Ländern die *Aufgabe des Obersten Gerichtes* des gegebenen Staates, der Föderation oder föderativen Republik bzw. autonomen Republik[178]. Diese Aufgabe lässt aber einigen der

---

172 Wie Fussnote 171.

173 So I. **Andrianov**, A felülvizsgálati eljárások formái polgári ügyekben, Magyar Jog, 1984/2, S. 170.

174 Vgl. den Art. 418 §§ 1-2 des polnischen ZVG.

175 Vgl. **Zilberstein/Ciobanu**, Nationalbericht, S. 24.

176 Vgl. **Zilberstein/Ciobanu**, Nationalbericht, S. 24 f.

177 Vgl. **Zilberstein/Ciobanu**, Nationalbericht, S. 25.

178 Vgl. den § 296 des albanischen ZVG; den Art. 227 des bulgarischen ZVG; den § 160 Abs. 1 der ZPO der DDR; die Art. 402 und 411 des jugoslawischen ZVG; den Art. 420 § 1 des polnischen ZVG; den Art. 329 des rumänischen ZVG; den § 321 des ZVG der RSFSR; den § 237 Abs. 1 des tschechos-

Obersten Gerichte - wie auch aus den wenigen, dem Referenten zur Verfügung stehenden Angaben ersichtlich - eine bedeutende, in gewissen Fällen mit der Erledigung der Berufungen identische oder diese überschreitende Arbeitslast zukommen. So führt z.B. das Oberste Gericht der rumänischen Sozialistischen Republik jährlich 2600-2900[179], das Oberste Gericht der Tschechischen[180] Sozialistischen Republik mehr als 600[181], und das Oberste Gericht der Ungarischen Volksrepublik annähernd 1000[182] Aufsichtsrevisionsverfahren durch. Demgegenüber haben in Jugoslawien 1985 die obersten Gerichte der föderativen Republiken nur 490 und das Föderative Gericht insgesamt 45 Aufsichtsrevisionen beurteilt, darunter auch - da es keine gesonderte Angabe bezüglich der Zivilsachen gibt - in Strafsachen[183].

In einigen Ländern können ausser dem Obersten Gericht auch andere, ebenfalls Rechtsmittelgerichte über die behandelten ausserordentlichen Rechtsbehelfe entscheiden und damit das Oberste Gericht einer gewissen Arbeitslast entlasten. Dieses Recht steht zu:

- in der DDR dem *Bezirksgericht*, wenn die Aufsichtsrevision von dem Staatsanwalt des Bezirkes oder dem Direktor des Bezirksgerichtes eingeleitet wurde[184];
- in Rumänien dem *Bezirksgericht*, im Falle einer Aufsichtsrevision, die gegen das von den Friedensgerichten in erster und durch Ausschluss der Berufungsmöglichkeit in letzter Instanz geholte Urteil eingeleitet wurde[185]; und schliesslich
- in der Sowjetunion den *regionalen, territorialen und Stadtgerichten*, den Gerichten der *autonomen Territorien* und den *Bezirksgerichten*, zur Beurteilung jener Aufsichtsrevisionen, die gegen die von ihnen getroffenen Entscheidungen sowie die Entscheidungen der Kreisvolksgerichte eingeleitet wurden[186].

3.5 DAS AUFSICHTSREVISIONSVERFAHREN

Das Aufsichtsrevisionsverfahren wird durch Einlegung der Aufsichtsrevision von Seiten des dazu Berechtigten eingeleitet. Zur Vorlegung setzt der Gesetzgeber in einigen Ländern - so in Albanien, Rumänien, der Sowjetunion und Ungarn- überhaupt keine Frist fest bzw. nur für bestimmte Ausnahmsfälle[187] oder

---

lowakischen ZVG; den § 271 der ungarischen ZPO.

179 Vgl. **Zilberstein/Ciobanu**, Nationalbericht, S. 16.

180 Bezüglich der Slowakischen Sozialistischen Republik hat der Nationalreferent keine Angaben mitgeteilt.

181 Laut des Berichtes des tschechoslowakischen Nationalreferenten werden 'jährlich rund 0,30 % aller entschiedenen Rechtssachen' durch Aufsichtsrevision angefochten (vgl. **Winterová**, Nationalbericht, S. 5). Das bedeutet, dass unter Inbetrachtziehung von 210 458 rechtskräftig entschiedenen Rechtsstreiten im Jahre 1986 in der Tschechischen Sozialistischen Republik die vom Obersten Gericht durchgeführten Aufsichtsrevisionsverfahren über 600 betragen mussten.

182 Wie Fussnote 171.

183 Vgl. **Rakic-Vodinelic**, Nationalbericht, S. 12.

184 Vgl. den § 160 Abs. 2 der ZPO der DDR.

185 Vgl. **Zilberstein/Ciobanu**, Nationalbericht, S. 28.

186 Vgl. den § 321 des ZVG der RSFSR.

187 Einen solchen Ausnahmefall stellt es in Albanien dar, wenn das rechtskräftige Urteil bereits vollstreckt worden ist. Dann kann nämlich die Aufsichtsrevision nur **innerhalb eines Jahres** gerechnet vom Vollzug an eingereicht werden (vgl. den § 292 des albanischen ZVG). In Rumänien kann der

Rechtsfolgen[188]. In anderen Ländern dagegen sind verschiedene, bedeutend voneinander abweichende Fristen[189] zur Einlegung der Aufsichtsrevision bekannt.

Über die an eine Frist Gebundenheit der Einlegung hinaus gestattet der Gesetzgeber in einem Teil der Länder die untersuchte Rechtsinstitution - im Interesse der Minderung derer Häufigkeit und natürlich der mit ihr einhergehenden und sich im allgemeinen auf die obersten Gerichte verlegenden Mehrarbeitslast zugunsten ein- und derselber Partei nur ein einziges Mal in Anspruch zu nehmen[190], bzw. schliesst sie gegen eine Entscheidung, welche vom in der Sache vorgegangenen Obersten Gericht bezüglich der Aufsichtsrevision getroffen wurde, völlig aus[191]. Das Verbot der Anfechtung der in Sache der Aufsichtsrevision getroffenen rechtskräftigen Entscheidungen der obersten Gerichte kommt übrigens fallweise auch dann zur Geltung, wenn das Oberste Gericht des gegebenen Landes die Kontrolle der einheitlichen Rechtsanwendung und Rechtsinterpretation zum bedeutenden Teil gerade durch die Aufsichtsrevisionsverfahren versieht[192]. In einigen Ländern aber - so z.B. in Rumänien und Ungarn - ist es möglich, dass unter Einhaltung der im Gesetz festgelegten Bedingungen und Fristen die dazu Berechtigten die Aufsichtsrevision auch mehrmals nacheinander gegen eine solche Entscheidung, welche vom Obersten Gericht im Laufe eines Aufsichtsrevisionsverfahrens getroffen wurde, in Anspruch nehmen[193].

Die vorgehenden Gerichte entscheiden über die Sache der eingelegten

---

Generalstaatsanwalt ausnahmsweise Aufsichtsrevision gegen die vom Obersten Gericht oder von den Komitatsgerichten in Rechtsstreitigkeiten 'zwischen sozialistischen Einheiten' getroffenen Entscheidungen einlegen, lediglich **innerhalb von sechs Monaten** seit Eintritt der Rechtskraft der angefochtenen Entscheidung gerechnet (vgl. **Zilberstein/Ciobanu**, Nationalbericht, S. 28).

188 In Ungarn erstreckt sich **die Wirkung der** im Aufsichtsrevisionsverfahren **getroffenen Entscheidungen nur dann auf die Prozessparteien**, wenn die dazu Berechtigten die Aufsichtsrevision **innerhalb eines Jahres** gerechnet seit Eintritt der Rechtskraft der Entscheidung, die in der Sache getroffen wurde, die als Grundlage des Verfahrens dient, unterbreiten (vgl. den § 273 Abs. 1 der ungarischen ZPO). Der nach einem Jahr rechtgebenden Entscheidung, die als Ergebnis einer eingelegten Aufsichtsrevision getroffen wurde, kommt ausschliesslich nur vom Gesichtspunkt der Leitung der Gerichtspraxis bzw. ihrer Vereinheitlichung Bedeutung zu.

189 Diese Frist, die seit Eintritt der Rechtskraft der angefochtenen Entscheidung gerechnet werden muss, beträgt in Bulgarien und in der DDR **ein Jahr** (vgl. den Art. 226 des bulgarischen ZVG; den § 160 Abs. 3 der ZPO der DDR), in Jugoslawien **dreissig Tage** bzw. **drei Monate** (vgl. die Art 401 und 312 des jugoslawischen ZVG), in Polen **sechs Monate** (vgl. den Art. 421 § 2 des polnischen ZVG),in der Tschechoslowakei dagegen **drei Jahre** (vgl. den § 238 des tschechoslowakischen ZVG).

190 Vgl. z.B. den Art. 417 § 2 des polnischen ZVG.

191 Vgl. die Art. 401 und 409 des jugoslawischen ZVG; den Art. 417 § 3 des polnischen ZVG; den § 236 Abs. 3 des tschechoslowakischen ZVG.

192 Vgl. **Rakic-Vodinelic**, Nationalbericht, S. 14 f.

193 Vgl. **Zilberstein/Ciobanu**, Nationalbericht, S. 9 sowie S. **Zilberstein**/V. **Ciobanu**, Intarirea legalitatii socialiste priu mijlocirea celor de atac in procesul civil român. Cîteva propuneri de lege ferenda în lumina unui nou sistem de judecatâ, Studii si Cercetari Juridice, 1979/2, S. 190; **Németh**, A törvényességi óvás elóterjesztése és elbirálása, in: J. **Farkas**/J. **Németh**/L. **Névai**/J. **Szilbereky**/Gy. **Varga**/I. **Vida**, Polgári eljárásjog II, Budapest, 1981, S. 85.

Aufsichtsrevision im allgemeinen in einer mündlichen Verhandlung[194]. In einigen Ländern dagegen ist die mündliche Verhandlung entweder nicht obligatorisch und hängt von der Entscheidung des Gerichtes ab[195], oder ist überhaupt nicht möglich, weil das Gericht infolge der gesetzlichen Bestimmungen über diesen ausserordentlichen Rechtsbehelf ohne mündliche Verhandlung entscheiden muss[196].

Die *Befugnis* des im Aufsichtsrevisionsverfahren vorgehenden *Gerichtes* ist in der entscheidenden Mehrzahl der europäischen sozialistischen Länder von *kassatorischem Charakter*[197], lediglich in Bulgarien verfügen die Gerichte über eine Befugnis von reformatorischem Charakter[198].

4 SCHLUSSBEMERKUNGEN

1. Die überlastung der Rechtsmittelgerichte kann mehrere, *allgemein zur Geltung kommende Gründe* haben. So vor allem den, dass infolge der Zunahme der Anzahl der Zivilprozesse - zwar nicht notwendigerweise, aber doch der allgemeinen Erfahrung gemäss die Zahl der Berufungen wächst. Die sich - oft gerade wegen der Zunahme der Anzahl der Prozesse - von fachlichem Gesichtspunkt aus verschlechternde Rechtsprechung der erstinstanzlichen Gerichte hat zumeist ein erhebliches Zuwachsen der Zahl der Berufungen zur Folge. Überdies kann im allgemeinen sehr vieles - angefangen von der missbräuchlichen, lediglich im Interesse der Verschleppung des Prozesses eine Berufung einlegenden böswilligen Verhaltensweise ganz bis hin zu dem in dem entsprechenden Land geltenden Rechtsmittelsystem - zur Überlastung der Berufungsgerichte beitragen.

Dieser Teil des Generalberichtes hat sich in erster Linie *mit jenen besonderen Gründen* befasst, welche in der Mehrzahl der europäischen sozialistischen Länder[199] - über die allgemein zur Geltung kommenden Gründe hinaus - zur

194 Vgl. z.B. den Art. 226 des bulgarischen ZVG; den § 161 Abs. 3 der ZPO der DDR; den Art. 420 § 1 des polnischen ZVG; den § 328 des ZVG der RSFSR; den § 272 der ungarischen ZPO.

195 Vgl. den § 240 des tschechoslowakischen ZVG.

196 Vgl. die Art 408 und 415 des jugoslawischen ZVG.

197 Vgl. die §§ 295-296 des albanischen ZVG; den § 161 Abs. 5 und den § 162 der ZPO der DDR; die Art. 405 und 415 des jugoslawischen ZVG. den Art. 422 §§ 1-2 des polnischen ZVG; den Art. 330 des rumänischen ZVG; den § 329 des ZVG der RSFSR; **Winterová**, Nationalbericht, S. 4; **Gáspárdy**, Nationalbericht II, S. 7.

198 Vgl. die Art. 228 und 229 des bulgarischen ZVG.

199 In der DDR - wie das der Nationalreferent ausser seiner in Fussnote 62 zitierten Meinung auch anderswo ausführt - kann bis heute von einer ernsthaften Überlastung der Berufungsgerichte nicht gesprochen werden (vgl. **Kellner**, Nationalbericht, S. 8). Diese Feststellung trifft besonders für das Oberste Gericht als Berufungsgericht zu, da der geltenden rechtlichen Regelung zufolge die Rechtsmitteltätigkeit des Obersten Gerichtes der DDR auf wenige Fälle pro Jahr beschränkt ist (vgl. **Kellner**, Nationalbericht, S. 4). Auch die rumänischen Nationalreferenten sind der Meinung, dass die Rechtsmittelgerichte in Rumänien nicht überlastet sind (vgl. **Zilberstein/Ciobanu**, Anlage des Nationalberichtes, S. 3). In anderen sozialistischen Ländern dagegen ist die Überlastung der Rechtsmittelgerichte - laut den Nationalberichten (vgl. **Braikow**, Nationalbericht I, S. 2; **Rakic-Vodinelic**, Nationalbericht, S. 23; **Gáspárdy**, Nationalbericht I, S. 17) sowie der Äusserungen in der Rechtsli-

Überlastung der Rechtsmittelgerichte und innerhalb derer der obersten Gerichte führen. Solche wichtigere, besondere Gründe sind, dass:

- die Rechtsmittelgerichte nicht nur in zweitinstanzlicher, sondern in gewissen Fällen auch in von irgendeinem unteren Gericht herangezogener oder übertragener erstinstanzlicher Zuständigkeit vorgehen;
- ausser den Parteien auch andere, das öffentliche Interesse vertretende Personen und Organisationen berechtigt sind, unter bestimmten Bedingungen sogar gegen den ausdrücklichen Willen der Prozessparteien eine Berufung einzulegen;
- in einigen Ländern die Rechtsmittelgerichte - besonders die obersten Gerichte - einen beträchtlichen Teil ihrer Arbeit auf die Beurteilung der Aufsichtsrevisionen, derjeniger ausserordentlichen Rechtsbehelfe, welche gegen die rechtskräftigen Gerichtsentscheidungen eingelegt wurden, verwenden.

2. Wichtiges Ziel jedes Rechtssystems ist die Beseitigung der allgemeinen und besonderen Gründe, die zur Überlastung der Rechtsmittelgerichte führen, zumindest aber die Verringerung ihrer Wirkung. Im Interesse der Verwirklichung dieses Zieles, der geeigneten Einschränkung des Sachverkehrs der Rechtsmittelgerichte sowie *ihrer wirksamen Tätigkeit* werden in den untersuchten Ländern verschiedene Lösungen bzw. Methoden angewandt.

Unter den unterschiedlichen Lösungen bzw. Methoden können - ihrer Bedeutung wegen - die folgenden hervorgehoben werden:

- *Die Erhöhung der Anzahl der an den Rechtsmittelgerichten urteilenden Richter.*

Diese Lösung - obwohl sie theoretisch sehr einfach und zweckmässig erscheint - stösst zumeist auf praktische Hindernisse. Solche Hindernisse sind unter anderem die beschränkten finanziellen Möglichkeiten der Gerichte oder der Mangel an Fachleuten, die zur Versehung dieser Aufgabe geeignet wären und über entsprechende fachliche Ausbildung und Fähigkeiten verfügten[200] usw. Trotzdem können unter den sozialistischen Ländern auch solche gefunden werden, wo *die Mitgliederzahl des Obersten Gerichtes* als Rechtsmittelgericht im Vergleich zu den übrigen Gerichten in relativ grossem Masse erhöht wurde, unter besonderer Hinsicht darauf, dass dieses Gericht die Last der Beurteilung der Aufsichtsrevisionen trägt. So kann es dann vorkommen, dass in Ungarn das Oberste Gericht über insgesamt 90 Richter verfügt, welche Zahl *6 % sämtlicher Richter des Landes* bedeutet.

- *Die Verringerung der Mitgliederzahl der an den Berufungsgerichten urteilenden Kollegien.*

Es ist eine zweifellose Tatsache, dass diese Lösung neben unveränderter Richterzahl die Ausgestaltung von mehr Kollegien an den Berufungsgerichten ermöglicht. Im Falle von mehreren Kollegien nimmt allerdings die Gefahr der Ausbildung einer abweichenden Gerichtspraxis zu, und die Verringerung der Mitgliederzahl der Kollegien kann eventuell die Qualität der zu treffenden

teratur (vgl. die Fussnoten 52 und 63) - eine Tatsache, mit der sowohl der Gesetzgeber als auch der Rechtsanwender rechnen muss.

200 Vgl. z.B. **Gáspárdy**, Nationalbericht I, S. 18.

Gerichtsentscheidungen negativ beeinflussen. Vermutlich spielen auch diese Gründe eine Rolle dabei, dass unter den untersuchten Ländern nur in Rumänien - im Falle bestimmter Voraussetzungen - anstelle von gewöhnlich drei Richtern das Berufungsgericht in einem aus zwei Richtern bestehenden Kollegium vorgeht, in anderen Ländern aber nicht[201].

- *Die Beschränkung des Rechts auf das Rechtsmittel.*

Die Überlastung der Rechtsmittelgerichte kann ausserordentlich schnell und einfach mit der Beschränkung des Rechts auf das Rechtsmittel verringert werden. In den europäischen sozialistischen Ländern jedoch wird diese radikale Lösung aus prinzipiellen Überlegungen heraus mit allgemeiner Gültigkeit nicht akzeptiert und auch unter den Nationalreferenten betonen einige, dass das Recht auf das Rechtsmittel 'ein solches *Garantieminimum* bildet, welches nicht beschränkt werden darf'[202], weder in Abhängigkeit von der Berufungssumme noch vom Gegenstand der Berufung[203].

- *Die Erhöhung der Zahl der den Richtern beistehenden sonstigen Bediensteten an den Rechtsmittelgerichten.*

Im Interesse dessen, dass sich die Richter mit der sachlichen Beurteilung der Berufungen, im gegebenen Fall der Aufsichtsrevisionen beschäftigen können und sie nicht gezwungen seien, einen bedeutenden Teil ihrer Zeit mit ausser ihrer tatsächlichen richterlichen Tätigkeit liegender, administrativer, vorbereitender Arbeit zu verbringen, muss ihnen eine entsprechende Zahl sonstiger Bediensteter gewährt sein, die über eine entsprechende Ausbildung verfügen. Das ist leider in den untersuchten Ländern heute noch nicht überall so. Daher wäre es begründet - dort wo erforderlich -, die Zahl dieser Bediensteten zu erhöhen, die ausser der mit der Funktion der Rechtsmittelgerichte verbundenen administrativen Arbeit, den Richtern auch beim Einsammeln der zur richtigen Gerichtsentscheidung unerlässlichen Informationen und derer Verarbeitung helfen könnten. Die Erhöhung der Zahl der nicht über juristische Bildung verfügenden Bediensteten ist ansonsten - auch von fachlichem und finanziellem Gesichtspunkt aus - eine viel leichter zu bewältigende Aufgabe, als die Erhöhung der Zahl der Richter.

- *Anwendung der modernen Bürotechnik und der elektronischen Datenverarbeitung.*

Bei der administrativen Arbeit der Rechtsmittelgerichte, dem schnellen, genauen und umfassenden Einsammeln und der gleichen Erarbeitung der zur zeitgemässen und begründeten Urteilsfindung notwendigen Informationen ist die Anwendung der modernen Bürotechnik sowie der elektronischen Datenverarbeitung heute immer unerlässlicher. Aufgrund der Berichte einiger Nationalreferenten und der vorhandenen Erfahrungen des Referenten auf diesem Gebiet kann jedoch festgestellt werden, dass in einem grossen Teil der sozialistischen Länder bei den Rechtsmittelgerichten - und bei den Gerichten überhaupt - von einer solch hochgradigen technischen Ausrüstung, welche bei der Verringerung

201 Wie Fussnote 37.

202 So **Gáspárdy**, Nationalbericht I, S. 18.

203 Vgl. **Braikow**, Nationalbericht I, S. 2.

der Arbeitslast eine wesentliche Hilfe bedeuten würde, heute noch überhaupt nicht gesprochen werden kann[204].
Ausser den obigen, zur Bewältigung der Überlastung der Rechtsmittelgerichte allgemein anwendbaren bedeutenderen Lösungen und Methoden gibt es natürlich auch noch solche, welche zur Verringerung der sich aus den besonderen Rechtsinstitutionen der sozialistischen Länder ergebenden Arbeitslast geeignet sind:

- die Aufhebung des Vorgehens der Rechtsmittelgerichte in erstinstanzlicher sachlicher Zuständigkeit,
- die Beschränkung der Berufungsberechtigung anderer Personen und Organe ausser den Parteien,
- die Erhöhung des Kostenrisikos,
- die Anwendung des kassatorischen Rechtsmittelsystems bei den Rechtsmittelgerichten,
- das Verbot der mehrfachen Anwendung der Aufsichtsrevisionen oder ihre Bindung an besondere Bedingungen[205] usw.

Die Teilfragen dieser Lösungen sind bereits an anderen Stellen des Berichtes berührt worden, ihre hier erfolgende Wiederholung erübrigt sich.

Die Entscheidung der Frage übrigens, welche allgemeinen oder besonderen Lösungen bzw. Methoden und in welchem Masse in einem gegebenen Land zur Verringerung der Überlastung der Rechtsmittelgerichte verwendet werden sollen, erfordert grosse Umsicht. Erst nach sorgfältiger Abwägung von Vor- und Nachteilen darf es entschieden werden und von keiner der Lösungen kann erwartet werden, dass sie in voller Gänze die Wirksamkeit der Arbeit der Rechtsmittelgerichte gewährleisten wird.

Der Standpunkt des Referenten ist übrigens - in völligem Einklang mit der Meinung mehrerer Nationalreferenten[206] -, dass *die Bewältigung der Überlastung der Rechtsmittelgerichte bei den erstinstanzlichen Gerichten begonnen werden muss*. Als grundlegende Lösung müssen die von den Richtern zu Recht erwarteten entsprechenden Arbeitsbedingungen sowie auch die Möglichkeiten ihrer fachlichen Weiterbildung gewährleistet werden, damit sich als Ergebnis dessen das Urteilsniveau der erstinstanzlichen Gerichte erhöht. In dem Falle nämlich, wenn die erstinstanzlichen Gerichte in grösserer Zahl von materiellrechtlichem und verfahrensrechtlichem Gesichtspunkt aus einwandfreie und überzeugend begründete Entscheidungen treffen, wird sich vermutlich die Zahl der Berufungen verringern. *Der Anspruch auf nochmalige Beurteilung der Rechtsstreite* ist nur *dann* wirklich *hoch*, wenn die Qualität der ersten Beurteilung unzureichend war.

---

204 Vgl. Rakic-Vodinelic, Nationalbericht, S. 27; Zilberstein/Ciobanu, Nationalbericht, S. 21; Gáspárdy, Nationalbericht II, S. 11.

205 In Rumänien kann der Generalstaatsanwalt - den neuen, im Interesse der Entlastung des Obersten Gerichtes getroffenen Bestimmungen zufolge - nur dann Aufsichtsrevision gegen in Rechtsstreiten zwischen sozialistischen Einheiten gefällte Entscheidungen einlegen, wenn das innerhalb von drei Monaten seit dem Eintritt der Rechtskraft an vom Leiter jenes Organes, unter dessen Aufsicht die mit der Entscheidung unzufriedene sozialistische Einheit steht, bei ihm beantragt wird und der Streitwert über eine Million Lei liegt (vgl. Zilberstein/Ciobanu, Nationalbericht, S. 28 f.)

206 Vgl. Braikow, Nationalbericht I, S. 2; Zilberstein/Ciobanu, Nationalbericht, S. 31 f.; Gáspárdy, Nationalbericht, I, S. 17.

REPORT OF THE DISCUSSION (WORKING-SESSION)

Chairman: *P. Gilles (Federal Republic Germany)*
Vice-Chairman: *U. Jacobsson (Sweden)*
Secretary: *H.J. Snijders (Netherlands)*[1]

The discussionpoints are to be found at pages 92 and 131.

WORKING SESSION

THE GENERAL REPORTS

Jolowicz. The General Report for 'Western' countries is in effect a sequel to the Reporter's General Report to the Congress held in Ghent in 1977 and Published under the title 'Appellate Proceedings' in Storme & Casman (ed.), *Towards a Justice with a Human Face*, 1978, pp. 127-165. What was said there is not repeated.

The 18 national reports received in time for incorporation in the General Report (a further report for India was received too late for consideration) show great differences in the caseload of appellate courts. They also show great differences in the appellate structure and in the style of proceedings, including proceedings at first instance. In order to keep the report within reasonable bounds certain assumptions are made and certain conventions adopted, in particular:

1. 'Appeal' includes not only the appeal properly so-called but also cassation. It does not include procedures (e.g. *opposition*) which come before the court of first instance or appeals which are handled outside the regular jurisdictional hierarchy. Only civil appeals are considered.
2. An appeal is introduced by a party to the litigation in question: the appeal in the interest of the law (*pourvoi dans l'intérêt de la loi*), where this exists, is mentioned only incidentally;
3. An appellate procedure has a purpose or purposes which is distinct from the purpose of the litigant who introduces an appeal on a given occasion. There is a 'private' purpose - that of meeting the desire of a defeated litigant to have his case reconsidered - and a 'public' purpose - that of controlling the conduct of the lower courts, of assisting the clarification and development of the law and of maintaining public confidence in the judicial system.
4. Save where the subject is specifically discussed in the General Report, the subject of abuse of the right of appeal is not taken into account. It is assumed that the right of appeal is exercised in good faith.

---

1 Assisted by Mr. R.W.Holzhauer (Netherlands).The secretary has consulted Prof. Jolowicz for the final text. This summary is not a transcript of the working session. Interventions are summarised and not all are reproduced.

fulfil the purposes for which it exists. From this point of view a paradox emerges. Courts of cassation, whose principal purpose is, theoretically, the public purpose of acting as 'guardian' of the law find themselves in many countries dealing with large numbers of cases which are of interest exclusively to the parties whereas the highest courts in common law countries, which are usually courts of appeal in the true sense and thus, apparently, exist to serve the private purpose of ensuring justice between the parties, have come to be acutely aware of the public purpose: in practice their caseloads are comparatively small and the cases that come before them are almost invariably such that their decision is of public interest. Thus, for example, the English House of Lords, which is a court of third instance, is not divided into Chambers and has but ten full-time judges, decides a mere fifty cases a year; the French *Cour de la cassation* has many more judges, is divided into a number of Chambers and decides approximately 16,000 cases a year.

The general increase in litigation, which is one reason for increase in the caseload of appellate courts is not the subject of the report. Its concern is the management of overload. Solutions might be found by increasing the total number of judges or decreasing the number of judges required to sit in a given case. Both solutions are found but there are limits to what is possible both in terms of public expenditure and in the danger that, if a supreme court sits in too many Chambers, conflicting decisions will be produced and the coherence of the law put at risk. Something can be achieved by the imposition of costs sanctions but, obviously, this must not be carried too far. Other solutions may also be found to have adverse effects on the ability of appellate courts to fulfil one or other or both of their purposes.

The most satisfactory solution, in theory, to the problem of overload is to reduce the demand for appeal by improvement of confidence in the decision at first instance. Where that decision is normally accepted as final there will be little demand for appeal but where, conversely, it is regarded simply as a stage in an ongoing procedure restrictions on the right of appeal will be resisted. On this aspect of the subject national reports reveal a cleavage between the common law and the civil law countries. In the common law countries the normal assumption is that the first word is also the last word; the appeal has no suspensive effect and a first instance judgment may be executed immediately unless a stay of execution is ordered. Of the civil law countries, only Austria is in a similar position. Elsewhere the decision at first instance tends to be downgraded and the demand for appeal is consequently great. This cleavage between the two legal families must be borne in mind when particular techniques for managing overload are considered, such as, in particular, exclusion altogether of the right of appeal in small cases. Further, common law courts of appeal may adopt self imposed limitations on the scope of the appeal: the English Court of Appeal is, theoretically, a court of fact as well as law but in practice the facts are not investigated a second time, and the Court contents itself with a transcript of the evidence given in the court below. Again in cases in which the decision is said to depend on the judge's 'discretion' the appellate court will not normally substitute its own opinion on the question for that of the judge below.

A different approach is to attempt to improve the 'efficiency' with which cases are handled, and particular attention is drawn to some efficiency devices mentioned in national reports such as the use of 'special' courts - the first instance court as a court of appeal or the creation of 'formations restreintes' for certain purposes - and the use of non-judicial staff in the preparation of cases or even of judgments as in the United States and Sweden.

Németh. Problems and solutions similar to those found in 'Western' countries are found also to a substantial extent in socialist countries. One of the main systematic differences lies in the power of the highest appellate court in a socialist country to cause a case to be transferred to itself for adjudication at first instance and in the possibility (e.g. in Poland) that a case may be voluntarily transferred from the court of first instance to a higher court when a serious problem of law arises.

It is not only the parties who may appeal. Certain third parties such as the procurator (the public prosecutor, 'le ministère public') may have a right of appeal which can be exercised even against the wishes of the parties. The procurator is seen as representing the public interest and acts in the interest of the law or for the protection of the state or its citizens. In most countries social organizations such as, in the German Democratic Republic, the Council for Child Protection in juvenile cases, and, in the U.S.S.R., labour unions, can appeal.

It is the reporter's opinion that one of the more important solutions to the problem of overload would be to limit or exclude such third party rights of appeal.

DISCUSSION

Chairman. Having summarised what had been said by the general reporters, attention was drawn to similarities of solution stemming from similarity of problems. The major differences in approach seem to stem from the party-oriented ideas of the West as contrasted with the more active judge and state control underlying the socialist systems.

To avoid the risk of confusion and to ensure concentration on the supra-national aspects of the subject three principal topics for discussion were proposed:

1. What is overload and by what criteria is it to be assessed? Overload implies more than the existence of a backlog in appellate courts. Perhaps overload is not the real problem.
2. What are the causes and origins of the problem? This topic must be limited to appellate courts: the causes and origins of overload in general are discussed at a separate working session (No:l).
3. Solutions to appellate overload:
(a) Expansion (more judges, more courts)
(b) Restriction (restrictions on the right of appeal; 'rationing' of appeals);
(c) 'Efficiency' in the management of appeals.

Wedekind (Netherlands). Overload may manifest itself in more than one form and is relative. Absolute numbers are not good indicators.

Ras (Netherlands. President of Supreme Court). Some countries such as France and Italy have a dramatic case-load but overload cannot be equated with backlog alone. It is essential to bear in mind the purposes and functions of appellate jurisdiction. Why does the President of the German Supreme Court (*'Bundesgerichthof'*) not complain? Is it because Germany has a restricted system of requiring leave to appeal and because the two main functions of the Supreme Court - guardianship of the law and the provision of recourse to the parties - are, in his opinion, well-served in Germany?

Bruzelius (Sweden. Retired judge). Numbers are an unreliable guide. The Swedish system is subject to both Anglo-American and continental influences. During the last ten years a Commission has studied the effectiveness of procedure and has produced numerous reports. The present procedure dates from 1948 and has been changed frequently. The right of appeal to the Supreme Court is now limited to cases of interest for the application of the law.

There does not seem to be a problem of overload, but the time taken for an appeal - approximately one year and a half - is considered to be too long. The entire process may take up to 3 years. In 1974 a simple procedure for small cases was introduced.

Leave is required for a case to be taken to the Supreme Court. Leave may be 'general' or 'partial'. The question is whether there are important legal questions in issue and especially whether there is need to create a precedent for the assistance of the lower courts. In the Supreme Court the public purpose is of principal concern but in the lower courts the private purpose is paramount.

Law clerks are used in preparatory work at all levels. In the Supreme Court every judge has a clerk. The system works satisfactorily.

Vice-Chairman. In disagreement with Bruzelius, overload does raise problems in Sweden.

Watson (Canada). Empirical work reveals that a desire for delay may actually provide a motive for appeals, which introduces the element of 'interest in interests.'

Perhaps the reversal rate rather than the number of appeals is the real cause of the overload problem: a 75% reversal rate may cause greater problems that a 10% appeal rate.

What is the effect of overload on an appellate court? Can it affect the court's interpretation of 'fact' and 'law'?

The denial of a right of appeal is potentially dangerous because it may lead to anarchy in the lower courts.

There is danger in the excessive use of law clerks but some delegation by the judges is proper and should be allowed.

In Canada the Supreme Court operates an effective control of its case-load and chooses approximately 60 cases - those which are the 'best' - for decision each year.

Dalsace (France. Judge). A restrictive attitude to appeals could usefully be adopted by the French *Cour de cassation* where there are now 30 Chambers.

The attitude of practitioners plays an important role and improvement of the quality of judgments at first instance would help. In particular judges should not be appointed too young.

There is abuse of the procedural system in the use of the appeal for the purpose of causing delay. Simplification of the rules of procedure and a stricter enforcement of time limits could help to improve the situation in France.

Jolowicz. Different attitudes of the legal profession in, for example, England and France can be significant to the problem of overload. Such different attitudes may be attributable to differences in the structure and training of the judiciary professional training in many continental countries and appointment from the Bar in common law countries.

Chairman. Problems created by the expansion strategy include the inflation of the appellate jurisdiction, reduction in the quality of appellate decisions and distortion (by the excessive number of judges) of the balance of power: in West Germany there are 75,000 judges.

Moons (Netherlands. Former President of Supreme Court). Many cases are of no interest from the public purpose point of view but nevertheless judges at the level of the Supreme Court have to give reasons for their decisions. Legislation is now in preparation to simplify the motivation of decisions in cases of this kind.

Jolowicz. In some jurisdictions of the United States a 'do not publish' notice can be appended to a decision. The public is then informed only that an appeal has been allowed or dismissed. Cases in which a 'do not publish' notice is used can be disposed of quickly.

Vihjalmsson (Iceland. Judge). Some countries have sought to overcome the problem of overload by the appointment for a limited period of additional judges at the highest level, but the experiment has not been successful. The judges concerned are not content to lose their offices and the independence of the judiciary is endangered. For these reasons the practice has been abandoned by three out of the five Scandinavian countries.

Goldstein (Israel). The causes of overload are associated with the legal culture of the society in question and with the incentives to appeal which exist. Sometimes the fear of overload is exaggerated and there may be no reason to introduce draconian remedies for what is not a real problem.

There are different methods of 'rationing' appeals. One is to require leave to appeal, another by the imposition of higher costs. Increasingly higher costs are now being imposed on the losing party by the Supreme Court of Israel. Care must, however, be taken to avoid making appeals too costly.

Rationalization is always good. The ideal position seems to be that there should be one appeal as of right to fulfil the private purpose and a second appeal, with leave, to fulfil the public purpose. Change will, however, always be difficult to achieve.

Watson. During the fifties and sixties the tendency was to increase resources; in the seventies the emphasis shifted to efficiency. Both are in fact necessary.

The problem is related to the phenomenon of the queue. If the length of the queue of people awaiting a hearing in court is reduced more people will seek access to the court. Further theoretical and empirical work on the relationship between supply and demand is necessary.

Perhaps the real cause of the problem is that there is no framework of responsibility. The independent judiciary which has no control over resources blames the lawyers who in turn blame the judges whereupon the judges complain that government fails to supply sufficient resources. In other institutions there is someone in charge and there is a sanction. In the judicial system each element blames the other.

Chairman. Some headings can be suggested for the restriction of appeals: exclusion of all rights of appeal; exclusion of appeal in small cases; exclusion of appeal against interlocutory decisions; barriers to appeal; simplification of judicial structure; reduction in size of appellate courts; abolition of full second instance; limitation of grounds for appeal. But the importance of appeals to the public purpose must not be overlooked.

Hansby (Norway. Judge). Norway has a three instance system and access to the Supreme Court is by way of an appeal selection committee of three Supreme Court judges. The committee can reject an appeal if it is manifestly ill-founded. This has solved the problem of overload in the Norwegian Supreme Court.

The number of judges required to decide an appeal has been reduced from seven to five, but it would not be politically acceptable to reduce the number of judges to three, still less to one.

Much of the overload is attributable not to the courts but to the Bar.

Snijders. Both general reporters have emphasised the importance of the first instance proceedings. Is not the main source of overload in the quality of the first instance? In the Netherlands there are many first instance courts with a single judge only and this might contribute to the overload of appellate courts. The introduction of a single judge at the appellate level might in turn influence the number of cases at the level of cassation. Is there any system with single-judge appellate courts? Does the fact that a lower court may act with only a single judge lead to problems of overload higher in the judicial hierarchy?

It may be noted that in Belgium experience of single-judge courts of first instance has led to a rise of 25% in appeals. In England, however, the application for leave to appeal is heard by a single judge, which means in effect that a single judge can dismiss an appeal.

Wright (Australia). In Australia there are three levels of civil court. The lowest level uses a single judge and appeal at the lowest level is also to a single judge. The system works reasonably well. Appeals are restricted to questions of law.

One approach to the overload problem is to consider the rate of reversals rather than of appeals. There are some empirical data in the national report. In one State (New South Wales) there is a separate court of appeal with judges who act only as appellate judges. In the other states the appellate court is made up of three judges of the first instance court who constitute the 'Full Court' and hear appeals from other judges of first instance. The data suggest that there is a higher rate of reversal in the New South Wales Court of Appeal than in the Full Court of Victoria. The explanation may be that a judge of the Full Court will have more respect for the work of a first instance judge than will a purely appellate judge and that the judge of a Full Court hearing an appeal will subsequently find himself again as a judge of first instance whose decisions may be appealed to the Full Court. Other facts are relevant, but the difference is striking. It is of the order of 300%: 60 reversals in the Victorian Full Court to 250 in the New South Wales Court of Appeal.

Chairman. Discussion of efficiency should consider devices such as the delegation of work to para-judicials, relief of judges from administrative work, greater co-operation between different professions, less ceremony, treating court organization more as a 'legal industry' with introduction of 'business administration'. The handling of files may be old fashioned and inefficient as may methods, behaviour and attitudes.

Greater specialization may be needed in appellate work. Introduction of written proceedings, written summaries and skeleton arguments should be considered to enable courts to dispose of cases more expeditiously and to dismiss hopeless cases more easily. Some kind of pre-appellate control may also be useful such as the use of appeal selection committees.

Andersson (Sweden. Retired Judge). The introduction of a small claims court has speeded up these cases.

A distinction in the use of law clerks must be made between the making of initial drafts before or after the hearing. The latter would be too dangerous.

In Norway there is a tendency to move away from written and towards an oral procedure. Experience shows that an oral procedure works better and faster than a written procedure. There used to be a problem of overload which has now disappeared.

The quality of the first instance decision is important. The decisions of first instance judges in Norway are highly respected; there is only a 10% appeal rate and a 1% cassation rate.

Watson. Devices such as the requirement of leave to appeal are satisfactory only in large countries and in small countries are unnecessary.

Jolowicz. By way of conclusion it may be said that the discussion has been good and interesting but also understandably disappointing since different legal cultures are involved. It is, however, significant that there is general agreement that overload in appellate courts starts with the first instance.

The discussion of efficiency devices was too brief though a number of approaches were mentioned. 'Efficiency' in the appellate process raises problems with procedural justice, and there may be greater problems in restricting the right of appeal in countries where the 'double jurisdiction' is considered to be fundamental than in common law countries where the requirement of leave to appeal is regularly employed.

Compromise solutions are inevitable and the question what may be sacrificed must be raised. Abandoning the idea of 'double jurisdiction' may be difficult in civil law countries; in common law countries, where it still tends to be thought desirable that the judge should enter the court room ignorant of the case he is to hear, it will be difficult to substitute written for oral procedures.

In all systems changes and compromises can be detected and it must be borne in mind that changes in one area often give rise to problems or disadvantages in another. The purpose of appellate procedures should be at the heart of the debate, but the ideal combination of the public and the private purposes is difficult to find. No two countries will settle on the same appellate system for the best combination of purposes, the best compromise, depends on the legal culture of the country in question.

PLENARY SESSION

INTRODUCTION

Chairman. Jolowicz based his general report on 18 national reports; Németh based his on 7 national reports.

Jolowicz opened the working session by stressing the differences between the national systems but considered that some common ground could be found. The working session thus sought to concentrate on the supra-national aspects of the subject and to define overload. Jolowicz suggested that overload exists when the purposes of an appellate system cannot be adequately achieved because of pressure of cases.

Another central theme was the need for a right of appeal. Individuals must have access to justice. It is therefore more important to consider the demand side rather than the supply side: proceedings at first instance must be improved so that parties are generally content with the first decision.

Dealing with European socialist countries, Németh pointed out the differences between the East and West European systems. In particular, in West European countries the appeal depends on the private initiative of the parties while in East European countries an appeal may also be initiated by the procurator (public prosecutor, 'le ministère public') and by a variety of administrative bodies.

Discussion at the working session centred on three principal matters:
1. The phenomenon of overload itself;
2. The causes and origins of overload;
3. Solutions to overload.

1. Overload is not merely a problem of justice, delay, manpower and the burdening of judges. It is not a problem on its own but has social, psychological, economic, political and, indeed, legal dimensions. Attention was also paid to the negative aspects of overload, notably the risk that justice becomes less accessible to individuals.
2. The causes and origins of overload are complex. Dissatisfaction of the parties to a decision is a factor, but other factors include the complexity of society, the tensions of the economic situation and the belief that a better judgment will be obtained in a higher court. In the Federal Republic of Germany, for example, the proceedings at first instance are regarded as little more than a transitional stage leading to appeal.

3. Solutions discussed included:
(a) Expansion of appellate resources (more judges, more courts);
(b) Protection of the courts against overload by restricting the right of appeal;
(c) Rationalization by making systems more efficient, seeking greater collaboration between Bench and Bar, the use of skeleton arguments to obtain shorter hearings, pre-appellate procedures such as appeal selection committees. Also, judges must themselves be able to work more efficiently; they must familiarise themselves with computers and other modern aids to their work.

DISCUSSION

Ganado (Malta). Overload is a serious and growing problem in many countries including Malta. Judges cannot cope adequately with more than 250 cases per annum but are compelled to do so. In Malta additional judges have been appointed for the hearing of evidence, but this is unsatisfactory: the evidence should be heard by the judge who is to decide the case. It is suggested that a maximum number of cases per judge should be fixed and also a minimum number of judges per million of the population.

Puccio (Argentina. Judge). How can the world-wide deficiencies of justice be combated? It is a question of attitudes in the legal profession. We need people committed to the profession, people who are fitted for it and who believe in law and liberty.

Perhaps the wrong people are educated for the profession and perhaps they are trained in the wrong way: lawyers must be trained not only for minor cases but also for difficult ones.

It is difficult to find the right people, but there is a need for more judges: a mere five judges must deal with thousands of cases.

Chairman. This introduces an interesting new element into the discussion, namely that education may also be a factor. German students get a good theoretical basis but not a practical basis. Once in practice they forget the theory.

Leipold (Federal Republic Germany). The problem is how to get better judges. It is not only a matter of idealistic attitude and education but of performance within the profession. Judges do not receive sufficient financial reward. If the reward can be increased judges will perform better. The difference in performance between judges and lawyers in private practice is to be remarked.

Another question relates to costs. Overload can be combated by application of the principle that all litigants must pay at least a part of the costs.

Cappelletti (Italy. President, International Association for Procedural Law). We must concentrate on the four main strategies for combating overload -increasing resources, limiting the possibilities for appeal, rationalising appeals and their procedure and, finally, improving the first instance.

Particular attention should be paid to limiting the possibilities of appeal: there is abuse in many countries. Nevertheless, before limiting appeals it is necessary to have a good first instance.

Improving the first instance is very difficult in countries where the judges of first instance are the younger and less experienced judges and where the selection of judges is not as it generally is in common law countries. Differences in judges must be kept in mind: some will be able to deal with more than 250 cases per annum; others, as Ganado has said, will not.

Greif (Uruguay): The training of judges is very important. Further, we must prevent overload, not cure it. But there must be a basic right of appeal. We must not only avoid an excessive number of appeals but improve the quality and the rapidity of appellate proceedings.

FINAL CONCLUSIONS

Németh. It is not easy to identify either the causes or the consequences of overload. We must, therefore, have further data concerning the population, the background of the judges (age, professional background, etc.), the number of cases judges can deal with in a year and the actual number of cases at first instance and on appeal. These data are not fully available in all East European countries. It is as if a doctor had to diagnose a disease without having the opportunity to examine the patient. Nevertheless, the data available allow some idea of the situation in socialist countries. Comparing the number of judges with the size of the population it emerges that Yugoslavia has, proportionately, the greatest number of judges (1:4,000). Czech. Socialist Republic/Bohemia (1:7,300), Hungary (1:7,100) and in particular the U.S.S.R. (1:25,500) are less well placed. The U.S.S.R. has 280 million inhabitants but only 11,000 judges. This may be compared with the Federal Republic of Germany which has 64 million inhabitants and 13,000 judges. The standard of the Soviet Ministry of Justice suggests that judges of first instance must deal with 400 cases per annum and the workload in some other East European countries is similar. There is no overload in the German Democratic Republic or in Rumania but there is overload in other East European countries.

What are the reasons for overload and what are the remedies? The main reason is the inadequacy of the first instance and the fight against overload must begin at that level. Judges must have adequate training and proper working conditions. Judgments at first instance must be well-founded and more convincing in order to reduce the number of appeals.

Jolowicz. The national reports show great differences between different countries. Overload is not just a problem of backlog and common ground can be found by concentration on the purposes for which the right of appeal exists. There is a problem in defining overload, but overload can be recognised where it exists.

A variety of approaches for combating overload were considered - expansion in the number of appellate courts and judges, 'rationing' and 'efficiency'.

1. There are obvious limits to what can be achieved by increasing the number of appellate judges;
2. Some kind of 'rationing' seems to be necessary as a general remedy. Each country has chosen, or will choose its own method such as the requirement of

'leave to appeal' which is wide-spread in common law countries or the use of 'formations restreintes' with power summarily to reject an appeal, as in France.

3. Improvement in 'efficiency' is, in principle desirable but must not be carried too far. The General Reporter was saddened to hear, in the working session, phrases such as 'the justice business' and 'productivity.' Our congress is not entitled 'Efficiency' but 'Justice and efficiency.'

4. No doubt empirical research is necessary to discover the causes of overload. Are the lawyers themselves to blame?

But the same solutions are not necessarily suitable for all countries. Each country must find its own compromises between the public and the private purposes of the appeal dependent on its own legal culture. The one suggestion that seems almost universally acceptable is to seek to improve the first instance and thus to increase confidence in and satisfaction with the decisions of courts of first instance.

IMPROVEMENT OF CIVIL LITIGATION BY LESSONS DERIVED FROM ARBITRATION

IMPROVEMENT OF CIVIL LITIGATION BY LESSONS DERIVED FROM ARBITRATION

W.J. Habscheid
Professor at the University of Zürich
Secretary-General International Association for Procedural Law
P. Schlosser
Professor at the Institut für Bürgerliches Recht und Zivilprozessrecht der Universität München

INTRODUCTION

It is questionable whether lessons really can be drawn from arbitration for the improvement of civil litigation. In any case, the fact that so many of the national reports initially promised to us never were delivered, seems to be due to pessimism regarding the assumption underlying the topic of our report. But even the few reports and brief statements which we received[1] reflect little hope for the outcome of our research. According to Professor Heuman from Stockholm, it is impossible to isolate the well-known advantages of arbitration and transfer them into the context of litigation[2]. In particular he rightly criticizes the view that arbitration laws lacking detailed procedural rules as they do in most countries provide appropriate models for statutory rules on civil procedures:

'It is incorrect to think that many procedural problems can be avoided if one refrains from regulating them'[3].

For the past two years Dr. Briner has been one of the three neutral arbitrators in the Iran-US Claims Tribunal. Consequently, he was the 'national' reporter from whom we had hoped to receive the most inspiration. However, like other reporters, Dr. Briner expressed considerable doubt whether the arbitration mechanism can provide inspiration for improving civil litigation. He states:

I ask myself .... seriously, whether arbitral practice is likely to teach lessons for the improvement of litigation ..... Some of the other praised advantages of arbitration such as discretion, flexibility of the

---

1 Dr. van den Berg and H. Rozemond NL; Dr. Briner CH; Prof. Calavros G; Dr. Dika JU; Prof. Fasching A; Prof. Heuman S; Prof. Kos-Rabczewicz-Zubkowski CAN; Dr. Ricci I; Prof. Schütze FRG; Dr. Steiner CSSR; Prof. Takakuwa JAP; Prof. Naón, ARG.

2 Sweden, 1.

3 Sweden, 11. On page 14 he refers to bad experiences the Swedes have had with certain special procedures designed to protect tenants which, regrettably, were based on the notion that proceedings in this context must be informal.

proceedings, free choice of places and languages are in principle incapable of being transferred into litigation'[4].

Dr. Briner further points out that arbitration is far from being a uniform institution and that the trend to increasing formalization of arbitration is tantamount to 'direct denial of the arbitration idea'. Professor Steiner from Czechoslovakia examined the topic in a report of over 40 pages in which he profoundly elaborated quite a number of issues. However, he made no proposal for improving civil litigation based on foreign trade arbitration or on the various forms of compulsory arbitration existing under Czechoslovakian law. Finally, some of the advantages claimed for arbitration, such as cheap and expeditious settlement of disputes, simply do not exist[5].

On the other hand four outstanding authorities express a contrary view. They are no lesser persons than British Law Lords. In 1973 in a 4:1 decision they abandoned the ancient legal rule prohibiting an English court from adjudicating amounts of money denominated in a currency other than sterling[6]. For many years prior to this decision arbitral tribunals had not conformed to this rule and British courts had always enforced their awards. Their Lordships did not fail to refer to that practice which never had raised difficulties. Therefore, they very convincingly pointed out that there was no reason whatsoever why courts of law should not follow arbitral practices in that respect. Lord Justice Michael Kerr[7] quite correctly stated that the decision was 'an interesting illustration of commercial arbitrators adopting a progressive and realistic practice in advance of the courts'. The decision is also an illustration what in other countries, such as for example, the U.S.A. could be achieved.

But in reality the decision is much more than a mere 'illustration'. It is a general model demonstrating how judges learn from arbitrators. Obviously arbitration does not provide an exclusive model for deriving measures to improve civil litigation. It would have been possible for the House of Lords to allow adjudication in a currency other than sterling without referring to arbitration practice in comparable circumstances. However, a lawyer generally tends to be very sceptical about venturing into unexplored fields. In seeking innovations for civil litigation, therefore, arbitration experiences may provide a somewhat familiar place for him to stand. In this context it is very instructive that the House of Lords not only pointed out what arbitrators do, but emphasized especially that their awards given in foreign currency had been enforced by British courts.

For minds trained in arbitration, however, the latter may provide other lessons than inspiring solutions to well-known deficiencies of litigation. Arbitration may rather create the very sensibility for what may be wrong with civil litigation.

Of course, all that presupposes that the administrators and judges responsible for the evolution of our legal civilization - not to speak of Members of Parliament - are familiar with arbitration practices. Although an English judge

---

4 Switserland, 2. Translation by the author.

5 Japan, 4.

6 Miliangos v. George Frank (Textiles) Ltd. (198^G76) A.C. 1007.

7 41 The Modern Law Review (1979), 1, 10.

cannot be appointed as a normal[8] arbitrator[9], the United Kingdom seems to be the country in which the judicial climate for interaction between judges and arbitrators is most favorable. Long years of advocacy prior to appointment to the High Court, frequent litigation about arbitration matters in the Commercial Court, together with the unique communication forum of the Chartered Institute of Arbitrators and the extreme concentration of the legal profession in London appears to suggest that British soil should be particularly fertile for our subject. This explains why much inspiration now comes from this country normally viewed as legally egocentric and tradition-minded. Once again, it was Lord Justic Michael Kerr[10] who first identified and described what is wrong with English litigation in complex matters: He acknowledges that the doctrine of the unprepared judge coming to the court room and listening to the party's testimony with a fresh mind functions well when the disputes are relatively small and transparent. In complex matters where difficult legal issues are often intertwined, the traditional common law system and particularly the English approach to litigation leads to endless hearings and the participants risk losing their overall perspective. Lord Justice Kerr candidly admits that civil law litigation is better equipped for managing such disputes. In such cases, effective management of the litigation depends on the ability of the judges to direct the proceedings and on the preparation of the main oral hearing by documents and extensive written pleadings, and this preparation must necessarily include the members of the decision-making body. It is quite clear that an English judge does not experience in continental-style litigation. But that is the very point of this report: Lord Justic Kerr has experience in continental-style arbitration which in itself reflects the main features of civil law litigation. As Lord Justice Kerr states in his own terms[11]:

> 'In long and complex cases the continental inquisitorial procedure is often more effective than our adversary system. It is often better for the tribunal to limit discovery in the first instance, to appoint its own experts, and then to exercise control over the volume of discovery and the witnesses whom it wants to hear. Our arbitrators will have to learn to be more imaginative than merely to follow the mirror image of the procedure in our courts'.

Of course, the direct focus of his observation is what English arbitrators and not judges should learn from civil law arbitrators, and we cannot ignore the particular incentive which had opened the mind of our English friends:

> The difficulties concerning the adoption of the inquisitorial procedure of the civil law in appropriate cases have been a secondary reason why the ICC has been reluctant to direct arbitrations to this country[12].

But we should not worry about special motives for a particular readiness to learn. What matters, is the readiness.

---

8 As distinguished from a judicial arbitrator see; I 1 b below.

9 Sect. 4 Administration of Justice Act 1970. See Mustill-Boyd, Commercial Arbitration (1982) 230.

10 Arbitration v. litigation in Journal of Business Law 1980, 164.

11 International Arbitration v. Litigation, in: Journal of Business Law 1980, 164, 180.

12 Kerr op. cit.

Lord Justice Kerr's observation coincides with what Professor Heuman states in his report[13]. It seems that the principle of orality is upheld in Sweden just as it is in common law countries. Apparently the Swedes suffer from the same shortcomings. Therefore, it may not be futile to overcome any initial scepticism you may feel and to stimulate your imagination in order to exhaust our topic. Viewed from a comparative law aspect it could be treated in three steps.

1. Which lessons can be learnt within the framework of a single legal order? How can Germans, French, British and Swiss apply lessons learnt from arbitration to improve civil litigation procedures in their own countries?

2. What lessons can be learnt in this respect within the context of each of the world's three primary legal systems? Could the British learn anything from American arbitration, the Germans from French arbitration and the Polish from Hungarian arbitration?

3. Can lessons be learned across legal systems? For example, could the Germans improve German civil litigation after having studied American arbitration?

The following discussion certainly does not ignore these three aspects. However, to avoid repetition they do not provide the primary basis for structuring our inquiry. In contrast we will examine each of the main phases of arbitration, keeping in mind that even then overlapping issues are unavoidable.

The following discussion begins by reviewing the types of activities that generally establish lis pendens in arbitral proceedings (1).

The discussion then turns to examining how facts are gathered in arbitration proceedings and what lessons can be drawn from this procedure (2). Of course 'investigation of facts' as used in this portion of the discussion is not synonymous with what common law lawyers refer to as 'taking of evidence'. The broader expression 'investigation of facts', however, may be acceptable also to common law lawyers. Even the famous treatise on commercial arbitration by Mustill-Boyd uses the term 'investigation of facts' to distinguish the procedure in arbitration practice from 'taking evidence' in the litigation setting.

The judgement of the House of Lords cited repeatedly above demonstrates that lessons for the improvement of civil litigation may be learnt from arbitration in the field of legal remedies as well. This will be the third topic in the discussion (3).

Finally the discussion focusses on particular aspects of international arbitration. In view of the extraordinary development of arbitration as a means for settling international commercial disputes, it would be quite astonishing if no lessons could be learnt in that context (4).

1 THE INITIAL PHASE OF ARBITRAL PROCEEDINGS

In discussing 'initiation' of arbitration proceedings we must first note that 'initiation' is a very broad concept, including much more than merely meeting

---

13 Sweden, 3.

the minimum requirements for achieving the legal status of lis pendens in arbitration. Initiation in this context includes every activity of the parties that is destined to give the dispute its particular identity. Two main steps are necessary in this respect. First, the body of the decision makers must be identified, and, second, claims and issues have to be clarified.

1.1 THE IDENTIFICATION OF THE DECISION-MAKING BODY

Unlike a court an arbitral tribunal does not simply exist, but must be constituted in the initiation stage of arbitral process. The parties may agree which person to appoint as sole arbitrator. In most cases either party appoints 'his' arbitrator and the two party-appointed arbitrators appoint a third to serve as chairman. We asked the national reporters whether this particular feature of arbitration provides a basis for improving civil litigation. The answer was an almost unanimous and categorical 'No!'[14]. Indeed, normal administration of justice would appear not to tolerate that parties appoint as 'their' judge whatever member of court they desire. The idea that two judges appointed by the parties should chose one of their colleagues to serve as the presiding judge certainly would be even more repugnant. Dr. Ricci from Italy pointed out in his national report that only compulsory arbitration would allow a system of ad-hoc-appointed decision makers; but this would be something very dissimilar of litigation. Nevertheless, we believe that it would be premature to conclude from this that arbitration cannot provide inspiration in this area.

a) From the German and Japanese national reporters comes the proposal to establish chambers specialized in international matters[15]. If this undoubtedly would help to have judges of special knowledge available, the idea, however, seems to only remotely derive from experiences in arbitration.

b) In many legal systems decision-making bodies consist of one professional judge who presides over the proceedings and two lay judges. The German 'chambers for commercial matters' and German labour law courts use such a system. What should dissuade us from giving the parties the power to select for their dispute one of the lay judges enlisted on the court's roll? Lay judges in German labour law courts are not neutral judges in the professional understanding of that term, because one is selected from a list of labour union proposals, and the other from a list of management nominations. The step to empower either party to select one member of the tripartite decision making body should not be enormous. If a lay judge selected in this manner is not entitled to receive any remuneration other than an reimbursement of costs and compensation for forgone income, the risk that he would act as a passionate advocate for one side rather than a third party, is not very great. Even if he feels particularly responsible to ensure that evidence and arguments introduced by the party who appointed him is not overlooked, this would not do any harm to justice. On the other hand, allowing the parties to participate in constituting the deciding bodies has considerable advantages. Of course, it would not enable

---

14 Austria, 5; Sweden, 4; Netherlands, 2; Italy, 10; Greece, 3; Argentina, 6.

15 Germany, 6; Japan, 7.

parties to designate somebody who has their particular personal confidence. In most cases no such lay judge would be available on the list. However, the parties could make their choice based on the appointee's knowledge of the particular industries in question and of other specific aspects relevant for the proper settlement of the dispute.

Our Yugoslavian reporter who for the safeguard, of democracy in justice would not allow parties to appoint members of the decision making body, has no objection to have parties in litigation granted the power to agree that their case be decided by a single judge rather than by a tripartite panel[16].

Only England allows the parties in litigation to agree to the appointment of a judge. The model is very different from the one outlined above. Under English law the parties may agree to have one of the puisne judges of the commercial court adjudicate their dispute, subject to the consent of the judge so selected. Finally, the Lord Chief Justice must authorize the appointment. This institute is called 'judicial arbitration'[17]. Sec. 4 of the Administration of Justice Act 1970 authorizes judges to accept appointments as a sole arbitrator or as an umpire. This sounds like arbitration. However, in this context the terms 'sole arbitrator' and 'umpire' should not be misunderstood. The institution differs significantly from normal arbitration. It could be called a very privileged kind of arbitration. Such arbitrations have to be fitted into the court's list of commercial matters in the same way as other fixtures. A judicial arbitrator is not entitled to receive personal remuneration: fees must be paid to the court. The arbitrators' 'awards' are binding and normally unappealable like other awards. An appeal on a point of law such as against arbitral awards sometimes opened under English law[18] must be lodged with the Court of Appeal and not with the first-instance Commercial Court like in normal arbitration cases. In many other respects a judicial arbitrator is viewed like a trial court judge[19]. The main difference between a judicial arbitrator and his colleague in the Commercial Court is the informal and private nature of the proceedings. Therefore, it does not seem to be accurate to designate judicial arbitration as an 'intermediate between litigation and conventional arbitration'[20]. More accurately, judicial arbitration is a particular kind of litigation rather than arbitration. Although acting as a judicial arbitrator does not provide a personal financial advantage, English judges are very much in favour of the idea[21]. This seems to be another indication of the inclination of our British friends to draw lessons from dispute settlement mechanisms developed in arbitration to improve the civil litigation process. It must be added, however, that parties do not often make use of this process. This is probably attributable to the fact that parties are not likely to agree to anything once a dispute has arisen. It is likely that the institution

---

16 Yugoslavia, 7.

17 For details see Mustill-Boyd op. cit. 230.

18 Arbitration Act 1979 Sect. 1 (2). With regard to the admissibility of exclusion agreements, see Sect. 1 (6).

19 For details see the tabulated survey in Mustill-Boyd, op.cit. 232.

20 Mustill-Boyd, op. cit., 230.

21 Mustill-Boyd, op. cit. 230; Kerr, Modern Law Review, op. cit. 5.

would be used more often, if parties could provide for judicial arbitration in their contracts. Why not allow parties stipulations like this:

'Judicial arbitration, the arbitrator to be appointed by the Lord Chief Justice if parties do not reach an agreement. Commercial arbitration, the arbitrator to be appointed by (e.g.) the Lord Chief Justice if judicial arbitration is not available.'

Also in other common law countries several types of 'judicial' arbitrations exist. The Canadian reporter[22] draws our attention to a decision maker called an 'arbitrator advocate'. In his view this person is a 'sui generis ad hoc judge'. He is bound to the statutory rules of civil procedure, and his decision is subject to normal appellate proceedings. Unlike small claims compulsory arbitration in the United States, the appointment of an 'arbitrator-advocate' necessitates an agreement between the parties. Unlike judicial arbitration in the United Kingdom, it grants special privileges to advocates rather than to judges. Nevertheless, both institutions are interesting attempts to reduce judicial overload without implementing compulsory devices and without deviating substantially from the framework of state-controlled administration of justice.

1.2 IDENTIFYING CLAIMS AND ISSUES

One of the main problems in any dispute settlement proceeding is the timely identification of claims and issues and, on the other hand, time needed to achieve reliability in doing so. It is not easy to make parties agree on what they disagree.

a) Various legal systems have developed various techniques to force participants in legal proceedings, including decision makers, to focus on what is relevant. Many legal systems require the claimant to clearly and specifically indicate the remedy he is seeking, including, if any, the judgment amount. Counterclaims and additional claims are not admitted unconditionally. Many statutory rules impose a formalized structure for factual allegations of the parties.

In common law countries the number of pleadings is limited, and their content is restricted to general allegations regarding the claim raised. The defendant must follow the systematical pattern of the plaintiff's brief precisely. The judge and other court officials have power to strike out briefs not complying with these requirements. All of these rules, however, are primarily intended to ensure concentration on the party's respective pleadings. Although the judge often has had little preparation for the proceedings, the rules ensure that the parties have clarified the relevant issues in the case.

West German, Austrian and multiple Swiss civil litigation patterns probably reflect the extreme counterposition. Prior to the oral hearing, the parties are free to submit as lengthy and as many written pleadings as they desire. No law whatsoever prescribes any systematic order for such pleadings. Factual contentions, legal explanations, evidence offered and to be offered, circumstances of indirect relevance not in dispute or to be proved by evidence offered,

22 He is referring to art. 382-394 of the Quebec Code of Civil Procedure. Quebec, however, certainly does not qualify as a common law country. Nevertheless, common law influence cannot be overlooked.

anticipated evaluation of evidence to be offered and general polemics are usually mixed together. The defendant need not follow the order of presentation the plaintiff follows. The main objective of each party in filing written pleadings is to convince the judge from the outset of the validity of his position. The skill of the advocate in trivializing weak points and overemphasizing insignificant details intended to cast a favorable light on the pleading, together with pure negligence in drafting pleadings make it particularly cumbersome for judges in these countries to identify the actual issues involved. Several years ago pre-hearing conferences were introduced in Germany[23]. However, these conferences function quite differently from pre-hearing conferences in common law countries. The judge is supposed to have already thoroughly studied the extensive briefs of the parties before opening the pre-hearing conference[24].

b) In this field it is certainly less appropriate than in others to view 'arbitration' as a uniform model for improving civil litigation. However, it is proper to consider what can be leart from specific institutional arbitration mechanisms and from other types of pre-established arbitration rules. In England[25], and under the Rules of the American Arbitration Association[26], in the USA, pre-hearing conferences between the arbitrators and the parties have become common. One of the main objectives of such conferences is to identify the issues to be dealt with in the main hearing. Naturally, arbitrators encourage the parties to agree on what issues the hearing will cover. Since the Federal Rules of Civil Procedure were amended in 1983, scheduling conferences[27] have become a standard feature in federal civil litigation in the USA. This is not due to lessons drawn from arbitration. Pre-hearing conferences in arbitration have rather become popular due to lessons drawn from litigation. It is, however, quite likely that the US experience with Iran-US claims arbitration in The Hague will further help to familiarize American lawyers with that modern litigation element of pre-hearing conferences. American lawyers appear to be very much impressed by the extensive pre-hearing management of the subsequent trial they learnt in The Hague[28]. As one American lawyer stated, 'the guidance afforded by comments at the pre-hearing conference is invaluable'.

c) In this context the 'terms of reference' procedure used in proceedings conducted under the arbitration rules of the International Chamber of Commerce should be mentioned[29]. This procedure has its historical basis in the French 'compromis'. However, the French 'compromis' is intended only to clarify the

---

23 §§ 272, 275 Code of Civil Procedure.

24 Regrettably the use which is made of rather extensive pre-hearing conferences is on the decrease. See Bender in Gilles and others (Ed.) Rechtsmittel im Zivilprozeß (1985) 44.

25 Mustill-Boyd, op. cit. 279; Hunter, Hypothetical Case Study question 24, to be published in ICCA, 8th International Congress, New York 1986 (edited by Pieter Sanders, Congress Series no. 3).

26 Hoellering in Sanders (Ed.) preceding footnote.

27 Art. 16.

28 Stanton P. Balland, Journal of International Arbitration, 237, 240 (1984).

29 Art. 13 ICC Arbitration Rules.

matter in dispute ('object du litige')[30]. In contrast, 'terms of reference'[31] identify not only 'the issues'[32], but also summarize the respective contentions of the parties. This forces the arbitrators and the parties not to allow the materials of the proceedings to accumulate in an uncontrolled manner. From the outset, they must seek to distinguish between what is relevant and what is not.

Nevertheless it cannot be overlooked that many ICC arbitrators are critical with the terms of reference. Our national reporters as well appear to be reluctant in drawing lessons from the ICC terms of reference[33]. In most cases the two month deadline, calculated from the handing over of the minutes to the arbitrators, for the setting up of the terms of reference can not be met. Almost invariably the Court of Arbitration in Paris has to extend the time. Tensions and difficulties regarding which matters to include as issues in dispute and how to formulate each party's contentions may already arise during the initial phase of arbitration. Moreover, it is unclear to what extent arbitrators are bound to the matters specified in the terms of reference. Apparently, the ICC arbitration rules are contradictory in this respect[34]. In many cases the arbitrators must propose the drafting of the terms of reference according to very brief pleadings of the parties, leaving the final identification of issues to subsequent extensive exchange of writings: Finally, not infrequently the places of business of the parties are far apart. The loss of time and other costs involved may dictate that a 'pre-reference' hearing is not worthwhile. Refusal of the defendant to collaborate in drawing up terms of reference after all even may be a dilatory device. Consequently, terms of reference frequently appear to be rather general[35]. Therefore, a procedure similar to the ICC 'terms of reference' would not appear to be appropriate for being applied as a mandatory element in the context of civil litigation.

Nevertheless, the ICC 'terms of reference' procedure may provide an optional useful mechanism for countries in which judges actively direct and manage litigation proceedings.

Many lawyers familiar with the ICC arbitration, as well as many arbitrators, do not share the above-mentioned scepticism regarding the terms of reference procedure. On the contrary, they commend that procedure pointing out that it provides an opportunity to force the parties to timely focus on the relevant points to be settled. The German Arbitration Institute recently commented on

---

30 Art. 1448 nouveau code de procédure civil corresponding to art. 1006 code de procédure civil (ancien) of 1806.

31 French: acte de mission.

32 The German translation 'Streitfälle' is incorrect.

33 For example Austria, 6.

34 Art. 16 provides...

35 See, for example, the model terms from SPP (Middle East) Ltd. v. Southern Pacific Properties and another published in Craig, a.a. in International Chamber of Commerce Arbitration, vol. II, app. 6, 1. The president of the Amsterdam District Court declared the subsequent partial award regarding the arbitrator's jurisdiction to be enforceable. See Yearbook Commercial Arbitration, Vol. X, 487 (1985). The Paris Court of Appeal. however, later vacated the award. See Revue de l'arbitrage, 86 (1986). One of the few issues specified in the terms of reference was 'whether defendants committed any and, if so, what breaches of those contracts'.

possible modifications of the ICC Arbitration Rules. They did not propose, however, anything which might weaken the requirement of terms of reference to be drawn up when arbitration is starting[36]. Precisely in situations where judges suffer from an overload of proceedings identifying relevant issues in the record in good time can help manage the proceedings. In such cases, the result of the pre-hearing conference could function like the drawing up of terms of reference. In other words, those results could be summarized in a document listing factual and legal issues and points on which the parties disagree[37]. If at the end of the pre-hearing conference the judge can require the parties to sign a document stating which issues are in dispute, this would represent an important step toward concluding the litigation. Procedural rules could prohibit subsequent modifications of claims and factual issues without court approval. In contemporary German and Austrian and to some extent in Swiss litigation as well, a single main hearing unfortunately does not follow the pre-hearing conference. By contrast, numerous subsequent hearings are not infrequently even something restricted to a series of formalities which really have nothing in common with judicial hearings will take place. Consequently, in the meantime the disputes may be reassigned to other judges. Sometimes even advocates may be substituted by others. In all such situations terms of reference may be useful to expedite proceedings and prevent delay.

This can only be achieved, however, if the principle of strict orality which continues to apply even today under some legal systems, is weakened to allow judges to manage the proceedings effectively. Of course, allowing judges broader powers in managing proceedings is by no means tantamount to granting 'inquisitorial judicial powers'. But having in mind what has been cited from Lord Justice Michael Kerr one may be hopeful in this respect - by lessons learnt and to be learnt from arbitration.

The foregoing discussion serves to introduce the second part of this study.

2 INQUISITION AND THE TAKING OF EVIDENCE

Every judgement concluding a legal proceeding is based on findings of fact, which may contain hypothetical elements. The parties' identical description of facts and what they intentionally omit is sacrosanct in many legal systems and not subject to any further clarification. Furthermore, rules establishing the burden of proof indicate which hypothetical facts should be the basis of the judgement, if the parties and judges are unable to achieve full clarification. Although they differ radically in approach, all legal systems strive to eliminate hypothetical elements based on disputed factual issues in their court decisions. Furthermore, it is submitted that in this respect some approaches are more efficient than others. Two main aspects of judicial fact-finding must be distinguished. Continental lawyers are inclined primarily to look for 'the proofs' for specific contentions set out by one of the parties and disputed by

---

36 See Schwab, in: Festschrift Kralik 317, 322 (1986).

37 An experienced German judge recently proposed that the courts should not summon parties for a pre-hearing conference without indicating what issues they deem not to be in dispute according to the written pleadings of the parties. See Bender op. cit.

his opponent (2). A glance at the common law system, however, indicates that a fundamental problem exists in that context, which is little familiar to civil law lawyers, although it exists everywhere in the world: How can parties obtain the information they need to decide whether litigating makes sense or not. It is not reasonable for a party to make any specific allegation until this problem is resolved. In common law countries the relevant device is pre-trial discovery, as opposed to taking of evidence. The Germans distinguish between 'Aufklärung' and 'Beweiserhebung'. Literally translated, 'Aufklärung' means disclosure in court, while 'Beweiserhebung' means proof in trial. The following two sections examine these two aspects of litigation in greater detail.

2.1 DISCOVERY AND DISCLOSURE

It seems normal that initial discovery and disclosure are basic problems within every legal system that each system must resolve in an appropriate manner, even if the means employed differ somewhat. In reality the most fundamental differences in worldwide rules of civil procedure can be found in this respect. Legal institutions are not only structurally and procedurally different, they also approach the problem with varying degrees of intensity and efficiency.

This is true even within related legal systems. In one of the last judgments of the English Court of Appeal in which Lord Denning presided[38], the Master of the Rolls stated:

> .....as a moth is drawn to the light, so is a litigant drawn to the United States. If he can only get his case into their courts, he stands to win a fortune.

US style pre-trial discovery is indeed unique in our world. It gives powers to the litigant's lawyers which in other legal orders not even public prosecutors possess. This of course provides plaintiffs a great advantage in litigation.

In civil law countries as well, rules of civil procedure differ substantially. What they have in common is the strict denial of party-directed pre-trial discovery and disclosure.

Compulsory general discovery, as opposed to discovery of specified materials, and party to party depositions and interrogatories do not exist at all in the civil law setting. No rule permits anything resembling a 'fishing expedition', in which a party can gain access to any information whatsoever in order to build up a potential claim. Civil law countries are even reluctant to permit discovery of well-specified documents. However, great differences exist in this respect. Judges in France[39] and Italy[40] have substantial power to order parties and witnesses to produce documents and to give access to other evidentiary materials. Although these powers are much more limited than those open to American or - with relation to documents - even English lawyers, they are much greater than those available to German judges.

---

38 Smith Kline & French Laboratoriesk, Ltd. v. Bloch (1983) 1 WLR 730. In a similar sense see the opinion of Lord Diplock in Britisch Airways Board v. Laker Airways Ltd. (1984) 3 All E.R. 413 A.C.

39 Art. 11 nouveau code de procédure civil.

40 Art. 117, 118 codice di procedura civile.

In Germany, a witness called into court to testify need not state anything more than that which he happens to remember. He is not bound to review his files before going to court, and he need not bring those files with him or make them available for the court[41]. Theoretically, the plaintiff is legally bound to substantiate his claim by providing detailed explanations of the facts underlying the dispute. The German Code of Civil Procedure, however, by no means establishes how the plaintiff can obtain such information. The defendant is not required to do anything more than contest the plaintiff's contentions[42]. The Code of Civil Procedure does not very much in order to bind either party to produce documents or tangible evidence, or to participate actively in clarifying factual issues. The Code of Civil Procedure in Germany does not even envisage anything similar to the limited type of documentary discovery available in the United Kingdom. A German judge generally cannot even order production of well identified documents. He may order production only of those documents[43] which a party referred in his pleadings. In practice, German judges already have broken the narrow confines of these rules. Nevertheless, even court made rules for documentary production are very strict in Germany. The court may order production of documents only if the documents to be produced are specified clearly, and necessary for the litigant to meet his burden of proof[44]. Legal theorists sometimes point out that documentary discovery is necessary in common law countries, because it functions as a substitute for the Judge's inquisitorial powers[45]. In reality, however, discovery of documents is much more than that. What common law lawyers often misunderstand is that a civil law judge does not have very many 'inquisitorial powers'.

Returning to our particular problem, two things must be conspicuous. In both civil law and common law jurisdictions lawyers complain about the shortcomings of their system. In arbitral proceedings they have come much closer together.

a) Let us first consider *common law proceedings*. Complaints about malfunctioning and even abuses of the US discovery procedure are manifold and extensive. It has been estimated that American corporations spend 80 billion dollars every year on intercorporate litigation and discovery[46]. Former Chief Justice Burger personally led the critics and argued against 'filing a complaint based almost on rumors and then embarking on months of extensive pre-trial discovery to find out if his client had a case'. He concludes:

For some disputes trials will be the only means, but for many trials by the adversary contest must in

---

41 A draft bill to modify the German code of civil procedure in this respect has not been adopted. See Bundesratsdrucksachen 522/84, which proposed replacing § 378 with the following rule: The witness must review and have available at trial his notes and other documents related to the subjects on which he will testify and legally available to him.

42 Naturally this does not apply where the defendant bears the burden of proof.

43 § 142 Code of Civil Procedure.

44 Stein-Jonas-Leipold, Kommentar zur Zivilprozeßordnung, 20th ed. § 273 no. 25 (1985); Schreiber, Die Urkunde im Zivilprozeß, 75, 78 (1982).

45 See Mustill-Boyd, op. cit. at 285.

46 Charles Rosenberg, referred to in: Abraham Ribicoff Arbitration Journal 1983. 4.4.

time go the way of the ancient trial by battle and blood. Our system is too costly, too painful, too distractive, too inefficient for a truly civilized people[47].

In the well-known Mitsubishi Case[48] the U.S. Supreme Court subsequently pointed out the advantages of arbitration:

'In any event, adaptability and access to expertise are hallmarks of arbitration... It is often a judgment that streamlined proceedings and expeditious results will best serve their needs, that causes parties to agree to arbitrate their dispute...'

Justice Burger and the Supreme Court are contemplating arbitration as an alternative to litigation rather than contemplating litigation to be improved by elements taken from arbitration[49]. If it is appropriate, however, to have the decision-maker reduce pre-trial discovery and 'digest evidence at his own time and pace without the expensive panoply of the judicial process' why not proceed to reorganize litigation itself rather than to look for alternatives?

A couple of years ago the relevant provisions of the Federal Rules of Civil Procedure relating to pre-trial discovery[50] were altered. Since then federal judges have the power (and the duty) to organize pre-trial conferences and thus to manage litigation. European observers predict that due to this innovation US federal litigation will change dramatically[51].

The British, too, have become more open minded. A high ranking British judge, endowed with an extraordinary gift of observation[52], recently stated:

On the other hand, if it is employed without discrimination, the procedure of discovery can have serious practical disadvantages. In complex cases, a full order for discovery may require the parties to list and produce large quantities of documents, all but a small fraction of which are of no interest or value to either party. If carried thoroughly, the preparation of a list of documents involves the parties and their legal advisors in a great expenditure of time and money, much of which could be more usefully employed in preparing the evidence for the hearing..... Many foreigners view with incredulity a system which requires then to produce (for example) documents passing in their own organization which were never intended for general distribution: and they point out with justice that the possibility of disclosure must serve to inhibit their freedom to express themselves frankly in writing.

Yet in both legal systems many practitioners still fight for discovery just as it is, arguing that otherwise the truth could not be found and justice would be severely hampered.

Viewed from that background, it is amazing that pre-hearing discovery is far less developed in common law arbitration than it is applied in common law litigation.

---

47 70 American Bar Association Journal, April 1984 p. 65.

48 Mitsubishi Motors Copr. v. Soler Chrysler-Plymouth, 53 Law Week (1985) 5069, 5075.

49 68 American Bar Association, March 1982 page 275.

50 Rules 16, 26 (b) (1) (applicable as of August 1, 1983).

51 Junker, Discovery im deutsch-amerikanischen Rechtsverkehr, 106 (1987); Heck, Zeitschrift für vergleichende Rechtswissenschaft, 84, 208, 210 (1985).

52 Mustill, in: Mustill-Boyd, op. cit. 285.

aa) Discovery is probably more important in *English arbitration* than it is in US arbitration, but even in England statutory rules[53] limit a party's obligation to produce documents to the arbitrator rather than to his opponent. Furthermore, he is free to wait until the arbitrator 'requires' him to do so. The most reputable British treatise on commercial arbitration[54] is full of warnings against useless efforts:

> The arbitrator should remember that he need not necessarily employ the full extent of his powers. A restricted form of discovery may be appropriate.

Apparently, everyone is satisfied with this system. Thus far, British courts have rarely had to rule either on access to evidence or on protection against excessive discovery in the arbitration context[55]. This is even more impressive in light of the fact that more than ten thousand arbitration proceedings are brought in the United Kingdom each year[56]. No recorded decision examines whether an arbitrator was guilty of misconduct when granting or refusing discovery orders, which sanction could easily have been contemplated under English law[57]. Apparently, discovery devices applied in arbitration are another 'interesting illustration of commercial arbitrators adopting a progressive and realistic practice'. This device has not yet been adopted 'in advance of the courts', but perhaps in anticipation of future practice in litigation.

bb) In the *United States* the contrast between arbitration and litigation is even greater. Whoever is familiar with the relevance of pre-trial discovery in US litigation must really be surprised to learn what US courts think about discovery in the context of arbitration. Court orders for discovery are available only in situations of utmost urgency[58]. This is similar to the 'Beweissicherungsverfahren' under German law, in which discovery is available only if there is a substantial risk that the evidence sought will have become unavailable by the time the litigation or arbitration proceedings begin[59]. Court ordered pre-arbitration discovery is viewed by many US-courts as being an undue combination of litigation and arbitration[60]. As one court stated:

> The availability of disclosure devices is a significant differentiating factor between judicial and arbitral

---

53 Arbitration Act 1950, Sec. 13 (1). This has correctly been pointed out by Morgan, J.Int. Arb. 1986.3.12.

54 Mustill-Boyd, op. cit. 286. For considerably more detail see Wetter, J. Int. Arb. 1985.2.16 pp; Morgan op. cit.

55 See the references given by Morgan op. cit. 12.

56 This figure is taken from Kerr, Modern Law Review, 6 (1978).

57 See Arbitration Act 1950, Sec. 23.

58 For examples including the following citations see McClendon-Goodman, International Commercial Arbitration in New York 90 (1986) and Morgan, J. Int. Arb. 1986.1.17. The most important precedents seem to be Coastal States Trading v. Zenith Navigation, S.A., 446 F. Supp. 430 (S.D.N.Y. 1974) and Mississippi Power Co. v. Peabody Canal Co. 69 F.R.D. 588 (S.D. Miss. 1976).

59 Thus, the test in Bergen Shipping Co. Ltd. v. Japan Marine Service, Ltd., 386 F. Supp. 430 (S.D.N.Y. 1974) where depositions were ordered from the crew of a vessel prepared to sailing away.

60 Matter of Katz, 3 A.D. 2d 238, 160 N.Y.S. 2d 159 (1st Department 1957).

proceedings..... The courtroom may not be used as a convenient vestibule to the arbitration hall so as to allow the party to build his own unique structure combining litigation and arbitration[61].

One circuit court went so far to say that when concluding arbitration agreements parties waive such 'niceties' as pre-trial discovery[62]. Recently, court ordered discovery in aid of arbitration has even been refused as a matter of principle which does not tolerate exceptions[63].

The American Arbitration Association (AAA) apparently fears that American style pre-trial discovery might damage the reputation of the United States as a good place for international arbitration. Hence AAA publications[64] repeatedly emphasize the distinction between litigation and arbitration in this respect. Even more remarkably, they do not see any need to assure their readers that access to evidence nevertheless is warranted in arbitration as well as in litigation. Apparently no doubt exists in this respect. However, how can access to evidence be realized in arbitration without pre-hearing discovery devices?

The US Arbitration Act grants powers to arbitrators not only to subpoena witnesses, but also to require them to bring with them 'any book, record, document or paper which may be deemed material as evidence in the case'. What is lacking, however, is comparable statutory power over the parties to the arbitration[65]. Even if pre-established arbitration rules, such as those of the American Arbitration Association[66], bind the parties to produce evidentiary materials, no means of direct enforcement exist. The only sanction is the possible adverse conclusion an arbitrator may draw from the party's refusal to produce documents and other papers specifically requested[67].

If this is so, the question inevitably arises whether it is sufficient for sound administration of justice to make adverse fact-finding the only sanction against litigants refusing to produce documents and other evidentiary materials.

It cannot be ignored that the legal position is not very clear as to court-ordered pre-arbitration discovery in general[68]. In one respect, however, the trend is very clear. Fishing expeditions as distinct from discovery for clarifica-

---

61 De Sapio v. Kohlmeyer, 35 N.Y. 2d 402; 321 N.E. 2d 770; 362 N.Y.S. 2d 843, 847 (1974).

62 Burton v. Bush, 614 F. 2d 389 (4th Cir. 1980). For additional references to decisions not allowing discovery orders, see McClendon-Goodman, op. cit. 91, note 85.

63 Thompson v. Zavin, 607 F. Supp. 780 (C.D. Cal. 1984).

64 McClendon-Goodman, op. cit.; Hoellering in Arbitration and the Law, AAA General Counsel's Annual Report 49 (1984).

65 US Arbitration Act, Sec. 7. The phrase used there is 'any person ... as a witness', which certainly does not refer to the parties themselves. Yet implied powers to order discovery is sometimes acknowledged: e.g. Crane and Rigging Co. v. Docutel Corp. 160 N.Y.S. 2d 159, 161. See Morgen (op. cit.), according to whom 'no party is under an obligation to produce evidence detrimental to his own case'.

66 See Rule 31, which provides 'the party ... shall produce such additional evidence as the arbitrator may deem necessary...'

67 Commercial Solvents Corp. v. Louisana Liquid Fertilizer Corp., 20 F.R.D. 359 (S.D.N.Y. 1957). The rule applied even in a case, where the party refused to present persons as witnesses over which he had directory powers.

68 Hoellering, op. cit.

tion of specifically identified issues[69] are not at all tolerable. In contrast to judges, arbitrators should not order discovery in order to aid parties in building up their cases[70].

b) Turning away from common law arbitration and litigation, the discussion will now examine *civil law litigation*.

Undoubtedly, legislation in many countries has gone a long way towards eliminating the shortcomings of civil law litigation. The powers of the court which may, however, not be called inquisitorial, have been strengthened. Yet the well known abuses of pre-trial discovery in the United States have discredited pre-trial discovery in general. Even the mere term is likely to give raise to emotions. Consequently, today it is no longer possible to make proposals for the improvement of civil litigation inspired by elements of common law pre-trial discovery.

Discovery in the context of arbitration, however, has never given rise to comparable irritations. Compared to the access to evidence common under the procedural rules of many civil law jurisdictions, rules regulating discovery prior to arbitral proceedings in the United Kingdom and in the United States, particularly those relating to production of documents are much broader. However, these rules have not been criticized as excessive or harmful. They appear to lack all the deterrent elements of pre-trial discovery such as applied in the context of civil litigation. Therefore, discovery practice in common law arbitration may provide guidance for civil law jurisdictions to improve their rules on the collection of information to the extent necessary to meet contemporary standards.

For example, nothing supports retaining the antiquated rule under Austrian[71] and German[72] law which provides that third parties cannot be required to produce evidence over which they exercise control.

Fewer problems arise regarding evidence within the control of the litigants, particularly the defendants, because the court has limited discretion to make adverse factual determinations if parties fail to cooperate and produce evidence[73]. However, the power to make adverse findings of fact does not always produce satisfactory results. Several years ago, a treatise over 400 pages in

---

69 For the distinction between the two meanings of 'fishing expedition', see Junker, op. cit. 120.

70 See Landegger v. Parsons § Whittmore, 54 N.Y.S. 2d 76, 77 mod. App. Div., 54 N.Y.S. 2d 701 (1945) where the court stated that discovery 'may not be used to enable a party or even arbitrators to search the records of another, merely to determine whether or not they disclose the existence of evidence'. See also U.S. Rubber Co. v. Polly Prentiss (N.Y.L.J.) June 2, 1954, p. 6 cit. acording to Domke-Wilner, On Commercial Arbitration 5th edition 375; Knickerbocker Textile Corp. v. Kingley Fashions 80 N.Y.S. 2d 425, 427 (1948); Commercial Metals Co. v. International Union Marine Corp. 318 F. Supp. 1334 (S.D.N.Y. 1970).

71 Fasching, Zivilprozeßrecht, no. 961 (1984).

72 See footnote no. 41.

73 In comparative law adverse fact finding in order to sanction a party's unwillingness to cooperate seems to be almost universally admitted. In his general report for the Würzburg VIIth International Congress of Civil Procedure Perrot thus called the question 'academic' whether the refusal to produce documents is equivalent to a formal admission of the opponent's respective contention. See Habscheid (Ed.), Effectiveness of Judicial Protection and Constitutional Order (1983) 101.

length was published in Germany examining numerous shortcomings in the German system for gathering information prior to hearings[74]. Paragraph 427 of the German Code of Civil Procedure and paragraph 316 of the Japanese Code provide that, subject to some important limitations, the court must order production in cases where the opponent of the moving party is unwilling to produce a specified document. However, a party cannot be held in contempt for refusing to comply with the order. The only sanction available for noncompliance with the order to produce is that the court may recognize as fact the allegations the moving party has made regarding the content of the document. These rules make no provision for the hypothesis that the moving party may not know what the documents actually provide. In this respect as in many others, experiences of civil law lawyers in common law arbitration may help them to overcome general distrust of discovery obligations and to accept them to an extent as can be found in English and American arbitration.

One does not have to be irritated by the fact that in common law countries discovery does not commence prior to formal initiation of arbitration and that arbitrators must order discovery to be presented to themselves rather than to the other party. Initiating arbitration or litigation proceedings in common law jurisdictions is not particularly expensive. Therefore, in such jurisdictions it is possible to initiate proceedings merely to obtain information. Particularly in Germany, but in other civil law jurisdictions as well, initiating proceedings is quite costly. A functional approach in comparative law analysis, therefore, entails that mutual discovery or disclosure rights civil law jurisdictions adopt from common law jurisdictions must also be in the form of access to information prior to the formal initiation of litigation[75].

Contemporary codes of civil procedure have implemented such rules to a limited extent. For example, French law allows 'mesures d'instruction in futurum'[76] the admissibility of which does not depend on the urgency of the request[77]. Amazingly enough, however, production of documents and other evidentiary materials in the possession of the prospective opponent and not subject to any expert analysis cannot be ordered 'in futurum'. Arbitration, therefore, may provide inspiration even for improving recent legislation on civil procedure.

Professor Calavros from Greece rightly points out that generally experiences in arbitration suggest that some civil law jurisdictions must provide judges with

---

74 Stürner, Die Aufklärungspflichten der Parteien des Zivilprozesses, 1976. For a criticism of Stürner's view, see Arens 96 Zeitschrift für Zivilprozeß 1 (1983).

75 Conform precisely in this respect Stürner op. cit. 266 who based his argument on common law discovery devices.

76 Perrot considers the contrary view to be anachronistic.

77 Art. 145 nouveau code de procédure civile; Cour de Cassation, chambre commerciale 25.10.1983 Bulletin Civil IV 237; Court of Appeal Paris 10.1.1979 Gazette du Palais 1979.1.166; Revue Trimestrielle de Droit Civil, 431 (1979). The latter case is particularly inistructive. It reveals great similarities with 'fishing expeditions' known in the framework of US pre-trial discovery: A bank was likely to be liable for having given excessive credit. An expert was appointed in order to find out whether the credit was useful for the bank's client.

more efficient means for regulating disclosure[78]. An example thereof has just been given.

2.2 THE TAKING OF EVIDENCE AS OPPOSED TO DISCOVERY AND DISCLOSURE

Procedural technicalities can give rise to endless disputes. This study cannot provide an exhaustive survey of all of these matters, which require further examination. Therefor I only refer to the very interesting proposal of our Argentine Reporter 'to allow party autonomy to determine the type of court proceedings in the course of which commercial or economic controversies are to be adjudicated' thus substituting e.g. summary proceeding for normal formal litigation. Furthermore, it is not worthwhile to examine issues which are no longer subject to substantial dispute. For example, hardly anyone would suggest that mandatory publicity of civil litigation proceedings is desirable. In England experienced lawyers, however, were not successful in their attempt to have proceedings in the Commercial Court conducted in camera[79]. However, all of our national reporters agree that at least where all parties consent, hearings should be conducted without the public having access[80]. After having noted this, the balance of our discussion will examine three aspects of the taking of evidence.

a) In common law jurisdictions, rules regarding *admissibility of evidence* are rather formalistic. As is the case regarding pre-trial discovery, US literature on commercial arbitration does not fail to point out the numerous advantages of arbitration in this context. For example, identity and authenticity of documents may be assumed if no party objects, and affidavits may be admitted in place of oral testimony. Furthermore witnesses can 'tell their story' rather than be examined, and hearsay evidence is common[81]. Leading questions on direct examination are allowed, and witnesses may even be interrogated about issues apparently established by documentary evidence. Arbitrators may accept expert reports without hearing oral testimony from the experts[82]. In the United Kingdom arbitrators are bound by rules of evidence, but parties may waive this requirement. In fact, British judges tend to infer such waiver from a party's conduct, even in the absence of clear indications[83].

All this is instructive, and apparently no one ever has complained that these liberal evidentiary rules in arbitration have been harmful. On the other hand, strict common law evidentiary rules sometimes produce strange results. A recent case concerning an American award and decided by the German Federal Supreme Court provides an interesting example of this[84]. In that case, the

78 Greece, 6.

79 See Mustill-Boyd op. cit. 230 note 9.

80 Austria, 5; Italy 17; Canada, 2; Sweden, 12; Federal Republic of Germany, 10; Greece, 3; Netherlands, 2.

81 Petroleum Separating Co. v. Interamerican Refining Corp., 296 F 2d 124 (2d Cir. 1962).

82 McClendon-Goodman, op. cit. 93; Domke-Wilner, § 24.02.

83 Mustill-Boyd loc. cit. 310 referring to judicial precedents.

84 BGH, Recht der internationalen Wirtschaft, 557 (1984).

defendant alleged that he had paid a debt by forwarding a check to the president of the creditor company. The check had been debited to his account, but the bank had destroyed the original check after making a microfilm copy of it. Because the defendant could not produce the original check, he was required to pay the debt again. On examination, the president of the company was not even allowed to testify whether the endorsement on the back of the check was his[85]. In view of modern communication and documentation facilities, such formal rules are no longer appropriate, and, as arbitration reveals, they no longer are necessary.

On the other hand, civil law evidentiary rules also have shortcomings. An especially egregious shortcoming in Germany is the inadmissability of evidence by party presented experts. Where a litigant desires to present 'his' expert witness the court may not go so far as to refuse to listen to his testimony or read his report, but the actual capacity in which he can testify is unclear. Occasionally, courts construe evidentiary rules in a strained, or perhaps excessive, manner to overcome shortcomings. Some commentators, however, express the view that the judge does not have authority to consider 'private expert testimony' if the opponent objects[86]. According to the German Federal Supreme Court, a party presented expert report may be admitted as 'documentary evidence', whatever this means in that context[87]. Approximately 25 years ago the same court ruled that either party is entitled to have his opponent's expert summoned into court for oral examination[88]. However, particularly in this context the capacity in which the expert testifies is troublesome, because the code of civil procedure deals only with court appointed experts. Furthermore, no right of a litigant exists to have the court appointed expert examined by his own expert.

Civil procedure statutes in other jurisdictions also fail to deal with testimony of expert witnesses. This, however, is a narrow view. The philosophy underlying the concept of party-selected expert witnesses is, due to the battle of experts, to illuminate little understandable circumstances. This concept may appear to be naive and costly if the deciding body has no power to appoint neutral experts in addition to hearing expert witnesses of the parties. General refusal to admit testimony of experts selected by the parties, however, is equally narrow-minded. Arbitration reveals that the coexistence of court-appointed and party-presented experts is the better solution. Because the civil law arbitrator has broad discretional powers, such coexistence is common in civil law arbitration[89]. On the other hand, in England arbitrators can appoint neutral experts to testify in

---

85 We do not dissimulate that the respective decision was given by an arbitrator who, for reasons we do not know, felt bound to strict evidentiary rules. The German Supreme Federal Court enforced the award. Of course, this just is not a lesson to be drawn from arbitration. Yet normally arbitrators, as opposed to judges, should not feel bound to strict rules of evidence.

86 Rosenberg-Schwab Zivilprozessrecht 14th ed., § 124 II 4; Bundesarbeitsgericht, Der Betrieb, 1104 (1961).

87 BGH, Neue Juristische Wochenschrift 2874, 2875 (1983). Conform for Austria Fasching, Lehrbuch des österreichischen Zivilprozessrechts no. 1008 (1984).

88 Versicherungsrecht 63 (1956); 450 (1984).

89 See in France: Robert-Moreau, L'arbitrage national et international, 5th ed. no. 179; David, L'arbitrage dans le commerce international no. 326 (1982).

addition to the experts the parties present[90]. The same applies to the UNCITRAL Arbitration Rules[91] and the UNCITRAL model law[92]. Finally, the new rules of the London Court of International Arbitration allow both types of testimony as well[93].

b) Our second point refers to particular problems of *litigation in complex matters*. How to make litigants and judges focus on what is relevant and what is not, when they have to decide for what issues to take evidence. Lord Justice Michael Kerr was not alone in criticizing common law litigation in this respect[94]. It has often been maintained that common law litigation and civil law litigation respectively are distinct and thoroughly balanced systems and that it is impossible and detrimental to justice to attempt to combine elements of both systems. This, however is a judgement springing from intellectual easiness. Arbitration experience demonstrates that it is completely wrong. Precisely in cases involving large sums of money and numerous intertwined legal and factual issues, international arbitration has emerged as a means of dispute settlement combining elements from common law and civil law proceedings. A variety of international arbitration models confirm this. The most important of these are the Washington Convention on the Settlement of Investment Disputes[95] and the UNCITRAL Arbitration Rules[96].

The Washington Convention adopted from civil law systems the use of extensive written pleadings to inform the arbitrators of all relevant issues and the surrounding circumstances relating to the proceedings[97]. As in common law systems, however, the Convention provides that, as a rule, the parties rather than the arbitrators examine witnesses and experts[98], and grants the arbitrators substantial discretion to accept affidavits or other written testimony[99].

The UNCITRAL Arbitration Rules are particularly instructive, because they have become the main basis for proceedings before the Iran-US Claims Tribunal in The Hague. Of course, the proceedings before this tribunal were not initiated through voluntary submission, as is ordinarily the case in arbitration proceedings. In contrast the proceedings before the Iran-US Tribunal constitute compulsory arbitration. However, this distinction is irrelevant in our context. The main feature distinguishing the Hague 'arbitral' proceedings is that the tribunal is not deciding a single case submitted to it by the parties, but has jurisdiction to settle more than four thousand separate disputes that have been assigned to three different chambers. More than any court in any country, this

90 Mustill-Boyd, loc.cit. 294.

91 Art. 27.1 see II Yearbook Commercial Arbitration 167 (1977).

92 Art. 26 no. 2 see XI Yearbook Commercial Arbitration 387 (1986).

93 Art. 11, 12 see X Yearbook Commercial Arbitration 157 (1985).

94 See e.g. for the United States Klingsberg in Böckstiegel (Ed.) Arbitration in US-German Business Relations (1985) 73, 79.

95 Of December 17, 1962.

96 Reprinted in II Yearbook Commercial Arbitration (1977) 161 ss, to be distinguished from the UNCITRAL model law, see XI Yearbook Commercial Arbitration (1986) 380.

97 See Art. 30 Arbitration Rules.

98 Art. 34 Arbitration Rules.

99 Art. 35 Arbitration Rules.

tribunal suffers from overload. Consequently, it provides a unique illustration of how arbitration techniques can apply to relieve overload in permanent courts. Keeping in mind the special circumstances surrounding the activity of that tribunal, it is possible to make a variety of observations in this regard.

aa) Tribunals handling a great number of matters simultaneously must insist on substantial *uniformity in the proceedings*. Therefore, the UNCITRAL rules were modified to ensure such uniformity[100]. This is particularly instructive, because the UNCITRAL rules originally were drafted for ad hoc arbitrators who normally are allowed to exercise wide discretion in structuring proceedings. In The Hague, however, strict standards have been developed even regarding deadlines fixed by court orders for the submission of pleadings and other procedural activities of the parties. These developments confirm the view of our Swedish and Greek reporters[101] who note that arbitration does not suggest granting judges curial discretion comparable to the discretionary powers arbitrators normally have.

bb) The Hague proceedings are a hybrid of European continental traditions and U.S. practice[102]. As under the Washington Convention, proceedings are initiated by *extensive written memoranda of the parties*. The number of pleadings to be exchanged, however, is restricted. In contrast, as in common law proceedings, the parties present their materials and witnesses to build their cases, while the members of the tribunal put additional questions.

cc) In the past, the tribunal has been reluctant to appoint *experts*, even if no legal obstacle exists for doing so[103].

In the meantime, however, the Iran-US Claims Tribunal has gained experience in applying the UNCITRAL Arbitration Rules. Apparently, it still does not favour experts appointed by the tribunal rather than presented by the parties. If it decides to appoint experts, at least in big cases the tribunal relies on thorough cooperation with the parties in preparing the terms of reference and in determining the number and the capacity of the experts. Draft terms of reference are submitted to the parties for comment and finally prepared with the assistance of an expert other than the one to be appointed ultimately[104].

dd) Another experience gained in The Hague is worth further examination. Although the UNCITRAL rules basically are framed according to civil law approaches, it was impossible for the tribunal not to accept what they call *'party testimony'* in one form or another[105]. This does not seem to be very

---

100 See report Briner 4. The respective instruments are to be found in VIII Yearbook Commercial Arbitration (1983) 234 ff.

101 Greece 6 s; Sweden 10 s.

102 Report Briner 4.

103 Report Briner 4.

104 Harza v. Islamic Republic of Iran 1 Iran-U.S.C.T.R. 234, 235. For a comment see Michael Straus J. Int. Art. 1986.4 = 57, 65.

105 See Leila Danesh Arfa Mochmoud v. Islamic Republic of Iran, Award Nr. 204-237-2 cited by Michael Straus loc. cit. 59.

innovative since contemporary codes of civil procedure such as the French n.c.pr.c.[106] also admit party statements and party examination as evidence. Nevertheless, some specific aspects of the Hague arbitration experience remain instructive. Most importantly, it suggests that party testimony should be admitted generally and not only to support other evidence. Additional rules of civil procedure should be developed with regard to the undeniable fact that officers and other high ranking staff members from disputing companies realistically can never be identified to normally witnesses.

ee) In The Hague they do accept *affidavits* though not foreseen in the rules[107].

ff) The most instructive element of The Hague procedure is the manner in which all *hearings are conducted*. Depending on the complexity of the particular case, the tribunal determines the number of days available for the hearing and how much time each party will have to present its case regarding any claim or counterclaim in it. Oral hearings generally are limited to one or occasionally two days. In the recent big oil cases, the tribunal allowed a week for oral hearings, in one exceptional case even more. One of the orders preparing the oral hearing has been made available to us. It provides:

'Each side is free to determine how much of the time it spends on the claim and how much time it spends on the counter-claims as well as the division it makes between legal argument and the presentation of witnesses.' "When the response has completed their (time) of presentation, the claimant will present its case with respect to the counter-claims in the time it has reserved." "While the tribunal is free to pose questions at any time, it may be anticipated that most questions by the tribunal will be posed following the initial presentations and prior to the rebuttals." "Time used by a party in examining witnesses presented by an opposing party will be deducted from the time allotted to the examining party." "As stated in previous orders, not further written evidence, including written testimony, will be received, except with the permission of the tribunal, and such permission should not be anticipated.'

One of the attorneys who had a case decided by the tribunal after a two and a half day hearing estimated that an U.S. court would have needed four weeks of continuous hearing before reaching its decision[108]. Of course, it is likely that more work is necessary to prepare a case for an oral hearing in The Hague than would be necessary for preparing an U.S. trial. However, the efficiency of The Hague proceedings is evident. It seems that the time spent for the oral hearing could even be shortened. In the oil field expropriation case to the hearing of which one of the general reporters attended, opening statements of counsel and a great part of direct examination were mere reiterations of what had already been briefed.

c) Our last point in the context of the taking of evidence involves *appellate proceedings*. Ordinarily, appellate review of arbitration decisions does not

106 Art. 184-198.

107 Briner S. 4.

108 Staton P. Belland, The Iran-United States Claims Tribunal: Some reflections on trying a claim Journal of International Arbitration 1984, 250 conforms to what U.S. lawyers told the reporter when he visited the tribunal.

occur. Does this not teach us to limit appellate proceedings in litigation? One is inclined to object that uniform interpretation and application of legal rules is indispensible and appellate courts must develop our legal civilization through judge-made law. Indeed, it appears that appellate proceedings in some form are indispensible. Nevertheless, arbitration may provoke contemplations about limiting appellate proceedings to points of law including rules of procedure. Professor Ricci[109] strongly supports such an inference from arbitration proceedings, adding that first instance judgments, like arbitral awards, must be enforceable immediately, even if only provisionally. We were somewhat surprised that the German national reporter[110] and the Greek national reporter[111] agree. However, not all of our national reporters shared this view. Professor Steiner from Czechoslovakia views a two level judiciary as an indispensable guarantee for the benefit of the citizens[112]. We feel unable to give a definite commentary on such proposals. Statistics from the Federal Republic of Germany reveal that a considerable number of appeals are successful on points of fact[113]. This, however, does not necessarily mean that the judgment rendered on appeal is better than the first instance rulings. Therefore, we conclude that the following lesson should be drawn from arbitration: reliable research about the efficiency of appellate proceedings as far as points of fact are concerned should be organized.

3 REMEDIES AND POWERS OF ARBITRATORS

The judgment of the House of Lords referred to frequently above demonstrates that arbitration also may offer guidance for improving civil litigation in the context of judicial remedies. The term 'judicial remedies' is difficult to translate into other languages. Germans probably would translate the term as 'Rechtsschutzformen'. It also is difficult for the French to find an adequate translation, although they share an important feature with common law systems in that judicial remedies take the form of monetary awards. Art. 1142 of the French Civil Code is very well-known. It reads:

> Toutes obligations de faire ou de ne pas faire ce résout en dommages et intérêts, en cas d'inexécution de la part du débiteur.

As is commonly known, this corresponds to the basic principle of common law adjudication. Specific performance, injunctions, declaratory relief and even adjudication of interest, consequential and punitive damages have emerged

---

109 Italy II page 6.

110 Federal Republic of Germany 15 ss.

111 Greece page 4.

112 Czechoslovakia 28.

113 About 100.000 first-instance-judgments of the 'Landgerichte' (as opposed to the 'Amtsgerichte') were rendered in 1985. More than 6.000 were subsequently vacated or altered in appellate proceedings after additional taking of evidence. 3000 appellate proceedings were amicably settled after additional evidence had been taken; statistical data delivered to us by the Federal Ministry of Justice.

primarily as 'equitable', or occasionally as statutory remedies[114]. In the early stages, this tended to have a negative impact on arbitration. Views differed greatly regarding whether arbitrators, like judges, have powers to grant such remedies. Such disputes are common today as well as is the power of arbitrators to grant injunctions. Furthermore, it is still questionable whether parties may grant powers to arbitrators that are not available to judges. For example, it is not clear whether an arbitrator could be empowered to fill gaps in contracts or adapt contractual relationships to changed circumstances in situations where judges could not be so empowered.

The American Arbitration Association apparently was not satisfied with the status quo and attempted to grant its arbitrators the most substantial powers possible:

> The arbitrator may grant any remedy or relief which the arbitrator deems just and equitable and within the scope of the agreement of the parties.....[115].

It is clear that the provision may not be a model for innovations in rules concerning civil litigation. Commercial law and other areas of the law relating to private relationships are subject to the principle of legality, just as are other branches of our legal systems. This is true also in common law countries, where courts are bound by judicial precedent. This, of course, does not preclude the claimant from specifying what remedy and, as the case may be, which amount he is seeking[116]. The central issue, however, is whether the number of judicial remedies should be increased. It is worthwhile to ask whether some of the remedies common in arbitration should be offered for improving civil litigation. In this regard it may be useful to distinguish between final judgments and interim judgments including partial judgments.

3.1 FINAL JUDGMENTS

In discussing whether to empower judges to grant particular remedies, a wide variety of issues is involved. To take just one example: Professor Ricci from Italy very convincingly proposes granting provisional enforcement to first instance court judgments by operation of law. He points out that arbitral awards are immediately enforceable, even if the parties can still apply to have the award set aside or even if proceedings to set aside the award are in progress[117]. However, it would exceed the scope of this study to attempt to list all the potential problems that could arise in the context within each legal system. In contrast, it is more productive to discuss three points of more general interest. The first point is what the French call *'amiable composition'*.

---

114 See for England Mustill-Boyd loc. cit. 343; for the US Hoellering Arbitration and the Law 1985, AAA General Counsels Annual Report, 37. A detailed comparative analysis has been given in Journal of International Arbitration... (1987), partialy reprinted in: Böckstiegel, Die Schiedsgerichtsbarkeit im deutsch-englischen Wirtschaftsverkehr, to appear in 1987.

115 Rule 43 1986 edition. Similarily Sec. 29 Maritime Arbitration Rules of the Society of Maritime Arbitrators 1983. Both reprinted in: McClendon-Goodman loc. cit. 191, 264.

116 Correctly pointed out in the Yoguslavian report, 11.

117 Italy, 6.

The second is whether parties may agree that judges should fill gaps in their contracts and adapt them to modified circumstances, and the third is whether the agreement of the parties generally may grant a judge powers he normally does not have.

a) One of the most salient features of arbitration is the ability of the parties to agree to *'amiable composition'*, usually translated as 'ex aequo et bono arbitration'. Parties are free to agree that the arbitrator should render a just and equitable decision without being bound to find a solution which rules of law would dictate in the circumstances. Today ex aequo et bono arbitration is accepted universally, England being the last country to join the ranks[118]. In the United States the predominant view is 'that arbitrators do not ordinarily consider themselves to be bound to decide according to legal rules'[119].

It is commonly known that Italian[120] and French[121] law provide that parties may, by mutual agreement, grant the judge the powers of an 'amiable compositeur'. However, any such agreement is invalid if it is conducted at the time the parties entered into their original agreement, rather than after a dispute has arisen. Due to that limitation this innovation was not successful. Once a dispute has arisen, the litigating parties are so distrustful of one another that they are not likely to agree to anything whatsoever. However, there appears to be no reason why contracting parties should not be free to agree in advance to allow the court to grant ex aequo et bono judgments if disputes should arise between them. Such a contractual provision would not increase the court's workload or make its task more difficult[122]. Therefore, arbitration suggests a liberal approach to this issue.

b) Dispute settlement ex aequo et bono is not the only example of special powers the parties may grant to arbitrators by agreement. Nowadays it is almost a matter of course that arbitrators may fill *gaps in contracts and may adapt contractual relationships* to altered circumstances if the parties grant them the power to do so. Parties may give arbitrators such powers even where courts do not have and could never be given similar authority[123]. An English court never has power to fill gaps in contracts or to adapt contracts to new circumstances, and this rule cannot be modified by a contrary agreement of the parties[124]. In arbitration, however, the English rule prohibiting arbitrators from modifying contracts is not mandatory and the parties are free to alter it

118 Eagle Star Insurance Co. Ltd. v. Yval Insurance Co. Ltd. (1978) 1 Ll Rep. 357, 361, C.A. See the comments on this judgement by Mann, 94 LQR 486 and Gastambide Q.C.M.A. Revue de l'arbitrage 1981, 195. In the USA many arbitrators feel empowered to decide as French 'amiables compositeurs' would decide. See Böckstiegel, Arbitration in US-German Business Relations 56 (1985); de Vries, Journal of International Arbitration 18 (1984).

119 Wilko v. Swan 201 F. 2d 439 (2d Cir. 1953).

120 Art. 114 codice die procedura civile.

121 Art. 12 Sect. 5 N.C.Pr.C.

122 As rightly pointed out by the japanese report, 8; conf. Argentina 6.

123 See Stahlinski v. Pyramid Electric Corp., 188 N.Y.S. 2d 541, 959; specific enforcement to ensure reemployment of a dismissed employee.

124 Schmitthof, Journal of Business Law 92 (1980).

by agreement[125]. Commentators seem to favour not only giving effect 'to such agreements, but also to inferring such agreements from the conduct of the parties[126].

However, no reason whatsoever appears to exist to distinguish between arbitration and litigation in this context. What harm may be done to justice if parties are free to grant judges powers to fill gaps in their contracts or to adapt them to changed circumstances? Our French friends appear to be more consistent. Like the English, they generally do not allow judges to fill gaps in contracts or to adapt contracts to changed circumstances. However, they do not grant arbitrators such powers either[127].

It is interesting to note that both in England and in France considerable dissatisfaction exists regarding the lack of judicial powers in this context. French courts have interpreted contractual stipulations regarding changed circumstances to oblige the parties to renegotiate and have enforced such obligations by appointing judicial observers to monitor the renegotiation efforts of the parties[128]. However, the relevant statutory provisions do not in any way provide for the appointment of a judicial observer. Moreover, judicial observation does not appear to be an effective enforcement device. International arbitration very easily could provide a model for improvement of domestic curial law, because, even if they are not frequently used, arbitration law at least widely acknowledges the filling of gaps in contracts or adapting contracts to changed circumstances as appropriate remedies[129]. German law clearly establishes the validity of stipulations for adapting contracts to changed circumstances in arbitration proceedings[130]. Today it is uncontested in Germany that respective powers also may be granted to courts[131]. Courts are willing to assume such powers even if one party fails to appoint his valuer according to the underlying contractual stipulations[132].

c) These examples can be generalized. In arbitration, *parties are free to grant particular powers* to the decision-making body. Occasionally, it has been argued that the arbitrators cannot be empowered to do anything which a judge in comparable circumstances could not do[133]. However, arbitral practice offers no

---

125 See Steyn, Yearbook Commercial Arbitraion Vol. VIII, 10 (1983); Horn, in Horn (Ed.) Adaption and Renegotiation of Contracts in International Trade and Finance 22, 180 (1985).

126 F & G Sykes (Wesses) Ltd. v. Fine Fare Ltd. (1967) 1 Ll Rep. 53.

127 De Boisséson-Juglart, Le droit français de l'arbitrage, Rnr. 233 (1983).

128 Cour d'Appel Paris J.C.P. 1978 II 18809 note Robert; award of mai 28 1982 rendered by the former president of the Cour de Cassation, unpublished, but discribed in de Boisséssson-Juglart op. cit. 196.

129 See Böckstiegel in Horn op. cit. 164; Homburger in Reymond-Bucher (Ed.), Swiss Essays on International Arbitration, Zürich 99, 101 (1984).

130 Federal Supreme Court, Konkurs-, Treuhand- und Schiedsgerichtswesen 42 (1977) = Wertpapiermitteilungen 910 (1976).

131 Federal Supreme Court, Der Betrieb 927 (1978); official collection of the Supreme Court decision 71, 276 = NJW 1371 (1978).

132 Federal Supreme Court Official Collecting Tom 74, 341 = NJW 1543, 1544 (1979).

133 See Wiget, 75 Schweizerische Juristenzeitung 17, 25 (1979); Homburger in Reymond and Bucher, Swiss Essays on International Arbitration, 89 (1984).

support for this view. Our research has revealed no decision in which a court has overturned a remedy granted in arbitration on the ground that the arbitrators exceeded their authority in situations where the agreement of the parties clearly authorized the remedy granted.

In the light of these observations, the question becomes inescapable what should prevent a court from following the stipulations of the parties giving the court power to grant remedies it otherwise could not grant. A few examples may illustrate this point.

aa) An English court does not have the power to grant *post judgment interest.* Rather, the judgement itself bears interest at fixed rates specified by law. This raises difficulties for extraterritorial enforcement, because courts in other jurisdictions may not enforce interest accruing on judgments[134]. Furthermore, the interest rate established by statute normally does not correspond to the market rate. For a long time, the same problem existed in arbitration. Recently, however, English arbitration practice began to grant interest at a rate the arbitration deems to be appropriate[135] which allows the arbitrators to take the market rate into consideration. It appears that this also is a practice that can be labelled a 'progressive and realistic (one) in advance of the courts'.

bb) Which party must bear the *costs of the proceedings* is not as unimportant as many commentators seem to think. Normally, strict rules apply in litigation to determine who bears the costs of the proceeding. In some legal systems, the rule applies as a matter of course that the costs follow the event. In other legal systems the successful litigant is not entitled to recover his costs in pursuing the case. Arbitrators have broad discretionary powers allowing them to avoid many of the unsatisfactory results to which litigation often leads. It would be encouraging if courts became more flexible in this respect.

3.2 INTERIM DECISIONS

In many countries binding interim decisions are rare. Consequently, the parties often do not have a reliable basis on which to make decisions regarding which course to pursue in litigation. For example, under German law a partial judgment is allowed only if one of several pending claims is mature for decision independently, or if it is clear that one party is entitled to judgment on a portion of the total amount in dispute in any event. Furthermore, under German law the court may enter an interim judgment to clarify that the claim is admissable or that it is well-founded in principle, leaving the amount to the final judgment. However, interim judgments cannot be entered under German law on particular issues of the case. A German court e.g. could not enter an interim judgment regarding whether a claim is time barred or otherwise extinguished. This is not the case in German arbitration, because it is within the discretion

134 For more details see my articles in Böckstiegel (ed.) Arbitration in German-English Business Relations (1987) and in J.Int.Arb. 1987.1.

135 See London Court of International Arbitration Rules, Art. 16.5.

of the arbitrators to determine how to proceed[136]. Apparently, it does not occur infrequently in common law countries that arbitrators issue interim decisions on central issues, and this practice often facilitates subsequent settlement of the entire dispute[137]. In international arbitration interim decisions have been issued regarding whether the 1955 or the 1975 International Chamber of Commerce Arbitration Rules applied to the reference[138] and which national law applied to the merits of the case[139].

Rules of civil procedure could become more flexible in this respect as well. It is obvious that interim judgments could be abused by parties who lodge hopeless appeals in order to postpone final adjudication. However, it exceeds the scope of this study to examine the measures that could be used to deter such dilatory practices.

4 SPECIFIC PROBLEMS OF DISPUTE SETTLEMENT IN INTERNATIONAL MATTERS

It is not necessary to point out the extraordinary significance arbitration has obtained in international dispute settlement. However, precisely this development should encourage us to examine what lessons could be drawn from international arbitration to improve international litigation.

One great advantage of international arbitration, however, appears not to be transferable to litigation. Even if the parties are permitted to participate in selecting the members of the court who will decide their case, it does not appear possible to conduct proceedings in a language other than the normal language of the court[140]. Our national reporters from the Netherlands[141], Greece[142] and Czechoslovakia[143], however, are more optimistic in this respect. In particular, the Czechoslovakian reporter pointed out that applicable Czechoslovakian law provides reassignment of cases to judges who speak the language spoken by the parties. On the other hand, the Canadian reporter[144] correctly emphasizes the difficulties appellate courts will face if trial court proceedings are conducted in a foreign language.

However, scepsism in this respect should not prevent us from considering the flexibility of the court somewhat in this context. Submitting translations of documents would appear to be unnecessary in many cases where the judges can read the original text. Moreover, some documents are incapable of being correctly translated into foreign languages. In such cases, submission of

136 § 1034 German Code of Civil Procedure. For futher explanations see Stein-Jonas (Schlosser)[20] § 1034 no. 42.

137 Mustill-Boyd, loc. cit., 331.

138 Mobil Oil Indonesia, Inc. v. Asamera Oil Indonesia, Ltd., 43 N.Y. 2d 276; 372 N.E. 2d 21; 401 N.Y.S. 2d 186.

139 Companie D'Armement Maritime S.A. v. Compagnie Tunésienne De Navigation S.A. (1971) A.C. 572.

140 See national Reports, Austria, 12; Switzerland, 3.

141 page 5.

142 page 11.

143 39.

144 page 3.

translations should be discretionary rather than mandatory. In many cases judges, like arbitrators, would abstain from ordering translations, particularly if such documents are drafted in English.

International arbitration has other advantages that could provide guidance for improving civil litigation. Three such advantages deserve closer examination. The first of these relates to the distinction between 'domestic' and 'foreign' law. The second is the ability to grant awards on agreed terms. The third is the service of claims and other materials.

4.1 THE DISTINCTION BETWEEN 'DOMESTIC' AND 'FOREIGN' LAW

Arbitrators never enter decisions in the name of a national sovereign. Therefore, they do not have any lex fori. This statement is a matter of unescapable logic rather than of experience. Although, in practice, arbitration proceedings almost invariably are conducted under the procedural law of the country in which the proceedings take place, this does not contradict the fact that no lex fori exists. Moreover, the domestic procedural rules the arbitrators apply do not necessarily correspond to those applicable in litigation. Consequently, the very absence of any lex fori in arbitration implies that arbitrators are not bound to apply rules of private international law applicable in the country whose procedural rules they apply[145].

Of course, in principle this approach is not suitable for litigation. National conflict rules must establish which law to apply. Arbitration, however, may suggest how to apply 'foreign' law in practice, because it is not uncommon for arbitrators to apply legal rules they are not accustomed to using.

a) In some jurisdictions establishing what the *'foreign' rules* are is a factual determination to be established through evidence. In England and Switzerland foreign law is even presumed to be identical to domestic law unless the parties prove otherwise[146]. To be sure, English arbitrators generally apply this presumption, too[147]. However, we venture to say that this is an antiquated position which may be explained by the fact that thousands of arbitration proceedings are conducted annually in England. The rule iura novit curia

145 Berthold-Goldman Rec. de Cour 1963 I 443; Derains in: Etudes offerts à Berthold-Goldman, 32 (1982), with further references; Derains, Revue de l'arbitrage 380 (1986); Lalive Ordre public transnational (ou réellement international et arbitrage international, to be published in: Sanders (Ed.), Arbitration and Public Policy (ICCA Congress Series no. 3) no. 41; Böckstiegel, Legal Rules ... in 60 Years of ICC Arbitration (Paris 1984) 152; ICC award no. 1512 of 1971 published in Vol. V YCA 74 (1980). The legal position may be different if national legislation orders arbitrators sitting within their territory to apply the state's conflict rules.

146 Mustill-Boyd, loc. cit., 318; Habscheid, Droit judiciaire privé Suisse, 2nd edition 1981, 367 with reference to the Federal Court decision published in the official record volume 60 II 433.

147 Mustill-Boyd, loc. cit., Art. 13.1 (a) of the LCIA Rules, however, seems to be different: 'the tribunal shall have the power, on the application of any party or of his own motion ... to determine what are the rules of law governing or applicable to any contract...'

appears to apply everywhere else in arbitration[148]. Applying the law of the country in which the arbitral tribunal sits to the merits in a proceeding merely because evidence is not sufficient to establish what is the content of the foreign law to be applied is arbitrary. The iura novit curia rule has not only proved to be reliable in arbitration, but also in German[149], Austrian[150], Swiss[151] litigation.

b) The most salient feature of contemporary international arbitration is the *trend to denationalization*. This trend has found its most characteristic doctrinal manifestation in the legal theory of the so called new lex mercatoria[152]. According to this theory, transnational commercial law has emerged as a new area of customary international law. Proponents of this theory contend that as this area of the law develops, it will render traditional private international law approaches increasingly superfluous. However, to say the least, this legal innovation is not yet based on solid ground[153]. Therefore, for the time being it would be wise not to suggest a lex mercatoria approach to our courts.

In a much less radical manner, however, judges may learn from arbitrators means for establishing the legal basis for decisions in international disputes. Arbitrators usually do not base their decision on the law of one particular state rather than of another one. They like to point out that the solution they have reached is consistent with the law in each of the various jurisdictions that could have an interest in the proceedings. If the law they apply does not provide a clear solution, they often consider case law and legal doctrine in other jurisdictions.

Encouraging judges to take a similar approach is not as revolutionary as it seems. Courts in common law countries generally acknowledge the persuasive authority of decisions of other courts from other common law countries, especially of high ranking courts. Swiss Federal Court decisions often cite legal provisions, court holdings and legal writers in Germany, Austria, Italy and France.

4.2 AMICABLE SETTLEMENTS IN ARBITRATION AND LITIGATION

Whether judges or arbitrators should initiate or otherwise encourage amicable settlements is subject to considerable dispute in legal literature. Common law tradition disfavours encouraging settlements. Consequently, lawyers in common law jurisdictions have tended to disapprove of efforts of arbitrators to promote

---

148 See Wetter, Journal of International Arbitration 1985.2.25; Schlosser, Das Recht der internationalen privaten Schiedsgerichtsbarkeit (1975) no. 618; Tallon, in: Schmitthoff, The sources of the law of international trade, 154 (1964).

149 See § 293 Code of Civil Procedure and commentaries to the provision.

150 See Fasching, Zivilprozessrecht no. 836 (1984).

151 See Habscheid, op. cit.

152 Its main supporter being Berthold-Goldman, 475 (1979) and Revue de l'arbitrage 379 (1983). See also many of the contributions published in Etudes Offerts à Berthold-Goldman (1982).

153 For critical commentaries of the theories see Schlosser in XIX Comparative Law Review (Japan) 1985.2.85 (105); Lagarde, Etudes Offerts à Berthold-Goldman 125 (1982); Werner Lorenz, FS (Liber amicorum) Neumayer 407 (1986); Mustill, Current Legal Problems 133, 140 (1984).

settlements. However, as discussed before, pre-hearing conferences have become frequent in US litigation and arbitration. One of the primary objectives of such conferences is to facilitate pre-trial dispute settlement. Unfortunately, no materials are available from which we can develop detailed proposals for improving court-supported settlements of disputes.

In arbitration, however, a method of promoting amicable settlements has been developed which is worth further consideration here. In arbitration, awards on agreed terms, in contrast with recorded agreements have become quite common. One should not be misled when reading that the following is supposed to be the legal starting point:

> The parties may not compel the arbitrators to incorporate their settlement in an award unless the applicable procedural rules so require[154].

There is no reason why parties should not be allowed to alter such rules to facilitate a settlement agreement. All of such 'applicable procedural rules' are simply elements of the parties' agreement, and domestic law generally does not prohibit arbitral awards on terms agreed by the parties. Indeed, the most important standard rules for international arbitration provide for awards on agreed terms[155].

This practice results from shortcomings in domestic law regarding enforcement of arbitral dispute settlement instruments. Although today arbitral awards are enforceable in almost every country, recorded settlements are not, at least not without further litigation.

The same shortcomings exist in the context of litigation. The Brussels Convention of 1968, in force in the European Economic Community, appears to be the only major instrument providing direct enforcement of court-recorded settlements[156]. Many other international treaties do not deal with this issue. In the majority of countries foreign judgments are enforceable according to unilateral legal provisions or according to international comity. In contrast, no equivalent rule exists for court-recorded settlements. Consequently, it seems that courts could achieve much progress if they adopted the practice common in arbitration.

Courts should adopt this practice at least in international litigation. However, it should also apply in domestic litigation. A court-recorded settlement does not acquire the finality of a res iudicata decision. Dispute settlements on agreed terms are private agreements. Consequently, such settlements are subject to all the challenges which normally can be raised against private agreements. However, there appears to be no reason not to deem dispute settlement on agreed terms to be res iudicata. In this context, the parties need no greater protection against negligence, error or pressure than in the context of any other conduct related to the litigation. In many countries, such as England, court orders 'by consent', specifying such matters as alimony, are common in

---

154 McClendon-Goodman, loc. cit., 131.

155 ICC Rules Art. 17; UNCITRAL Rules Art. 34 (1); AAA Commercial Arbitration Rules 44; London Court of International Arbitration Rules ARt. 16.7; UNCITRAL Model Law Art. 30.

156 See Art. 51.

family law. Consequently, introducing a similar practice in commercial litigation is not revolutionary.

4.3 TRANSNATIONAL SERVICE OF DOCUMENTS INITIATING OR FURTHER DEVELOPING LEGAL PROCEEDINGS

In arbitration, the technical aspects regarding communication between the parties themselves and between the parties and the tribunal do not generate significant problems. Of course, it may happen that the person to be sued has vanished without a trace. However, if his ordinary residence is known, arbitration usually is initiated by registered mail with a return receipt. If it appears that the defendant will continue to refuse to participate in the proceedings, further communications between the claimants and the tribunal usually also will be made in this manner. However, this is the limit of formality for communications in arbitral proceedings. Apparently, everyone agrees that this method meets the requirements of due process. Treatises and commentaries on arbitration do not even examine this issue, and judicial authority is limited. The only two recorded decisions of this area were entered by Mexican courts and provide that even service by ordinary mail is sufficient to ensure enforceability of the final award in Mexico[157].

In litigation, in contrast thereto, numerous complications arise for service of process, even under The Hague Convention of 1965 on the Service of Judicial and Extra-judicial Documents Abroad. With few exceptions, the countries consider it to violate their national sovereignty if foreign authorities were allowed to arrange transnational official communications to people residing within their own territory. This would be understandable, if not defendable in policy, if these countries were prepared to grant each other control over such communications. However, the policies of these countries are radically inconsistent in this respect. Each claims jurisdiction for courts and other authorities over certain persons residing in other countries. In order to exercise this jurisdiction, they have developed grotesque substitutes for service abroad which are really equivalent to legislation in fraudem legis internationalis[158]. Already we have become too accustomed to such rules!

Under French law, if the defendant lives abroad, the plaintiff can initiate litigation by delivering the appropriate documents to the public prosecutor. This process, known as 'signification au parquet' is equivalent to service of process, and lis pendens begins with the delivery of the documents[159]. Texas law seems to have adopted a similar approach[160]. Of course, this does not involve foreign territory, and, therefore, does not violate the sovereignty of any other state. But at what price! Legislation has created a monstruous fiction

157 Press Office (France) v. Centro Editorial Hoy S.A. (Mexico) 18th Civil Court of First Instance for the Federal District of Mexico IV YCA (1979) 301; Malden Mills Inc. (US v. Hilaturas Lourdes S.A. (Mexico) IV YCA (1979) 302.

158 For a closer study of the issue see Schlosser in Festschrift E. Stiefel, to be published in 1987.

159 Art. 684 and 653 n.c.pr.c.

160 Sec. 3 of Art. 2031 b Tex. Rev. Civ. Stat. Ann: '... acts of engaging in such business within the State shall be deemed equivalent to an appointment by such corporation ... of the Secretary of State of Texas as agent upon whom service of process may be made... '

which would conflict with the most elementary notions of due process if at least in the case of France the statute did not require the defendant to be given notice of service by registered mail[161] and if it did not provide that normally no judgment could be entered unless the defendant had a fair chance to argue his case[162].

The German method of circumventing international law is not as elegant as the French one. Service of process, indeed, may not occur in a way comparable to the French 'signification au parquet'. Service of further pleadings and service of judgments, however, may be deemed to occur when the bailiff deposits the respective document in a public mailbox[163]. Because service is completed when the document is placed in the mailbox, rather than when it is forwarded to the addressee, it is argued that the German procedure does not conflict with the view held in many European states that service of documents by mail conflicts with territorial sovereignty. According to the German theory, forwarding the document to the addressee in the cases referred to has no independent legal effect. It merely provides the addressee notice of the legal consequences that arose when the document was deposited in the mailbox in Germany. Furthermore, no specific requirements regarding the manner of delivery apply. The document need not even be sent with air mail if the addressee lives on another continent. In default proceedings, it is not unlikely that the filing deadline for challenging the judgment already will have expired by the time the mail arrives at the defendant's address. And all this is done to avoid infringing the sovereignty of one state through extraterritorial activities of another state's authorities! Adherence to such doctrine in state practice is ridiculous. The fact that this form of service of documents does not apply in Germany to the document initiating litigation does not make the practice any less egregious with respect to other documents. Furthermore, the German practice regarding service of documents initiating litigation is also extremely complicated and unclear[164].

Apparently similar rules exist in many states. Venezuela provides a striking example. The new code of civil procedure in Venezuela[165] does not even provide for service of documents at all if the defendant is not present within Venezuela. For that case the code merely requires the issuance of public notice of the proceedings and the publication of an accompanying announcement for a certain period of time in a newspaper.

The attempt to resolve problems of international service of judicial documents by reference to state sovereignty and its ridiculous consequences have a long tradition in civil law countries. This may explain why the West German national reporter even suggested expanding the scope of application of this doctrine to

---

161 Art. 686 in addition to the sometimes long-lasting official transmission of the document in conformity with the provisions of The Hague Convention of 1965.

162 Art. 685 n.c.pr.c. and Art. 15 The Hague Convention of 1965.

163 § 175 Code of Civil Procedure.

164 See e.g. the recent judgement of the Karlsruhe Court of Appeal, Recht der internationalen Wirtschaft 62 (1986). Not less than four important defects of the service of a Canadian writ had been identified there.

165 Art. 224.

fictitious substitutes for service of documents initiating the proceedings[166]. He correctly points out that otherwise litigation in Germany might really be impeded. The lessons we can draw from arbitration, however, are different and more innovative. States have to relinquish their childish concept of judicial sovereignty regarding service of documents in civil litigation. Giving priority to interests of state sovereignty in this context, as civil law states require, compromises fundamental due process interests of the litigants. In a democratic society prerogatives based on state sovereignty do not make any sense, unless they are invoked in a reasonable manner to protect citizens and domiciliaries. In our context, no such protection is involved. Arbitration practices demonstrate that in civil litigation nobody needs to be protected against service of documents. Control of awards and foreign judgments prior to enforcement is more than sufficient to protect these interests.

We candidly admit that the question we asked our national reporters was a leading one: Should states allow foreign courts to proceed to extraterritorial service of documents by registered mail with returnable acknowledgment of receipt? The answer was an almost unanimous 'Yes'[167]. Austrians[168] and Americans[169] have already empowered their courts to order service abroad by specified forms of mail. From this practice it may be inferred that they would accept similar proceedings in foreign courts as well[170]. Arbitration should further encourage this progress.

Of course, other issues of international collaboration in civil litigation could be raised here. Subject to one exception our national reporters agree, for example, that extraterritorial enforcement of judgments should not be more difficult or less expeditious than enforcement of arbitral awards, whether domestic or international[171]. As has been emphasized repeatedly, our topic conclusively demonstrates that experiences in arbitration provide valuable guidance for scrutinizing almost any method proposed for improving civil litigation. Nevertheless, our topic also has shown that experiences in arbitration alone are almost never sufficient to provide the definite solution. Thus, subject to this qualification, arbitration provides guidance for resolving numerous specific problems both in domestic as well as in international civil litigation. Furthermore, it should provide inspiration to all those who have not yet given up the endeavour to overcome the great shortcomings of contemporary litigation.

---

166 Federal Republic of Germany, 14.

167 Yugoslavia, 17; Canada, 3; Netherlands, 6; Greece, 12; Austria, 14.

168 Fasching, Zivilprozessrecht Nr. 531.

169 Federal Rules of Civil Procedure Rule 4 (i) (1) (D).

170 For Austria this inference is valid: Heller-Berger-Stix, Kommentar zur Exekutionsordnung I 777, additional letter of the Austrian reporter, Prof. Fasching, to the general reporter.

171 Yugoslavia, 18; Canada, 3; Federal Republic of Germany, 17; CSSR, 41; contra Austria, 15.

DISCUSSION POINTS

1 A Each party in litigation should have the possibility to select a lay assessor for participation in the deciding court; the parties should, however, be bound to a list of persons admitted as assessors.

B Courts should be encouraged to draft 'terms of reference' to be signed by the parties; a practice similar to that used in ICC-arbitration.

2 A Pre-arbitration discovery and discovery such as customary in the initial phase of common law arbitration is a good model for improving both common law an civil law litigation. Pre-trial discovery in common law countries could thus be substantially reduced to a more reasonable level. Reasonable pre-trial discovery could be introduced in civil law models of civil procedure.

B Arbitration practices demonstrate that the common perception that the taking of evidence, such as administered in common law countries or civil law countries respectively, is incapable of providing lessons for legal systems belonging to the contrasting legal family is mistaken. The coexistence of court appointed and party presented experts is one of the lessons to be derived from arbitration and can benefit both legal families.

3 Lessons can also be drawn from arbitration in expanding the scope of legal remedies available in litigation. One such lesson is the practice under arbitration to grant judges the power to revise contracts due to changed circumstances. A second lesson is to grant judges more flexibility in awarding costs.

4 Moreover, international arbitration is particularly instructive because of the many experiences thus for attained on how to reasonably settle transnational disputes. One lesson to be derived from the settlement of transnational disputes under international arbitration is that differences between domestic and 'foreign' law should not be overemphasized. Another, more specific lesson is that we should discard the dogmatic doctrine that transnational communication of judicial documents infringes upon the 'judicial sovereignty' of any state.

REPORT OF THE DISCUSSION

Chairman: *Z. Stalev (Bulgaria)*
Vice-chairman: *Z. Asikin Kusumah Atmadja (Indonesia)*
Secretary: *J.A. Freedberg-Swartzburg (the Netherlands)*

The discussionpoints are to be found at page 183.

Working Group 2, chaired by Prof. Stalev, Bulgaria, and Judge Asikin, Supreme Court Judge, Indonesia, as vice-chairman, on the subject of the 'Improvement of Civil Litigation by Lessons Derived from Arbitration', was first addressed by the General Rapporteur, Prof. Walther J. Habscheid, who, in turn introduced as spokesman for the Report, his co-rapporteur, Prof. Peter Schlosser.

Prof. Schlosser touched upon a number of the main points dealt with in the General Report, and the ensuing discussion referred to the Report, to the suggested discussion points, and to additional discussion points raised by participants.

Prof. Schlosser began his summary by referring to a 1973 decision of the British Law Lords, a decision which adjudicated in a foreign currency. This practice already had been successfully adopted by arbitration. Lord Justice Michael Kerr was quoted as stating that the decision was 'an interesting illustration of commercial arbitrators adopting a progressive and realistic practice in advance of the courts'. The decision indicated that arbitration, and in particular arbitrators, can and should provide the English judge with a vision of the advantages of continental civil law inquisitorial procedure, especially in long and complex cases.

The initial phase of the arbitral proceedings first entails the identification of the decision-making body - the constitution of the arbitral tribunal by the appointment of the arbitrators. Can this practice be transmitted to litigation? In general, the national reporters rejected the idea. However, mention was made of legal systems which provide for specialized tribunals composed of a member of the judiciary, assisted by lay judges. This was raised as the first discussion point which stated that 'Parties in litigation should each be given the possibility to select one of the lay assessors who will comprise the judicial tribunal, their selection being limited, however, to a list of pre-selected persons.' In the discussion of this point, attention was drawn (by Mr. Dolinar, Austria) to the tendency to rely on specialized expertise, both in lawyers and expert testimony - a tendency which goes beyond the distinction between arbitration and litigation. The suggestion was made that parties could nominate expert judges from lists of experts, who in turn would appoint a chairman. The presence of experts on the bench could help the judge to reach a more valuable decision.

Several participants gave instances in their national practice of such possibilities. The willingness shown in the USA to borrow from arbitration was illustrated (by Prof. Bundy, California, USA) by a description of the practice found in the procedural codes of most US states of appointing a 'special master', a voluntary procedure for complex cases. 'Special masters' are private persons with expertise in the relevant field who will make findings of fact. The 'rent a judge' procedure which allows parties to refer out after filing was also mentioned.

Several Scottish practices were described (by Mr. Robertson, Scotland): that of the assessor who at the request of a party can be appointed by the judge to assist him, and the possibility for the parties to request the judge to remit to a 'man of skill', for example, a surveyor, whose report will be binding barring any grave error.

The Chairman expressed his doubts regarding the usefulness of party-appointed lay assessors due to the danger of partyappointed arbitrators acting as advocates for the parties.

The initial phase of the arbitration is completed by the identification of claims and issues. The pros and cons of drawing up Terms of Reference as practiced in ICC arbitration were summarized and the Rapporteurs' conclusion that Terms of Reference or a pre-hearing conference, where issues in dispute are identified, would be useful mechanisms in litigation, drew no further special comment as a discussion point, at this time.

The issues having been identified, the highly charged question of the desirability of pre-trial discovery may arise, a question subject to virtually diametrically opposed points of view. This practice is widely used in common law countries, but civil law countries generally do not allow party-directed pretrial discovery. However, discovery in the context of arbitration does not in practice give rise to excesses and could give guidance for litigation in both common law and civil law litigation. With arbitration as a model, pre-trial discovery in common law countries could be substantially reduced to what is reasonable, and reasonable pre-trial discovery could be introduced to civil law models of civil procedure. These last statements, which formed a discussion point, were contested (by Mr. Dolinar) in the discussion where discovery was characterized as time consuming and undesirable for introduction into the continental legal system.

The discussion on evidence focused on the unique practice of the Iran-US Claims Tribunal in The Hague (as elaborated by Dr. Briner, third country arbitrator at the Tribunal) in regard to the testimony of high ranking officials of companies which are parties to the claim. At the Tribunal, most of the procedure is written and evidence may be submitted in the form of affidavits. Both sides in Tribunal cases now submit affidavits from high officials and these officials appear as witnesses. The Tribunal makes the final assessment of the weight of the evidence. Such practices are also allowed under the law of most Swiss cantons where the question of whether such officials are a 'party' or a 'witness' is determined by the procedural law in question.

On the subject of remedies, the General Report spoke favorably of allowing parties to give the court the power to grant remedies it would not otherwise grant, such as decisions *ex aequo et bono,* filling of contractual gaps and adapting of contracts. An opposite view was brought forward (by the Chairman in his concluding remarks) that the power to fill gaps in a contract or adapt a contract to drastically changed circumstances is rarely used in arbitration because parties fear the consequences, and this is even more so in the court of the defendant.

In regard to flexibility with respect to costs, arbitrators successfully use the discretion allowed to them in equitably awarding costs, a discussion point which engendered no further discussion.

Another discussion point which did not elicit extensive comment was the unsatisfactory situation which currently prevails for the transnational service of documents initiating or further developing legal proceedings. A lesson could well be derived from 'arbitration practice which demonstrates that in civil litigation nobody needs to be protected from the service of documents'. The Chairman recommended that service could be effected by registered mail against receipt.

The subject of awards on agreed terms was raised from the floor in the context of general remarks (by Prof. Sanders, The Netherlands). This possibility has been opened in the new Arbitration Act in the Netherlands which has also adopted a number of litigation practices for arbitration, i.e., the power to order a personal appearance of the parties to encourage a settlement, joinder of a party in proceedings and consolidation of arbitrations. The possibility to record settlements in the form of an award is one of the characteristics of an 'advanced' arbitration, a distinction which can be used to describe arbitration in some countries but, unfortunately, not yet in all countries where arbitration is practised.

In the USA (according to Prof. Bundy) 'consent judgments' have the effect of a court judgment. This is not the case in the Federal Republic of Germany (according to Prof. Schlosser). In the German Democratic Republic (as explained by Dr. Strohbach, GDR), an award on agreed terms can take two forms: (1) a settlement in the form of an award on agreed terms, which fulfills the requirements of the New York Convention, and (2) a settlement which is registered in the protocol of the hearing, which fulfills the terms of the 1972 Moscow Convention - neither form being possible in litigation.

A further intervention (by Dr. Briner) introduced the subject of dissenting and concurring opinions and their use in the Iran-US Claims Tribunal, and the similar practice in Zurich and in the Swiss Federal Supreme Court, where the judges deliberate in public, concluding that such practices can contribute to the development of law.

An additional discussion point (as described by Prof. Stalev) was the possibility to render documents-only awards, a practice which is encouraged in arbitrations at the Court of Arbitration in Sofia. This practice helps to eliminate unnecessary hearings and could also be transferred to litigation.

A number of observations arising from the specific discussion points and in the context of more general remarks may be mentioned briefly. The consensual nature of arbitration was observed (by Prof. Bundy) to be a guarantee that the procedure is just.

Several national reporters who had been rather pessimistic if such lessons existed were pleasantly surprised by the results of the discussions (Prof. Strohbach and Prof. Takakuwa, Japan).

The relationship between arbitration and litigation was described (by Prof. Carpi, Italy) as a 'love-hate-relationship'. To be effective, arbitration requires the cooperation of the parties, without which court intervention and assistance becomes necessary. Without cooperation of the parties or the support of judicial recourses, problems which arise, for example, in regard to multi-party arbitration or related procedures could become insoluble. Arbitration must remain flexible, limited by the principles of due process.

The question was raised (by Prof. Taniguchi, Japan) 'What cannot be borrowed?' That is to say, what cannot be adopted from arbitration into litigation because it would change the character of litigation. The answer was proposed (by Prof. Stalev) that, *inter alia*, party arbitration, when it entails an arbitrator acting for a party must not be transplanted, nor should the filling of contractual gaps or the adaption of contracts.

In his concluding remarks, General Rapporteur Prof. Schlosser recalled that arbitration is an individually framed procedure, whereas courts must provide uniformity of procedure, and added that the consensual nature of arbitration did not necessarily create an impediment to transplanting useful elements to litigation.

General Rapporteur Prof. Habscheid added that a dialogue has been opened whereby the courts are not seen as controlling arbitration, but learning from arbitration. Arbitration and litigation can be seen as equal routes for settling differences.

In a final observation to the Working Group (by Prof. Stalev) participants were reminded that the discussion referred to international commercial arbitration.

The Plenary Session was opened by Prof. Stalev who summarized the discussions held in the Working Group, as elaborated above. Several general conclusions could be drawn from the discussions. Litigation and arbitration are two separate forms of civil justice, having as their common goal the final and enforceable resolution of disputes. Secondly, a new approach is possible whereby the old process of arbitration borrowing from litigation can be reversed; this should occur in an atmosphere of mutual collaboration and enrichment, not isolation. Experience in international dispute resolution can be used to improve national legislation and practice. The solutions which are transferable are those which represent their functional similarity, i.e., the procedural devices used by arbitrators in order to resolve the dispute. Prof. Stalev concluded that, in looking to arbitration, this Conference has opened a new page in comparative civil procedure.

In the ensuing discussion from the floor, the possibility for parties to fill contractual gaps and adapt contracts if the parties have so agreed as provided in Art. 1020 of the new Arbitration Act of The Netherlands was supported as being both necessary in practice especially in the construction industry, and justified by general contract law (Mr. J. Rozemond, The Netherlands).

The Spanish arbitration legislation which provides for two forms of arbitration - arbitration according to law, which entails the use of lawyers, and *amiable composition* which does not - was described (by Mr. Miguel y Alonso, Spain) as not having achieved its aim of providing an alternative to legislation.

Although parties seem to prefer arbitration according to law, the shortage of experienced lawyers who are willing to accept being involved in arbitration proceedings leads to the same shortcomings as the judicial system. A possible means to make arbitration a more attractive alternative would be to set a time limit for the procedure, e.g., ninety days.

Mr. J. Alvaro Diaz elaborated on arbitration in Portugal and Brazil where the practice of arbitration is not presently of great importance. He predicted that in both countries, arbitration is about to become a burning issue and is currently receiving attention from the Ministry of Justice.

The discussion from the floor was concluded (by Prof. Sanders) with comments regarding the filling of gaps. The new Netherlands Civil Code will allow judges to fill gaps and adapt contracts, but the possibility for arbitrators to do so was expressly included in the Arbitration Act to remove any doubts. On the other hand, the practice of drawing up Terms of Reference was not to be recommended for use in litigation as it often created enormous delays. The practice of party arbitration, while acceptable and even desirable in international arbitration, should be avoided in domestic arbitration where list procedures are more suitable. In general, arbitration offered the advantage of ease of enforcement, thanks mainly to the New York Convention of 1958, adhered to by over seventy states, equality of the parties and the benefits of the recent good work of UNCITRAL which has a harmonizing effect.

Prof. Schlosser, speaking on behalf of both General Rapporteurs, concluded that arbitration may be seen as forming a bridge between civil law and common law concepts. These systems are separated by different approaches, which may be characterized as flexible or rigid, regarding details such as foreign currency judgments or judgments on agreed terms. An understanding of the origin or cause of these differences makes it possible to determine what can be borrowed from another system for the purposes of arbitration.

IMPROVING THE PROCEDURES FOR THE ENFORCEMENT AND RECOGNITION OF FOREIGN JUDGMENTS AND ARBITRAL AWARDS

IMPROVING THE PROCEDURES FOR THE ENFORCEMENT AND RECOGNITION OF FOREIGN JUDGMENTS AND ARBITRAL AWARDS

J.C. Barbosa Moreira
Professor at the University of the State of Rio de Janeiro (Brazil)

PRELIMINARY NOTE

This general report is based essentially on the information and opinions contained in national reports from twenty-five countries[1], not to mention Brazilian law, that the general rapporteur also took into consideration. It does not cover the systems of the member States of European Communities as they are the object of another general report submitted by Professor Konstantinos Kerameus, of Athens.

Invaluable was the contribution of the national rapporteurs, to whom the general rapporteur expresses his deepest gratitude, at the same time that the regrets that for obvious reasons it was not possible for him to include in this general report all the valuable data and critical considerations offered by them. Occasionally, the general rapporteur made use of elements gathered from doctrinal works and texts of laws and of international treaties and conventions. The general rapporteur assumes full responsibility and offers his excuses for possible inaccuracies of fact and eventually wrong interpretations of a national report or other text.

The proposed theme was 'Improving the procedures for the enforcement and recognition of foreign judgments and arbitral awards'. Such a formulation did not suggest to the general rapporteur an analysis in depth of the many questions of predominantly theoretical interest usually raised about extraterritorial extension of the efficacy of judgments and arbitral awards; they are,

---

1 In alphabetic order, with the respective national rapporteurs: Argentina (Gualberto Lucas Sosa), Austria (Franz Matscher), Bolivia (Gabriel Pelaez Gantier), Bulgaria (Theodor Tschipev), Cape Verde (Antonio Manuel Mascarenhas Gomes Monteiro), Colombia (Hernando Morales Molina), Costa Rica (Olman Arguedas Salazar), Czechoslovakia (Zd. Kucera), El Salvador (Francisco Arrieta Gallegos), German Democratic Republic (Rainer Kosewähr), Guatemala (Mario Aguirre Godoy), Hungary (Jozsef Farkas and Laszlo Kecskés), Israel (Celia Wasserstein Fassberg), Japan (Akio Takakuwa and Kaoru Matsuura), Mexico (Jorge Antonio Zepeda), Paraguay (Hugo Allen), Peru (Carlos Parodi Remon), Poland (Jerzy Jodlowski) Rumania (Savelly Zilberstein and Ion Bacanu), Switzerland (Hans Ulrich Walder), Turkey (Ergun Özsunay), United States (Freidrich K. Juenger, who also kindly supplied a copy of his general report on the theme The Recognition of Money Judgments in Civil and Commercial Matters, prepared for the XII Congress of the International Academy of Comparative Law, Australia, 1986), Uruguay (Enrique Vescovi, Bernadette Minvielle and Eduardo Tellechea Bergman), Venezuela (Aristides Rengel Romberg), Yugoslavia (Milan Pak).
Quotations in footnotes, not containing any specific indication, refer to these national reports.

therefore, only incidentally referred to. The general rapporteur was preferably concerned with the examination of the most important difficulties met by extraterritorial extension of efficacy and the possible means of mitigating or eliminating them. Hence the division of the central nucleus of the report into two parts entitled The 'restrictive mechanisms' of international extension of the effects of judgments (2) and Possibilities of abolishing or mitigating the 'restrictive mechanisms' (3). They are preceded by an introduction, consisting of A bird's view of the present situation (1). It was thought advisable that the set of problems relating to foreign arbitral awards should be treated separately (4). A special chapter was also dedicated to the role played in the context by international treaties and conventions (5). The paper was completed with the formulation of some general conclusions (6).

Since exhaustion is obviously out of the question both in the listing of the topics and in the handling of questions connected with each of them, the general rapporteur made a selection as a result of which he may understandably have overlooked or even completely neglected aspects which should be emphasized in the opinion of others. The general rapporteur is, furthermore, fully conscious that he was unable to give more than a cursory glance at very important questions in his own opinion. He is comforted by the thought that the main function of works of this kind is less that of offering a complete elaboration of a theme than that of suggesting points for a frank and open discussion - the supreme goal of a law congress.

1 A BIRD'S VIEW OF THE PRESENT SITUATION

1.1 THE TREND TOWARD FACILITATING INTERNATIONAL EXTENSION OF THE EFFECTS OF JUDGMENTS

Despite certain resistances there seems to be a generalized idea that it is desirable to permit the effects of judgments to be carried beyond the territorial limits of the States where they are rendered. In modern times, several obvious factors have been contributing to enhance such a trend: intensification of relationship among industrial, business and service companies located in different States; the movements of people from one country to another on a permanent basis (migration) or temporarily (international tourism, business, cultural voyages, etc); the more and more frequent cases of a person (individual or company) having property and interests within the territory of different States, and so forth. Take, for instance, the problem arising when someone does not succeed in having the annulment or dissolution of his marriage, as decreed in his country of origin, confirmed in the country where he decided to live; or when a creditor, having obtained judgment against the debtor, fails to receive his dues because satisfaction of the debt would imply disposal of property located in another State the Courts of which refuse to cooperate.

The drawbacks of an 'impervious' attitude against foreign judgments strike the eye. Such drawbacks are not merely personal in nature. Again examining one of the instances referred to above, the impossibility of a new marriage has socially harmful effects to the extent that it may, on the one hand, create or aggravate conditions of affective insatisfaction capable of originating anomalous behaviour or, on the other, encourage illegal unions with perhaps undesirable consequences from the point of view of the community. If the unpaid creditor, in turn, is forced to sue again before the Courts of a State for the same redress he had already obtained in another State, he will also contribute to increase the volume of work of the legal body that would, otherwise, be free from such a burden if it could take advantage of a work already done elsewhere. The systematic imperviousness of a country to judgments rendered in other countries endangers juridical certainty and in some cases causes a logically absurd breach in the necessary uniformity in dealing with the same juridical situation. It constitutes ultimately a source of serious injustices.

1.2 DIFFICULTIES AND PROSPECTS

Nevertheless, the prevailing inclination in favour of international expansion of the efficacy of judgments is not free from backcurrents. Historically, opposition to it has often been inspired by a kind of overemphasis upon the idea of sovereignty. Another cause, correlated in fact, may consist of a particularly vigorous intention to protect the natives, which would explain rejection of foreign judgments when unfavorable to any of them; here, the reaction mechanism sometimes uses indirect means, as when national jurisdiction is admitted on an exclusive basis in respect of any action brought against a citizen of the country, at the same time that the possibility is ruled out of recognizing efficacy to the judgment rendered by a foreign Court not having jurisdiction to decide upon the case.

Of course, ideas of this kind flourish more strongly in the case of States the legal systems of which are considerably apart from one another. They usually also reflect a feeling of distrust nurtured by an either true or illusory perception of great qualitative differences in the operation of the Courts of several countries. It's understandable, then, that resistances are much more easily broken in relations among countries of reasonably homogeneous development, culture, traditions and customs, at least from a legal standpoint. It's also understandable that more advanced solutions are sometimes being reached through bilateral or multilateral treaties rather than through changes in the internal legal system. It should be added that, in some cases, the discipline in treaties is absorbing most of the normative functions and assigning only a secondary, if not clearly unimportant, role to the domestic laws of signatory countries. This is what happens, as everyone knows, in European communities. For the time being, however, such a phenomenon is far from reaching universal dimensions: a good part of the world remains alien, or almost so, to such an evolution.

At any rate, it can hardly be denied that, under different shapes and despite occasional setbacks, legal systems in general are moving toward a greater receptivity to foreign judgments. Recent legislative reforms point in that direction[2].

---

2 E.g., Bulgaria, 1983: Tschipev, p. 1; Turkey, 1982: Öszunay, p. 2.

2 THE 'RESTRICTIVE MECHANISMS' OF INTERNATIONAL EXTENSION OF THE EFFECTS OF JUDGMENTS

2.1 THE EXISTENCE OF 'RESTRICTIVE MECHANISMS'

What has been said before does not carry the intention to deny the widespread and, in certain cases, immense practical importance of a series of 'restrictive mechanisms' of international extension of the effects of judgments. It should be noted that no legal system can, to a greater or lesser extent, do without such mechanisms: as a target 'the total and absolute free circulation' of judgments on an international level seems unattainable, at least over a short or medium term.

There are several kinds of 'restrictive mechanisms'. Without intending to offer a rigid and exhaustive classification, it's possible to point out a few more important classes. Needless to stress that the several kinds may appear in combined forms, and they, in fact, frequently do so, within the same legal system.

2.2 PRE-EXCLUSION OF THE POSSIBILITY OF TAKING THE FOREIGN JUDGMENT INTO ACCOUNT

The first idea that comes to mind is the existence of basic prerequisites the lack of which definitely eliminates for national Courts the very possibility of taking the foreign judgment into consideration. For instance: (a) the need for a treaty or convention in force, of which the rendition State and the State where the decision is to be recognized or enforced are signatories. This requirement can be softened and made to refer only to the enforcement of the judgment (and not to other possible effects): this is what occurs, for example, in the Soviet Union, according to article 63 of the Principles of Civil Procedure[3].

Another prerequisite, partly associated with the preceding one, is (b) reciprocity: judgments can only be allowed to produce effects in the territory of a State if originating from foreign States adopting an identical position in relation to that State[4]. Reciprocity can be *legislative*, when foreseen in law;

3 Cf. Lunz, Internationaler Zivilprozess, transl. Maskow, Berlin, 1968, p. 98.

4 For example: Austria (Exekutionsordnung, par. 79; cf. Matscher, p. 1); Bolivia (Código de Procedimiento Civil, arts. 553 and 554); Colombia (Código de Procedimiento Civil, art. 693); German Democratic Republic (Zivilprozessordnung, § 193, 1; cf. Kosewähr, p. 10/11); Guatemala (Código Procesal Civil y Mercantil, art. 344;; cf. Aguirre Godoy, p. 2); Japan (Code of Civil Procedure, art. 200, 4, and Civil Enforcement Act, art. 24, 3; cf. Takakuwa and Matsuura, p. 17); Mexico (Código de Procedimientos Civiles para el Distrito Federal, art. 604); Peru (Código Civil, arts. 2102, 2103 and 2104, No. 8; cf. Parodi Remon, p. 2); Poland (Code of Civil Procedure, art. 1146 par. 1; par. 3 excepts the cases within the exclusive jurisdiction of the State of origin, according to the Polish law; cf. Jodlowski, p. 11, 13); Rumania (Zilberstein and Bacanu, p. 5, 15/16); Turkey (Act on Private International Law and Procedural Law, art. 38, a; cf. Özsunay, p. 5, 7, 10); Uruguay (Código de Procedimiento Civil, arts. 512 and 513); Venezuela (Código de Procedimiento Civil, art. 850; cf. Rengel Romberg, p. 4); In Argentina, the requisite subsists in some provincial codes, but not in the national code (Sosa, p. 11/12). It also subsists in few American States, but is rejected by the Uniform Foreign Money-

diplomatic, when resulting from a treaty; and *de facto*, when founded on constant practice merely. The production of effects is sometimes (c) excluded *a priori* as to judgments rendered in certain kinds of actions; or, on the contrary, the possibility of such production is limited to certain classes. Furthermore (d), a clause is universally found permitting a State to refuse efficacy within its territory to judgments which, although bearing the required characteristics, conflict with fundamental principles of the system: mention is usually made of 'public policy' (*'ordre public'*), with or without the addition of other expressions ('good customs', 'national sovereignty')[5].

A certain relationship with the above topic is to be found in the kind of 'restrictive mechanisms' inspired by what could be called the principle of the 'preference for national jurisdiction'. What we have in mind here is not only the very obvious consideration that no judgment can be allowed to produce effects in the territory of another State where a final court decision already exists about the same action. In such cases, the *bis in idem* prohibition is the basic rule that prevails, preventing even the judges of the rendition State from hearing the case again, although a peculiarity can be observed in the fact that the *res judicata* of the 'importing' State is made to prevail regardless of its chronological priority, so that extension of the effects is prevented even when the foreign judgment precedes the national judgment. A step further, however, is occasionally taken: the mere circumstance that a pending suit exists in the national territory about the same subject-matter decided upon by the foreign judgment is held sufficient to bar the possibility of extension of effects[6].

Judgments Recognition Act (Juenger, p. 4, 6, 18).

5 E.g.: Argentina, Código Procesal Civil y Comercial de la Nación, art. 517, 4th (cf. Soza, p. 4, 15/17); Brazil, Lei de Introduçao ao Código Civil (Decree-law No. 4.657, of 9.4.1942, art. 17); Bulgaria (Tschipev, p. 6); Colombia, Código de Proced. Civ., art. 694, No. 2 (cf. Morales Molina, p. 2); Costa Rica, Código de Procedimientos Civiles, art. 1022, 4th (cf. Arguedas Salazar, p. 3); Czechoslovakia, Act on Private International Law and International Procedure, of 1963, art. 64, d, 67, and 68 (cf. Kucera, p. 3, 6); German Democratic Republic, ZPO, § 193, (2), 5 cf. Kosewähr, p. 11/12; Hungary, Private International Law Code, § 73, a, (cf. Farkas-Kecskés, p. 4, 12); Israel, Law No. 5718, of 1958, sections 3 (3) and 7 (cf. Fassberg, p. 8 and notes 53 and 54); Japan, Private International Law Code, art. 30 (cf. Takakuwa and Matsuura, p. 15/17); Peru, Código Civil, art. 2013, No. 7; Turkey, Act on Priv. Int. Law, art. 38, d (cf. Özsunay, p. 6, 7); United States (Juenger, p. 7; cf. Uniform Foreign Money-Judgments Recognition Act, section 4 (b) (3); Venezuela, Cod. de Proced. Civ., art. 851, 6th (cf. Rengel Romberg, p. 5). Also in Paraguay, by an analogical application of art. 14 of the Civil Code, efficacy is denied to the foreign judgment when contrary 'al derecho público del Estado, a la tolerancia de cultos, o a la moral y buenas costumbres' (Allen, p. 1). In Mexico, likewise, arts. 80 and 1830 of the Civil Code for the Federal District in common matters and for the whole Republic in federal matters are invoked (Zepeda, p. 20).

6 For example: Bulgaria (Tschipev. p. 4); Colombia (Código de Proced. Civ., art. 694, No. 5); Hungary (Priv. Int. Law Code, par. 73, e; cf. Farkas Kecskés, p. 5); Israel (Law No. 5718, of 1958, section 6 (5); the restriction is not applicable to the cases regulated by the common law: v. Fassberg, p. 7); Peru (Código Civil, art. 2104, No. 5). In the latter two countries it's necessary, for exclusion, that the national proceeding shall have been started before the foreign proceeding.

2.3 ESTABLISHMENT OF REQUIREMENTS TO BE MET BY THE PROCEEDING STARTED IN THE FOREIGN COUNTRY AND BY THE JUDGMENT RENDERED THEREUNDER

Another kind of 'restrictive mechanisms' refers to the requisites to be met by the proceeding started in a foreign country and by the judgment rendered thereunder. The intention here is mainly to deny the cooperation of the national Courts to the enforcement of decisions not offering, according to the conception prevailing in the State, the minimum necessary assurance that the rules essential to the seriousness of the judgement were complied with. Furthermore, it may be demanded that the foreign judgment be apt to produce effects in the country of origin, or have attained a certain degree of stability, meaning that it's not (or is less) subject to reversal or annulment. Finally, it may be a mere question of being sure about the authenticity of the act and its respective contents; for instance: a consular attestation and a certified translation of the judgment may be required.

This last class of prerequisites, relatively simple, usually offers no great difficulties, although they may eventually contribute to delay attainment of the envisaged goal and increase its costs. As for the rest, it's easy to detect a certain similarity among the relevant legal dispositions of the several countries. The basic points, common to almost all laws, refer (a) to the jurisdiction power of the Court that rendered the judgment, (b) to the participation of the party defeated in the foreign proceeding, (c) to the situation reached by the judgment in the country of origin. Such points deserve a brief explanation.

(a) The jurisdiction power requirement admits of different disciplines in more than one sense. First, different criteria can be adopted to check the jurisdiction power of the foreign Court involved: in the absence of a supranational criterion in the light of which the jurisdictional areas of each State would be delimited, the question can conceivably be settled by applying the law of the country of origin[7] or the country to the territory of which efficacy of the judgment is to be carried[8]. Both the latter and the former approaches can turn into a 'restrictive mechanism'. In what case this is to occur is something that depends on how the latter is regulated in the former and in the latter systems: if the system of the rendition State is more rigorous, its application will exclude extension of efficacy in cases where said extension would be possible according to the system of the 'importing' State, and vice versa. On the other hand, if the law of the rendition State is held applicable, it should be asked if the requirement is to be considered satisfied provided its jurisdiction power on an international level is recognized (*general* jurisdiction) or if, additionally, the judgment is required to have been rendered by a qualified Court of that State (*special* jurisdiction).

It should be seen finally how far the effects of the will of the parties are to be taken into account in the evaluation of jurisdiction. They may, by common

---

7 This is, in principle, the prevailing understanding in Brazil in view of the silence of the texts in force: v., for all, Haroldo Valladao, Direito International Privado, vol. III, Rio de Janeiro, 1978, p. 199; Federal Supreme Court, S.E. No. 2227, 4.23.1975.

8 For example: Argentina (Código nacional, art. 517, 1st.; cf. Sosa p. 2, 5); Japan (Takakuwa and Matsuura, p. 12/13).

agreement, have chosen a certain Court to decide upon the disputes arising from a contract; or, in the absence of such a covenant, the defeated party may pure and simply have submitted itself to the Courts of the rendition State, recognizing its jurisdiction power. Law systems vary in evaluating such facts, now admitting now denying that the behaviour of the parties lends jurisdictional power to the foreign Court that would otherwise lack such a power. To deny to a greater or smaller extent such an effect is an attitude that operates as a 'restrictive mechanism' in cases where no basis exists for establishing the power of the foreign Court other than the (express or implied) will of the parties. In most cases, in this context, one fears and tries to avoid the occurrence of fraud against the national law; and denial of efficacy in general finds its formal expression in the assertion of the incompatibility of the foreign judgment with the public policy of the State where said judgment is to produce its effects.

(b) Modern procedural systems, in general, contain rules intended to assure the parties the possibility of enforcing their reasons in court; the level of satisfactory guarantees may, however, vary from country to country. That explains the care in demanding certain requirements in the foreign proceeding which originated the judgment. As a rule, one is basically concerned with the certainty that the defeated party was given clear notice of the proceeding and a reasonable (even if eventually lost) opportunity of defense. The question naturally becomes particularly critical when the party is judged in default[9]. Although it's understood, in principle, that the manner of notifying the defendant is governed by the law of the State where the proceeding is started, some forms, unknown to national law, are sometimes held unacceptable, specially when considered less fit to assure the possibility of defense in an apt manner. Such a position is occasionally adopted in case law, even if not supported by a written legal text[10]. It may occur, on the other hand, that the law makes a distinction, being stricter in the case where the foreign judgment is rendered against a national of, or a person domiciled in, the 'importing' State[11].

(c) As far as it concerns the situation reached by the judgment in the rendition State, two distinct, although generally interrelated aspects, should be mentioned. A certain number of systems requires the foreign judgment to be final; others refer to the circumstance that it must be enforceable[12]. Requirements not always coincide in practice: it's well-known that in several cases judgments can be enforced even before they become final, whereas circumstan-

---

9 A radical attitude here is to pre-exclude the possibility of extending the efficacy of any judgment rendered in a proceeding where the defendant was in default: to this effect art. 452, 2nd., of the Código de Procedimientos Civiles of El Salvador, and art. 345, 2nd, 1st part, of the Cod. Proc. Civ. y Merc. of Guatemala.

10 Thus, e.g., in Uruguay (Vescovi-Minvielle-Tellechea, p. 8).

11 In Bulgaria, for instance, service of summons by publication is not considered sufficient if the defendant is a Bulgarian; the difference in treatment raises a problem the solution of which may be found, according to the national rapporteur, in the resort to the 'public policy' clause in favour of the foreign party (Tschipev, p. 3/4). A similar situation exists in Japan (Takakuwa and Matsuura, p. 14).

12 Thus, e.g. the Austrian law: Exekutionsordnung, par. 80, 3 (cf. Matscher, p. 6).

ces exist under which, though final, judgment enforcement cannot be started because it's subject to a term or condition.

The problem becomes complicated in view of the ambiguous notion of *res judicata*, that in some procedural systems presupposes the exhaustion of all appeals and in others of only a few of them. Consequently, in certain cases, the requirement will assume a variable meaning, depending on the adoption of the criterion of the rendition State (according to the prevailing tendency) or that of the national system. Of course, if the 'importing' State is satisfied with a relative degree of stability, it affords the possibility that a judgment eventually subject to reversal or annulment may produce effects in its territory. This is liable to offer practical hindrances; on the other hand, an absolutely rigid position in this respect is capable of preventing prompt attention to situations which, by their own nature, are not compatible with the generally long time required for attainment of absolute stability.

A further source of complications is the distinction, recognized in many legal systems, between a *material* and a *formal res judicata*: as it's well-known, the latter refers only to the stability of the judgment within the proceeding in which it is rendered owing to the exhaustion of appeals, whereas the former means the impossibility of arguing again in a new action the subject-matter of the judgment. A large legal tradition recognizes the existence of judgments which produce only a formal and not a *material res judicata*: thus, for instance, those granting provisional remedies. If taken to refer to a *material res judicata*, the pre-requisite we are discussing would completely deny, in the States where adopted, the possibility of producing effects within the national territory to judgments ordering the seizure of a debtor's property to assure the practical efficacy of a future enforcement against him, or to judgments regulating on a provisional basis the custody of a minor claimed by both parents. Partly analogous to this is the problem of judgments that part of the doctrine - with an expression of doubtful technical appropriateness - holds subject to the *rebus sic stantibus* clause; for instance: a judgment ordering the payment of alimony.

2.4 THE DISCIPLINE OF THE MANNER IN WHICH THE INTERESTED PARTY CAN RESORT TO THE FOREIGN JUDGMENT

Examination should now be made of the 'restrictive mechanisms' referring to the manner in which the interested party is permitted to resort to the foreign judgment in the country where it must produce effects. In principle, two basic possibilities can be thought of: (a) the interested party pure and simply presents the foreign judgment to the Court and the later - verifying the concurrence of requirements - gives the judgment the desired effect; (b) the interested party must obtain from the State a formal act and has to apply for it to the appropriate Court, causing the formation of a proceeding, however simple it may be, at the end of which the claim is accepted or rejected.

Solution (b) can be seen from more than one angle. From a theoretical standpoint, the proceeding can be conceived as exclusively destined to the examination of the foreign judgment and, if all requirements are present, to the granting of the *exequatur* (or 'homologation') that renders it efficacious in the national territory; or else one can see in the foreign judgment a source of an obligation of the defeated party with a basis on which the winner sues him before a national Court for compliance[13]. On the other hand, still in the first case, there is a large variation in the extent of the cognitive powers conferred upon the national Court: it's either invested with power to review the litigation decided upon in the country of origin and will only grant the *'exequatur'* (or homologation) if the adopted solution is considered correct[14]; or it must limit itself to the verification of the presence of certain requirements, and, in case of an affirmative conclusion, it cannot deny the *'exequatur'* (or homologation) even if the foreign decision seems unjust in its merits[15]. It's clear that the action of the national Court will operate as a 'restrictive mechanism' the more strongly the larger the latitude granted to it in exercising its cognition power.

Principles (a) and (b) may and usually appear in a combined form. In fact, several countries adopt a mixed system in which a formal act (and the proceeding intended to produce it) is only required when the interested party desires to enforce (in the proper sense of the word) a foreign judgment in the national territory. If, instead, it's a mere instance of using it for another purpose (for example: invoke its authority as *res judicata* against the claim of the other party), the national Court itself in charge of examining the issue will incidentally inquire into the existence of the requisites and will recognize (or not) the efficacy of the foreign judgment[16].

If a formal act is necessary - for enforcement only or for recognition as well - the power to perform it may be assigned to one Court[17] or, otherwise,

---

13 As it's known, the second conception is characteristic of the common law countries, although, from a certain time on, the described system has been losing ground, mainly in England, in favour of a mechanism based on the mere registration of the foreign judgment. Comparing the traditional system, still prevailing in the United States today, with that of the exequatur adopted in civil law countries, Homburger, Recognition and Enforcement of Foreign Judgments, in American Journal of Comparative Law, vol 18, no. 2, 1970, p. 378, maintains that, despite the difference in theory, 'the two devices are obviously functionally and operationally quite similar', emphasizing, among other points, that 'both afford the judgment debtor a limited opportunity to voice objections, directed mainly to the regularity of the foreign proceedings and the foreign court's jurisdiction'. In Israeli law, the two systems coexist: v. Fassberg, p. 1/2.

14 It's the system of the 'révision au fond', prevailing in France until 1964 (when the Cour de Cassation, in the famous Arrêt Munzer, changed its course of decisions to adopt the mere 'contrôle' of the foreign judgment).

15 This is the largely prevailing trend both in the Roman-Germanic countries and in those of the socialist area as well as in other parts of the world. A few qualifications, however, will have to be made in due time (infra, 3.6 and 3.13).

16 This clear distinction between the rules governing enforcement and those dealing with the mere recognition of the foreign judgment is sanctioned, among others, by the laws of Argentina (Código Nacional, arts. 518 and 519; cf. Sosa, p. 7), Austria (Matscher, p. 8/9), El Salvador (Arrieta Gallegos, p. 3), German Democratic Republic (ZPO, §§ 193, 195, 196; cf. Kosewähr, p. 6), Hungary (Farkas-Kecskés, p. 10/11), Japan (Takakuwa and Matsuura, p. 2), Peru (Código Civil, arts. 2106 to 2108 and 2110), Turkey (Act on Priv. Int. Law, art. 42, par. 1; cf. Özsunay, p. 4); Uruguay (Vescovi-Minvielle-Tellechea, p. 14).

17 For example: Bolivia (Pelaez Gantier, p. 1); Bulgaria, starting from the 1983 reform (Tschipev, p. 4/5); Cape Verde (Gomes Monteiro, p. 3); Colombia (Morales Molina, p. 1), Costa Rica (Arguedas Salazar, p. 2); Uruguay (for condemnatory, separation and divorce judgments: Vescovi-Minvielle-Tellechea, p. 15); Venezuela (save for decisions of a non litigious nature: Rengel Romberg, p. 1). The

granted to a group of Courts[18]. Besides, a period of time may be set at the end of which the possibility of obtaining efficacy for the foreign judgment in the national territory will cease[19].

3 POSSIBILITIES OF ABOLISHING OR MITIGATING THE 'RESTRICTIVE MECHANISMS'

3.1 IMPORTANCE OF POLITICAL FACTORS

It's time now to inquire into the possibilities of abolishing or at least mitigating the 'restrictive mechanisms'. A reservation - an obvious one in fact- should be made from the outset: the attitude of States in the matter is strongly influenced by considerations of a political nature. This is a phenomenon to be seen at several levels, from that of the division of the world into ideologically 'blocks' to that of regional constellations of interests. The degree of permeability to foreign judgment may not represent more than a particular aspect of the global position assumed by the country before the world community or a sector thereof, or before another country individually considered. And, as it's well understood, it will tend to increase or decrease as such a position evolves toward a political 'openness' of 'imperviousness'. Certainly, the relationship between the two variables will not always be reduced to a rigidly deterministic mechanism; but not even so is it less necessary to rely on it in any evaluation of expectations aiming at a minimum realism.

Thus, the supreme facilitation factor will always be a political one in the proper sense of the word. Although it may be an exaggeration in this field to refer to 'laws', logic suggests and historical experience confirms that the longest steps in that direction have been taken under the pressure of necessities or conveniences closely related to the situation at hand, mainly the international one. What the jurist must do is to show the appropriate ways on the presupposition of the existence of a political will to follow them.

---

same system may be said to be followed in Brazil where jurisdiction is vested upon the Federal Supreme Court or, if no opposition is offered, upon its Chief Justice (Internal Regulation, arts. 215, 222, 223).

18 E.g.: Argentina (Sosa, p. 8), Austria (Exekutionsordnung, par. 82; cf. Matscher, p. 9), German Democratic Republic (Kosewähr, p. 9), Israel (since 1977, when section 9 of Law No. 5718, of 1958, that assigned exclusive jurisdiction to the Court of Appeals of Jerusalem, was repealed: v. Fassberg, p. 9/10); Yugoslavia (Pak, p. 2), Japan (Takakuwa and Matsuura, p. 24); Mexico (Código de Proced. en mat. civ. y com., art. 494), Peru (Código de Proced. Civ., art. 1161; cf. Parodi Remon, p. 2), Poland (Jodlowski, p. 1), Switzerland (Walder, p. 2), Rumania (Zilberstein and Bacanu, p. 10), Turkey (Özsunay, p. 8).

19 Thus, in the Soviet Union, the period of three years established in art. 63, 2nd part, of the Principles of Civil Procedure; in Israel, the period of five years foreseen in section 5 of Law No. 5718, of 1958, in fact subject to change through agreement with the rendition State, or when the court considers that there are special reasons justifying such a change (cf. Fassberg, p. 7, where it's pointed out that the hypotheses governed by common law and not by statutory law are subject to the common prescription period).

3.2 THE REQUIREMENT OF A TREATY OR CONVENTION

The accuracy of what has just been said is perfectly apparent when we consider the 'restrictive mechanisms' first mentioned in this paper (*supra* 2.2 (a). If the system of a certain country subjects the possibility of 'reception' of foreign judgments to the existence of a treaty with the country of origin, or a convention of which both are signatories, there can be only two ways to facilitate attainment of the result: either the country waives the requirement totally or in part or intensifies the signature of treaties and conventions on the matter.

An example of evolution of the first type is given by the Polish law. According to the 1932 Code, only under the terms of an international convention was it possible to enforce a foreign judgment in Poland; and the course of decisions of the Supreme Court, despite doctrinal criticism, extended the requisite to cases of mere recognition. The serious practical hindrances of such a regulation led the legislator first to permit expressly the recognition of foreign decisions in civil and family matters, even in the absence of a convention; later on, in the 1964 Code, to expand this policy to all cases of recognition. A convention, however, is still required for enforcement of the foreign judgment, save for decisions granting alimony, on the condition of reciprocity (art. 1150, par. 1 and 3)[20].

Systems which make the possibility of foreign judgments producing effects in the national territory dependent upon the existence of a treaty or convention in absolute terms are exceptions today. This does not mean that the signature of such acts loses importance as a means of neutralizing 'restrictive mechanisms': well on the contrary. It only happens that they are called upon to act at another level: no longer just to make the production of effects *possible*, but to make it *easier* as well. Their role, from this standpoint, deserves special emphasis. A separate chapter of this report (infra, 5) will be dedicated to some main aspects of the present topic.

3.3 THE REQUIREMENT OF RECIPROCITY

Let us now consider the requirement of reciprocity. Theoretically, it could be seen, from a certain point of view, as a manner of stimulating 'openness': each State would be interested in 'receiving' foreign judgments in order to avoid 'rejection' of its own judgments by other States. In practice, however, reluctance to take the first step leads the mechanism to operate the other way around, as a hindrance rather than as an incentive. A rigid position in the matter may, ultimately, impair circulation of judgments of the very States that adopt it[21].

---

20 Jodlowsky, p. 1, 5/6.

21 Cf. Grunsky, Internationales Prozessrecht (general report for the International Congress of Civil Procedural Law of Gent, 1977, in Towards a Justice with a Human Face, edited by Storme and Casman, Antwerp-Deventer, 1978, p. 89); Juenger, general report on the theme The Recognition of Money Judgments in Civil and Commercial Matters for the 12th Congress of the International Academy of Comparative Law (Australia, 1986), p. 7.

Special registration in this context should be made of the Austrian case. Paragraph 79 of the Exekutionsordnung subjects the enforceability of foreign judgments to a reciprocity stipulated under a treaty or asserted by a governmental declaration. Declarations of reciprocity, however, ceased almost entirely after the first world war. Consequently, it became practically impossible, in Austria, to enforce foreign judgments with a basis on the EO, at least in respect of property matters[22]: it's the conventional law that supplies the basis for most of such enforcement. Save for that relief valve, the risk of total 'paralysis' would assume dramatic colors.

The 'restrictive mechanisms' we are dealing with admits of mitigations of different kinds and reach. For instance:

(a) instead of subordinating efficacy of the foreign judgment, in absolute terms, to the reciprocity clause, one could simply permit efficacy to be denied when the requirement is not met, thus leaving the decision *in casu*[23] to the discretion of the appropriate body;
(b) reciprocity of fact could be accepted as sufficient, dispensing with an express provision in some text[24];
(c) the requisite could be waived in certain matters[25];
(d) it could be waived under certain circumstances[26];
(e) it could be waived for certain purposes[27];
(f) compliance with the requirement could be presumed until evidence to the contrary[28].

In truth, however, the reciprocity requirement should be completely and immediately forsaken. From the litigants' standpoint, it will certainly sound absurd that the same judgment rendered in State A can be efficacious in State B but not in State C, owing to a circumstance entirely extraneous to the nature

---

22 Matscher, p. 1/2.

23 E.g.: ZPO of the Canton of Solothurn, of 9.11.1966, par. 323, 5; Code de procédure civile of the Canton of Vaud, of 12.14.1966, art. 507, 3rd part; ZPO of the Canton of Zürich, of 6.13.1976, par. 302 (cf. Habscheid, Droit judiciaire privé suisse, 2nd ed., Geneva, 1981, p. 336).

24 Thus in Bulgaria, starting from the 1983 reform (Tschipev, p. 1), Yugoslavia (Pak, p. 3); Poland (Jodlowski, p. 13), Rumania (Zilberstein and Bacanu, p. 16); Turkey (Özsunay, p. 5-6, 11).

25 As it occurs in Austria, according to Holzhammer, Österreichisches Zwangsvollstreckungsrecht, Vienna-New York, 1974, p. 77, with decisions concerning the marital status of foreigners; in Yugoslavia, when the judgment deals with marriage or acknowledgement of paternity or maternity, if the petitioner is a Yugoslavian citizen (Pak, p. 3); in Poland, with reference to actions not related with property, that fall within the exclusive jurisdiction of the Courts of origin, according to the Polish law (Code of Civil Procedure, art. 1164, par. 3; Jodlowski, p. 13).

26 E.g.: in Israel, when requested by the Attorney-General (Law No. 5718, of 1958, No. 4, b; cf. Fassberg, note 44, p. 26, showing that there are no actual cases); in Czechoslovakia, if the foreign judgment was not rendered against a Czechoslovak citizen or legal entity (Act on Private International Law and International Procedure, of 1963, art. 64, e; cf. Kucera, p. 3, 6).

27 The Hungarian law, for instance, limits the requisite to those cases where the foreign judgment is desired to be enforced, in the proper sense of the word, leaving it aside in case of mere recognition (Private International Law Code, par. 74, 1; cf. Farkas-Kecskés, p. 9, 11).

28 Thus in Austria, according to Neumann-Lichtblau, Kommentar zur Exekutionsordnung, 4th ed., vol. 1, Vienna 1969, p. 769/70.

of the suit and to the characteristics of the proceeding and of the decision itself. The winner will no doubt take as an arbitrary punishment an eventual impossibility of enjoying his victory for a reason not imputable to him and which he can do nothing to avoid. On the other hand, the practical difficulties frequently found in evaluating the precise position of foreign systems endanger legal certainty. Neither to be found is a serious justification for the requirement from the point of view of the State where the judgment is intended to produce effects: experience shows that by preventing such effects on a non-reciprocity basis, no greater 'receptivity' has been obtained abroad by national judgments.

Partial remedies seem quite inadequate here. Justly criticized, for instance, has been the discriminatory solution of limiting the application of the reciprocity principle to the cases where the party interested in enforcing in the national territory a judgment rendered in another State is a foreigner. It should be fully recognized that the reciprocity requirement unduly refrains the progress of legal interchange; it's an attitude deserving, like few, the label of reactionary. There has been lately a growing conscience of the respective evils. It does not seem rash to identify a clear tendency toward the abandonment of the requirement[29].

3.4 DISTINCTIONS CONCERNING THE KINDS OF JUDGMENTS

Legal systems which are, in principle, refractory to the 'importation' of foreign judgments can make an exception to those rendered in certain kinds of suits; we have here a mitigation of the restrictive system. Such a case of mitigation eventually assumes special importance. There are States which, although recognizing the reciprocity principle, do not require such reciprocity to cover *all* judgments of their Courts, but only consider the attitude of the foreign State in respect of domestic judgments of the *same nature*. Now, it may occur that country A - exceptionally - admits the production of effects in its territory by foreign judgments related to the status of persons[30], including those of country B, where the reciprocity principle prevails. A will be, thus, indirectly contributing to a larger 'receptivity' to foreign judgments by B, to the extent that B, satisfied with such a partial reciprocity, admits efficacy in its territory to status judgments rendered in A.

On the other hand, it can be observed that certain legislations exclude *a priori* the possibility of 'importing' certain classes of foreign judgments, or-which amounts to the same - they limit such a possibility to certain classes of judgments. There are very obvious instances, like that of the exclusion, generally admitted even the absence of a written provision, of judgments of merely procedural contents: these raise no important problems. Other hypotheses

---

29 It's becoming obsolete, e.g., in the United States: several state systems have ruled it out, and it's not foreseen under the Uniform Foreign Money - Judgments Recognition Act, adopted by a certain number of important States (Juenger, general report, cit., p. 35). In Mexico, difficulties encountered led judicial practice to disregard the reciprocity requirement despite the provision of art. 605 of the Cod. de Proced. Civ. para el D.F. (Zepeda, p. 17/18).

30 As it seems to be the case in Sweden since some time: v. Ginsburg and Bruzelius, Civil Procedure in Sweden, The Hague, 1965, p. 387-8.

of limitation refer to the nature and the object of the claim. It may be required, for instance, that the foreign judgment shall have decided upon a 'personal action' or a 'real action on movables' (therefore excluding judgments handed down in real actions on immovables)[31].

This kind of restriction often results in the pure and simple exclusion of foreign judgments rendered in actions falling under the exclusive jurisdiction power of domestic Courts[32]: the question relates intrinsically to another 'restrictive mechanism' we examined elsewhere (see supra, 2.3 (a) and infra, 3.8). In other cases, what seems to be at stake is the 'public policy' as conceived by the 'importing' State; the reader is, therefore, referred to the relevant topic (infra, 3.6).

3.5 EQUIVALENCE BETWEEN DECISIONS OF NON-JUDICIAL BODIES AND JUDGMENTS

The investigation area should be somewhat enlarged here. As a rule, 'foreign judgment' immediately brings to the mind the notion of a decision originated from a court of justice. However, the legal system may confer upon authorities outside of the field of the Judiciary the power to perform acts exclusively reserved to judges in other countries. Hence, the alternatives: either to adopt a strictly *conceptual* criterion, limiting the possibility of production of effects in the national territory to acts similar in their characteristics to the judgments of the 'importing' State or to consider as judgments for the purposes examined hereunder acts not performed by judges but functionally equivalent to them.

Solutions, of course, may vary in the silence of texts. Brazilian course of court decisions, for instance, is firm in favour of the equivalence. The Supreme Court has homologated divorce (a) decreed by the King of Denmark of (b) by Norwegian and Danish administrative authorities or still (c) registered before the mayor of a Japanese city[33]. In Poland, the position of the Supreme Court has fluctuated as it sometimes - but not always - liberally interpreted article 1145, par. 1, of the Code of Civil Procedure (where mention is made of 'foreign courts') in order to recognize divorce decisions rendered by administrative bodies[34].

---

31 Thus, in Argentina: Código nacional, art. 517, 1st. (cf. Sosa, p. 3). More restrictive, in Mexico, art. 605, II, of the Código de Procedimientos Civiles para el Distrito Federal, according to which only foreign judgments rendered in an 'acción personal' are allowed to produce effects (cf. Zepeda, p. 4/5).

32 The Brazilian Code of Civil Procedure, e.g., prescribes in art. 89, No. 1, that the national Courts alone, 'with the exclusion of any others', are qualified to decide upon actions 'referring to real estate located in Brazil'. Consequently, no foreign judgment on the matter can be homologated due to the lack of the jurisdiction power requisite. The goal is reached through another route.

33 Respectively: (a) S.E. No. 912, 1.30.1933, and S.E. No. 1943, 8.16.1967; (b) S.E. No. 1282, 5.30.1952; S.E. No. 2703, 12.14.1979; (c) S.E. No. 1312, 5.22.1953; S.E. No. 2251, 10.15.1975, and S.E. No. 2636, 2.27.1981. An equal directive is followed by the Yugoslavian law (Pak, p. 1). Likewise in Austria the name of the act or the authority it came from is not taken into account (Matscher, p. 2).

34 Jodlowski, p. 8-10, tells how this course of decisions evolved and concludes by saying that the question is still open. This is also the way it seems to be in Israel: Fassberg, note 25, p. 22, without mentioning precedents holds it improbable that Israeli courts should adopt in this case a strict interpretation of section 1 of Law No. 5718, of 1958.

A restrictive attitude in this connection does not seem reasonable. Also here, from the standpoint of the interested parties, it cannot help sounding strange if they are denied recognition because the decision did not come from a body other than the only one legally qualified to render it in the country of origin. It does not make sense, on the other hand, that the 'importing' State should, so to say, require the rendition State to have a political organization and a distribution of power among public bodies similar to its own.

Obviously, it is possible that a proceeding before an administrative body should seem less trustworthy than a judicial proceeding from the point of view of the guarantees offered to the interested parties. If the level of such guarantees is lower than that considered necessary to deserve the cooperation of domestic Courts, then there will be a legitimate ground for denial. This, however, is a point to be examined in each case; unjustifiable is an absolute rejection *a priori*.

3.6 THE 'PUBLIC POLICY' (OR OTHER SIMILAR) CLAUSE

The restrictive mechanism arising from the 'public policy' and/or other similar clause raises a multiform set of problems. It's understandable that it should be so considering the large degree of indetermination of the legal concepts expressed by means of such formulas. It's impossible to arrive at accurate definitions in this field, and the establishment of less vague criteria itself becomes extremely difficult. Courts, as a rule, avoid any compromise with the adoption of rigid positions, probably, among other reasons, with the intent to preserve for themselves a freedom of action that will permit them to readjust themselves in the light of the highly variable peculiarities of actual cases submitted to them. An argument in favour of such an attitude is the facility it assures to eventual changes in directives, forced by contingencies of a political order, in the broadest sense of the expression. Of course, a price is to be paid for that flexibility, in terms of legal certainty; however high it may sometimes seem, there's no indication of any significant change in the prevailing situation.

The limitative clause is often resorted to in connection with well-known situations, where the foreign judgment, in examining the merits of an action, applies a rule inconsistent with some principle considered as basic under the domestic system. There are classic examples in family law, as in the cases of divorce or polygamy, in relation to States that do not adopt such institutions. In this field, as some see it, resort to the clause can mean, in practice, the opening of a gap through which the judicial body is given a certain control of the foreign judgment in its contents, attenuating the proscription of the so-called *révision au fond* in countries where, as a rule, it is not adopted[35].

But the clause is also resorted to in connection with questions extraneous to the merits. Thus, for instance, it has been understood that the legal requirement of a reasoned decision causes the impossibility of admitting, without

35 The point is mentioned by more than one national rapporteur: Matscher, p. 10; Jodlowski, p. 1; Walder, p. 3; with an intimation of doubt, Arguedas Salazar, p. 2. Things carefully considered, when a foreign judgment is not held apt to produce effects in the national territory because it violates the 'public policy', this does not necessarily mean that the foreign judge did not hand down a 'fair' decision in the light of the premises on which he based himself.

offense to the public order, the validity in the national territory of a foreign judgment not containing an express indication of the reasons on which conclusion was based[36]. At other times, the clause is, so to say, called upon to reinforce some reason for rejection of the foreign judgment related with another legal requirement, as for example, the regular service of summons upon the defendant in the foreign proceeding[37].

The very heterogeneity of the aspects of the set of problems surrounding 'public policy' is a great hindrance to the formulation of an opinion about the possibilities of attenuating the restrictive mechanism. In certain cases the evolution of legal systems toward a greater uniformity is gradually undermining or eliminating situations traditionally in favour of resort to the clause. An example of this is the progressive weakening of resistances against the institution of divorce; as legislations assimilate it, in what seems to be an irreversible evolution, one of the classic hypotheses of rejection of foreign judgments with a basis on the preservation of the 'public policy' disappears or, at least, loses much of its importance.

As for the rest, it seems extremely improbable that any State would abandon that relief valve in absolute terms. And it can be safely forecast that it will go on being used in the way of *ultima ratio*, in the most different fields, in cases for which the feeling of aversion to foreign judgments, however explained, finds no adequate shelter in any of the specifically foreseen restrictive mechanism.

At all events, from a practical standpoint, the reach of the obstacle should not be overestimated. It's worthwhile noting that none of the national rapporteurs spoke of great difficulties related with the resort to the clause under discussion here; and several of them, on the contrary, expressly emphasized the moderation with which Courts usually apply it[38].

3.7 THE QUESTION OF 'PREFERENCE FOR THE DOMESTIC JURISDICTION'

Let's now turn our eyes to the phenomenon we call 'preference for the domestic jurisdiction'. Strictly speaking, the name is not quite fit to the case where no effects are permitted to be produced in the territory of a State by a

---

36 In Rumanian law, such a directive only prevails with all its strictness when the requisite is foreseen in the systems of the States of origin (Zilberstein and Bacanu, p. 17). But elsewhere a further step has been taken: in Brazil, the Federal Supreme Court, in more than one decision (e.g.: 9.3.1986, S.E. No. 3262), adopted the thesis that the lack of reasons is, in the light of the Brazilian system, a sufficient obstacle, despite the regulation of the matter in the country of origin.

37 Vide the decision of the Federal Supreme Court of Brazil, of 2.2.1983, in S.E. No. 2912, where the public policy clause was called upon to deny homologation to a judgment rendered in Belgium, in a suit where the defendant, known to be domiciled in Brazil, had not been notified by means of a letter rogatory according to the Brazilian law.

38 As in Austria, Matscher, p. 9/10; in Bulgaria, Tschipev, p. 6; in the United States, Juenger, p. 19; in Poland, Jodlowski, p. 20; in Switzerland, Walder, p. 2. In the German Democratic Republic and in Israel no cases are reported denying recognition or enforcement of foreign judgments for offense to the public policy (Kosewähr, p. 12; Fassberg, note 53, p. 27). Less optimistic in Brazil the appreciation of Jacob Dolinger, Brazilian Confirmation of Foreign Judgments, in The International Lawyer, vol. 19, No. 3, p. 876.

judgment rendered in another State in a suit already finally decided upon in the former. The phenomenon has nothing specifically connected with the international circulation of court decisions. It's a universally accepted principle that the same case should not be tried more than once. Thus, in the case under consideration it's not its condition as *foreign* that governs the destiny of the latter judgment; neither would it be acceptable that some *domestic* body could again judge the claim.

Such considerations, however, do not prevail when there's only a proceeding under way about the same action before the domestic Courts. Such a circumstance should not be held sufficient to preexclude the possibility of 'importing' the foreign judgment[39]. It can by no means be understood that the national sovereignty is at stake here, or that the 'importation' is against the prestige or dignity of the Courts of the 'importing' country. The question becomes particularly serious if the impediment subsists even when the domestic proceeding is subsequent to the foreign proceeding. The party defeated in State A will be tempted to start, in State B, a second proceeding referring to the claim, with the sole intent to prevent the effects of A's judgment from being produced in B, as would be necessary to satisfy the winner. No legal system should favour a tactic of this kind.

3.8 THE PROBLEM OF THE JURISDICTION POWER OF THE FOREIGN COURT

Several questions are raised by the requirement of the jurisdiction power of the foreign court to render a judgment the efficacy of which is to be carried into the national territory.

3.8.1 As said before, the basic inquiry deals with the choice of the system in the light of which it will be decided whether or not the Court that rendered the judgment had the jurisdictional power to do so. This inquiry could be easily answered if there were a supranational discipline regarding division of jurisdiction or, at least, if the several States would adopt uniform rules about the matter. This is not what happens. Treaties can, no doubt, establish a regulation binding upon all signatory countries in their mutual relationship; otherwise, the question is subject to the sometimes very large diversity of national legislation.

From a strictly logical point of view, it's possible to support with good reasons the preference for the criterion sanctioned in the system of the State originating the judgment. Indeed: this will obviously have been the criterion utilized by the adjudging body; and it seems strange, at least on a first approach, that its decision should be submitted to a control based on rules not necessarily coincident with those it applied. It's as if the Court of the rendition State, when examining its jurisdiction power, were required to do it not only according to the rules of its own law but also bearing in mind the system of the foreign country where the judgment may have to produce effects.

---

39 In Brazil, where the question is doctrinally controversial (v. Barbosa Moreira, Comentários ao Código de Processo Civil, vol. V, 5th ed., Rio de Janeiro, 1985, p. 99 and note 134), the Supreme Court has already ruled in the sense indicated in our text (S.E. No. 2727, 4.9.1981).

Two considerations, however, are usually superimposed here to the suggestions of pure logic. The first one arises from the fact that, not infrequently, domestic law reserves to the courts of a State, on an exclusive basis, the power to decide upon certain litigations (for instance: those referring to real property situated in the national territory), with the consequence that the former is prevented from recognizing any other court as competent and is, therefore, forced to deny efficacy to a judgment rendered by a foreign Court on the matter[40], regardless of any provision of the law of the other country in that respect. The second consideration is that, even out of such cases, the Court of the 'importing' State may oppose recognition of the power of the Court of the rendition State, established according to the respective system, with a basis on a criterion inconsistent with the fundamental principles of the national law: for instance, the mere temporary stay of spouses in a country of which they are not citizens and where they are not domiciled will not be regarded as sufficient to justify recognition of the power of the respective Court (even if sanctioned by the local system) to decree the divorce of the couple. In such a case, it is common to resort to the 'public policy' or other similar clause to justify denial of efficacy.

On the other hand, the solution consisting of adopting the criterion of the system prevailing in the rendition State is far from avoiding difficulties. As already seen[41], the principle is at the same time too narrow and too broad: the law of the 'importing' State may be excessively restrictive - in which case it will impose undue limitations to the recognition of judgments rendered with a basis on a jurisdiction power having a reasonable legal ground -, or, on the contrary, excessively liberal - in which case there is an immediate risk of the 'importation' of some judgment from a Court the action of which might not be justified in the light of the relation between the foreign State and the litigious matter or the parties. It's certain that the 'importing' State, ultimately, will have no one but itself to complain of, in such an emergency. This does not mean that, in practice, it will not hesitate to give free course to the corollaries of its own basic option.

The truth is that, in this matter, States are not generally inclined to keep an attitude fully consistent with the purity of rigid principles. Whatever the concept they adopt, they take the care to soften it with reservations and exceptions more or less extensive in reach. Thus solutions often tend to approximate to a good extent, despite the diversity of the premises. It would be unrealistic to expect a complete waiver of any kind of control over the power of the foreign Court. The problem will be extremely simplified to the extent that conventional solutions gain a larger space. In the absence of a treaty, and the systems of the rendition State and of the State where production of effects is desired being divergent, the most favorable suggestion for the international circulation of judgments would clearly consist of an option for the system that, in the case under consideration, would permit justification of the jurisdiction power.

This, of course, would not solve everything. It's easy to foresee the permanence of difficulties related with the cases where the rendition State would

40 This is not an absolute rule: Hungarian law, for instance, admits of exceptions (Farkas-Kecskés, p. 3/4).

41 Juenger, general report cit., p. 15/16.

consider itself qualified to decide on matters included by another State within the exclusive jurisdiction of its own Courts. For these, there would still be the resort to a generic restrictive clause ('public policy', 'national sovereignty', or the like). The same tactic would permit exclusion of judgments coming from States the jurisdiction power of which would seem to rely upon an excessively weak element, clamorously insufficient in the eye of the Courts of the 'importing' State. In this connection, however, an exception should be made: even if the 'importing' State rejects as inconsistent with the 'public policy' the reason adopted by the rendition State to recognize the jurisdiction of its Court, it should not, on that account, reject the judgment rendered there if, according to this own system, that jurisdiction could be otherwise justified[42].

3.8.2 At any rate, it seems clearly advisable to limit control of the 'importing' State to the general jurisdiction of the foreign Court, without allowing it to examine whether or not the rules governing the internal distribution of jurisdiction in the rendition State were complied with[43]; neither is it to presume that its Courts are more qualified than those of the rendition State to interpret those rules correctly. Furthermore, if the foreign judicial system has exclusive jurisdiction and since it cannot, obviously, be compelled to judge through the body held competent by the 'importing' State, the situation would ultimately constitute a clear denial of justice to the interested party.

It is conceivable, however, that in some exceptional hypotheses the circumstance that the suit was decided upon by a clearly unqualified body would justify denial to the foreign proceeding of a minimum guarantee to the parties (or to one of them) necessary to assure the cooperation of the domestic Courts. In such an extreme case, resort to the 'public policy' clause in order to reject 'importation' of the judgment will always be available.

3.8.3 Finally, there is the problem of jurisdiction power being granted to the Courts of a State by the will of the parties. It may happen, in fact, that the parties shall have made an express agreement in that direction; it may also be that, even without such an agreement, the defendant voluntarily accepts the jurisdiction of the State where the suit was started, either expressly or by failing to act in the manner foreseen in the respective system to raise the question.

In similar cases, the State to which efficacy of the judgment is to be carried can only be interested in objecting to such judgment if the parties acted in such a manner as to withdraw from its Courts an action which, according to the domestic system, would fall within its exclusive jurisdiction; or if the granting of jurisdiction to the foreign State is repugnant to the domestic concept beyond any acceptable limit because of the lack of some important element relating the suit with that State, so that the choice of its Courts can be taken as a fraud against the law or as an arrangement intended to submit the defendant to less favorable defense conditions. Such cases permit the classic solution of rejecting efficacy to the foreign judgment because it offends the 'public policy' or the 'national sovereignty'. Aside these, as a rule, the option

---

42 Rightly Juenger, general report cit., p. 17/8.

43 Cf. Jodlowski, p. 16/7.

of the parties should not by itself be a reason not to recognize the efficacy of the foreign judgment in the national territory.

It should be noted that the principle of respect for the will of the parties, if rigidly applied, could eventually operate in a direction opposed to that of the international circulation of judgments. For instance: if the parties had validly chosen the Courts of State A, but the suit was started and decided upon in State B, the convention would prevent 'importation' of B's judgment for failing to meet the jurisdiction requirement. The choice of jurisdiction here would indeed operate as a 'restrictive mechanism' ... At all events, it would have to be seen if the defendant, sued in a State other than the one indicated in the agreement, would not have expressly or implicitly accepted submission to the respective Court and what effects such an acceptation would produce. To probe further into the question would not be opportune in this context.

3.9 EXAMINATION OF THE REGULARITY OF THE SERVICE OF SUMMONS AND OF THE POSSIBILITY OF DEFENSE

Basically justified is the concern as to whether the foreign proceeding assured the parties an effective possibility of presenting their reasons and evidences to the judicial body. Strictly speaking, in fact, we are not dealing here with a problem peculiar to the treatment of judgments rendered in other States: more than one procedural system know some means of controlling domestic decisions in that connection, admitting, for instance, opposition to enforcement with a basis on the fact that the defeated party could not defend himself either because he was given no notice about the suit or because summons service was made in an irregular manner capable of rendering it null and void[44].

Obviously, the question concerning the regular notice to the defendant is placed on an instrumental perspective as concerns the guarantee of good defense. Therefore, an eventual inexistence or nullity of the act should not constitute an obstacle to the production of effects by a judgment within or without the territory of the State where it was rendered, if, despite such inexistence or nullity, the defendant appeared in Court and was given all normal chances to defend himself. On the other hand, the mere fact that some sort of notice was given does not necessarily, by itself, remove suspicion of disregard of the guarantee of defense: there may be a reason to doubt whether the summons, such as it was served, was apt to give the defendant the possibility of effectually contradicting the plaintiff's claim[45]. For example: the defendant was not fully informed of the contents of the claim and its respective ground, or the period of time assigned to him was clearly insufficient to permit a reasonable preparation of the defense, and so forth.

Considering all this, it can be well understood that the 'importing' State should exercise some control in this matter and deny efficacy to the foreign judgment in its territory, if the requirements it deems essential do not seem to have been met. What admits of discussion here is the extent to which such a control is justifiable. It's natural that attitudes should vary considerably here

44 Brazilian law, for instance: Código de Processo Civil, art. 741, No. 1.

45 This is stressed, among others, by Juenger, p. 12, and Zepeda, p. 9.

according to the more or less restrictive directives adopted in the juridical policy area.

Some constants undoubtedly exist. It's difficult today to find a State willing to permit a judgment to produce effects within its frontiers when such a judgment was rendered in another State against a defendant that received no notice of the suit or was given no opportunity to defend himself. In other points, however, differences are considerable: thus, for instance, with regard to the form of notification.

The general principle in that connection is to accept notice of the suit to the defendant as regular, provided formalities laid down by the systems of the country where said notice was given were complied with (*locus regit actum*). In the light of that principle, irrelevant is the objection that the defendant was notified, in the State or origin, in a manner different from that which would be adopted in the 'importing' State. Neither consistent with said principle, *a fortiori*, is the requirement that summons always be served upon the defendant personally[46].

The question becomes more delicate when, although the case was decided upon abroad, summons was served in the territory of the State where the judgment is intended to produce effects later. The strict application of the *locus regit actum* principle would cause here the necessity of following the procedure foreseen in the law of the 'importing' State - let's say, summons requested through a *letter rogatory* and effected by the local Court. From this approach, there will be no possibility of admitting efficacy, within the national territory, of a foreign judgment rendered in a suit where - for instance - the defendant was notified of the proceeding through diplomatic route, if such a modality is extraneous to the law of the 'importing' State[47]. It doesn't seem, however, that a thoroughly rigid position should be adopted here. There's no sufficient reason to put away, a priori, the possibility of any and all means not coincident with the one sanctioned by the domestic system. The decisive criterion shall ultimately be that of the appropriateness of the route chosen to give the defendant notice of the suit under the conditions and with the elements necessary for a good preparation of the defense.

Examination of the regularity of the summons served in a foreign country involves clear risks. The Courts of the 'importing' State cannot always easily form a opinion about the compliance with formalities peculiar to the system of another country. A practical way to avoid such a trouble, with favorable effects to the international circulation of judgments, consist of presuming the regularity of the act, provided the other pre-requisites for recognition and/or enforcement have been proven, granting the interested party the chance to submit eventually evidence to the contrary[48].

---

46 As is the case, for instance, in Argentine law: national Código, art. 517, 2nd (cf. Sosa, p. 3). It seems reasonable, however, to repudiate summons service by publication when the residence of the defendant was known (v., for Brazilian law, Haroldo Valladao, op. cit., p. 200).

47 In a case of the kind, the Chief Justice of the Brazilian Supreme Court denied homologation of a German judgment on the ground that performance of a typically jurisdictional act in Brazilian territory by a foreign consular authority offended the national sovereignty (S.E. No. 2730, 1.26.1981).

48 As in the Colombian law: v. Morales Molina, p. 2.

Nothing justifies the difference in treatment based on the nationality or on the domicile of the defeated party. The principle according to which nobody can be tried unless previously notified of the proceeding and given an opportunity to defend himself is not a privilege of those born or domiciled in the territory of any State. Distinctions of this kind attempt against equality and should be completely eliminated.

A last observation of generic reach: most of the problems faced in connection with this topic will probably find a satisfactory solution in the intelligent use of the 'public policy' (or other similar) clause. It would be useless to multiply specific rules, as they generally raise several reservations or even establish a number of exceptions, unnecessarily complicating the situation. It's better, in principle, to accept the procedure adopted provided it can be considered appropriate to reach the basic purposes; and to settle dubious cases according to the criterion of the respective consistency of inconsistency with the public policy of the State where the judgment is invoked.

3.10 THE LEGAL SITUATION OF THE FOREIGN JUDGMENT

It's understandable that the 'importing' State should hesitate in extending the cooperation of its Courts of law for the production of effects in the national territory by a foreign judgment that has not yet reached a certain degree of stability. Furthermore, it would not be reasonable that effects could be produced in another State by a judgment still incapable of producing said effects in the very country where it was rendered. It's understandable, then, that legislations should be concerned, on the one hand, with the eventuality of appeals capable of reversing or annulling the judgment in the country of origin; and on the other, in case of enforcement, with the aptness of the judgment to be enforced in the country of origin.

At any rate, it seems worthwhile to maintain this last requirement. As concerns the other one, some attenuation is conceivable. If the legal system of the rendition State does not demand exhaustion of all appeals in order to establish said aptness, the Courts of the 'importing' State should be satisfied with that concept. The Israeli law, under the system of law No. 5718, of 1958, goes even further: without referring to the judgment becoming a *res judicata*, it demands no more than the fact that the foreign judgment is no longer questionable by means of one appeal: other possible attacks upon the judgment are not important[49].

The prerequisite now under examination must be taken as referring to formal *res judicata* (the unappealable character of the decision). There's no ponderable reason to demand the existence of a material *res judicata*: the question here is to admit in the territory of the 'importing' State the production of effects by *that particular* judgment; it doesn't matter much whether or not the object of the decision can be discussed in another proceeding.

Neither justified would be an absolute refusal to 'import' judgments granting provisional remedies. Sometimes, the enforcement of such remedies constitutes the only possibility of assuring effective jurisdictional protection. Any objection based on the eventuality of reversal or modification of the judgment may lose

49 Law No. 5718, section 3 (2); cf. Fassberg, p. 5/6.

importance when confronted with the interest in attaining that objective. The alternative of applying for the provisional remedy directly in the country where its effects are to be produced[50] doesn't seem apt to give a satisfactory solution to all cases. Restrictions must, of course, be thought of with a view to protecting the party affected by the remedy.

As to judgments ordering alimony, it would be very little reasonable to deny them the ability to produce effects outside of the rendition State with a basis on the mere consideration that the system established in said judgments is subject to changes if circumstances are altered later. On the contrary, there's a considerable tendency toward facilitating the 'circulation' of such judgments: article 2, No. 2, of the New York Convention, of 6.20.1956, for instance, provides for the cooperation of the signatory countries through the appointment of a 'Receiving Agency' in charge of taking 'all appropriate steps for the recovery of maintenance', according to article 6, No. 1, including 'the execution of any order or other judicial act'. The possibility of 'importation' should cover judgments granting provisional alimony[51].

The unappealable character being maintained, the possibility of attenuating the strictness as regards evidence that the judgment has become final should not be laid aside. It may be unnecessary when the decision is unappealable because of the mere circumstance that it came from an authority (judicial or otherwise) located at the top of the hierarchic pyramid, save if that same authority can legally review its own decision. Another possible hypothesis is that the judgment may be presumed to have become final if an act is performed for which said condition is a prerequisite established by the law. Circumstantial evidence will, then, be admitted[52].

3.11 THE MANNER TO CONFORM A FOREIGN JUDGMENT

It's now time to examine the main aspects of the *modus faciendi* to be utilized when a judgment is desired to produce effects outside of its State of origin. As noted before (supra, 2.4), solutions have varied in more than one point.

Maximum simplicity would obviously be attained by waiving in any case a formal act (and the proceeding intended to produce it) and accepting that the prerequisite of the 'importation' of efficacy were examined by the body before which the foreign judgment is intended to produce its effects. Legislations, however, have not gone so far: those that go farthest only waive a formal act in the case of recognition of efficacy of a foreign judgment for a purpose connected with a pending suit - if, for instance, there has been resort to the *res judicata* resulting from said judgment. This is not so when the intention is to promote in the 'importing' State the enforcement of the foreign decision: in such a case, a national Court must render a specific decision.

A general evolution of the several systems toward an unconditional waiver of a formal act to lend automatic efficacy to a foreign judgment in the 'importing'

---

50 Referred to by Matscher, p. 12.

51 The Federal Supreme Court has already recognized it in Brazil: 'Embargos' in S.E. No. 1763, 3.9.1964.

52 Paulo Cezar Aragao, Comentários ao Código de Processo Civil, v. V, Sao Paulo, 1975, p. 224, with indication of precedents in note 244.

State[53] seems improbable. Up to now the practical possibility of such a step seems to be limited to the context of bilateral or multilateral treaties. Less unrealistic is the perspective of extending to other legal systems the adoption of the 'incidental' method in checking the prerequisite in the case of a mere recognition of that efficacy for purposes other than enforcement. The requirement of a formal act (and the respective proceeding) would be limited to the cases where the foreign judgment should be enforced (in the proper sense of the word).

A brief remark is in order on the alternative: *exequatur* (or homologation) proceeding - or 'an action on the foreign judgment' (v. *supra*, 2.4). In theory, at least, the first solution seems to present a clear advantage from the standpoint of simplicity; and it's opportune to note that none of the reports from countries that adopt said solution criticizes the procedure as being unnecessarily complex: on the contrary, its simplicity is almost unanimously proclaimed[54]. The comparison, however, is not always unfavorable to the system of the 'action on the judgment': in a State where both models exist, as in Israel, it can often offer in many cases a quicker and simpler route[55]. It seems meaningless, to a certain extent, to defend the replacement of any of the two schemes by the other: even if the superiority of either of them could be demonstrated with unquestionable arguments, it's highly doubtful, to say the least, that such a demonstration could by itself determine the fate of the evolutional process, clearly subject to the influence of other factors and delimited by national tradition.

There's no justification for the establishment of a temporal limitation to the initiative of the interested party in enforcing the foreign judgment. No legitimately founded interest of the 'importing' State calls for the assignment of a period of time for such an initiative. From the point of view of the winning party, it can easily be conceived that the necessity of taking it will not appear but at a very late date subsequently to the trial. The interest of the other party will be sufficiently protected by the opportunity it may be given to oppose the recognition and/or enforcement of the foreign judgment with a basis on some extinctive effect the applicable system may assign to the lapse of time. As a rule, in fact, such an eventuality will only confirm itself with reference to enforcement: if, for instance, the claim of limitation following the foreign judgment is admissible; the other effects it may produce, as well as its authority as *res judicata*, usually are not affected in the same manner by the course of time.

---

53 As portended by Sosa, p. 18, with the reservation that anyone interested should be allowed to oppose enforcement.

54 Tschipev, p. 7; Gomes Monteiro, p. 3; Arguedas Salazar, p. 2; Aguirre Godoy, p. 2; Allen, p. 1; Parodi Remón, p. 2; Zilberstein and Bacanu, p. 11; Walder, p. 2; Vescovi-Minvielle-Tellechea, p. 16; Rengel Romberg, p. 3. In Colombia, Morales Molina, p. 1, criticizes the customary assignment by the Supreme Court of an excessively long period of time for probative procedure. In El Salvador, according to Arrieta Gallegos, p. 4, the procedure can be complex if the other party opposes recognition of the foreign judgment.

55 Fassberg, p. 13. In Homburger's opinion, op. cit., p. 378, the procedure followed in many U.S. States for the action on the foreign judgment 'compares favorably with the exequatur of the civil law'. Juenger, p. 5, on the other hand, criticizes it as 'inefficient, costly and time-consuming'.

3.12 THE QUESTION OF THE AUTHORITY TO EXAMINE A FOREIGN JUDGMENT

This question can obviously be put in different manners, according to the method adopted: the 'incidental' checking or the specific declaration through an individualized procedure. To the extent that the first method is used, the question loses its own importance: in each actual case, authority to recognize or deny efficacy to the judgment in the 'importing' States will be incumbent upon the judicial body deemed qualified to settle the dispute the decision of which will be affected by the foreign judgment. The alternative would be to submit to the (only) theoretically qualified body the question regarding the efficacy of the foreign judgment whenever it is resorted to in any proceeding, similarly to what occurs in some systems with the problem of the unconstitutionality of a law. Clear are, however, the practical hindrances that such a regulation would bring about; and it doesn't seem that any eventual advantages, whatever they could be, would be enough to offset them, as witnessed by the fact that such a mechanism doesn't appear to have been used by any legal system.

If, on the contrary, a formal act is the option, then, to the extent that it is required, it becomes necessary to define what bodies would be qualified to perform it. As far as it concerns the countries covered by the present report, a certain preference can be detected for the system of 'diffuse' jurisdiction, that is, jurisdiction distributed according to variable criteria among a plurality of judicial bodies: the number of States adopting it is somewhat higher than that of countries that would rather concentrate the authority in one sole body (invariably the highest in judicial hierarchy).

It doesn't seem easy to identify constant relations between the choice of either system and the characteristics of the ideology, geography or political and administrative structure of the several countries. There are socialist countries (example: Poland) and non-socialist countries (example: Argentina) among those that adopt the diffuse authority rule, just as there are socialist countries (example: Bulgaria) and non-socialist countries (example: Colombia) among those that prefer the concentrated authority method. The latter is observed in federal States (like Venezuela) and in unitary States (like Uruguay); the same as to the former (Mexico is a federation, Peru is not). Contrary to what might be conceived *a priori*, countries of large territorial extension adopt the concentrated jurisdiction method (example: Brazil); other less extensive countries the diffuse system (example: Israel).

In view of the foregoing, relative is the range of any discussion about the advantages and disadvantages of each of the systems. Preference for either of them seems to be subject to local peculiarities or variable historical circumstances that do not conform to classical schemes. At all events, with all appropriate exceptions, a few observations of a generic nature are justified.

The diffuse authority system, in many instances, is undoubtedly capable of facilitating for the interested party the attainment of the envisaged target: if he is permitted to validate the effects of a foreign judgment through the mere presentation of that judgment to the body qualified to decide on the action it's supposed to affect, the party is clearly saved the time and the money he would have to spend to obtain the decision of another body not infrequently situated in a far place. On the other hand, there's a risk of different decisions with serious consequences for legal certainty, if the foreign judgment is invoked in more than one proceeding before different courts - although such an inconvenient can be corrected by means of some sort of appeal permitting review of conflicting decisions by one sole higher court. Similar considerations would be appropriate in connection with the necessity to assure a certain uniformity in the manner of understanding and applying clauses such as the 'public policy' and other similar provisions.

3.13 LIMITATION ON THE POWERS OF THE COURTS IN THE 'IMPORTING' STATES

A point of the utmost significance is the one dealing with the extension of the powers conferred on the Courts of the 'importing' States in deciding upon the party's petition to confirm a foreign judgment. The large majority of systems nowadays are frankly averse to the possibility of reviewing a suit in its substance to see whether the solution given to it in the State of origin was fair or unfair. Exceptional are the cases where such a possibility is admitted[56].

Seen from a closer range, however, this seems to be only a half-truth. Several systems permit an investigation, although a limited one, concerning the cause of action decided upon in a foreign country, when they sanction clauses such as, for instance, the one including among the prerequisites of the production of effects by the judgment the lawfulness (or validity) of the obligation, under the laws of the 'importing' State[57]. Mention was also made here (*supra*, 2.6) of the opinion of some, according to which the examination of the compatibility of the foreign judgment with the domestic public policy would, under certain aspects, open an opportunity to attenuate the prohibition of the '*révision au fond*'.

It doesn't seem possible to eliminate completely the eventuality of more or less significant (and more or less dissimulated) concessions to the review principle. Courts will always find one way or another to justify theoretically the rejection of a foreign judgment when some serious circumstance appears to be sufficient to convince them that the production of the respective effects in the national territory must be prevented at all costs. It has already been emphasized how deceitful it would be to expect States to renounce resort to the 'public policy' (or other analogous) clause, including - let it be added - for the purpose of prohibiting the 'importation' of a foreign judgment denoting an unbearable teratology from the standpoint of justice.

Desirable here is that the use of the technique should not go beyond limits held as strictly necessary to preserve the legal and ethic values considered fundamental in States where the judgment is to produce effects. In this particular, however, the risk of intolerable excesses doesn't seem too great[58].

---

56 In Israel, Fassberg, p. 8-9, identifies two of them: the allegation of fraud in the foreign proceeding and the fact that the petitioner based himself 'on the original cause of action' as permitted by the common law; the latter hypothesis, however, is not really a case of enforcement of the foreign judgment, strictly speaking.

57 Examples: Guatemala, Cód. Proc. Civ. y Merc., art. 345, 3rd; Paraguay, Cód. de Proc. en mat. civ. y com., art. 573, d.

58 Cf. supra, note 37 to No. III, 6.

4 FOREIGN ARBITRAL AWARDS

4.1 GENERAL CONSIDERATIONS

Certain sectors entrust the settlement of disputes preferably to arbitration, as it is, from the simplicity and rapidity (if not from other) standpoints, considered superior to State jurisdiction. This tendency is mainly clear in the international trade world, and it renders the problem of the extraterritorial extension of efficacy, to a certain degree, more critical in relation to arbitral awards than with reference to judgments.

It must be admitted, on the other hand, that the state of things referring to arbitration is, from several angles, less satisfactory, specially if viewed in the light of national legislations. Uncertainty is such that, in many cases, in order to induce the defeated party to comply with the award, one has to rely on the pressure of the litigant's interest rather than on the coercive means of the State where the award is to produce the desired effects: the company that submits itself to an arbitration usually fears the economic consequences of an eventual reluctance to voluntary compliance with the arbitrator's award and is aware that such an attitude could bring the company discredit and isolation in the international trading community[59].

Several factors contribute to the insufficient development reached by the regulation of the matter so far. In many circles, it should be pointed out, a diffuse feeling of distrust stimulates a resistance, which does not seem easy to break, against the 'importation' of awards. If the appropriateness of the foreign judicial proceeding is not always to be relied upon, even less tranquility is often experienced in relation to the ability of an arbitration held somewhere else to offer impartiality and correctness guarantees capable of justifying the 'opening' of the territory to its decision. Intuitively, such an attitude tends to become worse in the case of awards unfavorable to national citizens or companies; that is, just in those cases where it's most necessary, as a rule, to permit the production of effects within the frontiers of the country.

If the existence of some ground for this kind of fear is admitted, and considering the scarce probability of a radical change in the evolution of events, when everything shows that the arbitral phenomenon tends to occupy larger and larger space, the correct solution cannot be to leave the matter immersed in juridical uncertainty, subject to the hazards of never-ending controversies. Most of the national systems, however, have not yet grasped the need to clarify the situation: the sources of law remain extremely laconic, if not silent, in a great number of countries. This has been probably contributing to a certain increment in initiatives envisaging the regulation of the matter by means of treaties and conventions: such treaties and conventions are intended, among other things, to fill the normative gap in national legal systems.

---

59 Cf. Fouchard, L'arbitrage commercial international, V. II, Paris, 1965, p. 464/5; David, L'arbitrage dans le commerce international, Paris, 1982, p. 545.

4.2 THE PREVIOUS QUESTION OF QUALIFICATION

As it is well known, there's not among scholars a uniform concept about the arbitral phenomenon. The award is sometimes seen as a act assimilable or equivalent to the judgment by a judge, sometimes as a decision that takes all its strength from a contractual bond between the parties. This contraposition is apt to create practical problems, specially when there's no coincidence between the notions prevailing in the State where the arbitration was held and in the State in the territory of which the award is to be recognized or enforced.

Legal texts are usually less exacting with reference to compliance with contracts entered into elsewhere than in connection with the recognition and/or enforcement of foreign judgments. In Brazil, for instance, article 5 of the Introductory Law to the Civil Code expressly subjects the production of effects by such judgments to a number of requirements, whereas other acts carried out abroad are only subject to the clause of conformity with the 'national sovereignty, the public policy and the good customs' (art. 17). Legal systems in general do not require a formal act by national Courts of law to authorize the creditor to demand from the debtor in court compliance with an obligation under a contract signed elsewhere, even when such a formality is necessary for enforcement of a judgment from a foreign Court.

If an award from State A is to be carried out in State B, and the concepts prevailing in both States are different from each other, a question is raised from the outset as regards qualification, that is, it must be established, before anything else, if State B will accept the award as an act of the nature assigned to it by State A or if, on the contrary, it will assign to it the nature the State itself lends to domestic awards. Intuitively, the discipline will vary with the position adopted, should treatment reserved to judgments differ from that given to contracts. The list of possibilities can be broken down into several items: such as it was observed in connection with the jurisdictional power problem regarding judgments (*supra*, 2.3 (a), application of the foreign system or of the national system may be more favorable or less favorable.

Maximum simplification would, of course, be attained by establishing that, in any case of divergence, the less rigid system would be applied, whether it corresponded to the concept of the rendition State or to that of the 'importing' State. To the best of our knowledge, this point has not been reached so far. It's even possible to say, at least in general, that States where awards are considered equivalent to judgments do not hesitate to maintain that equivalence in respect of foreign awards even if coming from States where the contractual concept of arbitration prevails. Consequently, any award from abroad, in order to become efficacious in the national territory, must meet the same requirements and be subject to the same formalities imposed upon a judgment from a foreign Court.

4.3 FOREIGN AWARDS PUT ON THE SAME LEVEL WITH FOREIGN JUDGMENTS. CONSEQUENCES

In most countries, for the purpose of recognition and/or enforcement, arbitral awards rendered elsewhere are fully or partially put on the same level with foreign judgments[60]. Several procedural systems expressly sanction such an equivalence, ordering the same rule adopted for the former to be applicable to the latter[61]. But the concept prevails even in the absence of a legal regulation governing the matter[62].

Consequently, and to a good extent, the list of 'restrictive mechanisms' and the set of problems concerning the means that can be used to eliminate or mitigate them can, *mutatis mutandis*, be referred to what was said about foreign judgments. Still valid here are, therefore, and to a large degree, the considerations drawn on the requisite of a treaty or convention (*supra*, 3.2), on the reciprocity requirement (2.3), on the 'public policy' and other similar clauses (3.6), etc. If, in certain cases, the nature of the cause decided upon abroad affects the treatment applicable to the foreign judgment in the 'importing' State (*supra*, 3.4), a similar remark can be made as concerns the award: the respective ability to produce effects may, for instance, be limited to cases where the matter therein decided upon could also be decided upon by arbitration according to national law[63]. As it's easily understood, some questions assume a peculiar colour in this context. Thus, for example, the question of the arbitrators' powers, that can be based on the will of the parties rather than on some rule of the legal system of any State.

Equivalence of the award to the judgment could lead the Courts of the 'importing' State to a radically negative position in the absence of an act performed by a judicial body in the State of origin. Admittance into the country will be denied to an award that has not received abroad the *exequatur* (or homologation) by a judge[64]. We face here a 'restrictive mechanism' of great importance in certain cases: it's very possible, indeed, that the award, in the State of origin, does not need that official confirmation to acquire efficacy, or that, because it emanates from an international entity, it does not even admit of any control of the kind; this raises the risk of impossible compliance with the requirement, thus absolutely ruling out the eventual production of effects in the country where said requirement is necessary. The operation of this 'restrictive mechanism' can be reduced to a less serious magnitude by a simple distinction, namely: to take into account the rules in force in the rendition State, in order to waive the requirement whenever, under those rules, the award is not subject to the *exequatur* (or homologation).

The rules governing the extension of the powers conferred upon the Courts of the 'importing' State in the examination of a foreign award open the way for a number of alternatives. Of course, the lesser the amplitude of control, the

60 V. David, op. cit., p. 537.

61 E.g.: in the German Democratic Republic (ZPO, par. 198, 1), in Bolivia (Cód. de Proced. Civ., art. 556), in Chile (Código de Procedimiento Civil, art. 246), in Colombia (Cód. de Proced. Civ., arts. 693 to 695).

62 This is what occurs in Rumania, for instance, where the dispositions of art. 375 of the Code of Civil Procedure with the required adjustments are considered analogically applicable to foreign arbitral awards (Zilberstein and Bacanu, p. 6).

63 The question of the ratione materiae inadmissibility is not infrequently examined from the standpoint of the 'public policy': v. Fouchard, op. cit., p. 114; Zilberstein and Bacanu, p. 7.

64 To this effect the course of decisions of the Brazilian Federal Supreme Court: S.E. No. 1982, 6.3.1970; S.E. No. 2006, 11.18.1971; S.E. No. 2178, 6.30.1979.

easier the production of effects by the awards. For instance, if control is allowed to go down to the examination of requirements that should have been satisfied under the arbitral agreement, the possibilities of denying efficacy to the award will be enlarged: the agreement may, indeed, have a defect such as the lack of capacity of one or of both parties to undertake obligations or the non-observance of an essential formality, and so forth. Such an eventuality is excluded beforehand when control is restricted to the formal aspects of the award itself or of the procedure followed by the arbitrators.

5 THE ROLE OF TREATIES AND CONVENTIONS

In due time reference was made to the importance that the role of international treaties and conventions can assume in the matter of recognition and enforcement of foreign decisions. This is specially true for the member-States of European Communities; but the phenomenon, obviously, is not restricted to that area.

Observing it in Latin America, for instance, we see that since the past century a tendency has appeared toward sanctioning in conventional texts understandings, the need for which was very early felt, among the States of that region. Hence the appearance in 1889 of a treaty signed in Montevideo by several South-American countries on the extraterritorial efficacy of foreign judgments and awards. The requirements stipulated thereunder are among those traditionally foreseen in connection with the matter. Another treaty, now in force among a smaller number of countries, was signed in 1940 in the Capital of Uruguay, eliminating the requirement of the *exequatur* for judgments rendered by the Courts of the signatory States[65].

Of greater importance, in view of the number of countries that ratified it (though with reservations on the part of several of them), is the Havana convention, of 1928, that sanctioned the International Private Law Code, known as Bustamante Code. It cannot be said, however, that it contains far-reaching innovations. As to the extraterritorial efficacy of judgments, article 423 thereof lists in traditional terms the prerequisites of enforcement, referring to the jurisdiction power of the adjudging Court, the summons of the parties (personal service or service upon the party's legal representative), the compatibility with the public policy and the public law of the State where enforcement is to take place, the enforceability of the judgment in the country of origin, and requirements of a formal nature (translation, when necessary; authenticity of the document). Article 431 refers to judgments the provisions of which are not enforceable, stipulating that they will produce the 'effects of a *res judicata*' in case they fulfil the conditions therefor as foreseen in the Code, save those related with enforcement. Article 432, in turn, makes the same rules governing judgments applicable to arbitral awards, provided the subject-matter decided upon could be the object of a compromise according to the laws of the 'importing' State.

More recently, the following are worth mentioning: the Inter-American Convention on the Extraterritorial Efficacy of Foreign Judgments and Arbitral

65 Vescovi-Minvielle-Tellechea, p. 4.

Awards (Montevideo, 1979) and the Inter-American Convention on Jurisdiction in the International Field For the Extraterritorial Efficacy of Foreign Judgments (La Paz, 1984), signed in the second and in the third Inter-American Conference on International Private Law, respectively, promoted by the Organization of American States. A few innovations were introduced by the Montevideo Convention, e.g.: any of the signatory countries can, through a declaration in the moment of ratifying the act, extend its applicability to the decisions of non-judicial bodies, provided they perform jurisdictional functions, as well as to sentences of criminal judges condemning the defendant to the payment of damages resulting from his crime (art. 2); expressly provided for is the possibility of admitting the *partial* efficacy of the foreign decision in case it's not possible to admit it in full (art. 4); the benefit of assistance *in forma pauperis* granted in the country of origin is guaranteed to subsist in the 'importing' country (art. 5).

The 1979 Convention took position about the problem of the international jurisdiction of foreign Courts, prescribing that this requisite will be examined in the light of the laws of the State where the decision was rendered (art. 2nd, d) - a solution that, as already shown (*supra*, 2.3 (a), can be more favorable or less favorable to the extension of efficacy, as the case may be. The matter, however, was again regulated in the La Paz Convention, article 1 of which lists a number of situations considered sufficient to establish the international jurisdiction of the Courts of the rendition State, specifically mentioning the cases of personal actions (A), real actions on movable property (B), real actions on immovable property (C) and actions arising out of commercial contracts (D).

Particularly interesting is the provision of art. 2 of the La Paz Convention according to which the requirement of jurisdiction power in the international field will be considered satisfied if, at the discretion of the jurisdictional body of the party State where the judgment is to produce effects, the jurisdictional body that rendered the judgment declared itself qualified in order to avoid denial of justice owing to the inexistence of a qualified jurisdictional entity. On the other hand, it maintains for the 'importing State' the possibility of refusing the extraterritorial extension of efficacy to a judgment rendered with invasion of the jurisdiction of the State where said extension is requested. Let it be noted, at any rate, that several matters of great importance were expressly excluded from the applicability area of the 1984 Convention: status and capacity of individuals, divorce, nullity of marriage, property system in marriage, alimony, *causa mortis* descent, bankruptcy and composition with creditors, liquidation of companies, labour and social security disputes, arbitration, extracontract liability, maritime and air questions (art. 64).

Returning to the 1979 Convention, an observation is in order regarding the clause on the notice of the claim to the defendant. Art. 2nd, e, prescribes that summons must have been served upon the defendant in the due form of law 'in a manner substantially equivalent' to that accepted by the 'importing' State. Not excluded, therefore, is the occasional utilization of a specific modality of summons, different from the one that would have to be used in that State. The 'substantial equivalence' will be measured by the degree of aptitude of the act to transmit to the defendant full notice of the claim, with all the elements required for the preparation of the defense. Such a degree cannot be lower than that of the modality of summons that would be used in the 'importing' State. It's an intelligent solution that satisfactorily reconciles the advisability of avoiding excessive formalism with the necessity of preserving one of the basic guarantees of the proceeding.

Specifically in connection with foreign arbitral awards, it should be noted that a good number of countries the legal systems of which are examined in this general report, are signatories to the New York Convention, of 1958. More recently, mention should be made of the Inter-American Convention on International Commercial Arbitration, signed in Panama, in 1975. The dispositions of both conventions are remarkably similar to a large degree. Both seek to avert problems of a technical and juridical nature related with the distinction sanctioned by many systems between 'compromising clause' and 'compromise', denying it any importance for practical purposes (art. 11, 2, of the New York Convention; art. 1st of the Panama Convention). The cases permitting rejection of the extraterritorial extension of efficacy are foreseen in very similar terms (art. V of the New York Convention; art. 5th of the Panama Convention). A disposition equally common to both conventions, intended to favour the extension of efficacy, assigns to the party opposing the recognition or the enforcement of the award the burden of proving the absence of the prerequisites of the extension or efficacy (art. V, No. 1, of the New York Convention; art. 5th, No. 1, of the Panama Convention); the cases of impossibility of submitting the matter to arbitration according to the law of the 'importing' State, and of incompatibility with the public policy of that State are exceptions (art. V, No. 2, of the New York Convention; art. 5th, No. 2, of the Panama Convention). Art. 4th of the Panama Convention expressly established that arbitral awards not impugnable under the applicable law or procedural rules will prevail as a Court judgment, and enforcement or recognition thereof can be claimed similarly to what occurs with judgments handed down by courts.

In the area of the socialist countries, mention should be made of the Moscow Convention, of 1972, referring to the arbitral settlement of disputes arising from economic and technical and scientific interchange. As stressed by the Rumanian rapporteurs[66], said Convention made a significant progress toward simplification, to the extent that it made awards originated from other signatory States equivalent to national awards and eliminated the need for *exequatur*. Such elimination, in fact, had already been sanctioned in another field by the Washington Convention, of 1965, only applicable to investment relationships.

Of course, there's still a considerable number of bilateral treaties, on which not even a brief comment is possible here. We will only say that some of them have extremely facilitated the extraterritorial extension of judgments by admitting, at least in certain matters and under certain circumstances, that Court decisions of each of the signatory countries can produce effects in the territory of another State without any formality[67].

---

66 Zilberstein and Bacanu, p. 29/30.

67 Also in this connection, v. Zilberstein and Bacanu, p. 22/23, who give several examples of treaties between Rumania and other socialist and non-socialist States.

6 GENERAL CONCLUSIONS

Reports of this kind are not sets of dogmatic theses, geometrically demonstrated. Therefore, it wouldn't seem appropriate to organize a list of conclusions about each of the varying topics of the several problems we are dealing with. A certain number of them, in fact, have been enunciated in this paper, under the items specifically destined to the examination of each question. It's for us now to summarize the impression at which we arrived after reading the national reports and reviewing legal and conventional texts and other important data.

In the area covered by this report the situation suggests no pessimistic appreciation. According to almost all national rapporteurs, requests for the recognition and/or enforcement of foreign judgments are, as a rule, granted in their majority[68]. This might indicate, on the one hand, that the requirements for the extraterritorial extension of efficacy are not usually excessive, and, on the other - a constant assertion expressly made in most reports - that the competent bodies are inclined to give them a liberal interpretation. At all events, a predictable argument would claim that no notice is being taken of the eventual existence of foreign judgments (in a perhaps significant number) the recognition and/or enforcement of which are *not* requested by the interested parties. If such an abstention can be related with the firm belief that difficulties are great and chances of success are small, any conclusion will become extremely uncertain.

At any rate, it's remarkable to note that more than one national rapporteur declared themselves satisfied with the system of their countries and abstained from offering any *de lege ferenda* suggestions[69]. As to those actually put forward, some are short-ranged as they are limited to peculiarities of the national system: this is the case of Israel, where the coexistence of different systems is a source of confusion and juridical uncertainty[70]. Something similar occurs in countries still adopting to a larger or lesser degree the requirement of reciprocity, the elimination of which has been recommended[71]. Other defects are pointed out in national systems, not infrequently consisting of omissions such as the lack of an express regulation of the country's jurisdictional power in the international field[72]. As for the rest, it's easy to detect a preference for the system of incidental checking of the prerequisites for the extension of efficacy, as compared to that of the specific formal act[73]. Very small is the

---

68 A few rapporteurs do claim the absence of statistical data, that would prevent a decisive opinion (e.g.: Sosa, p. 17; Arrieta Gallegos, p. 5; Walder, p. 3). In Turkey, courts have recently tended to a restrictive attitude, especially in respect of enforcement of foreign judgments on personal status of Turkish citizens (Özsunay, p. 12).

69 V., for Guatemala, Aguirre Godoy, p. 3; for the German Democratic Republic, Kosewähr, p. 12; for Hungary, Farkas-Kecskés, p. 12; for Poland, Jodlowski, p. 3 (with the express statement that other Polish specialists have a different opinion).

70 Fassberg, p. 15.

71 V., for Austria, Matscher, p. 11-12; for Uruguay, Vescovi-Minvielle-Tellechea, p. 18.

72 As in Rumania, Zilberstein and Bacanu, p. 18.

73 E.g.: Zepeda, p. 26-7; Walder, p. 2; Vescovi-Minvielle-Tellechea, p. 18 (in connection with foreign judgments granting alimony).

number of rapporteurs to whom it seems necessary to simplify the procedure leading to such an act.

Less satisfactory is the situation as concerns the extraterritorial extension of the efficacy of arbitral awards. Known obstacles seem capable here of more actively barring the 'importation' of decisions. At any rate, it would be a mistake to underestimate the strength of the movement in its favour.

There's a general desire that treaties be more frequently signed, as they are seen as a more efficient instrument to remove difficulties. Some examples suggest that, in this sector, it's easier to reach a high degree of efficiency by means of bilateral treaties (mainly between States having related legal systems) than through multilateral conventions with a large number of signatories, in which the outstanding difference in particular directives brings about the danger of reducing the agreement to excessively generic dispositions.

Of course, along with the *de iure* situation, it would be necessary to consider the problems that make it impossible or difficult *de facto* for the interested party to plead recognition and/or enforcement of a foreign judgment. But few data are available on this matter. The U.S. report points out that lawyers, mainly those practicing away from metropolitan centers, may lack the linguistic knowledge and the technical and legal background required for an efficient defense of rights of the winning party under the foreign proceeding; it also mentions the high fees that aggravate the cost of the initiative particularly in a system that does not provide for the reimbursement of said fees by the loser to the winner[74]. These observations are in part applicable to other countries. Undoubtedly, the very choice of a lawyer to represent him before the qualified body may be highly problematic for a foreign interested party having no personal contacts in professional circles.

Other difficulties will not be necessarily peculiar to the sphere of 'importation' of decisions, but mere signs of a more generic deficiency in the field of 'access to Justice'. The respective analysis would clearly transcend the limits of this report.

TOPICS FOR DISCUSSION

1. Does a general trend toward facilitation of recognition and enforcement of foreign judgments and arbitral awards exist in your country? If so, which are the main recent landmarks of such an evolution?

2. Which are the most important *de iure* and *de facto* obstacles that still prevent or retard the attainment of an entirely satisfactory situation in that respect?

3. Do the recognition and/or enforcement of foreign judgments in your country depend on reciprocity? In such case, should this requirement be abolished, or at least attenuated? In what way could such a goal be reached?

---

74 Jenger, p. 19.

4. To what extent is an *exequatur* necessary for the recognition and/or enforcement of a foreign judgment in your country? Are the proceedings complex? If so, how could the main difficulties be removed or lessened?

5. Are there any surviving traces of a direct or indirect *révision au fond* in the way courts deal with foreign judgments in your country? Could they be completely eliminated?

6. In what way and to what extent is it desirable and possible to reduce difficulties in the recognition and/or enforcement of foreign judgments due to requirements such as jurisdiction of the rendition State, notice of the proceedings, opportunity of defense, and the like?

7. How is the 'finality' requirement to be understood? Is it reasonable, under any circumstances, to exclude the possibility of recognition and/or enforcement regarding provisional remedies?

8. Does the public policy (*ordre public*) clause create a serious obstacle to the recognition and/or enforcement of foreign judgments? Should courts, in your opinion, make more liberal or more rigorous use of such clause?

9. How does the situation of a foreign arbitral award compares in your country with that of a foreign judgment as to the chances of being recognized and/or enforced? Which are the main problems specifically concerning recognition and/or enforcement of arbitral awards? What measures should be taken to solve them?

10. In your view, are the best chances to improve the situation of recognition and/or enforcement of both foreign judgments and arbitral awards connected with changes in domestic law or rather likely to arise from bilateral or multilateral treaties and conventions?

IMPROVING THE PROCEDURES FOR THE RECOGNITION AND ENFORCEMENT OF FOREIGN JUDGMENTS AND ARBITRAL AWARDS

K. D. Kerameus
Professor of Civil Procedure at Athens University School of Law

TABLE OF CONTENTS

I INTRODUCTION

1. This paper is the other part of the general report to subject 7 on the list of the 8th World Conference on Procedural Law held in late August 1987 in Utrecht (The Netherlands). The subject bears the title 'Improving the procedures for the recognition and enforcement of foreign judgments and arbitral awards' and has been divided into two parts: this part deals with the legal situation in the twelve member States of the European Communities, while Professor José Carlos Barbosa Moreira of the University of the State of Rio de Janeiro has assumed a similar task with respect to the rest of the world. Obviously, the separation of the subject has been implicitly induced by the impact of the Brussels Convention of September 27, 1968 on Jurisdiction and the Enforcement of Judgments in Civil and Commercial Matters. This Convention is now binding on eight out of the twelve member States of the European Communities: the six original members (Belgium, Federal Republic of Germany, France, Italy, Luxembourg, the Netherlands) since February 1, 1972, and in addition Denmark since November 1, 1986 and the United Kingdom of Great Britain and Northern Ireland since January 1, 1987. Ireland and Greece have acceded to the Brussels Convention but have not yet ratified it[1], while Portugal and Spain are expected to enter into negotiations for accession to the Convention.

2. This general report is almost exclusively based on the twelve national reports which, in the period between October 1986 and August 1987, came in and were written in six languages by the following colleagues (mentioned in alphabetical order of their last names): Professor Valentin Cortés of the University of Madrid (for Spain); Professor André Huet of the University of Strasbourg (for France); Professor Harald Koch of the University of Hannover (for the Federal Republic of Germany); Professor Jean Laenens of the University of Antwerpen (for Belgium); Professor David Gwynn Morgan of the University College of Cork (for the Republic of Ireland); Judge Georges Ravarani of the Tribunal d'arondissement of Luxembourg (for Luxembourg); Professor T. Svenné Schmidt of the University of Aarhus (for Denmark); Lecturer P.A. Stone of the University of Exeter (for the United Kingdom); Professor A.M. Pessoa Vaz and Mr. J. Alvaro Dias, LL.M., of the University of Coimbra (for Portugal);

1 In the meantime, Ireland implemented the Convention on March 5, 1988.

Professor J.P. Verheul of the University of Leiden (for the Netherlands); Professor Vincenzo Vigoriti of the University of Siena (for Italy); and Professor Sp. Vl. Vrellis of the University of Athens (for Greece). I am deeply thankful to the distinguished colleagues for their valuable contributions which, in a brilliant way, stressed various and interesting aspects of the wide topic.

3. Although the Brussels Convention may have been the origin of splitting up the general report on subject 7 into two parts, this paper must go beyond the limits of the Convention in many respects. First of all, the paper covers legal systems in which the Brussels Convention is not - or not yet -in force: Greece, Ireland, Portugal, Spain. Secondly, even in the countries already bound by the Brussels Convention, all other legal sources pertaining to recognition and enforcement are dealt with: in the first place the respective systems of domestic law, but also bilateral conventions or other multilateral conventions besides the Convention of Brussels. Thirdly, matters explicitly left out of the scope of application of the Brussels Convention, like family matters or arbitration, have been taken into account; special attention has been paid to the recognition and enforcement of foreign arbitral awards, which figure even in the title of the general report. Therefore, the Brussels Convention constitutes only a point of reference, a sort of potential geographical delimitation of the legal systems to be covered. This text is not meant to offer a detailed study of the Brussels Convention[2], but rather to envisage the functioning of the recognition and enforcement of foreign judgments in an area of the world in which, *inter alia*, an important multilateral convention has been in force for fifteen years. Since the Brussels Convention does not cover, both actually and potentially, the whole of Europe, this general report should not be understood as *the European response* to a major problem in the law of international civil procedure. Much more modestly, an attempt is being made to identify and understand advantages and disadvantages connected with the coexistence of a modern multilateral convention and various other rules governing the recognition and enforcement of foreign judicial activity.

4. A further remark should be added. The very title of the report focuses on *improving* the relevant procedures. Thus, an element of legislative policy may not be ignored in the following developments. After all, this feature is in line with the general theme of the Utrecht Conference, striving to achieve 'Justice and Efficiency': both parameters call for considerations *de lege ferenda* as well. However, no improving mechanism can be meaningfully set in motion without a good knowledge of existing law. Therefore, an effort should be made to analyze the actual structures and procedures in the member States of the European Communities with respect to recognition and enforcement of foreign judgments and arbitral awards. Policy considerations should be promoted by stressing recent changes in legislation and in case law, or by discussing developments in preparation.

---

2 Among the abundant literature see the official reports to the original 1968 Convention by P. Jenard, Official Journal of the European Communities, No. C 59 of 5.3.1979, p. 1-70; to the 1978 Accession Convention (Denmark, Ireland and United Kingdom) by P. Schlosser, ibid. p. 71-151; to the 1982 Accession Convention (Greece) by D. Evrigenis and K.D. Kerameus, OJ C 298/24.11.1986, p. 1-27.

5. Finally, this general report is only a tentative approach. It tries to offer a synthesis of the twelve national reports, often inserting the author's personal observations and putting some central questions. In this form, the general report has been delivered by the Convention Bureau to all Conference participants and could serve as a discussion basis in both the working and the plenary sessions. The author has been happy to benefit from the national reporters' observations and corrections, the discussions in Utrecht as well as from his own further elaboration. Building upon all that, he altered in some points the original report in order to establish this text for publication.

6. The plan of this general report has been partly imposed by the elements contained in the title of the subject. It has been further expanded in a lengthy questionnaire consisting of 53 topics and sent out to all national reporters as a guideline for their contributions. In accordance with this preparation, the following parts of the text will successively deal with the domestic law of the twelve European states under consideration (part II), with the bilateral or multilateral conventions (other than the Brussels Convention) binding upon them (part III), with general aspects of the Brussels Convention (part IV), with specific issues of the Brussels Convention (part V), and with the recognition and enforcement of foreign arbitral awards both under domestic law and under international conventions (part vI). The last part of the report (VII) will be devoted to some general conclusions.

II THE DOMESTIC LAW OF THE EC-MEMBER STATES ON RECOGNITION AND ENFORCEMENT OF FOREIGN JUDGMENTS

7. The area of law concerning the recognition and enforcement of foreign judgments deals in essence with the integration of the latter into the domestic legal order[3]. This integration may take on different faces and develop on various levels. Often, four kinds of effects attributable to foreign judgments are distinguished: (a) a factual effect, resulting from the existence of a foreign judgment as such; (b) an evidentiary effect; (c) a binding effect; and (d) an enforcing effect[4]. Most important are the two latter effects. They are most often resorted to, and they give expression to the very function of judicial decisions: to establish in a binding way legal relationships under dispute among the parties (*res judicata*); and to set the coercive mechanism of the state in motion against the reluctant judgment debtor in order to bend his will and to realize the contents of the judgment (enforcement). A theoretical question (which may have some practical implications, too) arises here with respect to the intrinsic meaning of inserting or accepting a foreign judgment into one's own domestic legal order: Does this integration merely extend the legal consequences, that ensued from the foreign judgment abroad, over the state

---

3 See Huet p. 2. Names without other specification indicate the national reports submitted by the respective authors (see the text **supra**, para. 2).

4 Cf. Laenens p. 1-2; Vaz and Dias p. 7, 29.

border into our own system, or does it compel - beyond that or regardless of that - a treatment equal to similar domestic judgments[5]?

8. A further question pertains to the mechanics rather than to the nature of recognition. Traditionally, the common law view has been not to let the original cause of action merge with the foreign judgment but to permit instead a new action in a domestic forum based on the foreign proceedings. By contrast, the civil law system tends to adopt the foreign judgment as such, that is to integrate it into the domestic legal order as soon as certain requirements are met, without having recourse to a new action. However, here as well as in many other areas of comparison between the two legal systems, the distinction has begun to get blurred and trends of convergence have emerged. Article 431 of the Dutch Code of Civil Procedure seems to impose, in the absence of an international treaty, a new action in a Dutch court[6]. The situation in Denmark is similar[7]. Even in France such a direct action on the foreign judgment has been envisaged under exceptional circumstances[8]. On the other hand, in a common law jurisdiction like Ireland, both theories seem actually to be available[9].

9. In most countries under review, the provisions governing recognition and enforcement of the foreign judgment are to be found in the Codes of Civil Procedure (Belgium, Federal Republic of Germany, France, Greece, Italy, the Netherlands, Portugal, Spain). Even in the United Kingdom, common law has been supplemented by the Administration of Justice Act 1920 and by the Foreign Judgments (Reciprocal Enforcement) Act 1933[10], while in Ireland there exist very few statutes as well as cases, and an assumption of similarity to English law is adhered to[11]. Case law seems to be the preponderant source in this area of law in Luxembourg[12]. Danish law presents in this respect an original evolution[13]. While until 1932 foreign judgments were regularly recognized, provided that the foreign court had jurisdiction according to the Danish rules on international jurisdiction, the preparation of the 1932 Nordic Convention induced the Danish legislator to refrain from recognizing non-Nordic judgments under less requirements than Nordic ones. Therefore, under a new section 223a inserted 1932 in the Administration of Justice Act, recognition was made dependent on an international treaty or a Royal Ordinance, and at any rate on reciprocity. An amendment of the same section in 1976 authorized the Minister of Justice to lay down rules on recognition, in the absence of which a new action in a Danish court remains the only possibility.

---

5 Cf. Koch p. 3 and notes 5, 6.

6 Verheul p. 1.

7 Schmidt p. 4.

8 Huet p. 27 note 6.

9 Morgan, p. 9.

10 Stone p. 1.

11 Morgan p. 1.

12 Ravarani p. 1-2.

13 See Schmidt p. 1-4.

10. Recent or expected changes in the rules governing recognition and enforcement are twofold. The most important ones refer to those countries in which the Brussels Convention came of late (Denmark, United Kingdom) or is about to come into effect (Greece, Ireland). A second range of changes occurred in other countries within a purely domestic framework. Thus, the Federal Republic of Germany, in the process of its major private international law reform, has amended since September 1, 1986 § 328 I Nos 2 and 3 of the Code of Civil Procedure[14]. And Spain introduced, through the Law 30/1981, the recognition of Spanish ecclesiastical decisions concerning nullity of marriage and separation under a judicial review of conformity with the law of the state[15]. On the level of case law, it is worth mentioning that the leading decision of the French Court of Cassation of February 6, 1985 greatly limited jurisdictional impediments to the recognition of foreign judgments[16].

11. The question of what kinds of foreign judgments are susceptible to recognition and/or enforcement is an issue of both convergence and divergence among the various legal systems. There seems to be a high degree of agreement as to the need for a 'final' judgment[17] and as to the prevalence of the nature of the matter adjudicated over the denomination or the quality of the authority which rendered the judgment[18]. Under the latter aspect, even civil claims adjudicated by a penal tribunal to a 'partie civile'[19], or decrees of voluntary jurisdiction[20] seem to be susceptible to recognition. Thus, Italian courts recognize measures taken by the *conseil de prud'hommes*, decisions of rabbinical tribunals, and a divorce decree pronounced by the Canadian Senate[21]; and Greek courts recognize decisions by ecclesiastical courts abroad as well as by foreign civil status services[22]. However, under German law acts of a foreign administrative authority would not be recognizable[23]. And whether foreign provisional decrees may be recognized, is also a point of divergence[24].

12. With regard to the competent court for purposes of recognition and enforcement, there exists almost uniformity as far as venue is concerned. The

14 See Koch p. 2.

15 Cortés p. 1-2. For the situation in Portugal under Legislative Decree 30615 of July 27, 1940 see Vaz and Dias p. 28-29.

16 See Huet, p. 8, 24, 26. Cf. **infra**, para. 15.

17 See, for example, Cortés p. 3; Koch p. 3; Morgan p. 5-6; Stone p. 2; Verheul p. 2; Vigoriti p. 3; under article 797 (4) of the Italian Code of Civil Procedure the foreign judgment must be final in accordance with the law of the place where it was rendered. In Portugal, the final character of the foreign judgment seems to be presumed: Vaz and Dias p. 40-41.

18 Koch p. 2-3; Laenens No. 28; Ravarani p. 3-4; Vaz and Dias p. 30; Vigoriti p. 3.

19 Laenens No. 28; Stone, The recognition and enforcement in England of foreign personal and proprietary judgments, [1983] 1 Lloyd's Maritime and Commercial Law Quarterly, 1 at 15. Doubts in Luxembourg: Ravarani p. 3-4.

20 Huet p. 27 note 2; Koch p. 2; Ravarani p. 4; Vrellis p. 3.

21 Vigoriti note 1.

22 Vrellis p. 8 and notes 26, 27.

23 Koch p. 2 and note 3.

24 Cf., for instance, the opposite views by Vigoriti p. 3 and Vrellis p. 28/29 note 13.

request may be brought either in the domicile of the foreign judgment debtor or in the place where enforcement proceedings are to follow. By contrast, uniformity ceases to exist as soon as the question of subject-matter competence comes up. In most countries, it is true, the request has to be lodged with the first instance court having general jurisdiction; in systems in which more than one first instance courts exist, there may be some split of competence among them according to type and value of subject matter[25]. However, in Italy and Portugal the respective competence is allocated to the court of appeals[26], in Spain even to the Supreme Court[27]. On the basis of the national reports one can only conjecture as to whether this wide discrepancy among the totality of the judicial fora from the one-member first instance court all the way up to the Supreme Court is mainly influenced by tradition rather than by the rarity and ensuing solemnity of recognizing or enforcing foreign judgments.

13. All systems under review try to adopt proceedings for recognition and enforcement that are as simple as possible. Some of them, like Greek law, adopt the special procedure of voluntary jurisdiction[28], while others like Belgium[29], Luxembourg[30] and Spain[31] adhere to regular adversary proceedings. In some systems, the public prosecutor may[32], or even must be made a party[33], while in Spain the request has to be served not only to the defendant but to the Ministry of Finance as well[34]. The general feeling is that the proceedings are not particularly complex. However complaints become loud in Luxembourg as to the length of time needed[35], and in the Netherlands as to the financial burden of barrister's fees calculated anew on the amount involved[36]. Some national reporters opt for the adoption of *ex parte* proceedings in the first place, according to the model of the Brussels Convention[37], which seems to be already the case in Ireland[38].

14. Some sharp divisions among the national systems become observable with regard to the extent to which an incidental recognition of a foreign judgment is available. To be sure, all systems allow the defendant, who has been successful abroad and is now sued on the same cause of action in a domestic forum, to

---

25 Cf. Koch p. 4; Morgan p. 9-10. Greece goes even further down in the ladder of judicial hierarchy, granting exclusive competence to the one-member rather than to the three-member court of first instance, which is the court of general jurisdiction; see Vrellis p. 5.

26 Vigoriti p. 7-8, 9; Vaz and Dias p. 30, 41, 51.

27 Cortés p. 9.

28 Vrellis p. 5-6.

29 Laenens Nos. 29-30.

30 Ravarani p. 8.

31 Cortés p. 10.

32 Greece: art. 905 I 2, 748 II, 750 of the Code of Civil Procedure.

33 Italy: Vigoriti p. 7.

34 Cortés p. 10, 11.

35 Ravarani p. 8: about a year, and an additional year if the request goes on appeal.

36 Verheul p. 3, 4.

37 Koch p. 7; Ravarani p. 8-9; Verheul p. 3. Cf. also Vaz and Dias p. 68 No. 2.

38 Morgan p. 11.

present the foreign judgment as a valid defense. In such a case the domestic court would incidentally check the requirements needed in order for the foreign judgment to be recognized as binding; only Italian law seems to suspend the main proceeding and to refer the issue to the competent court of appeal as soon as one of the parties asks for re-examination of the merits[39]. However the systems diverge as far as the incidental recognition of status judgments or judgments in family matters is concerned. While France[40], Belgium[41] and Luxembourg[42] seem to recognize incidentally even the judgments mentioned, the Federal Republic of Germany[43] and Greece[44] require a special procedure for this purpose. One may be surprised at the fact that obviously the same need for legal certainty has brought about diametrically opposite results.

15. A crucial problem in any domestic system of recognition and enforcement of foreign judgments are the criteria under which the foreign court's jurisdiction is evaluated. The issue is called indirect jurisdiction (compétence indirecte, Anerkennungszustaendigkeit), since it emerges only as a condition of recognition or enforcement by the judge of the second state. In the absence of international treaties, most Continental systems have approached the problem by explicitly projecting their own rules of jurisdiction to the foreign country in which the judgment originated; so, for example, the Federal Republic of Germany[45], Greece[46], or Italy[47]; some countries demand existence of jurisdiction according to the law of the state of origin as well, although this additional requirement does not seem to have become relevant in practice (Ireland[48]; Luxembourg[49]). But also common law is not different in substance. If it does not expressly extend its own jurisdictional concepts, it assumes in a self-explanatory way that only those foreign judgments could be relied upon which were rendered in a forum acceptable under common law notions; neither the judgment debtor's domicile nor the cause of action arising in the foreign country belong thereto[50]. Recently, some legislative or case law developments have begun to become discernible in the search for 'internationally accepted' fora, which would not in any way include plaintiff's domicile[51]. Yet, taken apart some international treaties and especially the Brussels Convention, the degree of agreement as to which fora are internationally acceptable is still extremely low.

---

39 Vigoriti p. 9.

40 Huet p. 4, with reference to the judgment of the Court of Cassation of March 3, 1930.

41 Laenens Nos. 13-14, with reference to the judgment of the Court of Cassation of March 29, 1973.

42 Ravarani p. 4, 9.

43 Koch p. 4, 5.

44 Vrellis p. 4-5 and 28 not 9, with reference to the judgment 569/1972 of the Supreme Court (**Areios Pagos**).

45 Koch p. 1.

46 Vrellis p. 4 and 26-27 note 4.

47 Vigoriti p. 3. Also Portugal: Vaz and Dias p. 42.

48 Morgan p. 3-5.

49 Ravarani p. 1 No. 2.

50 Stone (**supra**, n. 18) at 13.

51 In Belgium by virtue of article 570 (3) of the Code Judiciaire: Laenens No. 24; in the Netherlands by virtue of recent case law: Verheul p. 2 and notes 4-5.

16. Prorogation certainly figures among the widely accepted bases of jurisdiction. Nevertheless, the national reports deal only scantily therewith. The question has risen to eminent practical importance under articles 17 and 18 of the Brussels Convention, and has brought about some of the most interesting judgments of the Court of Justice of the European Communities. As regards the national reports, the remark may be made that English law is still more reserved vis-à-vis prorogation as compared to the Continental systems. Perhaps under the traditional common law disapproval of parties 'ousting' the courts of their jurisdiction[52], English law requires that the agreement be express and not implied, while on the other hand the party may enter an appearance - not amounting to submission - for the limited purpose of contesting the jurisdiction of the court[53].

17. In the area of indirect international jurisdiction as a condition for recognition and enforcement of foreign judgments a certain progress has been made recently through the wider acceptance of the notion of exclusive jurisdiction. The notion conveys the concept of limited connecting factors which are considered sufficient for the purpose of submitting by all means some clearly defined disputes to domestic jurisdiction and beyond which national courts are in principle open to admit other meaningful connecting factors leading to foreign fora. The notion was explicitly adopted by the Spanish law of 1985[54]. But probably the most interesting development happened here in French case law. The traditional position of French courts based on articles 14 and 15 of the Civil Code was that the French nationality as such of any party would establish exclusive jurisdiction of the French courts; therefore, absent a choice-of-forum clause, no foreign judgment rendered against a French party could in principle be recognized or enforced in France. Now the leading judgment of the Court of Cassation of February 6, 1985 seems to indicate that, absent any specific French rule of exclusive jurisdiction, the foreign court is deemed to have had indirect jurisdiction if the dispute was connected in a characteristic way to the foreign country[55].

18. A common and fundamental requirement for both recognition and enforcement of foreign judgments consists in the safeguard of the right of defense in the foreign court. The requirement, which has also constitutional underpinnings[56], becomes essentially relevant in foreign default judgments. In such cases, the question arises whether the defendant was notified of the proceedings properly and in time sufficient to prepare his defense. Both appropriateness and time of the service of process are evaluated in the first place according to the law of the state of origin. However, this first evaluation is usually subject to a discretionary review against basic principles of domestic law. Thus, in Italy a period of sixteen days for the filing of an appearance in an Austrian court was

52 See, for example, Vagts, Transnational Business Problems 179-181 (1986).

53 Stone (**supra**, n. 18) at 12.

54 Cortés p. 6-7.

55 Huet p. 8, 24, 26.

56 Cf. Cortés p. 8.

held to be sufficient[57]. Greek law seems to be rather liberal in this respect: neither the lack of financial means to support a journey abroad and the appointment of an attorney nor the growing of a foreign default judgment into res judicata without further service of the judgment itself nor the initial service of process *in a foreign language* in Greece for the purposes of foreign litigation were considered to have actually deprived the party of the right to be heard[58].

19. Formal prerequisites do not cause serious problems to the recognition or enforcement of foreign judgments. Of course, the authenticity of the foreign judgment must be established[59]. English law requires, in addition, an affidavit by the applicant[60]. And English as well as Irish law is oriented to foreign judgments *for a definite sum*[61]. The final character of the foreign judgment could also be regarded as a formal prerequisite but has been already indicated[62].

20. The idea of reciprocity, highly praised in the 5-4 *Hilton* v. *Guyot*[63] decision of the United States Supreme Court in the late 19th century, is now in an unmistakable decline. To be sure, reciprocity is still followed by common law jurisdictions, like the United Kingdom[64] and Ireland[65]. From the Continental countries only the Federal Republic of Germany[66] and Spain[67] adhere to reciprocity, the latter country surprisingly by reiteration of the principle in article 278 of the recent law of 1985. The rest of the systems under review have never adopted reciprocity, and Denmark abolished it through the 1976 amendment[68]. But even in the countries which have incorporated reciprocity into the conditions for recognition, the practical relevance of the issue seems to be limited. In most instances, the question is answered in the affirmative, while German law has inserted a series of exceptions to the rule.

21. The relation of recognition and enforcement to a *lis pendens* in a domestic forum or abroad presents many aspects. On the basis of the national reports, it can only be said that a domestic decree on provisional measures does not prevent the recognition of a foreign unchallengeable decision[69]. Further, a do-

57 Vigoriti p. 4 and note 4. The period of appearance may of course be extended by virtue of international treaties; for example, ninety days under the Greek-Lebanese Convention of April 5, 1975: Vrellis p. 44 note 150. On the other hand, domestic law may become relevant by way of exception or restriction: Vaz and Dias p. 43-45.

58 Vrellis p. 4 and 31 notes 30-33.

59 See, for example, Laenens No. 26. Cf. also Cortés p. 13; Vaz and Dias p. 36-37.

60 Stone p. 2 No. 6.

61 Stone p. 2 No. 4; Morgan p. 6.

62 **Supra**, para. 11 and n. 16.

63 159 U.S. 113 (1895).

64 Stone (**supra**, n. 18) at 4; see also Stone p. 2 No. 10.

65 Morgan p. 12 No. 10.

66 Koch p. 5.

67 Cortés p. 2, 11-12.

68 Schmidt p. 2.

69 See Vrellis p. 27 note 7.

mestic *lis pendens*, before res judicata ensues, will probably not interfere in most cases with recognition, even though Italian and Portuguese law espouse the opposite view[70]. On the other hand, an appeal pending abroad against the judgment under recognition will normally lead to staying the recognition or enforcement proceedings in a domestic court. However, the Queen's Bench Division decided in *General Textiles* v. *Sun and Sand Agencies* (1978) that the court will not exercise its discretion to set aside the registration or adjourn the application in favour of a party engaged in unmeritorious procedural maneuverings with a view to postponing the evil hour of payment[71].

22. In most systems, there is no time limitation as regards the application for recognition and/or enforcement of a foreign judgment. It can be inserted into the domestic legal order as long as it stands and remains enforceable in the state of origin. There exist nevertheless exceptions, induced probably by the idea that recognition or enforcement is a quasi-continuation of the original proceedings. Thus, under the 1933 English Act an application must be instituted within six years of the foreign judgment[72], while in Italy, under article 2946 of the Civil Code, this period extends to ten years from the date the foreign judgment became final in the country of origin[73].

23. The outstanding example of a system permitting re-examination of the merits, which stimulated the United States Supreme Court in *Hilton* v. *Guyot* to deny reciprocity[74], had been until 1964 French law. But the leading *Munzer* decision of the Court of Cassation of January 7, 1964 abolished this requirement[75]. Thereafter, only Italy and Belgium adhere to the so-called 'révision au fond'. Italian law grants to the court of appeals an exceptional authority to re-examine the merits in cases of default judgments or of evidence recognized as being false under article 395 of the Code of Civil Procedure[76]. And article 570 II pr. of the Belgian Code Judiciaire is construed - although in legal doctrine rather than in practice[77] - as to permit a new examination by the Belgian judge only if the foreign judge's way of dealing has destroyed the presumption of truth accorded to the foreign judgment[78]. What the other systems, while following the principle of non-review of the merits, understand as an eventual exception to the principle is the authority to either consider posterior facts, like subsequent reductions of the judgment debt[79], or to examine allegations of

70 Vigoriti p. 4; Vaz and Dias p. 42-43.

71 Stone (**supra**, n. 18) at 9.

72 Stone (**supra**, n. 18) at 6-7.

73 Vigoriti p. 7.

74 See **supra**, para. 20 and n. 62.

75 See Huet p. 6.

76 Vigoriti p. 8. A similar, document-based obstacle to recognition is erected in Portugal under article 771 (c) of the Code of Civil Procedure: Vaz and Dias p. 33-35, 51.

77 There is no opinion of the Court of Cassation as of now: Laenens No. 11 p. 4.

78 Laenens No. 12.

79 See Ravarani p. 6.

fraud or violations of public policy[80]. The last two points will be examined below[81].

24. The review of the foreign judgment for fraud is again a characteristic feature of common law. Both English[82] and Irish[83] law permit such a review, the former perhaps in a broader sense than the latter. The report for the United Kingdom indicates that extrinsic as well as intrinsic fraud may open a re-investigation of the merits, and adds that it will probably be necessary to refer to the Court of Justice of the European Communities to get a definite ruling that the traditional English review for fraud is contrary to the Brussels Convention[84]. Besides the common law world, only Italy admits fraud on the part of the parties as a ground for re-opening the merits under article 395 of the Code of Civil Procedure. At any rate, here as well as there, the cases in which fraud was actually proven and could support a judgment refusing recognition seem to have been rare.

25. A review on the merits can as well take the more restrained form of checking whether the law applied by the foreign court would have also been held applicable by virtue of the domestic conflict rules. Many systems have given up this additional requirement[85], most recently the Federal Republic of Germany since the reform of private international law which came into effect on September 1, 1986[86]. In other countries, the law chosen by the foreign court becomes relevant as a condition for recognition only within the sphere of voluntary jurisdiction[87]. The problem is mostly discussed in France[88], where case law insists on the identity of applicable law under both the domestic and the respective foreign system of conflicts. The theory supporting this requirement consists in preventing the French judge from implementing foreign rules of conflicts. Therefore, the requirement is satisfied as soon as the same law would have been applied by means of the French rule on *renvoi*, or the same solution would have been reached by virtue of the law applicable under the French conflict rules (*théorie de l'équivalence des solutions*)[89].

26. Public policy, a notion 'mysterious, relative and mutable over time'[90], constitutes a classic topic in the law of recognition and enforcement. There

---

80 Cf., for example, Cortés p. 5; Koch p. 3 No. 5.

81 Paras. 24 and 26.

82 Stone p. 2 No. 5.

83 Morgan p. 8.

84 Stone p. 5 No. 8.

85 Cf., for example, Verheul p. 1 and 9-10 note 1. Partially also Portugal: Vaz and Dias p. 47; but see infra n. 87.

86 Koch p. 2 No. 2.

87 So in Greece under article 780 (1) of the Code of Civil Procedure: Vrellis p. 5 and 29 notes 16, 17.

88 See Huet p. 9-10. Portugal adheres to a similar principle under article 1096 (g) of the Code of Civil Procedure, as far as the party defeated abroad is a Portuguese: Vaz and Dias p. 31-33, 47-50. Hereby connotations of public policy reappear.

89 The same limitation prevails equally in Luxembourg: Ravarani p. 2 No. 5.

90 Vigoriti p. 4.

seems to exist a wide concord among the systems as to (a) the more restrictive scope of international public policy as opposed to domestic public policy, which includes all domestic rules of *ius cogens*[91]; and (b) the division of public policy into a procedural and a substantive segment[92], whereby the former presents a broader scope but largely coincides with the right of defense[93]. Substantive public policy mainly used to protect domestic notions of divorce but in recent years, under the impact of the sweeping family law reform, even this area has become much more open-minded and less sensitive (Belgium[94], Greece[95], the Netherlands[96], Ireland[97], Spain[98]). Beyond these points of progressive and convergent restriction of international public policy, two recent developments seem to take slightly the opposite direction. On the one hand, the English Protection of Trading Interests Act 1980 enables money, under a theory of public policy, to be recovered back in England if awarded abroad within a scheme of multiple damages[99]. On the other hand, the judgment No 18 of February 2, 1982 of the Italian Constitutional Court considered the public policy defense to fulfill even a constitutional mandate and to consist of the entirety of the 'fundamental rules imposed by the Constitution and the laws shaping legal institutions in which the legal system in its perennial adaptation to the evolution of society is articulated'[100].

27. Most systems reserve a special treatment to foreign judgments rendered in family matters. It is difficult to locate a common denominator to the various special provisions. It may suffice here to refer to the discrepancies indicated above during the discussion on the availability of incidental recognition[101]. At any rate, some countries follow easier patterns in recognizing foreign judgments in family matters. Danish law belongs hereto, by broadening the bases for international jurisdiction, by limiting recourse to the public policy defense and by trusting recognition, in sequence to the 1931 Nordic Convention on marriage, adoption and guardianship, to administrative authorities[102]. The last feature is

---

91 Significant in this respect is the progressive restriction of the notion in Spain (Cortés p. 13-14) and the new wording of §328 I of the German Code of Civil Procedure (Koch p. 5-6). See also Laenens No. 16; Ravarani p. 11-12; Vaz and Dias p. 45-46; Vrellis p. 10 and 31 note 34. An analogous restriction of international public policy **with respect to recognition** as opposed to the same notion **with respect to application of foreign law** is expressed in France as the 'effet atténué de l'ordre public' (Huet p. 11).

92 See Huet p. 10-11.

93 Cf. Laenens Nos. 20, 23. See **supra**, para. 18.

94 Laenens Nos. 17, 20-22.

95 Vrellis p. 10-11.

96 Verheul p. 10 note 1.

97 Morgan p. 2, 12-14.

98 Cortés p. 14.

99 Stone p. 3 No. 12. Considerations of restraint of trade have equally influenced Dutch legislation (Verheul p. 2).

100 See Vigoriti p. 5-6.

101 **Supra**, para. 14 and n. 39-43.

102 Schmidt p. 8-12.

also espoused by German law[103]. An appeal against an administrative decision may of course be, but in practice very rarely is, lodged with a court of law[104].

28. It goes without saying that some judgments, e.g. declaratory judgments, are capable of recognition as res judicata but not of enforcement as well. This diversification, which lies in the nature of judicial remedies, is drawn further in English law; there, judgments awarding non-monetary relief, for example an order for specific performance of a contract, are only apt to be recognized[105]. But this distinction apart, the requirements for recognition and enforcement of a foreign judgment largely coincide[106]. This means that the legal systems in principle do not regard the res judicata effect of a foreign judgment as a minor intrusion into the domestic legal order as compared to an actual enforcement; therefore, the material conditions for the latter do not go beyond the ones required for the former. Since, however, recognition presupposes in general res judicata and enforcement enforceability (both times in the state of origin), there may arise some discrepancy to the extent that, under the foreign legal system, the judgment does not mature to res judicata and to enforceability precisely at the same time[107].

29. As regards the question whether a strict or liberal interpretation prevails in the systems under review, the national reports seem to support the idea that jurisdictional requirements are dealt with rather strictly[108], while the other conditions, including public policy[109], foreign procedural irregularities[110] and reciprocity[111], are more open to a liberal treatment. In Spain, under the 1978 Constitution, recognition of foreign judgments has equally become more flexible[112].

30. Understandably, the national reports contain only scanty information about statistical data. It seems that the vast majority of requests for recognition and/or enforcement are granted[113]. About 5% are declined in France[114], and the same is true in the Federal Republic of Germany with respect to family matters[115], while as far as judgments on pecuniary matters are concerned, the refusal percentage may amount to 10-15%[116]. For Greece, it is reported that the

103 Koch p. 4 No. 8b.

104 Cf. Koch p. 6 No. 13a: in less than 0,5% of all cases; Schmidt p. 10: never.

105 Stone p. 2 No. 4.

106 Cortés p. 4-5; Koch p. 3 No. 4; Laenens Nos. 11, 15; Morgan p. 7; Ravarani p. 4.

107 See, for some discussion, Koch p. 3 and notes 5, 6; Vrellis p. 5 and 28-29 note 13.

108 Cf. Huet p. 6-8; Stone p. 3 No. 11.

109 E.g. Ravarani p. 11; Stone p. 3 No. 11.

110 Stone p. 3 No. 11.

111 Koch p. 5 No. 11.

112 Cortés p. 13.

113 Ravarani p. 13 speaks even of the 'immense majority'.

114 Huet p. 11.

115 Koch p. 6 No. 13a: out of 3.000 cases a year!

116 Koch p. 6-7: out of about one hundred cases a year.

public policy defense is rejected in a percentage higher than 71%[117]. It should be nevertheless kept in mind that in some countries the whole number of enforcement cases is extremely low, e.g. five in Ireland during the period 1982-1985 as opposed to 301 cases in Belgium only in 1982[118].

31. Proposals for improvement on the existing law have been made by the national reporters on two levels, a substantive and a purely procedural one. On the former, the recommendations are mainly directed towards extending jurisdictional bases[119], enforcing provisionally enforceable judgments[120] and judgments for specific performance[121], and eliminating the reciprocity requirement[122]. On the purely procedural level, the general feeling in favour of initial *ex parte* proceedings has already been mentioned[123].

III BILATERAL AND MULTILATERAL CONVENTIONS ON RECOGNITION AND ENFORCEMENT OF FOREIGN JUDGMENTS

32. Number and density of bilateral conventions on recognition and enforcement of foreign judgments binding upon the member States of the European Communities vary greatly: from apparently none in the case of Ireland[124] to about forty in the case of France[125]. Those existing among the States bound by the Brussels Convention and in principle repealed thereby are enumerated in article 55 of the same. These conventions deal mainly with international jurisdiction, recognition and enforcement, sometimes also with arbitration and bankruptcy. In other instances, relevant provisions are inserted into broader conventions on judicial assistance or even, more generally, on friendship, commerce and navigation[126]. Some countries have concluded just one convention, as Luxembourg with Austria (1971)[127]. But even in countries bound by several bilateral conventions it may well be that only one such convention has reached practical relevance, for example Spain with regard to France (1969, 1974)[128], or Greece with regard to the Federal Republic of Germany (1961)[129].

33. Some recent bilateral conventions signed by member States of the European Communities are worth mentioning. An Anglo-Canadian Convention, signed after the United Kingdom acceded to the Brussels Convention, contains a clause

117 Vrellis p. 9.

118 For Ireland: Morgan p. 11; for Belgium: supplementary letter by Prof. Laenens of January 5, 1987.

119 Stone p. 3 No. 14; Vrellis p. 7.

120 Koch p. 7.

121 Morgan p. 4, 11-12.

122 Koch p. 7.

123 **Supra**, para. 13 and n. 36.

124 Morgan p. 15A-16.

125 Huet p. 17. Belgium has also concluded a high number of bilateral conventions (Laenens Nos. 32-34).

126 See Vrellis p. 18 and 37-38 notes 95-105.

127 Ravarani p. 15. See also **infra**, para. 38 and n. 152.

128 Cortés p. 16, 17.

129 Vrellis p. 22 and 46 note 165. See also **infra**, para. 38.

giving Canada the benefit of article 59 of the latter[130]. Greece has concluded a series of bilateral judicial assistance conventions with Eastern European or Middle East countries[131], while Belgium moves in a similar direction, although limited to maintenance obligations[132]. The Federal Republic of Germany ratified 1981 two bilateral conventions with Israel and Norway, and is about to ratify the 1983 Convention with Spain, as well as to sign a convention with Egypt[133].

34. The way by which a bilateral recognition and enforcement convention takes effect in the domestic legal order is not uniform in the systems under review. In most countries the normal parliamentary ratification is followed, which adds nothing to the conventional text but its transformation into national law. However, in the United Kingdom all bilateral conventions take effect in accordance with the detailed provisions of domestic enactments, namely the Administration of Justice Act 1920 and the Foreign Judgments (Reciprocal Enforcement) Act 1933. The same pattern has been put into operation as regards the Brussels Convention through the Civil Jurisdiction and Judgments Act 1982[134]. In a perhaps similar vein, the Federal Republic of Germany tends to add to the ratification of such conventions a sometimes lengthy domestic 'Ausfuehrungsgesetz'.

35. In the area of the requirements for the recognition or enforcement of foreign judgments, three lines of improvement in the domestic legal systems emerge out of the national reports. Most important is the establishment of rules on indirect international jurisdiction, so as to eliminate or reduce a major impediment to recognition and enforcement[135]. In the second place, some conventions enlarge the scope of judgments apt to be recognized or enforced, e.g. expressly including provisionally enforceable judgments[136] or decrees rendered in voluntary jurisdiction[137]. The third line of improvement consists in doing away with re-examination where it still existed under domestic law[138].

36. The procedural aspects of improvement result in making the mechanics of recognition and enforcement easier in many respects. First, there is a tendency to generalize the recognition of foreign judgments without any previous proceedings (so-called automatic recognition)[139]. Secondly, the judicial body competent to grant the exequatur is simpler, easier accessible and not subject to all usual methods of appeal[140]. Surprisingly, some conventions concluded by

130 Stone p. 3 sub II (1), 4 sub (5).

131 Vrellis p. 18.

132 Laenens No. 34.

133 Koch p. 10.

134 Stone p. 1, 3 sub II (1).

135 Cf., for example, Cortés p. 18-19; Koch p. 8 No. 2 b; Ravarani p. 15; Vigoriti p. 9-10; Vrellis p. 20, 23, 42 notes 137, 138.

136 Koch p. 8 No. 2 b.

137 Cortés p. 18 b.

138 Laenens No. 36; Vigoriti p. 10.

139 Huet p. 18 and 32 note 68; Laenens Nos. 36-37; Vigoriti p. 10; Vrellis p. 23 and 46 notes 166, 167.

140 Cortés p. 9; Huet p. 18; Koch p. 8 No. 2 a.

Greece provide even for the possibility of lodging the request for recognition and/or enforcement in a court of the state of origin[141]. Of course, international conventions become eminently important in countries in which a genuine exequatur can be granted only on the basis of such a convention, like the Netherlands[142]. On the other hand, it is reported for the United Kingdom that international conventions make little difference as compared to domestic law[143].

37. The national reports could identify only slight repercussions by the bilateral conventions on the construction or application of the domestic systems of recognition and enforcement[144]. Mainly in the Federal Republic of Germany, the recent amendment to § 328 of the Code of Civil Procedure seems to have been influenced by the conventions[145]. A similar trend is discernible in Greece, although with respect to the new law of arbitration included in the Code of Civil Procedure of 1968[146]. Interestingly, a recent Dutch decision recognized, outside of any convention, a Liechtenstein judgment 'since Liechtenstein has a legal system that does not differ essentially... from the legal systems of those countries with which the Netherlands has enforcement treaties'[147].

38. In most systems under review, the majority of recognition and enforcement cases have been dealt with under international conventions rather than under domestic law[148]. Greece and Spain make an exception to this principle, although upon varying amounts of statistical data. For Greece, in the period 1950-1986 out of 211 reported decisions dealing with recognition or enforcement of foreign judgments 16,6% were rendered under bilateral conventions, which means - except one case - under the Greek-German Convention of 1961[149]. For Spain, in the period 1983-1985 the corresponding total number of cases is five, all of them pertaining to divorce, and decided the four of them under domestic law while the fifth one under the Spanish-French Convention of 1969[150]. Interesting data come from the Federal Republic of Germany: against about 100 exequatur decisions under domestic law per year, more than 2,000 are rendered under (bi- and multilateral) international conventions. Since, however, about half of the conventions do not apply to family matters, the percentage of judgments in pecuniary matters enforced under the conventions rises up to more than 96% as against 3,11% under domestic law[151]. In the Netherlands, during the period 1970-1986, out of a selective series of 128 decisions on foreign judgments, 80 pertained to an international convention, mainly the Brussels Convention, and only 48 to domestic law; but here again, if one disregards the family law cases,

---

141 Vrellis p. 23 and 44 note 151, 47 note 170.

142 Verheul p. 1, 3, 5. For the somehow analogous situation in Denmark see **supra**, para. 9.

143 Stone p. 3 **sub** II (2).

144 Cf. Stone p. 3 **sub** II (4).

145 Koch p. 9 No. 4.

146 See Vrellis p. 47 note 172 a.

147 Verheul p. 5.

148 Cf. Vigoriti p. 2.

149 Vrellis p. 22.

150 Cortés p. 20.

151 Koch p. 6 No. 13 b, 9 No. 3.

the percentage of decisions rendered under domestic law comes down to less than 20%[152]. From Luxembourg it is reported that against 150-200 decisions rendered per year under the Brussels Convention, less than six pertain to the Luxembourg-Austrian Convention and only up to thirty to domestic law[153]. Thus, the quantitative preponderance of international conventions over domestic law becomes impressive in the countries in which the Brussels Convention is in force.

39. Besides the Brussels Convention, most of the countries under review are also parties to many other multilateral conventions pertaining to specific areas and including provisions on recognition and enforcement. There is no point in enumerating them or the states which have signed or ratified them[154]. However, many of the Hague conventions, especially on maintenance, the 1952 Brussels Convention on the arrest of seagoing ships, the 1980 Luxembourg Convention on guardianship of children, the international transportation conventions etc. cover most of the relevant countries, even though the extent of practical application does not appear to be large. A special case is the 1977 Nordic Convention on the recognition and enforcement of judgments, which replaced the older one of 1932 and has been in force since January 1, 1978 between Denmark, Finland, Norway and Sweden, whereas Iceland is still bound by the old convention[155]. Due to the high degree of legal similarity and cooperation among the Scandinavian countries, the Nordic Convention does not include positive provisions on international jurisdiction but only eliminates some exorbitant fora. It applies regardless of nationality or domicile of the parties and allows the judgment creditor to go directly to the enforcement authority of the state of execution, without requiring an exequatur. The convention has been implemented through almost uniform domestic statutes of all four member States.

40. In spite of the improvements which have been brought about by many international conventions[156], their growing age in addition to the progressive amendments of domestic legal systems has made the latter, in some instances, more liberal than the respective international conventions. Therefore, in almost all systems, the question arises whether the requesting party may disregard the convention and opt instead for the application of domestic law. The systems under review are deeply split over this question. Some of them adhere to a strict exclusivity of the convention, which is meant to do away with domestic law (Luxembourg[157], Belgium[158], United Kingdom[159]). English law would even

---

152 Verheul p. 4, 6.

153 Ravarani p. 16 No. 3, 22.

154 Cf. Cortés p. 20-21; Huet p. 17 and 31 note 59; Koch p. 10; Laenens No. 35; Morgan p. 6, 15A-16; Ravarani p. 17; Schmidt p. 7-8, 9 in f.; Stone p. 4 No. 6; id. (*supra*, n. 18) at 28; Verheul p. 3; Vigoriti p. 9 and note 16; Vrellis p. 18.

155 See Schmidt p. 4-5.

156 See **supra**, paras. 35, 36.

157 Ravarani p. 18.

158 Laenens Nos. 38-39, with reference to the judgments of the Court of Cassation of May 27, 1971 and January 27, 1977.

159 Stone p. 4 No. 7.

penalize with the burden of costs an applicant who proceeds at common law to enforce a judgment falling within the 1920 Act. In France, the issue is under hot debate at least since *Bartin,* with the national reporter favoring rather the exclusive character of the conventions unless they offer an option[160]. On the other hand, the Federal Republic of Germany[161], Greece[162], Italy[163] and the Netherlands[164] allow the requesting party to meet the requirements either of the applicable international convention or of domestic law, whichever seems in the particular case to be more favorable. Under a theory that 'the treaties prescribe a minimum, not a maximum'[165], the countries just mentioned follow the 'rule of the maximum efficiency'[166]. However, they require the party to choose one or the other system, without allowing a selective mixture of several rules[167].

IV GENERAL ASPECTS OF THE BRUSSELS CONVENTION ON RECOGNITION AND ENFORCEMENT OF FOREIGN JUDGMENTS

41. By contrast to all other bilateral and multilateral conventions, the Brussels Convention on Jurisdiction and the Enforcement of Judgments in Civil and Commercial Matters of September 27, 1968 (in force since February 1, 1972), as amended in 1978 and 1982, presents two major different features. First, it contains a detailed set of rules on *direct* international jurisdiction. By this means, uniform and precise bases of original jurisdiction are established throughout the member States, and the judge called upon to recognize or enforce a foreign judgment under the Convention is in principle not allowed to investigate any more the jurisdiction of the court of origin (art. 28, especially 3). Thus, a major impediment to recognition and enforcement is removed from the very beginning[168]. How practically useful is the determination of jurisdictional issues under uniform rules by the court of origin, is exemplified by the fact that over two thirds of the total number of judgments by the Court of Justice under the Brussels Convention pertain to direct jurisdiction as compared to only one third concerning recognition and enforcement[169]. The second important element of the Brussels Convention consists in the safeguard of its uniform interpretation by the Court of Justice of the European Communities, which became effective on September 1, 1975. The rulings of the Court are binding on the national courts in the case at bar. The Convention is thus put under the interpretive authority of a supranational court and within the

---

160 Huet p. 22-26, against Francescakis, Rev.crit.dr.int.pr. 1985. 270.

161 Koch p. 11.

162 Vrellis p. 17.

163 Vigoriti p. 10-11.

164 Verheul p. 5.

165 **Id.**

166 Koch p. 11: 'Günstigkeitsprinzip' or 'Regel der maximalen Wirksamkeit'.

167 Vrellis p. 17 and 46 note 165, with reference to Court of Appeals Athens 7143/1977.

168 For a comparison to domestic systems see **supra**, para. 15. Cf. in particular Vaz and Dias p. 10-16, 54-56.

169 See Koch p. 12.

framework of an organized economic community under article 220 of the Treaty of Rome. This function of the Convention may explain the exclusive character of its application, as declared in the *De Wolf* v. *Cox* case by the Court of Justice[170] against the rule of the maximum efficiency[171].

42. In accordance with the institutional position of the Court of Justice, the national courts of the member States follow now its case law conscientiously and loyally[172], even though the interpretive rulings do not have, in legal terms, an absolute but only a relative binding force, that is limited to the case at bar[173]. From the Federal Republic of Germany it is reported that no German court has up to now expressly deviated from the case law of the Court of Justice[174]. The initial nationalistic interpretation of the Convention by the Italian Court of Cassation has been overcome[175], and the resistance of some tribunals in Antwerpen as regards the choice-of-forum clause appears by now a past episode[176]. Across the board, the references to the case law of the Court of Justice in the opinions of the national courts are growing[177]. Two Greek appellate courts have already relied on the Brussels Convention, even though the Convention has not yet taken effect in that country[178].

43. The extent to which national courts refer under the Brussels Convention preliminary questions to the Court of Justice varies greatly. The national reports indicate six references from Belgium[179], more than twenty from the Federal Republic of Germany, whereby more than 50% originated with the *Bundesgerichtshof*[180], two from Italy[181], nine from Luxembourg[182], and eight from the Netherlands[183]. Of course, these figures pertain to the whole of the Convention of Brussels and not only to its Title III on recognition and enforcement[184].

44. The national reactions (on the level of legislation, doctrine and judicial opinions) to the Brussels Convention are basically positive. Luxembourg[185] and

170 See Verheul p. 5 and 11 note 12.

171 See **supra**, para. 40 and n. 165.

172 Ravarani p. 19 **sub** III 1; Stone p. 4 **sub** III 1; Verheul p. 5, in spite of criticism.

173 Koch p. 12 and notes 38, 39.

174 Koch p. 12 No. 1.

175 Vigoriti p. 11 and note 20.

176 Laenens Nos. 40-44, especially 41.

177 See Koch p. 12 No. 2; Laenens No. 44; Vigoriti p. 11.

178 See Vrellis p. 38 note 110.

179 Laenens No. 44 in combination with his supplementary letter of January 5, 1987.

180 Koch p. 12/13.

181 Vigoriti note 20 at p. 5.

182 Ravarani p. 20 No. 3.

183 Verheul p. 5.

184 See, for the corresponding percentage, **supra**, para. 41 and n. 168.

185 Ravarani p. 21. The Luxembourg Court of Appeals allows even so the enforcement of foreign judgments rendered in violation of art. I of the additional 1968 Protocol.

already Spain[186] have partially amended their domestic legislation along the lines of the Convention, the former with respect to the procedure of enforcement, the latter with respect to direct international jurisdiction. The Italian reaction praises the disconnection, under article 28 III[187], of recognition and enforcement from the jurisdiction of the court of origin as well as the general availability of incidental recognition[188]. The German reaction approves of the uniform jurisdictional bases and of the simpler exequatur proceedings, but raises some criticism of several provisions[189]; a similar criticism comes also from the Netherlands[190]. The most serious complaints address a question which lies actually outside the scope of this report, and only indirectly influences recognition and enforcement of foreign judgments, namely the survival, under articles 3 and 4 of the Convention, of the exorbitant bases of jurisdiction against defendants domiciled outside the Communities. According to the British report, this discrimination 'is scandalous and invites retaliation'[191], whereas American indignation is still stronger[192]. Some remarks on this point will be made in the last part of this general report.

45. The frequency of application of the Brussels Convention as opposed to any other legal sources (other international conventions or purely domestic sources) has been already indicated above when discussing the portions of recognition and enforcement granted under international conventions and under domestic law[193]. In addition, it is reported from the Federal Republic of Germany[194] that in the field of direct international jurisdiction well over 50% of the cases with a foreign connection are decided under the Brussels Convention. By contrast, this rate may come below 50% in the field of enforcement, since non-Community fora may be for various reasons attractive and chosen, although no meaningful enforcement could ever take place there. In such cases, the resulting judgment will have to get enforced in the Federal Republic under rules other than the Brussels Convention.

V SPECIFIC ISSUES OF THE BRUSSELS CONVENTION ON RECOGNITION AND ENFORCEMENT OF FOREIGN JUDGMENTS

46. The Brussels Convention deals with recognition and enforcement in titles III

---

186 Cortés p. 24-25. For Ireland cf. Morgan p. 16.

187 See **supra**, para. 41.

188 Vigoriti p. 16, 11-12.

189 Koch p. 13.

190 Verheul p. 5 and note 14.

191 Stone p. 4 **sub** III (4).

192 See, for instance, A.T. Von Mehren, Recognition and enforcement of foreign judgments - General theory and the role of jurisdictional requirements, 167 Recueil des Cours 9, at 100, 101 (1980 II); 'Shock becomes outrage'; 'the single most regressive step that has occurred in international recognition and enforcement practice in this century'.

193 **Supra**, para. 38.

194 Koch p. 13a.

and IV (art. 25-49 and 50-51). As mentioned before[195], the purpose of this general report is not to discuss in detail the relevant provisions of the Convention, nor even to present the case law developments brought about by the fifty or so interpretive rulings of the Court of Justice[196]. Instead, this part will examine some specific issues of recognition and enforcement under the Brussels Convention, as viewed by the national courts and pointed out in the national reports. Of course, the discussion will more or less be limited to the six original member States, in which only the Convention had been in force up to October 31, 1986. But even there, some questions put by the general reporter[197] did not seem to be interesting enough, so they have to be left out of this report.

47. Under article 25 of the Convention 'judgment' means any judgment given by a court or tribunal of a contracting State, whatever the judgment may be called, including a decree, order, decision or writ of execution, as well as the determination of costs or expenses by an officer of the court'. In accordance with this broad definition, national courts have considered that provisionally enforceable judgments[198], summary judgments upon adversary proceedings[199], or voluntary jurisdiction decrees[200] met the requirement. Even the determination of counsel's fees by a French *bâtonnier*[201] or a German *Rechtspfleger*[202] as well as the assessment of legal expenses involved in a judgment which was pronounced on a matter excluded by article 1 of the Convention[203], may equally be recognized and enforced. The United Kingdom would by now enforce a foreign personal judgment awarding non-monetary relief[204]. And Denmark has taken care, by inserting article Va to the 1968 Protocol, of getting maintenance orders granted by a Danish administrative authority enforced abroad[205].

48. Article 26 of the Convention, besides allowing the incidental recognition of a foreign judgment, provides for the recognition of the same as a principal issue as well. One is reminded here of the French *action en opposabilité*[206]. However, all national reports[207] including the French one[208], declare that almost no use has been made of this 'principal' recognition. According to the

---

195 Para. 3.

196 This has been done in the official report by Evrigenis and Kerameus (**supra**, n. 1).

197 See **supra**, para. 6.

198 Koch p. 14 with note 64; Laenens No. 46; Vigoriti p. 12 and note 13.

199 Koch p. 14 and notes 61-63; Verheul p. 6.

200 Laenens No. 46.

201 Laenens No. 46.

202 Verheul p. 6.

203 Vigoriti note 23.

204 Stone (**supra**, n. 18) at 26, also 24 **sub** (b) (i). The conclusiveness of a foreign judgment is not any more dependent upon the condition that the judgment was unsatisfied abroad; **id.** at 25 **sub** (ii).

205 Schmidt p. 6-7.

206 Huet p. 5.

207 Koch p. 15; Laenens No. 48; Ravarani p. 23-24; Verheul p. 6.

208 Huet p. 19 with note 70.

British report[209], tradition and costs are in favour of incidental recognition, *i.e.* by way of defense.

49. The public policy defense, provided for in article 27 (1), is distinguished, under the Brussels Convention as well as under domestic law[210], in a substantive and a procedural segment[211]. Under both aspects, public policy is understood very restrictively, so that in most countries, as far as substantive public policy is concerned, hardly any application has ever been identified.[212]. Doctrinal contemplation would locate a possible violation of public policy in the field of economic law, as in the Federal Republic of Germany[213] and in the Netherlands[214], while in the United Kingdom obtaining the judgment by fraud or discovering new evidence could become relevant issues[215].

50. Under article 27(2) a default judgment shall not be recognized, 'if the defendant was not duly served with the document which instituted the proceedings or with an equivalent document in sufficient time to enable him to arrange for his defence'. The first check on regularity of service is submitted to the law of the state in which the service of process has taken place[216]. However, under the guidance of the Court of Justice in the cases *Klomps* v. *Michel* (1981), *Pendy Plastic Products* v. *Pluspunkt* 1982) and *Debaecker* (1984), the sufficiency of time for the purposes of defense has also to be evaluated by the enforcing court[217]. While the Italian report approves of this subsequent evaluation as a method of filling a gap in the Convention[218], the German one distrusts the recess of objective criteria in favour of particular considerations[219].

51. Two further impediments, under articles 27 and 34 (2), to recognition and enforcement have not, as by now, risen to practical relevance. If the judgment debtor presents[220] an opposite domestic judgment for his defense, the irreconcilable character of the two judgments would probably mean that the results of both are in conflict with each other, if only in the evaluation of a preliminary relationship[221]. On the other hand, the reviewability of the choice of law under

---

209 Stone p. 4 **sub** IV (2).

210 See **supra**, para. 26 at note 91.

211 Huet p. 21-22.

212 Huet p. 22 and 33 note 84; Koch p. 16-17; Laenens No. 51; Vigoriti p. 13 and note 26.

213 Koch p. 16 **sub** c.

214 Verheul p. 6.

215 Stone (**supra**, no. 18) at 21-22.

216 See Koch p. 17; Verheul p. 6; Vigoriti p. 14 at note 28.

217 Koch p. 18 **sub** b; Verheul p. 26/27, especially Vigoriti p. 13-14: art. 27 (2) 'assumes a central role with respect to recognition and enforcement' and is the only norm 'which allows the Italian judge some control over the insertion into the Italian legal system of foreign judgments'. Cf. also Stone (**supra**, n. 18) at 18. Doubtful about this double-checking Laenens No. 52.

218 Vigoriti p. 14-15.

219 Koch p. 17-18 and note 87.

220 Cf. Verheul p. 7.

221 See Koch p. 18-19. Cf. Stone (**supra**, n. 18) at 26.

the close conditions of article 27 (4), including the theory of equivalent results[222], gives mandatory form to a requirement which used to be approached in English law under the head of public policy[223]. However, article 27 (4) has in most countries never been applied[224]. Only one case is reported from the Netherlands, where the 'injure grave' supporting a French divorce between Dutch spouses was found by the Dutch courts not to be equivalent to 'permanent breakdown' required by Dutch Law[225].

52. As it was said before[226], one of the main features of the Brussels Convention is to limit the examination of jurisdictional issues to the court of origin and then to relieve, in principle, recognition and enforcement from jurisdictional impediments. The exceptions to this principle accepted by article 28 (1) refer mainly to matters for which the Convention reserves more or less exclusive jurisdictional bases, that is insurance and consumer matters as well as the exclusive jurisdiction properly speaking (article 16). Subject to these exceptions, 'the jurisdiction of the court of the State in which the judgment was given may not be reviewed' (article 28 (3)). This objective of the Convention has been indeed carried out, if some decisions of inferior French courts are disregarded[227]. Even a jurisdictional violation of article I of the 1968 Protocol is usually not reviewed[228]. However, as regards the reviewability of exclusive jurisdictions, especially in insurance matters, several German voices seek to grant to the weaker party only the right to plead lack of jurisdiction[229].

53. Under articles 30 and 38, the proceedings of both recognition and enforcement may at the discretion of the court be stayed if an ordinary appeal against the judgment has been lodged in the state of origin. Therefore, finality of the judgment is, strictly speaking, not any more required[230]. In the leading case of *Industrial Diamond Supplies* v. *Riva* the Court of Justice brought up a really autonomous notion of the 'ordinary appeal': any appeal which is such that it may result in the annulment or the amendment of the judgment under appeal, and the lodging of which is bound to a period which is laid down by law and which is linked to the judgment itself. Under this definition, cassation which traditionally is not considered in the Romanic legal systems (France, Belgium, Luxembourg, Italy, Greece) an ordinary method of appeal[231] has to qualify as an ordinary appeal under the Convention[232].

---

222 See **supra**, para. 25 with notes 87-88.

223 Stone p. 5 No. 6.

224 Huet p. 21; Koch p. 19 No. 6; Ravarani p. 26 No. 6.

225 Verheul p. 7. For a somewhat analogous Portuguese case decided by the Court of Appeals of Coimbra see Vaz and Dias p. 32-33.

226 Para. 41.

227 See Huet note 73.

228 See **supra**, n. 184. This solution is approved of by Laenens No. 53. Ravarani p. 26 No. 7 hints at a further limitation with respect to art. 7-16.

229 See Koch p. 19-20 and note 94, with doctrinal references against BGHZ 74, 248.

230 Stone (**supra**, n. 18) at 9.

231 Cf. for example, Ravarani p. 27 No. 9.

232 Koch p. 20-21 and note 99; Laenens No. 55.

54. To counterbalance the *ex parte* enforcement proceedings in the initial phase, the Convention provides in articles 36 to 41 for a system of appeals going in most countries up to the respective supreme court. Of special interest is the first attack against the decision authorizing or refusing enforcement. This first attack is not lodged in all countries with the same court in both cases of authorization and refusal. What is more, if enforcement is authorized, an appeal is lodged under article 37 in some countries with the first instance court, like a quasi-*tierce opposition*, while in others to the court of appeals, like a regular appeal[233]. At any rate, an appeal 'cannot regard a re-examination of the merits, but only the review of the existence of the prerequisites for the granting of recognition' or enforcement[234]. Italian courts tend to disconnect the protective measures of article 39 (2) from the requirements of national law[235], while the German report expresses some reservation about the amount of security upon which enforcement may be made conditional under article 38 (3)[236]. As regards frequency, the number of appeals actually lodged varies from a very low- almost always unsuccessful at that - in Luxembourg[237] to a not insignificant in the Federal Republic of Germany[238].

55. The ruling of the Court of Justice in *De Wolf* v. *Cox* about the exclusivity of recognition and enforcement under the Brussels Convention as opposed to domestic law, has been followed by national courts, yet not without dissatisfaction and a certain reaction. The Dutch report finds the reasons of the ruling 'not quite convincing'[239]. The German report still adheres to the rule of the maximum efficiency[240]. The Italian Court of Cassation recently required that the enforcement proceedings under the Convention be of an adversarial nature in order to produce an exclusive effect[241]. And Luxembourg would apply domestic law as soon as the application for enforcement includes as well some claims falling outside the scope of the Convention[242].

56. As regards the enforceability of foreign authentic instruments and court settlements under articles 50 and 51 of the Convention, the general feeling is one of unreserved approval[243]. Here the Convention has been able to bring about a simple and progressive unification with respect to existing domestic laws. Some systems, like English law[244], did not previously have a concept of an authentic instrument, while others did not provide for the enforcement of

233 Cf. Laenens Nos. 64-65.

234 In the words of the Italian Court of Cassation (June 25, 1986), reproduced by Vigoriti p. 16/17 and note 36.

235 See Vigoriti p. 17.

236 Koch p. 22.

237 Ravarani p. 29 No. 12.

238 Koch p. 22.

239 Verheul p. 5. See, however, Stone p. 5 No. 13.

240 Koch p. 22 No. 13. See also **supra**, paras. 40, 41 in f.

241 See Vigoriti note 37.

242 Ravarani p. 29-30.

243 Cf. Ravarani p. 30 No. 14.

244 Stone p. 6 No. 14.

foreign authentic instruments and court settlements[245], or did so only by virtue of an international convention[246].

57. The 'General provisions' of articles 52 and 53 as to the law applicable to the domicile of a party and to the seat of a company or other legal person are not generally considered to have produced any substantial change or improvement[247]. Most critical is German doctrine which detects the failure of the drafters to establish a common notion of domicile and seat, and deplores the resort to a complicated conflicts mechanism[248].

VI RECOGNITION AND ENFORCEMENT OF FOREIGN ARBITRAL AWARDS

58. The whole and increasingly expanding area of recognition and enforcement of foreign arbitral awards deserves, and has been in many places granted, a full scale treatment. It is not the purpose of the general report to reiterate such an interesting and complicated discussion, but rather to indicate striking similarities and differences as compared to foreign judgments[249]. Thus, the following developments are only meant as a supplement to the main subject of the report, and they are equally based on information and thoughts contained in the national reports[250]. Most of the latter are governed by the assumption, or reach the conclusion, that the recognition of awards is more liberal as compared to judgments, because awards have a purely contractual basis and are not pronounced in the name of any state authority[251].

59. On the question of the criterion distinguishing foreign from domestic awards, *i.e.* attributing awards to a particular legal order, the national systems under review are almost equally split. Belgium[252], France[253], Italy[254], Luxembourg[255] and the Netherlands[256] look to the place where the award was rendered, while Denmark[257], the Federal Republic of Germany[258], Greece[259],

245 For German law Koch p. 23 No. 14.

246 For Belgian law Laenens No. 66; cf. also No. 56 in f.

247 See Stone p. 6 No. 15.

248 Koch p. 23 and notes 110-112.

249 Cf., for example, Cortés p. 26-27; Vaz and Dias p. 59.

250 See **supra**, para. 5.

251 Characteristically Huet p. 2 and note 5, p. 11 in f.

252 Laenens No. 68.

253 Huet note 4.

254 Vigoriti p. 18 and note 43.

255 Ravarani p. 33 No. 1.

256 Verheul p. 8.

257 Schmidt p. 14, stressing that 'among the contacts a special weight shall be placed on the law which governs the arbitral procedure (the **lex arbitri**)'.

258 Koch p. 25 and notes 123-125, with reference to BGHZ 21, 365.

259 Vrellis p. 13 and 34-35 notes 65-68.

Ireland[260], Spain[261] and the United Kingdom[262] prefer as a connecting factor, more or less, the law which governed arbitral procedure. Nevertheless, under international conventions, the place where the award was rendered becomes primarily relevant[263]. Most interesting is, in this respect, the new French law of arbitration which proceeds actually to a trichotomy of awards: (i) awards rendered abroad, which are subject to exequatur proceedings but not to annulment in France; (ii) awards rendered in France which, by contrast, are subject to annulment but not to exequatur proceedings in France; (iii) awards rendered in France *but in matters of international arbitration*[264], which are subject both to annulment and exequatur proceedings in France[265]. Under present French law, the place of rendition remains the principal criterion followed, however by the subject matter of arbitration if the award was rendered in France.

60. The validity of the arbitration agreement and the arbitrability of the dispute are the elements most close to the jurisdictional requirements as regards foreign judgments. Both of them benefit from a high degree of consensus in the legal systems under review. The validity of the arbitration agreement is evaluated according to the private international law of the forum of recognition or enforcement, and in most cases governed by the proper law of the contract[266]. The arbitrability of the dispute is usually governed by the *lex fori*[267], which thereby limits towards all directions the extent to which parties are allowed to repulse the jurisdiction of the courts. German law seems to be more liberal, by not considering arbitrability as a special requirement for recognition but by having recourse to the general notion of public policy[268].

61. The right of defense to be granted to the parties as a requirement for recognition and enforcement of the ensuing award is not substantially different to the one examined already with respect to judgments[269]. Here again, the period conceded for the preparation of defense is not prescribed in precise terms of time but rather depends on the particular situation[270]. Quite a number of systems insist on the fully adversarial character of arbitral proceedings, including the disclosure to the parties of any element of arbitrator's personal

---

260 Morgan p. 17 **sub** (a).

261 Cortés p. 27-28.

262 Stone p. 6 **sub** V (1), for the purpose of the common law.

263 Cf. Morgan p. 17-18; Stone p. 6 **sub** V (1); Vrellis p. 24 and 47 note 174.

264 Under the new article 1492 of the French Code of Civil Procedure, arbitration is qualified as international as soon as it involves 'interests of international commerce'.

265 Huet p. 12, 14, 30 note 46.

266 Cf. Huet p. 13; Koch p. 26 No. 2a; Morgan p. 19; Stone p. 6 **sub** V (2); Vrellis p. 14.

267 See Laenens No. 72 at p. 25, No. 76, with reference to the judgment of the Court of Cassation of June 28, 1979. Schmidt p. 14; Stone p. 6 **sub** V (2); Vigoriti p. 18; Vrellis p. 14 and 34 note 74. Cf. also Cortés p. 28.

268 Koch p. 26 with note 130.

269 See **supra**, para. 18.

270 See Vigoriti p. 19 and note 49, with reference to the judgment of the Court of Cassation of October 7, 1980.

knowledge[271]. On the other hand, no distinction is made in most countries between a domestic and a foreign defendant with respect to the requirement of a full and fair trial[272]. Greek law goes even as far as to recognize a foreign award with no actual participation of the parties or their counsel but with the party-appointed arbitrators taking up counsel's function[273].

62. Public policy as an impediment to recognition and enforcement of foreign awards plays a minimal role[274], perhaps still more limited in comparison to foreign judgments[275]. Recent amendments to both French[276] and German[277] law require that the violation of the forum's international public policy be *manifest*. It is further acknowledged that only the operational part of the award, and not its reasons are to be reviewed against public policy standards[278]. Therefore, even the lack of reasons is not considered to constitute a violation of public policy[279].

63. A number of national reports show that, quite apart from the implementation of the New York Convention, recent domestic law developments have improved the status of foreign arbitral awards. In Denmark, the Arbitration Act of May 24, 1972 authorized the Minister of Justice to lay down rules as to the conditions for the recognition and enforcement of foreign arbitral awards, which was promptly done through order No 117 of March 7, 1973[280]. In France, the decree of May 12, 1981 has widely strengthened the effect of awards rendered in matters of international arbitration; these awards are subject under article 1504 of the Code of Civil Procedure to an action for annulment, but all other methods of appeal have been eliminated[281], and one has to keep in mind that at any rate we are in face of awards rendered, after all, within France[282]. In Luxembourg, the decree of December 8, 1981 enumerates and limits the grounds for annulment of a foreign award[283]. The Federal Republic of Germany has since September 1, 1986 reduced the ambit of article 1044 II (2) of the Code of Civil Procedure[284] and has also simplified the arbitral procedure[285]. The Netherlands has by virtue of article 1076, introduced to the Code of Civil Procedure on December 1, 1986, provided for a general exequatur proceeding as

---

271 Ravarani p. 35 No. 3. Especially Huet p. 13 and 30 note 43; Supreme Court of Greece 1509/1982.

272 Koch p. 27 No. 3; Morgan p. 25 No. 3; Stone p. 6 **sub** V (3).

273 Vrellis p. 15-16 and 36 note 85, with reference to the judgment of the full bench of the Supreme Court 1572/1981.

274 Stone p. 7 No. 4.

275 Cortés p. 30; Koch p. 27 and note 134, with reference to BGH NJW 1986, 3027.

276 Huet p. 15.

277 Koch p. 27 No. 4a in combination with p. 6.

278 Vigoriti p. 20.

279 Vrellis p. 16 and 36-37 note 89. For Belgium see Laenens Nos. 79, 80.

280 Schmidt p. 13.

281 Huet p. 12-16, especially at 16.

282 See **supra**, para. 59 (iii).

283 Ravarani p. 36 No. 5.

284 Koch (**supra**, n. 276).

285 Koch p. 28 No. 5.

regards foreign awards, whereas such a proceeding may take place with respect to judgments only by virtue of an international convention[286]. In Spain, the 1953 Arbitration Act has been already overstepped in practice, and in Portugal the relevant provisions of the Code of Civil Procedure were amended in 1984 and 1986[287]. In Greece, article 903 of the Code of Civil Procedure provides even for incidental recognition of foreign arbitral awards[288].

64. The proceedings for recognition or enforcement of foreign awards are in many countries similar to those related to foreign judgments[289]. Many systems (Belgium[290], France[291], Greece[292]) do not provide for a mandatory summoning of the award debtor, while in most instances the application is addressed to a one-member court of first instance[293]. However, in Italy the subject-matter competence belongs to the court of appeals[294], and in Spain to the Supreme Court[295].

65. Bilateral conventions have had a rather limited impact on recognition and enforcement of foreign awards[296]. After all, reference is often made to the existing multilateral conventions, and mostly to the New York Convention[297]. Even the European Convention on International Commercial Arbitration of April 21, 1961 does not seem to have been applied very often. The German report finds that the European Convention is specially relevant to the East-West Trade[298]. For the rest, as advantages of this convention are considered the elimination of the form in writing for the arbitration agreement[299] as well as the limitation of the grounds for refusal of recognition in connection with the setting aside of the award abroad[300].

66. By contrast, both the impact and the degree of frequent application of the New York Convention are quite considerable. In common law[301] as well as in civil law jurisdictions[302], the Convention is regarded as a significant improve-

286 Verheul p. 1. See also supra, para. 8.

287 Cortés p. 31; Vaz and Dias p. 61.

288 Vrellis p. 13 and 35 note 69.

289 See Vigoriti p. 18, 20; Vrellis p. 13, 24 with note 173.

290 Laenens No. 71.

291 Huet p. 14.

292 Vrellis p. 13 in combination with 5 and 29 note 18.

293 Cf., for instance, Laenens No. 69; Verheul p. 8; Vrellis p. 5, 13 and 35 note 71.

294 Vigoriti p. 19 and note 47.

295 Cortés p. 27.

296 Cf. Stone p. 7 No. 6.

297 See Koch p. 28 No. 6; Vrellis p. 24 and 47-48 notes 175-177, with reference to the judgment 759/1980 of the Supreme Court.

298 Koch p. 29 with note 137.

299 Koch p. 29 with note 139.

300 Koch p. 28; Laenens No. 80; Vigoriti p. 21.

301 Morgan p. 23; Stone p. 7 No. 9.

302 Cortés p. 31-33; Koch p. 30. However, Portugal has not yet adhered to the New York Convention: Vaz and Dias p. 61, 67, 69.

ment, especially with respect to the inversion of the burden of proof[303]. Figures related to enforcement under the New York Convention vary of course from country to country. From Spain only one case is reported for the period 1983-1985[304], while in the Federal Republic of Germany the percentage amounts to about 80%[305], and the Italian report speaks of the Convention as the almost exclusive source in practice for recognition and enforcement of foreign awards[306]. In Greece, in the period 1950-1986 out of 44 reported cases dealing with recognition or enforcement of foreign awards, 21 were decided under domestic law, 17 under the New York Convention, 5 under the older 1927 Geneva Convention, and 1 under the bilateral Greek-U.S. Convention[307].

VII CONCLUSIONS

67. At the end of this general report based on national reports of such value and richness, one might inquire whether any general trends emerge. I would try to identify three of them, and reserve the rest for full discussion in Utrecht.

68. Both the progressive reduction of the public policy defense and its concentration on the procedural rather than on the substantive side should be hailed. An unexpected feeling of satisfaction comes out of the national assessments about the surprisingly declining numbers of cases in which violation of public policy was successfully pleaded. On the other hand, locating public policy considerations mainly on its procedural aspects is apt to enhance highly valued guarantees of the parties during litigation in the court of original jurisdiction.

69. Both under domestic and conventional law, the practice of first instance *ex parte* proceedings for recognition and enforcement has been expanding. In this respect, the impact of the Brussels Convention is unmistakable. The advantages in terms of time and efficiency of such a method of recognizing and enforcing foreign judgments or awards are obvious. Almost all disadvantages may be overcome by providing for adequate ways of appeal.

70. A trend from bilateral to multilateral conventions is easily discernible, with the New York and the Brussels Conventions as the two most conspicuous examples. The comparison between them seems instructive on several levels. International unification appears to be feasible in a higher degree with respect to foreign arbitral awards than to foreign judgments. The Geneva Conventions of the 1920's on the same area may confirm this evaluation. The reasons for such a different approach to judgments and awards seem to be connected to the less national character of the latter which are thus apt to circulate more easily

303 See Morgan p. 23 **sub** (iii); Vigoriti p. 19 and note 48, with reference to the judgment of the Court of Cassation of December 15, 1982.

304 Cortés p. 33.

305 Koch p. 29-30 and note 140.

306 Vigoriti p. 19.

307 Vrellis p. 25.

in the world and are likely to stimulate national sensitivities and to invite retaliation only to a limited extent. Any direct involvement of state activity potentially enhances the chances of non-recognition. Characteristically enough, the major impediment to recognition and enforcement of judgments has always consisted in jurisdictional requirements, which are again immediate emanations of state authority. Therefore, the major contribution of the Brussels Convention has been to establish uniform rules of direct international jurisdiction, and primarily by this means to facilitate recognition and enforcement. But such a radical method of lowering state borders, when viewed from a world perspective, has its own limitations and disadvantages. Establishing common rules of direct international jurisdiction presupposes a close cooperation in many fields of state activity. In today's world, such a cooperation is unfortunately possible only on a regional basis. The Brussels Convention, fitting well into the entirety of the Community mechanisms, is to be understood under the same point of view as all other Community policies, so to say as the quasi-judicial policy of the European Communities. Advantages and shortcomings of the Brussels Convention appear thus as an intrinsic result of contemporary regional integration.

SUGGESTIONS FOR DISCUSSION

1. To what type of court should be granted subject-matter competence for the recognition and/or enforcement of foreign judgments and arbitral awards?

2. Advantages and disadvantages of an incidental recognition of foreign status judgments or judgments in family matters as opposed to a principal application for this purpose.

3. How are *ex parte* proceedings for recognition or enforcement evaluated by the legal community in your country?

4. Would you approve the availability of a final appeal to the Supreme Court in matters of recognition and enforcement?

5. To what extent should the law applied by the foreign court influence recognition or enforcement of the foreign judgment, and what is the relationship of this requirement to the theory of renvoi (since under both approaches foreign conceptions of conflict rules may become relevant)?

6. How do you explain the clear decline of the public policy defense against recognition and enforcement? Possible emergence of new sensitive areas (economic law, 'lois d'application immédiate')?

7. A comparison between the Brussels Convention and the 1977 Nordic Convention (e.g. with respect to the applicability of the latter regardless of nationality *or domicile* of the parties).

8. Foundations, justification and limitations of the exclusivity of conventions

as against domestic law (also with regard to the *De Wolf* v. *Cox* case of the Court of Justice of the European Communities).

9. Is it desirable to expand the applicability of the Brussels Convention to non-EC countries (through accession, through a 'parallel' convention, or otherwise)?

10. To what extent does the behaviour of party-appointed arbitrators have an impact on recognition and enforcement of a foreign arbitral award?

REPORT OF THE DISCUSSION

Chairman: *J. Laenens (Belgium)*
Vice-chairman: *J. Jodlowski (Poland)*
Secretary: *R.Ch. Verschuur (the Netherlands)*

The discussionpoints are to be found at pages 224 and 257.

1 INTRODUCTION

For this subject two elaborate and excellent general reports had been prepared: for the countries which are members of the European Economic Community by prof. K. Kerameus from Athens and for the rest of the world by prof. J. Barbosa Moreira from Rio de Janeiro. While a practical division for the subject matter had been made this way, it must be understood that the two reports do not complement each other in the sense that they deal with different aspects of the matter; the division is merely geographical. Both reports deal with enforcement and recognition of foreign judgments and arbitral awards according to domestic law and according to international treaties. The report by prof. Kerameus only differs from the report by prof. Barbosa Moreira in the respect that it also deals with perhaps the most far advanced international treaty on the subject viz. the Brussels Convention of 27 september 1968 on jurisdiction and enforcement of foreign judgments in civil and commercial matters, as amended by the treaty of 9 october 1978. It must be stressed, however, that this treaty does not apply yet to all EEC-members[1].

A synthesis of the two reports could not be made during the short time of the congress. General trends emerge from both reports, from which I mention:

a. as to arbitral awards international unification seems to be feasible to a higher degree than as to foreign judgments. Kerameus offers as an explanation that arbitral awards seem to circulate more freely, because they are less connected with the national character of judgments. Of course the New York Convention and before the Geneva Convention much facilitated international unification. Still, Barbosa Moreira finds in some countries some distrust with respect to foreign arbitral awards and dissatisfaction with respect to present developments.

b. restrictive mechanisms of international extension of foreign judgments are as yet inevitable. Barbosa Moreira discerns the following
- the need for a convention or a treaty;
- reciprocity;
- conflict with public policy ('ordre public');
- res iudicata.

1 At present the convention applies to Belgium, Denmark, France, Ireland, Italy, Luxembourg, the Netherlands, the United Kingdom of Great Britain and Northern Ireland and West-Germany.

Of these the public policy defence seems to be in recline. Nowadays public policy will mainly be invoked either if fundamental principles of procedure have been violated (for instance the rule 'et altera pars auditur') or if a foreign judgment clearly conflicts with rules of social-economic law of the state concerned.

c. international conventions greatly facilitate the recognition and enforcement of foreign judgments.

d. in general the present situation is appreciated.

2 WORKING SESSION

Both the working session and plenary session were ably presided by prof. Jean Laenens from Antwerp.

During the working session most participants confirmed the optimistic view as to the present situation, as it had been expressed already by the general reporters. Though generally the liberal attitude towards foreign judgments, as found by the general reporters, was confirmed, some negative voices were heard. Prof. J.P. Verheul from Leyden University pointed to a decline of this liberal attitude in some Western European countries in family law matters, where foreigners from countries as Morocco and Turkey are concerned. In this respect prof. Jodlowski from Warsaw expressed the opinion that in family law matters the national judge must have some control on foreign judgments. Kerameus was of the opinion that the present situation in family law matters is only a minor element, since in general the public control defence is clearly loosing importance.

Reciprocity of recognition and enforcement is still a subject under discussion. Some prefer complete abolishment of this condition as an obstacle of inflexibility and rigidity. Jodlowski declared that in Polish jurisprudence reciprocity is still advocated as a mean to prevent discrimination from capitalist countries.

Most participants acclaimed the conclusion of worldwide treaties, or more realistically on a regional basis. Kerameus remarked in this respect that regional treaties have indeed the effect of extension of foreign judgments within the region, but that such conventions may result in discrimination towards other states. A preference for more international conventions, rather multilateral than bilateral, was expressed, though it was acknowledged that also under the present conventions problems remain to be solved.

3 PLENARY SESSION

During the plenary session much of the discussion of the working session was continued. Several speakers emphasized the importance of the Brussels Convention of 1968, concluded between members of the EEC. An extension of this convention was advocated; an important extension will indeed be made, because negotiations between the members of the EEC and the EFTA on the conclusion of a parallel convention seem to lead to a favorable result. Mme Weser from

Belgium recollected the criticisms from the USA against the Brussels Convention, because of its undesirable effects against the citizens of non member-states. Mmw Weser invited the USA to start negotiations with the members of the EEC on another parallel convention. Mme Weser also wondered how the English courts will receive the supremacy of the International Court of Justice of the EEC in Luxembourg in view of the English abhorrence of foreign and supranational law.

A member of the delegation of the People's Republic of China announced, that this country has decided to join the New York Convention on arbitral awards; this treaty will thus be extended to about one third of the world's population.

Again a general wish for a liberal circulation of foreign judgments was expressed; further conclusion of conventions which reduce restrictive mechanisms is held to be desirable.

In his final word prof. Kerameus illustrated that such conventions specially will have the result of improving the rules and procedures for recognition and enforcement, if such conventions will contain also international rules of jurisdiction as the Brussels Convention of 1968.

IMPROVEMENT OF CIVIL LITIGATION BY LESSONS DERIVED FROM ADMINISTRATIVE PROCEDURES

IMPROVEMENT OF CIVIL LITIGATION BY LESSONS DERIVED FROM ADMINISTRATIVE PROCEDURES: GENERAL REPORT ON COUNTRIES OTHER THAN IBERIAN PENINSULA AND LATIN AMERICA

B.G. Garth
Dean, Indiana University School of Law, Bloomington, Indiana

This topic assumes that students of courts and civil procedure have something to learn from administrative procedures. As the national reports[1] indicate, however, most of our procedural histories have run in precisely the opposite direction[2]. Progress --at least in the view of legal scholars -- has generally been defined as bringing the administration under the control that comes with courtlike machinery and the transcendent legal principles of natural justice and due process[3]. National reporters for this topic thus have some difficulty in

---

1 National Reports used in preparation of the General Report include: Argentina (Augusto Mario Morello); Belgium (M. Paul Martens); Brazil (Antonio Carlos de Araujo Cintra); Canada (W.A. Bogart); Colombia (Hernando Devis Echandia); England and Wales (Neil Andrews); Federal Republic of Germany (Harald Koch); France (Franck Moderne); Greece (Pelayia Yessiou-Faltsi); Hungary (Miklós Kengyel); Italy (Aldo Travi); Netherlands (H. Bolt); New Zealand (G.D.S. Taylor); Poland (Mieczyslaw Sawczuk); and Spain (Adolfo Carretero Pérez). Because of difficulties in correspondence and pressures of time, this report has been mailed before receipt of the General Report on the Iberian Peninsula and Latin America, prepared by Professor Enrique Vescovi of Montevideo, Uruguay.

2 Typical is the remark of Dr. Taylor with respect to New Zealand: 'the movement of reformers of tribunals...[is] towards emulation of courts.' National Report on New Zealand, p.30.

3 According to Aldo Travi's report on Italy, 'Mentre risulta molto rilevante l'incidenza della disciplina del codice di procedura civile sul processo amministrativo, si deve escludere che in Italia la disciplina del processo amministrativo abbia influenzato il processo civile.' National Report on Italy, p. 7.
The 'tendency toward legalism' is found also in the British Report of Mr. Neil Andrews. National Report on England, p. 7.
Dr. Taylor makes a similar observation about New Zealand: 'The Rules Revision Committee (unsurprisingly) looked at other superior courts, particularly the Federal Court of Australia and the New South Wales Supreme Court in Australia, and not to tribunal procedures....[The Secretary to the Committee advised] that possible lessons to be learned from tribunal procedures were never considered.' National Report on New Zealand, p. 28.
Professor Yessiou-Faltsi, the National Reporter for Greece, also states about recent reforms in the Code of Civil Procedure: 'These modifications did not consciously attempt to adopt any experience gained through administrative procedures.' National Report on Greece, p. 16.
Professor González Perez reflects the tradition by stating: 'El proceso administrativo es una manifes-

pointing conclusively to any movement by court reformers to look for lessons from administrative procedures. Typical are the comments of Professor Moderne:

> Dans la mesure où la procédure civile est codifiée depuis longtemps et bénéficie des avantages que procure une pratique particulièrement riche, il est inévitable qu'elle ait peu de raisons de s'aligner sur la procédure administrative, plus jeune, moins éprouvée, moins nuancée...[4].

One might suggest, therefore, that our topic is merely academic: the question could be not what has been learned so far but whether civil procedure should in the future borrow from administrative courts and procedures. That is one way of defining the topic, but it appears in fact to sell our topic short. Important forces are ensuring that administrative procedures will have a strong contemporary impact on the reform of civil procedure.

First, civil court reformers in the future are likely to become a little more adventurous than they have been in the past. Public complaints about the court systems are coming from many directions. Many individuals complain about the cost, congestion, and formality of the regular court procedures. Others complain about the inability of courts in many countries to handle the highly technical and specialized disputes characteristic of modern commerce and industry. And still others assert that courts must become more involved in issues of important public policy. Given these concerns, the flexibility and expertise permitted by administrative procedures will no doubt attract the attention of future critics and reformers of courts.

Second, courts and administrative procedures affect each other in ways that are not always recognized. The two kinds of proceedings are usually defined in opposition to each other[5]. Both are products of long histories that vary substantially among regions and countries, but a substantial part of each history revolves around the assignment of disputes to one category of procedure or another; and that assignment of disputes then inevitably affects how the procedures for each category develop. Just as no historian of British legal history can understand courts of equity without understanding courts of law, and vice versa; and no historian of the procedure of the *jus commune* can understand civil justice without understanding religious courts and procedures; no modern student can understand civil courts without seeing them in the context of today's more or less celebrated alternative -- administrative courts and procedures. There does not need to be an explicit interchange for there to be a reciprocal impact. Put in the terms of the topic of this report, civil litigation is *inevitably* affected by lessons derived from administrative procedures. Neither could exist in its present form, however varied among national court systems, without the other.

Finally, the relationship between courts and administrative procedures must be reconsidered for another reason. The two general models of dispute processing

---

tación del fenómeno procesal, como lo son el proceso civil y el penal.' J. González Perez, Derecho procesal administrativo hispanoamericano 10 (1985).

4 National Report on France, p. 13.

5 'It is not unreasonable to suggest that the Appeals Act was an attempt [in 1902] to establish a procedure which could be regarded as the exact opposite of the existing civil procedure.' National Report on the Netherlands, p. 5.

discussed in this report can be traced to certain assumptions about courts and about administration[6]. In simple terms, we often have assumed that courts exist to apply the law to private disputes, while administrative procedures exist in order to see that public policies are applied fairly and effectively. Obviously this dichotomy is very difficult to sustain. Lines between public and private are notoriously hard to draft with precision. At the very least, the public-private rationale for distinguishing administrative proceedings from civil proceedings has become the subject of considerable debate and discussion, with implications both for civil courts and for administrative procedures.

The lesson, however, is not necessarily that there will be movement toward a series of converging trends in legal reform. We can point in this general report to evidence of convergence, but we cannot stop there. It may be more useful to take another step and see this topic in terms of converging dilemmas and problems. National histories frame the problems in somewhat different ways, and different settings provide different social and legal resources for addressing the problems. But the dilemmas apply generally. The relationship between courts and administrative procedures will be as difficult to decide as the relationship between private and public, and that relationship will in turn determine which lessons, if any, are likely to be borrowed by civil courts from administrative courts and procedures.

1 HISTORICAL BACKGROUND: ADMINISTRATIVE PROCEDURES IN CONTEXT

National reporters have pointed out the difficulty of defining what is meant by administrative procedures. In one sense administrative disputes involve the formulation of policy by governments, with the question of how citizens should participate in the process. Another sense concerns how individuals obtain redress when they are victims of some governmental action, even including traffic accidents involving governmental employees. Dr. Taylor's observation on the basis of the situation in New Zealand and Australia thus applies generally: 'The question of whether a tribunal is viewed as a form of administration or of adjudication is vital to this paper'[7]. One view emphasizes the importance of effective social policies, while the other tends to focus on dispute resolution akin to that in traditional courts[8]. Combining these two concerns -- administration and adjudication -- and a model of courts, we can point to several possible relationships between administrative and court procedures that have been described in national reports. These relationships, while necessarily oversimplified for purposes of discussion, will provide the setting for the exploration of the possible impacts of administrative procedures on the courts.

---

6 For a different but useful way of conceptualizing those differences, see M. Damaska, The Faces of Justice and State Authority (1986).

7 National Report on New Zealand, p. 10.

8 This is the distinction in Germany between the administrative court system (**Verwaltungsgerichte**) and the procedures for decision-making within the administration (**Verwaltungsverfahren**).

1.1 VARIATIONS ON THE FRENCH MODEL

Relationships between administration and adjudication are anchored in ideas about the separation of powers. One view of separation of powers, traceable to the French Revolution and Article 12 of the Law of August 16-24, 1790, is that traditional civil courts must avoid making any decisions involving the public administration. Courts are not supposed to restrain the government. They did too much of that prior to the Revolution. The French *Conseil d'Etat* and the *Tribunaux Administratifs* enforce this distinction rigorously according to a *'tradition fortement établie'*[9] that can be stated simply: 'acts which fall within the domain of private law are not administrative acts and cannot be made subject to the jurisdiction of administrative courts'[10]. And the other side is that public law must be in a jurisdiction outside civil courts.

While there are national variations, this basic idea informs the systems found in Belgium, the Federal Republic of Germany, Greece, Italy, and the Netherlands. It can be traced further into doctrinal tests such as that distinguishing between 'subjective rights' and 'legitimate interests'[11]. The subjective rights are associated with private law, while the legitimate interests are associated with 'diverse positions'[12] respecting the acts of the public administration. Civil courts are not supposed to take sides among various positions one might take with respect to public acts.

1.2 VARIATIONS ON THE BRITISH MODEL

The principal difference between the French and British models stems from a different historical attitude toward courts underlined by the lack of a French-style revolution in Britain. In the undisrupted common law tradition, individuals could seek redress against the government through writs available in the courts of law[13]. In contrast to the rigid separation of powers found in the post-Revolutionary French model, therefore, the British model contemplates using the regular courts to hold the public administration accountable. As noted by Mr. Neil Andrews, the British National Reporter, since 1977 these remedies have been grouped together and termed 'applications for judicial review'[14]: 'When hearing such an application, not only does the court possess the power to issue one of the special remedies of prohibition, *mandamus*, and *certiorari*, but it can also issue the ordinary civil remedies of declaration, injunction and damages'[15]. Traditional public law finds its way into the courts through this procedure. Indeed, '[i]t is now established that questions of public law in the courts must be considered exclusively under this procedure'[16].

---

9 National Report on France, p. 2.

10 Z. Nadjati and J. Trice, English and Continental Systems of Administrative Law 36 (1978).

11 See,e.g., National Report on Italy, p. 1; National Report on the Federal Republic of Germany, p. 11-13.

12 National Report on Italy, p. 1.

13 National Report on England and Wales, p. 8.

14 National Report on England and Wales, p. 8.

15 National Report on England and Wales, p. 8.

16 National Report on England and Wales, p. 8.

This public law remedy helped to prevent the development of a separate administrative *court* system, but other notable developments did occur. Administrative *tribunals* outside of the courts became a major twentieth century phenomenon. According to Dr. Taylor, for example, only six such tribunals existed in New Zealand before the First World War, while by 1965 there were some sixty-three administrative tribunals[17]. A comparable statistic could be cited for Britain, Canada, and the United States.

The rationale generally offered for these developments is a familiar one:

> ...social legislation of the 20th Century demanded tribunals for purely administrative reasons: they could offer speedier, cheaper and more accessible justice, essential for the administration of welfare schemes involving large numbers of small claims. The process of courts of law is elaborate, slow and costly. Its defects are those of its merits, for the object is to provide the highest standard of justice. Generally speaking, the public wants the best possible article and is prepared to pay for it. But in administering social services the aim is different. The object is not the best article at any price but the best article that is consistent with efficient administration. Disputes must be disposed of quickly and cheaply for the benefit of the public purse as well as for that of the claimant[18].

One point that emerges strikingly from this quotation is that the model for tribunals was conceived of specifically as *something different* from the courts in procedure as well as workload. The issue is not simply separation of powers in the formal sense. Courts could continue to handle judicial review of administrative action, but dispute processing needs of the welfare state were to be concentrated more in the tribunals than in the courts. As Mr. Andrews observes, tribunals at the outset could both 'insulate the courts from issues of economic policy and consumer protection...and spare them the heavy caseload generated by these matters'[19].

The relative success of this insulation can be debated, but it is clear that ordinary courts in this system are entrusted with a relatively limited role in controlling public activities[20]. That is more of a role than the French civil courts, but it is still quite circumscribed. As a recent British treatise on administrative law stated,

> In relation to the affairs of private citizens the courts are the primary organs for interpreting, applying, and enforcing the law. But when they are dealing with matters involving other branches of government the courts take a more restrained view of their role. The legislature is almost entirely free of judicial control and, under the doctrine of ultra vires, the executive enjoys a considerable degree of autonomy

---

17 National Report on New Zealand, p. 6.

18 National Report on New Zealand, p. 7-8 (quoting H.W.R. Wade, Administrative Law 779 (5th ed. 1982).

19 National Report on England and Wales, p. 2.

20 While the Canadian situation is in flux and is described in more detail below, Professor Bogart's description of the development of administrative procedures is apt: 'The exclusion of the courts from a particular sphere occurred because the legislature decided that the task to be accomplished was too repetitive and burdensome (because of numbers) to require the courts' attention or because it concluded that the judiciary lacked the expertise or was simply too hostile to the policy being implemented to be entrusted with the task.' National Report on Canada, p. 4.

and immunity from judicial control. This judicial restraint is partly a function of the doctrine of separation of powers ..[21].

The emphasis on the British Constitutional role of the courts as contrasted to the executive and legislative branches of government points to the next model. When there is a greater Constitutional role entrusted to the courts, it is inevitable that 'public law' will be 'interpreted, applied, and enforced' to a much greater extent in the courts. Neither of the kinds of 'separation' enshrined in the French and British models can survive this kind of mixing.

1.3 VARIATIONS ON THE MODEL FOUND IN THE UNITED STATES

While we have defined another model, we should not exaggerate its uniqueness. The model found in Great Britain, Australia, and New Zealand is not very different in basic outline from the model which can be associated with the United States. The history is again comparable, and a substantial piece of the welfare state has been carved out and assigned to administrative machinery subject to a relatively minimal standard of review in the courts. The Canadian situation reported by Professor Bogart aligns Canada mainly with the British model. For purposes of understanding trends and contrasts, however, it is more instructive to put the United States and, to a lesser extent, Canada in a different category. Judicial review as long practiced in the United States, and as newly established by the Canadian Charter of Rights and Freedoms enacted in 1982, helps to put the courts in a different political situation[22].

Put simply, the battles over law in the welfare state in Great Britain may be fought in the legislature and in various administrative fora, but in the United States, at least, the courts are heavily involved. According to Professor Richard Stewart,

> Federal courts' relaxation of standing, reviewability, and ripeness doctrines and expansion of various procedural rights invited litigation of developing social issues before political momentum could generate congressional legislation to create new programs of administrative regulation[23].

Courts have not backed off from public administration in the manner largely accepted in Britain. Rather, courts have been the subject of both lavish praise and excoriating criticism for their role in public administration in the United States[24]. Not a few commentators have pointed to an analogy especially notable for the purposes of this report. Courts appear to resemble administrative agencies much more than traditional courts in their approaches to many of the disputes that reach them[25]. Professor Bogart makes this point explicitly in his

---

21 P. Cane, An Introduction to Administrative Law 5 (1986).

22 As discussed below, this is not to imply that comparable movements in what courts do cannot be found in countries like the Federal Republic of Germany and Italy.

23 R. Stewart, 'Reconstitutive Law,' 46 Maryland Law Review 86, 97 (1987).

24 **Compare** Chayes, 'Public Law Litigation,' 89 Harvard Law Review 1281 (1976) and D. Horowitz, The Courts and Social Policy (1977).

25 **See, e.g.,** Clark, 'Adjudication to Administration: A Statistical Analysis of Federal Courts in the Twentieth Century,' 55 Southern California Law Review 65 (1981); M. Shapiro, Courts (1981).

report on developments in Canada: 'I hope courts would become more flexible as a result of looking at administrative actors and the various ways they carry out their different mandates'[26]. The separation of courts and administrative machinery becomes much more problematic in this model.

1.4 JUDICIALIZATION IN THE SOCIALIST COUNTRIES

While the erosion of the theoretical distinction between public and private helps to account for the U.S. model, the ostensible eradication of the distinction forms a starting point for discussion of the Socialist countries[27]. This eradication could in theory lead to the elimination of adjudication in favor of administration or vice versa. The terms could become meaningless.

The Socialist countries have taken the position that the courts -- with some greater implication of independence -- should be the primary forum for state-sponsored dispute processing. According to Professor Rácz, for example, the ideal is the 'fuller realization of the principle of the unity of socialist jurisdiction,...since the non-judicial adjudicatory instances will cease to exist or will be restricted to a negligible scale'[28]. As stated by Miklós Kengyel, the Hungarian National Reporter, 'Im Gegensatz zur Lehre von Montesquieu wird die Trennung der Staatsmächte durch die sozialistische Staatstheorie nicht anerkannt, anstatt dessen wird *das Prinzip der Einheit der Staatsmacht verkündigt*'[29]. Not separation of powers but unity is the starting point.

This basic point, which is not without exceptions, is consistent with an approach to courts which borrows many of the features commonly associated with administrative procedure and with an approach to administrative procedure that is courtlike -- 'judicialized'[30]. According to Professor Sawczuk in the National Report on Poland, 'The theory of administrative procedure treats [in a] parallel...[fashion] primary principles of judicial procedure and general principles within the administrative procedure sphere'[31]. And both administrative and judicial procedure work with the 'dominating' principle of 'objective truth'[32], which affects in significant ways the relative roles of the parties and the decisionmakers[33]. The Socialist model favors courts, but the courts themselves take on much of the character of what might be termed administrative procedures elsewhere.

---

26 National Report on Canada, p. 25.

27 National Report on Poland, p. 5.

28 A. Rácz, Courts and Tribunals 238 (1980).

29 National Report on Hungary, p. 6.

30 National Report on Poland, p. 11-12.

31 National Report on Poland, p. 14.

32 National Report on Poland, p. 17.

33 'In practice, it turns out to be hard to decide whether any case is civil from the very nature, especially when mixed legal relations combining civil and administrative elements are involved, the tangible subject and result being the decisive factor as regards admissibility of judicial recourse to the law.' National Report on Poland, p. 26.

2 CHARACTERISTICS OF ADMINISTRATIVE PROCEDURE

The line between courts and administrative procedure is not necessarily easy to locate,[34] and it varies in different countries. Each of the systems described above, for example, asks courts to perform somewhat different functions. Nevertheless, discussions of administrative procedures in the national reports tend to highlight certain features associated with administrative procedures and administrative courts. These features are typically different from those found in civil courts. We can begin with the most flexible of the administrative procedures and then ask what is different about administrative courts. These descriptions will then lead to the question of what civil court systems really can learn in a positive way from these features.

The first set of distinguishing features stems from the fact that administrative procedures are typically designed to serve some particular public policy. They are not designed merely to resolve a dispute or apply a formal law to the product of a formal procedure. This more substantive orientation implies first that administrative decision-makers must approach their work in light of certain public policy implications; second, that procedures will be flexibly defined, depending on the ends to be served; and, third, that they are likely to be organized to promote a particular technical expertise. Traditional courts tend to have a relatively inflexible procedure, an ostensibly neutral, non-policy oriented approach applicable to all claims, and decision-makers who are generalists lacking specialized expertise[35].

Second, since many administrative procedures are designed to serve programs directed to large segments of the public, such as persons who are disabled or unemployed, they tend to be adept at handling large numbers of claims efficiently; and they tend also to emphasize accessibility and informality to allow ordinary people to pursue their claims. Ease of access in turn leads to more use by individuals, more prosecution of claims, and a greater ability to see that the public policy is very widely enforced.

Finally, since administrative procedures may require new interpretations of public policies, they often have mechanisms to involve interested members of the public in that process of decisionmaking. As noted before, administrative procedures tend to mix adjudication of claims and the setting of public policy. The question of participation inevitably surfaces in any policy-setting agency, whether informal or formal in approach.

Administrative *courts* as exist in France or the Federal Republic of Germany have similar characteristics to the administrative procedures but without as much procedural diversity and flexibility as the huge variety permits in jurisdictions like England and Canada[36]. The German system even goes beyond

---

34 A useful discussion of judicial processes which points to links between these two kinds of process and the 'activist state' is M. Damaska, **supra** note 6. **See** also M. Shapiro, **supra** note 24; National Report on England and Wales, p. 1.

35 Max Weber's description is useful and found in 2 Economy and Society 812 (G. Roth and C. Wittich eds. 1978).

36 According to Andrews, 'The most secure ground for making the distinction [between tribunals and courts] is that tribunals possess a greater degree of specialisation and expertise than the ordinary civil courts.' National Report on England and Wales, p. 1.

the French in promoting specialization and expertise. There are tax, labor, and social courts in addition to courts specifically denominated as administrative courts[37]. In general, however, administrative courts resemble regular courts, although that does not mean that they necessarily follow precisely the same procedures.

Quite a number of national reporters emphasize the remaining differences. In particular, some of the specific historical problems of courts, the targets of the 'orality movement' on the Continent and in Latin America[38], are addressed in the administrative courts. The administrative courts for the most part have more active judges, freer evaluation of the evidence, and more concentrated proceedings[39]. The procedures may be predominantly written, but they nevertheless overcome some of the deficiencies that inspired the orality movement. And they tend to be more accessible to potential litigants and more solicitous of individuals who must face the government on the other side[40]. The general theme of administrative procedures and administrative courts is flexibility, informality, and sensitivity to governmental policy. There are important reasons for this theme, which has explanatory power in quite a number of different settings. The question then becomes whether the factors are universal enough and the reasons sufficiently universal to point toward specific lessons for civil courts. We can respond to that question, but the response must proceed in descending levels. Each level, described in subsequent sections, complicates and builds on the previous one.

3 INITIAL LESSONS FOR CIVIL PROCEDURE: FUNDAMENTALS AND FLEXIBILITY

Two obvious lessons for civil procedure emerge from the previous discussion[41]. First is the lesson of flexibility, since administrative procedures offer a rich variety of tested models for processing disputes. Many reformers are unhappy with traditional aspects of civil procedure, which seem designed for an era when disputes involved individuals concerned with such matters as who should pay when a farm animal escapes and causes damages, or how to assess responsibility when a small enterprise fails to deliver goods on time to another

37 National Report on the Federal Republic of Germany, p. 1a-1b.

38 See, e.g., National Report from the Federal Republic of Germany, p. 9 (discussing §139 of the ZPO). For a recent discussion of the orality movement, see M. Cappelletti & B. Garth, 'Policies, Trends, and Ideas in Civil Procedure,' Volume XVI, Ch. I of the International Encyclopedia of Comparative Law (in press).

39 National Report on Belgium, p. 23; National Report on France, p. 7; National Report on Greece, p. 12; National Report on the Netherlands, p. 4, 16-21.

40 See, e.g., National Report on the Netherlands, p. 11.

41 Professor Bogart makes a comparable description of the lesson as follows:

> Tolerance because administrative procedures demonstrate that there are many ways to respond to issues and to resolve disputes which do not follow court procedures and which, nevertheless, are capable of reaching satisfactory decisions by methods which can be respected.
>
> National Report on Canada, p. 24.

comparable enterprise. These are disputes that everybody agrees are treated wel as private matters for courts.

The reformers wonder if traditional civil procedure is suited for disputes involving huge corporations intimately connected with the prosperity of the national economy, or involving private individuals pitted against one or another of the large organizations that characterize modern life. It is much more difficult to look at these disputes as merely private matters. As Professor Koch notes, 'Von Lehren des Verwaltungsverfahrens und des Verwaltungsprozesses für den Zivilprozess ist hier insofern zu sprechen, als immer deutlicher zutage tritt, dass es auch im Zivilprozess nicht lediglich um den Streit zweier Privatpersonen geht'[42]. It is unfortunate that critics of civil procedure who make comparable observations too often fail to draw on the variety of models and approaches associated with administrative procedures and administrative courts.

The second lesson goes well with the first. If moving away from traditional court procedures is desirable, it necessarily raises concerns about how far to go. Again the various experiences with administrative procedures are instructive. With respect to the basic fundamentals, for example, the French Report speaks of the need to preserve the *'principe du contradictoire.'* The Report on England and Wales emphasizes the challenge, taken up in the 1957 Francks Report on the system of administrative tribunals, 'to achieve the traditional standards of adjudication associated with the courts and at the same time preserve flexibility for tribunals'[43]. And the United States can point to a more than fifteen-year evolution in Supreme Court jurisprudence with respect to the application of principles of due process to administrative procedures[44]. We can therefore look toward administrative courts and procedures for help with two of the most essential concerns: making courts more flexible on the one hand, but not too flexible on the other. The next question, however, is whether there are specific trends that make this lesson timely today.

4 CONVERGING TRENDS?

A relatively straightforward reform agenda might now be proposed on the basis of the insights derived from administrative courts and procedures. We certainly can begin with the calls for more flexibility in the courts, recognizing that the basic fundamentals of procedure need not be interpreted too rigidly. It is not easy to find the point where flexibility becomes excessive and violates procedural fundamentals, but we might conclude in any event that a little more flexibility would not hurt. We need a better social and political understanding,

---

42 National Report on Federal Republic of Germany, p. 14.

43 National Report on England and Wales, p. 2; see National Report on New Zealand, p. 17-27; National Report on Canada, p. 20 (describing 'minimal procedural decencies').

44 **See, e.g.,** Goldberg v. Kelly, 397 U.S. 254 (1970); Mathews v. Eldridge, 424 U.S. 319 (1985); **See also** National Report on Italy, p. 7: 'In conclusione, si sostiene che il codice di procedura civile avrebbe un valore generale di disciplina del procedimento giurisdizionale, e pertanto sarebbe senz'altro utilizzabile per colmare le lacune della normativa sul giudizio amministrativo.' Also Italy speaks of Constitutional principles as 'criteri di coerenza generale del sistema processuale.'; **Cf.** National Report on the Federal Republic of Germany, p. 2.

however, to make any sense of such an agenda. Reform proposals that call abstractly for some but not too much flexibility may beg the question. What is the public dimension that makes us *want* to push beyond traditional civil procedure?

A plausible assumption, found in many of the reports, can take the reform agenda farther and continue the discussion of convergence. The assumption-- most pronounced in the Socialist countries -- is that the traditional line between public and private cannot be maintained, and that therefore certain values not recognized traditionally in courts need to be accommodated. Neither administrative courts nor administrative tribunals of one sort or another, according to this assumption, will insulate the civil courts from matters of important public concern. None of the models of separation of powers will keep courts really separate from the welfare state. If civil courts are becoming more involved in these public matters, it will then be natural that they look toward the experience of the administrative procedures and administrative courts that have been concerned with public matters all along.

One place to look, given that assumption, is in the range of persons and groups allowed access to the courts. Liberalized standing to sue for individuals and groups, and greater opportunities for intervention in existing litigation, are characteristic of administrative proceedings and courts. As civil courts become involved in the setting of policies and as the public interest in law enforcement increases, it makes sense to expand opportunities to bring disputes to court and to participate in the judicial process[45]. Again the German situation is instructive:

> In einer wachsenden Zahl von Ausnahmefällen wird allerdings die Bindung der Klagebefugnis an die Individualbetroffenheit gelöst: im gewerblichen Rechtsschutz, im Wettbewerbsrecht, im Umweltrecht und im Verbraucherrecht begegnen wir Verbandsklagen, teilweise sogar Popularklagen, jeweils in Rechtsgebieten, in denen die Durchsetzung des objektiven Rechts nicht als blosses Nebenprodukt dem Individualrechtsschutz überlassen bleiben kann[46].

A second place to look is at procedures designed to make sure that *outcomes* of the procedures are consistent with the public policies embodied in the substantive law. For example, a more active role for the judge is certainly

---

45 **See, e.g.**, National Report on Belgium, p. 8-13; National Report on France, p. 10. According to Professor Bogart,

> [T]he courts' acknowledgment of interests not driven by laissez-faire individualism, their willingness to break the control of the immediate parties to the litigation to admit others in order to explore the ramifications of their decisions beyond the immediate parties, and their recognition that the values to be advanced may have little to do with traditional common law rules, all strike a chord familiar to the goals of administrative tribunals.

National Report on Canada, p. 22. **See generally** M. Cappelletti, 'Vindicating the Public Interest Through the Courts: A Comparativist's Contribution,' 25 Buffalo Law Review 643 (1976). Of course, effectiveness of social goals and expansion of participation are not always harmonious goals. **See, e.g.**, Stewart, **supra** note 23, at 102.

46 National Report on Federal Republic of Germany, p. 13.

consistent with this social welfare perspective[47]. In terms used recently by Professor Damaska in his book on 'The Faces of Justice and State Authority,' the 'activist state' is consistent with a more active and inquisitorial judiciary[48]. Many models could be found to translate an activist state into a judicial role, but certainly an important place to look will be at the inquisitorial features described as aspects of general administrative courts and procedures. The Socialist countries' emphasis on truth as an outcome, for example, points to a synthesis of administrative and judicial modes of dispute processing.

Third, it begins to make sense also to emphasize specialization and access to expertise if public policy is going to be affected more by the decisions of courts. And again it would be natural to look for lessons from administrative procedures. There are many models from which to choose, ranging from the specialized German administrative courts to diverse British administrative tribunals, where expertise is actively sought in decisionmakers. Is it time to admit that generalist civil courts make too many mistakes at too high a social cost? If the social cost is too high to have a generalist *administration* in charge of questions of detail, why should we have generalist *courts* overseeing precisely those details?

Finally, one can add the realization that another traditional assumption of courts, that litigating parties are roughly equal in resources, is highly questionable. If public policy includes a desire for correct outcomes, then that inequality must be addressed. Since the basic assumption underlying many administrative procedures is that the parties are often *unequal* in resources, again the lessons of those procedures have implications for court procedures as well. This may again point toward a more active judicial role, but it may also be accommodated in other ways borrowed from administrative courts and procedures[49].

These converging trends in the reform agenda for civil courts have a certain plausibility. They imply a more or less uniform development whereby the recognized successes of administrative courts and procedures are used to improve civil procedure and adjust it to some of the public policy requirements of today's world. It would be misleading, however, to overdo these lessons for civil procedure. In the first place, our national reports do not permit one to evaluate systematically just how successful the various administrative approaches have been in accomplishing the purposes that have been attributed to them.

---

47 National Report on Greece, p. 17: 'a strong power of the court in managing the civil proceedings does not always include a non-permitted intervention in private personal freedom and free development, when the idea of this procedure possessing a social welfare function is adopted.'

48 M. Damaska, **supra** note 6; according to Koch,

Einer der Gründe für die Annäherung der zivilprozessualen Richterrolle an die des Verwaltungsprozesses ist die ungenügende Berücksichtigung sozialer Schutzerwägungen und öffentlicher Interessen durch die Parteien. Daneben beginnt sich die Erkenntnis durchzusetzen, dass die Prozessfunktionen im Zivil- und Verwaltungsprozess sich nicht grundsätzlich voneinander unterscheiden, wenn man sie allgemein mit Streiterledigung oder Konfliktlösung beschreibt: Darunter lassen sich sowohl subjektiver Rechtsschutz als auch objektive Rechtsbewährung fassen, die mit je unterschiedlicher Intensität im Verfahren der einen wie der anderen Art wahrgenommen werden.

National Report on Federal Republic of Germany, p. 10-11.

49 **See, e.g.**, National Report on England and Wales, p. 13.

More research, national and comparative, would certainly be necessary before we start calling for wholesale borrowing.

More fundamental, however, is another question about the agenda we have constructed. The entire reform enterprise may be challenged. One of the reasons to look toward the experience of administrative courts and procedures is a pervasive uneasiness today about courts and civil procedure. Many commentators perceive a crisis in the courts, requiring dramatic reforms. What they often miss, however, is that both the definition of crisis and the prescription for solution are controversial matters that require a more sophisticated analysis. As will be seen below, it may make more sense to speak of converging dilemmas than converging trends.

5 CONVERGING DILEMMAS

The starting point is that the expansion of the state in recent decades has brought with it new demands on state-supported dispute processing machinery. In the United States, for example, there is much discussion of a 'litigation explosion'[50]. The pressure of increased caseloads is felt both in regular court systems and in administrative court systems[51]. In France the situation is notable:

> [L]es lenteurs de la justice, souvent dénoncées, prennent des allures inquiétantes dans le domaine du contentieux administratif. L'encombrement du prétoire ne permet guère de régler définitivement une affaire, en moyenne, avant quatre ou cinq moins, pour peu qu'il y ait appel. Le faible nombre des juridictions administratives de droit commun (une trentaine au total) et l'engorgement au Conseil d'Etat (malgré des efforts récents), l'augmentation des litiges liée à l'interventionnisme croissant de l'administration dans le champ social, le rôle des associations de défense des consommateurs ou des usagers de services publics, des associations de protection de la nature et de l'environnement, des syndicats etc... et une meillure connaissance de la justice administrative expliquant une situation de plus en plus préoccupante[52]

There is enormous political pressure to solve these problems, but there is some debate about the appropriate approach to take.

In countries where administrative matters are not allocated to courts, for example, there is pressure to cut costs by further tinkering with the administrative processes. Thus in England the absence of legal aid for representation in

---

50 See, e.g., Galanter, 'The Day After the Litigation Explosion,' 46 Maryland Law Review 3 (1986) (criticizing the sport of lamenting U.S. litigation).

51 See, e.g., National Report on Greece, p. 15, 'In Greece both civil and administrative judicial proceedings have a rather long duration. Normally a civil law case needs about 3-4 years in order to reach the stage of final decision of the first instance. Administrative proceedings are delayed even more, as the continuously developing branch of the ordinary administrative courts is highly overloaded.' National Report on Italy, p. 5, 'Presson numerosi Tribunali amministrativi si ha...un notevole accumulo di arretrato, e cio significa che numerosi ricorsi non riescono ad avere una decisione.' National Report on the Netherlands, p. 19, 'administrative proceedings...are beginning to rival civil proceedings as regards the length of time they take.' Cf. National Report on Belgium, p. 14, 26.

52 National Report on France, p. 10.

administrative matters can be justified in the interest of access and informality, but it certainly has another explanation as well: 'One obvious means of saving public money is by creating or preserving tribunals in which legal representation is declared to be not merely unnecessary but also positively deleterious'[53]. It is difficult to predict the outcomes of 'reforms' produced by a coalition of groups pushing for better processes and groups preoccupied with costs to the state, but an understandable skepticism seems justified.

The more general dilemma is of course the question of how much of the 'trappings' or 'protections' of formal due process in administrative procedures can be exchanged in the name of the efficient processing of caseloads. It is no surprise that there is still considerable controversy, for example, in the United States over just how flexible the Supreme Court should be in interpreting the Constitutional boundaries of procedural due process as applied to administrative proceedings[54]. The trend in recent years has been toward greater informality and less of an emphasis on courtlike procedural protections, but the trend has not gained any real social consensus.

One simple response to a perception of crisis would be to promote cost savings from the point of view of the state, by tailoring each administrative procedure to the kind of disputes likely to arise,[55] but that kind of response raises new problems. The resultant lack of uniformity can easily confuse disputants and a public concerned with monitoring the performance of these institutions. Precision tailoring sounds better in the abstract than it works in practice.

This dilemma applies to regular courts as well as administrative dispute processing machinery. Larger caseloads and cost consciousness can lead to the same kind of ambiguous 'reforms' in civil courts. The National Report of the Netherlands worries, for example, about 'longstanding and valuable safeguards enshrined in civil procedure'[56]. As the Dutch Reporter, Mr. Bolt, explains, 'It is increasingly argued that changes are needed in the form of civil procedure on grounds of efficiency and economy, under which approach normative considerations would be permitted to recede into the background somewhat'[57]. The danger is that the value of efficiency, which too often is translated simply into the variable of state costs, is taken for granted as equal to or greater in importance than the need to preserve longstanding and valuable safeguards in procedure. We might call this the simple meaning of a trade-off between efficiency and justice.

These dilemmas, in sum, are relatively straightforward. If we cheapen administrative procedures or court procedures, we might make them more accessible or able to process larger numbers of proceedings; but cheaper means of processing disputes may neglect certain values fundamental to a fair

53 National Report on England and Wales, p. 8.

54 See, e.g., Cass, 'Looking With One Eye Closed: The Twilight of Administrative Law,' 1986 Duke Law Journal 238, 253.

55 See, e.g., National Report on the Federal Republic of Germany, p. 1a. For a thoughtful middle ground favoring 'particular procedures attuned to each jurisdiction within a broadly phrased set of procedural provisions,' see National Report on New Zealand, p. 26.

56 National Report on the Netherlands, p.23.

57 National Report on the Netherlands, p. 10.

procedural system. One lesson from administrative procedure is simply that, while there is much to learn about how to balance concerns of economy and fairness, there is no easy answer to which policymakers or reformers can turn with confidence.

The dilemmas of this topic can also be approached from a different perspective, focusing on the relationship of administration and courts. Lessons are not simply questions of how far to go in certain reforms of courts and/or administrative machinery. If there is going to be delay, for example, it is possible to take action to ease the burden or transform the burden placed on *one or another* dispute processing institution: administrative procedures, administrative courts, courts. The relationship becomes crucial, and the allocation of burdens will determine the effectiveness of each such institution.

The question, moreover, is not simply what one does with a case burden in terms of allocating it among the designated institutions. The question becomes what belongs in courts and what belongs elsewhere. Ultimately the dilemma of what to borrow from administrative procedures stems from the difficulty of deciding how much courts ought to be deciding the kind of policy matters typically associated with administrative proceedings. And this question inevitably will get very different approaches within countries and certainly between them. It is a matter of very significant debates taking place even now in national political circles.

Liberalized standing, broadened participation, relatively activist judges, mechanisms for providing specialized expertise, and the like, have been associated with a transformation of courts more into equal partners with the other branches of government in the interpretation and formulation of policy. One might say that the trend is inevitable, and that the United States is simply a little farther along than most other countries because of its long history of Constitutional adjudication. It might then follow, for example, that the legal system of England and Wales need not borrow much *yet* from administrative procedures because to date the welfare state is still for the most part kept out of the courts. There is evidence from many national reports, including Canada and the Federal Republic of Germany, that the welfare state and questions of Constitutional principle do push the courts to a greater policy making role.

This assumption of a predictable movement, however, is much disputed, even or perhaps especially in the United States. On the one hand, there is an understandable fear of what happens if courts become too 'uncourtlike.' As the National Report for Belgium states,

> Enfin, il faut redouter une tendance de nos démocraties pluralistes qui consiste à ne plus trancher au parlement les questions essentielles -- éthiques ou économiques -- et à laisser au juge le soin de les apprécier sans lui donner une loi pour limiter son arbitraire, avec cette conséquence paradoxale que, quand le juge a tranché, ceux-là memes qui sont chargés de faire les lois crient au gouvernement des juges[58].

More is at stake, however, than the legitimacy of judicial authority.

Many commentators simply want courts to retreat. This means, first, to back away from administrative proceedings and allow the administration to implement

58 National Report on Belgium, p. 15.

policy as it sees fit. Such commentators want maximum flexibility in administration and minimal judicial review[59]. Let the government make its policies, in other words, and keep the courts away. Commentators in the U.S. are thus urging the adoption of something more like the British model. Courts should refrain from any aggressive review of the welfare state as translated into administrative tribunals and proceedings. In some respects this retreat is defensible because it maximizes freedom for the 'democratic' institutions of representative government. But it raises the concern of just how much the governmental bureaucracy should be insulated from the kind of oversight traditionally provided by courts. The dilemma is thus the trade-off between the flexibility and potential tyranny of unfettered policy making and the somewhat intrusive meddling of courts.

A still more fundamental debate is also taking place. Many commentators and judges would like to redefine the mission of the courts, even in the United States, away from the implementation of the public values discussed above and more towards a renewed emphasis on decision of essentially private disputes[60]. Thus, while the private-public line was once accepted as a matter of course, and subsequently eroded because of the development of the activist state, it now has become an affirmative program for those who have not been happy with the activist state. They want courts to play an active role in ensuring that disputes get resolved according to principles of economic efficiency and traditional private law. They are strongly opposed to governmental regulation, which takes for granted a public interest in the regulation of business and commercial relationships. If we reject any public interest other than the enforcement of private economic arrangements, then courts have absolutely nothing to learn from administrative procedures. Indeed, administrative procedures would also have to be rethought and reformed.

The contest over what courts should do is thus ultimately a debate about the activist state. More activism suggests more involvement by courts in administrative and public policy matters. Less activism, as the trend now points in the United States and several other countries, points toward a retreat from concerns about public policy and the control over its implementation. If justice mainly means private justice, economic efficiency, and a minimalist state regulatory apparatus, civil courts face one reform agenda. If we are concerned with the social justice of the activist state, however, lessons from administrative procedure assume more importance.

This political dilemma about the activist state sounds rather striking; and it reflects some very fundamental debates now taking place. The conclusion, however, must urge some caution. Debates in the United States frame the issues nicely, but any comparativist writing about the United States must acknowledge some cultural peculiarities. National debates in the United States focus the issues and make them sound extreme: an emphasis on eliminating the activist state and changing dramatically the role of the courts. In fact, the reality

---

59 See, e.g., Scalia, 'The Doctrine of Standing as an Essential Element of the Separation of Powers,' 17 Suffolk University Law Review 881 (1983); Smith, 'Judicialization: The Twilight of Administrative Law,' 1985 Duke Law Journal 427.

60 See, e.g., Easterbrook, 'The Supreme Court 1983 Term, Foreword: The Court and the Economic System,' 98 Harvard Law Review 4 (1984); R. Posner, The Federal Courts (1985).

shifts much less notably than public debates imply. There are dilemmas and trade-offs that are vitally important in determining how much court reformers might draw on administrative experience. That much is true. But the activist state appears to remain with us today in the United States, despite nearly seven years of the Reagan era. It is probably reasonable to suggest that civil courts in most countries will retain enough of the activist state to draw on the lessons of administrative procedures and courts.

DISCUSSIONQUESTIONS

1. Why has there been so little improvement of civil litigation by lessons derived from administrative procedures?

2. Are there converging trends that make civil courts more like administrative decisionmakers in the work that they do?

3. If so, can civil courts learn lessons from administrative courts and procedures?

4. Which kinds of lessons can be learned? Efficiency? Specialization? Broaden participation?

5. What are the limits in the lessons civil courts can take from administrative procedures?

6. How does the direction of reform relate to the political question of what decisions and problems can be handled by civil courts as opposed to other branches of government, including the public administration?

IMPROVEMENT OF CIVIL LITIGATION: LESSONS FROM ADMINISTRATIVE PROCEDURES: EN EL ÁREA IBEROAMERICANA

E. Vescovi[1]
Professor, University of Montevideo, Uruguay

SUMARIO

---

1 Por solicitud del Comité Organizador del Congreso y con el generoso acuerdo del Profesor Bryant Garth, hemos aceptado actuar de co-relatores en el tema del epígrafe. Lamentablemente, el tardío nombramiento nos impidió solicitar -y a veces recibir- en tiempo, varios relatos nacionales, así como efectuar un más adecuado y cuidadoso tratamiento del tema.

I EL TEMA

1 EFFICIENCY ON THE PORSUIT OF JUSTICE

Es natural que el Relato General para el Congreso de Utrecht se inscriba dentro del marco del lema del evento, cual es el de la búsqueda de una mayor eficiencia de la Justicia.

Tarea en la cual los juristas (políticos, sociólogos, etc.) están empañados desde hace mucho tiempo, pero que resulta más apremiante en nuestra época de cambio social en la cual la situación del Poder Judicial, frente a la modernización general del Estado, presenta un mayor contraste. Es así que el burocratismo, la dificultad de acceso, la lentitud de los procedimientos, el excesivo planteo de problemas formales (procedimentales), va conformando un cuadro que coloca nuestra Justicia en posición desairada ante los justos y precisos reclamos de una sociedad en muy rápida evolución. Frente a cuyos problemas más modernos (del medio ambiente, de la protección al consumidor, de la resolución de cuestiones técnicas, de la situación de la familia y los menores ...) no encuentra una adecuada y rápida respuesta. Como debe ser, pues la finalidad del procedimiento resulta en definitiva lo esencial en el servicio al justiciable.

Por eso el enfoque de cualquiera de los temas que se plantean a este VIII Congreso Internacional de Derecho Procesal, se relacionan todos con la búsqueda urgente de una mayor eficiencia (eficacia) en el Servicio de Justicia[2].

---

2 Este tema constituye uno de los más importantes que ha encarado la comunidad internacional, en la cual resulta significativo el aporte de la doctrina procesal. Resulta de interés destacar, en tal sentido, el programa realizado, bajo la dirección de Mauro Cappelletti sobre el Acceso a la Justicia, en el Centro de Derecho Comparado y Estudios Judiciales de Florencia y, a partir de 1976, en el Instituto Universitario Europeo (también con sede en Florencia). Estos proyectos culminaron con la publicación, en 1978-79, de cuatro volúmenes (seis libros) bajo dicho título (Acceso a la Justicia): 'The Florence Access to Justice Proyect' (M. Cappelletti, gen. ed.) Vols. 1-4. Alphen aan den Rijn (Holland) & Sijthoff and Noordhoft & Giuffre, 1978-1979.
Vide también Access to justice and the welfare state. Mauro Cappelletti (ed) Sijthoff, Bruylant, Klett-

En ese sentido y sin perjuicio de los trabajos que se realizan en otras áreas- tal como sucede en la Comunidad Europea, lo cual queda fuera del ámbito de este Relato- en Iberoamérica se han multiplicado los esfuerzos en los últimos tiempos.

Es de hacer notar que, sin perjuicio de los adelantos realizados en los países en particular, cuyas modificaciones legislativas y administrativas de códigos procesales y servicio de Justicia son innumerables, debemos señalar que a nivel general, se ha trabajado, en equipo, con ese fin. Que, por sobre todas las cosas, coincide con un esfuerzo denodado -aunque solo con pocos resultados y en los últimos tiempos- por crear una región comunitaria (Asociación de Libre Comercio, Parlamento Latinoamericano, Pacto Andino, Pacto de San José de Costa Rica y Tribunales supranacionales...) dentro de la cual aparece la necesidad de derechos y procedimientos comunes.

En esa labor colectiva por la mejora de la Justicia en el área, que presentamos a este Congreso como un eslabón más del esfuerzo universal que aquí se procura, nos parece del caso destacar la tarea de dos Instituciones, que mucho están haciendo, con las dificultades que, entre otras, las carencias de las naciones en vías de desarrollo encuentran para su progreso, en este mundo convulsionado por el mejoramiento de la Justicia. Nos referimos tanto a la Organización de Estados Americanos (O.A.E) como al Instituto Iberoamericano de Derecho Procesal. La primera ha creado un verdadero Derecho comunitario, para facilitar la cooperación judicial en América, especialmente a través de las Conferencias especializadas organizadas por su Comité Jurídico, tales como la CIDIP I (Panamá, 1975), la CIDIP II (Montevideo, 1979) y la CIDIP III (La Paz, Bolivia, 1984) (preparándose ya la IV), cuyos diversos tratados sobre exhortos y cartas rogatorias, arbitraje comercial, cooperación en materia de medidas cautelares, prueba, ejecución de sentencias y laudos extranjeros, dictado de normas generales, etc. van abriendo un importante camino en América toda.

A su vez el Instituto Iberoamericano de Derecho Procesal, creado en Montevideo en 1957, en sus Ias. Jornadas (en memoria de Eduardo J. Couture), ya en la IVas (Caracas, Valencia, Venezuela, 1967) dispuso que se prepararan BASES UNIFORMES PARA LA LEGISLACION PROCESAL CIVIL Y COMERCIAL EN LATINOAMERICA (que luego se amplían a Iberoamérica) las cuales son consideradas en las Vas Jornadas de Bototá (1970) y a partir de allí se dispone la preparación de Anteproyectos de códigos procesales (Civil y Penal) Modelos para Iberoamérica, los cuales están prácticamente prontos y han sido considerados en diversas Jornadas (VIIa, Guatemala, 1981; VIIIas, Quito, 1982 y serán presentados en las XIas Jornadas (Río, 1988).

Ultimamente en el área se ha puesto el acento en el Servicio de Justicia, enfocando, en especial, la infraestructura necesaria para el marco procesal

---

Cotta, Le Monnier, 1981.

El tema ha sido encarado a fondo también en Latinoamérica y es objeto de tratamiento en diversos Congresos, como decimos en el texto. Podríamos decir que todos los países del área tienen en marcha proyectos de investigación en ese sentido. Para citar uno, como modelo, nos queremos referir al realizado por la Universidad de la Plata, su Colegio de Abogados y la fundación Jus. Más ampliamente: R. Berizonce, 'El funcionamiento concreto del servicio de Justicia; necesidad de investigaciones empíricas', Rev. Urug. Der. Proc., 1984, pág. 135. También, 'La organización de la asistencia jurídica', Rev. Urug. Der. Proc., 1986, pág. 432.

referido, atacando el problema desde su base. Tratando de utilizar, de alguna manera, los modernos medios técnicos a ese fin. No es extraño, entonces, que en las recientes Jornadas Uruguayas de Derecho Procesal (IVas Jornadas, Punta del Este, marzo de 1987) con participación de juristas de nuestro país, pero también de Argentina y Brasil, uno de los cuatro temas fuera dedicado al análisis de esta cuestión y en las XIas Jornadas del Instituto Iberoamericano de Río de Janeiro (Mayo de 1988) el tema nro. 1 será: 'Medios de aumentar la eficiencia del Servicio de Justicia'.

La Eficiencia de la Justicia como tema global es, sin duda, tema prioritario y muy bien han hecho los organizadores del Congreso en colocarlo como lema de nuestras labores en Utrecht.

Dentro de este corresponde analizar, en este Relato, la cuestión de qué experiencias puede aportar el proceso administrativo para mejorar le eficiencia de la Justicia en general.

El Relato general ha contado con la invalorable colaboración de los siguientes relatos nacionales: de Argentina, del profesor Augusto Mario Morello, de Brasil, del profesor Antonio Carlos de Araujo Cintra, de España, magistrado Adolfo Carretero Pérez (estos tres designados originalmente por el profesor Bryant Garth), de Ecuador, el profesor Isaac Lovato, de Colombia, el profesor Hernando Devis Echandia, de Perú, el profesor Carlos Parodi Remón y de Costa Rica, el magistrado Olman Arguedas Salazar. Estos relatores, los últimos con el poco tiempo que mi nombramiento tardío me permitió otorgar para sus informes, me han aportado una información invalorable para la preparación del trabajo, por lo cual deseo expresarles mi más efusivo agradecimiento.

2 DELIMITACION DEL TEMA EN EL AREA: PROCESO ADMINISTRATIVO Y PROCESO CONTENCIOSO ADMINISTRATIVO EN IBEROAMERICA

En el área iberoamericana -así como en otras- es necesario distinguir el procedimiento administrativo puramente dicho, del proceso contencioso administrativo.

Es decir, el procedimiento puramente administrativo, realizado por la Administración en cumplimiento de esta función, que puede asumir formas más o menos procesales (V. Infra, nro. 2.1) y el proceso contencioso administrativo que regula la Justicia referida a la Administración, ya sea cuando esta es parte en un litigio judicial o, especialmente, cuando tiene por objeto anular y/o reformar los actos administrativos ilegales dictados por la Administración o reparar los perjuicios derivados de dicha ilicitud (Infra nro. 2.2).

Es decir, por un lado, el procedimiento que realiza la Administración por sí y ante sí, naturalmente con referencia a los administrados y sus derechos y por otro el proceso que se organiza para *juzgar* a la Administración.

Regímenes que, en Iberoamérica -en general- están separados, obedecen a principios distintos y se realizan por órganos diferentes, aun cuando puedan, en algunos puntos, tender a confluir.

2.1 EL PROCEDIMIENTO ADMINISTRATIVO

El procedimiento administrativo es el que realiza la Administración actuando en su típica función (administrativa), tomando decisiones, dictando actos (administrativos) inclusive decidiendo peticiones y/o recursos de los administrados, pero siempre dictando resoluciones a través de sus diversos órganos.

Esto es totalmente diferente de la actividad (jurisdiccional) por la cual se juzga a la Administración por órganos que, naturalmente, ejercen otra función diferente a la administrativa. Ese es el campo del contencioso administrativo.

En el primer caso estamos dentro de la Administraticón, pues se trata de dictar y luego examinar, juzgar, anular (o confirmar) los actos dentro de ella, mientras que, por el contrario, las acciones o recursos jurisdiccionales, contra los actos administrativos, constituyen Justicia y no administración[3].

Esta delimitación no excluye que, dentro de la propia Administración, se noten dos tendencias trascendentes, a veces confundidas en una sola que, desde cierto punto de vista, hacen más borrosas las diferencias y hasta permitirían extraer lecciones para el proceso civil, no solo del contencioso administrativo, sino del propio procedimiento administrativo. (Aunque, como veremos, la principal tendencia es la contraria, Infra nro. 3).

Es así que (sobre todo en países fuera del área, en especial los del Common Law) se crean tribunales que no pertenecen al Poder Judicial y que deciden los litigios administrativos en materias determinadas y específicas, a veces con carácter definitivo. La adopción por la Administración de los principios del 'due process' (entre otras la obligación de los órganos públicos de 'notice and hearing', que es considerada como 'fundamental of fairplay', como una 'rule of natural Justice') llevó a considerar los procedimientos administrativos como 'a quasi judicial functions' y a las autoridades respectivas como 'administrative tribunals', no obstante la resistencia general a reconocerle la naturaleza de órganos de Justicia. La presencia de estos 'offices', 'boards', 'commissions' con amplios poderes normativos o reglamentarios (rule making) y de decisión (adjudication) en las controversias entre la Administración y los particulares, levantó gran resistencia, pero el camino estaba marcado y por él se seguiría transitando (Infra, nro. 3)[4].

En el área iberoamericana, por el contrario, se proclama, en general y con base constitucional, que debe excluirse la función jurisdiccional dentro del ámbito de la Administración.

---

3 En principio el procedimiento administrativo es el destinado, dentro de la propia Administración, a resolver los requerimientos contínuos e impostergables de la vida administrativa, sin perjuicio de su revisión jurisdiccional posterior. En este procedimiento, como es sabido, no se enfrentan partes iguales, la Administración no es juez independiente, juzga en causa propia, no hay cosa juzgada...
Desde hace mucho tiempo el procesalismo distingue claramente ambas actividades. Entre otros: P. Calamandrei, 'Límites entre jurisdicción y administración en la sentencia civil', en Estudios sobre el Proceso Civil. Trad. Sentís Melendo, Buenos Aires, 1961, págs. 19 y ss.

4 Más ampliamente: H. Giorgi. 'El contencioso administrativo de anulación', Montevideo, 1959, págs. 100 y ss. Asimismo E. Vescovi. El proceso contencioso administrativo. Contribución al estudio del Derecho comparado, con especial referencia al régimen latinoamericano y del Uruguay', en libro de homenaje a Amílcar Mercader, La Plata, 1971.

2.2 EL PROCESO CONTENCIOSO ADMINISTRATIVO

2.2.1 Generalidades

El proceso contencioso administrativo, en cambio, se puede ubicar dentro del género de las acciones impugnativas[5], pues tiene como fin la queja (impugnación) contra las decisiones (definitivas) de la Administración.

En este campo tenemos que distinguir los litigios comunes en los cuales la Administración es parte (El Estado como órgano público, pero actuando en la actividad privada, los organismos estatales, para-estatales, etc.). Y los que llamamos contencioso-administrativos (propiamente dichos), en los cuales se juzga la actividad de la Administración, bajo el ángulo de la Justicia, con el fin de anular (o confirmar) los actos administrativos, disponer su revocación (o reforma) o la reparación, como consecuencia de dicha anulación o simplemente en virtud de los daños y perjuicios ocasionados (En cuya ocasión se pueden incluir en el primer caso).

En ambos casos no estamos dentro de la actividad administrativa, sino jurisdiccional (Infra, nro. 3); en el primero, juzgando litigios comunes, con la única particularidad que una de las partes es la propia Administración; en el otro, juzgando a esta, a sus propios actos[6].

2.2.2 Diversos sistemas de Justicia Administrativa

En el dictado de la Justicia Administrativa, esto es en el juzgamiento de la Administración, existen diferentes sistemas que pueden ubicarse dentro de tres principales. (Que no son puros y responden solo a la necesidad de la exposición, como todas la clasificaciones en Derecho).

A Justicia Administrativa a cargo del Poder Judicial

En este sistema, el Poder Judicial, compliendo su natural función, imparte la Justicia, inclusive la administrativa. Se considera que en tal virtud la Administración no tiene ninguna razón para quedar excluida. Estando bajo el imperio del Derecho y a partir de que se reconoce este principio, debe estar también bajo el control de los jueces naturales del Estado.

---

5 Así lo hemos hecho en un libro reciente: E. Vescovi, 'Tratado de los Recursos. Teoría General de la Impugnación'. Cap. XV, Editorial Depalma. (En prensa).

6 En varios países se ha buscado superar las dificultades derivadas de las varias jurisdicciones para juzgar a la Administración, estableciendo el sistema de unidad. Para los litigios en los cuales una de las partes del proceso es el Estado o uno de los Entes Públicos, así como en aquellos en que se juzga (revisa) la actividad de ellos. Entre estos países, en nuestra área, podríamos citar a los de Costa Rica y Venezuela, a los cuales nos referiremos en el curso de este trabajo. En el primero se incluyen, en el ámbito llamado contencioso administrativo, las cuestiones civiles, en el sentido amplio del Derecho privado (no penales, ni laborales) en el que sea parte la Administración Pública (ley de 12 de marzo de 1966, art. 40). En Venezuela, el ámbito del orden jurisdiccional contencioso administrativo se extiende a todo litigio en que sea parte o una Administración pública o una empresa estatal. En Uruguay, a esos efectos, se crearon los Juzgados Letrados de Hacienda y lo Contencioso o Administrativo, pero para la anulación de los actos de la Administración se crea el Tribunal de lo Contencioso Administrativo.

Es el sistema que se desarrolló en Inglaterra, España (hasta cierto momento) Suiza, Noruega y Dinamarca, entre otros países de Europa. Y en los países latinoamericanos tales como Cuba, Argentina, Brasil, Venezuela, Perú, Bolivia, Uruguay (hasta 1952), etc. En algunos de estos países se han creado, sin embargo, regímenes especiales para ciertas materias (en especial, la fiscal); así sucede con el Tribunal Fiscal en México, creado en 1936.

Nace históricamente en el principio de separación de poderes, en el cual juzga solo la Justicia y en la afirmación tradicional, por ejemplo del Derecho inglés, de que la Administración está siempre sometida al contralor de los tribunales ordinarios, lo mismo que los paticulares[7].

Sin embargo, por virtud de ese mismo principio (separación de poderes) el sistema encuentra dificultades en cuanto a la limitación de las facultades del órgano jurisdiccional (Infra nro. 2.2.3). Por eso, en general, no se desarrolla demasiado. En Uruguay, por ejemplo, siempre se consideró que la única facultad de la Justicia era la de disponer la reparación (indemnización) por acto ilegal, sin poder revocar, ni anular los actos administrativos.

En principio, en este régimen, o juzgan todos los órganos del Poder Judicial o se crea una Justicia especializada, ciertos jueces y tribunales de lo contencioso administrativo.

Como variante de este sistema (con tendencia a insertarse en el régimen de tribunales especiales: Infra letra C) podemos señalar que en ciertos países la competencia de juzgar a la Administración se otorga a un solo tribunal especializado del Poder Judicial (a una Sala de alguno de los órganos supremos, por ejemplo, la Suprema Corte de Justicia).

B Justicia Administrativa, a cargo de órganos del Poder Administrador

Este sistema se originó y desarrolló en Francia, cuna del contencioso administrativo, Portugal (en la esfera nacional) y en parte en Italia, Bélgica, Grecia y los países de Africa de origen francofono (Egipto, Siria, etc.). El mismo ha influido en los países latinoamericanos como los de Ecuador, Colombia y Panamá. Pero se puede afirmar que actualmente no existe en ningún país de nuestra área.

Este sistema se origina en Francia -cuya evolución es demasiado conocida y queda fuera de este Relato- curiosamente también al amparo del principio de la separación de poderes, aunque su explicación radica, fundamentalmente, en una razón de desconfianza a los tribunales judiciales (parlements) que habían caído en enorme desprestigio al momento de la Revolución Francesa[8].

Es el llamado sistema de la Justicia retenida, del que luego se pasa a la Justicia delegada, pero siempre dentro de la Administración. Se funda en la

---

7 Conforme Robson, 'Justice and administrative law', 3a. ed., London, 1951. Murillo Ferrol, 'El régimen jurídico de la Administración inglesa', en Rev. de Adm. Públ., Madrid, 1950, nro. 1, págs. 39/78.

8 Es curioso observar cómo las mismas razones determinan orientaciones opuestas, en Inglaterra y en Francia, con influencia en el Continente. Es que en Inglaterra, la circunstancia histórica determinó que al organizarse el sistema, el régimen que estaba en mayor desprestigio era justamente el de la Justicia impartida por la propia Administración y el recuerdo de la 'Cámara estrellada' influyó negativamente sobre la posibilidad de darle a la Administración la facultad de dictar Justicia administrativa. En Francia, como decimos en el texto, lo más desprestigiado era la Justicia dictada por los tribunales judiciales (Parlements).

especialización del Derecho administrativo (inclusive lo hace nacer y provoca su desarrollo) y en la indudable autoridad que ejerce el órgano especializado: el Consejo de Estado. Este se convierte en verdadero rector de la actividad de la Administración (expresa su parecer sobre proyectos de leyes, su opinión es necesaria en materia de reglamentos, evacúa consultas de los Ministerios ...). Su independencia y autoridad lo convierten en un pilar del Derecho administrativo francés y de su Justicia administrativa.

También en este sistema se nota una evolución (en Francia y demás países, con ciertas diferencias) que lo acercan, por muchos de sus caracteres, a los tribunales judiciales (Infra, nro. 3).

C Justicia administrativa a cargo de órganos especializados independientes del Poder Judicial y del Administrador

Se crea un Tribunal especial que no se ubica ni dentro del Poder Judicial, ni de la Administración, también invocando el principio de la separación de poderes; se trata de deslindar, tanto del Poder Ejecutivo, para que no sea Juez en causa propia, como del Judicial, para que no interfiera, sustituyéndose, a la Administración. Es el triunfo de la especialización del contencioso administrativo, en base a la idea de que dado el desarrollo que ha tomado (como lo puramente administrativo) debe someterse a principios especiales.

Es el régimen de Alemania Occidental, también el que existe en Latinoamérica, en Uruguay y Panamá, entre otros.

En Iberoamérica, fuera del sistema en el cual la Justicia administrativa se realiza dentro de la propia Administración, según el sistema francés, que no aparece, los demás existen en variadas formas. No obstante podemos decir que predomina una tendencia a crear tribunales independientes y especializados para juzgar la actividad de la Administración.

Tema muy relacionado a este de la organización de la Justicia administrativa es el de la competencia de los órganos, sobre el cual haremos, también, una breve puntualización.

2.2.3 La Competencia de los Tribunales Contencioso Administrativos

La jurisdicción contencioso administrativa puede tener competencias diversas.

El primero de los contenciosos a mencionar es el de *plena jurisdicción*; en él el administrado puede obtener tanto la anulación o reforma del acto administrativo ilegítimo, como la reparación.

Aparece, predominantemente, en el régimen francés de Justicia administrativa impartida por la propia Administración; en los demás regímenes el principio de la separación de poderes pone alguna limitación al juzgamiento de la Administración, en cuanto la decisión pueda implicar una intromisión en la actividad del Poder Administrador (o poder político).

Sin embargo, en Alemania, existe una acción que permite dictar una orden que obligue a la Administración, por lo que, en parte se puede decir que se realiza este contencioso en un régimen con tribunales fuera de la Administración[9].

---

9 Más ampliamente H. Cassinelli Muñoz, 'Confrontación entre los sistemas de lo contencioso administrativo en Alemania Federal y en Uruguay', Rev. D.J.A., t. 66, pág. 160.

El segundo contencioso que existe, este sí en varios países del área que abarcamos, es el *anulatorio*, que persigue la reparación del derecho o interés lesionado, destruyendo la fuente misma que causó el agravio o perjuicio: anulando el acto administrativo.

Es el más común entre los países del área, como también, en prácticamente, la mayoría de los contenciosos del mundo.

La *indemnización* es en algunos países, como Uruguay, una consecuencia de la anulación. También puede ser independiente si se admite que, aun dejándose el acto en pie, se disponga la indemnización[10].

Existe tembién la *jurisdicción represiva* y el *contencioso de interpretación*, que no creemos del caso analizar en el marco de este Relato.

En definitiva la conclusión que puede sacarse es que los sistemas son variados y el concepto acerca de la naturaleza y las competencias, dependerá de los sistemas diversos.

No obstante, dada la finalidad del trabajo, debemos analizar principalmente los procedimientos con el fin de considerar la posibilidad de extraer lecciones en nuestra búsqueda por la mayor eficiencia de la Justicia civil.

3 LOS PROCEDIMIENTOS ADMINISTRATIVOS (PROPIAMENTE DICHOS)

En el análisis de los procedimientos administrativos estrictamente hablando (excluyendo la Justicia administrativa, el contencioso administrativo) no parecen encontrarse principios que puedan inspirar las reformas al proceso civil. Más bien aparece una tendencia a la influencia de este en aquel, dentro de lo que se ha llamado la tendencia a la *juridización de la Administración*. Fenómeno que creemos del caso analizar, aunque fuera muy someramente, en este Relato, por cuanto, en definitiva, se trata de confirmar la validez de los principios que inspiran al proceso civil y que si fueran aplicados correctamente, permitirían, de seguro, una más eficiente Justicia.

Como consecuencia de la característica del procedimiento administrativo, en el cual no se enfrentan partes iguales -como en el proceso- sino que el administrado está sujeto a la Administración, que realiza actos de autoridad fundados en el interés general, predominan en el procedimiento administrativo la unilateralidad y el autoritarismo[11].

Con la proclamación del Estado de Derecho se reclamó (inclusive en la doctrina alemana, como una consecuencia de este) la necesidad de tribunales para juzgar a la Administración, ya fueran judiciales o especiales, pero

---

10 En Uruguay, según la Constitución, el Tribunal de lo Contencioso Administrativo puede declarar la nulidad del acto por cuatro votos conformes (de los cinco miembros) pero, en cambio, por tres votos puede reservar la acción por indemnización (aunque no se anule el acto).

11 Más ampliamente, A.R. Real, 'Rasgos generales de la evolución contemporánea del procedimiento administrativo. Atenuación del originario autoritarismo napoleónico por el debate contradictorio'. En Nuevos estudios de Derecho Administrativo, Montevideo, 1976.

Nos encontramos dentro de las conocidas concepciones, especialmente del Derecho francés, de la **Justicia retenida** y del **Ministro Juez** (Auby-Drago, 'Traité du contentiaux administratif' 2a. ed., 1975, parágs. 117, 126 y ss, 532, etc.).

independientes del gobierno. Este movimiento se encuadra dentro del más amplio de reclamar jueces imparciales para juzgar la regularidad jurídica de todas las funciones del Estado, incluidas, también, la legislativa y jurisdiccional[12].

Esta tendencia ha conducido a cambiar el enfoque clásico del procedimiento administrativo no contencioso, a valorizar su regulación jurídica y sus garantías. Sin alterar sus rasgos específicos dicho procedimiento ha adoptado ciertas normas propias del Derecho procesal, en especial las grantías del debido proceso legal. Metafóricamente, entonces, se ha hablado de la *jurisdiccionalización* del procedimiento administrativo. También se habló de *procedimentación* o *procesalización*[13].

Las principales manifestaciones de esta juridización que aparece en los procedimientos administrativos del área iberoamericana, siguiendo la línea de los sistemas de otras áreas, tales como las leyes de Alemania y España, consiste en la utilización de los principios que regulan el proceso, en especial el debido proceso[14].

Esta tendencia coincide en la expedición de códigos administrativos que abarcan una gama muy grande de países y en los cuales, casi generalmente, se incluyen estos nuevos principios jurídicos[15]. Inclusive en la propia Francia se señala esta misma tendencia, aunque en forma menos amplia y solo parcial, pero que marca la misma línea[16]. Semejantes conceptos pueden ser aplicados a los países del Common Law[17].

Son múltiples los principios procesales que ingresan al procedimiento administrativo.

---

12 Dentro de este mismo orden de ideas es que aparece la teoría de la responsabilidad por acto legislativo, la declaración de inconstitucionalidad de las leyes, la responsabilidad por actos jurisdiccionales y, desde luego, la posible anulación de los actos ilegítimos, aunque provengan del propio Poder Legislativo o Judicial (con tal, naturalmente, que se tratan de actos administrativos).

13 Ya Duguit señaló la jurisdiccionalización ('Traité de Droit constitutionnel', 3a. ed., T. II, págs. 287/288).

A.R. Real, entre nosotros, es quien usó el término **juridización**, que aparece adecuado (Procedimiento administrativo comparado. Su juridización. En Rev. Urug. Der. Proc., 1982, págs. 103 y ss).

Se ha hablado también de **procedimientación** o **precesalización** (A. Gelsi Bidart, 'Límites actuales entre jurisdicción y administración' en Estudios de Derechto Administrativo, Publ. Fac. Der. de Montevideo, T. II, págs. 208/209). R.B. Stewart, 'Le procéduralisme dans le Droit administratif. Etudes et documents de Conseil d'Etat, nro. 30, 1979, pág. 303).

Dromi, en Argentina, más bien en tono despectivo y con intención crítica habla de '**judializació** (J.R. Dromi, 'Derecho subjetivo y responsabilidad pública', Bogotá, 1980, pág. 139, etc.).

14 Se menciona como la primera normativa en tal sentido la ley austríaca de 21 de julio de 1925 dictada en la época más influyente de la escuela vienesa (C. Wiener, 'Vers une codification de la procédure administrative', Paris, 1975, págs. 77 y ss). La ley española a la cual nos referimos es la de 17 de Julio de 1958 y la ley alemana la que entró en vigencia el 1o. de Enero de 1977.

15 Los administrativistas han destacado que estas nuevas leyes no solo se dan en los países democráticos (Estado de Derecho), sino que aparecen en la España franquista, en la Argentina de Lanuse. En Uruguay, el decreto 640/973, fue dictado en pleno gobierno de facto.

16 Es así que la ley francesa de 11 de julio de 1979 impone la necesaria motivación de una serie de decisiones administrativas.

17 E. Soto Kloss, 'Notas sobre el procedimiento administrativo inglés', en Rev. Der. Publ., nro. 16, 1974, págs. 59 y ss.

Así podemos mencionar el *derecho de defensa*, a través del derecho a tener conocimiento y a ser oído. Estas garantías aparecen, especialmente, en la ley alemana, pues en Francia solo se requiere respecto de las medidas tomadas a título de sanción, lo cual es mucho más restringido[18], pues en Alemania se extiende a todos los casos y comprende al peticionante o su eventual oponente (si se discute sobre derechos exclusivos) o al destinatario del acto. Inclusive si la petición, de ser acogida, pudiera ocasionar un efecto favorable a un tercero, se le debe dar la oportunidad de intervenir. Y cuando la Administración se propone preparar planes que afectan a una colectividad de individuos, o al público en general, el procedimiento previo mediante el cual se ejerce aquel derecho asume formas semejantes a la audiencia o encuesta pública[19].

Otro aspecto importante es la posibilidad de ver el expediente y aún los dossier de los interesados. Recientemente, leyes francesas, alemanas y estadounidenses, consagren el derecho de los ciudadanos a conocer las constancias sobre ellos en los ficheros públicos[20]. Se establece también la obligación de motivar las resoluciones administrativas.

Estos principios son recogidos en Iberoamérica en varios países. Inclusive en Uruguay, por disposición constitucional, se establece 'la carrera administrativa', la 'destitución solo ... de acuerdo con las reglas establecidas en la ... Constitución ..' y dispone que le ley deberá establecer 'las condiciones de ingreso ... el derecho a la permanencia en el cargo, el ascenso ... las condiciones de suspensión o traslado... (arts. 60 y 61 de la Constitución de 1967 vigente).

El relator nacional brasileño Antonio Carlos de Araujo Cintra, hace notar cómo los principios del debido proceso se deben observar, según la más moderna doctrina de su país[21] en todos los procedimientos, inclusive los propiamente administrativos, notándose una tendencia hacia la flexibilización de dichos procedimientos, que van tendiendo a su juridización, pese a la heterogeneidad de los mismos (págs. 6, 7 y 8 de su Relato) destacando la influencia de los procesos, tanto civil como penal, en los procedimientos administrativos, como lo venimos explicando (pág. 9 del Relato nacional de Brasil).

Lo mismo podemos decir de España, como vimos, y también de Argentina y Uruguay, donde existe una amplia regulación de dichos procedimientos administrativos. como en la mayoría de los países del área, donde se nota la influencia procesal (judicialización).

Leyes o decretos administrativos (cuando no códigos, como dijimos) han ido

18 Conforme, M. Fromont, 'La codification du Droit administratif par la loi de 25 mai 1976', Rev. de Droit Pub., 1977, nro. 6, págs. 1290/1291.

19 Más ampliamente A.R. Real, 'Procedimiento administrativo ...' en Rev. Urug. Der. Proc., cit. y bibliografía allí referida, en la que nos hemos inspirado.

20 El tema ha dado lugar a grandes polémicas comprobándose la existencia de fichas secretas que, en distintos países, eran manipuladas por las autoridades de gobierno en forma ilegítima; así sucedió en Francia, con la famosa ley de 1905, luego que el 'escándalo de las fichas' se desatara. Más ampliamente, A.R. Real, 'Publicidad de los archivos administrativos en la legislación norteamericana y francesa', en Rev. 'Arquivos del Ministerio de Justicia', Brasilia, abril, junio 1970, nro. 150, págs. 20/23. También en 'Procedimiento administrativo comparado', cit, pág. 107.

21 Entre ellas cita el conocido libro de Ada Pellegrini Grinover 'O procéso en sua unidade', Sao Paulo, 1978 y II ed. Rio, 1984.

regulando la actividad procedimental de la Administración, en general conforme a dichos principios.

Esto no hace mas que conformar que, en materia procesal, en cuanto proclamamos doctrinariamente estos principios o los volcamos en leyes y códigos, estamos en la buena senda; lo esencial será que los mismos se cumplan efectivamente.

Resulta, en definitiva, que en lugar de que los procedimientos típicamente administrativos puedan influir en el proceso, la situación es la contraria: los principios de este están impregnando, como forma de mayores garantías, a la actividad de la Administración.

II EL SISTEMA PROCESAL ADMINISTRATIVO (EL CONTENCIOSO ADMINISTRATIVO) EN IBEROAMERICA. EVENTUALES PRINCIPIOS Y PROCEDIMIENTOS APLICABLES AL PROCESO CIVIL PARA OBTENER UNA JUSTICIA MAS EFICIENTE

4 LOS SISTEMAS CONTENCIOSO ADMINISTRATIVOS EN IBEROAMERICA

Como hemos dicho, en Iberoamérica no existe el sistema en el cual un órgano de la propia Administración imparte la Justicia administrativa, como sucede en el Conseil d'Etat de Francia[22].

Se dice que el sistema referido influyó en algunos países de Latinoamérica y se menciona el caso de Colombia y Ecuador, donde si bien existieron Consejos de Estado, originariamente órganos administrativos, la evolución, desde hace tiempo. los llevó a convertirse en verdaderos tribunales independientes.

El relator colombiano, Hernando Devis Echadía, nos señala en su Relato Nacional que, en su país, a partir de 1916 los Tribunales Administrativos forman parte del Organo Judicial, existiendo una verdadera Justicia especializada e independiente (pág. 2) y agrega que el Consejo de Estado colombiano, 'formado de siempre por verdaderos magistrados, tuvo a partir de dicho año de 1916 el derecho de designar sus vacantes por los restantes magistrados del mismo Consejo, así como también de designar a todos los magistrados de los Tribunales Administrativos seccionales. Lo que ha hecho escogiéndolos entre los juristas que considera mejor preparados y de una pulcra honestidad' (pág. 3). 'En estos aspectos, concluye el profesor Devis Echandía, hay una igualdad total entre el Consejo de Estado, cabeza de la Justicia judicial contencioso administrativa y la Corte Suprema, cabeza de la Justicia judicial civil, comercial, penal y laboral' (pág. 3).

En Ecuador, según nos expresa el relator nacional Isaac Lovato, existe un Tribunal de lo Contencioso Administrativo independiente, compuesto por tres

22 Además de los relatos nacionales mencionados, seguimos, en la exposición, dos importantes obras generales del área, la de Briseño Sierra, desde México, que fuera pionera y la más moderna del magnífico profesor y especialista español Jesús González Pérez, fuera de otras obras especiales sobre los diversos temas. H. Briseño Sierra: 'El proceso administrativo en Iberoamérica', México, U.N.A.M., 1968. J. González Pérez, 'Derecho procesal administrativo hispanoamericano', Bogotá, 1985.

magistrados elegidos por el Congreso Nacional de una terna presentada por la Suprema Corte de Justicia con facultades de plena jurisdicción y anulación.

También se ha mencionado a México, en cuanto a su Tribunal Fiscal, como régimen contencioso dentro del Poder Administrador[23], pero la situación es mucho más compleja. En primer lugar, debemos señalar, que estos tribunales tienen una gran independencia y están formados como en Colombia, por verdaderos magistrados[24]. En segundo término, debemos mencionar la introducción de sistemas contencioso administrativos con tribunales independientes en varios Estados, inclusive en el propio Distrito Federal[25].

La mayor parte de los países restantes en Latinoamérica tienen un sistema judicialista, en los cuales es la jurisdicción común (a veces dentro de una rama especializada de tribunales) quien juzga a la Administración, igual que a cualquier persona privada.

Así sucede en Argentina, aunque allí, en virtud del régimen federal, existen tribunales contencioso administrativos en algunas provincias[26], en Brasil[27], en Bolivia (Constitución, art. 122 y 127) Paraguay (Constitución, art. 199), etc.

También en Perú, donde el relator nacional, Carlos Parodi Remón, nos expresa claramente que, lo que sí ha quedado claro, es que en el Perú será el Poder Judicial y no un Tribunal de lo Contencioso Administrativo el que conozca y resuelva de las acciones contencioso-administrativas, en vía de impugnación de las resoluciones que expida la Administración y que causan estado. La solución judicialista responde a diversas causas, entre ellas que no existe en el Perú

---

23 J. González Pérez, cit., pág. 45.

24 Briseño Sierra señala que en México el contencioso administrativo está identificado como el proceso seguido ante dos tribunales especiales: el Tribunal Fiscal de la Federación y el Tribunal Federal de Conciliación y Arbitraje, para conocer los conflictos de los trabajadores del servicio del Estado (ob. cit., pág. 319). Ambos están dentro de la Administración. El Tribunal Fiscal dictaba sus fallos en representación del Ejecutivo de la Unión (art. 146 de la ley originaria de 1936), pero luego, por su ley orgánica, que entra en vigor en 1967, se dice que es 'un Tribunal administrativo dotado de plena autonomía para sus fallos' (art. 1o).

Más ampliamente: H. Briseño Sierra, 'El proceso ...', cit., págs. 325/335. J. González Pérez, 'Derecho procesal...', cit., págs. 45/46.

25 Nos referimos, en este caso, a la ley de 28 de Enero de 1971. Más ampliamente: H. Fix Zamudio, 'Introducción a la Justicia administrativa en el ordenamiento mexicano', México, 1983. J. Carpizo, 'Bases constitucionales de los tribunales contencioso administrativos', en Rev. del T.C.A. del Distrito Federal, nro. 1, Mex., 1972, págs. 31 y ss.

26 Dromi, 'Procedimientos administrativos provinciales', Mendoza, 1977, págs. 14 y ss.

27 Nos explica la profesora brasileña Ada Pellegrini Grinover que en Brasil, aunque la Constitución (de 1969 y enmienda 7/977) continúa hablando de 'contencioso administrativo', en puridad, el único sistema que merece ese nombre es el contralor de la Administración por el Poder Judicial y que en Brasil la revisión de la decisión administrativa está reservada al Poder Judicial' ('O proceso em sua unidade', S. Paulo, 1978, págs. 55 y ss).

Inclusive en recientes conversaciones nos expresaba dicha profesora que entre los proyectos de enmienda para la nueva Constitución que ha de aprobarse en Brasil, no existe ambiente para la creación de tribunales contencioso administrativos.

tradición respecto de la acción contencioso-administrativa con esa denominación y los alcances que se le reconoce en la doctrina y en otras legislaciones[28].

En otro grupo de países -cuyo número parece aumentar- existen tribunales contencioso administrativos independientes. Así sucede en España, Panamá, Costa Rica, Guatemala y Uruguay, por ejemplo.

Otro grupo de países puede incluirse dentro de aquellos que tienen una Justicia administrativa con tribunales independientes, aunque en algunos de ellos estos integren los cuadros del Poder Judicial. Son, entre otros, España, Panamá, Costa Rica, Venezuela y Guatemala. Así como los de ciertos Estados mexicanos y Provincias argentinas que crean tribunales contencioso administrativos.

Nos resulta claro el ejemplo de Uruguay, donde el Tribunal de lo Contencioso Administrativo es absolutamente independiente y no se encuentra dentro de ninguno de los tradicionales Poderes (Legislativo, Ejecutivo y Judicial, en especial en estos dos, donde normalmente encontramos dichos órganos, como vimos). Junto a la Corte Electoral (Justicia Electoral) y Tribunal de Cuentas (Corte de Cuentas) forman tres órganos absolutamente independientes (semi-poderes) con total autonomía. Sus integrantes, como los miembros de la Suprema Corte de Justicia, son nombrados por el Parlamento Nacional (Asamblea General, reunión de ambas Cámaras). La Constitución establece la absoluta asimilación de los miembros del T.C.A. con los de la Suprema Corte de Justicia (jerarquía, remuneraciones, independencia...).

En España se crea el Tribunal de lo Contencioso Administrativo, en esta etapa, por ley de 27 de diciembre de 1956 (complementada por la ley de protección de los derechos fundamentales de la persona de 26 de diciembre de 1978) que sigue vigente pese al estatuto de las Comunidades Autónomas en materia de derecho sustantivo (Gonzáles Pérez).

En Costa Rica la ley vigente de 1966[29] encomienda dicha jurisdicción a los Juzgados especializados (de lo Contencioso Administrativo y Civil de Hacienda) pero en alzada y casación a las Salas Civiles de la Suprema Corte de Justicia y Tribunales Superiores (art. 7 de la ley).

5 LOS PRINCIPIOS PROCESALES REGULADORES DEL CONTECIOSO ADMINISTRATIVO

En materia de principios procesales no encontramos mayores especialidades en el proceso contencioso administrativo.

En general se afilia, la organización de este proceso, a los principios proclamados por los procesalistas para todas las materias.

El relator nacional argentino, profesor de La Plata, Augusto Mario Morello, señala, entre los 'Basamentos comunes' a los procesos civil y contencioso

28 Tal normativa resulta del Código Procesal Civil de 1912 (con enmiendas) del Decreto Legislativo nro. 127 y del Decreto Ley nr. 21.773).

29 La legislación costarricense reguladora de la jurisdicción contencioso administrativa es la siguiente: Ley nro. 3.667, de 12 de marzo de 1966, reformada por leyes nros. 3.830, de 3 de diciembre de 1966, 4.191, de 17 de diciembre de 1968, 4.957 de 16 de febrero de 1972, 5.052 de 17 de agosto de 1972, 6.160 de 25 de noviembre de 1977, 6.175 de 12 de diciembre de 1977 y 6.872 de 16 de junio de 1983 (Información a Diciembre de 1986).

administrativo, el de la garantía de defensa en jucio, el de igualdad, el de garantías de seguridad jurídica y lo que llama suficiente y último contralor judicial necesario, entre lo que incluye el deber de motivación razonada, desarrollando, con su habitual magisterio, la labor de la Suprema Corte de la Nación Argentina en aplicación y defensa de dicho principio. Tratando los originales y trascendentes institutos de la gravedad institucional y exceso ritual manifiesto, que dieran lugar a una verdadera doctrina de casación constitucional, que es ejemplo de dicho país[30].

Jesús González Pérez coincide en la apreciación de que en el proceso contencioso administrativo se cumplen los principales principios procesales y Ada Pellegrini los coloca, en su mayoría, por su raíz constitucional, como aplicables a todos los procesos, incluyendo los procedimientos administrativos[31].

A todo ello podríamos agregar un refuerzo de los poderes del Juzgador que analizaremos en detalle en cada uno de los momentos del procedimiento.

6 EL DESARROLLO DEL PROCESO CONTENCIOSO ADMINISTRATIVO Y LAS LECCIONES A EXTRAER PARA LA ORGANIZACION DEL PROCESO CIVIL

6.1 LOS PROCESOS PRELIMINARES. PRESUPUESTOS DEL PROCESO

6.1.1 El agotamiento de la vía administrativa. Su relación con la conciliación en el proceso civil

Como se sabe, los procesos contenciosos administrativos, prácticamente en todos los países, requieren, como presupuesto para su iniciación, que el administrado recurrente haya agotado la vía administrativa. Esto es, que haya reclamado ante la Administración misma la revocación del acto (o indemnización ... anulación ...) que pide al Tribunal, utilizando, en su debido tiempo y forma, todos los recursos que los procedimientos administrativos le ofrecen.

En general los administrativistas reconocen que esto representa, en ciertos casos, una traba al ejercicio del derecho, en virtud de la complejidad de dichos recursos administrativos (con sus plazos, sus variedades ...). Inclusive, para evitar lo que se ha denominado como verdadero calvario en ciertos sistemas, como en España (ley cit., art. 122, 2) se establece el principio de que cualquiera sea la autoridad de que emane el acto se puede plantear la alzada ante el Superior (último), saltéandose los recursos intermedios ante autoridades a las cuales por regla general se debía recurrir (omisso medio).

El relator nacional de Costa Rica, Olman Arguedas, entiende que esta instancia se puede asimilar a la conciliación en materia procesal. Y el relator español Adolfo Carretero Pérez asimila también a este remedio extrapocesal, que

30 A.M. Morello, 'Relato nacional argentino', págs. 3 a 6. También en 'Los recursos extraordinarios y la eficacia del proceso', T. 2, Buenos Aires, 1981.

31 J. González Pérez (ob. cit.) habla de los principios de 'dualidad de partes' (Pág. 11), es decir bilateralidad, de 'contradicción' (págs. 111/112), de 'igualdad' (pág. 112), de 'defensa' (pág. 127), de 'concentración' (pág. 222), y de 'preclusión (págs. 232/233 y 291). También Ada Pellegrini Grinover destaca la necesaria aplicación de los principios ('O proceso en sua unidade', pág. 56 y ss., esp. págs. 64/65).

tanto desarrollo tiene en el mundo contemporáneo, la consulta que el particular puede formular ante la Administración y en virtud de la cual esta debe precisar su posición respecto del caso concreto consultado, lo que favorece la actuación del administrado[32].

6.1.2 La suspensión del acto administrativo como medida cautelar anticipativa

En la mayoría de los procesos contencioso administrativos iberoamericanos se admite la suspensión del acto administrativo como medida cautelar.

Puesto que, si bien los recursos puramente administrativos pueden tener efecto suspensivo, en cambio la acción de nulidad ante el contencioso administrativo no la tiene y el acto se cumple, por regla general, igualmente.

La suspensión se admite con la excepcionalidad que requiere la adopción de medidas cautelares, resultando de interés señalar la especialidad (y quizá el progreso) del sistema español que, a partir de la ley de 1978, dispone que dicha suspensión se convierte en regla cuando se trata de la protección de los derechos fundamentales de la persona.

Consideramos que esta solución puede aplicarse (o se aplica ya) al proceso civil como forma de mayor eficacia de la Justicia, ya sea a través del instituto de la ejecución provisional de la sentencia, que existe desde hace tiempo en el Derecho francés y también el italiano y se ha incluído en el Código Procesal Civil Modelo para América Latina, pero, fundamentalmente, a través de la medida cautelar anticipada.

Es conocida la tendencia moderna del procesalismo de admitir este tipo de medidas (anticipativas) que constituyen, a nuestro juicio, un género de la especie medida cautelar y que permite anticipar la decisión del Juzgador en los casos graves y urgentes, dictando una providencia provisional que no tiene por fin asegurar el cumplimiento de la futura sentencia (cautela), sino anticipar la decisión, permitiendo que el demandado entre a disfrutar (provisionalmente) de la situación jurídica que reclama (alimentos, jornales ...)[33].

---

32 Dice así el relator español Adolfo Carretero Pérez: 'Las consultas vienen a funcionar a modo de una conciliación entre la Administración y los ciudadanos. A pesar de que aquella no puede transigir porque defiende el interés público, un modo de evitar que surja una cuestión discutible dentro del procedimiento administrativo es contestar a una consulta previa, donde sea conocida de antemano su postura. Los principios procesales que favorecen la eficacia del acto de conciliación, pueden jugar el mismo papel de las consultas en las cuales los defectos formales en que hubiera podido incurrir la Administración, no deben repercutir sobre la sustancia de la materia o problema que haya sido objeto de la consulta, mas que en la medida indispensable, como sucede en Derecho procesal'.

33 F. Baur, 'Tutela jurídica mediante medida cautelar', G. Arrieta 'I provedimenti d'urgenza', Padova, 1982. A Proto Pisani, 'Appunti sulla giustizia civile', Bari, 1982. A. Pellegrini Grinover, 'La tutela preventiva de la libertad en el ordenamiento brasileño'. 'En Studi in onore di Tito Carnacini'. Theodoro Junior, 'Proceso cautelar', 4a, ed., S. Paulo, 1980.
Ver asimismo 'I processi speciali' Studi oferti a Virgilio Andrioli, Napoli, 1979. Espec. La China Sergio, 'Quale futuro per i provedimenti d'urgenza', pág. 151; A Proto Pisani, 'Appunti sulla tutela sommaria', págs. 309 y ss.; A. Tizzano, 'I provedimenti urgenti nel processo comunitario'; G. Verde, 'Considerazioni sul procedimento d'urgenza', págs. 407 y ss.

6.2 LOS ACTOS DE INICIACION DEL PROCESO. DEMANDA Y CONTESTACION. LA AGREGACION DE PRUEBA

Considerando solamente las especialidades que pueden determinar alguna enseñanza para el proceso civil, nos detendremos a analizar la documentación que debe agregarse con la demanda y la contestación.

En muchos de los ordenamientos del régimen iberoamericano, se requiere que a la demanda se acompañe la copia del acto objeto de impugnación o, al menos, una precisa indicación de dónde está contenido (diario oficial en que fuera publicado, etc.). Así como los documentos que prueben las alegaciones de hecho. Y, como resulta esencial, que la Administración, con la contestación, acompañe el expediente administrativo del cual procede el acto o disposición impugnada.

En la mayoría de las legislaciones, sobre todo las más modernas, se establecen estos deberes (o cargas) con escasas variantes. Así sucede en la ley española, en el Código contencioso administrativo de Colombia (art. 139), en los códigos de las Provincias Argentinas, en la ley de Costa Rica (arts. 36 y 40), en el Código Fiscal de la Federación de México (art. 214), ley de lo Contencioso Administrativo uruguaya, etc.

Respecto de la demanda se otorgan, en general, amplios poderes al Tribunal para rechazarla si no se cumplen las formalidades requeridas; en algunos sistemas más modernos el Tribunal debe establecer cuáles son los errores a corregir y fijar un plazo al efecto.

En cuanto a la carga de acompañar la prueba, hay sistemas que para el actor impiden presentar la documental posteriormente y para la Administración se faculta al Tribunal a considerar como ciertas las afirmaciones del actor, salvo que resulten contradichas por otros elementos de juicio[34].

También el moderno proceso civil tiende a establecer la carga de acompañar con la demanda, al menos la prueba documental y, en algunos casos la prueba toda (salvo los hechos nuevos, o la prueba que resulte de la contestación del demandado). Así lo establece el Código Procesal Civil Modelo para Iberoamérica.

6.3 LA PRUEBA. SUS ESPECIALIDADES

Podemos señalar, a través de los relatos nacionales iberoamericanos la existencia de algunos (muy pocos) preceptos especiales.

---

34 La ley uruguaya (nro. 15.524 de 9-1-1984) establece, entre otras normas, que la parte demandada junto con la contestación deberá remitir 'todos los antecedentes administrativos', entre los cuales se menciona 'el texto del referido acto, todos los elementos (dictámenes, informes, actuaciones sumariales, etc) que hayan precedido a su formulación ...' excluyendo solo los casos de 'secreto administrativo que la ley determine' (arts. 64 y 65). Y concluye disponiendo que, en caso de no cumplirse con este mandato legal 'el Tribunal podrá considerar como ciertas las afirmaciones del actor, salvo que resulten contradichas por otros elementos de juicio'.

Esta consagración legal no es mas que la solución que indicó la doctrina, desde mucho antes y la propia jurisprudencia del Tribunal. V.E.J. Couture, 'Sobre el precepto nemo tenetur aedere contra se'. En 'Estudios de Derecho Procesal Civil', Buenos Aires, 1946, t. II, págs. 129 y ss. E.T. Liebman 'Efectos de la negativa injustificada a la exhibición de prueba documental en poder de la parte' en L.J.U., t. II, sec. dotr. pág. 5. También, L. Torello y E. Vescovi, 'El nuevo régimen judicial', Montevideo, 1984, esp. págs. 63/64.

En primer lugar existe una ampliación de los poderes inquisitivos del Juez, dentro siempre del proceso dispositivo, lo que analizaremos por separado (Infra, nro. 7).

Existe alguna especialidad en cuanto a medios de prueba se refiere.

Resulta de interés señalar que las más modernas leyes regulan lo relativo a los informes de la Administración, prohibiendo que se cite a los miembros de los organismos públicos a absolver posiciones (ley uruguaya, art. 78; ley de Costa Rica, art. 54; códigos provinciales argentinos; ley de Ecuador (relato nacional, pág. 3); Códigos Fiscales de México (Federación, Hidalgo, etc.)). Es decir, como dice Morello, se está preferenciando por razones justificadas la prueba de informes (Relato nacional argentino, pág. 11). A lo que se agrega, en la ley uruguaya, la posibilidad de 'solicitar la exhibición y entrega de cosas o documentos en su poder, cuando su conocimiento se estime necesario a los fines del proceso' (Supra, nota nro. 33).

También Morello señala normas especiales en su país (Argentina) para la prueba pericial, disponiendo que el particular podrá solicitar peritos a su costa, pero la Administración se abstendrá de designarlos, debiendo recabar informes de sus agentes y oficinas técnicas (pág. 11).

6.4 LOS MODOS EXTRAORDINARIOS DE CONCLUIR EL PROCESO

El proceso contencioso administrativo, siguiendo la regla general, termina normalmente por la sentencia, pero tiene modos anormales de finalización (extinción) que ameritan, al menos algunos, subrayar sus principales caracteres.

La primer forma extraordinaria de extinguirse el proceso es a través del *desistimiento*, que es frecuente en este juicio, especialmente cuando se ha satisfecho extraprocesalmente la pretensión del titular. Como sucede cuando la propia Administración revoca el acto administrativo impugnado (de acuerdo a una facultad inmanente según casi toda la doctrina, que sostiene que no hay cosa juzgada en la Administración). En cuyo caso el proceso administrativo queda sin objeto. (Así suele declararlo el T.C.A. uruguayo, aun cuando no haya desistimiento).

El desistimiento es incluido en varias legislaciones modernas (Ecuador, Colombia, España, Costa Rica, Provincias Argentinas, etc.) y en algunas de ellas se dice que necesita ser aceptado. En efecto, como estamos frente a un desistimiento de la pretensión (del derecho) se trata de un desistimiento unilateral.

Mayor problema crea la *transacción*, que según algunos autores no puede darse, puesto que se trata -al menos, de parte de la Administración- de derechos indisponibles. González Pérez afirma que no cabe la transacción, que es contrato de derecho privado, en estos casos[35], lo cual sin embargo es admitido en los códigos de las Provincias argentinas, por ejemplo[36].

En cuanto a la caducidad (perención) de la instancia, no solo se regula, sino que existe una tendencia a disminuir los plazos (a 6 meses, en lugar de un año, como en el proceso civil) y a establecer la facultad del Tribunal de declarar de oficio dicha caducidad (Infra, nro. 7).

35 J. González Pérez, 'Derecho procesal....', cit. págs. 358/361.

36 Dromi, 'Proceso Administrativo Provincial', cit.

También la muerte del actor termina el proceso, pero solo en caso de pretensión intrasmisible, pues siempre queda a salvo la acción resarcitoria que pasa a los herederos.

6.5 LA SENTENCIA. LA COSA JUZGADA. LA EJECUCION

En esta temática queremos destacar, en primer término, en cuanto representa una especialidad, lo relativo a la cosa juzgada, al menos respecto de algunos ordenamientos. Puesto que, en general, se aplican los principios ya conocidos de los límites objetivos y subjetivos de la sentencia que dicta el Tribunal, que lo hace, en ejercicio de función jurisdiccional.

Sin embargo, se pueden señalar algunos casos en que la eficacia de la sentencia excede de dichos límites tradicionales.

Así la ley mexicana del Contencioso Administrativo del Distrito Federal dispone que la sentencia dictada en un juicio con relación a determinado acto administrativo tiene eficacia en otro juicio 'aun cuando las violaciones reclamadas sean diversas' (art. 49 de la ley de 25 de febrero de 1971); en Colombia cuando se trata de pretensiones de anulación de actos de carácter general tiene efectos erga omnes (relato nacional de H. Devis Echandía, pág. 14); en Uruguay existe una norma que establece que cuando la decisión 'declare la nulidad del acto en interés de la regla de derecho o de la buena administración producirá efectos generales y absolutos' (Constitución nacional, art. 311). En Costa Rica, lo que ya entra dentro de principios generales aceptados por el moderno procesalismo, se admite el efecto extensivo de la sentencia de nulidad frente a los demás interesados que se encuentren en la misma situación jurídica que el actor (Relato nacional, págs. 3/4).

En todo caso se trata de principios que modifican el régimen procesal de la cosa juzgada y que ameritarían un estudio más profundo, que no podemos realizar en este Relato General. No obstante ello, podemos señalar que, como hemos dicho, por lo menos el efecto extensivo de los recursos (o medios de impugnación entre los que colocamos esta acción impugnativa de nulidad) constituye un instituto receptado por la doctrina y aun la legislación procesal, para ciertos casos especiales[37].

En cuanto a la ejucución de la sentencia, dado que el ejecutado es el Estado o una administración estatal o paraestatal, los problemas que se plantean son específicos y las soluciones variadas. Frente a la posible resistencia a dicha ejecución y a la dificultad del uso de medios compulsivos contra las personas estatales.

Esta dificultad ha pretendido ser superada -en defensa del imperio del Derecho y el acatamiento a las decisiones jurisdiccionales- buscándose diversos mecanismos en las más modernas leyes contenciosas administrativas del área.

---

37 El tema del efecto extensivo se ha estudiado especialmente en los recursos del proceso penal. G. Leone, 'Tratado de derecho procesal penal', Buenos Aires, 1963, t. III, págs. 112/113. J. Clariá Olmedo, 'Tratado de derecho procesal penal', Buenos Aires, 1966, T.V. págs. 312/317. También en Enciclopedia Omeba 'Efecto extensivo ...', pág. 661. A. Pellegrini Grinover, 'Condena paralela y efecto extensivo de los recursos', Rev. Urug. Der. Proc., 1984, pág. 251. J.C. Barbosa Moreira, 'El litisconsorcio unitario', Rio de Janeiro, 1972. E. Vescovi, 'Tratado de los Recursos', cit., (en prensa), Cap. II, nro. 9.4, y bibliografía citada.

En Alemania Federal se prevé la posibilidad de imponer coactivamente el pago de sumas de dinero a la Administración y se prevé la responsabilidad del funcionario incumplidor que podrá ser condenado al pago de daños y perjuicios. En Italia el decreto de 1924 (28 de junio, art. 24) preveía la posibilidad de recurrir ante la jurisdicción de mérito del Consejo de Estado, en caso de incumplimiento de la autoridad administrativa.

En el área iberoamericana se ha avanzado más en la búsqueda de soluciones que no resultan fáciles de efectivizar[38].

En Costa Rica hay un régimen detallado para obtener el cumplimiento compulsivo de la Administración (ley cit., arts. 76/81) y se establece que el Tribunal dispondrá la ejecución directa dictando medidas precisas; las legislaciones de las Provincias argentinas también disponen la adopción de precisas medidas; también en Ecuador se dispone que el Tribunal, a petición de parte, dispondrá de todas las medidas que considere adecuadas para hacer ejecutar las sentencias.

En definitiva se trata de una amplia problemática que aún no ha tenido soluciones totalmente efectivas[39].

7 EL AUMENTO DE LOS PODERES DEL TRIBUNAL Y SU APLICACION AL PROCESO CIVIL

Consideramos que la tendencia al aumento de los poderes del Juzgador en el proceso contencioso administrativo responde a la tendencia general del proceso (en su unidad) hacia ello.

En efecto, en el proceso civil, sin abandonar el sistema dispositivo, se ha admitido el aumento de poderes del Tribunal, en general, lo que se ve reflejado en el proceso contencioso administrativo. Que, a su vez, en este tráfico de doble mano, nos servirá para proyectar en las reformas a la Justicia, buscando una mayor eficiencia.

En materia de iniciación de la acción sigue rigiendo el principio dispositivo en cuanto a que es el titular el único que puede promover la demanda, no pudiendo el Tribunal proceder de oficio.

Solo puede señalarse, como excepción a la promoción de la defensa de su interés directo, personal y legítimo (como requiere la Constitución uruguaya) el caso de la *acción popular*. La cual se prevé en forma específica para los procedimientos contencioso administrativos en Colombia y Perú y en forma más genérica en Brasil y España, lo que permite a parte de la doctrina admitir este tipo de acciones en la materia que aquí tratamos. Lo cual viene a llenar un

---

38 En nuestro país, si bien las decisiones del Tribunal de lo Contencioso se cumplen, dado el prestigio del órgano, los autores expresan que solo existen los siguientes medios para obligar a la Administración: a) interposición de recursos administrativos y jurisdiccionales contra los actos que contrarían la cosa juzgada; b) petición al superior jerárquico para que ordene dicho cumplimiento y haga efectivas las responsabilidades y c) responsabilidad, especialmente penal de los funcionarios, inclusive por desacato (H. Giorgi, 'El contencioso ...' cit., pág. 294; H. Casseinelli Muñoz, 'El ajuste de la Administración a las sentencias jurisdiccionales', En Rev. D.J.A., t. 55, págs. 70 y ss.

39 Más ampliamente, J. González Pérez, ob. cit., págs. 382/404.

vacío que se nota en defensa de los intereses superindividuales en estos momentos de nuestra sociedad de consumo y de masas[40].

En cuanto a la demanda ya vimos los poderes del Tribunal para rechazarla y/o ordenar su rectificación.

En materia de excepciones la mayoría de los regímenes contencioso administrativos modernos admite el relevamiento de oficio de la falta de los presupuestos procesales específicos de la acción de nulidad, como son los de caducidad (del plazo) o falta de agotamiento de la vía administrativa. En algunos países, dando un paso más adelante, se permite también relevar de oficio las excepciones dilatorias de falta de personería, incompetencia ... inclusive las de cosa juzgada y litispendencia[41].

El relator nacional español Adolfo Carretero Pérez reclama la mayor actividad del Juez para comprobar la correcta constitución de la relación procesal, evitando nulidades posteriores. Una especie de despacho saneador sería aconsejable en esta etapa.

En materia de prueba, ya hemos visto, que el Tribunal tiene amplios poderes, en general, en los nuevos regímenes, para recabar, especialmente de la Administración, las pruebas necesarias.

También se permite (por ejemplo en la ley uruguaya nro. 15.564) el rechazo in limine no solo de las pruebas inadmisibles, sino, aun, de las inconducentes, lo que significa un avance induscutible.

Por último hemos visto cómo en materia de caducidad de la instancia, también prodomina el impulso de oficio bien entendido, facultando al Tribunal a declararla, sin necesidad de pedido de parte, requerido, en general, en el proceso civil de la mayoría de nuestros países.

En cuanto a la sentencia no hay mayores variantes, manteniéndose el principio de congruencia (emanción del dispositivo). Solo por excepción puede citarse algún caso como el del Distrito Federal mexicano, en el cual el Tribunal de lo Contencioso Administrativo puede fallar basado en motivos distintos a los pedidos por las partes.

En cuanto a la ejecución de la sentencia los amplios poderes que se dan al Tribunal de lo contencioso administrativo son originados en la dificultad generalizada para ejecutar las sentencias contra la Administración, lo que es

---

40 Entre la abundantísima bibliografía (muy reciente) referida al tema, en reconocimiento a la continuidad de la labor de estos Congresos, nos limitaremos a citar el Relato General de los profesores Mauro Cappelletti y Bryant Garth para el VII Congreso Internacional celebrado en Würzburg (1983) tibulado: 'The protection of diffuse, fragmented and collective interest in civil litigation', Bielefeld 1983 (Libro con la publicación de relatos generales) págs. 117/159.

41 La ley uruguaya establece que 'si entre las exceptiones dilatorias no se encontraran la falta de jurisdicción, la de agotamiento de la vía administrativa, ni la de caducidad, el Tribunal igual se pronunciará de oficio sobre tales presupuestos del ejercicio de la acción de nulidad, si del examen de los antecedentes administrativos resultare de modo inequívoco y manifiesto su carencia o incumplimento' (art. 67).

El art. 670 de la ley de Costa Rica establece que se declarará la 'inadmisibilidad de la acción en los casos de falte de jurisdicción, incapacidad del actor o falta de legitimación del representante, actos no susceptibles de impugnación, cosa juzgada, caducidad de los plazos, defectos formales que impidan un pronunciamiento sobre el fondo'.

común a los procesos comunes en que la Administración es una de las partes y resulta condenada.

III LECCIONES PARA EL PROCESO CIVIL EXTRAIDAS DEL CONTENCIOSO ADMINISTRATIVO. LAS MODERNAS TENDENCIAS EN IBEROAMERICA

8 CONCLUSIONES DE LO DICHO RESPECTO DEL PROCESO CONTENCIOSO ADMINISTRATIVO

A manera de conclusión podemos decir (o reiterar) que existe una interacción entre el proceso civil y el proceso contencioso administrativo (y aún el administrativo puro).

Y quizá que por encima de ambos planean los principios generales del proceso, expuestos por la Teoría General que es válida tanto para uno como para otro proceso.

Es decir que reivindicamos la unidad procesal y la de sus principios, entendiendo que el proceso es uno y sus principios aplicables a todos los procedimientos, sean estos civiles, penales, administrativos, laborales, agrarios ...

No obstante reconocer que, siendo el procesal un Derecho secundario, debe estar al servicio del Derecho sustantivo (de fondo) y, por consiguiente, adecuar sus fines al de este y establecer las especialidades que se requieran para mejor servir a los fines de él.

Este enfoque, indiscutible, ha llevado a los distintos especialistas del Derecho de fondo a reclamar un proceso especial para su sistema (sean los penalistas, con el proceso penal, los laboristas, los agraristas, los administrativistas ...) Perdiendo de vista la unidad esencial del proceso que, de alguna manera, refleja la unidad esencial del Derecho.

Resulta entonces que las lecciones que podemos extraer del proceso administrativo, nada despreciables en esta búsqueda de una mayor eficiencia de la Justicia, obedecen, a nuestro juicio, a los principios generales del proceso. Y en tal sentido a la Teoría General del proceso debemos recurrir para beber en la fuente común de todas las organizaciones procesales.

No obstante ello, no debemos desaprovechar la lección de los procesos contencioso administrativos, para lograr una mayor eficiencia de la Justicia en todo el mundo, naturalmente en el área iberoamericana, desde el enfoque que debo dar a mi Relato (co-relato con referencia dicho ámbito exclusivamente).

Interesa, entonces, para concluir, analizar muy someramente las principales tendencias y las orientaciones para la reforma del proceso civil en Iberoamérica, a la luz de los principios estudiados extraídos del proceso contencioso administrativo (o no, pero en principio coincidentes con dichos datos).

9 LAS GRANDES LINEAS PROYECTADAS PARA EL PROCESO CIVIL: HACIA UN CODIGO MODELO PARA IBEROAMERICA

Hemos explicado las tareas para la preparación de sendos Códigos Modelos para Iberoamérica, tanto para el proceso penal, como para el civil.

Ateniéndonos al tema de nuestro Congreso y en lo estrictamente procesal (sin desconocer, como dijimos que el Servicio de Justicia necesita reformas estructurales y de base) nos referiremos a las líneas principales del proceso civil proyectado para el área. Y para no salirnos del tema, lo haremos con especial referencia a los principios que estudiamos en el contencioso administrativo.

9.1 PRINCIPIOS GENERALES

En cuanto al principio dispositivo, si bien este se mantiene, tanto en el proceso administrativo como en el civil iberoamericano, sin embargo sufre algunas atenuaciones que hacen decir a algunos autores que se tiende al principio inquisitivo. (Punto que no es del caso discutir aquí, pero que la doctrina iberoamericana, en su mayoría resuelve en el primer sentido).

Lo cierto es que existe un importante aumento de los poderes del Tribunal (Juez) que aparece en múltiples manifestaciones.

Sin perjuicio de que el proceso solo se inicia a pedido de parte -y no de oficio por el Tribunal- sin embargo aparece el impulso de oficio, sea a través de plazos perentorios, dirección del procedimiento por el Juzgador (que sin ser dictador, tampoco es espectador, sino director, según la terminología del maestro Alcalá Zamora y Castillo) así como la posibilidad de decretar de oficio la caducidad de la instancia.

También existe una clara manifestación del poder del Juzgador a través de la posibilidad de oponer de oficio ciertas excepciones, así como prevenir nulidades y complementar los presupuestos procesales indispensables (inclusive integrando el litisconsorcio en los casos en que este es necesario o unitario). Alcanzando un poder que le permite el saneamiento del proceso, conforme al instituto recogido en nuestro Código Modelo del despacho saneador de origen lusitano.

Resulta, sin embargo, de excepción, el poder fallar más allá de las pretensiones que las partes plantean en el proceso (ultrapetita, extrapetita) lo que, como vimos, aparece en forma muy excepcional en el proceso contencioso administrativo (Mexico), como es excepcional en el proceso civil iberoamericano, recordando solo el caso del Código de Cuba (1970 y 1978) que sigue el sistema soviético; el resto de los países y el Código Modelo se atienen al principio de congruencia y del tantum devolutum quantum apellatum para la segunda instancia.

El aumento de los poderes del Tribunal encuentra su máxima expresión en los procesos contencioso administrativos, como en los nuevos códigos procesales civiles iberoamericanos, a través de la facultad del Juzgador de buscar pruebas (verdad real) con mayor amplitud y no solo a través de las que solicitan las partes. (Naturalmente, que dentro de lo alegado por estas, de acuerdo con el principio dispositivo). Aquí es, quizá, donde se encuentran elementos del proceso inquisitivo.

También aparece, en las más nuevas leyes contencioso-administrativas del área iberoamericana, una tendencia a la aplicación de los principios de inmediación y concentración, aunque no de oralidad, ni del proceso mixto por audiencia, que ha sido el modelo que utilizamos para la preparación del Anteproyecto de Código

Procesal Civil para Iberoamérica[42]. Es que quizá el proceso contencioso-administrativo sea uno de los que menos se presta al régimen de audiencia oral, dado que, en su mayor parte, plantea cuestiones de Derecho y no de hecho.

Como consecuencia de estos principios y el aumento de los poderes del Juzgador, se busca crear un procedimiento en el cual predomine la regla moral y los principios de lealtad y buena fe, excluyendo la 'chicana' y las argucias de los malos litigantes.

También ha sido esta la preocupación en el Código Procesal Civil Modelo, estableciendo la condena en costas preceptiva, la exclusión del fraude, las sanciones y responsabilidades de las parte y de sus abogados, etc., así como la mayor simplificación y sencillez de los procedimientos. Estableciendo, por ejemplo, plazos uniformes, un lenguaje simple y claro, un número muy limitado de procesos y un sistema de recursos también simplificado.

9.2 MEDIDAS CAUTELARES Y ANTICIPATIVAS. EJECUCION DE SENTENCIA

Como una forma de aseguramiento de la Justicia y de búsqueda de su eficacia, se toma, como en el procedimiento administrativo, la precaución de admitir medidas cautelares y aún anticipativas (Supra, nota nro. 32).

Asimismo se introduce, en el Código Modelo, la ejecución provisoria de la sentencia de primera instancia (prestando fianza) y se le quita el carácter de suspensivo a algunos recursos (apelación diferida, casación ...) de modo de

---

42 El proceso por audiencia es un poco el pivot sobre el cual gira toda nuestra proyectada reforma del proceso civil iberoamericano. Es decir la introducción de un proceso mixto, en el cual la demanda y contestación (o reconvención) son escritas y también lo son los escritos introductorios de los recursos, pero el proceso gira a través de la audiencia. En general el proceso ordinario (plenario, de conocimiento) se organiza en base a dos audiencias. La principal es la audiencia preliminar. Esta, cuyo origen semántico provendría del derecho austríaco (erste tagsatung) como idea de primera o previa (aun cuando este derecho la ha convertido en facultativa, luego de su reforma de 1983). E.J. Couture la incorpora en su proyecto de Código de Procedimiento Civil para Uruguay (1945), el cual ha sido tomado como modelo por varios países (y ahora también del Anteproyecto de Código Procesal Civil Modelo para Iberoamérica) quien la habría tomado del régimen norteamericano (pre trial) y de la Conferencia Preliminar del Juicio de Puerto Rico. Guasp, al proyectar su 'Sistema de una ley procesal iberoamericana', también la incluye, dándole, como origen, la concordantia dubiorum del Derecho Canónico. Cappelletti menciona como su origen el Summon of direction del Derechto inglés (En 'La testimonianza della parte nell sistema dell'oralitá', Milano, 1962, T. II, págs. 421 y 485).
Otros la atribuyen al sistema del Regolamento legislativo e giudiziario del Papa Gregorio VI de 1834.
En todo caso la incorporamos con tres funciones principales: a) tentar la conciliación, sea total o parcial por el Juzgador reunido con las partes y conociendo ya el planteo de la litis (similar al Modelo de Stuttgart); b) sanear el proceso de excepciones, defectos, nulidades, de modo de permitir, en adelante, avocarse a la cuestión de mérito (fondo) y c) diligenciar la prueba o preparar su desahogo, fijando el objeto del proceso para la segunda audiencia. Que será, entonces, de prueba, alegatos y sentencia.
Resulta rescatable que en dos de las más trascendentes reformas del área, en España y México se haya incorporado este instituto. En España, a través de la ley de reformas urgentes, a través de la comparecencia para los asuntos de monto menor y en México en la reforma del Código del Distrito Federal de 1985, que es siempre modelo seguido por otros Estados.

permitir el cumplimiento de las sentencias, sin perjuicio de estos y otros recursos (revisión). Como contrapartida se admite que el recurrente (en casación, por ejemplo) pueda su vez -prestando fianza- obtener la suspensión de la ejecución mientras no se resuelve el recurso de su contraparte.

En materia de ejecución de sentencias contra el Estado, tema específico del proceso contencioso administrativo (ya que todas las de condena lo son contra aquel y otras entidades públicas) se establecen algunas soluciones inspiradas, también, en los sistemas estudiados, disponiendo que el Tribunal de ejecución, en casos de condenas líquidas (al menos) pueda ordenar al Banco del Estado que entregue la suma adeudada, debitando en la cuenta del Estado, Ente público, etc. la referida cantidad. Así como el establecimiento de sanciones conminativas (astreintes) y la eventual responsabilidad del funcionario desobediente.

9.3 LOS PODERES DEL TRIBUNAL EN LA ETAPA DE INICIACION DEL PROCESO

En esta etapa también en el proceso civil, coincidiendo con el contencioso administrativo, en los modernos códigos, se dan amplias facultades al Tribunal para controlar la demanda en sus aspectos formales, principalmente, pudiéndola rechazar si no se adecua a los requisitos debidos.

Los contralores van más allá en la doctrina iberoamericana y en el Código Modelo, permitiendo también rechazar la pretensión en caso de improponibilidad manifiesta, o si la falta de legitimación en la causa surge también de modo claro e incontestable, así como para ordenar le integración del contradictorio en casos de litisconsorcio necesario.

Estos poderes, de ordenación y dirección del proceso constituyen una afirmación de las facultades del Tribunal, así como un elemento indispensable para depurar el procedimiento de defectos, de modo que, en las etapas posteriores de prueba, alegaciones y sentencia solo se considere el mérito de la causa.

Inclusive, en el contencioso administrativo, en algunos países se avanza un paso más, permitiendo el relevamiento de oficio de otras excepciones previas (caducidad, litispendencia, cosa juzgada, falta de jurisdicción), algunas de las cuales también se receptan en esa forma en ciertos sistemas procesales civiles de Iberoamérica, aunque excepcionalmente también.

9.4 LA PRUEBA

En materia de prueba, quizá, las innovaciones más importantes las constituyen las facultades del Tribunal para procurar la verdad dentro de las afirmaciones de las partes, así como para rechazar pruebas no solo inadmisibles, sino también inconducentes (de plano y antes de la sentencia, donde también) rechaza las impertinentes) y el deber (carga) de las partes de acompañar toda la prueba con los escritos introductorios.

En varios códigos latinoamericanos se estableció, desde hace tiempo, la carga de acompañar con la demanda (y la contestación) la prueba documental (en su poder, indicando dónde se encuentra el resto) bajo sanción de no poderse agregar luego; ahora el Código Modelo -y en esto hay cierto parelelismo con el contencioso administrativo, como vimos- exige que se acompañe la prueba documental, pero también se solicite el diligenciamento de todo el resto de la prueba con dichos escritos. Salvo la que resulte de hechos nuevos, o posteriores alegaciones de las partes que sean permitidas, como en la contestación o reconvención.

Estas innovaciones son coherentes con el principio de lealtad y probidad que se proclama y permiten realizar en la audiencia al Juez y las partes, una labor constructiva en la búsqueda de la sentencia (Supra, nota nro. 41).

9.5 LA JUSTICIA CONCILIATORIA

Resulte parecido o no, el agotamiento administrativo a la conciliación extraprocesal, lo que no cabe duda es que la tendencia del proceso civil iberoamericano, de nuestros días, tiende a receptar el movimiento mundial hacia la Justicia conciliatoria.

Naturalmente que esta excede en mucho el marco de este Relato[43], pero de cualquier manera queremos reafirmar la confianza en especial de la doctrina de nuestra área en la difusión de esta forma práctica de la solución de muchas causas que, en general, no tienen cabida en la Justicia formal y organizada de nuestros países y en especial para los nuevos problemas y las pequeñas causas[44].

Además de esta conciliación extraprocesal, hemos proclamado la necesidad de realizar la intraprocesal con activa participación del Tribunal en la audiencia[45].

IV CONCLUSIONES Y RESUMEN

10 RESUMEN CONCLUSIVO

Hemos realizado en este Relato (co-relato para el área iberoamericana) sobre las lecciones del proceso administrativo en la búsqueda de una más eficiente Justicia, un análisis previo del procedimiento administrativo propiamente dicho, así como del proceso contencioso administrativo. Porque, como hemos explicado, en nuestra área, el procedimiento administrativo es realizado exclusivamente

---

43 Sería inagotable señalar la amplísima bibliografía sobre la Justicia conciliatoria, solo nos referiremos a los trabajos del Coloquio de Pau, de donde surgió la mayor llamada de atención y al tratamiento del tema en nuestros anteriores congresos y la amplia bibliografía citada en ambos trabajos.
H. Kötz, R. Ottenhof, 'Les conciliateurs. La conciliation. Une étude comparative', Paris, 1983. V. Denti y V. Vigoritti, 'Le rôle de la conciliation comme moyen d'éviter le procès et de résoudre le conflit'. Relato al Congreso de Würzburg ... cit., págs. 291/344.

44 El tema de los tribunales de pequeñas causas también ha ocupado la atención de los procesalistas de los países iberoamericanos, siendo objeto de tratamiento especial en el Congreso de Punta del Este (Uruguay, noviembre de 1986) donde se presentaron varios trabajos, inclusive una ley brasileña y la reciente experiencia de ese país (Rev. Urug. Der. Proc., 1987, nro. 1). E. Oteiza, 'Los tribunales de menor cuantía como respuesta actual basada en los principios de la Justicia de Paz'.

45 En dicha audiencia (Supra, nota nr. 41) el Tribunal que ya conoce la demanda y contestación está en condiciones de lograr un acuerdo entre las partes. Y si no lo logra, al menos de delimitar (generalmente reduciendo) el objeto del proceso y el de la prueba.
En especial, y siguiendo la línea de continuidad de nuestras labores ya indicada, ver: H.W. Fasching, 'Small claim courts', Relato al VI Congreso Internacional de Derecho Procesal Civil en Ghent, Bélgica. Libro de los relatos generales. 'Towards a Justice with a human face' Kluwer, Antwerpen/Deventer, 1978, págs. 343/375.

dentro de la Administración, mientras que el contencioso administrativo solo se efectúa fuera de ella, a través de la función jurisdiccional, sea por la Justicia común, sea por organismos especializados (Tribunales de lo contencioso administrativo).

En cuanto al procedimiento puramente administrativo en función administrativa (no jurisdiccional) analizamos su evolución y la tendencia hacia su judicialización (jurisdiccionalización) que se percibe a través de las más modernas leyes (y códigos) administrativos en los cuales se incluyen, en garantía para el administrado, los principios del debido proceso, del derecho de defensa y de motivación razonada de la sentencia.

El proceso contencioso administrativo (jurisdiccional) se caracteriza por la introducción -en forma similar y con efecto de doble mano para el proceso civil- de los principios de ampliación de los poderes del Tribunal, de lealtad y buena fe, de concentración y simplificación, de impulso de oficio y de reforzamiento de la ejecución de las sentencias de los jueces.

Así hemos analizado algunas etapas del proceso contencioso administrativo-que luego comparamos con las tendencias de los modernos códigos iberoamericanos y el Código Modelo del proceso civil- para poner de resalto la aplicación de dichos principios.

El Tribunal contencioso administrativo en los más modernos sistemas puede rechazar la demanda que no se adecue a las formas debidas, puede, también, disponer, que se reparen los defectos y se complete la legitimación. Como el Juez civil, según la doctrina latinoamericana, debe poder rechazar la demanda, además, por manifiestamente improponible o por falta notoria de legitimación en la causa.

Se requiere que el actor, con su demanda, acompañe sus elementos de prueba y que la Administración en la contestación agregue todos los antecedentes administrativos en su poder, bajo pena de tener por válidas las afirmaciones del actor. Como en el Código Modelo se requiere que en los escritos introductorios se acompañe la prueba documental y se solicite toda la restante que se proponen las partes producir en el proceso, salvo excepciones.

El proceso contencioso administrativo admite la adopción como medida cautelar, de la suspensión del acto administrativo. Este tipo de medida cautelar anticipativa es receptada ya por varios códigos procesales civiles.

Se faculta al Juzgador para rechazar pruebas inadmisibles e inconducentes y para disponer el interrogatorio de partes y testigos y otros medios para la averiguación de la verdad. (En el proceso administrativo no cabe el interrogatorio de partes, ni las posiciones, lo que se sustituye por la prueba de informes).

También se faculta al Tribunal contencioso administrativo a disponer de oficio la conclusión del proceso por caducidad de la instancia y a admitir las otras formas extraordinarias de extinguir el proceso, tales como el desistimiento (que es unilateral, pues resulta de la pretensión) así como la transacción. Esta última resulta discutible en el proceso contencioso administrativo, pero no en el civil. Por el contrario, en este, la conciliación cumple, en el moderno proceso civil, una función primordial. Tanto la extraprocesal, a través de la moderna Justicia conciliatoria, tan difundida y analizada por toda la doctrina y puesta en práctica en muy diversos países para la resolución de conflictos, sobre todo los producidos a raíz de las modernas formas de vida en nuestra sociedad de consumo y macificada. Pero también la procesal, en la audiencia, dirigida por el Tribunal ya instruido de la causa, en la cual se tienen grandes esperanzas.

Resulta, entonces, bastante clara la conclusión que por los diversos caminos, sea del proceso administrativo como del civil (en general, esto es, el no penal) llegamos al mismo objetivo de mejoramiento de la Justicia, a través de un proceso inspirado en los modernos principios aquí analizados y que se dan -o se tratan de incorporar- por el procesalismo contemporáneo con pocas discrepancias en las ansiadas reformas del Derecho positivo de todos los países y para nosotros, en especial para nuestra Iberoamérica.

En definitiva, si a esta reforma procesal -en cuyas líneas generales existe acuerdo- se agrega (o anticipa) una reforma estructural de todo el Servicio de Justicia, creando los órganos indispensables, inclusive los juzgados de las pequeñas causas, y proporcionando al Poder Judicial -el más desvalido y pobre de todos- los elementos necesarios, tenemos la esperanza de obtener para los justiciables, que son los reales protagonistas (y consumidores), una Justicia más verdadera y más eficiente.

SUMMARY

We have in this Report (co-report for the Iberoamerican area), referred to the lessons derived from administrative procedures in search of a more efficient justice, studying not only the administrative procedure properly understood but also the contentious administrative procedure as well. Administrative procedure appears only within the administration, while the contentious procedure is carried on only outside of it, by function, through common civil justice or by specialized organs (contentious administrative courts).

With reference to the proceedings properly administrative, we analyzed its evolution and its tendency towards a judicial status ('jurisdictionalization') perceived through the more recent administrative laws (and codes), which include, as guarantees of the parties' rights, the principles of due process, of the right to defense, and of decisions reached through judicial reasoning and the application of the law.

The contentious administrative proceedings are characterized by the introduction, parallel to developments in civil procedure, of the principles of enlargement of the court powers, of loyalty and good faith, of concentration and simplification, of court initiative, and of the strengthening of the enforcement of judicial decisions.

We thus analyzed some stages of the contentious administrative procedure and compared them with the tendencies of the recent Iberoamerican codes and with the Model Code of Civil Procedure, in order to underline their application.

In the more recent systems, the contentious administrative courts can reject a claim inadequately complying with proper forms, but they can also mend the defects even with respect to the standing to sue. And according to Latin American doctrine, the contentious administrative courts. like the civil courts, must be able to reject an obviously unfit claim or a claim brought with a notorious lack of standing.

It is also required that the complaint be accompanied by all the evidence of the complaining party and that the administration do the same for its defense: it must bring together all of the administrative antecedents in its power. If not, the plaintiff's assertions will be deemed validated. As in the Model Code, the parties are required to join, with the pleadings, all their documentary evidence and to ask for the ones they intend to produce during the procedure, with some exceptions.

The contentious administrative proceedings admit the suspension of the administrative act, as a cautionary measure. That kind of anticipatory cautionary measure is already received by some procedural civil codes.

The judge is empowered to reject inadmissible and nonprobative evidence. to promote the examination of parties, defendants and witnesses, and to act in other ways conducing to the ascertainment of the truth. (In the contentious administrative proceedings the defendant cannot be examined: he must give a written statement).

The contentious administrative courts are also empowered to conclude 'ex officio' proceedings in case of the expiration time of deadlines for the instance and to recognize other extraordinary ways of extinguishing the procedure. such as the dismissal (that is unilateral) and the transaction or settlement, reached by discussion in the contentious administrative procedure, but not in the civil one. On the contrary, in this one the conciliation procedure performs a primordial function. The extra procedural procedures of the modern conciliatory justice have been much noted and analyzed by the doctrine and applied in a great number of countries in order to resolve disputes, especially those produced by the modern ways of life of our consumers and mass society; we also have high hopes for procedural mechanisms within the procedure including hearings presided over by the court, which at that point has already and adequately been instructed about the lawsuit.

In conclusion, if to this procedural reform - about whose general lines everybody agrees - we associate a structural reform of the service of justice, creating the indispensable organs, included the courts of small claims, and furnishing the judiciary - the most unprotected and poorest of all the three state powers - with all the elements it needs, we hope to be able to obtain for claimants and defendants, who are the real protagonists (and consumers) a true and more efficient justice.

Our conclusion, then, is quite clear: by way of the many changes to introduce (and already introduced) in the contentious administrative procedure and in the civil one (that is, excluding the criminal proceedings), we are going to arrive to the same objective of bettering of the justice. By means of a procedure inspired in the modern principles which appear in or will be incorporated in contemporary proceduralism, we hope that with very few discrepancies the reforms will be successful, needed by the positive law of every country and, for us, especially in Iberoamerica.

REPORT OF THE DISCUSSION

Chairman: I.L. Backer (Norway)
Secretary: H. Bolt (the Netherlands)

The discussionpoints are to be found at pages 281 and 307.

The working session started with a short introduction by both general rapporteurs. Prof. Vescovi briefly sketched the historical and political background against which his report, relating to the Latin American countries, should be read. In these countries the diffidence about making statutory regulations for the citizen's protection from the authorities is gradually being overcome. Administrative procedures (before the courts) are currently being developed. Besides, Prof. Vescovi observed a converging trend: civil procedures and administrative procedures are growing towards each other. For instance: administrative procedures tend to become more formal while in civil procedures the aspect of orality is at present gaining prominence again. With respect to the developing administrative procedure he pointed to the following features:
- a preliminary procedure, preceding the contentious proceedings. The functions of the former include: opportunity of conciliation; establishing the scope of the dispute. During these preliminary proceedings provisional measures, such as suspension of the disputed government decision, are possible.
- development of the contentious procedure, with observance of the requirements of due process (e.g.: equal distribution of the burden of proof).

Subsequently, Prof. Garth gave a summary of his report, focussing on the following line of reasoning. (Wherever both procedures exist), civil procedure and administrative procedure have developed into *different procedures*, because they deal with *different disputes*. This then raises the question whether there is a great difference between public and private disputes? If public and private disputes are growing towards each other (are coming to have the same characteristics, e.g.: inequality of the parties), then it is only logical that the two types of procedures are growing (can grow) towards each other and (can) begin to show the same characteristics as well. In this connection one can think of: efficiency, specialization, broadening of standing (group actions), orality, preliminary procedures. Finally, he puts the question: What are the limits to the process of converging trends? Would it ever be possible to arrive at one comprehensive theory of procedures in general?

For discussion purposes Prof. Garth had drawn up a number of questions (see his general report). The last of these had a (rich) sociological background and read: What belongs in the courts? This question, however, did not emerge very clearly any more in the discussions; probably because the subject matter it broached was too complex (including, e.g.: legal economy, privatization of the settling of disputes, etc.).

The working session - with some 20 participants - yielded a lively and interesting discussion. A great deal of interesting material was put forward by the participants. The contribution on the side of Hungary and Russia, for example, made it clear that in these countries, too, work is being done on the improvement of the citizens' protection from the authorities. In these countries, however, the nature and the scope of this protection is (often) considered to be a political/ideological issue.

It is impossible to give a full-length report of the discussion. A selection will have to suffice, therefore.

It was pointed out that the discussion of this subject is not restricted to a comparison between the own (national) civil procedure and the own administrative procedure. Lessons can also be derived from the system for administrative procedure in another country. One particular example which was mentioned was the French administrative procedure, which, among other things, proceeds on the hypothesis that the two parties are not equal. What are the consequences for the procedure's system? Another interesting suggestion was, to spend some thought on the question to what extent the need for improved efficiency is reinforced by the fact that judges cannot be called to account for their working methods. When judges are called to account for their working methods (the amount of the work in hand; the duration of the proceedings) their usual response is that they are overloaded and that more judges are needed. By way of illustration, reference was made to those agencies/tribunals which do fall under a minister's responsibility and which pay far greater attention to a speedy and efficient way of dealing with the work.

Moreover, participants were in favour of further specialization within the civil procedure (for administrative proceedings often take place before specialized judges or agencies/tribunals). Such specialized civil proceedings, however, should be conducted before the courts (independent and professional) and not before administrative bodies. The wider possibilities of participation which apply in administrative proceedings ('broadening of standing in court') were also pointed out; it might be worth while to adopt this feature.

A number of participants, on the other hand, warned against too much optimism about the lessons which civil litigation might derive from administrative procedure. For there are great differences between the two as well, which makes it far from simple to draw such lessons. There are, e.g., various types of administrative procedures (mass-line procedures as opposed to complicated, technical procedures). Besides, administrative procedures have a different starting-point from civil procedures; the former always start with a decision, in which the legal relationship is established. It was suggested that there may be possibilities to make civil procedures more similar to administrative procedures in this respect. Finally, it was observed that informality and cheapness of procedure may also entail a heavy pressure on the courts, which have to cope with the consequences of these aspects.

During the plenary session, the discussion was opened by the chairman with a brief summary of the discussion at the working session. This was followed by some further remarks.

It was observed, for instance, that it seems that developments are not taking the same direction in all countries. In Eastern Europe developments move in the direction of more formal and more independent procedures. In the Western countries the trend is rather towards informality and specialization; in these countries the courts tend to adopt a more 'administrative' line (more informal, more efficient). Whatever the development, one must always keep certain limits well in mind: a procedure may not become too technocratic and it must continue to meet the requirements of due process. Another example of developments in opposite directions seemed to be those of specialization (a greater number of judicial bodies) and unification (towards a uniform model). In Latin America the trend is towards unification, in which, however, modifications are again introduced depending on the disputes which are being heard; in the Western countries the trend seems to be rather towards specialization (small claim courts, consumer disputes, etc.).

Generally, the existence of a converging trend (the growing towards each other of civil and administrative procedures) was recognized. Emphasis was laid on the need therefor, even from the side of the administrative procedure: in this procedure, too, it is important to make the requirements of due process. It seems that this converging trend causes the procedures to develop in the direction of the so-called Stuttgarter Modell: not too formal in character, active role of the court, orality. All participants unanimously subscribed to the notion that judicial bodies must be manned by independent and professional judges.

In conclusion, attention was drawn to the two sides of the conference theme. The central point in all developments must be to ensure, that the citizen's need for protection from the authorities be met *fairly* and *efficiently*. Efficiency is more than just cutting costs!

SIMPLIFYING THE TAKING OF EVIDENCE

SIMPLIFYING THE TAKING OF EVIDENCE

V. Denti et M. Taruffo
Université de Pavie (Italie)

REMARQUES PREALABLES

1. Etant donné que le thème général du congrès a pur but d'envisager les causes de la surcharge de travail des tribunaux et d'indiquer les moyens qui, dans les différents systèmes juridiques et aux différents niveaux de la protection des droits, ont été indiqués pour accélerer les temps de la justice civile, le problème de la simplification de l'administration de la preuve c'est surtout le problème de réduire la complexité et le formalisme de la procédure dans ce domaine. Dans ce cadre général, nous avons signalé aux collègues rapporteurs régionaux ou nationaux les points suivants:

(a) Avant tout, il s'agit de sélectionner les moyens de preuve qui doivent être soumis à l'appréciation du juge et à l'aide desquels doit être établie la vérité des faits allégués par une partie et contestés par l'autre. Dans les systèmes contemporains, entre les deux principes qui se partageaient les législations, celui de la preuve légale et celui de l'intime conviction, c'est le deuxième qui l'emporte, et l'on voit restreindre de plus en plus les cas où c'est la loi qui détermine la force probante des moyens de preuve. Il appartient au juge, par conséquent, là où la loi n'apporte pas de restrictions à l'admissibilité de la preuve, d'en apprécier la pertinence, c'est à dire l'aptitude de la preuve à une démonstration appropriée des faits invoqués par les parties à l'appui de leurs prétentions. Il faut ajouter qu'une évolution semblable se produit dans les systèmes de *common law*, étant donné que les règles d'exclusion de la preuve ont été sensiblement assouplies dans les réformes les plus récentes, notamment en ce qui concerne l'inadmissibilité de l'*hearsay* et la production des documents. Il est fort probable que l'élargissement des pouvoirs discrétionnaires du juge soit une source de complication, et non pas de simplification dans l'administration de la preuve.

(b) Un deuxième point concerne la réglementation des mesures d'instruction dans le but d'en accélérer le déroulement, comme l'exige l'encombrement croissant des tribunaux. On se trouve ici face à plusieurs problèmes, qui vont de la forme et des effets des décision qui ordonnent les mesures d'instruction, à la procédure d'exécution de ces mesures, aux conséquences de la nullité des actes d'administration de la preuve. On est, en général, d'accord sur le point que les procédures d'administration de la preuve sont trop complexes: il suffit de rappeler, par exemple, les véritables monuments de formalisme constitués par le faux incident civil et la vérification d'écriture. Il faut cependant souligner que la simplification des procédures probatoires trouve sa limite dans l'exigence de respecter le principe de la contradiction, que le juge doit faire observer en toutes circonstances.

(c) Le problème de la concentration de l'administration de la preuve marque la différence entre les systèmes de *common law*, qui sont caractérisés par l'exécution des mesures d'instruction dans le *trial* unique par le juge même qui prononce le jugement, et les systèmes de *civil law*, dans lesquels, en général, l'exécution se déroule en une série d'actes qui se disposent dans le temps, tels que l'enquête, l'interrogatoire des parties, l'expertise, etc., mesures qui peuvent être exécutées par un juge qui n'appartient pas à la formation de jugement. Il faut ajouter que dans les pays de *common law* la concentration de l'instruction dans le *trial* est facilité par les *pretrial procedures*, au cours desquelles les parties ont la possibilité d'obtenir des reinsegnements sur les faits du litige et sur les moyens de preuve. S'il est incontestable que la concentration peut simplifier, dans une certaine mesure, l'administration de la preuve, il faut reconnaître que la condition préalable de cette simplification est la prévision d'une phase préparatoire, dans le but d'éviter des surprises injustifiées pour les parties pendant l'execution des mesures d'instruction. Il s'agit alors de décider si cette phase préparatoire doit se dérouler avant l'introduction de l'instance, ou bien dans son cours, sous la direction du juge auquel l'instance est confiée.

(d) Enfin, on a souligné le problème de l'accroissement des pouvoirs du juge, comme moyen de simplification de l'administration de la preuve. Lorsqu'il s'agit des pouvoirs qui visent à limiter les mesures d'instruction à ce qui est suffisant pour la solution du litige, on ne peut pas douter que le but est de retenir ce qui est le plus simple et le moins onéreux pour la preuve des faits nécessaires à trancher le litige; mais peut-on dire la même chose du pouvoir d'ordonner d'office les mesures d'instruction? Il ne s'agit pas d'une complication, plutôt que d'une simplification de la procédure? En d'autres termes, le but de la recherche de la vérité des faits au delà des allégation des parties semble allonger, plutôt qu'abréger, la durée de l'instance. Peut-être le problème se pose d'une façon différent dans les différents systèmes: là où le preuve des faits, suivant la tradition, est surtout une affaire des parties, les pouvoirs d'initiative du juge peuvent simplifier l'instruction de l'affaire, en tranchant l'exaspération du combat judiciaire; au contraire, là où le juge jouit d'un pouvoir de contrôle sur l'administration de la preuve, de nouveaux pouvoirs d'office élargissent le champ de la recherche, si dans le même temps on ne réduit pas le domaine des parties. Encore une fois, on se retrouve face au principe de la contradiction et au droit des parties à la preuve, comme un aspect de la liberté de la défense.

2. Nous sommes très reconnaissants à tous le collègues rapporteurs régionaux ou nationaux qui ont donnée leur collaboration pour l'élaboration de notre rapport général, à savoir les professeurs:
- Robert Boman (Suède)
- Sergio Chiarloni (Italie)
- Jacques Elders (Hollande)
- Wolfgang Grunsky (République Fédéral d'Allemagne)
- Eliahu Harnon et Alex Stein (Israël)
- Juan C. Hitters (Argentine) pour les pays de l'Amérique Latine
- André Joly (France)
- Shozaburo Yoshino (Japon)
- Zbigniew Resich (Pologne) pour les pays socialistes.

Malheureusement, nous n'avons pas reçu les rapports des pays de *common law*, tels que l'Angleterre et les Etats-Unis, qui auraient pu élargir le tableau de l'évolution du droit des preuves dans le monde contemporain. On a essayé de remplacer ce défaut avec les renseignements qu'on a pu obtenir par d'autres sources à propos de réformes qu'on souhaite dans le but de simplifier l'administration de la preuve. Ce qu'on peut remarquer et qui nous a paru quelque peu étonnant c'est que dans les pays de l'oralité dans le sens le plus classique du terme on souhaite l'introduction la plus ample du témoinage écrit (*affidavit*) au lieu de l'audiction directe des témoins par le juge, tandis que dans les pays de *civil law* on souhaite l'application la plus rigoureuse de l'oralité suivant le modèle du *trial* de la *common law*. D'où la leçon qu'il faut se méfier des modèles abstraits de justice civile et qu'il faut, ou contraire, s'en tenir à l'expérience concrète de l'administration de la justice dans les différents milieu, politiques et sociaux. Si l'on peut constater, en général, le regret pour l'inefficacité de la justice, et surtout la lenteur des procédures, il est très difficile de généraliser les causes de ce phénomène, au-delà de l'engorgement des tribunaux dû à la multiplication des affaires. Et il ne faut pas oublier que les règles de preuve n'ont pas une valeur seulement technique, étant donné qu'en arrière des règles il y a la tradition, la coutume, les croyances des peuples: dans un seul mot, leur histoire.

L'ADMISSION DE LA PREUVE

Dans le domaine de l'admission de la preuve, la première question qui se pose concerne les critères selon lesquel les preuves sont admises. Comme on sait, il s'agit de la pertinence et de l'admissibilité de la preuve.

En ce qui concerne la pertinence, il va sans dire que ce critère est présent dans tous les systèmes procéduraux, sur la base d'exigences élémentaires d'économie processuelle. En soi, ce critère est une règle de simplification du procès, puisqu'il produit l'exclusion préalable des mesures d'instruction qui provoqueraient des complications inutiles. Mais s'il n'y a pas de problèmes sur le critère abstraitement considéré, des questions se posent au niveau de son application concrète. En effet, il peut produire une simplification réelle du procès seulement s'il est appliqué par le juge d'une façon rigoureuse, dans le but d'éviter l'administration des preuves non pertinentes ou dilatoires. Au contraire, son efficacité simplificatrice va être perdue si le juge applique ce critère d'une façon trop élastique, ou s'il ne l'applique pas du tout, en admettant toutes les preuves produites par les parties. Il est précisément ce qui arrive dans plusieurs systèmes, comme il est souligné en particulier par le collègue Hitters pour l'Amérique Latine (tandis que la question ne se pose pas, paraît-il, en France et en Allemagne). Il va sans dire que s'il n'y a pas une véritable sélection préalable des mesures d'instruction selon un critère rigoureux de pertinence, des conséquences très graves en dérivent sur le déroulement du procès. L'instruction probatoire se dilate, et devient longue, compliquée et coûteuse, puisqu'on permet l'administration des preuves qui sont tout à fait inutiles pour le jugement sur les faits.

On dit parfois qu'une application souple du critère de la pertinence, ou même son inapplication, sert à éviter que le juge exclut préalablement des mesures d'instruction qui pourraient se revéler utiles pour l'établissement de la vérité.

On a d'ailleurs l'impression qu'il s'agit d'une fausse justification. En effet, lorsque le juge n'exerce pas effectivement son pouvoir de ne pas admettre les preuves non pertinentes, la raison essentielle est qu'il ne connaît pas assez bien l'affaire, et donc il n'est pas en état d'évaluer raisonnablement la pertinence des preuves.

Il s'ajoute, en plus, la tendence générale des juges au 'laisser faire', c'est à dire à ne pas interférer dans l'administration que les parties font du procès, et en particulier de l'instruction probatoire (tendance qui est signalée en particulier par les collègues Chiarloni et Hitters). Donc il ne s'agit pas de mettre en discussion le critère général de la pertinence de la preuve, mais d'assurer qu'il soit effectivement appliqué par les juges. Evidemment le problème ne se pose pas au niveau des règles du procès; il concerne plutôt l'idée que le juge a de son rôle dans le fonctionnement du procès (voir surtout le rapport latino-americain).

En ce qui concerne l'admissibilité des preuves on se situe proprement au niveau des normes. A ce propos il faut d'ailleurs distinguer entre les systèmes de *civil law* et les systèmes de *common law* (et ceux qui s'inspirent du modèle de *common law*).

Dans les premiers il y a des règles qui concernent surtout l'inadmissibilité de la preuve par témoins, et qui visent en particulier à exclure la preuve orale des contrats. Le rapporteur italien souligne justement que le problème de l'admissibilité des preuves n'est pas vu, d'habitude, comme une question concernant la simplification du procès. En plus, la doctrine de *civil law* place les règles qui privilègent la preuve littérale dans le domaine de la reglémentation des obligations privées, plutôt que dans le domaine de la reglémentation procédurale de la preuve, ce qui entraîne une certaine manque de considération pour le côté processuel du problème.

D'ailleurs on ne peut dire (et encore le collègue Chiarloni le souligne) que le domaine des règles d'exclusion de certaines preuves, et en particulier du témoignage, soit tout à fait depourvu d'importance du point de vue de la simplification du procès. Bien sûr la question de renforcer ou de réduire les limites probatoires concerne surtout le *quantum* et le 'type' de vérité qu'on veut atteindre dans le procès civil, ainsi que le droit à la preuve des parties. On pourrait même considérer qu'une réduction substantielle des limites probatoires, qui augmenterait la protection du droit à la preuve et la capacité du procès d'établir la 'vérité réelle' des faits, peut être à effet contraire du point de vue de la simplification, puisqu'elle augmenterait le nombre des preuves admissibles.

Toutefois, il y a un côte de cette question qui concerne la simplification du procès, et qui est indiqué dans le rapport italien. En effet, une réduction des limites probatoires entraîne une réduction correspondante des occasions d'application de la loi au moment de l'admission des preuves: ça signifie moins de question de droit sur ce point, c'est à dire moins de contestations des parties, et moins de risques de nullité du jugement pour des raisons remontant à la reglémentation légale des preuves. De ce point de vue, on comprend bien que le collègue Elders signale l'importance d'un projet hollandais récent, qui vise à réduire et à simplifier les limites probatoires qui concernent le preuve littérale et notamment la preuve par témoins.

Dans les pays de *civil law*, il y a encore un autre problème. Il s'agit des décisions relatives aux mesures d'instruction, puisque le procès est plus ou moins simple selon qu'on admet ou non la possibilité des parties d'attaquer immédiatement ces décisions. On constate une tendance assez forte à éliminer cette possibilité, en prévoyant que ces décisions soient insusceptibles d'opposition en elles mêmes, et qu'elles ne puissent être attaquées qu'avec la décision sur le fond (voir en particulier les rapports français et allemand). L'exclusion des voies de recours directes contre les décisions sur l'admission des preuves entraîne évidemment une simplification importante du procès. D'ailleurs, dans plusieurs systèmes on admet que ces décisions soient attaquées directement en elles mêmes, ce qui provoque des complications et des dilations considérables (voir les rapports italien, latino-americain et hollandais). Dans ces systèmes se pose donc la question d'éliminer les voies de recours autonomes contre les décisions sur l'admission des mesures d'instruction, ou au moins de les reglémenter de façon qu'elles soient limitées au minimum, et qu'elles ne provoquent pas de dilations inutiles.

Dans les pays de *common law* le problème de l'admissibilité des preuves se pose d'une façon tout à fait différente. Il est bien connu que le système des *exclusionary rules* est arrivé, dans le XIXe siècle, à un degré extrème de complication et de difficulté. Cette situation a d'ailleurs produit une forte tendance contraire, visant à une simplification radicale de la *law of evidence*, qui a sorti des résultats considérables. Dans les *Federal Rules of Evidence* nordamericaines, et notamment dans le *Civil Evidence Act* anglais de 1968, il y a en effet des simplifications remarquables de la *hearsay rule*, et la *best evidence rule* perd aussi beaucoup de son importance.

Il faut dire toutefois que la simplification et la réduction des *exclusionary rules* ne concernent pas la simplification du procès, bien qu'elles soient importantes pour la réalisation du principe selon lequel toutes les preuves pertinentes doivent être admises. Le rapport israélien signale donc una tendance à multiplier les exceptions à la *hearsay rule*, mais elle n'a pas beaucoup d'importance du point de vue de la simplification de la procédure.

De l'autre côté, il faut considérer que les *exclusionary rules* ont vigueur dans la phase du *trial*, mais elles ne sont pas appliquées dans la phase du *pre-trial*, tandis que la plupart des *civil cases* trouve une solution dans cette phase. Il en derive que la réduction des *exclusionary rules*, bien que souhaitable pour d'autres raisons, est une question marginale du point de vue de la simplification du procès.

Plutôt, si on considére la phase du *pre-trial*, on découvre des questions très graves, mais qui sont tout à fait différentes. Elles concernent surtout la *discovery*, c'est à dire le moyen par lequel les parties peuvent connaître en avance les preuves de l'adversaire. Il s'agit d'un technique essentielle, soit pour la préparation du *trial* que pour évaluer la convénance d'une solution conciliative. En particulier de ce deuxième point de vue, un bon fonctionnement de la *discovery* est important, puisqu'il permet aux parties de résoudre l'affaire sans aller à la phase compliqée et coûteuse du *trial*. Mais il est sur ce point qu'il y a beaucoup de problèmes, en particulier aux Etats Unis: la *discovery* est devenue à son tour très compliquée et coûteuse, de sorte qu'elle est très souvent un moyen pour provoquer des obstacles et des dilations, plutôt qu'un moyen raisonnable pour bien préparer le *trial*, ou même pour l'éviter.

En général, on peut faire deux observations fondamentales à propos du rapport entre l'admission des preuves et la simplification du procès.

La première observation est que la réduction des limites probatoires peut être justifiée par des raisons diverses, mais qu'elle ne parait pas destinée à produire de conséquences considérables sur le déroulement du procès. Le seul point qui parait vraiement important concerne l'exclusion de la possibilité d'attaquer immédiatement et d'une façon autonome les décisions relatives à l'admission des mesures d'instruction.

La deuxième observation est que la réduction ou l'élimination des limites probatoires est en soi même problématique. D'un côté, en effet, elle permet de mieux établir la 'vérité réelle' des faits, mais de l'autre côté on peut douter que ça favorise la simplification de l'administration des preuves. De ce point de vue, il y a une opposition évidente entre la valeur de la vérité et la valeur de la simplification du procès. La question essentielle est donc de trouver - en ce qui concerne les limites probatoires - le point du compromis idéal entre ces deux valeurs, selon les principes qui règlent chaque système juridique.

A ce propos il faut encore ajouter que, en tout cas, une réduction considérable des limites probatoires impliquerait une importance croissante du problème de la pertinence de la preuve. En effet, là où les règles légales d'inadmissibilité viennent à manquer, le rôle de critère de sélection préalable des mesures d'instruction est joué seulement par la critère de la pertinence. En principe, il s'agit d'une situation tout à fait raisonnable, mais du point de vue du déroulement du procès tout vien à dépendre de la façon dans laquelle le juge emploie ce critère. Une application rigoureuse de la règle de la pertinence pourrait en effet assurer un procès assez simple, au moins par rapport à l'exigence d'établir la vérité; au contraire, la mauvaise application qu'on fait de cette règle dans plusieurs pays pourrait produire des conséquences très graves. Une réduction des limites probatoires est donc souhaitable, mais l'exigence d'assurer un degré suffisant d'efficacité de l'instruction probatoire demande que le critère de la pertinence de la preuve soit effectivement appliqué en fonction de filtre préliminaire.

L'ADMINISTRATION DES MESURES D'INSTRUCTION

Le problème qui est plus directement lié avec la simplification du procès concerne évidemment les procédures d'administration des mesures d'instruction. Les rapports nationaux mettent d'ailleurs en évidence des questions assez différentes, par rapport aux divers modèles de l'instruction probatoire.

Il faut donc distinguer trois situations fondamentales.

a) La première concerne les pays comme l'Italie, l'Espagne et ceux de l'Amérique Latine, où l'instruction probatoire se déroule dans de nombreuses audiences, où il n'existe aucune distinction rigoureuse entre une phase préparatoire et une phase d'administration des preuves proprement dite, et où l'instruction probatoire se mêle avec d'autres activités processuelles. Dans ce cas, le problème fondamental vient de la structure même de l'instruction probatoire, qui n'assure pas - en principe - la concentration de l'administration des preuves. Ce qui manque est la règle de 'l'audience unique', tandis que l'administration des preuves demande de nombreuses audiences, parfois très éloignées dans le temps. C'est justement ce qui arrive en Italie, avec la seule exception du procès en matière de travail, et dans les pays qui suivent le modèle espagnol. Le collègue Hitters souligne en effet que le défaut principal vient du fait que la concentration de l'instruction probatoire - bien qu'abstraitement prévue par la loi - n'est pas effectivement réalisée.

Il faut dire d'ailleurs qu'il ne s'agit pas seulement de modèles généraux. En effet, bien que le modèle de l'audience unique puisse encourager la concentration du procès, il ne paraît pas absolument nécessaire, pourvu que l'administration des preuves soit reglée d'une façon assez simple. Cette conclusion se dégage du rapport français, qui souligne que le nouveau code de procédure civile de 1976 a simplifié l'administration des preuves d'une façon remarquable, bien qu'il n'ait pas adopté le système de l'audience unique. Même au dehors de ce système, donc, il y a beaucoup de possibilités de simplification, en éliminant des complications formalistes inutiles (par ex. en ce qui concerne l'administration de la preuve par témoins et les contestations relatives aux preuves littérales).

b) En tout cas, le problème général de la structure de l'instruction probatoire n'est pas insignifiant. Il est assez clair, en effet, qu'il y a beaucoup moins de questions dans les systèmes, même de *civil law*, qui suivent le modèle fondé sur la distinction d'une phase préparatoire et d'une phase d'administration des preuves dans une seule audience orale. Ce point est bien demontré par l'exemple de l'Allemagne, où ce modèle a été renforcé par la *Vereinfachungsnovelle* de 1976. Le collègue Grunsky souligne que cette loi a augmenté l'efficacité de la phase préparatoire en ce qui concerne la sélection des mesures d'instruction, et que par conséquent elle a beaucoup simplifié l'administration des preuves, qui est faite dans une audience orale devant le juge. Des exemples semblables viennent des pays socialistes, où, comme il est signalé par le collègue Resich, l'administration des preuves est concentrée dans une audience orale, et où on envisage seulement l'exigence de renforcer ce système en prévoyant des délais brefs.

Encore, un exemple intéressant vient de la Suède: selon le rapporteur suédois, l'administration des preuves dans une audience orale assure un niveau satisfaisant de simplicité et de rapidité. On vise d'ailleurs à améliorer ce système, en prévoyant que le témoin soit interrogé par téléphone, s'il ne peut pas être présent à l'audience.

Ces exemples confirment que le système de l'audience unique présente des avantages considérables. D'un côté, il assure en soi même que les preuves soient administrées rapidement, avec des ajournements d'audience réduits au minimum. De l'autre côté, il implique que les procédures pour l'administration des diverses mesures d'instruction soient simplifiées et déformalisées au maximum.

c) La troisième situation qu'on doit considérer est donnée par les pays qui suivent le modèle de *common law*. Ce modèle se caracterise aussi par une distinction très marquée entre une phase préparatoire (dite de *pre-trial*) et la phase du *trial*, dans laquelle les preuves sont administrées oralement. Il faut d'ailleurs considérer que ce modèle est suivi dans plusieurs pays, comme Israël et Japon, et pas seulement en Angleterre et aux Etats-Unis. Il faut aussi souligner que l'institution fondamentale du *trial*, c'est à dire l'interrogation des témoins, des parties et des experts, conduite par les avocats des parties et centrée sur la *cross examination*, existe aussi ailleurs, comme par ex. en Suède.

Dans le cadre général du *trial* il y a un lieu commun traditionnel, selon lequel les interrogatoires directs et croisés sont la meilleure méthode pour établir la vérité. Il y a d'ailleurs des problèmes remarquables qui concernent le déroulement du *trial*, et surtout le fait que c'est d'habitude une procédure très compliquée, longue et difficile à conduire.

Le problème principal paraît dependre de la structure fondamentale du *trial*, c'est à dire du fait qu'il est empreint des principes de *l'adversary system*, étant donné que le rôle essentiel est joué par les avocats des parties. La conséquence est que l'administration des preuves orales devient très longue et compliquée. La *cross examination*, qui en principe est un moyen efficace pour vérifier la crédibilité des témoins, se transforme dans un moyen d'obstruction et de complication du *trial*.

Ces graves inconvénients sont signalés par les rapporteurs israëliens, japonais et suèduois, qui les ramènent au caractère excessivement *adversary* du *trial*, c'est à dire à la prédominance des parties et à la faiblesse du rôle qui est joué par le juge. Ces inconvénients sont encore plus graves là où, comme il arrive au Japon, le *trial* se déroule dans l'absence d'une phase préparatoire qui fixe préalablement le *thema decidendum* de l'affaire. Dans ce cas, ce qui vient à manquer c'est la concentration même de l'administration des preuves, puisqu'elle se mêle avec la détermination progressive de l'objet du litige.

En présence de ces problèmes, les rapports nationaux indiquent des remèdes, qui en partie ont été réalisés, et en partie sont seulement envisagés. On souligne par ex. que la simplification du *trial* peut venir de l'efficacité du *pre-trial*: le rapport israëlien signale cette fonction du *pre-trial*, qui vient du fait qu'il a un caractère décidément inquisitoire, et donc permet un'efficace *discovery* préalable des preuves et une sélection réelle des points qui vont être discutés au *trial*. Le rapport japonais est dans le même sens, mais il remarque qu'au Japon la phase préparatoire écrite est très rarement employée, ainsi qu'il n'y a pas de véritables forclusions, et on arrive au *trial* sans avoir fixé l'objet du litige et sans avoir choisi les preuves qu'on doit administrer.

On dit en outre qu'un remède pourrait être une réduction du caractère *adversary* de l'administration des preuves, mais il s'agit d'un point très problématique. Parfois elle peut être réalisée assez aisément: par ex., le rapport israëlien souligne l'utilité du pouvoir du juge de nommer des experts indépendants, dans le but d'éliminer la 'bataille des experts' des parties. En outre, on pourrait envisager l'interrogation des témoins par le juge, qui selon le rapporteur suèdois pourrait faire épargner beaucoup de temps et d'argent. S'il est d'ailleurs indéniable, comme souligne le rapporteur japonais, que le noeud du problème est la passivité excessive du juge dans le *trial*, on pourrait même penser à lui donner un rôle actif dans l'administration des preuves.

Mais contre une transformation inquisitoire du *trial* il y a des objections très fortes. D'un côté, comme il est souligné par le rapporteur suèdois, il y a la traditionnelle conviction selon laquelle la *cross examination* est la meilleure méthode pour l'administration des preuves orales. De l'autre côté, on doit considérer que l'*adversary system* n'est pas tout simplement une technique procédurale, mais il est fondé sur des bases idéologiques très solides. Ce n'est pas par hasard, en effet, que les tentatives d'introduire des éléments *nonadversary* dans le système nordaméricain ont substantiellement échoué, en présence de l'idée fondamentale du *trial* comme 'chose des parties' ou des avocats.

Dans la difficulté de dépasser l'idée centrale du procès *adversary*, les systèmes qui suivent ce modèle cherchent d'autres solutions au problème de la simplification du *trial*. Une solution qui paraît en train de se repandre est fondée sur la réduction du caractère oral de l'administration des preuves. Il y a en effet une tendance, signalée par ex. par le rapport israëlien, à remplacer le témoignage oral par la présentation d'*affidavits* qui contiennent des témoignages écrits.

Bien sûr l'emploi d'un *affidavit* est beaucoup plus simple et rapide qu'un témoignage administré par l'interrogation orale et la *cross examination*. Il entraîne donc une simplification radicale de l'administration de la preuve. Mais il faut remarquer qu'on arrive ainsi à éliminer des caractères importants de la preuve par témoins. Elle perd en effet son caractère oral, et si on visait à la substitution complète du témoignage par les *affidavits*, on devrait constater la disparution du *trial*, puisqu'il s'agirait seulement d'acquérir des documents. En plus, dans l'*affidavit* les faits sont fixés, tandis que l'interrogation orale permet d'approfondir l'analyse des faits et de vérifier la crédibilité du témoin. Même de ce point de vue, donc, la valeur de la simplification du procès entre en opposition avec la valeur de l'établissement de la vérité sur la base des preuves.

Du panorama des rapports nationaux il ressort qu'il y a des situations assez diversifiées. La procédure d'administration des mesures d'instruction est considérée adéquate dans les pays où des réformes récentes ont introduit des simplifications remarquables: c'est le cas de la France, et spécialement de l'Allemagne. Même dans ces cas on peut avoir des problèmes en ce qui concerne la durée du procès civil, mais le rapporteur français souligne qu'ils remontent à d'autres raisons, comme par ex. le nombre insuffisant des juges.

Des questions considérables se posent, au contraire, dans les autres pays de *civil law*, où il s'agit de simplifier les procédures d'administration des mesures d'instruction, ou même de changer la structure générale de l'instruction probatoire. Ainsi le rapport hollandais remarque la tendence, qui a donné lieu à un projet récent, à simplifier de nombreux aspects de l'administration des preuves. Selon d'autres rapports (voir en particulier ce du collègue Hitters) l'exigence fondamentale est de réaliser une concentration réelle de l'instruction probatoire, en modifiant sa structure suivant le modèle de l'audience unique et orale. Dans le même sens il y a des projets en Italie, où ce modèle est réalisé dans le procès en matière de travail. L'exigence de concentration émerge d'ailleurs même dans les pays socialistes, comme il est souligné par le collègue Resich.

Mais il faut aussi dire que le modèle de l'audience orale ne paraît pas suffisant à résoudre tous les problèmes de simplification. L'expérience des pays qui suivent le système de *common law* montre en effet que ce modèle peut être excessivement compliqué, surtout à cause du caractère *adversary* de l'administration des preuves. De ce point de vue, la question se déplace sur un autre plan, qui concerne proprement le rôle du juge, par rapport au rôle des parties, dans l'administration des mesures d'instruction.

LES POUVOIRS DU JUGE

En abordant le thème des pouvoirs du juge dans l'administration de la preuve, il est classique d'opposer les systèmes de *civil law*, que l'on considère inspirés du principe de la recherche de la vérité au delà des initiatives des parties, et les systèmes de *common law*, qui considérent la preuve des faits comme un affaire exclusif des parties, suivant les règles de l'*adversary system of litigation*, dont l'idée centrale est la neutralité et la non-intervention du juge. A vrai dire, cette façon d'envisager le problème nous semble quelque peu démodé, étant donné que les limites traditionnelles de l'*adversary system* dans le sens classique vont se restreindre de plus en plus, en raison directe de l'expansion du domain des juridictions d'exception qui n'appliquent pas les règles de preuve du *trial* ordinaire (*administrative tribunals*, *agencies*, etc.). Et il faut ajouter que même dans les juridictions de droit commun on voit s'accroitre les pouvoirs du juge surtout dans le cadre de la *public law litigation* dans le sens large du terme: il suffit d'indiquer les litiges qui concernent l'environnement, les consommateurs, les *mass-media*, etc.

Mais si l'on se borne à considérer le problème du point de vue du thème de notre rapport, la question est la suivante: est ce que l'augmentation des pouvoirs du juge donne lieu à une simplification dans l'administration de la preuve? Dans le but de donner une réponse à cette question il faut examiner séparément: (a) les pouvoirs du juge d'ordonner d'office les mesures d'instruction; (b) le pouvoir du juge de limiter le choix des mesures d'instruction; (c) le pouvoir du juge de concentrer dans le temps l'administration de la preuve.

(a) En général, on peut remarquer que l'attribution au juge du pouvoir d'ordonner d'office les mesures d'instruction n'est plus aujourd'hui un principe typique de la procédure civile des pays socialistes, puisqu'on le retrouve affirmé à l'occasion des réformes les plus récentes dans les pays de *civil law*, dont l'expression la plus large est donnée par l'art. 10 du nouveau code de procédure civile français: 'Le juge a le pouvoir d'ordonner d'office toutes les mesures d'instruction légalement admissibles'. Il est vrai que dans certains systèmes le pouvoir d'office est limité à des procédures déterminées, en raison des droits que l'on vise à protéger (comme, par exemple, les droits des travailleurs), mais on ne peut nier qu'il existe une ligne de tendence générale dans cette direction, comme nous le témoigne, entre autres, le rapport du collègue Hitters pour les pays de l'Amérique du Sud. Il ne s'agit pas, bien sûr, d'effacer totalement le principe suivant lequel les parties ont la charge d'alléguer les faits propres à fonder leurs prétentions, mais plutôt d'établir un principe de *collaboration* entre le juge et les parties dans le but de la connaissance des faits nécessaires à la solution du litige.

Sur l'appui des rapport régionaux et nationaux, on peut douter du fait que l'exercice des pouvoirs d'office du juge produit une simplification de l'administration de la preuve. Même si le juge se borne à suppléer au manque d'initiative des parties, il y a quand même une intégration des éléments du débat, qu'on aurait pu trancher à l'appui de la règle de la charge de la preuve. Et il faut ajouter que parmi les mesures d'instruction que le juge peut ordonner d'office, c'est l'expertise qui occupe la première place; la complication croissante de l'expertise dans plusieurs matières est fort bien connue (il suffit de citer l'examen du sang pour la recherche de la paternité), et, par ailleurs, il y a l'exigence qu'on n'oublie pas le respect du principe du contradictoire au cours des opérations d'expertise.

(b) Il en est autrement en ce qui concerne la sélection par le juge des mesures d'instruction, suivant la règle qu'on a très bien énoncée dans l'art. 147 du nouveau code de procédure civile français: 'Le juge doit limiter le choix de la mesure à ce qui est suffisant pour la solution du litige, en s'attachant à retenir ce qui est le plus simple et le moins onéreux'. Dans cette règle on peut voir consacré un principe général d'économie processuelle (*Prozessökonomie*) qui est tipique de la justice civile moderne, dans le cadre d'une conception qui confie au droit judiciaire privé la tâche d'assurer le fonctionnement correct du service public de la justice. Dans ce cadre, on n'hésite pas à conférer au juge un rôle prépondérant dans la direction de la procédure, et donc les pouvoirs nécessaires à réaliser l'économie de procédure indispensable pour que, dans le respect du droit de défense, l'efficacité du service public judiciaire soit assurée. Il ne s'agit pas seulement de sélectionner les mesures d'instruction en faisant application du critère de la *pertinence* de la preuve par rapport aux faits desquels dépend la solution du litige, mais aussi bien de trancher l'exécution des mesures d'instruction lorsque le juge décide qu'on a acquis des éléments suffisants pour la connaissance des faits. Enfin, il s'agit d'évaluer le coût de la mesure, par rapport à son utilité; par exemple, lorsqu'on peut décider de faire établir un enregistrement sonore, visuel ou audiovisuel des opérations d'instruction.

Le principe de l'économie de procédure dans l'administration de la preuve représente une règle commune à tous le systèmes, étant donné que dans la *common law* on connait les *Simplificative Rules*, qui visent à l'exclusion des moyens de preuve qui provoquent une 'undue consumption of time' (on peut voir, à ce propos, la *Rule* 403 des *Federal Rules of Evidence* des Etats-Unis). D'où la règle de *l'economy of trial*, qui suppose un *judicial activism* au-delà des principes classiques de l'*adversary system*, puisqu'il s'agit de confier au juge des pouvoir qui limitent la maîtrise des parties sur le déroulement du *trial* et sur le *factfinding process*.

Dans la même perspective de simplification de l'administration de la preuve on peut considérer l'emploi des *pre-trial procedures* dont nous parle le rapport des collègues Harnon et Stein pour le droit israëlien, sur l'appui de la *Rule* 143 des *Israeli Rules of Civil Procedure*, suivant laquelle le juge dans le *pre-trial* peut 'give every direction as to procedure which may simplify or ease the trial': par exemple, ordonner la preuve testimoniale par *affidavits* au lieu de la *direct examination;* désigner un expert 'on behalf of the court' au lieu des experts présentés par les parties, etc.

(c) La concentration de l'administration de la preuve est sans doute le moyen le plus important pour la simplification de la procédure d'instruction. Il s'agit, par ailleurs, d'un des grands principes de la justice civile moderne, qui a inspiré les mouvements de réforme les plus importants dans tous les pays. Le collègue Resich nous rappelle que la concentration est un des principes directeurs du procès civil polonais et des pays socialistes en général et il affirme que 'afin d'accélérer la procédure des preuves il faut un système reconnaissant le principe de concentration des matériaux du procès avec tout un régime de délais de production des preuves sous peine de leur élimination et des sanctions'. Il faut ajouter, d'après l'expérience des réformes de la procédure civile allemande, dont nous informe le collègue Grunsky, que la concentration de l'administration de la preuve exige une phase préliminaire et préparatoire, dans laquelle il faut déterminer exactement le *thema probandum*. Il s'agit de la *Vorbereitung der mundlichen Verhandlung* prévue par le § 273 de la Z.P.O. de la République Fédérale Allemande, suivant le fameux *Stuttgart Model* expérimenté avant la réforme de la *Vereinfachungsnovelle* de 1976. La procédure préparatoire nous est signalée, pour le code japonais, par le rapport du collègue Yoshino, qui nous rappelle la dérivation de la législation de son pays du code allemand de 1877, en soulignant néanmoins que la phase prépatoire de l'instance a été réformée en 1950 sous l'influence du droit américain de la *pre-trial procedure*.

Il est difficile de réaliser une véritable concentration de l'administration de la preuve sans une augmentation des pouvoirs d'office du juge, puisqu'il s'agit de fixer des délais et des déchéances à l'activité des parties: en un seul mot, de diriger la marche de l'instance, dans le but que le procès s'achève dans un laps de temps acceptable pour l'efficacité de la justice. Et il faut ajouter que dans les réformes les plus récentes dans le domaine de l'administration de la preuve, on retrouve même la tendence à sanctionner les obligations processuelles des parties au moyen de mesures de condamnations pécuniaires telles que les astreintes, qui jouent le rôle de véritables peines privées (voir, pour la production forcée des preuves en justice, l'art. 11 du nouveau code de procédure civile français).

On peut donc conclure que les pouvoir d'office du juge jouent en général un rôle décisif pour la réalisation du principe d'économie de procédure dans l'administration de la preuve.

CONCLUSION

Le panorama qui se dégage des rapports nationaux et régionaux est très riche, et il montre qu'il y a beaucoup de questions au niveau des rapports entre l'administration des mesures d'instruction et la simplification du procès civil.

En particulier il est évident que ce rapport est positif là où des réformes récentes ont visé à une simplification globale du procès, en prévoyant même une réduction considérable des formalités et des complications dans l'administration des preuves. On a déjà vu que c'est surtout le cas de la France et de l'Allemagne.

La situation est d'ailleurs tout à fait différente dans les systèmes qui sont encore caractérisés par de nombreuses limites probatoires, par une concentration insuffisante de la phase d'administration des mesures d'instruction, et par le rôle fondamentalement passif du juge. Dans ces domaines, il y a la possibilité et l'exigence d'améliorer la structure et le fonctionnement du procès dans la direction d'une simplification remarquable. Dans ce sens il y a d'ailleurs des projets intéressants; en tout cas, on souligne la nécessité d'introduire des changements.

Toutefois, on constate aisément qu'il ne s'agit pas d'une question simple.

D'un côté, la simplification de l'administration des preuves n'est pas un problème isolé. De plusieurs points de vue, en effet, il est strictement lié, souvent par opposition, à d'autres problèmes généraux qui concernent la fonction et la structure du procès civil. On doit par ex. considérer que la valeur de la simplification du procès est importante, mais que sa réalisation doit être en accord avec la valeur de l'établissement de la vérité dans le procès. On doit aussi considérer que les problèmes de l'administration des preuves concernent en réalité les structures fondamentales du procès dans les divers systèmes, et donc qu'il ne s'agit pas tout simplement de modifier quelques normes secondaires. Enfin, il faut remarquer que ces problèmes concernent directement le rôle du juge dans le procès, et donc qu'ils mettent en question les idéologies fondamentales qui sont la base de la structure et du déroulement effectif du procès civil.

De l'autre côté, il faut aussi remarquer que la simplification de l'administration des preuves est bien sûr importante, mais qu'elle n'est qu'un aspect de la simplification du procès et de l'efficacité de la justice civile. On a vu en effet que beaucoup de problèmes concernant l'administration des mesures d'instruction ne remontent pas proprement à la réglementation légale des preuves et de leur administration, puisqu'ils sont par contre la conséquence d'autres problèmes qui concernent plus en général le fonctionnement de la justice civile. Il s'agit surtout de la surcharge du travail des cours, du nombre insuffisant des juges, du rôle qui est joué par les avocats et par les juges, et des idéologies qui influencent l'administration de la justice civile. De ce point de vue, la simplification de l'administration des preuves est utile, mais elle n'est pas décisive.

La conclusion qu'on peut tirer est donc que la simplification de l'administration des preuves peut contribuer à l'efficacité de la justice civile, mais elle n'est pas la solution du problème: dans une certaine mesure elle est nécessaire et souhaitable, mais bien sûr elle ne suffit pas à assurer une justice rapide et efficace.

POINTS DE DISCUSSION

1. La simplification de l'administration des preuves et la sélection préalable des mesures d'instruction selon le critère de la pertinence de la preuve.

2. Réduction des limites probatoires légales et conséquences sur l'administration des preuves.

3. Forme et effets des décisions qui ordonnent les mesures d'instruction; possibilité de recours autonome; conséquences sur le déroulement des procès.

4. Techniques pour assurer un niveau suffisant de concentration dans l'administration de la preuve. Phase préparatoire et administration des mesures d'instruction.

5. Formes d'administration de la preuve: preuve orale et preuve par affidavit; administration de la preuve par le juge ou par les parties. Leur conséquences sur la simplification du procès.

6. Le faux incident civil et la vérification d'écriture: exigences de déformalisation.

7. Les pouvoirs du juge d'ordonner l'office d'administration des mesures d'instruction non demandées par les parties.

8. Le rôle du juge dans la direction de l'administration des preuves.

9. Simplification de l'administration des preuves et recherche de la vérité.

10. Simplification de l'administration des preuves et garanties procédurales des parties.

REPORT OF THE DISCUSSION

Chairman: *J.L. Bergel (France)*
Vice-chairman: *W.H. Rechberger (Austria)*
Secretary: *J. Elders (the Netherlands)*

The discussionpoints are to be found at page 329.

In his introduction, the general reporter prof. Denti stressed that the law of evidence at first sight seems to be just a set of technical rules but behind this rules we find various traditions, historic, religious and ideological. Therefore in his opinion it will not be possible to ignore this background. There are differences in the various legal systems that can't simply be bridged.

We must distinguish two great lines of development in procedural law the line of constitutional law by means of which the rights of the litigants are protected and the trend to enlarge the power of the judge in the search for truth. Where legal systems don't belong to the same law family, it seems impossible to have the same rules of procedure. An aspect of great importance is the trend to increase the power of the judge to take an initiative as to the facts to be established by means of evidence and as to the weighing of the evidence submitted.

The general reporter prof. Taruffo mentioned in his summary two problems in connection with the theme of the section, the pertinence and the admissibility of the evidence to be taken. In this respect, not the legal rules are determinant but the way the judge will apply these rules. If procedural rules are applied very strictly, many complications may be the result and therefore there is a general trend towards a more flexible approach of procedural rules. It is the attitude of the judge that counts most. Who wants to renew the law of evidence, will have to renew the basic principles of procedural law too. An example from the common law system may make this clear.

In the adversary system, the judge is like a arbiter and the litigants play a game. The technique of cross-examination is based on the oral character of the procedure. Nowadays this oral character will find its counterpart in the growing importance of the affidavit. Use of affidavits may mean gain of time and simplification of the procedure but the disappearance of cross-examination might cause a loss in credibility. We should not forget that the adversary system is closely connected with the common law system itself, with specific roles of judge and litigants which means that a small reform does not seem possible.

After the summary, given by the general reporters, the discussion was opened by S. Mukhtar, Indonesia. He warned against simplification and he mentioned the trend to eliminate oral evidence. The pursuit of justice should be guaranteed by procedural rules. In the Indonesian system, the judge plays an active role in speeding up proceedings without simplification.

R. Boman, Sweden, defended the trend to increase to power of the judge. He made a distinction between the formal competence of the judge and the way the judge should operate. In Sweden, the judge is allowed to exclude non relevant means of evidence but non-pertinence must be evident.

K. Uff, United Kingdom, mentioned that in his country the hear-say rule was abolished to a large extent in 1968. The result of this has not been a great success. The reason is that the law has become more complicated and therefore barristers prefer the old rule. Another point to be mentioned is the disclosure of the means of evidence in the pretrial stage. Members of the bar fear this might contradict orality. In their view the element of surprise in oral examination is vital.

Z. Stalev, Bulgaria, stated that simplification in civil procedure has to do with a comparison of various values. It should be clear, that the search for truth is a primary value but endless trial is no value at all. Therefore in the field of law, the sense of measure is predominant. Orality in evidence can't be applied without exception.

S. Wagner, Belgium, called attention to the problem of evidence by experts in case of serious delay in reporting. The Belgian law provides no sanction against such delay which causes in many cases an urgent problem.

Ferreira da Silva, Portugal, discussed the problem of interpretation of oral evidence. He presented the opinion that declarations should be recorded in full to prevent problems in interpretation. Therefore, the use of recorders during oral examination seemed to him indispensable.

J. Elders, Netherlands, regretted the in some way pessimistic conclusions of the general reporters. He deemed it possible to simplify proceedings by a number of general rules that would not endanger fundamental values of the various legal systems. Among his points, he stressed particularly the rules that proof might be established by all means, that contestation by a litigant of facts asserted by the other party with sufficient ground, should imply the grounds for dispute and the discretionary freedom of the judge to weigh the evidence submitted.

In his overall review of the discussion about the theme, the chairman of this section, stressed the difficulty of harmonizing the procedural rules of civil law, common law and socialist countries. Conflicts may arise between the values of efficiency and thoroughness. Simplification might endanger certain values. On the other hand, among the participants there was much approval of the trend to enlarge the power of the judge with reference to the distribution of the burden of proof, the choice of the means of evidence and the weighing of the evidence submitted, and finally the control of the terms to present witnesses.

In the plenary discussion, Ferreira da Silva, Portugal, remarked that, even if the law of evidence might be elaborate, new problems will arise in the course of litigation. Therefore he warned against to much confidence in legal systems. Further on he expressed the opinion that the litigants should have the right to lodge an appeal against in interlocutory judgment without exception because there is always a danger that judges of the first instance will not admit the taking of evidence by one of the litigants.

Greger, Germany, put that evidence by experts had drawn too little attention of the participants so far. He opposed to the view that experts are the cause of long delays in litigation. He pleaded a preliminary appointment of experts and he was also in favour of an oral explanation by experts.

Finally, he wanted to reenforce the position of the expert in general considering him as an technical counsel of the judge.

Vescovi, Uruguay, pleaded to exclude inadmissible means of evidence in an early phase of litigation.

Boman, Sweden, contested the opinion of Taruffo about exclusion of indirect evidence. In his opinion the judge should be free to use any indirect evidence as corroborative evidence in connection with established facts.

Morello, Argentina, stated also that the judge is confronted with the crisis in values. He warned against simplification but he defended rationalization in stead.

Fettweis, Belgium, put that some judges might ignore some procedural rules and therefore the right to lodge appeal from interlocutory judgments should be maintained.

In their conclusive speech, the general reporters Denti and Taruffo pleaded prudence as to major restatements of the law of evidence. They again stressed the importance of historic situations and cultural differences, and finally, the protection of the position of the weak and the poor in civil litigation. In their opinion there is no other aim in litigation but the search for justice and truth.

INFORMAL ALTERNATIVES TO OR WITHIN THE ORDINARY LITIGATION

INFORMAL ALTERNATIVES TO AND WITHIN FORMAL PROCEDURES

E. Blankenburg
Professor at the Vrije Universiteit, Amsterdam
and
Y. Taniguchi
Professor at the University of Kyoto

1 INTRODUCTION TO THE TOPIC

It is obvious that 'alternatives' can only be defined with respect to a model of the 'ordinary'. What is to be considered an 'informal alternative' procedure depends on the notion of a 'formal procedure'. Thus, among lawyers on the European Continent, we find the characteristic of 'informality' attributed to any form of conflict solving which does not engage the parties in a full fledged procedure, that is to say: with the right to counsel, with an independent judge who decides on the basis of taking evidence, and with the possibility of having a first instance decision checked in a second instance of appeal. If a judge mediates a conflict between the parties in place of deciding it by final judgment, this will be regarded as an 'informal solution' according to this definition, even if an attempt to conciliate may by procedural code be prescribed as a first step within the procedure. It is only a minor step from conciliation *within* the procedure to the proposal of either the judge or the parties to interrupt the formal procedure for the sake of out-of-court conciliations. From here it is only a minor step again, if parties and their lawyers negotiate informally out of court while the formal procedure is going on; parties might present the judge with a negotiated settlement, or they might simply notify the court that they will no longer pursue the procedure. In all of these cases, there is a gradual informalization of what was initially a formal procedure.

Apart from the relativity of legal systems and consequently of what is considered to be 'alternative' to them, we meet with different directions of alternativity where deviations from a full fledged formal procedure model are being sought. Mostly they start off from criticism of what is considered to be 'too costly' in formal procedures. 'Costs' can be coined in terms of time and effort spent to reach a decision, they can also be seen in substantive formalizations of law. Both types of criticism lead to a different type of deviation from a full fledged formal procedure:

- The first one simplifies procedures for minor matters to be handled in a quicker, more efficient and less costly manner. Such *summary* procedures usually adopt the same substantive law as would be applied in full fledged procedural models, but replace some of the procedural guarantee for the defending party by enabling the demanding party to move reliably and quickly to acquire a legal title. Summary procedures are typically adopted when substantive law and matters of evidence are not in doubt. They tend to promote standardized forms and routine procedures.
- On the other hand 'alternative procedures' can be adopted in order to achieve more *informal justice* on substantive issues. Such alternatives typically try to avoid the standardizations inherent in formal regulation by allowing arbitration by a judge and negotiation among the parties involved to enter the decision making process. Elements of arbitration may gradually emerge as 'alternatives *within*' formal procedures, or they may be institutionalized outside of courts as 'alternatives *to*' them.

Summary as well as informal procedures are found in any of the legal systems we compare. In some they are statutorily recognized in the procedural *codes*, in others they exist as the procedural *practice* of lawyers and courts. In practice we find everywhere *gradual* distinctions of informality within formal procedures. However, some systems develop more simplifying and informal alternatives than others. Alternatives generally develop more, the more formal the procedural codes are. This will be obvious, if we introduce a general distinction between 'adversarial' and 'inquisitorial' procedural traditions. Adversary trial procedures in the Anglo-American tradition, being more formal than Continental Civil law procedures, call for more informal ways around formality. Most Continental judges enjoy more discretion in handling the procedure, in initiating interactions and in the ways parties present evidence than would be the case in Anglo-American systems. Numbers of detailed differences among Continental procedural codes as well as among English, Scottish or American civil courts notwithstanding, they have summarily been typified as *'inquisitorial'* on the one hand and *'adversarial'* on the other, according to the relative power of the judge on the one hand and the parties with their lawyers on the other. As adversarial trials have been developed with regard to a possible participation of lay benches or lay juries, trial procedures have developed a detailed set of rules on evidence as well as on the course of the procedural interaction should take. As a consequence, the full trial procedure in Anglo-American models imposes far more formal restrictions on the participants than would the Continental model of procedure. Therefore, informal alternatives are more important as a method of getting around adversarial trials than they are on the Continent. They have been institutionalized partly in the form of pre-trial handling of cases, partly in the form of out-of-court bodies handling those types of conflict for which courts might potentially be invoked.

All of the gradual alternatives of more informality within or of informal procedures out-of-court have a common element of conciliation and of settling conflicts. However, even though conciliation allows for some discretion as to the substantive decision to be reached, 'alternative' procedures are not free from the consideration of what a formal procedure and formal decision would be like. Every 'alternative' to formal procedures operates under the threat of potentially invoking a judicial decision within the full-fledged model of a formal procedure. As long as the possibility of invoking a formal procedure is maintained, informal alternatives work 'under the shadow of a formal procedure and of formal law'. This can be seen as a justification for legal scholars viewing 'alternatives' from the perspective of the model of a full-fledged procedure. In such a view 'alternatives' are described as a deviation from the full fledged model. A radically different perspective is adopted by those scholars who look at a set of similar conflict situations in the first place, and from here consider judicial procedures as one of the many alternatives in handling them. Often such a view is justified by the existence of long standing traditions of handling conflicts. Traditionalists among lawyers have again and again pointed at *folk law* as a predecessor to judicial institutions in the historical sense. Very often such a view has been developed under the conditions of the imposition of law by either a ruling class or a colonial power, with folk institutions resisting superimposed courts. However, sociologists of law in developed countries have found that similar patterns of official and unofficial legal institutions exist side by side. Wherever social relations are regulated in *semi-autonomous* fields capable to some degree of autonomous conflict handling, they have observed a tendency of invoking the official institutions with their formality as an ultimum remedium. To the degree to which semi-autonomous fields are considered to be effective and legitimate agencies for handling conflicts, invoking formal procedures becomes more exceptional. On the other hand, the more formal and costly court procedures become, the more there might develop more informal agencies and procedures outside of courts. This thesis shall be elaborated upon in our report.

Before going into the details of the many 'alternative' procedural forms to be found, a general remark on the suppositions of comparativity should be made.

It should be immediately clear that what is considered to be 'alternative' to the model of formal procedure must vary from one legal system to the other as well as from the perspective of one observer or another. In comparing a number of national reports, we cannot always distinguish between the variations of the legal systems which are reported upon and the perspective of our rapporteur. A comparative survey becomes even more difficult, if we do not restrict ourselves to describing different regulations and institutions, but try to grasp some of their empirical relevance.

In some countries the reports state that there are no exceptions from certain procedural principles. This might either be a statement strictly on normative grounds or it might be a statement on the practice of courts, or even on the practice of parties and advocates who try to avoid such formalities. In some other countries such practice has been incorporated into legal thinking and into the discussions among lawyers on procedural questions. In such cases our reports will state considerable national differences. They have to be taken as an indication of the awareness among legal procedural lawyers of the plurality of formal and informal meanings of conflict handling, rather than as an indication of their empirical relevance.

With such careful reservation in mind, we may now give a summary of the national reports seen through the selective eye of those aspects which seem to be comparable throughout the respective legal systems.

2 COUNTRY REPORTS

2.1 COMMON LAW COUNTRIES

2.1.1 United States of America (Prof. Bundy, Berkeley California)

If there is a *movement* towards developing alternatives to formal procedures, it originated in the United States of America. It was fed by the discontent with trial procedures. As a matter of fact, more than 90% of all civil litigation in the United States trial courts of first instance are settled before going to a full trial. 'Settlement' in American courts can mean everything from mere threats of one party by first filing a law suit and thereby bringing the other party to give in, to negotiating in pre-trial procedures of the courts or to using arbitration out of court while the threat of a law suit pending is hanging above the parties. Inquiry in the American procedure puts such a heavy burden on the lawyers of both parties, and the rules of evidence during the trial impose so many formalities, that every party concerned will do its best to avoid as much of it as possible while at the same time threatening with the costs and uncertainties of an adversary procedure.

Recently there has been much talk about an alleged 'litigation explosion'. Even though long-term litigation statistics do not show any such spectacular growth, the perceived problem and the rhetoric around the litigiousness of Americans indicates a discontent with the adversariness of lawyers and the functioning of the courts. In order to meet these discontents, a variety of dispute resolution projects have been set up by communities, by foundations and by action groups, others (such as labour arbitration) have been discovered and further developed as part of the 'alternative dispute resolution movement' (ADR). Some of these projects are provided as a public service adjunct to the public system of formal adjudication, others are supplied pursuant to agreement by the disputants either by contract before, or after the dispute has arisen; some operate as an element of internal regulations of institutions (university, hospitals, prisons, large corporations) devising procedures for handling complaints either of clients or of organization members. In a few cases, free-standing community institutions have been set up for neighborhood conflicts of all sorts: these, however, seldom have a considerable caseload unless serving as a referral institution which helps to avoid more formal and more costly adjudication.

Alternative dispute resolution reform in the United States responds to perceived flaws of the civil justice system: high caseloads and long delays; lack of access; the limited competence of the courts to resolve matters that are intimate or technically complex or that involve continuing relationships among the litigants; and excessive contentiousness. More fundamentally, enthusiasm for alternatives often reflects distrust of legal regulation and the legal profession.

Public interest law alternatives which center on arbitration and mediation programs are designed to promote settlement short of judicial resolution. Most such programs are court annexed and operate only after suit has been filed (e.g., court-annexed arbitration, court annexed mediation of divorce, small claims and neighbor-neighbor disputes). Other programs operate prior to court filing (e.g., medical malpractice screening, mediation of certain environmental disputes). Apart from formal alternative schemes, trial judges are devoting increased attention to the expansion of their informal role in mediating pre-trial settlements.

Outside the courts, disputant-controlled dispute settlement processes have assumed increased importance. With strong judicial and legislative support, the use of arbitration has been expanded to fields like medical malpractice and patent disputes where it had preciously been available. Mediation has been heavily promoted in family, environmental and complex business disputes, although the actual extent of its use is uncertain. Finally, many public and private institutions frequently involved in litigation have adopted mediatory internal dispute management processes to forestall or settle claims short of formal adjudication.

Available evidence from publicly sponsored alternative programs indicates that voluntary programs have failed to attract sufficient participation to be economic. Compulsory programs have a better record, but studies suggest that even the most successful programs have had at best a modest impact on reducing costs and delays or improving outcomes. The reporter argues that the modest impact of reform can be traced to three principal factors: First the civil justice system already contained substantial elements of compromise and mediation: often reform merely formalized those agreements. Second, a combination of concerns for procedural fairness and for the economic interests of the legal profession have sharply moderated the thrust of reform: even 'compulsory' programs normally do not bar resort to full adjudicatory procedures. Third, in practice the goals of reform have often proven incompatible and self-canceling.

2.1.2 Australia (Prof. Williams, University of Melbourne)

While the general discontent with delay, expense and procedural complexity of formal adjudication applies in Australia as well as in the United States, our reporter points out that alternatives to formal procedures have developed especially in certain areas of law. Small claims tribunals which limit their jurisdiction to contract matters up to A$.3,000 have been established by national legislation. They have, however, not achieved a considerable case load in comparison to the magistrates courts; and much to the surprise of the reformers, they have not attracted many consumer cases but rather been used to obtain title by relatively middle class plaintiffs. A similar function is performed by a summons procedure for monetary claims up to A$.20,000 in Victoria: here the claimant sends a letter of claim to which the recipient can respond by entering into structured negotiations; if the recipient does not respond, the claimant receives a summons within two months. Thus, in this Australian state we observe an offer of mediation combined with a summary procedure for debt enforcement.

The second area of law where court procedures are drawn before a specialized tribunal concerns landlord-tenant disputes. Residential tenancy tribunals are constituted by a chairman who is legally qualified; while procedure they follow is discretionary. They are competent in deciding on rental price, modifying the terms of a periodic tenancy, and award compensation for damage by either landlord or tenant. Chairmen will encourage the parties to settle the matter before starting a hearing.

In a few places in Victoria and South Wales local neighborhood mediation services have been set up to handle more widely dispersed neighborhood grievances, noise or pollution. Surveys however show that satisfaction with the cases handled by neighborhood mediation remains low as most parties feel that conflicts are escalated rather than resolved. It may also come as a surprise that the parties invoking the service were local government, police, lawyers, estate agents and landlords rather than tenants or other private people voicing their disputes. Other reports from New South Wales, however, give a much more favorable evaluation based on the fact that in most of their cases a settlement was mediated and that the system provided more acceptable and comprehensible options for day to day conflicts.

A step away from adversary litigation in divorce procedures is made by changing substantive law. The introduction of no-fault divorce together with specialized family courts has initiated a development away from litigating about the grounds of divorce towards negotiating the conditions of separation. Specialized family mediation projects and mediation services by divorce lawyers try to come to agreements before court procedures are in progress. They however led to the need for drawing a borderline of lawyer ethics between representing one party and mediating between two.

Commercial arbitration has been a traditional field for out-of-court procedures. Statutory law in 1984 gives wide powers to an arbitrator in a party-controlled arbitration procedure. Even more autonomy of the parties is enjoyed in 'mini-trials' between commercial parties which choose to follow a procedure of mutual presentation of evidence without even invoking a third party as mediator, but rather relying upon the mutual interest of reaching a settlement. As a matter of course the case loads for such procedures remain unknown, as the use of such 'private mini trials' comes to light only in case of breakdown and pursuant litigation. As in many of our national reports, we might be focussing attention on customary and regular modes of conflict handling which we call 'alternatives' only because they eventually show up at the tip of the iceberg in publicly known court litigation.

2.1.3 Great Britain (Prof. Wilson, Warwick)

In diffuse interest matters such as consumer protection courts inherently present too high a threshold of access for the individual claim while the collective interest would require legal remedy. Therefore *representative* interest organizations develop strategies of handling individual grievances out of court and at the same time involving courts for test cases and occasionally to 'show-off' their enforcement power. This interest constellation has led to institutions such as the 'Office of Fair Trading' and a number of local schemes for 'simple justice'. They usually treat complaints in the most direct fashion possible, resorting to arbitration only when necessary. Their verdicts are usually enforceable by the local courts.

A rather large section of the British report is devoted to conflict handling in labour disputes, as these have only recently (since the 1970s) been drawn before 'unindustrial tribunals' with a mandatory Arbitration and Conciliation Service (ACAS) to be passed before invoking the tribunal. Again, we here find a combination of conciliation procedures followed by an adversarial procedure in case of failure (with the proviso that tribunals are not as formal as a regular Crown Court would be). And again, we here have an example of mediation being integrated into formal litigation in an area in which trade unions heretofore have been violently anti-legalistic and therefore opposed substantive regulation as well as handling of disputes by court-like institutions.

A further area where thresholds of invoking the courts have been considered to render substantive law ineffective is that of race-relations. Therefore a 'Race-Relations Board' was introduced by statutory law in 1965 to implement anti-discrimination rules in employment situations. The policy-making function of the board can be seen by following the kinds of grievances and the enlargement of competence of the board throughout the history of its existence. Rather than applying a static body of rules, the board has actively sought to innovate the perceptions of lawyers as well as rule-making with regard to equality of opportunity. Alternative modes of handling grievances have in this case paved the way for cases of discriminatory treatment to be brought before regular courts.

2.2 CIVIL LAW COUNTRIES

Some of the qualms about the formalities of trial procedures in Common Law countries do not apply to courts of justice in Civil Law countries. Judges in Civil Law procedure enjoy much more discretion in shifting back and forth between mediation and adjudication than they would in a trial procedure. They often use this for moving back and forth between mediative and adjudicative styles in their hearings. We therefore find many more in-court alternatives to full adjudication which in Common Law countries have to be externalised. This holds true for informal ways of arriving at in-court settlements as well as introducing summary procedures for cases in which courts are invoked for enforcement functions rather than adjudication between adversary arguments.

In some countries (such as West-Germany and Austria) courts are comparatively well equipped and efficient so that qualitative arguments for informalism are stressed rather than relief from high caseloads. Some country reports restrict themselves to alternative modes of adjudication within the framework of their civil procedural codes (like largely the Austrian, Greek and Italian reports), others are explicitly looking for alternatives outside of the legal system (like the Brazilian or the Dutch report). And finally, some reports (like the Danish) start out from the theoretical notion, that judicial procedure is only one (rather exceptional) mode of dispute resolution, while others start out from the judicial model and see informalism as an 'alternative' deviating from it.

2.2.1 Federal Republic of Germany (Dr. Gottwald, Stuttgart)

The different point of departure in the problems of court reform leading to the discussion of 'alternatives to formal procedures' in civil law countries is most apparent in the German report. In comparison to common law countries, civil procedure here lies much more in the hands of judges than of parties and their lawyers. And even though there are complaints about the long duration of procedures, civil law suits are remarkably fast in every instance in West Germany. The number of judges in relation to the population is higher than anywhere else, and the costs of court and lawyer fees are low compared to Common Law practice. Therefore, 'alternatives' to the full adjudicatory procedure are more likely to be sought within courts rather than outside them. A number of recent publications have stressed the advantages of settlements in court as compared to full adjudication with the imminent risk of de novo appeal. It is also stressed that settlements in court provide the judge with some discretion in integrating considerations outside of the substantive law applying to the case in litigation leaving some room for equity rather than pure applications of the law.

On the other hand a highly standardized dunning procedure is used widely for debt enforcement producing an almost automatized executory title for creditors unless the debtor contradicts explicitly within two weeks. The ease and efficiency of debt enforcement by court order leads to a high volume of procedures, encouraging risky credit as well as mail-order deliveries which, without such court service, would have to take more careful prevention.

Also preliminary court orders have been used as an efficient way of obtaining executory title without going through the pains of taking full evidence.

Compared to the summary and the informal alternatives within court, out-of-court conciliation has not taken on a considerable case load. Institutions like the 'Schiedsmann' are faced with declining demand and are rightly called a 'dying institution'. Complaints commissions in consumer matters on the other hand are increasing their case loads.

Local traditions such as the Arbitration and Conciliation Board (OeRA) at Hamburg are carefully restricted by the Advocates Associations in order not to be followed up in other parts of the Federal Republic.

Commercial arbitration, however, is spreading as well as attempts of professional organizations and chambers of commerce to handle conflicts internally. Many of the German judges resent that the courts of justice are handling an increasingly high volume of petty cases, while vital social conflicts choose forums outside of the court system of justice.

2.2.2 Austria (Dr. Mayr, Dr. Schmidt, Innsbruck)

The Austrian report, too, addresses settlement as a mode within the civil procedural code. Parties have the choice of submitting a settlement before court rather than litigating on the way to adjudication. In some issues such as divorce the judge is obliged to attempt conciliation before entering adversary procedure. Parties may also by contract agree on conciliation in case of conflict, however, this is used more often in an international contract than in a national one, because, courts provide the parties with a relatively speedy and efficient procedure.

This is one of the reasons why the conciliation service which communities are obliged to render (Gemeindevermittlungsaemter) are seldom used. However, more use is made of professional conciliation in complaints against lawyers, doctors or engineers. Also public administration offers conciliation such as in rental conflicts and hunting damages. In all of these mandatory conciliation precedes a possible law suit. Parties are free to invoke courts, if an amicable settlement has failed.

Especially insurance companies make use of conciliating claims, usually with the help of expert opinions. However, the attempt to establish conciliation for damages in traffic accidents failed, apparently because the advocates associations opposed it.

2.2.3 Greece (Dr. Orfanidis, Athens)

Also the Greek reporter stresses the very points that have been paramount in the German report. An 'alternative dispute resolution movement' has not developed in Greece, even though overburdening of courts is a constant complaint. Instead, there has been increased emphasis on settlement *within* court as an alternative mode of adjudication. On the other hand, simplified procedure for debt enforcement (comparable to the German Mahnverfahren) was introduced in 1953 enabling creditors to enforce their claims without due process guaranteed to the defendant. Also landlords are provided with a simplified procedure in order to prevent tenants from exploiting new long durations of court procedures when threatened by eviction. In divorce cases a similar tendency towards simplified adjudication rather than mediation is to be observed: the regulation that divorce is to be preceded by a conciliatory attempt aimed at preventing the separation (dating back to clerical procedures) has been abolished, a simplified procedure in case of consent rather enables the divorcees to separate without adversary hearings.

Other courts of arbitration and conciliation met with suspicion by the legislation of the 19th century, but have recently been up-valued in light of the overburdening of the courts. Not much is known about the use of conciliatory agreements in contracting, but it can be assumed, that it is used among business partners to avoid court litigation and that lawyers attempt to settle out of court before filing a law suit.

A special procedure for petty cases (with a value up to 30,000 dinars) is handled by the judges of the peace. Designed for consumers, it is not quite clear however, whether they are not primarily invoked by debt enforcers but procedures are terminated by adjudication even though there should be a mandatory attempt for a settlement. Most likely out-of-court settlements are more frequent than those before the courts.

Judicial institutions stressing settlement rather than adjudication are more typical for labour disputes. Civil procedure demands a mandatory attempt at conciliation in labour cases. Furthermore, labour administration provides a conciliation service in disputes between individual workers and bargaining committees in collective labour law cases. The caseloads of these administrative conciliation procedures demonstrate that they serve as a court-avoiding institution.

2.2.4 France (Dr. Bonafé-Schmitt, Lyon)

Our French reporter restricts himself to alternatives *to* the courts which are to be found with respect to consumer complaints, landlord-tenant problems and in neighborhood relations. The latter are sometimes connected to alternative measures replacing penal sanctions (especially for violent crime if it occurs within longstanding relations or if victims of violence are to be reimbursed). The report differentiates between the guiding ideas of alternative institutions:

- the idea of *efficient management* gave rise to the institution of 'conciliators' in 1977 who have the task of handling to mass of petty cases which in earlier times have been treated by 'judges of the peace'. Even though their caseload of 22756 cases (half of them were settled by conciliation) is not sizable in comparison to the caseloads of civil courts, same already fear the rise of a 'parallel system of justice'.

- the idea of *social integration* gave rise to projects of 'direct medication' such as the association 'ACCORD' in Strasbourg which treats neighborhood conflicts concerning civil as well as penal disputes, or the 'Conciliation Committees on Violence' at several places which try to 'civilize' the reactions on violent acts by conciliating between the violator an the victim.

- the idea of *redistribution of social power relations* gave rise to interest representation of tenants, consumers or advice services of law shops. They explicitly act in a partisan way in favour of socially underprivileged groups in mobilizing diffuse interest groups and representing test cases. The same issues are also subject to more neutral services such as the 'Post Box 5000' for consumer arbitration which treated 27.385 cases in 1981 or the 'Landlord-Tenant Commissions' which were institutionalized by the socialist governments in 1982 treating a caseload of (only) 1294 cases in 1984.

All of these institutions are mediatory and settle about half of their cases. They do not always preclude the danger of putting pressure upon the parties to come to an agreement, especially if their procedures are being formalized, and if they act according to professional ideologies of the mediators rather than according to the (opposing) interests of their clients. In such cases 'alternative' institutions do not escape the very problems that lead parties to avoid adjudication by courts. The reporter concludes with an appeal to look for a pluralism of conflict treatment which is sufficiently differentiated to meet the problems of relations specific to different areas of social life.

2.2.5 Belgium (Dr. Demeulenaere, Ghent)

The Belgian report concentrates on complaints boards for consumers such as furniture, travel agencies and the cleaning industry. Two recent experiments with complaint boards in Belgium show that arbitration offers are not used by many, if participation remains voluntary. Both schemes provided the mediating court clerks with rudimentary rights to information, but did not provide them with any powers in case one party did not appear or did not consent. Therefore, professional litigants never invoked the procedure, and private individuals often return from it disappointed.

2.2.6 The Netherlands (Prof. Hondius, Utrecht)

The Dutch report stresses that courts never had a monopoly to settling conflicts. Commercial arbitration in national as well as international trade has traditionally taken place outside the court. Consumer complaints are represented by special organizations which handle a high caseload, but only occasionally resort to litigating test cases. Special procedures outside of court are regulating rental as well as labour conflicts. Dutch society, being highly regulated by welfare provisions, has not drawn many of the conflicts resulting thereof into the courts. The reform of judicial procedure which is now under way might change that by increasing the attractiveness of courts by introducing more simple procedures and stressing oral hearings. Our reporter sees the pluralism of procedures inside and outside of courts as a system of competition stimulating the supply side of the court system as well as of private arbitration and other forums offering the public a wide range of choices in seeking justice.

2.2.7 Denmark (Prof. Blegvad, Kobnhavn)

The Danish report concentrates on some of the theoretical considerations underlying the difficulty of comparing national legal systems. In a comparison of litigation rules for West Germany, The Netherlands and Denmark it becomes quite apparent that the volume of litigation per 100,000 of the population varies widely even though the northern European countries are very much alike in terms of economic development, welfare provisions and thereby societal conflict potential. The variations from one country to the next can be explained by looking into the semi-autonomous fields from which conflict originates. The availability of conflict handling institutions in these fields on the one hand, the efficiency of courts on the other determine how large a share of potentially legal conflict gets to be treated by court. Debt enforcement provides the largest share of civil court procedures in Denmark, while family law and divorce as well as labour cases are largely handled outside the judicial system. Non-judicial treatment of conflict is not even considered as being 'alternative' to court procedures, but rather as the normal way with judicial proceedings being considered as the rather unusual 'alternative'.

2.2.8 Italy (Dr. Silvestri, Pavia)

There could be no more radical difference in point of view than that between the Danish and the Italian reports. While the Danish report looks from societal conflict and thus regards the selective crew of judicial procedures as an exception, the Italians report looks at alternatives from the point of view of the judicial procedure. Particularly it comes to the conclusion that 'an alternative dissolution movement has not yet arisen'. Even though the Italian code of civil procedure obliges the judge to try and conciliate between parties, this is seldom put into practice. In landlord-tenant cases and labour disputes, a conciliation attempt is mandatory, but if declared unsuccessful judges and parties feel free to enter into the adjudicatory procedure.

There are lay conciliators outside of court and there is the possibility of trying conciliation in labour disputes before going to court. No information on their use is given, however, as the reporter considers them a means to avoid adjudication rather than leading to subsequent proceedings.

2.2.9 Spain (Prof. Nosete, Madrid)

It is no doubt due to the reform impulse of the post-Franco modernization in Spain and stimulated by American alternative institutions that a multitude of initiatives towards alternatives within different civil procedures are being discussed. Traditional elements which we have seen in other civil law countries reoccur: summary procedures in debt enforcement of smaller amounts enjoy a longer tradition, arbitration in commercial conflicts has been established outside of the courts. Special courts are set up for individual as well as collective labour disputes with mandatory conciliation before adversary procedures is entered. Conciliation also prevails in landlord-tenant cases in which district as well as cases about land-lease in rural districts. As much as the procedural forms of alternative disputes mirror those in other civil law countries, there is a spirit of reform in the presentation of our reporter which emphasizes changes in the direction of reformalization rather than those forces aiming at preserving the prerogatives of full adjudication.

2.2.10 Brazil (Prof. Grinover, Sao Paulo)

Most enthusiastic about alternative dispute resolution is our Brazilian reporter. When from 1982 on conciliation councils were introduced in several Brazilian jurisdictions, this can be seen as a breakthrough for improved access to justice. Neighborhood quarrels are being brought before these courts as well as damages arising from traffic accidents, consumer cases and rental conflicts. Their invocation is optional and might lead to a form of court procedure if conciliation failed. Its guidelines are equity rather than codified law and the procedure is informal. Mediators who need be jurists are recruited. If ratified by a judge, a mediated settlement can be executed by force of a legal title. The experiment that in 1984 led to the institution of petty claims courts: they are chaired by professional judges and may decide on rates up to a value of 20 times the minimal wage. The procedure is informal and conciliation is preferred to adjudication. As petty claims courts are considered to be successful, it is to be expected that the range of their competence is gradually going to be extended to higher stakes and to other areas of law.

International disputes in commercial relations are largely referred to arbitrators, but hardly ever domestic commercial disputes. Arbitration is widely used, however, in collective labour disputes since 1985 since the former ban on collective agreements had been levied. Also procedures regarding mortgages for the purchase of a home, have been deformalized; but it must be admitted that this gives the creditor speedy access to executionary titles without giving the debtor sufficient time for due legal defense. Informality is here instrumentalized for enforcement efficiency rather than for conciliatory settlement.

2.3 EAST ASIAN COUNTRIES

All of our reporters from east-Asian countries stress the importance of the traditional ideology of keeping an amicable face and conciliating for a settlement rather than engaging in open conflict and litigating adversarily. Modernization in the 19th century, however, introduced European codes of law in many countries, and recent modernization after the 2nd World War brought with it the procedural ideology of American adversariness on the one hand, socialist lay justice on the other. East-Asian countries have merged such divergent traditions in various ways, often keeping seemingly contradictory systems side by side. Almost invariably they stress the obligation of first conciliating before litigating; invariably they also state that an imminent trend towards adversariness has caused courts to be crowded and legal policy makers to look for the virtues of traditional ways of mediation. Litigation is nevertheless offered as a last resort after conciliatory procedures have failed.

2.3.1 China (Prof. Wei-Dong, Beijing)

The contemporary Chinese legal system is a product of many centuries of indigenous legal tradition merging with socialist ideology both attempting to maintain a pluralism of ways of resolving conflict.

a) Alternatives within formal procedures

In civil litigation the adversarial principle which prevails in Western civil procedures is limited. The court supervises the disposition of litigation on behalf of the government. Representation by lawyers is minimal. There is a strong emphasis on mediatory settlements. 80% of civil suits are resolved through mediation by court.

Mediation, institutionalized or otherwise, has a long history and is encouraged by the present socialist regime. Emphasis is also given on mediation within the court. Institutionalized mediations are:

1) Mediation by administrative agencies such as ABIC and the Labour Management Department provide mediation of labour disputes. Also offices of local government conduct mediation.
2) Community mediation by Mediation Committees: There is a well organized network of systems for mediation involving towns, villages, factories, etc. under Judicial assistance. Mediation Committees are autonomous bodies and its members are elected by the people concerned. The practice of 'one mediator for ten households' has spread as as of 1985 there were 4,700,000 mediators who mediated 6,330,000 cases. Mediators serve without renumeration. A success rate of mediation of over 95% is being reported.
3) Consumer protection through National Consumer Association (NCA) set up in 1984. There are 239 associations receiving complaints from consumers, which lead to mediation, arbitration or disciplinary sanction.

b) Alternatives outside of formal litigation in court

4) Arbitration is widely used in economic relations. There are three arbitral organizations: the Administration Bureau for Industry and Commerce (ABIC),

the Foreign Economic and Trade Arbitration Commission (FETAC) and Maritime Arbitration Commission (MAC), the latter two being set up within China Council for the Promotion of International Trade (CCPIT) and concerned with international trade.

Arbitration dealing with disputes arising from domestic trade is administered by a commission with the central and local ABIC and not an arbitration in the true sense of the word because it does not require any arbitration agreement. Dissatisfied parties may sue in court after receiving the award. In essence, it is a compulsory preliminary to a litigation. Moreover, a mediation is a prerequisite for arbitration. Emphasis upon mediation applies also to the international trade arbitration by FETAC and MAC.

2.3.2 India (Prof. Mehra, New Delhi)

Common law based on civil procedure in India is considered to be too slow and too costly. Culturally and historically the people are more familiar with procedures aiming at settlement of disputes by community intervention rather than with adjudicated decision. Mutually agreed settlement is generally regarded as far superior to long drawn-out, expensive litigation.

a) Alternatives within the court system

- Family Courts: In view of the special considerations in dealing with family disputes, the Family Court Act of 1984 set up Family Courts: Here women are preferred as judges; the procedure is more informal than civil procedure in general with fewer technical rules of evidence; appeals are limited; court records are confidential; lawyers may be excluded; evidence is provided by court investigation rather than of adversarial trial; social welfare institutions and organizations are involved in the proceedings, etc.
- Small Claims Courts: Provincial Small Claims Courts Act of 1887 set a special procedure for claims, where an unreasoned judgement can be rendered immediately after one hearing and no appeals therefrom.

b) Para-judicial alternatives

- Lok Adalat (or People's Court) is a recently developed para-judicial institution. During 1982-86 over 256 of such courts were introduced in 11 states, they settled a great number of cases. It is particularly popular among automobile accident claimants and insurance companies. Lok Adalat is not a court in a technical sense, but may be perceived as such by people. It is a forum formed by volunteering lawyers and others. Its procedure is necessarily flexible and informal, pleasant and friendly. Cases are brought from legal aid agency, law college legal aid clinic and social action groups. The legal profession and the government have shown no hostility to this movement.
- Nyaya Panchayats are a traditional system analogous to English Justice of Peace or Russian People's Court, trying cases according to common sense justice, which is a part of the formal judicial system of the country, although the way to handle cases is very different from that of the ordinary courts. Conciliation and compromise are stressed.

c) Alternatives outside the legal system

- Commercial arbitration: Use of commercial arbitration has been growing, but not yet to the extent desired by the reporter. 10% of cases concern international disputes. Arbitration is often just as costly and time consuming as court litigation. Review of award by the court is also used as a dilatory tactic by the losing party. Certain government agencies have stopped using the arbitration clause recently, an expression of lack of faith in commercial arbitration.
- Conciliation officers for labour disputes form an independent agency created by law to promote industrial peace by making available governmental facilities in the process of collective bargaining.
- Bankruptcy legislation is instrumental for protecting debtors and solving disputes.
- A Tenant Protection Statute is intended to protect tenants from unjust eviction and to control rent, but this has not been working as satisfactorily as desired.

2.3.3 Japan (Dr. Yamamoto, Kyoto)

a) Alternatives within formal procedures

The volume of litigation in court is smaller than that of most Western countries due to a tradition heavily influenced by the Confucian ethics. But it should be admitted that the number of law suits is due to certain inadequacies inherent to the judicial system, namely delay and high costs. Accordingly, the need for alternatives inside and outside of the courts has been felt strongly. Some alternatives have a long tradition, others have been devised more recently.

Settlement during litigation under the Code of Civil Procedure occurs in one third of the cases at the District Court level.

For money claims and cashing of checks a simplified and swifter procedure is provided.

A summary payment procedure (comparable to the German Mahnverfahren) helps collect undisputed debts. In 1985 688,335 applications were made, more than three times as many than civil suits.

Non-contentious cases, dealing with a variety of matters including, among others, family disputes and certain landlord-tenant disputes with a summary procedure.

An attempt to settle amicably prior to asking for legal action is considered favorably by judges in giving an execution title quickly.

Conciliation in court includes civil conciliation for all kinds of civil disputes. It is conducted by a Conciliation Committee composed of two conciliators appointed from among citizens (lawyers and experts included depending on the nature of the dispute). Family disputes are handled by family conciliation in Family Courts. Conciliation is certainly the most popular court procedure among the people. It is accessible and inexpensive in addition to the benefit of avoiding confrontation.

b) Dispute settlement undertaken by administrative agencies

There are several commissions, local and central, given power under specific statutes to conduct mediation/conciliation, arbitration or adjudication in respective areas of dispute, such as environmental pollution, building contract, labour relations, etc. In addition, most local governments offer counselling services to citizens and this often functions as a dispute resolution mechanism. The police do the same with respect to traffic accidents as well as other disputes.

c) Alternatives outside of courts

Automobile Accident Dispute Settlement Centers operate under the sponsorship of the insurance industry. Lawyers are employed as arbiters and give non-binding assessment of damages. Since insurance companies have given an advance consent to it, it is the claimant's prerogative to accept or not. If not, he is free to bring a suit in court but most claimants do accept. Since this system was instituted, the number of automobile accident cases brought to conciliation in court has been decreasing. Local Bar associations compete with the Centre by establishing their own Automobile Accident Dispute Counselling Service, independently from the insurance industry.

Arbitration, however, is not popular except for international trade and shipping business. The Japanese Arbitration Association (JAA) and the Japanese Shipping Exchange (JSE) are active in these fields.

2.3.4 Korea (Prof. Sang Hyun Song, Seoul)

Litigation is not the principal means of dispute resolution in Korea. If there is litigation, inadequacies of the formal litigation system are strongly felt such as long delay and high costs. Courts prefer to act as mediators rather than adjudicators. As of January, 1987, the Supreme Court plans to utilize conciliation even more actively than before.

a) Alternatives within formal procedure

- Settlement as a way of ending litigation is possible under the Code of Civil Procedure. Judges normally stimulate the parties to arrive at a settlement.
- Payment order procedure for a summary collection of debt.
- Special statutory procedure for providing an executable deed through a notary or otherwise.
- Reference of single judge cases of conciliation.
- Special procedure under Small Claims Act (oral pleading, representation by a relative, reference to conciliation and decision by the court in lieu of conciliation to be avoided by objection of a party).
- Special procedures for family matters (family conciliation succeeds in 30% with devices to secure payment of money, conciliation being required before filing an action concerning family relation). The quality of judges and probation officers is questioned, however.

b) Alternatives outside of courts

Conciliation schemes are envisaged by a variety of statutes: In a culture which tries to avoid confrontation institutionalized conciliation plays an important role. Sometimes conciliatory attempts are at the disposition of the party in the sense that a party may choose adversary litigation from the outset but in other cases conciliation attempts are mandatory so that a party must first resort to conciliation before suing. In any event, conciliation can be regarded as a court of equity in Korea and channels a number of disputes which otherwise would result in litigation. Conciliation fills the gap between legal norms and actual life.

Voluntary Conciliation is provided for under the Land-Lease and House-Lease Conciliation Law, Environmental Preservation Law, Small Claims Adjudication Act, Domestic Affairs Adjudication Law, State Compensation Law, Labour Disputes Mediation Law, Insurance Law, etc. Conciliation is mandatory under the State Compensation Law, among others.

Under the Arbitration Act of 1966, the Korean Commercial Arbitration Board (KCAB) was formed and has been actively engaged in commercial arbitration. In the business community, arbitration has gained popularity.

2.3.5 The Philippines (Prof. Coquia, Manila)

Court congestion is a serious problem in the Philippines. Between 1967 and 1986 the number of civil cases pending before the trial courts has more than doubled from 80234 cases to 166,778. At the lowest level court a summary procedure has been introduced by recent legislation. But the problem of delay and high cost are still felt strongly, thus motivating a search for alternative methods of conflict resolution.

a) Alternatives within formal procedure

Mandatory pre-trial conferences are used to promote settlements and, when it fails, to simplify litigation procedure. 50% of all cases can be settled by pre-trial conferences.

Discovery procedures are used to eliminate unnecessary evidences.

Trial is delegated to commissioners who treat some or all issues to a 'commissioner' and report to the court. Judgement based on the pleadings and summary judgments are used to eliminate trials.

b) Alternatives outside of Court

- Katarungang Pambarangay Court (or Village Court) started in 1978 reviving the pre-Spanish tradition of amicable dispute settlement process. They try to achieve a conciliatory settlement rather than adjudication, as a precondition to a court action; no lawyers are allowed, and no fees levied; conciliators are chosen from neighborhood by the village head. Mediation is first attempted by the village head, and when this fails there follows either arbitration or conciliation by a panel or by a captain written agreement of the parties. Proceedings are open to the public and informal. 87% or 179,358 cases brought to this 'Court' during the first two years were settled. As this institution became popular, the number of cases filed with municipal courts rapidly decreased (it had been increasing) from 148,611 (1976) to 174,929 (1978, after the institution of the 'Court') it dropped to 138,810 (1979), and 111,784 (1982)).

Commercial arbitration has been becoming popular among merchants. Labour dispute settlements are mediated by a Labour Relations Commission, Labour Arbiters attempt to conciliate, but arbitrate if consent cannot be achieved.

2.3.6 Taiwan (Prof. Jung Tsung, Taipei)

As in other East Asian countries, the tradition of Taiwan is to avoid litigation in court. Suing is considered as evil and people tend to resort to more amicable ways of settling disputes.

a) Alternatives within formal procedure

Taiwan follows the Civil Law tradition. But courts always handle civil and family cases by attempting to conciliate. In divorce cases conciliation is mandatory before entering the divorce action.

b) Out of court alternatives

- A Consumer Protection Foundation was established in 1980 in order to mediate consumer disputes.
- The Commercial Arbitration Act of 1961 provides for arbitration but is practically unknown in the domestic business community.
- Land Tenancy Committee: Disputes between landlord and tenants of agricultural land are mediated. The system is intended for protection of agricultural tenants.
- Conciliation of labour disputes: Act for Disputes Settlement of Labour and Management of 1943 provides for a tripartite conciliation committee. The Committee may also give a binding decision.
- The Act of Conciliation in Villages and Towns of 1955 provides for a conciliation committee for civil and minor criminal cases under a supervision by the court throughout the country.

2.4 SOCIALIST COUNTRIES

Unfortunately, we did not receive any reports from European socialist countries. They might have provided us with still another view on conflict resolution embedded in other institutions of neighborhood and work life while at the same time the traditions of European legal systems are continued. Not only from the point of view of theoretical interest, we hope that in our final report it would have been desirable be able to incorporate some reports from these countries.

3 AREAS OF LAW WHERE THE TOPIC OF 'ALTERNATIVES' IS RELEVANT

From the outset of our comparative enterprise we identified a number of areas of law where alternative procedures are most likely to occur. Summary procedures are to be found wherever legal claims tend to be unambiguous so that a summary check of their validity is considered to be sufficient, and where such claims are very numerous so that routine handling methods are to be recommended in order to relieve courts from high case-loads. Debt collection is the most frequent task to be performed by such summary procedures. Although the stakes here show a zero-sum constellation, the defendants in debt collection cases often do not contest the claim, so that a summary procedure seems feasible.

Informal procedures occur wherever parties are engaged in a conflict whose interest constellation is not exclusively zero-sum but includes elements of mutual interest so that at least partial compromise becomes possible. The compromise often lies in consequences of the judicial decision which are not within the realm of the substantive law to be applied to the case, but rather flows from extra-legal considerations such as the concerns of parties not directly involved, or simply in considerations of time and costs inflicted by the procedure per se.

3.1 SMALL CLAIMS, DEBT COLLECTION VERSUS CONSUMER PROTECTION

In many countries the biggest share of the volume of court cases deals with debt collection. Even though the procedure might be contentious, the fact remains that defendants do not generally offer any defense, with the result that the procedure often ends with a default judgement. In consequence, many countries have introduced summary procedures summoning the debtor to pay after unilateral action by the claimant unless a defense is brought forward. An ordinary contentious procedure is usually initiated in cases where the defendant protests against the summons. Summary procedures for debt collection are found only in countries with a civil law tradition, always allowing the debtor to protest against the summons which forces the claimant to resort to the full procedure before the ordinary civil courts (such is the case in the German 'Mahnverfahren', which serves as a model for summary proceedings in the Netherlands, Korea and Japan: It is also the case with summary proceedings which come before the Danish bailiff's court; no summary debt collection proceedings are to be found in France, Belgium, Italy or in the Hispanic countries).

Debt collection is usually connected to strict executory powers of bailiffs ('Gerichtsvollzieher') who render a very reliable service for the implementation of the legal entitlement. However, even though the Netherlands and Japan explicitly formed their summary procedures on debt collection according to the German model, the use of it falls far short of its high-frequency usage in Austria and the Federal Republic of Germany. The explanation for the different levels of actual usage of procedures so similar in design are to be found in out-of-court institutions of debt enforcement, as well as in the more preventive patterns of credit management which are prevalent in Japan and the Netherlands as part of a 'culture' of avoidance of judicial involvement.

Small claims courts in Common Law countries were designed with a different purpose in mind. These are usually installed to allow consumers to raise complaints and to allow small shopkeepers to claim minor debts. But whether they are installed as particular tribunals (as in several jurisdictions in Australia or in several states of America) or offered as a simplified procedural alternative in the pre-trial stage (as in several local schemes in Great Britain), small claims procedures reduce the formality of the full adversarial trial procedure. Rules of evidence are largely at the discretion of the judge (or 'registrar' as they are called in the British schemes), lawyer representation is either discouraged or inadmissable, and settlement attempts are often required as part of the procedure.

Levying many of the procedural formalities of the full-trial procedure with its complicated rules of evidence, is mostly based on the assumption that these form a barrier to access for consumers and small shopkeepers. Small claims schemes thrive on the rhetoric of compensatory justice. Empirical studies of small claims courts in the Unites States, however, showed that they were largely used by sales organizations and professionals for the enforcement of small debts. The low costs, together with the short duration of the procedure, renders small claims courts attractive to routine litigants rather than lowering the barriers to access for the occasional client seeking compensatory justice.

Generally speaking, consumer protection is more effectively achieved by out-of-court settlements through such mediators as complaints boards, ombudsmen and conciliatory commissions. All the countries in our survey report some such institution which might have been initiated by voluntary organizations, trade unions, local government bodies or, possibly, by newspapers or television stations. The raison d'etre for the large number of out-of-court alternatives for consumer protection stems from the diffuse character of the interest constellation: each individual complaint case being too insignificant for a single consumer to endure the costs and the harassments involved in mobilizing the judicial institutions. The aggregate interests of all consumers jointly however, in view of the considerable collective interest, the idea of *representative* action inside and outside of court is lying at hand. Furthermore, there are a number of voluntary organizations such as trade unions and automobile clubs which see consumer representation as a membership service which increases their attractiveness. Trades organizations on the other hand occasionally respond by forming their own complaints boards thus preventing outsiders from developing the more aggressive strategy of collective interest representation. However, out-of-court handling for consumer complaints does not function entirely outside the legal system. On the contrary, as a rule they use litigation in court for test cases, which evokes an implicit threat of the possibility of a formal procedure if the informal route should meet with an unresponsive counter-party. 'Under the shadow of the formal procedure' they can effectively handle conflict cases informally. This is usually done by a combination of strategies: providing information and advice to consumers as well as offering arbitration in case of conflict, and resorting to formal litigation where informal conflict handling and arbitration has failed.

3.2 COMMERCIAL CONCILIATION AND ARBITRATION

Conflicts arising from commercial contracts and from 'unfair' competition are an everyday experience among businessmen. There are many ways of renegotiating the terms of trade and of out-of-court conciliation or arbitration. Certain sectors adopt conciliation or arbitration clauses as a standard clause in all contracts. International trading largely avoids the national court systems, but rather resorts to international arbitrators such as are provided by International Chambers of Commerce.

Courts in most Civil Law countries respond to the needs of the business world by having competent and time effective bodies for handling conflicts about commercial transactions by providing specialised courts for litigation among businessmen. Usually they provide a bench with so-called 'lay judges' who are experts in commercial practice but who are not necessarily trained in legal matters. Common law countries tend to provide out-of-court conciliation or arbitration schemes for committed disputes, often offering an appeal to the courts in case the attempts at settling the dispute fail.

The borderline between specialised courts and out-of-court conciliation or arbitration can be fluid. Established arbitration practice in sectors such as shipping, international transport and insurance rely on publishing precedent cases in specialized 'arbitration journals' thus approaching a private system of case law jurisprudence. Other sectors such as construction, use arbitration boards for conflicts among firms as well as between contractors and clients on a case-by-case basis. Professionals such as doctors, practicing lawyers, architects and journalists typically resort to internal boards for the control of professional conduct, sometimes using the courts as an appeal instance (such is the case with the control of professional conduct of attorneys in many countries).

Some reports stress that arbitration is a traditional form of dispute resolution increasingly being replaced by court-centered jurisdiction. With an increased interference of state authorities more and more disputes in many business communities were attracted to the court. Arbitration has always been a special method peculiar to highly specialized business relations like international trade, conflicts around construction projects and collective issues of labour relations. With courts in many countries being increasingly overcrowded, there is a trend towards a revival of arbitration in many areas of life as a general method of dispute resolution.

Arbitration is properly defined as a method of dispute resolution by agreement of the parties to a-priori acceptance of the decision of a third party which they appoint as arbitrator. Being based on agreement of the parties on the one hand and arriving at a binding decision on the other, it is halfway between *adjudication* which implies that the procedure can be enforced also against the consent of any party involved, and *conciliation* which implies the procedure as well as the decision to be valid only on consent of the parties involved.

The word 'arbitration' is often, however, used in a wider sense. In some Anglo-American jurisdictions (the United States, United Kingdom and Australia) the term is used to depict statutory adjudicatory proceedings by which small claims are handled. Typically, the court refers litigation in certain enumerated categories to a member of the bar who has been registered for such a purpose. Where an agreement of both parties is required for the court to do so, it is something closest to the true idea of arbitration. But, sometimes it is compulsory for certain small claims to be handled by an 'arbitrator.' Although truly conciliatory solutions (that is decisions based on mutual consent) are always encouraged, the procedure is often not even arbitration in the true meaning of the term because in the event of unsuccessful conciliation the 'arbitrator' will enforce a decision.

On the other hand, a procedure not called 'arbitration' may in fact function as arbitration. If one of the disputing parties had given a unilateral blanket consent to a decision of a certain organization of its trust, it is up to the other party to accept such a decision in order to end the dispute. No previous agreement between the parties is necessary for such arbitration. The. agreement is offered by one party from the beginning and can be said to be fully completed by the other party's acceptance of a decision. Where, for some reason, an acceptance is highly likely, such an institution would in fact function like an arbitration though technically it is not. This type of dispute resolution can typically be seen with consumer grievances. An industrial group may set up an organization to process consumer grievances and give a blanket advance consent to any decision resulting from the organization's panel. Consumers who resort to such an organization are free not to accept the decision, if they think it unreasonable, but normally they do accept because the only alternative would be costly litigation in court. Such seems to be the case of the American Better Business Bureaus (BBB). In many countries, similar mechanisms have been adopted by sales organizations, insurance companies or travel agencies.

Arbitration presents a wide variety of procedures. A basic distinction is that between *ad hoc* arbitration and *institutional* arbitration. While *ad hoc* arbitration can be set up by anybody in any dispute, the institutionalized forms of arbitration by permanent organizations such as chambers of commerce or trade organizations gain a para- legal status. The practice of the institutional arbitration can be regulated by procedural rules of the respective arbitral organization, and there may be substantive jurisprudence based on published arbitration cases.

Well known commercial arbitral organizations are the International Chamber of Commerce (ICC), the American Arbitration Association (AAA) and the London Court of Arbitration. Furthermore, there are many organizations specializing in international commercial arbitration or arbitration of domestic disputes. The choice of an arbiter can vary widely. In *ad hoc* arbitration it is left to the parties to agree on a procedure. For the international commercial arbitration the UNCITRAL Arbitration Rules of 1976 are gaining popularity among arbitral organizations. Usually, each party appoints one arbiter and the two arbiters consequently appoint a third one. The arbitral organizations usually prepare a comprehensive list of arbiter candidates. Sometimes, an arbitral organization itself appoints arbiters on the basis of the nature of the dispute and according to their estimation of acceptability. Arbitration clauses are standard in international trade referring usually to one of the above mentioned arbitral organizations, International traders want to avoid the possible bias of any national court and they rather trust the expertise of arbitrators who are versed in the practice of international trade. Arbitration is also used in areas where a specialised expertise is required for a proper handling of dispute, such as shipping disputes and architectural disputes. Arbitrators are chosen with respect to their expertise in the respective field. They are felt to be better bridge discrepancies between law and the practice in their fields than a court could because a court judgment would be required to apply a law which is felt not to solve disputes realistically. Also lower costs or higher speed are often mentioned as an important reason to choose arbitration, even though this expectation often does not seem to be based on facts. Large international commercial arbitrations are extremely costly and prolonged. Domestic arbitration organized by a trade association, however, may be used free of cost, if it is maintained by the membership fees and if the arbitrator's services are honorary.

How much arbitration is used in a country or in particular sectors of a society very much depends on the relative strength of the merit of arbitration *vis a vis* other methods of dispute resolution including litigation in court.

3.3 LABOUR RELATIONS, ESPECIALLY EMPLOYMENT PROTECTION

Historically, the handling of labour relations is a newcomer to court litigation. In Common Law countries with a rather anti-legalistic trade union tradition, labour relations, and especially conflicts centering around dismissal, are handled by arbitrators. If arbitration fails in the first instance, specialised tribunals are usually resorted to (United Kingdom, Denmark) or arbitration boards (United States, Canada) which as a rule institutionalize some element of collective representation of both trade unions and employers' associations.

Civil Law countries (such as France, Belgium and Germany) have a tradition of specialized labour courts. Representation of the collective organizations on the bench is the rule in these courts as well as some element of mediation as a particular obligation of the court laid down in procedural law. Thus, we meet in labour courts of Civil Law countries the same elements of collective interests being intertwined with the individual interest conflict. So-called lay representation by expert judges recruited from both collective parties, and emphasis on mediatory rather than adjudicatory tasks of the court, are included within judicial institutions rather than being institutionally separated as is the case in the arbitratory schemes of the Common Law countries.

Preservation of a continuing relationship is said to be an important factor in the active use of arbitration in the field of labour relations in the Anglo-American world. In Japan, however, labour arbitration is almost unknown although it is clearly provided for in law. The intention not to endanger continuing relationships here is felt to leave no choice but to conciliate without any binding decision to be enforced against any of the parties is considered to be just as confrontational as litigation because of its threat of enforcing a binding decision. In Asian cultures in general, people want to avoid confrontation, but once they dare confront each other, litigation is preferred because the decision will enjoy the prestige of a court and will provide a second and even third chance to challenge the outcome by an appeal.

The popularity of arbitration is determined by its relative usefulness in comparison with conciliation on the one, and litigation on the other hand. Arbitration's great popularity in the Anglo-American jurisdictions, including India, can be explained by the limited character of their appellate system. The competence of their appellate courts is limited to review of points of law, whereas in Civil Law countries the first appellate instance normally provides a *denovo* trial of facts. The intricacies of the rules of evidence in a trial procedure lead to the Anglo-American tendency of looking for competent arbitrators instead of court litigation. Wherever arbitration is actively used, arbitral organizations are eager to conduct training programs and provide competent arbiters. In some countries and fields, professional arbiters such as the labour arbitrator in North America, can make a living by working on a fee basis. Professionalization and regulation of arbitration render their use more reliable and thereby more popular.

3.4 LANDLORD-TENANT RELATIONSHIPS

Similar to labour disputes collective interest conflicts hiding behind the individual conflict may have led to landlord-tenant relations in many countries being regulated by mediation or conciliation boards, often with a resort to formal court procedures, if conciliation has failed (such as is the case of administrative conciliation in Austria, as well as tenant complaint boards in The Netherlands).

Complaints about the standard of housing as well as the amount of rent to be paid can lead to such high case-loads that courts are often relieved by informal procedures, filtering out only the more serious cases for the formal court procedure. Among the latter we usually find the claim for eviction. This confirms the general rule of the theory of mobilization of courts: if the two parties are likely to continue their social relationship in the future, they generally prefer informal institutions and try to avoid court and lawyer involvement; if, however, they are prepared to break up their social relationship, the involvement of judicial instances and formal procedures becomes more likely.

3.5 FAMILY AND DIVORCE RELATIONSHIPS

Family relations are, of course, notorious for occupying the courts when separation is at stake. Many divorce cases are consensual, at least in the sense that both parties have reached agreement out of court as to how to handle the separation. Countries differ widely as to how consensual divorce is to be treated procedurally: they range from the Federal Republic of Germany on the one hand, which requires every divorce to pass through a full procedure with an oral hearing and a decision by a judge, to the simplifying treatment of using court procedures in a notary fashion (such as is the case with default judgments in divorce cases in The Netherlands, or in the British schemes for a 'do-it-yourself-divorce'). At the other extreme divorce cases can be handled by a similar administrative body as that which registers the marriage and resorting to courts only, if conflict issues are so adversary that a formal court procedure seems unavoidable (such as is the case in Denmark and in Japan).

Divorce often brings about long-term legal obligations for the ex-spouses. This is especially true where children are involved. Such obligations as child support have to be altered in case of changes in the financial circumstances of an involved person. Ex-families therefore often have to re-appear before family courts for quasi-notary acts. If uncontested, such court actions may be mere routine, but if legal entitlements have to be enforced against the will of one of the parties involved (mostly the father who has to pay alimony), such procedures may turn adversary with an element of adjudicative decision making. In such cases, the notary functions which courts may have to perform may slip into adversary procedures.

4 SUMMARY

Over-generalization is unavoidable in a comparative report as short as this one. Many procedural differentiations have to be simplified and a terminology adopted which does not apply precisely to any of the procedural systems discussed. Therefore, we prefer to talk in terms of over-arching 'functions' of courts. As an 'ordinary model', or ideal type of function of courts we consider *adjudication* in adversary procedures with a neutral bench of one or more judges as the deciders. This model presupposes a zero-sum conflict where the defendant will lose what the plaintiff hopes to win.

Many conflict constellations before judicial bodies, however, contain at least some element of mutual interest. This allows the possibility to negotiate a settlement. Procedural systems differ to which degree they incorporate *mediatory* functions within the court procedure or tend to externalize them out of court.

Furthermore, the ideal type model presupposes that the outcome of litigation is uncertain beforehand: why should parties engage in costly procedures if they know from the beginning how the judges will decide? Factually, however, courts have to handle a high volume of cases in which the plaintiff has an overriding chance of success, mostly because the other party does not even turn up to defend his position. In such cases the courts perform the function of helping to *enforce* uncontested claims rather than to adjudicate or mediate.

Lastly, there are many court cases which neither present a zero-sum conflict constellation nor is there any uncertainty about the court's decision. Courts often have the task of registering and rendering legal validity to uncontested decisions. We call such a function *'quasi-notary'*.

This leaves us with three directions in which 'alternatives' to the ordinary model of adjudication are being sought:

	Zero sum interest conflict	interests of parties partly in common
outcome of litigation unforeseeable	adjudication	mediataive function
outcome predictable from the outset	enforcement function	quasi-notary function

As we have seen there is a growing tendency of developing 'alternatives' to the adjudicatory model in all three directions: stressing the mediating function which allows for procedural as well as substantive informality, introducing summary procedures which simplify executory functions of courts mostly at the cost of due process, and treating cases in a notary fashion if the parties involved are in at least partial agreement. Elements of these alternative functions are very often incorporated in adjudicatory procedures, so that recent tendencies of stressing the alternative procedures take the form of shifting emphases rather than revolutionizing the adjudicatory mode of courts altogether. It is also quite clear that for many of the alternative forms of procedure, the possibility (that is to say: the *threat*) of returning to the full adjudicatory model stays present.

In this sense we may consider the shifting emphasis from adjudication to alternative functions of courts as feasible only *'in the shadow of full adjudicatory justice'*. Both, the correction of various dysfunctions of formal procedures as well as the possibility for the parties involved to return to them, form the essentials of what we call 'alternatives'.

Our comparative reports might astonish the reader in two ways: while there are very divergent traditions of what 'full procedure' and 'adjudicatory model' of handling conflicts by courts means from one country to the next, there is an international tendency to look for a cure in the same direction of 'informal alternatives'. It might appear as if there were one medicine for divergent ailments. However, most of the 'alternative' recipes point at indigenous ways of conflict resolution, thus being even more culturally specific than formal procedural traditions. In a growing convergence of legal procedures throughout the world, and relative to the growing use of court procedures (at whatever high or low level of judicial involvement in different countries), the search for 'alternatives' to formal adjudication can only be a mitigating countertrend with respect to the dominant trend of increasing formalization and growing use of formal procedures in many walks of life and in all of the countries we know.

DISCUSSION POINTS

1. There is a basic policy question about the alternatives: is it a necessary vice to save the judiciary from overload or should 'alternatives' be promoted regardless of the functioning of formal procedures? It is recommended from our position *not* to overemphasize mutual exclusiveness.

2. 'Alternatives' to formal procedures are relative to the *qualms* about the judicial process. It is to be recommended that these points of critique be handled by improving the formal procedures *as well as* by providing alternatives *forums* to avoid them.

3. Informal forums of conflict resolution are 'normal' in many areas of law. The recourse to courts in many cases is chosen only after other attempts of solving a conflict have been *exhausted*. It is to be recommended to leave the clients seeking justice a *choice* of either forum.

4. Informal forums can work more effectively, if working 'in the shadow of the formal procedure', and formal procedures increase their impact if *avoidance* remains a possibility. Therefore, it is to be recommended that formal procedure leave *exits* to informal handling, while informal procedure should leave possibility of recourse to formal procedure.

5. It is often mentioned that Asian cultures are characterized by a strong preference for informal conflict handling. It is to be questioned how relevant the 'cultural' element is to our problem. It is recommended not to talk categorically in terms of 'East and West' or 'North and South', but to seek some common paradigms for comparison.

REPORT OF THE DISCUSSION

Chairman: *S. Goldstein (Israel)*
Vice-chairman: *J. Saleh (Netherlands Antilles)*
Secretary: *E.H. Hondius (Netherlands)*

The discussionpoints are to be found at page 360.

Mr Goldstein (President) opens the session and explains the procedure. He first gives the floor to the General Reporters, Professors Erhard Blankenburg (Amsterdam) and Yasuhei Taniguchi (Kyoto).

Mr Blankenburg (General Reporter) has put himself in the position of a customer of the justice system. From this point of view formal procedure is the real alternative. Informal handling of grievances is the normal thing. In this regard there are basic similarities between such diverse countries as the Netherlands and Japan, whereas Germany and the Netherlands are very different (see E. Blankenburg, J.R.A. Verwoerd, The Courts as a Final Resort?: Some Comparisons between the Legal Cultures of the Netherlands and the Federal Republic of Germany, 35 *Netherlands International Law Review* 7-28 (1988)).

What explains these similarities and dissimilarities? According to mr Blankenburg this is not the culture or the mentality of the people - the General Reporter is later to be challenged on this point by mr Taniguchi and Ms Quisumbing but rather the institutions.

Mr Taniguchi (General Reporter) submits that there exists an assumption that Asia has quite a different legal culture with regard to the settlement of conflicts from that in Europe. Mr Blankenburg has tried to refute this and instead maintained the differences are a question of different institutions that Mr Taniguchi is not in complete accordance with this view. He believes cultural differences do play a role.

The General Reporter has observed a legalization taking place in the West. This has certainly been good for business in bringing certainty. But human relations are not limited to business. In Asia, adjudication is not considered appropriate for each situation. A compromise is sometimes considered more important. Mediation and conciliation lead to better social results. Even business relationships are sometimes too delicate for adjudication.

Mr Goldstein (President) raises the point - later to be discussed in more detail by mr Bonafé-Schmidt and mr Bundy - that in Israel the vast majority of cased filed are settled before a judge is involved. So perhaps we should measure which parties seek outside help.

Mr Bonafé-Schmidt (France) also stresses that many cases are settled out of court, but he points to the changing way of such conciliation. Fifty years ago many conflicts were settled within the family. Urbanization and mobility have weakened the role of the family as a provider of conciliation. Instead the state has intervened. Mr Bonafé-Schmidt gives three examples: the 'conciliateurs', the Post Box for consumer grievances and the departmental commissions. There is a strong movement for more mediation. The ordinary courts are more often used for debt collection.

Mr Briers (Belgium) explains that as a 'huissier de justice' (bailiff) his main aim is to make people respect the law.

Mr Goldstein (President) challenges the idyllic view of mediation and conciliation. The parties sometimes both lose the satisfaction of having their day in court. Small claims procedures violate some of the basic procedural rights, such as the right to counsel and the right to appeal.

Ms Pellegrini-Grinover (Brasil) distinguishes between deformalization of procedure and deformalization of conflicts. Deformalized procedure should not be used for all types of cases. Deformalization of conflicts, the upsurge of conciliation, should not only be seen from the point of efficiency, of helping courts to handle their overload. Conciliation also helps to solve cases which otherwise would remain unheard. Many neighbour and consumer complaints would remain undealt with, were it not for informal conciliation schemes.

Ms Borucka (Poland) relates Poland's 20-year experience with conciliation, which is mainly negative. The only positive results have been booked in the villages, where people are close. In 1985 labour law conciliation, which until then had been compulsory, became voluntary. Now only 5% of the complaints are submitted to conciliation, the others prefer the courts.

However, Ms Borucka observes a major problem. Once a court is efficient, it will be trusted. This in turn will lead to more cases, which will make the judicial system less efficient.

Ms Wang (China) strongly supports mediation. In China, mediation is offered by retired teachers etc., who know the people and find it easier to arrive at the heart of the conflict. Many Chinese think it a shameful thing to go to court anyway.

Mr Wilson (England) raises several points. He distinguishes between alternatives that are necessary because of ineffectiveness of the traditional legal system and alternatives which challenge the legal system. An example of such challenge is the establishment of a local legal order instead of a national one. Such challenge goes well beyond the domain of civil procedure: it raises questions of constitutional law. The speaker mentions two developments which so far have not been brought up in the discussion. First, there is not only a trend towards more informal alternatives, but also a countertrend towards more formality in civil procedure. Second, what begins as an informal alternative, usually ends up becoming more formal. A conference such as this is a part of that very process.

Ms Quisumbing (Philippines) thinks it is an oversimplification to speak of Asia as one group. The Philippines, as opposed to some other Asian countries, is a highly litigious society with many lawyers. But like Mr Taniguchi, the speaker thinks culture does play a rule. With regard to the ideas exposed by Mr Blankenburg, she ventures that institutions are a part of a country's culture.

Ms Quisumbing observes that a society is not always homogenious. The Philippines, for instance, incorporate various legal systems, among which are adat and the sharia. The speaker gives information as to the village courts, which are between a formal and an informal system of conflict settlement. They form a part of the formal process, but they operate in an informal manner.

Mr Bundy (United States) raises two points. First, he stresses - as did mr Goldstein - that a lot of what comes to the court is not litigation. There is no serious dispute, rather bringing a case to court serves as a last - often succesfull - step in the negotiation process. Second, mr Bundy observes a conflict between the two stated goals of alternatives, i.e. encouraging access to the courts and reducing the court's overload. As was already stated by Ms Borucka, many alternatives have self-cancelling effects.

Ms Demeulenaere (Belgium) disagrees with the basic assumptions of the General Report, especially with the idea that adjudication is not appropriate for complex relationships. If there is equal bargaining power, conciliation and mediation may perhaps work. In the absence of equal bargaining power, conflict settlement should be left to the courts. Mediation has always been a very poor method for consumer disputes.

Mr Blankenburg (General Reporter) replies that formal procedures do not always help the weaker party; rather the opposite is true. Consumer tribunals actually help the consumer more than do the courts.

Ms Demeulenaere (Belgium) answers that the criticism of formal procedure is not always justified. In Belgium the recent pilot-projects in Deinze and Marchienne-au-Pont show that the courts may work well (see Marcel Storme and Bernadette Demeulenaere, Innovations in the Judicial and Extra-Judicial Resolution of Consumer Disputes in Belgium, 36 *American Journal of Comparative Law* 217-234 (1988)).

Mr Kojima (Japan), like before him ms Borucka, warns against the misreading of statistics. He points to the fact that the Japanese like to be seen as mythic and unique, yet when they go to the United States they change and become more litigious.

Mr Chen (Taiwan) points out that fifty years ago, the Chinese did not know what a court was not what was law.

Mr Öszunay (Turkey) says that in Turkey the alternatives are considered necessary to help fight the overload of the courts. Contrary to the Polish experience as related by ms Borucka, Turkish experience with conciliation in labour cases is that it works very well. This, however, is not the case in family law. Conciliation before divorce simply did not work and was therefore abolished. The speaker refers to a draft act on consumer protection, which provides for the establishment of conciliation boards.

Mr Williams (Australia) raises the point of quality. There is no dissatisfaction with the quality of court decisions, but rather with the delays. In theory, alternatives offer a choice. In reality there is no alternative but to resort to the alternative. The quality of the alternative usually is inferior to that of the court. The alternative usually does not operate in public, so there is no public scruting. There is no publicity, so any deterrent value is absent. Legal representation is absent. All this should be bourne in mind when alternatives are advocated.

Mr Schlosser (Federal Republic of Germany) observes that nowhere in the world does pre-trial conciliation work. He points to conciliation procedures after the trial, such as those in California - on which mr Bundy gives some additional information - and in France.

Mr Vilhjalmson (Iceland) points to the danger that special interests try to take the problems out of the courts.

Mr Saleh (Netherlands Antilles) looks at the alternatives within the court system. He points to the necessity of good management.

Mr Blankenburg (General Reporter) was stuck in a traffic jam travelling to Utrecht this morning. He compares the overload of the courts with such traffic jams. He recommends to provide as many alternatives as possible to arrive at justice. There is a problem involved, however: the more freeways we construct, the more traffic we get. Justice is a supply side service. The demand is expandible.

Mr Taniguchi (General Reporter) observes that mediation sometimes serves justice in a better way than does litigation. The danger, however, is that the State tends to exert pressure to take away legal guarantees.

Mr Goldstein (President) thanks the participants and closes the Working Group's session.

In the Plenary session, on Thursday 27 August 1987, mr Goldstein sums up the main points discussed in the Working Group. Mr De Miguel (Spain) declares that labour conciliation works very efficiently in Spain.

Ms Pellegrini (Brasil) again distinguishes between the two principal objectives of the alternatives: providing a better access to justice, and having more efficiency. For the latter objective, the type of the cases is important. Ms Quisumbing (Philippines) observes that what is informal in the West may well be formal in the East. Mr Stalev (Bulgaria) points to the tendency towards formalization in arbitration. Mr Kujima (Japan) states that small claims procedure in Japan is not an alternative. He also distinguishes between arbitration and mediation. Mr Blankenburg (General Reporter) finally observes that formal procedure may be regarded as a conciliation attempt which failed.

THE (AB)USE OF SUMMARY PROCEEDINGS

USAGE ET ABUS DES PROCÉDURES SOMMAIRES

P. Meijknecht
professeur extraordinaire à l'Université d'Utrecht
et
R.Ch. Verschuur
chargé de cours à l'Université d'Utrecht

LISTE DES ABREVIATIONS

acpc	ancien code de procédure civile français
AO 1977	Abgabeordnung 1977, RFA
CJ	Code Judiciaire/Gerechtelijk Wetboek, Belgique
cpc	code de procédure civile, suivant divers pays
EO	Exekutionsordnung, Autriche
FGO	Finanzgerichtsordnung, RFA
kpc	kodeks procedury cywilnej, Pologne
LEC	Ley de enjuiciamiento civil, Espagne
mp	mesure provisoire
ncpc	nouveau code de procédure civile français
NRv	Nieuw Wetboek van Burgerlijke Rechtsvordering. Code de procédure civile néerlandais, après introduction des livres 3, 5 et 6 du nouveau code civil
RFA	République fédérale d'Allemagne
Rv.	Wetboek van Burgerlijke Rechtsvordering, code de procédure civile néerlandais
UWG	Gesetz gegen den unlauteren Wettsbewerb, RFA

VwGO Verwaltungsgerichtsordnung, RFA
Wet AROB Wet administratieve rechtspraak overheidsbeschikkingen, Pays-Bas
ZPO Zivilprozessordnung, RFA

1 INTRODUCTION

Les données utilisées pour l'élaboration du présent rapport sont en grande partie reprises des réponses au questionnaire envoyé en 1986. D'une manière générale, le questionnaire a donné lieu à d'excellents rapports nationaux fort détaillés, que nous citons ci-après par ordre alphabétique:

Allemagne, Rép. fédérale	d'Dieter Leipold
Belgique	Dirk Lindemans
Chili	Miguel Otero Lathrop
Espagne	Francisco Ramos Mendez
Etats-Unis	Geoffrey C. Hazard
Finlande	Irma Lager
Grèce	K.D. Kerameus et K.P. Polyzogopoulos
Israël	Stephen Goldstein
Italie	Giuseppe Tarzia, Vincento Varano et Andrea Proto Pisani
Pays-Bas	Jeanine ten Berg-Koolen
Pologne	Tadeusz Erecinski
Portugal	Carlos Ferreira da Silva
Suisse	Isaak Meier
Uruguay	Jaime Greif

Nous avons en outre puisé dans les excellents rapports publiés sous le titre 'Les mesures provisoires en procédure civile', Milan 1985, à l'occasion du colloque international organisé les 12 et 13 octobre 1984, sous la présidence de Guiseppe Tarzia. Nous avons avant tout utilisé les rapports présentés à l'époque par les pays suivants:

Autriche (Frans Matscher)
Brésil (Ada Pelligrini Grinover)
France (Roger Perrot).

Les autres rapports publiés dans cet ouvrage ainsi que les considérations finales de Guiseppe Tarzia nous ont également fourni de nombreuses informations utiles.

Par ailleurs, nous avons reçu du Canada un aperçu des mesures provisoires dans le cadre des procédures de divorce dans la province du Québec.

Certains pays nous ont communiqué que leur droit national offrait une base insuffisante pour l'établissement d'un rapport en la matière.

C'est ainsi que Zh. Stalev nous a fait savoir qu'en Bulgarie les procédures sommaires sont pratiquement inconnues, exception faite des mesures provisoires dans le cadre d'une procédure de divorce. Selon Stalev, la raison en est que dans la pratique les procédures se déroulent assez rapidement, ne sont pas très coûteuses et moins formelles, de sorte que la nécessité des procédures sommaires se fait moins sentir.

József Farkas a communiqué que les procédures sommaires visées dans le cadre de cette étude n'existaient pas en Hongrie.

Antonio Gomes Monteiro a communiqué que ce genre de procédure n'est pas très développé au Cap-Vert. En ce qui concerne l'Inde, le rapport établi par M.A. Qureshi sur les Cours Publiques (Lok Adalats) n'a pas permis de conclure à l'existence d'une telle procédure dans ce pays.

Selon nos informations, les *districts courts* en Indonésie ne connaissent pas non plus de procédure sommaire; la Cour suprême de ce pays a explicitement établi ce fait en 1976[1].

Nous avons utilisé occasionnellement d'autres publications auxquelles nous renvoyons chaque fois expressément dans le présent rapport général. Nous avons pu constater que la Suède connaît une forme de mesure provisoire[2] mais nous n'avons toutefois pas pu obtenir d'autres informations complémentaires à ce sujet.

La notion de procédure sommaire pouvant être interprétée de façon très diverse, nous avons dû, afin de permettre une comparaison utile, apporter dans le questionnaire envoyé aux rapporteurs nationaux certaines restrictions en rapport avec notre étude qui a pour objectif de recueillir des données sur les procédures sommaires dans les divers pays afin de pouvoir en examiner l'utilité dans le cadre des efforts en vue d'accroître l'efficacité de la Justice. Cet objectif orienté sur la pratique ne pouvait que déboucher sur une délimitation de la matière. L'accent de l'étude doit en définitive porter sur les domaines où l'application des procédures sommaires soulève, pour des motifs divers, certains problèmes ou sur ceux dans lesquels l'absence de la possibilité d'utiliser pleinement ce genre de mesures est ressentie comme une (pénible) lacune.

Dans cette optique, notre intérêt s'est surtout concentré sur la mesure provisoire, connue dans plusieurs pays sous l'appelation 'procédures sommaires'. Ces deux notions se recouvrent d'ailleurs en grande partie. La mesure provisoire fait suite à une procédure ayant un caractère plus ou moins sommaire et une durée relativement courte. La caractéristique de la mesure provisoire est toutefois qu'elle a un certain rapport avec la procédure au fond qui peut, et dans beaucoup de cas, qui doit suivre. La mesure provisoire peut généralement être exécutée immédiatement et n'est valable que jusqu'à ce que le jugement sur le fond est passé en force de chose jugée.

Il existe nombre de procédures sommaires qui débouchent sur une décision judiciaire ne pouvant pas être considérée comme mesure provisoire en ce sens; c'est notamment le cas des procédures sommaires connues aux Etats-Unis en tant que *summary proceedings*. Nous citerons comme autre exemple la possibilité fort connue d'obtenir de façon simple un titre exécutoire pour une créance dans les cas où le débiteur ne comparaît pas ou ne se défend pas (tel que le 'Mahnverfahren' connu en Allemagne fédérale ou la 'provisorische Rechtsöffnung' connue en Suisse). Il convient également de citer dans ce contexte la

---

1 Mme Marianna Sutadi S.H., L.J. Ferdinandus S.H., H. Achmed Intam S.H., Civil Court System in Indonesia, 1985, p. 13, Indonesisch Procesrecht, Université de Leyde, Faculté de droit.

2 C.C.A. Voskuil, on 'Giving a hand' in Swedisch law of civil procedure, dans Essays on International & Comparative Law in honour of Judge Erades, Martinus Nijhoff Publishers, p. 230.

procédure qui aux Pays-Bas est désignée par le terme 'bref délai': il s'agit de procédures auxquelles s'appliquent des délais plus courts et dans le cadre desquelles les actes de procédure sont limités, même en cas de défense à la demande, mais qui débouchent néanmoins sur un jugement sans caractère provisoire. Ce type de procédure justifie certainement une étude comparative mais nous estimons que les risques de confusion sont toutefois trop grands lorsque toutes ces procédures 'sommaires' sont réunies côte à côte dans une même étude. Cela entraverait toute comparaison et toute discussion sensée et ne permettrait guère de tirer des conclusions utiles. Il y a lieu de se reporter également dans ce contexte au sujet 4: Alternatives informelles pour la procédure ordinaire. Signalons également que, comme le droit de procédure administratif fait spécifiquement l'objet du sujet no. 3, nous n'en traiterons qu'occasionnellement et de façon non systématique. Notre étude mettra également en évidence qu'en ce qui concerne les mesures provisoires, il n'y a pas de frontières bien délimitées et qu'il existe en la matière diverses formes transitoires. Notre décision d'orienter cette étude principalement sur les mesures provisoires s'explique par les problèmes actuels et pratiques qui se posent à grande échelle dans ce domaine et par le fait qu'une étude comparative peut contribuer à cerner l'inventaire de ces problèmes et à les inventorier.

C'est à juste titre que Perrot souligne dans son excellent rapport que 'l'apparante simplicité de la mesure provisoire dissimule en réalité de très sérieux problèmes' et que 'la croissance de cette fillette indisciplinée ne va pas sans difficulté'[3].

Il est évident que les problèmes pratiques sur lesquels nous souhaitons nous concentrer ne se présentent pas de la même façon pour les différents types de mesures provisoires. Dans ce domaine également il y a lieu de faire une différenciation. Nous nous félicitons donc de la masse d'informations utiles que nous avons pu tirer des rapports nationaux. Les distinctions que nous voulons faire sur la base de ces informations ont pour seul objectif de permettre d'approfondir le phénomène de la mesure provisoire sans tomber dans une stérile énumération. La quantité d'informations reçues était tellement grande qu'il a d'abord fallu les structurer clairement afin de déterminer les éléments principaux et les points sur lesquels il convenait de mettre l'accent dans le cadre de cette étude axée sur la justice et l'efficacité. Ceci présuppose une classification des mesures provisoires qui dépasse les frontières nationales, voire les frontières d'un groupe de pays connaissant un système plus ou moins identique, de sorte que la classification ait une portée universelle et non pas une portée uniquement régionale ou déterminée par des aléas historiques.

Les rapports nationaux bien documentés ont mis en évidence que dans le cadre de cette étude il est à la fois utile et sensé de distinguer les trois catégories suivantes de mesures provisoires:

1. les mesures provisoires qui tendent à garantir l'exécution du jugement sur le fond;
2. les mesures provisoires à caractère exclusivement régulateur;
3. les mesures provisoires qui anticipent sur le jugement sur le fond.

---

3 Perrot, Les mesures provisoires en droit français, dans Les mesures provisoires en procédure civile, Atti del colloquio internazionale, Milano 12-13 octobre 1984, a cura di Giuseppe Tarzia, Milano, Dott. A. Giuffrè Editore, 1985, p. 150.

Pour cette classification, nous avons pu suivre dans une large mesure celle préconisée par Perrot dans son rapport[4] et celle qui, selon Matscher, est faite dans la doctrine allemande et autrichienne[5]. Le rapport suisse fait également état de cette subdivision en trois types[6].

Perrot distingue:
1. les mesures provisoires du type classique que sont les mesures d'attente;
2. les mesures provisoires qui anticipent sur le jugement;
3. celles qui anticipent sur l'exécution.

Les types que distingue Matscher sont:
1. les mesures de garantie (Sicherungsverfügungen);
2. les mesures d'ordre ou de réglementation (Ordnungs- oder Regelungsverfügungen);
3. les mesures de prestations (Leistungsverfügungen).

La différence dans le domaine de la terminologie semble plus grande qu'elle ne l'est en réalité. Il existe en fait une base commune suffisante qui justifie à notre avis la classification que nous allons suivre dans la partie descriptive de ce rapport (chapitre 2). Le fait que l'on retrouve cette différenciation dans la doctrine de divers pays appartenant à différentes familles juridiques justifie davantage encore notre choix. Nous avons ainsi trouvé pour notre étude une ligne directrice qui est utilisable pour pratiquement tous les rapports nationaux.

Nous tenons à signaler d'emblée qu'à notre avis le groupe des mesures provisoires qui anticipent sur le jugement sur le fond est le type le plus intéressant dans le cadre de notre étude. Une description des deux premières catégories de mesures provisoires est néanmoins indispensable puisque l'intérêt de chaque catégorie spécifique, et en particulier celui de la troisième catégorie de mesures, ne peut être mis en évidence que si on dispose d'une vue d'ensemble. Par ailleurs, les délimitations ne sont pas toujours aussi nettes que ne le souhaiteraient les experts. Les relations qui, tant du point de vue de l'évolution historique que de la teneur même, existent entre les divers types de mesures provisoires sont souvent fort marquées. C'est à plusieurs reprises que par la suite nous soulignerons ce fait.

2 LES DIVERS TYPES DE MESURES PROVISOIRES

2.1 LES MESURES PROVISOIRES QUI TENDENT A GARANTIR L'EXECUTION DU JUGEMENT SUR LE FOND

La plupart des systèmes juridiques connaissent la saisie conservatoire dont l'objectif est de permettre au créancier d'empêcher que son débiteur ne laisse

4 Perrot, idem.

5 Matscher, Les mesures provisoires en droit de procédure civile autrichien, dans Les mesures provisoires en procédure civile (cf. note 3), p. 112.

6 Meier, rapport, chapitre III.1.

dépérir ou ne fasse disparaître des éléments du patrimoine sur lesquels il souhaite recouvrer sa créance.

Bien que les formes de saisie conservatoire ne retiennent pas en premier lieu notre intérêt, il est, pour des considérations de systématique et de compréhension, néanmoins nécessaire de les aborder brièvement. Cela vaut en particulier pour le groupe de pays qui connaissent en la matière des règles juridiques apparantées à la ZPO allemande parce que l'on fait dans ces pays tant dans la législation que dans la doctrine, un lien étroit entre les mesures provisoires en général et la garantie de l'exécution du jugement sur le fond. C'est pour cette raison que dans ce groupe de pays les mesures provisoires qui visent à garantir cet objectif ont une signification particulière. Elles doivent être considérées comme la forme 'primaire' des mesures provisoires. C'est donc par ce groupe de pays que commencera notre analyse.

La garantie de l'exécution du jugement sur le fond est à son tour intimement liée avec l'exécution forcée du jugement sur le fond. Dans le groupe de pays visé, la notion générale de mesures provisoires est par conséquent liée au droit d'exécution. En ce qui concerne la République fédérale d'Allemagne, cela ressort du paragraphe 5 (Arrest und einstweilige Verfügung) portant sur les paragraphes 916-945 du livre 8 (Zwangsvollstreckung) ZPO. Seul le 'Arrest' est réglé en détail: la 'einstweilige Verfügung' découle, quant à sa systématique et sa définition, du 'Arrest'[7].

Nous constatons chose analogue en Pologne et en Autriche. En Pologne, les dispositions pertinentes se retrouvent dans le premier livre (mesures conservatoires) renfermant les articles 730-757 de la seconde partie (mesures conservatoires et exécution) du Code de procédure civile polonais[8]. En Autriche, il s'agit avant tout des articles 379-388 EO, qui figurent dans la partie II, intitulée 'Sicherung' (Garantie). A l'origine, la mesure provisoire avait dans ces pays essentiellement pour rôle d'assurer la conservation des biens litigieux en attendant le jugement définitif. L'objectif est avant tout le maintien du statu quo. Pour ces pays il importe de ne pas perdre de vue ce point de départ.

Les moyens par lesquels cette conservation peut être assurée dans ces pays de même que dans les autres pays auxquels s'étend notre analyse, sont en premier lieu les formes de saisie conservatoire en cas de créance d'argent ou de créance pouvant être évaluée en argent, formes ayant des appellations et des portées diverses mais dont le seul objectif est de garantir le paiement dès que le créancier a obtenu un titre exécutoire. Pour une saisie conservatoire, le créancier n'a pas besoin d'un titre exécutoire; d'une manière générale, il lui suffit de démontrer la vraisemblance de l'existence de sa créance sur le débiteur (RFA, article 920 ZPO; Pologne, article 730 kpc; Autriche, article 378 EO, France, articles 48, 53 et 54 ncpc; Belgique; Pays-Bas, notamment article 727 Rv. et article 700 par. 2 NRv; Italie, article 671 cpc). Cette 'démonstration' de l'existence de la créance se fait sans l'application des règles générales en matière de preuve, par exemple par la présentation de déclaration écrite de

7 Leipold, rapport, chapitre A2.

8 Erecinski, rapport chapitre I, attire en outre l'attention sur les conceptions prédominantes dans la littérature polonaise selon lesquelles les procédures conservatoires sont plus liées au procès ordinaire qu'à l'exécution.

témoins[9]. Dans la plupart des pays on pose en outre comme condition qu'il y ait des raisons sérieuses de craindre la disparition d'éléments du patrimoine à saisir (en France: urgence, péril dans le recouvrement[10]). Le droit de procédure israélien qui correspond d'ailleurs en grande partie au droit de procédure anglais connaît la saisie conservatoire comme mesure provisoire en plus de la 'preliminary injunction'; en Israël, la saisie conservatoire trouve son origine dans le code de procédure ottoman de 1879 qui suit le système français de droit de procédure et qui était applicable en Palestine sous la dénomination turque[11]. En Autriche, en Pologne et en RFA cela est formulé de façon plus générale: la mesure provisoire n'est prise que si autrement les droit du créancier risqueraient d'être perdus ou s'il y serait sensiblement porté atteinte (Autriche, article 379 EO et suiv.; Pologne, article 730 kpc; RFA, article 917 ZPO). D'une manière générale, il faut l'autorisation du juge pour procéder à une saisie conservatoire; quelquefois il est également possible de procéder à une saisie conservatoire sans l'intervention du juge (aux Pays-Bas, saisie-gagerie, saisie entre les mains d'un tiers lorsqu'il y a des documents concernant la créance. L'article 700 par. 2 NRv exige toujours l'autorisation du président du tribunal). Dans la phase d'octroi de l'autorisation d'une saisie conservatoire, le principe du contradictoire n'a pas besoin d'être appliqué[12]. Toutes les législations prévoient la possibilité pour le juge compétent de donner son autorisation *inaudita altera parte* à condition qu'il y ait risque de soustraction des biens par le débiteur[13]. D'une manière générale on considère que le principe du contradictoire est garanti par la possibilité de recours contre les décisions unilatérales du juge[14]. Dans le cas d'une saisie conservatoire, le juge n'examinera que très sommairement les preuves de l'existence de la créance dont le recouvrement est demandé, et ce de façon encore plus sommaire que ce n'est le cas pour les autres mesures provisoires.

Une saisie conservatoire doit pratiquement toujours avoir lieu pendant une procédure au fond ou être suivie d'une telle procédure au cours de laquelle le créancier devra obtenir du juge civil un titre exécutoire afin que la saisie conservatoire devienne saisie-exécution.

En plus de la saisie conservatoire, les législations de la plupart des pays connaissent le séquestre, à savoir le transfert de la détention d'une chose meuble, immeuble, ensemble d'objets ou entreprise à un séquestre par garde.

Le droit en Autriche, en Pologne et en RFA prévoit, outre la saisie, une possibilité générale de garantie d'une demande, indépendamment de sa nature, qui ne vise pas au paiement d'une somme en argent (Autriche, article 381 EO;

---

9 Voir en ce qui concerne la Pologne, Erecinski; rapport paragraphe 13, et pour la RFA, Leipold, rapport C 10.

10 Perrot, pp. 175-176.

11 Goldstein, rapport, pp. 53-54.

12 Le juge peut dans certains cas convoquer les parties lorsque cela n'a pas pour effet de frustrer la mesure conservatoire demandée; cf. par exemple l'article 152 kpc traité par Erecinski dans son rapport, chapitre I.3.

13 Perrot, page 176; Kerameus et Polyzogopoulos, Les mesures provisoires en procédure civile hellénique, dans Les mesures provisoires en procédure civile (cf. note 3), p. 70.

14 Perrot, p. 176; Ramos Mendez, Les mesures provisoires indéterminées dans le procès civil espagnol, dans Les mesures provisoires en procédure civile (cf. note 3), p. 205.

Pologne, article 755 kpc; RFA, par. 935 ZPO). La mesure qui peut être demandée à cette fin ne fait l'objet d'aucune limitation légale[15]. La parenté avec la saisie apparaît, pour ce qui est de l'objectif (à savoir garantir ultérieurement l'exécution forcée d'un titre exécutoire), clairement du fait que dans ce cas il doit être question, dans une mesure pratiquement identique, du risque de disparition des possibilités de recouvrement et que le bien-fondé d'une action au fond ne doit pas être sérieusement contestable. La parenté avec la saisie ressort également du fait que la 'einstweilige Verfügung' peut également être accordée sans examen oral (artcle 937 ZPO).

Il importe enfin de s'arrêter au droit de procédure administratif et aux procédures engagées contre les pouvoirs publics. Dans la mesure où, en attendant une décision définitive sur la légitimité, il est possible de suspendre une décision administrative, il est question d'une mesure provisoire qui tombe entièrement dans la catégorie que nous examinons actuellement (sauvegarde de droits). En fait, la suspension de l'effet d'une décision administrative en attendant une décision du juge saisi du fond, maintient le *statu quo* et empêche que la décision du juge ne puisse plus avoir d'effet du fait qu'elle intervient trop tard.

Le rapport national allemand cite dans ce contexte l'effet suspensif de l'opposition contre des décisions administratives (par. 80 VwGO); dans certains cas, la suspension provisoire exige une décision spécifique (par. 361 AO 1977 et par. 69, alinéa 2 et suiv. FGO)[16].

Malheureusement, le rapport de Perrot ne contient pas de données en la matière en ce qui concerne la France où le droit administratif a peut-être plus évolué que dans tout autre pays. Matscher signale l'existence de mesures provisoires dans le droit administratif autrichien, mais les informations contenues dans le rapport sont insuffisamment spécifiées[17]. Le rapport national suisse se limite également au droit civil. En Belgique où le droit administratif connaît une réglementation fort détaillée en ce qui concerne les procédures au fond contre les pouvoirs publics, il n'est pas possible de prendre une mesure provisoire, à l'exception d'une demande de sursis à l'exécution d'un arrêt de renvoi ou d'expulsion d'un étranger[18]. Une action en référé contre les pouvoirs publics est toutefois possible; le juge ne peut toutefois évaluer que de façon marginale l'action des pouvoirs publics, l'hypothèse de la voie de fait, par laquelle il faut entendre: 'une opération matérielle dans l'accomplissement de laquelle l'administration commet une irrégularité grossière portant atteinte au droit de propriété ou à la liberté du public'[19].

Pour une partie importante des décisions des pouvoirs publics, le droit administratif néerlandais prévoit depuis 1976 la possibilité de demander au Président de la Section Juridiction du Conseil d'Etat de suspendre l'effet de la

---

15 En ce qui concerne l'Autriche, cela ressort de la remarque faite par Matscher à la page 92 (cf. note 5): 'Ici le code ne donne que quelques exemples de mesures admises.' Se reporter également pour les Etats-Unis à la Rule 65 du Federal Rules of Civil Procedures, traitée par Hazard, rapport, A.b.

16 Rapport Leipold, chapitre A.3. Leipold relève que ces mesures provisoires ont exclusivement pour caractère de garantir le jugement au fond et n'anticipent pas sur ce jugement.

17 Pour l'Autriche, voir avant tout Matscher, p. 91.

18 Lindemans, rapport C.1.

19 Lindemans, rapport C.15.

décision incriminée ou de prendre une mesure provisoire sur la base de la loi relative aux recours administratifs (AROB).

Par ailleurs, le législateur néerlandais a prévu la possibilité de s'adresser au Président de la Section Contentieux du Conseil d'Etat pour les recours administratifs et au tribunal de la fonction publique pour les litiges concernant des agents de la fonction publique[20]. Dans les cas où la loi ne prévoit pas la possibilité de demander une mesure provisoire administrative, le président du tribunal de grande instance qui aux Pays-Bas est toujours le juge des référés est compétent en la matière; d'une manière générale il ne procédera qu'à une appréciation marginale des actes des pouvoirs publics; cette appréciation marginale qui s'est développée dans la jurisprudence ne s'applique pas spécifiquement aux actions en référé contre les pouvoirs publics mais d'une manière générale lorsque le juge civil est appelé à se prononcer sur les actes des pouvoirs publics.

Il existe en Italie un double système: le juge civil est compétent dans les affaires contre les pouvoirs publics lorsqu'il est question d'une violation d'un 'droit' alors que le juge administratif est compétent en tant que violation d'un 'intérêt légitime'. Au cours des dernières décennies, la juridiction a évolué en ce sens que le juge ordinaire peut ordonner une mesure provisoire contre les pouvoirs publics mais doit s'abstenir de prendre des décisions portant suspension, annulation ou modification d'une décision des pouvoirs publics ou d'ordonner des mesures en ce sens. Les tribunaux administratifs qui ont compétence pour juger de la violation d'intérêts légitimes peuvent suspendre une décision administrative lorsque sa mise en application risque d'entraîner un préjudice grave et irréparable. La jurisprudence récente de la Cour Constitutionelle semble offrir la possibilité au juge ordinaire qui, au lieu du tribunal administratif, est compétent lorsqu'il est question d'une violation d'un droit, de prendre une mesure provisoire portant suspension de la décision incriminée lorsque la durée de la procédure ordinaire risque d'entraîner pour le plaignant un préjudice irréparable[21].

En Grèce il n'est pas possible de demander une mesure provisoire dans les domaines pour lesquels il existe des tribunaux administratifs. C'est notamment le cas en matière fiscale. Le juge civil n'est pas non plus compétent lorsque des mesures provisoires concernent l'exécution de jugements contre les pouvoirs publics parce qu'en Grèce l'exécution contre des organes des pouvoirs publics n'est pas autorisée[22].

En Pologne, l'article 749 kpc interdit les mesures conservatoires contre l'Etat; de telles mesures sont toutefois autorisées dans certaines limites contre des entreprises d'Etat[23].

Le droit administratif portugais prévoit la possibilité de demander par mesure provisoire la suspension de la décision administrative incriminée dans une cause principale. L'exécution de cette décision doit, d'une part, entraîner pour le plaignant un préjudice difficilement reparable, mais d'autre part, la suspension ne doit pas porter sérieusement préjudice à l'intérêt général. En dehors de ce

20 Ten Berg-Koolen, rapport no. 2.

21 Proto Pisani et Varano, no. 5.

22 Kerameus et Polyzogopoulos, p. 61.

23 Erecinski, rapport, chapitre I.2.

cas, les pouvoirs publics peuvent être attaqués de la façon normale à l'exception de l'opposition à nouvel oeuvre[24].

Au Brésil également, le juge civil peut ordonner diverses mesures provisoires contre les pouvoirs publics, et ce malgré le fait qu'au Brésil on admet qu'un acte administratif est en soi légitime. L'article 119 de la Constitution offre en outre la possibilité de demander au procureur général de la République près du Supremo Tribunal Federal une mesure provisoire lorsqu'une loi viole la Constitution[25].

2.2 MESURES PROVISOIRES A CARACTERE EXCLUSIVEMENT REGULATEUR

Perrot caractérise ces mesures comme suit:

> 'Les mesures provisoires qui, avant tout litige ou en cours d'instance, ont pour objet de sauvegarder ou d'organiser temporairement une situation conflictuelle sans impliquer le moindre jugement sur le fond'[26].

Il ne s'agit plus avant tout de maintenir un *statu quo* mais plutôt de créer temporairement une nouvelle situation qui, dans bien des cas, a un caractère définitif.

Tous les pays connaissent l'une ou l'autre possibilité de demander par mesure provisoire une pension alimentaire. E.M. Meijers écrit que le droit romain prévoyait déjà la possibilité d'ordonner par mesure provisoire le paiement par le père ou le grand-père, ou encore ses héritiers, une pension alimentaire à un enfant légitime. Dans les textes pertinents en la matière il était déjà fait expressément mention du fait que la mesure provisoire ne préjugeait pas la décision sur le fond du litige (*nihil ex hoc praeiudicium generare*). Meijers mentionne encore dans ce contexte que dans la pratique française l'octroi d'une pension alimentaire s'est fait pendant longtemps encore par l'application de cette forme de mesure provisoire[27]. A l'heure actuelle, la mesure provisoire la plus fréquente porte toujours sur une pension alimentaire, notamment au cours d'une procédure de divorce. Il existe souvent à cet effet une procédure particulière (France, Pays-Bas, Italie, Espagne, Portugal, Grèce, Israël, Brésil, Bulgarie, Québec, Autriche, Uruguay, RFA et Pologne); en Uruguay, il s'agit en l'occurrence d'une des rares possibilités prévues par le droit de procédure pour demander une mesure provisoire. En Belgique, il est possible de demander l'octroi d'une pension alimentaire par une mesure provisoire en référé, à peu près de le même manière que les autres mesures provisoires[28].

La possibilité de demander une pension alimentaire (ou d'autres mesures provisoires) dans le cadre d'une procédure de divorce dépend toujours de

---

24 Ferreira da Silva, IIc.

25 Pellegrini Grinover, La tutela cautelare aticipa nel processo civile brasiliano, dans Les mesures provisoires en procédure civile (cf. note 3), p. 142

26 Perrot, p. 154

27 E.M. Mijers, Het Kort Geding, 2e impression, adapté par J. Th. Vermeulen, Zwolle, Tjeenk Willink, 1967, pp. 3-4.

28 D. Lindemans, Kort Geding; Kluwer rechtswetenschappen, Anvers, p. 199 et suiv.: Le caractère d'urgence n'est dans ce cas pas une condition à la compétence du président du tribunal.

l'introduction d'une action principale demandant le divorce. La règle principale est que la requête est introduite pendant la procédure, mais dans un certain nombre de pays la mesure provisoire peut également être ordonnée en dehors d'une telle procédure. Elle cesse d'avoir effet si la procédure principale n'est pas intentée dans un délai légalement fixé.

D'une manière générale, l'urgence n'est pas posée comme condition à la recevabilité d'une requête en vue d'une mesure provisoire pour l'octroi d'une pension alimentaire ou d'autres mesures provisoires pendant une procédure de divorce. Il est d'usage qu'avant la décision du juge, le défendeur soit mis en mesure d'être entendu. En Belgique et en France, on peut toutefois demander au juge, en cas d'urgence particulière, d'ordonner une mesure provisoire *inaudita altera parte*. L'urgence est alors une condition formelle.

En ce qui concerne la preuve, les règles normales ne s'appliquent généralement pas. Le juge se contente le plus souvent d'une appréciation sommaire qui ne doit d'ailleurs pas être placée au même niveau que celle dans laquelle il procède en cas d'autorisation d'une saisie conservatoire.

Il n'est pas nécessaire qu'il y ait un risque en rapport avec la demande principale, c'est-à-dire qu'il n'est pas nécessaire de démontrer ou de rendre admissible que les droits risqueraient d'être lésés en l'absence d'une mesure provisoire. Sur ce point la requête est exclusivement examinée sur ses propres mérites.

Dans les systèmes juridiques examinés dans le cadre de cette étude nous n'avons pas non plus pu trouver en ce qui concerne la demande principale une condition aux termes de laquelle le bien-fondé de la demande principale doit être admissible ou probable. Il y a donc toujours un pouvoir discrétionnaire (pratiquement) illimité du juge.

Les mesures provisoires dans les procédures de divorce ne visent pas, ou ne visent que dans une moindre mesure, à garantir la demande dans la procédure au fond. Elles ont un caractère plus autonome que les mesures examinées dans le paragraphe 1. Une des caractéristiques particulières est que bien souvent le juge a la compétence d'ordonner d'office une mesure ou d'adjuger plus qu'il n'est demandé.

Nous signalons a toutes fins utiles l'existence de mesures provisoires qui font fortement penser aux mesures dans les procédures de divorce mais qui tombent néanmoins dans la catégorie des mesures qui sont traitées dans le chapitre 3: il s'agit de mesures qui concernent également et avant tout des pensions alimentaires et qui anticipent sur le jugement sur le fond et qui sont donc intimement liées au résultat de la procédure au fond. Nous faisons allusion par exemple à la possibilité de demander dans le cadre d'une action en reconnaissance de paternité une allocation provisoire ou le paiement des frais d'accouchement. La différence nette par rapport aux mesures provisoires dans une procédure de divorce est que dans les cas auxquels nous avons fait allusion les montants doivent être remboursés si la demande principale est rejetée ultérieurement sur ces cas.

La possibilité de mesures provisoires dans le cadre d'une procédure de divorce existe dans la plupart des pays parallèlement à celle, plus générale, de mesures provisoires. Certains pays connaissent en outre des réglementations spécifiques, notamment dans le domaine du droit du travail (Italie, Portugal, Uruguay). Seul l'Uruguay ne connaît pas de réglementation générale, mais uniquement des mesures spécifiques concernant les mineurs, les affaires familiales, les affaires du travail et les litiges en matière de loyer.

Dans la plupart des pays, la procédure générale est inspirée par le référé français. Les législations belge et néerlandaise sont directement basées sur le référé français et connaissent cette procédure depuis l'epoque napoléonienne. Mais les réglementations de date plus récente (Italie, 1942; Espagne, 1984) s'inspirent, elles aussi, largement du référé français. Au Portugal, les mesures provisoires sont réglées ensemble et en rapport avec les procédures conservatoires. Le Code français de procédure civile de 1806 règle dans les articles 806-812 les référés qui trouvent leur origine dans la possibilité de demander dans la France prérévolutionnaire au lieutenant civil près le Châtelet de Paris une ordonnance par provision; avec le code de procédure civile de 1806, cette procédure de mesures provisoires qui était réglementée par l'édit de janvier 1685 et limitée à la région de Paris, a été étendue à l'ensemble de la France et aux régions annexées.

Le Code de procédure français de 1806 distingue principalement deux manières selon lesquelles une mesure provisoire peut être demandée:
- au cours de la procédure principale;
- en dehors d'une telle procédure.

Dans le nouveau Code de procédure civile, les articles pertinents ont été adaptés mais en soi la réglementation n'a pas été profondément modifiée. Pendant la procédure principale dont est saisi un tribunal de grande instance, c'est le juge de la mise en état (article 771) qui est compétent, un juge d'instruction qui appartient à la chambre chargée de l'examen de l'affaire au fond (article 763 cpc)[29]. En dehors d'une procédure, une mesure provisoire doit être demandée au Président du tribunal de grande instance. Il n'existe pas de grande différence entre les deux procédures. En Belgique et aux Pays-Bas, une mesure provisoire doit en principe toujours être demandée au Président du tribunal de grande instance (Belgique, article 584 CJ; Pays-Bas, article 289 Rv.). Dans d'autres pays, les règlements de compétence correspondent souvent à ceux existant en France.

L'urgence (*periculum in mora*) est en règle générale, et en dehors des réglementations particulières dont nous venons de parler en cas de divorce, une conditon requise. Dans quelques cas seulement, l'urgence n'est pas posée comme condition (Pays-Bas, articles 53 et 100 Rv)[30]. Il est intéressant de relever que le degré d'urgence peut également déterminer le déroulement de la procédure: en France, en Belgique, en Grèce, en RFA et en Italie, le juge peut prendre sa décision *inaudita altera parte* en cas d'extrême urgence[31]. Le juge est toutefois tenu d'entendre l'autre partie de sa propre initiative (Italie) pour examiner si la mesure peut être maintenue ou la partie qui n'a pas été entendue peut faire opposition (Belgique, RFA, France). Rappelons toutefois dans ce contexte que le droit à une procédure contradictoire est un principe essentiel d'une bonne administration de la justice. En rapport avec ce principe il y a lieu de citer la 'Schutzschrift' avec laquelle il est possible en RFA de se protéger d'emblée

---

29 Perrot, pp. 162-163.

30 Voir projet de loi 19 976 (modification de la procédure civile des tribunaux cantonaux), article 118 Rv.

31 Perrot, p. 159; Lindemans, Kort Geding, pp. 116-117; Kerameus et Polyzogopoulos, p. 70; Proto Pisani et Varano, 4.2 et 4.1.2.1.

contre les risques que quelqu'un demande une mesure provisoire[32]. En cas d'extrême urgence il est possible en Suisse de ne pas entendre le défendeur dans le cadre de la mesure dite 'superprovisorische'[33]. En Grèce, le droit d'être entendu est, depuis la Constitution de 1975, considéré comme un droit fondamental (article 20, alinéa 1er) sur la base duquel la jurisprudence et la doctrine veulent limiter la possibilité d'obtenir unilatéralement une mesure provisoire à des cas très exceptionnels parmi lesquels est mentionnée explicitement la saisie conservatoire qui en fait relève de la catégorie I 'au cas où il serait fort probable que le débiteur, dès qu'il prendrait connaissance de la requête visant à une saisie conservatoire de ses biens, s'efforcerait de faire disparaître ces derniers[34].

Une autre condition posée en plus de l'urgence est celle du risque d'un danger irréparable. L'exigence du *periculum in mora* a toutefois une autre teneur que dans le paragraphe (1). Cela est normal puisqu'il s'agit à présent d'une autre sorte de danger qui n'a que dans une moindre mesure ou même pas du tout de rapport avec les possibilités d'exécution en ce qui concerne le litige au fond. La mesure provisoire doit apparaître nécessaire pour un préjudice substantiel, de prévenir le risque de violence ou de prévenir le risque d'une dommage irréparable. La possibilité d'une mesure provisoire n'est pas subordonnée dans tous les pays à une instance au fond. La France, la Belgique et le Pays-Bas ne connaissent pas cette condition, bien qu'aux Pays-Bas le référé se soit probablement développé de façon plus autonome à l'égard de l'introduction d'une action principale que ce n'est le cas en Belgique. Le rapporteur belge Lindemans mentionne dans ce contexte que 'L'introduction d'une action en référé ne doit, en droit, pas nécessairement être concomittante à l'introduction d'une action principale bien que cela s'avère en général nécessaire ou, à tout le moins, opportun'[35]. Dans d'autres pays où il est possible d'obtenir une mesure provisoire en dehors d'une instance, une action principale doit toujours être introduite dans un délai déterminé sous peine de nullité de la mesure provisoire[36].

Le créancier qui souhaite qu'une mesure provisoire soit prise doit rendre admissible sa créance, et démontrer le *fumus boni iuris*. D'une manière générale, les preuves n'ont pas besoin d'être aussi élaborées que ce n'est le cas dans une action principale. Il existe dans les divers pays un éventail de conceptions quant à l'étendue de la preuve et à l'applicabilité des règles normales de la charge de

32 Leipold, rapport, chapitre C.4. Selon Leipold, cette pratique ne repose pas sur une base légale.

33 Meier, I.7.

34 Kerameus et Polyzogopoulos, p. 70. Dans ce contexte, il y a lieu de relever que la Cour CE à Luxembourg qui a compétence pour se prononcer au sujet de la Convention CE du 27 septembre 1968 concernant la compétence judiciaire et l'exécution des décision judiciaires en matière civile et commerciale, modifiée par la Convention du 9 octobre 1978 relative à l'adhésion du Danemark, de l'Irlande et de la Grande-Bretagne, a stipulé que la procédure simplifiée d'exécution prévue par la Convention ne s'applique pas aux décisions judiciaires qui, comme l'autorisation de saisie, sont prises en l'absence du défendeur et exécutées sans signification préalable à ce dernier. Cour de Justice CE, 21.5.1980 publié notamment dans le revue Nederlandse Jurisprudentie 1981, 184.

35 Lindemans rapport C.6. citation de son livre Kort Geding (cf. note 28).

36 Italie: voir Proto Pisani et Varano, 4.2; Kerameus et Polyzogopoulos, pp. 79-80; Ramos Mendez, p. 201; Ferreira da Silva, III.2; Pellegrini Grinover, p. 131.

la preuve. Au Brésil, lorsqu'une mesure provisoire est demandée dans le cadre d'une action principale, la phase d'instruction de la mesure provisoire et de l'action principale sont combinées. Cela peut déboucher sur un jugement cumulatif et simultané dans les deux procédures. Ce qui explique que la mesure provisoire perd beaucoup sinon tout de l'effet recherché [37]. Le rapporteur portugais Ferreira signale que si la preuve reste limitée à des déclarations de témoins à des preuves écrites, il n'en demeure pas moins qu'il reste possible d'entendre au maximum huit témoins et que le juge a en outre la possibilité de recueillir des informations auprès d'autres juges[38]. Dans la plupart des pays, le juge se contente toutefois d'une preuve plus sommaire et n'est pas lié aux règles concernant la preuve valable formellement pour l'action principale.

En ce qui concerne les mesures provisoires à caractère exclusivement régulateur, il existe en Autriche, en Pologne, en RFA et également en Suisse une étroite parenté avec les mesures qui tendent à garantir l'exécution du jugement au fond (cf. paragraphe 1). Dans les codes de procédure civile de ces pays, les dispositions concernant ces mesures provisoires figurent toujours à la suite de celles qui tendent à garantir l'exécution du jugement au fond traitées sous le point (1) du chapitre 2. Il en résulte qu'ils ont en commun nombre de conditions et de caractéristiques et qu'il est parfois même impossible de tracer de façon très nette la frontière entre les mesures provisoires qui tendent à garantir l'exécution du jugement au fond et les mesures provisoires à caractère exclusivement régulateur. Et ce, malgré l'existence de différences bien évidentes.

Il y a lieu de signaler d'emblée que le droit de procédure civile de ces pays prévoit la possibilité de demander une mesure provisoire quel que soit le type de litige ou d'affaire. En RFA, cette possibilité vaut *expressis verbis* également en droit administratif (article 123 VwGO, qui ressemble fort à l'article 940 ZPO). Il doit toutefois y avoir une relation avec l'action principale; cf. par exemple l'article 940 ZPO. Cet article ainsi que l'article 382 EO mettent encore clairement en évidence qu'à l'origine ces mesures provisoires avaient surtout, voire exclusivement le caractère d'une mesure tendant à garantir l'exécution de jugement au fond. En Pologne, ce caractère est encore si fort qu'il est permis de douter si, vu la place et la teneur des articles 730 et 755 kpc, il est effectivement question d'une mesure qui se distingue de celle traitée au point (1) du présent chapitre.

Il y a lieu de relever que les possibilités de demander ces mesures provisoires sont limitées d'une certaine manière sur le fait de prévoir dans les dispositions applicables la nécessité d'ordonner la mesure; on retrouve une disposition analogue dans l'article 755 kpc qui enjoint au juge 'de ne pas imposer le débiteur plus que nécessaire'.

Nous soulignons enfin que le système d'une mesure provisoire à caractère exclusivement régulateur s'étend en RFA à l'ensemble de la juridiction gracieuse (c'est ce qui est du moins admis dans la littérature) ainsi qu'à la juridiction des tribunaux non civils (en vertu d'un grand nombre de dispositions particulières)[39].

---

37 Pellegrini Grinover, p. 145.

38 Ferreira da Silva, III.5.

39 Leipold, B.2.

En ce qui concerne l'exigence que la demande principale doit être susceptible d'être adjugée, nous n'avons pas trouvé de différence nette entre ces mesures provisoires et celles faisant l'objet du point (1) de ce chapitre.

2.3 LES MESURES PROVISOIRES ANTICIPANT SUR LE JUGEMENT SUR LE FOND

C'est sur ce type de mesures provisoires que les conceptions juridiques dans les divers pays diffèrent le plus. Dans certains pays on est d'avis que les mesures provisoires ne peuvent d'aucune manière anticiper sur le jugement au fond et que par conséquent seules les mesures provisoires traitées aux points (1) et (2) sont admissibles. La question à laquelle il faut répondre est celle posée par Ramos Mendez: 'Une partie peut-elle recevoir par voie provisoire ce que normalement elle doit uniquement recevoir par voie principale et à fin du procès?'[40] Ramos Mendez ne laisse planer aucun doute quant à la réponse qui s'impose: 'Une mesure provisoire peut anticiper les effets d'une exécution future et ne doit pas se borner seulement à la conservation d'une situation juridique ou de fait'[41]. Nous avons déjà relevé que les mesures provisoires à caractère exclusivement régulateur ont elles aussi parfois un caractère définitif. En ce qui concerne la Suisse, Meier considère par conséquent que la différence entre les mesures provisoires traitées aux points (2) et (3) n'est pas essentielle[42].

La législation grecque par contre stipule expressément dans son article 692, alinéa 4 cpc hellénique 'que les mesures provisoires ne doivent pas donner pleine satisfaction au droit dont la protection est demandée'. Reconnaissons toutefois que les tribunaux et la doctrine s'efforcent d'adoucir l'effet de cette disposition, ce qui dans la pratique est notamment le cas dans le domaine de la propriété intellectuelle et industrielle[43].

En Belgique et en Italie, le juge peut en principe ordonner par une mesure provisoire les mêmes mesures que celles qui sont possibles dans le jugement au fond; c'est là une compétence à laquelle le juge italien recourt de plus en plus souvent: de plus en plus souvent la mesure provisoire produit non seulement les mèmes effets que le jugement au fond mais aussi des effets irréversibles; elle réalise donc une protection des droits qui est autonome de celle assurée par le jugement sur le fond et qui peut même préjuger ce dernier[44].

Au Brésil, en France et aux Pays-Bas on considère avant tout, comme c'est de plus en plus le cas en Italie, la mesure provisoire comme une mesure autonome: Pellegrini Grinover mentionne que les limites à la juridiction du juge sont fixées pour chaque procès par le législateur. Selon Perrot, le juge des référés n'a sans doute pas plus de pouvoir que le juge ordinaire, il en a même moins si l'on considère qu'il ne statue qu'à titre provisoire. Cela ressort également du rapport néerlandais dans lequel Ten Berg-Koolen relève qu'à certains égards la compétence du juge en référé est plus grande que celle du juge du fond du fait que le juge des référés peut toujours déclarer sa décision exécutoire par

40 Ramos Mendez, p. 191.

41 Ramos Mendez, p. 192.

42 Meier, rapport, chapitre III.1.

43 Kerameus et Polyzogopoulos, p. 75.

44 Tarzia, rapport, p. 29.

provision, même d'office, ou ordonner la publication de son jugement[45]. Le rapporteur néerlandais fait également mention de la discussion fondamentale qui a lieu actuellement aux Pays-Bas au sujet de la question de savoir s'il est possible d'imposer au défendeur par mesure provisoire une injonction ou interdiction sans qu'il y ait pour cela une base juridique mais uniquement sur la base d'une appréciation des intérêts en jeu ou de considération d'efficacité. Le rapporteur constate que dans la doctrine la majorité défend le point de vue selon lequel une injonction ou une interdiction doit en principe s'appuyer sur une base juridique mais que certains auteurs estiment néanmoins que dans des cas exceptionnels, le juge des référés est compétent pour ordonner sur demande une injonction ou une interdiction, même en l'absence d'une base juridique[46].

La RFA, la Pologne, l'Autriche et la Suisse occupent une position nettement différente et autonome. Il est intéressant de relever qu'en ce qui concerne ce type de mesures provisoires, les conceptions et le droit dans ces pays s'opposaient à l'origine contre de telles mesures. Cela s'explique par les conceptions qui dans le système juridique sont à la base de ces mesures provisoires, conceptions sur lesquelles nous avons déjà attiré l'attention. Il s'agit en effet de garantir le recouvrement de la créance faisant l'objet de l'action principale. Pour la RFA, Leipold en tire comme principe que la protection juridique provisoire ne doit pas avoir pour but d'assurer la pleine satisfaction de la demande de l'action principale[47]. Nous constaterons toutefois par la suite qu'en RFA il y a néanmoins des exceptions à ce principe.

C'est à la lumière de ces conceptions que selon la jurisprudence et la doctrine suisses les créances ne peuvent pas faire l'objet de ce genre de mesures provisoires et que pour tous les autres cas il doit y avoir explicitement une base légale[48].

Il importe certainement de citer dans ce contexte l'article 731 du kpc polonais qui s'énonce: 'Une mesure provisoire ne peut avoir pour objet la satisfaction de la demande'. Nous constaterons néanmoins par la suite que malgré cette disposition explicite ce principe n'est pas appliqué à 100% en Pologne et qu'il y a des exceptions même si elles ne sont pas nombreuses[49].

Bien qu'il n'y ait pas en Autriche une telle limitation légale et que le rapport de Matscher n'en fasse pas non plus explicitement état, l'idée qui se dégage à la lecture du rapport autrichien est que cette catégorie de mesures provisoires n'est en Autriche qu'un phénomène marginal. Leur base est dans tous les cas très vague[50].

En résumé, on peut signaler pour ce groupe de pays l'existence d'une contradiction entre les conceptions théoriques et les besoins ressentis dans la

45 Ten Berg-Koolen, 1.1.2.

46 Idem, 1.1.3.

47 Leipold, rapport, A.2.

48 Meier, rapport, chapitre III. 1 et 3. La base même doit exister dans le droit confédéral et donc pas seulement dans le droit du canton concerné. Par ailleurs, Meier et d'autres auteurs suisses cités par lui plaident pour la révision de cette conception, ce qui a déjà été fait par la jurisprudence dans le canton de Zurich.

49 Comme le mentionne Erecinski à la fin de son rapport.

50 Matscher, pp. 96-97 et 99. Matscher ne voit des possibilités pour une 'Leistungsverfügung' que dans des cas urgents ou des situations exceptionnelles; p. 111.

pratique par les tribunaux. Leipold relève à juste titre que cela peut entrainer des tensions internes[51]. Il en résulte que ces pays ne connaissent pas la possibilité générale de prendre des mesures provisoires anticipant sur le jugement au fond et que, contrairement à ce qui est le cas pour les provisons faisant l'objet des paragraphes (1) et (2) de ce chapitre, de telles mesures provisoires ne sont possibles que dans des domaines juridiques strictement délimités.

La Suisse occupe à notre avis une place particulière puisque ce pays connaît une gamme variée de mesures provisoires anticipant sur le jugement au fond. Certaines de ces variantes sont fort intéressantes et témoignent de conceptions très originales. Nous reviendrons ultérieurement sur une de ces variantes, à savoir le 'Verfahren zur Handhabung klaren Rechts' (l'usage rapide du droit évident).

Prévoir la possibilité d'anticiper d'une manière ou d'une autre sur la demande au fond est en soi la méthode la plus directe et la plus efficace de garantir l'exécution du jugement au fond. Mais, plus la mesure anticipe sur le fond, plus elle perd de son caractère provisoire et dépendant. Elle devient en d'autres termes plus autonome et moins temporaire. Le lien avec l'action principale se relâche ou disparaît même entièrement. Les conditions à imposer doivent par conséquent avoir une autre teneur que celles s'appliquant pour les mesures provisoires discutées aux paragraphes (1) et (2).

L'exemple le plus connu dans le droit de la République fédérale d'Allemagne est fourni par le paragraphe 25 de la loi contre la concurrence illicite (UWG), exemple qui est en même temps caractéristique de l'approche à laquelle conduisent les conceptions existant dans ce pays et que nous venons de décrire ci-dessus. Il n'est en effet pas directement stipulé qu'en cas de concurrence illicite il soit possible d'anticiper entièrement ou partiellement sur le jugement au moyen d'une mesure provisoire. Ce résultat n'est rendu possible que de façon indirecte du fait que le paragraphe 25 de l'UWG stipule que les conditions que les paragraphes 935 et 940 ZPO posent à la prise d'une 'Einstweilige Verfügung' n'ont pas besoin d'être réunies dans les cas relevant de l'UWG. Formellement, il s'agit encore toujours d'une 'Sicherung' mais en fait la voie est laissée ouverte à une mesure provisoire autonome. S'il n'y a plus par la suite de jugement au fond, il n'y a plus rien 'à garantir'. Leipold souligne dans son contexte que dans les cas couverts par le paragraphe 25 UWG on admet une 'présomption d'urgence'. Il souligne que généralement une procédure au fond n'a plus lieu[52,53].

Selon la justice allemande, les 'Leistungsverfügungen' peuvent être ordonnés sans base légale dans les cas où une telle mesure est indispensable pour prévenir un préjudice sensible, par exemple en cas de créance alimentaire ou salariale. Ce critère crée à notre avis un lien avec le paragraphe 940 ZPO d'autant plus qu'on pose l'exigence d'une situation d'urgence du créancier.

---

51 Leipold, A.2.

52 Leipold, E.6. 'Du point de vue juridique, la procédure n'est que provisoire mais dans la pratique les parties renoncent souvent à faire suivre la procédure sommaire par une demande au fond'.

53 Meier, rapport, chapitre III.9, examine lui aussi spécialement l'utilisation des mesures provisoires en matière de concurrence où elles sont un moyen de pression effectif. En Suisse, elles ont dans la pratique le caractère d'une mesure définitive.

L'article 123 VwGO peut être la base d'une 'Leistungsverfügung' dirigée contre les pouvoirs publics[54].

On trouve dans le droit familial des exemples de 'Leistungsverfügungen' plus spécifiques, en particulier lors d'action en reconnaissance de paternité. Les codes allemand et polonais mentionnent explicitement ce cas; dans le code polonais, les dispositions en la matière figurent toutefois dans le cadre d'une réglementation plus générale concernant les mesures provisoires relatives aux pensions alimentaires qui englobent également les demandes de dommages-intérêts pour acte illicite entraînant une invalidité ou le décès (article 641 ZPO; articles 753 et 754 kpc). En ce qui concerne l'Autriche, on trouve des dispositions analogues dans le EO. Il est intéressant de constater que l'on retrouve également dans ces dispositions spécifiques des dérogations explicites aux limitations prévues par ailleurs; citons à titre d'exemple la suppression de la condition qu'il doit être rendu admissible qu'à défaut de mesures provisoires le créancier peut perdre en définitive, totalement ou partiellement, les possibilités de recouvrement. Dans ces cas spécifiques également, il faut qu'il soit vraisemblable que le juge puisse adjuger la demande dans une procédure au fond (par exemple que le défendeur est le père de l'enfant). Une particularité intéressante de la réglementation polonaise est enfin qu'en cas d'invalidité ou de décès par suite d'un acte illicite l'indemnisation accordée par mesure provisoire peut uniquement porter sur une pension alimentaire minimum indispensable. Il est de cette façon fait quelque peu droit au point de départ de l'article 731 kpc[55].

Les procédures à suivre pour obtenir une mesure provisoire de cette catégorie correspondent dans l'ensemble aux procédures générales décrites plus haut au point (2). Il n'y a rien d'étonnant à cela puisque les mesures provisoires anticipant sur le jugement ont été en majeure partie développées dans le cadre des réglementations générales des mesures provisoires. Il n'en est pas de même de l'exécution provisoire, 'la mesure qui permet à celui qui a obtenu un jugement en sa faveur de le faire exécuter immédiatement dès qu'il a été signifié, ... comme une dérogation exceptionnelle à l'effet suspensif des voies de recours ordinaires (l'appel ou l'opposition)'[56]. Perrot désigne cette exécution provisoire en tant que mesure de la première catégorie qui vise donc à garantir l'exécution du jugement. Contrairement au point de vue adopté par Perrot, nous considérons que l'exécution provisoire tant d'un jugement dans une procédure au fond que d'un jugement ordonnant une mesure provisoire est une mesure par laquelle le créancier reçoit avant même le jugement définitiéf, ce à quoi il pense avoir droit ou, pour paraphraser Perrot, 'une mesure qui devance ce que pourra éventuellement décider le juge'[57]. Bien que cette possibilité d'une mesure provisoire ne soit pas traitée dans tous les rapports, nous avons l'impression qu'elle figure dans pratiquement toutes les législations des pays concernés[58]. En règle générale, l'exécution provisoire sera demandée simultané-

54 Leipold, C.15.

55 Erecinski, rapport, chapitre I.5.

56 Perrot, p. 171.

57 Perrot, p. 161.

58 L'Autriche fait en tout cas exception. Le droit autrichien ne connaît pas l'exécution provisoire d'un jugement. En Autriche, l'exécution provisoire (Exekution zur Sicherstellung) remplit une fonction analogue, mais elle ne sert que pour garantir l'exécution forcée de dettes pécuniaires et elle ne

ment à la demande dans l'action principale ou dans la procédure provisoire. L'article 515 du nouveau Code de procédure civile français permet d'ordonner l'exécution provisoire 'chaque fois que le juge l'estime nécessaire'. L'urgence n'est donc plus exigée comme c'était le cas dans l'article 135a de l'ancien code de procédure civile. Selon le droit néerlandais, le juge est toujours tenu d'ordonner l'exécution provisoire dans certains cas spécifiques désignés dans la législation (article 52 Rv.). Dans d'autres cas (article 53 Rv.) il a en la matière pouvoir discrétionnaire. Selon la jurisprudence fixe, le juge ne peut toutefois pas ordonner d'office l'exécution provisoire du jugement mais uniquement si celle-ci est expressément demandée. Le juge des référés a, sur la base de l'article 293 Rv. toujours la possibilité d'ordonner, même d'office, que le jugement sera exécutoire par provision.

Il convient de mentionner spécialement cette réglementation connue dans de nombreux cantons suisses que constitue la procédure appelée 'schnelle Handhabung klaren Rechts', procédure ayant pour objectif d'apporter rapidement une solution dans les cas où les droits sont évidents. Dans la plupart des cantons qui connaissent cette procédure, la décision a formellement un caractère provisoire, ce qui justifie qu'elle soit examinée dans le cadre de notre étude. D'autre part, cette procédure a en principe un caractère autonome et son introduction ne dépend pas de conditions particulières telles que l'existence du risque que les droits se perdent. Une limite importante est toutefois posée par le fait que la procédure ne peut pas porter sur une créance d'argent. Il y a lieu de relever que la littérature considère cette limitation comme non fondée. Dans la plupart des cantons, le juge du fond n'est pas tenu par une telle mesure visant à garantir des droit évidents mais dans la pratique une procédure à cet effet devant le juge du fond n'a selon Meier que peu de chance de succès.

La mesure est prise après audition des parties, les documents, présomptions et déclarations des parties étant utilisés comme moyens de preuve. La procédure dure de un à trois mois et le plus souvent des voies de recours sont ouvertes. Il s'agit en grande partie d'affaires concernant l'expulsion de locataires ne payant pas le loyer, de restitution d'objets ou de documents et d'affaires dans le domaine de la concurrence déloyale, en somme d'un grand nombre d'affaires civiles. Une telle mesure est toutefois plus difficile à obtenir qu'une mesure provisoire 'normale' qui est donc très souvent demandée en même temps. En effet, pour une mesure provisoire il suffit que la prétention apparaisse vraisemblable, ce qui est moins difficile que de prouver un 'droit évident'. L'inconvénient d'une demande de mesure provisoire est qu'en Suisse il faut qu'il y ait ultérieurement une procédure au fond. Meier attire notre attention sur le fait que dans la pratique un avocat habile du défendeur peut (trop) facilement frustrer une telle procédure sur la base d'un 'droit évident' par une défense qui apparaît sérieuse mais qui en fait ne l'est pas. Il faut donc que le juge réponde à des critères très élevés[59].

---

conduit qu'à des mesures conservatoires, comme un droit de gage ou de priorité; cf. Matscher, rapport, pp. 88-89. En Autriche les mesures provisoires sont également immédiatement exécutoires; Matscher, p. 91

59 Voir Meier, rapport, chapitre II. Il semble y avoir quelque ressemblance avec l'article 7.24 (Eviction) d'une loi finnoise de 1895, mentionné par Lager, rapport.

La plus ancienne forme de mesures provisoires de cette troisième catégorie est sans aucun doute l'action possessoire que l'on rencontre dans la législation de pratiquement tous les pays. Il ressort du rapport d'Erecinski qu'en Pologne les actions possessoires jouent encore un rôle important[60]. La mesure a force de chose jugée mais est provisoire en ce sens qu'elle ne vise qu'à rétablir rapidement une situation de fait sans qu'il y ait un jugement sur le droit de propriété. Les présomptions jouent un grand rôle en la matière. A l'heure actuelle, l'intérêt pratique de cette action semble moins grand qu'il ne l'était dans le passé. Greif de l'Uruguay mentionne dans son rapport: 'Evidemment et pour des raisons de développement économique, les actions possessoires sont presque tombées en désuétude'[61]. En Suisse, les actions possessoires jouent encore un rôle important mais Meier considère qu'en raison du système actuel des mesures provisoires ce type d'action pourrait être supprimé[62].

L'un des plus grands problèmes en ce qui concerne les mesures provisoires est celui qui se pose lorsque le tribunal saisi du fond s'écarte dans son jugement de la décision prise par la mesure provisoire. Bien que ce problème puisse également se présenter pour les mesures de la première et de la deuxième catégorie, il ne prend toute sa signification que pour les mesures de la troisième catégorie puisqu'il sera bien plus souvent impossible de redresser les conséquences qu'a eu la mesure provisoire, ce problème mérite donc que l'on s'y arrête. Les décisions prises dans l'action principale peuvent s'écarter de celles prises dans la mesure provisoire puisqu'on admet généralement que le tribunal saisi du fond n'est pas lié par la mesure provisoire. Ce problème prend toute sa signification en cas d'exécution provisoire d'une créance.

Il existe en France depuis 1973 une procédure particulière appelée le référé-provision. Selon Perrot c'est 'l'innovation la plus remarquable' dans le cadre des référés. Dans le référé-provision, le juge - le juge de référé et le juge de la mise en état - a la faculté d'accorder tout de suite à celui qui se prétend créancier une provision à valoir sur le montant de la condamnation qui sera éventuellement prononcée par le tribunal[63]. La seule et unique condition est que 'l'obligation ne soit pas sérieusement contestable', l'urgence n'étant pas une condition requise. En principe le juge peut accorder à titre de provision le montant total de la créance. Depuis 1981, la loi a prévu que le juge peut exiger du demandeur une garantie pour le remboursement éventuel du montant en cas de décision différente du juge au fond. Le domaine d'application du référé-provision est en principe limité aux obligations ayant pour objet le paiement d'une somme d'argent; il importe peu que l'obligation ait une source légale, conventionnelle, délictuelle, quasi-délictuelle ou quasi-contractuelle. La provision peut être demandée tant au cours d'un procès qu'avant même l'introduction d'une instance au fond, en toute matière du droit, exception faite du droit administratif. Le Conseil d'Etat français s'est en effet fermement opposé contre

---

60 Erecinski, rapport, chapitre III. En Pologne, ces affaires ont représenté au cours des dix dernières années 2 à 3% du nombre total des affaires en première instance auprès des juridictions d'instance (sady rejonowe). En 1985, il s'agissait par exemple de 5000 demandes et de quelque 2000 ordonnances.

61 Greif, rapport, 1. Cf. également Lager, rapport E1: 'The self help in a modern country is of course very rare', etc.

62 Meier, chapitre IV.

63 Perrot, p. 162.

l'introduction d'une telle provision dans le droit administratif[64]. Perrot[65] signale que cette forme de référé est parfois désignée par le terme de référé au fond puisque le juge anticipe sur ce que pourra décider le juge du fond. Il n'est pas nécessaire que le référé-provision soit suivi d'une procédure au fond; sans procédure au fond, la mesure provisoire devient définitive en fait[66].

En Belgique, l'action en référé en matière de créance semble s'être moins développée que ce n'est le cas en France. Il n'existe pas de dispositions spéciales en la matière; Lindemans signale que les tribunaux et la doctrine admettent de plus en plus la possibilité de l'octroi d'une provision à titre d'avance sur ce qui est demandé au fond dans la mesure où l'exigibilité de la somme ne peut pas être sérieusement contestée et où l'affaire revêt un caractère urgent. Lindemans signale en outre que le juge du fond peut également ordonner par la voie de mesures provisoires le paiement d'une avance en vertu de l'article 19 du Cj mais que l'application de cette procédure est peu développée[67].

Les Pays-Bas ont, tout comme la Belgique, adopté initialement une attitude réservée en ce qui concerne le recouvrement d'une créance par mesure provisoire, à l'exception du paiement d'une avance sur dommages-intérêts notamment aux victimes d'un accident de la circulation et de l'octroi d'une pension alimentaire par mesure provisoire dans une affaire de droit familial. A partir du moment où en 1979 le président du tribunal d'Amsterdam a fait savoir qu'en ce qui le concerne il ne voyait aucune objection à ordonner le paiement d'une créance en tant que mesure provisoire en référé, cette question a fait pendant quelque temps l'objet de discussions animées. Il ressort d'arrêts rendus entre-temps par la Cour suprême que les actions en référé en vue du recouvrement d'une créance existant sur la base de biens ou services livrés ne doivent pas satisfaire à d'autres conditions que celles valables pour les autres actions en référé, à savoir l'urgence et l'intérêt légitime des parties[68]. La Cour suprême signale toutefois qu'il y a lieu d'accorder une attention particulière aux risques de restitution mais que ce facteur n'est pas à considérer comme une condition mais plutôt comme un des éléments qui doit jouer un rôle lors de l'appréciation des intérêts des parties. Bien que l'article 293 Rv prévoit expressément que le juge peut imposer une caution, cette possibilité n'est que rarement utilisée dans la pratique.

Dans le cadre de l'assurance obligatoire responsabilité civile en cas d'accident de la route, la législation italienne contient depuis 1969 une disposition particulière en ce qui concerne les actions en vue du paiement d'une avance sur les dommages-intérêts aux victimes d'accidents de la circulation. L'article 24 de la loi du 24 décembre 1969 n° 990 stipule que les quatre-cinquièmes du montant évalué du dommage peuvent être accordés au cas où la victime est dans le besoin. La mesure provisoire qui doit être demandée dans le cadre de l'action principale peut être révoquée par le jugement au fond. Les salariés ont

64 Idem, p. 164.

65 Idem, p. 165.

66 Idem, p. 169.

67 Lindemans, Kort Geding, p. 320.

68 Cour suprême des Pays-Bas, 29 mars 1985. Revue néerlandaise de jurisprudence 1986, 84.

également la possibilité de demander par mesure provisoire le paiement d'une somme d'argent dans une procédure devant le juge des affaires du travail[69].

Il semble qu'en Grèce le paiement de créances en tant que mesures provisoires ne pose pas de problème particulier. Kerameus et Polyzogopoulos signalent que malgré la disposition contenue dans l'article 692, alinéa 4 du Code de procédure civile hellénique qui stipule que les mesures provisoires ne doivent pas entièrement donner satisfaction au demandeur, ces dispositions ne s'appliquent en aucun cas aux créances puisque dans l'article 723, alinéa 1er, la loi stipule par ailleurs que les mesures provisoires portant sur les pensions alimentaires peuvent être adjugées[70].

Dans son rapport écrit en 1984 au sujet de la nouvelle réglementation espagnole entrée en vigueur le 1er septembre 1984, Ramos Mendez signale qu'en vertu de l'article 1428 LEC une condamnation par mesure provisoire au paiement d'une somme d'argent n'est pas entièrement exclue mais doit se limiter aux cas où il y a un rapport plus ou moins direct avec une obligation de faire ou de ne pas faire ou une obligation de livrer une certaine chose[71]. Ramos Mendez cite expressément la nécessité pour le juge d'ordonner une caution, étant entendu que le juge doit avoir en la matière la latitude nécessaire[72].

Pellegrini Grinover ne fait pas de remarques particulières au sujet de la possibilité d'obtenir par mesure provisoire le paiement d'une créance. Bien qu'elle signale que les possibilités de mesures provisoires prévues dans les articles 798 et 799 du code de procédure brésilien sont très générales[73], cette mesure spécifique ne figure pas dans l'énumération détaillée des mesures provisoires possibles[74].

Dans le cadre de l'analyse du problème esquissé plus haut, à savoir la relation entre une mesure provisoire et une décision (divergente) dans la procédure principale, nous devons également aborder la relation entre une décision exécutoire par provision et un jugement divergent en appel. Dans les deux cas il y a le risque que le second juge qui sera appelé à se prononcer sur l'affaire jugera différemment la position des parties que ce ne fut le cas lors de la mesure provisoire initiale ou lors du jugement rendu à l'origine en première instance. Quelles sont pour le plaideur qui fait procéder à l'exécution provisoire les conséquences d'un jugement infirmé ultérieurement?

En ce qui concerne le droit français, Perrot signale que l'exécution provisoire a toujours lieu aux risques et périls du gagnant, ce qui signifie qu'il peut se voir condamner à des dommages-intérêts si l'exécution provisoire d'un jugement ultérieurement infirmé a entraîné un préjudice pour son adversaire[75]. Perrot souligne dans son contexte les problèmes sérieux auxquels peut se voir confronter celui qui a été condamné au paiement d'une provision lorsque par la suite il peut obtenir restitution de ce qu'il a payé indûment. Dans un arrêt

69 Proto Pisani et Varano, rapport 4.1.2.3 sous ii et iii; Tarzia, rapport, p. 11.

70 Kerameus et Polyzogopoulos, p. 75.

71 Ramos Mendez, p. 199.

72 Idem, pp. 201-202.

73 Pellegrini Grinover, p. 139.

74 Idem, pp. 141-142.

75 Perrot, p. 174.

rendu en 1984[76], la Cour suprême néerlandaise a qualifié la responsabilité de celui qui fait procéder à l'exécution comme étant une responsabilité découlant d'un acte illicite. Cette conception de la Cour suprême a été critiquée par W.H. Heemskerk qui qualifie cette responsabilité de responsabilité sans faute; le rapporteur belge Lindemans est du même avis, mais fait remarquer dans son rapport que: 'L'on s'accorde généralement pour dire que la partie condamnée en référé aura le droit de pouvoir mettre fin à la mesure provisoire. Par contre, la possibilité d'obtenir réparation du dommage subi par l'exécution de ces mesures provisoires est largement controversée'[77].

Sans porter de jugement de valeur, Tarzia constate que certaines mesures provisoires ont par définition des conséquences sur lesquelles il est impossible de revenir en arrière[78]; c'est le cas de mesures ordonnant la réintégration dans l'emploi d'un membre du personnel suspendu ou la destruction d'objets; il en résulte que le juge du fond ne peut prendre une décision que pour l'avenir et ne peut en fait pas revenir sur les effets de la mesure provisoire. Dans certains cas une mesure provisoire peut même avoir des conséquences plus importantes que la décision au fond parce que l'efficacité d'une mesure provisoire est plus grande en raison du court délai dans lequel elle peut être obtenue. Tarzia n'attend que peu de salut d'une responsabilité ou d'une caution étant donné que très souvent il est impossible de les concrétiser. Proto Pisani et Varano estiment qu'il y a là une tâche pour le juge qui est appelé à ordonner une mesure provisoire: a) il doit apprécier autant que possible le *fumus boni iuris* et b) il doit examiner de façon approfondie les intérêts de chacune des parties[79].

En Grèce, l'article 730, alinéa 2 cpc hellénique stipule qu'après une décision au fond qui s'écarte de la mesure provisoire, la partie intéressée a droit au rétablissement de la situation antérieure. De plus, lorsque l'action principale est jugée non fondée, la partie qui a fait exécuter la mesure provisoire sera tenue à des dommages-intérêts, mais uniquement si elle savait ou si elle ignorait par une faute grave de sa part l'existence du droit subjectif à la protection duquel visait la mesure provisoire[80].

Ramos Mendez qui, en ce qui concerne les mesures provisoires visant le paiement d'une créance estime que l'exécution d'une telle mesure provisoire devrait généralement être subordonnée au dépôt d'une caution, soutient que le dommage causé par l'exécution d'une mesure provisoire infirmée par la suite doit être recouvré sur cette caution[81].

Au Portugal, la partie contre laquelle est ordonnée une mesure provisoire peut, dans certains cas, en prévenir l'exécution grâce à une caution; dans d'autres cas, celui qui fait exécuter la mesure provisoire a l'obligation de déposer une caution. L'article 387 cpc portugais stipule que lorsqu'une mesure provisoire est jugée non fondée ou est devenue caduque, le demandeur est tenu

---

76 Cour suprême des Pays-Bas, 16 novembre 1984, Revue néerlandaise de Jurisprudence 1985, 547.

77 Lindemans Kort Geding, p. 226.

78 Tarzia, rapport, pp. 6 et 29.

79 Proto Pisani et Varano, rapport, réponse à la question 19 du questionnaire.

80 Kerameus et Polyzogopoulos, p. 78.

81 Ramos Mendez, p. 206.

à des dommages-intérêts lorsqu'il agit sans faire preuve de la sagesse requise et qu'il n'a aucune chance d'obtenir une mesure provisoire analogue[82].

En Uruguay, une mesure provisoire devra céder le pas à une décision ultérieure sur le fond qui s'en écarte. Ce qui a été payé en exécution d'une telle mesure provisoire devra être restitué en exécution des règles générales du droit des obligations; le rapporteur cite dans ce contexte la réglementation concernant l'enrichissement sans cause; ce point n'a toutefois retenu que peu d'attention dans la jurisprudence et la doctrine en Uruguay[83].

Au Brésil, l'exécution d'une mesure provisoire peut être empêchée par le dépôt d'une caution. Le demandeur a néanmoins la possibilité de déposer à son tour une caution pour assurer l'exécution de la mesure provisoire. Selon Pelligrini Grinover, ce système assure dans la pratique l'équilibre indispensable. Le dommage entraîné par la mauvaise foi lors de l'exécution d'un jugement doit être réparé en vertu de l'article 16 du Code de procédure pénale; sur la base de l'article 311 cpc on admet que les procédures concernant les mesures provisoires et leur exécution ont lieu, comme c'est le cas dans chaque procès, au risque du demandeur[84].

En RFA, l'article 945 ZPO prévoit l'obligation d'indemnisation au cas où le juge saisi au fond annule la mesure provisoire. Cette obligation ne dépend pas de la question de savoir si le débiteur est en faute. Leipold part dans ce contexte d'une sorte de responsabilité sans faute pouvant être considérée comme compensation pour le fait que la mesure d'urgence peut être obtenue sur la base de la simple vraisemblance[85]. Dans le droit administratif, le principe de l'article 945 ZPO ne s'applique pas en cas de suspension d'une mesure mais bien en cas de mesure sur la base de l'article 123 VwGO ('einstweilige Anordnungen').

Le droit à dommages-intérêts existe également en Autriche. Le juge autrichien peut déterminer librement le montant des dommages-intérêts lorsque le dommage ne peut pas être calculé[86].

La Suisse connaît des dispositions particulières qui établissent la responsabilité également en l'absence de faute mais à défaut de telles dispositions il faut prouver la faute, ce qui selon Meier ne sera possible que rarement. Pour les mesures provisoires étudiées sous ce point, on exige en Suisse souvent le dépôt d'une caution en raison précisément des risques relativement grands de dommages entraînés par la mesure provisoire[87].

En Israël, la Cour suprême a décidé en 1973 qu'une pension alimentaire provisoire que l'homme doit payer à sa femme pendant une procédure de divorce peut être recouvrée par l'homme lorsque la décision prise au fond établit que l'homme n'était pas obligé de survenir aux besoins de la femme[88].

---

82 Ferreira da Silva, rapport, III.1.1.

83 Greif, rapport, 20.

84 Pellegrini Grinover, pp. 146-147.

85 Leipold, chapitre C. 18 et 19. Leipold plaide pour l'extension des possibilités de prendre des mesures transitoires qui ne sont pas rendues caduques en cas de décision différente dans la procédure au fond ('Materielles Zwischenrecht').

86 Matscher, p. 105.

87 Meier, rapport, chapitre III, 5 et 6.

88 Goldstein, rapport II.G.

3 CONSIDERATIONS FINALES, CONCLUSIONS ET QUESTIONS

3.1 PORTEE

La première question qui se pose dans le cadre d'une étude portant sur l'usage et l'abus des procédures sommaires est celle de savoir si, et dans l'affirmative dans quelle mesure les systèmes juridiques des différents pays autorisent l'usage des procédures sommaires. Une réponse affirmative à cette question devient de plus en plus problématique au fur et à mesure des mesures provisoires traitées dans le chapitre précédent et *a fortiori* pour celles de la troisième catégorie.

En ce qui concerne les mesures provisoires qui tendent à garantir l'exécution du jugement au fond, il n'y a entre les divers pays que de faibles différences qui se situent davantage sur le plan de la systématique que sur celui des principes. Nous considérons en effet que dans la pratique il importe peu qu'il y ait - comme c'est le cas dans un certain nombre de pays - une possibilité générale de prendre en rapport avec une saisie conservatoire toutes sortes de mesures de sûreté ou que - comme c'est le cas dans de nombreux autres pays- il y ait une telle possibilité générale sans rapport avec le réglementation concernant la saisie conservatoire. Dans le premier cas on procédera peut-être moins souvent à un examen oral - en raison du lien avec la saisie conservatoire - mais quoiqu'il en soit nous n'avons pas pu constater l'existence de différences significantives ou de problèmes dans ce domaine.

Nous n'avons malheureusement pas pu recueillir suffisamment de données pour pouvoir répondre à la question de savoir si dans le droit de procédure administratif la garantie des droits, notamment par le truchement d'une suspension d'une décision administrative, est assurée et réglée de façon satisfaisante. L'impression qui se dégage du rapport est que tel n'est pas toujours le cas. Dans les pays où cette possibilité existe en principe, la compétence de prendre en la matière des mesures provisoires revient tantôt au juge civil, tantôt au juge administratif, parfois aux deux. Sur la base des données dont nous disposons il n'est pas possible de se prononcer en faveur de l'un ou de l'autre système ni de tirer des conclusions quant aux autres modalités. Une étude approfondie exige des données plus complètes. Il nous semble donc préférable de ne pas aborder ce sujet dans nos discussions.

En ce qui concerne les mesures provisoires à caractère exclusivement régulateur, il est utile de faire tout d'abord une différence entre d'une part les domaines spécifiques et les réglementations spécifiques correspondantes et d'autre part les possibilités générales de prendre de telles mesures provisoires. Pout ce qui est des mesures spécifiques, le droit de procédure en matière de divorce peut servir de modèle. Les mesures provisoires existent partout en matière de divorce. Elles ont un caractère relativement autonome par rapport à la procédure au fond. Bien que nous n'ayons pas demandé explicitement des informations détaillées au sujet de la portée des mesures provisoires en cas de divorce, les commentaires fournis justifient néanmoins les questions suivantes:

- La loi doit-elle, en plus des mesures provisoires en matière de pension alimentaire, énumérer de façon limitative d'autres mesures pouvant être demandées?
- Le juge doit-il avoir la compétence d'ordonner également d'office des mesures provisoires ou bien d'ordonner une mesure provisoire autre que celle qui a été demandee?

- Doit-il toujours y avoir des voies de recours et, dans l'affirmative, lesquelles?

En ce qui concerne la possibilité générale de demander une mesure provisoire à caractère exclusivement régulateur, possibilité qui existe pratiquement partout, il importe à nouveau de savoir si dans la systématique de la loi cette possibilité est oui ou non liée aux mesures provisoires tendant à garantir l'exécution du jugement sur le fond. Si tel est le cas, l'exigence qui'il y ait un rapport avec une procédure au fond peut entraîner dans la pratique une importante restriction; quelquefois une mesure provisioire ne peut être demandée que si une procédure au fond est pendante. Si tel n'est pas le cas, les possibilités de prendre une mesure provisoire sont généralement beaucoup plus vastes. Dans certains cas, la condition d'une procédure au fond n'est même pas prévue. Le point de discussion le plus important en ce qui concerne la portée de ces mesures provisoires peut donc être formulé comme suit:

Est-il utile ou souhaitable de prévoir une possibilité générale permettant de demander une mesure provisoire à caractère exclusivement régulateur, indépendamment de l'introduction d'une procédure au fond?

Sur la base des informations reçues nous avons tendance à répondre affirmativement à cette question.

La possibilité d'anticiper sur le jugement du fond par une mesure provisoire est de loin la plus problématique. Bien que dans certaines législations cette possibilité soit implicitement ou même explicitement exclue, les impératifs de la pratique semblent toujours l'emporter sur la doctrine, ce qui explique que ces mesures provisoires sont de plus en plus admises. Mais lorsqu'on considère l'ensemble de tous les pays concernés on constate néanmoins sur ce point de très fortes divergences.

Une fois de plus nous sommes confrontés à cette importante question de savoir si oui ou non il est question d'un lien avec le système légal des mesures conservatoires. Si tel est le cas on se trouve en présence de deux conceptions contradictoires: le système légal et les besoins ressentis dans la pratique qui dans certains cas semblent d'ailleurs l'emporter[89]. Pour les pays concernés on est naturellement en droit de se demander si le point de départ légal n'est pas trop contraignant et ne devrait pas faire place à une conception plus libérale en ce qui concerne la possibilité d'anticiper sur le jugement au fond par une mesure provisoire.

On constate qu'il y a également de grandes différences en la matière dans les pays qui connaissent un système apparenté au référé français. Le système dans ces pays évolue d'ailleurs encore constamment et cette évolution va toujours dans le sens d'une extension des possibilités[90]. Apparemment les besoins ressentis dans la pratique de pouvoir disposer de telles mesures provisoires l'emportent sur les éventuelles objections contre leur introduction.

Signalons d'emblée qu'il n'existe dans aucun pays une possibilité générale et illimitée d'obtenir en fait par une mesure provisoire ce que l'on recherche à travers une procédure au fond. Parmi les pays qui connaissent le système du référé, les Pays-Bas sont peut-être bien le pays où dans la pratique les référés

---

89 Voir en ce qui concerne la RFA, par exemple note 93 et pour la Suisse, Meier, rapport 3.10.2 et suiv.

90 Notamment Meier, fin du rapport: 'Die Tendenz geht jedoch in der Richtung der uneingeschränkten Zulassung aller Vollstreckungsverfügungen'.

sont le plus largement appliqués, bien que la condition de l'urgence, qui continue à être posée par la Cour suprême, impose quand même certaines limitations. Le caractère provisoire de la mesure joue encore un rôle puisque l'effet obligatoire dépend en définitive de la volonté des parties d'accepter le jugement rendu par le juge des référés et ne découle pas du jugement même. Il en résulte qu'aux Pays-Bas le référé ne remplace en fait pas le jugement ordinaire mais satisfait plutôt à un besoin spécifique ressenti dans la pratique. Il est étonnant que les référés en matière de recouvrement de sommes d'argent ne connaissent pas dans la pratique un grand essor bien qu'ils soient admis par la Cour suprême[91].

Dans certains domaines spécifiques d'autres pays vont d'ailleurs plus loin que les Pays-Bas, notamment dans des domaines particulièrement importants dans la pratique où l'urgence n'est pas posée comme condition à la mesure provisoire. Nous citons dans ce contexte le référé-provision français qui est limité aux créances d'argent, et à la mesure suisse (l'usage rapide du droit évident) dont l'application est curieusement limitée dans pratiquement tous les cantons à des demandes ne portant pas sur le paiement d'une somme d'argent. Ces deux règlements sont à notre avis fort intéressants. Mis à part leur domaine d'application, ils semblent avoir quelques caractéristiques communes puisque la mesure provisoire ne peut être prise que s'il s'agit d'une demande qui à première vue n'est pas sérieusement contestable. L'apparence de légitimité est donc à l'avantage du créancier, en dehors du cas où le défendeur fait défaut. Il y a pour ainsi dire un renversement de la charge de la preuve: le débiteur doit rendre admissible (par les moyens qui cadrent avec cette procédure sommaire) que sa défense est vraiment sérieuse. Nous pensons qu'il est permis de faire également dans ce cas un parallèle avec cet institut respectable qui est l'action possessoire même si dans la pratique actuelle elle a perdu de son importance. Le référé-provision français ne remonte d'ailleurs qu'a 1973 alors que sa soeur suisse a un âge beaucoup plus vénérable[92] (s'agit-il des 'fillettes indisciplinées de Perrot?).

Les procédures que nous venons de mentionner vont dans le sens des 'summary proceedings' connues dans les pays anglo-saxons. Le rapport américain mentionne qu'un 'summary judgement' est rendu immédiatement après les plaidoyers et l'administration des preuves lorsqu'il est démontré qu'il n'existe pas réellement de litige et que le demandeur a droit à un titre exécutoire. Un 'summary judgement' est d'ailleurs une mesure définitive et non une mesure provisoire[93]. Le droit israélien connaît lui aussi des 'summary judgement proceedings', notamment pour des demandes concernant le paiement de sommes d'argent[94].

---

91 Ten Berg-Koolen, rapport I.13.

92 Meier, rapport, mentionne que l'origine de cette forme de procédure est inconnue mais qu'elle se retrouve certainement dès le siècle dernier dans le codes cantonaux.

93 Hazard, rapport, n° 1.2.

94 Goldstein, chapitre III, notamment le passage suivant: 'If the plaintiff files such a summary judgement proceeding, the defendant has no right to defend the action unless and until he receives leave of court to do so; a defendant's application for such leave must be supported by an affidavit showing that he has a **prima facie** defence on the merits and verifying the facts on which this defence is based'.

Nous estimons que ces formes juridiques méritent toute notre attention, mais il n'a malheureusement pas été possible de les traiter en détail dans ce rapport. Les expériences faites dans les pays cités sont positives dans l'ensemble. Il semble donc qu'elles offrent pour certaines affaires une solution de rechange acceptable et utilisable pour les procédures au fond qui durent trop longtemps. Ces solutions permettraient donc de réaliser un important gain de temps et pour les parties et pour le juge[95]. Il est concevable que des procédures vraiment sommaires mais définitives se créeront ainsi également en dehors des pays anglo- saxons.

En considérant le groupe quelque peu amorphe des mesures provisoires dans divers domaines spécifiques (par exemple le droit de concurrence, le droit du travail et naturellement le droit de la famille) on est en droit de se demander ce qui justifie le fait que la possibilité de pouvoir anticiper sur une procédure au fond soit précisément limitée à ces domaines spécifiques. Serait-il question d'arbitraire et partant d'inégalité devant la loi?[96]

La dernière remarque concernant la portée des procédures sommaires concerne la question soulevée dans le rapport néerlandais, à savoir s'il est possible d'imposer à quelqu'un par mesure provisoire une injonction ou une interdiction uniquement en tant que mesure d'ordre, et ce en l'absence d'une base juridique (acte illicite, etc.). Tarzia soutient qu'il n'existe pas de base juridique pour prendre une mesure provisoire *ultra* ou *contra ius*[97].

Il est intéressant d'étudier si cette question fondamentale a également été soulevée dans d'autres pays et quelles sont les conceptions à ce sujet.

3.2 LIEN ENTRE LA MESURE PROVISOIRE ET LA DEMANDE

Dans la plupart des pays il découle de la nature même du droit de procédure civile que le juge ne prend pas ses décisions d'office mais uniquement à la suite d'une demande expresse à cet effet. Dans certains pays, le juge a toutefois la compétence d'ordonner d'office des mesures provisoires dans le cadre d'une procédure au fond; c'est notamment le cas en Autriche au cours d'une procédure possessoire[98].

En France, le juge peut ordonner d'office l'exécution provisoire[99]. L'Italie ne connaît pas la possibilité légale d'ordonner d'office une mesure provisoire; Tarzia fait toutefois mention de jugements dans lesquels le juge considérait que la demande d'une mesure provisoire était implicitement renfermée dans la demande introductive d'instance de la procédure au fond[100].

On admet toutefois d'une manière générale que le juge ne peut pas prendre de

95 Cf. expressément Meier dans ses conclusions. Lorsqu'il est question d'un 'klares Recht' (droit évident), une procédure au fond est exceptionnellement rare.

96 Leipold, rapport, chapitre E.3., conçoit des modifications de la législation, surtout à l'égard des 'Leistungsverfügungen' bien qu'il estime que la pratique juridique répond déjà dans une mesure acceptable aux besoins.

97 Tarzia, rapport, p. 23.

98 Matscher, p. 101.

99 Perrot, p. 172.

100 Tarzia, p. 22.

sa propre initiative une mesure pour assurer provisoirement la protection des droits.

Dans de nombreux pays, le juge a toutefois une certaine latitude en ce qui concerne le choix de la mesure provisoire, à condition que celle-ci lui ait été demandée. Cela vaut également en dehors du cas des mesures provisoires en cas de divorce dont nous avons déjà traité plus haut. On estime souvent que le juge n'est alors pas tenu à la demande introductive; dans beaucoup de rapports on constate que le juge peut ordonner la mesure qu'il estime la plus appropriée dans le cas de l'affaire soumise[101]. Kerameus et Polyzogopoulos définissent comme suit l'objectif de la demande introductive: 'Celle-ci a pour seul but d'orienter le tribunal vers la mesure provisoire propice au cas d'espèce'.

L'efficacité de l'intervention du juge qui doit ordonner une mesure provisoire exige que, également en dehors des affaires de divorce, le juge ne soit pas trop strictement lié à la demande introductive. Mais du point de vue de la protection de la partie contre laquelle est requise une mesure provisoire il peut également être souhaitable que le juge ait un certain pouvoir discrétionnaire de sorte qu'il puisse choisir la mesure la moins lourde[102]; il peut par exemple opter pour le dépôt d'une garantie ou pour l'inscription provisoire d'une hypothèque et non pour une saisie conservatoire.

De toutes les informations que nous avons recueillies il ressort toutefois d'une manière générale que le juge est lié à certaines règles même si la loi ne lui impose pas de limitation en ce qui concerne l'étendue des mesures provisoires.

On avance souvent le point de vue que le juge ne peut en aucun cas accorder par une mesure provisoire plus que ne pourrait accorder le juge saisi de la procédure au fond[103]. Mais il faut que le juge ait aussi la possibilité d'accorder moins que ce qui est demandé. Dans ce cas aussi, il devra être conscient du fait qu'il est lié par le caractère spécifique de sa compétence. Le rapporteur belge Lindemans critique dans ce contexte l'attitude des juges qui subordonnent une mesure provisoire à l'introduction dans un certain délai d'une procédure au fond au sujet de leur litige.

En résumé, la question se pose de savoir si d'une manière générale un juge qui prend une mesure provisoire doit être lié ou non par la demande introduite à cet effet.

3.3 USAGE ET ABUS

Comme nous l'avons déjà signalé, on constate dans beaucoup de pays un accroissement du nombre des demandes de mesures provisoires. Selon les données statistiques intéressantes et fort détaillées dans certains rapports, la situation dans quelques pays est stable; dans aucun cas il n'est question d'une régression du nombre de mesures provisoires. Les données diffèrent fortement en ce qui concerne le rapport entre le nombre de mesures provisoires et le nombre

---

101 Matscher, pp. 94, 96; Tarzia, p. 22; Ramoz Mendez, p. 196; Kerameus et Polyzogopoulos, pp. 73-74.

102 L'article 755, deuxième paragraphe du kpc polonais est très clair en la matière: 'Dans son choix des méthodes de garantie, le juge tient compte des intérêts des parties en garantissant les droits du créancier ou en lui offrant une protection suffisante et en n'imposant le débiteur pas plus que nécessaire'.

103 Tarzia, p. 23.

de procédures au fond. Dans certains pays, il y a incontestablement un lien de cause à effet entre l'accroissement du nombre des mesures provisoires et la durée excessive des procédures au fond[104]. Pour d'autres pays par contre, les statistiques ne mettent pas en évidence l'existence d'un tel lien[105]. Il est donc impossible de tirer une conclusion générale en la matière.

Selon certains rapports il ne saurait être question d'un usage abusif des mesures provisoires. On estime dans tous les cas que l'utilisation massive de la mesure provisoire ne saurait en soi être qualifiée d'abus[106]. Les rapporteurs font généralement preuve de compréhension pour ce phénomène et soulignent par exemple que le fait de faire preuve d'une trop grande réserve avantagerait unilatéralement les débiteurs[107].

Dans la mesure où il est question d'abus, on fait surtout allusion aux possibilités d'abus offertes par le législateur. Tarzia met particulièrement l'accent sur les lacunes qui existent dans la réglementation légale en Italie; certains rapporteurs relèvent dans ce contexte le fait que le législateur traite trop à la légère le principe du contradictoire[108]. Même s'il n'existe pas de données statistiques en la matière, il n'en demeure pas moins que nombreux sont ceux qui estiment que le législateur doit prévenir le risque d'abus inhérent à l'inobservation de ce principe fondamental du droit de procédure.

Un 'abus' tout différent relevé à plusieurs reprises est que même les procédures en vue de l'obtention d'une mesure provisoire durent souvent trop longtemps[109].

Cette forme 'd'abus' ne peut pas être mise sur le compte des parties ou du législateur mais uniquement sur le compte des autorités judiciaires par trop surchargées de travail.

3.4 PRINCIPE DU CONTRADICTOIRE

Comme nous l'avons déjà signalé dans le chapitre 1, le terme procédures sommaires désigne des procédures ayant un caractère plus ou moins sommaire et une durée relativement courte en comparaison avec la durée normale des procédures au fond. Selon les conceptions générales, la procédure normale doit satisfaire à un certain nombre d'exigences élémentaires: il doit y avoir un 'jugement équitable'. Le droit à un jugement équitable est pratiquement partout considéré comme un droit fondamental; Schwab et Gottwald ont mis l'accent sur

---

104 Selon les rapports nationaux, c'est le cas en Grèce, en Italie et en Israël.

105 Lindemans (p. 23): 'Cette influence est difficile à prouver mathématiquement'. Ten Berg-Koolen, rapport, p. 15, signale que les données statistiques ne permettent pas de conclure que l'augmentation du nombre de référés est allée au détriment du nombre des procès ordinaries; selon elle, il est plutôt question d'une évolution autonome.

106 Cf. Ferreira da Silva, Lager, Leipold et Lindemans.

107 En particulier Meier, p. 62.

108 Tarzia, rapport p. 21 et suiv.; Lindemans, rapport p. 23 et Leipold, p. 43. Ces auteurs soulignent que les dérogations au principe du contradictoire doivent être limitées au strict nécessaire, ce qui n'est toutefois pas le cas. Leipold estime que l'on peut envisager le cas échéant d'entrer téléphoniquement en contact avec les parties.

109 Notamment Meier, rapport p. 62: 'L'efficacité de ces mesures est le plus souvent compromise par la durée excessive de la procédure'.

ce point dans le rapport général 'Verfassung und Zivilprozess' publié en 1983[110]. Ce droit figure comme tel dans l'article 10 de la Déclaration universelle des droit de l'homme, dans l'article 6, paragraphe 1 de la Convention européenne pour la protection des droits de l'homme et dans le XIVe Amendement à la Constitution des Etats-Unis de l'Amérique du Nord. Bien que dans les divers pays ce droit à un 'jugement équitable' a été concrétisé de façon différente, on admet d'une manière générale que le principe du contradictoire *audi et alteram partem* constitue un élément important de ce droit fondamental.

Le second chapitre de notre rapport a toutefois mis en évidence que des mesures provisoires peuvent souvent être ordonnées *inaudita altera parte*. On est dès lors en droit de se demander si cela ne constitue pas une violation du principe du contradictoire. Nous considérons comme erroné le point de vue adopté par un juge néerlandais selon lequel il ne saurait être question de violation de ce droit basé dans ce cas sur l'effet direct de l'article 6, paragraphe 1 de la Convention européenne pour la protection des droits de l'homme parce qu'une mesure provisoire n'établit pas de droit ou d'obligation mais ne donne à ce sujet qu'un jugement provisoire[111]. Pourtant, une mesure provisoire fixe souvent des droits et des obligations, même si ce n'est qu'à titre temporaire. Schwab et Gottwald sont d'avis qu'en cas de mesures provisoires *inaudita altera parte*, il n'est pas toujours nécessairement question d'une violation du principe du contradictoire parce que:

a) la garantie des intérêts en jeu du demandeur de la mesure provisoire peut exiger une telle marche des affaires et
b) il peut être fait droit au principe du contradictoire après la mesure provisoire[112].

Il découle des informations dont nous disposons que Schwab et Gottwald adoptent en la matière un point de vue général. A l'instar de Tarzia, Lindemans et Leipold[113] il est permis de se demander si le juge n'a pas trop tendance à ignorer le principe du contradictoire lorsqu'il prend une mesure provisoire. Dans la pratique il apparaît que le juge n'apprécie pas toujours de façon approfondie l'intérêt du demandeur et il va de soi qu'en l'absence de la contradiction une telle appréciation peut soulever des problèmes. C'est pour cette raison d'ailleurs qu'en Grèce la possibilité d'obtenir *inaudita altera parte* unilatéralement une mesure provisoire est expressément limitée à des cas exceptionnels[114]. La discussion pourrait donc porter sur la question suivante: Est-il possible d'énumérer de façon limitative les cas dans lesquels au cours d'une procédure visant à une mesure provisoire il est autorisé de faire exception au principe du contradictoire?

Divers rapports signalent également que le juge devrait utiliser plus largement sa compétence d'ordonner le dépôt d'une caution pour les dommages éventuels

---

110 Voir Verfassung und Zivilprozess, rapport général de K.H. Schwab et P. Gottwald, dans 'Effektiver Rechtsschutz und verfassungsmässige Ordnung, Gieseking-Verlag, Bielefeld 1983, pp. 66 et 67.

111 Tribunal de grande instance de La Haye, 12 février 1987, Rechtspraak van de Week in Kort Geding 1987, 129.

112 Voir Verfassung und Zivilprozess (cf. note 110), pp. 67-68.

113 Voir note 108.

114 Voir note 38.

que peut subir le défendeur à la suite de la mesure provisoire[115]. Le juge devrait accorder une attention particulière à cette question certainement lorsqu'il s'agit d'une mesure provisoire *inaudita altera parte*. Bien que d'une manière générale les conséquences d'une mesure provisoire *inaudita altera parte* de la première et de la deuxième catégorie seront moins grandes que celles pouvant résulter d'une mesure provisoire de la troisième catégorie, nous considérons que d'une manière générale la question suivante devrait faire l'objet d'une discussion: Le juge qui ordonne une mesure provisoire *inaudita altera parte* doit-il en principe imposer le dépôt d'une caution pour les dommages éventuels que la mesure provisoire peut entraîner pour le défendeur?

3.5 ADMINISTRATION DE LA PREUVE

Une question intimement liée au principe du contradictoire dans les procédures sommaires est celle qui concerne la possibilité offerte aux deux parties d'étayer leurs prétentions par des preuves. Bien que les réglementations en matière de preuve dans les procédures sommaires diffèrent d'un pays à l'autre - allant des réglementations générales en matière de preuve en Uruguay[116] à une réglementation plus libérale dans la plupart des pays - nous avons constaté que dans la pratique des procédures sommaires on ne pose pas des conditions très strictes à l'administration de la preuve par le demandeur: il devra démontrer la vraisemblance de ses prétentions. Il faut ne jamais perdre de vue que les conditions moins strictes posées en matière de preuve au demandeur de la mesure provisoire ne doivent pas desavantager le défendeur en ce sens que ce dernier soit confronté à un trop grand alourdissement de la charge de la preuve. Mais nous sommes entièrement conscients du fait qu'en raison de la durée limitée dans le temps d'une procédure sommaire il est difficile de tenir toujours en équilibre les intérêts des deux parties. Nous proposons donc de faire porter la discussion sur la question suivante:

L'absence dans ce type de procédure d'une réglementation spéciale en matière de preuve doit-elle être considérée comme une lacune?

3.6 VOIES DE RECOURS

Nous avons déjà relevé auparavant que d'une manière générale les législations des divers pays prevoient des voies de recours.

En ce qui concerne les mesures provisoires obtenues dans le cadre de procédure prevoyant la contradiction, nous pouvons grosso modo distinguer deux possibilités:

a) modification de la mesure en raison de nouveaux faits ou circonstances;
b) l'appel.

La législation de la plupart des pays permet au juge ayant ordonné la mesure provisoire de la modifier. Nous n'avons pas pu constater l'existence de problèmes en la matière. En ce qui concerne la possibilité d'appel on constate

---

115 Cf. notamment Ramos Mendez, pp. 200-201.

116 Greif, rapport, n° 10.

toutefois des différences importantes quant aux possibilités prévues dans les divers pays, à savoir:

a) l'appel n'est pas possible;
b) l'appel n'est possible que simultanément avec le recours contre la décision au principal;
c) l'appel est toujours possible.

Nous n'aborderons pas les possibilités de cassation qui ne presentent pas un intérêt direct dans le cadre de cette étude.

Parmi les trois possibilités citées ci-dessus, celle mentionnée au point a) apparaît, et de loin, comme la moins sympathique. Au sujet de la possibilité d'appel simultanément avec l'appel contre le jugement au fond, Perrot signale: 'A quoi bon un appel lorsque le tribunal aura rendu son jugement définitif si l'on considère que, par hypothèse, ces mesures provisoires sont destinées à ne s'appliquer que durant l'instance? Après, un appel ne sert plus à rien'. Nous partageons en principe le point de vue adopté par Perrot qu'il aurait fallu admettre la possibilité d'un appel immédiat dans tous les cas[117].

A tous ceux qui sont néanmoins partisans d'une limitation des possibilités d'appel, nous soumettons la suggestion de Leipold[118] de combiner en partie les moyens de recours et également la procédure en matière de mesures provisoires avec la procédure au fond. Cette même idée a été lancée aux Pays-Bas en 1985 par H.J. Snijders[119].

3.7 LA MESURE PROVISOIRE, UN DROIT?

Lors du Septième Congrès mondial de droit procédural tenu en 1983, K.H. Schwab et P. Gottwald ont déjà souligné le rapport entre les mesures provisoires et le droit à une protection juridique effective[120]. On peut penser dans ce contexte au principe de l'état de droit ou à un droit constitutionnel explicite ou encore à l'article 6 de la Convention européenne pour la protection des droits de l'homme. Divers rapporteurs ont souligné l'existence d'un lien avec l'un ou l'autre de ces principes[121]. Cela nous amène à poser la question de savoir si d'une manière générale le droit fondamental à ce que la cause soit entendue par un juge indépendant qui d'une manière ou d'une autre est ancré dans la

117 Perrot, pp. 160-161.

118 Leipold, rapport, pp. 44-45.

119 H.J. Snijders, Troubles en doubles in het burgerlijk procesrecht, Kluwer 1985. Snijders propose que le juge qui est appelé à ordonner une mesure provisoire obtienne la possibilité de declarer que sa décision est un jugement au fond lorsque, à son avis, l'affaire ne nécessite plus aucun examen substantiel au fond. L'appel et la cassation sont ensuite dirigés contre ce jugement au fond de sorte que les doublures des mesures provisoires et des causes principales dans plusieurs instances soient limitées autant que possible.

120 Voir Verfassung und Zivilprozess, rapport général de K.H. Schwab et P. Gottwald (cf. note 110), pp. 66-67.

121 Cf. Kerameus et Polyzogopoulos, p. 85; Matscher, p. 109; Leipold, pp. 9 et 40; Varano et Proto Pisani, p. 45. En Suisse où le droit de procédure relève en principe les cantons, des directives écrites et non écrites de droit confédéral s'appliquent sur la base de considérations analogues; cf. Meier, chapitre III.2.

législation des divers pays, entraîne également un droit à une mesure provisoire dans l'hypothèse où les circonstances justifient une telle mesure. Sans mesure provisoire adéquate, ce droit fondamental deviendra rapidement un droit illusoire. Le présent rapport permet d'ailleurs de conclure qu'en soi les mesures provisoires répondent à tous les critères qui s'appliquent généralement aux jugements.

Lorsque le système juridique d'un pays n'autorise pas une mesure provisoire déterminée, le demandeur a probablement peu de chances de succès en invoquant l'existence d'un droit à une telle mesure provisoire en vertu des droits fondamentaux. La discussion fondamentale de cette question peut, à supposer qu'elle débouche sur un résultat concret, être néanmoins utile aux législateurs des pays qui envisagent d'introduire une réglementation plus étendue en matière de procédure sommaire. Si l'on admet que le droit à une mesure provisoire découle du droit à une protection juridique effective, il est difficile de soutenir que ce droit ne s'appliquerait uniquement qu'à certaines mesures provisoires et non par exemple à des mesures provisoires ayant un caractère plus ou moins définitif. Nous considérons comme trop stricte la conception selon laquelle des possibilités légales de mesures provisoires ne doivent pas être crées en tant que remède à la lenteur et à la durée des procédures au fond[122]. Par le fait de refuser sur cette base la création de certaines mesures provisoires (par exemple pour les créances) on risque de sacrifier les intérêts légitimes du demandeur pour une utopie, à savoir celle d'une procédure allant jusqu'au fond et qui est en même temps rapide. Dans ce contexte, Leipold et Perrot soulignent à juste titre que les possibilités d'accélérer les procédures au fond sont limitées[123].

Reconnaître ce fait revient à ne pas rejeter d'emblée la recherche de solutions pragmatiques, conscient du fait que la fonction première du droit de procédure est de servir la pratique judiciaire[124]. Dans la pratique, la rapidité de la procédure revêt un intérêt de plus en plus grand. La discussion ne doit pas non plus porter sur la question de savoir s'il est autorisé de rendre rapidement un jugement lorsque les droits et faits sont évidents et ne sont pas sérieusement contestés mais plutôt de savoir dans quelle mesure, dans quelles conditions et en présence de quelles garanties cette possibilité doit être offerte. En posant cette question, nous abandonnons en fait le terrain de la mesure provisoire et entrons dans le domaine de la *summary non-provisional relief*[125]. Il appartiendra à un prochain congrès mondial de déterminer s'il existe également un droit à un tel recours.

QUESTIONS A LA SUITE DU RAPPORT GENERAL

1. Est-il utile ou souhaitable de prévoir une possibilité générale permettant de demander une mesure provisoire à caractère exclusivement régulateur, indépendamment de l'introduction d'une procédure au fond? (3.1)

---

122 Voir à ce sujet Goldstein, p. 101, Kerameus et Polyzogopoulos, pp. 85-86; Matscher, p. 109.

123 Leipold, rapport, p. 42; Perrot, p. 179.

124 Cf. également les considérations finales de Tarzia, dans le livre cité dans la note 3, pp. 309 et suiv., en particulier p. 312.

125 Cf. Proto Pisani et Varano, rapport, p. 44.

2. Dans quelle mesure l'urgence doit-elle être une condition à l'obtention d'une décision judiciaire dans une procédure sommaire? (3.1)

3. Doit-il être possible d'une manière générale d'anticiper sur le jugement au fond par une mesure provisoire? Dans l'affirmative, une procédure qui suit celle du référé-provision français ou de l'usage rapide du droit évident suisse est-elle une variante acceptable et utilisable? (3.1)

4. Doit-il être possible d'ordonner par mesure provisoire une injonction ou une interdiction en tant que simple mesure d'ordre, même en l'absence d'une base juridique (par exemple un acte illicite ou la menace d'un tel acte)? (3.1)

5. Le juge qui ordonne la mesure provisoire doit-il d'une manière générale être lié ou non à la demande introduite à cet effet par le demandeur? (3.2)

6. Est-il possible d'énumérer de façon limitative les cas dans lesquels au cours d'une procédure visant à une mesure provisoire il est admis de faire exception au principe du contradictoire? (3.4)

7. Le juge qui ordonne une mesure provisoire *inaudita altera parte* doit-il en principe imposer au demandeur le dépôt d'une caution pour le dommage éventuel que peut subir le défendeur à la suite d'une telle mesure? (3.4)

8. L'absence d'une réglementation spéciale en ce qui concerne l'administration de la preuve dans cette procédure doit-elle être considérée comme une lacune? (3.5)

9. Dans quelle mesure des voies de recours doivent être ouvertes contre les mesures provisoires? (3.6)

10. Le droit fondamental à ce que la cause soit entendue par un juge indépendant entraîne-t-il d'une manière générale l'existence d'un droit à une mesure provisoire, en admettant que les circonstances du cas justifient en soi une telle mesure? (3.7)

REPORT OF THE DISCUSSION

Chairman: *C.H. Ferreira da Silva (Portugal)*
Vice-chairman: *A. Aguda (Nigeria)*
Secretary: *J. ten Berg-Koolen (the Netherlands)*

The discussionpoints are to be found at page 400.

The basis for the discussion, which was led by prof. C. Ferreira da Silva, was formed by the General Report on this subject by prof. Mr P.A.M. Meijknecht and Mr R.Ch. Verschuur. At the end of their report they had formulated ten discussion points, which all came up for more or less detailed discussion.

The debate concentrated on those summary proceedings which end in a provisional judicial measure. Such proceedings were found to exist in all legal systems; their application is also steadily increasing everywhere. Generally, a connection is assumed between this increased use and the long duration of the ordinary procedure. As a result of the increase in provisional measures, the ordinary proceedings are losing ground; one or two people feared that they will be completely superseded. Yet nobody reported actual abuse of summary proceedings.

The rapporteurs had raised the important question whether the fundamental right to a judicial decision implies the right to obtain a provisional measure as well. The meeting did not express a clear opinion on this issue. It was pointed out, however, that in certain circumstances a provisional measure might well be the only way in which legal protection can be effected. This is also true for the future; reducing the long duration of ordinary proceedings will be possible to a certain extent only. It was also put forward that refusal of a requested provisional measure does not mean that consequently the court is not intervening; a refusal implies protection of the defendant and sanctioning of an existing - possibly unlawful - situation. Therefore, the court must not be too wary of granting a requested provisional measure.

A warning was expressed, in particular by the participants from France, against the dangers which the wide use of summary proceedings may entail. Preferably, provisional measures should be pronounced by judges with special qualifications and great experience, in order to avoid incorrect decisions. One must, moreover, bear in mind that a provisional measure may in practice become a final decision. In cases in which the temporary custody of a child is to be decided, it may be a considerable time before a final decision can be taken; in such case the court will not easily give a different decision in the main proceedings. Besides, the parties may also decide not to go through with the main proceedings.

Furthermore, the possibility was discussed of ordering a provisional measure in the absence of a - specific - legal ground therefor. Such order was held to be acceptable in exceptional cases only; in any case great caution is required. The same applies to the ordering of provisional measures which have not been applied for. Before ordering such measures, the judge should at least discuss this with the parties; a provisional measure which is desired by neither plaintiff nor defendant is of no use whatsoever.

Another issue which came up for discussion was the question whether urgent interest is necessarily a condition for ordering a provisional measure. Urgency proved to be held of less importance than the apparent need for the requested provisional measure.

Attention was paid, furthermore, to the question whether it is warranted- e.g. in connection with the urgency of the claim - not to hear the other party; the general opinion was that this is acceptable only in exceptional cases. In any case the defendant who has not been heard must in some way or other have the opportunity to take objection to the measure as soon as possible after it has been granted.

Subsequently, the discussion turned to the consequences if the decision in the main proceedings goes against the provisional measure; there is the danger that the execution of the provisional measure will have created an irreversible situation. This risk can be obviated by ordering the party applying for a provisional measure to give security, e.g. in the form of a deposit; the difficulty is precisely that often the plaintiff in question will not be in a position to do so.

Finally, the question was discussed whether it must always be possible to appeal from a provisional measure. An important factor in this connection is the question whether the execution of the measure will be suspended by the appeal, which may badly impair the effectiveness of the measure. Besides, several of the participants emphasized the fact that the possibility of appeal is very important, particularly in cases involving children.

Summarizing: the outcome of the discussions appeared to be that summary proceedings for obtaining provisional measures, if wisely applied, constitute an important and welcome complement to the arsenal of ordinary proceedings. It was also proposed to put up the subject for discussion again at a subsequent conference.

THE USE OF TECHNOLOGY AND INFORMATICS IN COURT ADMINISTRATION

INFORMATION TECHNOLOGY AND COURT ADMINISTRATION

A.W. Koers
Professor law faculty, Utrecht

W.D. Pelger
Manager Berenschot Informatica, Utrecht

CONTENTS

1 SCOPE OF PAPER

Due to unforeseen circumstances the request to organize the session on 'The Use of Technology and Informatics in Court Administration' was received by us at a rather late stage (February 1987). Caution should have made us decline the request, but we decided to undertake the task anyway in view of our interest in the topic and its importance. If, however, the reader finds fault with this paper, he or she is kindly asked to keep in mind the restrictions of time - and length! - under which it had to be prepared.

In February 1987 the information base available to us was rather small. We therefore decided to send out a questionnaire to a number of individuals in Europe and North America, asking them to answer a range of questions on information systems in court administration in their respective countries - and this at rather short notice. We wish to express our gratitude for the co-operation we received.

Apart from the information collected through the questionnaires we also made use of the materials presented to the 'Fifth Colloquy on the Use of Computers in the Administration of Justice', organized by the Council of Europe from 14-

17 October 1986 at Madrid. We are grateful that these materials were made available to us.

As to this paper's structure: in part 2 we examine in a rather freewheeling fashion the impacts - present and future - of information technology on court administration. Part 3 then provides an analysis of the developments and trends as they emerge from the answers to our questionnaire and the documents of the Council of Europe. Part 4 concludes the paper with some final observations.

With this paper we hope to serve two objectives: (a) to contribute towards a better understanding of the potential and the pitfalls of applying information technology to court administration; and (b) to provide a basis for productive discussions at the Conference.

2 IMPACTS OF INFORMATION TECHNOLOGY

So far, automation has not yet made a large-scale appearance in the world of justice, neither to facilitate administrative matters nor in the actual judiciary.

Therefore the experience acquired in other sectors with both computers and software will be of use. It might even serve to predict future changes where the function of computer technology in the area of justice is concerned.

We shall provide a description of the developments in 4 stages, which can be briefly characterized as follows:

stage 1: the first system
stage 2: subsequent systems
stage 3: application on a larger scale
stage 4: 'first' mature stage.

STAGE 1. THE FIRST SYSTEM

Inspired by the fast and accurate data processing capabilities of computers, one would like to apply this technology to carry out large-scale routine work.

The pioneering quality of the very first implementation of computers in a particular area may be seen in the following: a limited number of mainly technically oriented specialists tackle a specific, isolated problem. Attention is concentrated exclusively on this problem, and especially on design of the necessary software.

This process alone usually causes quite enough difficulties. The struggle to translate administrative procedures into a systematized analysis fit for computer consumption is a hard one. After all, computers do not really think, and all sorts of things which are obvious to a human need to be explicitly clarified to a machine. People do not make appointments to meet yesterday; with computers, that 'possibility' needs to be explicitly excluded.

The introduction of the first application poses many different problems:

- Technical problems.
  Programme stopping, wrong calculations, lengthy response times, missing files etc. (a more detailed or extensive enumeration of technical difficulties is not relevant here).

- Problems of a functional nature.
  Limited or incorrect applicability: it may become apparent that the computer (actually: the software) is unable to perform certain tasks which were possible with the old system, and is moreover inadequate in its execution of other jobs. Hindsight will then tell us that this is not at all remarkable. After all, the users of the system will have had hardly any part in the definition of its specifications and functional requirements. Emphasis has been placed mostly on the difficulties of the technical aspects: programming and operating the computer.

- Organization, education and training.
  In many cases, new computer systems were applied first of all in an effort to simplify matters that were causing great problems on a day-to-day basis. Automation was thought to be the solution to everything. We now know that computerization of chaos leads to double chaos or worse. But even where there was no chaos the introduction of computers caused great changes, not only of a procedural nature, but also where the importance, size and difficulty of the jobs was concerned.
  Insufficient (or total absence of) anticipation gave rise to great problems, not to mention the fact that employees need training to be able to work with the new system.
  Even if this is taken into consideration, the time and effort that is required is usually very much underestimated.

After an eventful period, entailing considerable delay, the first application will generally have become operational. Enormous effort, irritation and drastic measures serve to create temporary solutions to the problems mentioned above. The result is a far cry from that which was originally envisaged. The users of the system acquire a feeling for its peculiarities; the sense of dissatisfaction remains, in spite of the advantages of the new excuse: 'it is the computer's fault'. After a while, the new system is seen to be better than no system: an encouraging thought, which leads to the tackling of new projects, and so to stage 2.

STAGE 2. SUBSEQUENT SYSTEMS

In this stage the set-up of automation projects becomes somewhat more professional. One's own mistakes will have proved to be of educational value, and during seminars teachers will have elucidated the proper ways of approach. Last but not least a visit may have been organized by (potential) suppliers to some company or other, during which the success story of that company will have been extensively reviewed.

Steering committees and workgroups are set up, aiming to increase the extent to which future users can be involved in specifying their new systems. Anticipation, where the implementation of those systems is concerned, will therefore improve.

However, it is a rare thing, on the whole, to find users of large-scale applications who have the ability and the necessary knowledge of present day technologies to envisage future, computerized situations.

If such people can be found, it will prove to be practically impossible to reserve their capacities for the purpose of a automation project, or to have their ideas accepted by the project group and the management.

This implies that the involvement of top level management constitutes one important factor with regard to the success of automation projects. The management should show initiative, should make the right people available for the job, should be actively engaged in planning at management level, and therefore be able to take the right decisions at important moments, and be able to provide effective leadership and guidance during the introduction process.

A large measure of common sense is another, very useful, contribution which the management can make, rather than fear and/or unbridled enthusiasm. Another problem, in many cases, is the role played by the computer expert, who will often be labouring under the impression that his or her expertise is a licence to tell others exactly what the computer can do and dictate how it should be used in a particular situation. This sort of recommendations is rarely supported by the necessary empathy with the users' situation; most often, the users do not (yet) put up sufficient resistance, and so help to lay the foundation for inadequate new systems. In those cases where users are able to provide counterpressure, an unpleasant atmosphere will often result. Nevertheless, practice shows that the latter situations (if there is sufficient ability on both sides) may give rise to a particular synergy which will lead to a successful automation project.

Another thing which may cause dissatisfaction is consistent overoptimistic planning and its corollary, budget deficits. The danger here is that, in order to comply with the plans, one may decide to round off the definition stage and the functional design stage although the investigations may be (as yet) too shallow. On paper, anything will work; however, during the testing or, worse, when the systems have been introduced, the user will pay as the deficiencies become apparent.

Computer applications, during this stage as well as in the first, tend to be approached in isolation; the systems are insufficiently interrelated. As soon as several different systems have become operational, one is confronted with the fact that there is no possibility to exchange data; confronted with the fact that there may be different definitions to indicate the same concept, and there may be one name to refer to several different quantities (such as price, cost price, factory price, stock price, retail price, standard price etc.).

The acceptance of the system will increase in proportion to its success, and dislike and fear on the part of its users will change into active participation, and the launching of ideas towards improvement and innovation.

In general, applications concern routine processes. In this way, manual operations of a repetitive nature are taken over by the computer. The result is a considerable efficiency improvement: the requirements in terms of (hu)manpower and processing time will have substantially decreased. Moreover, the constant accuracy of the computer ensures a considerable decrease of the number of mistakes, and therefore the quality of the output will be higher. These results have generally been used to realize a large increase in the number of transactions, eg. in banking, travel reservations etc.

STAGE 3. APPLICATION ON A LARGER SCALE

In this stage the organization learns to make better use of computers and acquires better control. User participation becomes a normal thing; users of computer systems start to take initiatives; new applications will be proposed, and the number of proposals for improvement of the systems that are already in use will steadily increase. Causes are: poor efficiency (as indicated above), the lack of integration of the different systems, and changes in the running of the company which have a bearing on the computerized systems.

In most companies automation is anything but a smooth process. Top level management is not always successful in its leadership; necessary improvements to the systems in operation may be more and more postponed (the automation departments' maintenance backlog may involve more than 2 years' work); dealing successfully with the rapid developments in the field of computer technology is a difficult thing. The scarcity of well-trained automation personnel does not improve the situation.

In this stage the applications concern more than just routine aspects. The computer will now be trusted to take certain simple decisions. For example, the computer orders replacements as soon as stocks have fallen below a certain level. Clearly, this attitude of trust needs to grow. During the first stage the computer was certainly not trusted to such an extent: one even kept duplicate accounts to be able to check the computer. The mere idea that the computer could be used to take such decisions seemed very far off. All kinds of matters were brought up, of which it was said that they would never occur to a computer, but certainly would to a human intelligence. That may have been right at the time, but it was exactly this process which gradually caused solutions to be found to those problems, so that the capacities of computers could be used to the full. Automatic ordering of fresh supplies, for example, proved feasible if the computer first generated a provisional order, which the buyer would then only have to read through and correct in special cases, such as special offers, obsolete products etc.

This meant that most calculations, and the responsibility of accurate stockkeeping were left to the computer. It is hardly necessary to say that, at first, all kinds of things went wrong: supplies, ordered by the computer and delivered before the purchase department had had even a chance to see the order; orders cancelled by the computer because payment for previous deliveries had not yet come through; automatic issue of reminders while - terrible, this- deliveries had not yet been completed, and many, many other examples, all proving the creed that 'automation means organization'.

Furthermore, this stage shows the beginnings of so-called management information. The fact that many operational data were now on file as a result of computerization caused the awareness that these data can also be used for management purposes.

In the first instance these data serve to monitor, quickly and effectively, all current affairs. The monitoring process does, however, require a highly accurate definition of the information concerned.

This is anything but simple, and it often goes wrong: once per day, per week or per month office desks in many companies are covered with great stacks of paper which appear as management information, only to be carried out again, unread, as waste paper.

The next step is to include this data in simulations of future scenarios; a forn of use which heralds the next stage of computer use for management decisioı taking on several levels.

In this stage companies of all kinds are willing to start working witł standard packages. Independent software suppliers develop material to suit many companies which make use of rather similar processes. These software packages can then be used by different companies (which, of course, have to pay for each separate package).

Another characteristic element during this stage is the growing awareness of the need for integration of related systems. Systems built during this stage are usually designed to meet the requirements towards this end. In this respect, the many shortcomings of systems built during earlier stages constitute as many obstacles which, for a long time, make it impossible to realize full-scale integration of data systems on a desirable level. In order to realize the necessary integration, special programmes are built and existing systems are altered.

STAGE 4. THE 'FIRST' MATURE STAGE

In the title of this section the word 'first' is put between inverted commas because Information Technology itself has not yet evolved beyond its initial stage of development.

This means that, in time, many different forms of information technology will be applied by companies and organizations.

That which is seen to be mature according to present day views and experience may be seen in a totally different light in 5 to 10 years time.

During this stage information technology is used in accordance with a policy which is formed on the basis of the company's aims and which includes all data facilities.

A division is made between the computer(-technology) and the actual data (which may in turn be split up into the actual applications on the one hand and data management on the other).

Users will be less and less concerned with technical aspects, in the same way as they do not have to bother about the telephone exchange for making telephonecalls. The decision which applications must be stand alone and which are to be integrated will be taken on the basis of the policy mentioned above.

Questions of centralization and decentralization are also decided within the framework of that policy.

In this stage integration of several new techniques takes place, for instance document processing. In the judicial world document processing will be highly applicable, though the problem of the legal validity of such documents may delay the introduction for quite some time.

Meanwhile, users will have become very well informed as to what automation can do for them, and what it cannot. Their contribution to the planning of new systems (really new, or renovations) meets the demands, both qualitatively and quantitatively speaking, to be able to build and introduce good information systems.

This stage too has its various problems (in additions to general human problems) in spite of its 'maturity'. For example: limited staff capacity in relation to the number of changes that have to be implemented (backlog); the users' own developments; the position of the central automation department and its apparently degenerating attitudes where service is concerned; incompatibility of new and existing equipment; the introduction of new - fourth generation-languages in order to achieve quicker system development, in combination with old systems written in old languages; limited documentation with regard to existing systems; ageing of computer staff.

CONCLUSION

The above descriptions of the learning process with regard to the introduction of automation serve above all to indicate that such a process exists and to show stereotype mistakes which may now be avoided. Scientific publications in this field also indicate that the various stages of growth must be passed through. The mistakes of one company department, it seems, sometimes need to be repeated by other departments within the same company. For example, we have seen companies which had passed through all four stages where the administrative side was concerned, but it emerged that in the automation of their production process they had bought robots without taking into account the production environment as a whole, without drawing up their own specifications first, entirely depending upon the information provided by the supplier of the machines; not to mention neglect of organizational aspects, and training and education of the relevant personnel.

Nevertheless, the writers of this report hope that it will be possible for the judicial system to profit from the fact that it has been relatively lagging behind (technologically) in that it will avoid a number of the mistakes we mentioned, and so suffer fewer disappointments while developing towards the fourth stage.

3 DEVELOPMENTS AND TRENDS

3.1 THE DATA BASE

Although the response to the questionnaires was quite satisfactory considering the deadlines imposed by us on the respondees, it must be acknowledged that it did not result in a data base of sufficient quality for presenting a complete and reliable picture of the developments and trends in the use of information technology in court administration in Europe and North America. A principal shortcoming is that there remain great differences among countries in the information available to us: of some countries we received a wealth of information, while for others the picture is still sketchy, or even blank.

We think that these differences are mainly due to our success - or lack thereof - in reaching the right individuals. Accordingly, if in the following paragraphs some countries are only briefly discussed - or even not mentioned at all - this must not be interpreted as an indication that they are less active.

Finally, it was not always clear to us if - or to what extent - there were overlaps between the answers received from different sources within the same country. Time did not permit us to check with the respondees.

These observations imply that the following should be understood for what it is: an incomplete and subjective thumbnail sketch of a field that is rapidly changing every day. A planned follow-up should improve the data base, thus making a more in-depth analysis possible in future publications.

3.2 SURVEY

Canada

In Canada a large number of projects have been - and are being - implemented, both at the federal and the provincial level. In fact, the number of projects on which information was received, was so large that it is not possible here to discuss them all with the degree of detail they deserve.

The Canadian Supreme Court is in the process of establishing a case management system. Its primary functions will be:

a. court docket maintenance
b. response to inquiries
c. case monitoring and control
d. court scheduling
e. management and statistical reporting.

The project is still in the design phase, but for hardware a minicomputer is anticipated.

At the provincial level there are already several systems in operation. This is the case with:

a. the 'Alberta Court Automated Information System'
b. the 'British Columbia Court Management Information System'
c. the 'Ontario Provincial Court Information System'
d. the 'Quebec Court Information System'
e. the 'Saskatchewan Justice Automated Information Network'.

Most of these systems were developed in the period 1975 to 1982, but they continue to evolve. As a general rule they were first established in the criminal law field (especially at the high volume provincial courts) and they were expanded to the area of civil law only where the number of cases justified such action.

Generally, the main functions of these systems are:

a. to identify the current status of cases
b. to increase throughput and efficiency
c. to improve the scheduling of cases
d. to improve the capacity (in terms of quality and quantity) for the production of documents.

The more recently established systems place greater emphasis on the management information component (e.g., workload and statistics). The Quebec system is unique in that it provides access to (parts of) the system to law firms and even the public at large through terminals. So far most systems operate at the level of a single (high case-load) court, with the largest systems (British Columbia and Quebec) handling 2 to 3 million cases a year. As to hardware: mainframe computers are being used or installed.

Under development are:

a. the 'Alberta Criminal Justice System'
b. the 'Newfoundland Law Courts Information System'
c. the 'Nova Scotia Provincial Court Information System'
d. the 'Ontario Supreme Court (York County) Information System'
e. a system at the Federal Court of Canada.

Although each of these systems has certain unique characteristics, they fall within the same overall class as the systems outlined above.

The above survey is far from complete. There are, for example, a number of systems (operational or under development) to keep track of financial activities. This may relate to the payment of fines (e.g., the 'Summary Offence System' of the Department of the Attorney General of Nova Scotia), as well as to other financial obligations resulting from a court decision (e.g. New Brunswick's 'Maintenance and Enforcement System' in respect of court ordered family support).

Insofar as systems are operational they appear well accepted, although it is noted that the importance of initial and follow-up training must not be underestimated. In some cases it was necessary to alter the administrative procedures of the court involved.

Finally, the Canadian Centre for Justice Statistics supports the development of court administration systems by providing subject matter and technical assistance.

Belgium

In the area of court administration Belgium has a project on the 'Automation of Crown Counsels' Offices and Registries of the Police Courts'. In early 1985 certain elements of this system became operational. So far the system runs on minicomputer equipment and it makes use of data communication facilities.

One operational element of the system concerns the management and supervision of the payments of fines for traffic offenses for the cities of Brussels, Nivelles and Namur. So far the system deals only with the out-of-court settlement of traffic offenses by the offices of the Crown Counsel, but there are plans to expand the scope of the system to other areas (on-the-spot fines; the serving of summonses and judgments).

Another operational element deals with the management of files holding information on persons accused of crimes. So far pilot projects have been undertaken at Namur and Ghent, but it is anticipated to expand these systems, both geographically and functionally.

More comprehensive plans were developed when the Belgian government, in 1984, allocated about 280 million francs towards a plan of the Ministry of Justice to equip the judiciary with an integrated data processing and office automation system.

As a first step a pilot project will be carried out at the Brussels Court of Appeal. This project is designed to set up a comprehensive system of word processing, data processing and data communication in the offices of the Crown Counsels, the registries of the criminal, civil and juvenile court sections and the central police records office.

The final systems analysis reports were submitted in September 1986 and (elements of) the system are to become operational in 1987.

The implementation of this project will require certain changes in the organizational structure and/or administrative procedures. Certain data will be open to lawyers and the public.

Federal Republic of Germany

Several systems are in operation in the Federal Republic of Germany and many more are in various stages of implementation. It is not possible here to discuss all these systems and projects and a brief description of some must suffice.

The Federal Court for Social Matters introduced automation as early as 1973. At present the Court uses information technology for a range of purposes:

a. to provide documentation and information services
b. the processing of the text of decisions
c. to generate input for the 'Juris' legal data bank
d. photosetting
e. the processing of litigation fees
f. to generate statistics
g. the mailing of decisions.

These applications were developed by employees of the Court in direct cooperation with the judges and they are continuously being expanded. The Court has its own minicomputer.

In the Federal Republic the responsibility for the administration of the courts rests with the states ('Länder'), the federal government being responsible only for the federal courts.

Some examples of systems/projects at the state-level:

a. the administration of fees and other financial aspects of civil procedures
b. the administration and control of prison sentences (including statistics)
c. the support of public prosecutors in cases concerning white collar crime.

Some of these systems have been developed under a cost-benefit sharing arrangement with other states.

The 'Sojus' project is designed to result in a (minicomputer based) system for case registration and tracking, first in respect of civil law and at a later stage for criminal law. There also are functions for document production, the generation of statistics and data communication. A prototype is operational and the system is available for other courts.

Finland

The Ministry of Justice operates (on a central mainframe computer) a system for the enforcement of summary penal orders. The system also provides statistical and management information.

Under development is a 'Judgement Pronouncement and Payment Collection System' which is aimed at:

a. collecting data concerning decisions in criminal cases
b. the collection of fines and damages
c. generating statistics.

The system provides judges with on-screen reminders of matters to be covered in their decisions. The system is operational at five courts and the plans call for expanding it to approximately 100 courts in the early 90's. It operates on a central mainframe computer connected to remote terminals.

One court of appeal and about ten lower courts use a microcomputer based system for word processing and data processing (case registration), both for the purpose of improving efficiency and for the purpose of providing management information. These systems are linked to the central information system of the Ministry of Justice. Plans call for expansion to all the courts.

France

Under the guidance of a 'Schema Directeur de l'Informatique 1984-1988' the French Ministry of Justice has undertaken an ambitious plan to introduce information technology in the judicial system. Some figures illustrate that so far the execution of this plan has had most significant results:

- In the period 1981 to 1986 the budget for computer equipment increased by 185 percent.
- In the same period the number of special word processing units increased from 25 to more than 300, while in addition approximately 160 microcomputers, 40 minicomputers and 140 data bank terminals were installed.
- It is estimated that at present productivity increases each year by six percent, whereas before it was limited to three percent.

From these few figures it can also be deduced that within the scope of this paper it is not possible to even mention all the activities that have been undertaken. Therefore, some general observations must suffice.

At the 'Cour de Cassation' integrated systems of word processing and data processing have been installed to handle the administration of cases and decisions. Additionally, the GIMO (Gestion Intellectuelle des Moyens) system is designed to ensure the consistency of decisions. These systems utilise a central mainframe computer at Versailles, a linked minicomputer at the 'Cour' and several terminals or stand-alone microcomputers.

The largest 'Cours d'Appel' have been provided with systems (hardware: minicomputers) to automate the principal functions of the administration of civil cases, including the production of documents and the generation of statistical data. Plans are being implemented to establish links between these systems and those of the Bar.

At the level of the 'Tribunaux de grande instance' a number of projects have also been realized. In the Paris region systems have been established for the administration of criminal cases and the production of documents and statistics. These systems utilize the central mainframe computer at Versailles, as well as linked minicomputers and they process large volumes of data (about 700.000 cases a year). The larger 'Tribunals' outside the Paris region have been equipped with similar systems (also for civil cases) on minicomputers. At the smaller 'Tribunals' microcomputers are used for the administration of civil and criminal cases.

The 'Tribunaux d'instance' use microcomputers for civil cases, while at the 'Conseils de prud'hommes' microcomputers are used for personnel management and the registration of cases.

Somewhat outside the area of court administration, but interesting nevertheless, are systems for the registration of the sentences imposed throughout

France (at the 'Casier judiciaire national') and for the administration of the penal system. Finally, access to legal data banks (of which there are many in France) has become universal.

Great Britain

Responsibility for the courts in England and Wales rests with the Home Office and the Lord Chancellor's Department. So far two systems in the area of court administration have become operational, while another two systems are in the design stage.

Of the 630 Magistrate Courts in England and Wales about 200 have now introduced computerization, mostly without central coordination. The systems so developed cover most aspects of the administration of the courts, both in relation to the pre-adjudication and the post-adjudication phase.

They also aid in the production of documents. In some cases the introduction of these systems had a minimal effect on working procedures, while in other cases computerization was used to make changes.

Also operational are microcomputer based systems at a number of the 260 County Courts in England and Wales. These systems are used for monitoring case flow, the production of documents and accounting. New software is introduced so as to enhance their functionality.

Under development is the 'Claims Registry' system. This system would automate the routine administrative work at the County Courts in connection with claims for fixed amounts. The system would produce summonses; receive the replies of defendants; enter the judgment; and administer any payments due. Also under development is a system to provide computer support to the Crown Court (which deals with the more serious crimes and which operates through about 70 regional offices in England and Wales). This system is designed to:

a. administer pending cases
b. produce documents and court orders
c. support the scheduling of cases and accounting
d. provide management information.

Introduction of both systems is scheduled at the end of the decade.

In Scotland the Procurator Fiscal Service operates in Glasgow a criminal tracking system for record keeping, management information and document production. The system utilizes a minicomputer and it is to be introduced in Edinburgh in 1987. Under development are systems for legal research (access to legal data banks) and for supporting the staff of the Scottish Sheriff Courts in the handling of criminal cases.

In Northern Ireland the Crown Court uses an automated system for the recording of evidence (evidence is encoded on tape and then transcribed by computer). There are plans for computerization in respect of the enforcement of judgments and the registration of cases before the Belfast Magistrates' Court.

Ireland

In Ireland priority was given to the District Court level in view of the large volume of cases at that level. Using a minicomputer a case registration system has been set up that supports not only daily operations (such as: the issue of summonses, the scheduling of hearings, court records of decisions, the issue of fines notices and fines warrants), but also long term management and policy decisions. The data stored in the system may be retrieved in a variety of formats so as to suit specific needs.

The system was initially established for the Dublin area and it made it possible to accommodate a significant increase in summonses applications as a result of the appointment of additional police officers and traffic wardens in Dublin. The system is now being extended to the Provinces.

For the higher level courts feasibility studies are being conducted:

a. for the Circuit Court on an automated system for the preparation of court orders, lists of jurors and court hearings
b. for the High Court on a system for the processing of civil cases, the filing and retrieving of documents and the electronic recording and reproduction of oral evidence
c. for the Supreme Court on introducing some elements of the High Court system.

Italy

In 1982 the Italian Ministry of Justice set up a special office for the introduction of information technology in the legal services; a coordinating committee was also established. Since then a number of systems have been implemented, both centralized and distributed.

As to centralized systems: apart from the well-known legal data bank of the Supreme Court, a feasibility study has been carried out with a view towards automating that Court's civil and criminal administrative procedures. This study should result in an operational system in 1987.

Another centralized system concerns the 'Judicial Records Office' and its branches throughout the country. It is designed to issue the criminal record of every individual in real time through terminals installed in each of the 159 State Prosecutors' Offices. Ultimately, every Italian may be able to obtain his or her criminal record directly through terminals open to the public.

The 'Prison Population Register' - another centralized information system- not only deals with prison admission registers, but also with financial and administrative matters (including prisoners' wage payments).

The Ministry itself operates a system for managing information relating to examinations, elections, career profiles and the workload of the various courts.

In the area of distributed systems work is in progress on the setting up of legal data banks (especially in respect of commercial law) and the administration of civil and criminal cases in specific courts. In the Rome region this has resulted in a Data Processing Centre under the responsibility of the President of the Rome Appeal Court.

Also in the distributed category fall the systems set up in offices dealing with the prosecution of organized crime (minicomputer based). In other instances microcomputer based systems are being used to facilitate the handling of information and documentation in the preparation of specific criminal cases. At the local level there are also operational systems for managing criminal records and suits pending against individuals. Lastly, the Genoa Judicial Records Interregional Centre collects statistics on caseloads, by subject matter and by judge.

In Italy the Juvenile Courts are considered autonomous, which has had an effect on the introduction of information technology. A first experiment on automating the functions of the courts' clerk has been completed successfully.

Luxembourg
Luxembourg is introducing a system for the administration of criminal cases throughout all stages of the procedure. The system is operational insofar as traffic offenses are concerned.

The Netherlands
Apart from the introduction of word processing, the Netherlands took its first steps towards the use of information technology in the administration of justice in October 1978: the 'Interim Fines Collection System' became operational in that month. The various Public Prosecutors' Offices and the Central Fines Collection Office (responsible for the collection of fines) send data to a government computer centre, which then produces the necessary documents, tables and notifications. The collection of fines is also monitored. The system was updated in 1983.

During the 70's the provision of legal aid grew very rapidly, both in term of cases handled (from 40.000 assignments in 1970 to almost 250.000 in 1980) and in terms of the cost to the government (from 45 million guilders in 1975 to some 240 million in 1985). Thus, a system was set up to monitor the form, nature and costs of legal aid. Data are entered at the local level and processed at a government computer centre. The Ministry of Justice is using the system as a management and policy-making instrument. At present the system is being redesigned.

'Mitra' - operational since 1987 - is a system designed to assist in making a more efficient use of prison cells. It contains data on the size and mix of present and prospective prison populations.

Two, more comprehensive systems are still under development: one in the area of criminal law, another in the area of civil law.

The 'Compas' project is designed to result in a system to assist the various Public Prosecutors' Offices not only in their day-to-day administrative work, but also in the formulation of management and policy decisions. The system to be built (based on distributed minicomputers) will have three main components:

a. 'Compas-kanton' will deal with the full range of administrative steps involved in the handling of minor offenses
b. 'Compas-district' will deal with more serious crimes and appeal cases
c. 'Compas-management' is to provide management and policy information. A first prototype of 'Compas-kanton' is scheduled to become operational at the end of 1987.

A 1984 study concluded that in the civil courts three areas of activities were especially suitable for computerization:

a. the registration of cases
b. the maintenance of records in respect of guardianship and trusteeship over minors
c. the payment order records in civil debts cases.

For each area functional design studies have been completed and a first prototype of the registration system is being built. It is estimated that the introduction of all systems in all courts will take at least six years.

Other projects being considered or in development deal with:
a. the calculation of child support
b. the clerical work involved in bankruptcy proceedings
c. the registration of cases pending before Administrative Law Tribunals
d. the administrative procedures of the Bureaus for Legal Aid
e. the storing and retrieval of criminal records
f. the setting up of a data bank on sentencing practices.

Norway

Norway is unique in that - excluding criminal cases - its court system generates net income for the government; this mainly as a result of the fees charged by the Districts Courts for land registration services.

The fact that most Norwegian courts have few judges and a small staff explains why the use of information technology is mostly restricted to word processing. However, one of the five High Courts is also using its minicomputer for administrative purposes (registration of case records and the production of statistics and documents).

Recently it was decided to computerise the land registration function of the District Courts, the aim being that the system to be established be self-financing. At particular District Courts centralized data bases have been set up (or are being set up) for the recording of documents creating liens on private property and for the registration of firms and companies. There is a project under development to provide all courts with information systems within a five year period.

Portugal

In 1970 Portugal's Ministry of Justice established a data processing centre for the purpose of storing en retrieving large volumes of data in such areas as:
a. national identity cards
b. registration of automobiles
c. cases being handled by the police
d. registration of persons sought.

In 1985 a plan was adopted for the introduction of information technology in court administration. Priority is given to the following projects:
a. the administration of cases at the 'Tribunal de Police' at Lisbon
b. the introduction of computerization at the Registry of the 'Palais de Justice' at Lisbon (also for statistical purposes)
c. personnel management.

These projects are still in the planning stage. The 'Bureau de Documentation et Droit Comparé de l'Office du Procureur-Général de la République' is in the process of establishing a number of legal data banks.

Spain

Spain completed the automation of the public records of the Ministry of Justice (prison and police records, wills and testaments, etc.) in 1982. In that same year it defined the 'Inforius' project for the use of information technology in court administration. This project was approved in 1984 and implementation began in the same year. Implementation was accelerated in 1985: in that year new legislation consolidated the new structure of the judiciary.

Generally, the Inforius project is designed to use information technology to reduce the time spent by the administrative staff on the preparation of documents and the searching for information concerning ongoing cases; it was estimated that these tasks - if performed manually - required 60 percent of staff time.

Accordingly, a system was defined integrating word- and data processing. Data on cases are entered into the system, which then generates the necessary documents, listings and statistics.

The main functions of the system are:
a. to maintain a general register of cases
b. to distribute cases among the various courts
c. to provide a follow-up of cases
d. to produce documents
e. to retrieve data
f. to generate statistics and reports
g. to archive sentences.

The same overall approach was followed when introducing the system at the various courts, albeit with some modification. The systems operate on minicomputers. Priority was given to the Police Courts in large cities and the Courts of First Instance and Preliminary Investigation. Insofar as the system deals with criminal law, it places great emphasis on filing and retrieving, as well as the preparation of records and statistics. On the civil law side the system reflects the greater complexity of (the procedure in) civil cases, e.g., in the generation of documents. Some of the higher level courts have also developed a data base on the legal principles involved in their decisions. This is also true for the Supreme Court.

At the end of 1986 about 30 percent of all Courts of the First Instance and Preliminary Investigation had been computerised, while this was also the case with 23 of the 55 Offices of the Public Prosecutor. Planning calls for a rapid expansion of the system.

Switzerland

In Switzerland two more notable projects are those at the 'Tribunal fédéral suisse' (including the 'Tribunal fédéral d'assurances') and at the courts of the Canton of Geneva.

In 1984 the 'Tribunal fédéral suisse' decided to use information technology so as to facilitate the work of its judges, law clerks and administrative staff. It consists of the following elements:
a. the registration and management of cases
b. the creation of multilingual thesauri

c. the computerization, indexation and retrieval of decisions, legislation and literature.

A minicomputer was installed in 1985 and the case registration and management system became operational in 1986 (although it is still evolving). The multilingual thesauri are designed to allow access to the data bases of decisions, legislation and literature in any of the three official languages. The objectives of the system are not only to assist with administrative work, but also to improve the consistence of the decisions.

The Geneva 'Palais de Justice' houses 19 separate (cantonal) courts. Word processing was introduced in 1982 and in 1983 a first report came out on computerised management of cases. In early 1986 the hardware was selected (minicomputer) and in June 1986 work began on a prototype. The first stage of the project is concerned with criminal procedures, the second with civil procedures and the third stage with a number of special procedures. Although for reasons related to the separation of powers it was decided not to establish links with other computer centers, it is considered that at some point the system must be interfaced with the data bases of other governmental agencies.

United States

In the United States much of the impetus towards the introduction of information technology in the courts was provided - and continues to be provided - by the Federal Judicial Centre, established in 1967 and charged with conducting research and development work on the application of computers in the (federal) courts. It should, therefore, be no surprise that as early as 1975 almost every major court in the United States had initiated some form of automation.

At present the use of information technology is even more widespread and this explains why it is impossible here to even mention all the systems in operation. Thus, the following discussion will be mainly limited to some of the major projects at the federal level as set forth in the present five-year plan.

The 'Federal Courts Civil Case Management System' is operational (either in whole or in part) at a number of courts; older versions are also still being used.

It provides the following functions:

a. a docketing module for case registration, case queries and case transactions
b. an editor module for adding, deleting and correcting docketing data
c. a reporting module for generating documents, reports, tables and statistics.

The system is not limited to the automation of administrative procedures, but it also provides management information. It is designed as an integrated system for about 100 federal district, appellate and bankruptcy courts and it uses distributed minicomputers (as do the systems mentioned below).

The 'Bankruptcy Automation System' follows the same overall approach. However, it takes account of some special features of bankruptcy proceedings (such as: high-volume notice generation; and different informational requirements). Experiments are conducted with the optical scanning of documents and voice synthesis for answering telephone queries. The system is installed in a number of prototype courts.

The main purpose of the 'Probation Information Management System' is to track offenders released under suspension of sentence for good behaviour. A prototype is operational.

Other systems (sometimes operational, sometimes under development) are:

a. the 'Central Violations Bureau' processes all minor offenses within federal jurisdiction
b. the 'Civil On-line Statistical Summary System' keeps track of civil case openings and closings
c. the 'Court Reporter Management System' supports the courts in managing information on court reporters and audio operators
d. the 'Criminal Caseflow Management System' provides automated docketing for about 45 percent of all criminal cases
e. the 'Jury System' supports the selection of jurors
f. the 'Stars/Index Replacement System', the 'Naturalization System' and the 'Notice, Docket and Index Card System' are smaller systems to provide certain courts with specific information
g. the 'Office Automation Project' is designed to improve performance levels of office computing (including electronic mail facilities)
h. the 'Computer-assisted Legal Research' project is concerned with the capability to access legal data banks
i. the 'Microcomputer Project' is designed to introduce general purpose microcomputer applications
j. the 'Telecommunications Project' purports to set up a data network between the federal courts, while it also looks into computer-aided transcription of oral evidence (technically, testimony can now be transcribed for almost immediate viewing on a computer monitor).

Not only the federal courts make extensive use of information technology, but also the offices of federal prosecutors. Generally, the prosecutors' systems are strictly separated from the court systems (there even is no sharing of hardware).

The 'Prosecutor's Management Information System' is installed in all large U.S. Attorneys' Offices (hardware: minicomputers).

It provides the following functions:

a. to track criminal, civil and collection cases
b. to provide information used by attorneys in litigation and investigation management and by supervisors to monitor cases and subject matters
c. to provide caseload statistics for allocating resources
d. to provide data for accounting and debt collection purposes.

The U.S. Attorneys' Offices also use 'Automated Litigation Support' to organize and manage large volumes of the evidentiary materials involved in complex litigation. Documents (including computer transcribed testimony) are converted to files for full text retrieval.

4 FINAL OBSERVATIONS

4.1 TRENDS IN THE PROCESS

If the survey of projects and systems suggests one general observation, it is that the introduction of information technology in court administration - in terms of process, as well as in terms of outcome - differs from country to country and that these differences reflect the peculiarities of the organization of the judiciary, of the legal system and indeed of society as a whole. Examples of this phenomenon range from the fact that in states with a centralized system of government the Ministry of Justice seems to play a more dominant role than in states with decentralized government, to the fact that in multilingual societies court administration and legal information systems must be multilingual too. And in countries with a tradition of making verbatim records of testimony in court, computer-aided transcription methods enjoy great interest.

However, one overall trend seems to be that automation is first introduced at high volume courts. The reasons for this are obvious: in those courts the workload is heaviest, while at the same time there usually is a strong routine element. In most countries this trend implies that priority was - and is being- given to the administration of criminal law. And within criminal law to minor offenses. Indeed, it is in respect of the administration of traffic offenses that in most countries automation was introduced for the first time.

Another general characteristic is an awareness that the introduction of information technology in court administration presents some unique features. One such feature is the emphasis given to training and education: it is realized that the level of know-how among the users is relatively low and that in most cases they encounter computers for the first time. There also is a great deal of attention for the aspect of confidentiality of data and the need to minimize any risks of systems being accessed by non-authorized individuals. There can be little doubt that this aspect will gain in importance now that the use of data communication - which makes computer systems necessarily more open - is increasing. Finally, the doctrines of the separation of powers and of the independence of the judiciary also have an impact: in many cases the choice in favour of distributed - or even: stand-alone - systems was a direct result of these doctrines.

The judiciary may have been late in accepting information technology, but in most countries the point of no return appears to have been passed. There can be no doubt that the increased workload of the courts in virtually all countries has been the driving force behind this development and that - faced with this reality - the legal profession has shed its traditional reluctance to make use of advanced technology.

Although specific figures are rare, the overall impression is that automation has indeed increased efficiency and that without it courts would have fallen even further behind. And the fact that the judiciary was late in accepting automation has the clear advantage of enabling it to learn from the mistakes of others: automation is introduced at a time when the technology has matured.

A final observation is that many countries began with specific projects, but that there now is an observable tendency towards integration. Some of the more recent projects are rather large-scale precisely because they treat the introduction of information technology in the administration of courts as a whole, i.e.

they are not directed towards automating specific functions, but towards automating all those functions for which this is profitable. This new approach is also clearly linked to the fact that more and more countries have developed master plans for the introduction of information technology in the judiciary and that - as result? - significant funding is made available. The step-by-step approach - in some cases: trial and error - appears to be disappearing.

4.2 TRENDS IN APPLICATIONS

There are several areas in the field of justice in which computers can be brought into action. They can be helpful in administrative facilitation, jurisprudence and the facilitation of the decision making process.

Administrative facilitation

Looking first of all at criminal justice, this sector may be subdivided into elaborate legal proceedings on the one hand and simple fines on the other. Several countries have already started to apply this distinction. Trials contain many routine processes, paperwork is usually voluminous, and therefore straightforward computerization is easily applied. A first area of application can be found in the preclusion of criminal prosecution. In case of certain offenses, such as parking fines, the computer may even be used to fill in the ticket. Automation may then be extended to the second step of the process, i.e. the trial itself. Good use can then be made of the data recorded during the first phase. A further extension will consist of the filing of sentences other than fines. The execution of verdicts too is facilitated by computers.

The application of computers in these cases frequently starts off on a small scale, locally, independently, even though they are very much interrelated. Not all courts make use of computers, and those that do will not use them in all cases. These forms of computer application are very characteristic of stage 1.

In both criminal law and (especially) civil law, case tracking and registration is a rewarding automation subject. This concerns monitoring the successive phases of current cases and the concatenate actions of parties, and surveillance with regard to the time limits involved. Preparing the lists and processing the decisions of a cause-list sitting entails mostly routine work.

Word processing is another computer application. It is widely used, on a large scale. Many messages and letters (such as subpoenas, summonses to appear in court, hearings of witnesses, proceedings upon default, notifications) are largely standardized, so that word processing may save a great deal of time and money. Judgments are largely composed of standard texts. If there is a problem to implement word processing in this area, it is caused by the fact that not every judge is fully conscious of his own standard texts; those judges who are able to explicitly formulate their texts find it hard to mutually agree upon them.

Integration of case tracking systems and word processing would be a very natural thing to do, as it would ensure that registration of basic facts like name, address, domicile of parties, lawyers needs to be performed only once. Moreover, a great many texts can then be generated directly as a result of cause-list decisions.

Further integration of various related areas of justice such as legal aid and provision for guardianship in divorce cases, is to be expected.

Also the integration of document processing may be mentioned as an application in the near future.

A somewhat more futuristic development which is expected to happen in the civil sector is the automatic exchange of data (i.e. computer to computer, via the public network) between courts and lawyers. After all, most lawyers also store their information on computer files.

In the criminal law sector the same development is bound to happen between the court and the public prosecutor. Even parts of the case registration system are stored in a joint computer system. In a case like this it is crucial to ensure the maintenance of a rigid separation of powers.

Computerized registration of current cases creates the possibility to simply and effectively gather additional information. For example, there may be several simultaneous cases on the same subject, past and present cases can be compared, one and the same party may be involved in several cases, or cases may be related, eg. bankruptcies. The principal requirement here is for the subjects of these cases to be clearly and unambiguously defined and recorded.

The reasons for automation of the administrative aspects of the legal system may be summed up as follows:

- a growing workload makes it imperative to find ways to improve efficiency
- automation takes care of dull administrative work
- the result is an improvement of both efficiency and effectiveness (more time available for complicated affairs, less time required for routine matters)
- quality improvement of administrative facilitation, because of decrease in the number of mistakes.

With an automated system the data on file may be used to compile the information required for surveillance and control of judicial processes. It will become possible to quickly acquire an insight into the periods of time needed for different kinds of cases, into present and future workloads of the court and individual judges, into the frequency with which time limits are exceeded, the number of witness statements, court summonses, etc.

The need for management information must be determined on the basis of the general management principles of the courts. Only then can the information be handled in the right way; can strong and weak points be recognised as such, and can specific measures towards improvement be taken. Without the framework of such general management principles computer-aided management information, which in itself is completely random, may come to resemble a time bomb, placed equally at random.

Reports of cases

This is an area in which computers have been in use as a source of information for some time. Legal data base systems contain reports of cases and law texts, and are usually run by a (commercial) third party. The more online computer facilities become available to the courts of justice, the more they will be used.

Facilitation of the decision making process

A totally different way to bring the computer into action is the facilitation of the preparation of judgments; computer science employs the terms 'artificial intelligence' and 'expert systems'. The thought processes and considerations of the judge are analyzed and made into a programme, so that the computer itself, as it were, becomes able to build up its own conclusions.

Artificial intelligence is a development which is still in its infancy, but some of its applications (mainly outside the field of justice) show that the process of deliberation gains either in speed or in quality.

It should be emphasized that these applications cannot be a substitute for a human judge, but they can facilitate his job. The extent of the facilitation depends on the nature of the case: if it is a frequently occurring, not very complex case there can be much more help from the computer than if it concerns a complex case with many intricate and idiosyncratic features.

Objections like 'computers can never be a substitute for human thought' or 'we do not want computer justice' are theoretically correct, but, first and foremost, they betray a lack of understanding where the use of these applications is concerned.

4.3 POTENTIAL IMPEDIMENTS

As shown by the source material described in chapter 3, and also in accordance with our own experience, automation in the field of justice is as yet in the initial stages 1 and 2. For the moment the facts do not indicate a quick and painless journey through these stages.
The following aspects support this statement:

- The management of the courts is conducted by judges and their knowledge of this field is inadequate, and it may even be said that considerable suspicion is felt for these technical developments.

- It follows from the above that the automation process is an uphill struggle, performed with a shortage of means, i.e. user capacity and technical capacity are too limited, with all sorts of problems as a direct consequence.

- The long-term result is an anti-automation environment which will be very averse to further adventures after a first disaster. Whatever may have been learned during the first stage will therefore be wasted. In addition, automation personnel, older and wiser, will have no trouble in finding jobs elsewhere, given the present shortage on the labour market.

- In many countries courts of justice are not allowed to decide about automation. In itself, this fact may be an advantage as it excludes the influence of the anti-automation ecology; on the other hand, when the use of these systems is enforced from above there is no reason to expect the sort of warm welcome and user support which are needed for a successful implementation. This is all the more valid if specifications have been drawn up without sufficient consultation of future users.

- Though, generally speaking, the attitude of judges seems to have very little in common with the attitude and affinity which are needed for effective widespread implementation of computers, it is true to say that there is a growing realization that automation is inevitable.

Furthermore, in different places, project teams can be put together of groups of people of sufficient authority, weight and quality to be able to realize and introduce computer applications on a larger scale.

RESPONDEES AND AUTHORS OF DOCUMENTS USED

We express our gratitude to the following persons:

Canada
R. Carter, Office of the Attorney General Alberta
G. Clarke, Supreme Court of Canada
A.M. DiGiacinto, Court of Queen's Bench New Brunswick
W. Dunlop, Supreme Court of Ontario
B. Grainger, Department of Justice of Canada
M.P. Harvey, Government of the Northwest Territories
J. Jamieson, Court of Queen's Bench Saskatchewan
A.E. Rennie, Department Attorney General of Nova Scotia
M. Veskimets, Department of Justice of Canada
W. Wendt, Federal Court of Canada

Our thanks also to M. Felsky (Canadian Law Information Council) and G. Goulard (Supreme Court of Canada).

Belgium
J.R. Waterplas, Office Public Prosecutor, Court of Appeals, Brussels

Federal Republic of Germany
H. Klein, Association for Mathematics and Data processing
P. Reichelt, Association for Mathematics and Data processing
Langner, Ministry of Justice
J. Volkmann, Federal Court for Social Matters

Finland
M. Leistén, Ministry of Justice

France
M.F. Stoliaroff, Ministry of Justice

Great Britain
R.G. Donaldson, Crown Office Edinburgh
P. Waugh, Lord Chancellor's Department

Ireland
E.M. Barnes, Office of Public Prosecutions
F. Dunne, Ministry of Justice

Italy
M.C. Sarzana, Ministry of Justice

Luxembourg
L. Prussen, Office of the Public Prosecutor

Norway
J. Bonnevie Hoyer, Ministry of Justice and Police

Portugal
J. Ferreira Dias, Ministry of Justice
J.M. Santos Pais, Office of the Prosecutor General

Spain
J. Martin Ostos, University of Cadiz

Switzerland
R. Mahler, Geneva Law Courts
P. A. Müller, Federal Tribunal

United States
R.D. Fennell, Federal Judicial Centre
J.J. Lane, Department of Justice

TRENDS IN USE OF INFORMATION TECHNOLOGY (INTRODUCTION)

W.D. Pelger
Manager Berenschot Informatica, Utrecht

Ladies and Gentlemen,

The majority of you will be aware that the use and implementation of Information Technology is not just buying a computer. It is much more, it is a process in an organization in which many people are involved and in order to get skilled the organization has to pass through a learning process. That is what the experiences in companies and organizations which are ahead in the use of computers have taught us.

As to the learning process, one may recognise four subsequent stages:

The first could be called *'The first system'*. Inspired by the fast and accurate data processing capabilities of computers, one would like to apply this technology to carry out large-scale routine work. The pioneering nature of the very first implementation of computers in a particular area may be seen in the following: a limited number of mainly technically oriented specialists tackle a specific, isolated problem. Attention is concentrated exclusively on this problem, and specially on designing and writing the software and making it running on the computer. A great variety of problems is met: technical ones, problems about a too limited or incorrect functionality of the system and problems with respect to the organization of the development and introduction of an application, such as training and education. Although the implementation and the use of the application will generate quite some deception and frustration, the advantages of using the computer are still felt to be greater than not using it.

And so we enter the next stage, which may be labelled as: *'Subsequent Systems'*. In this stage the set up of automation projects becomes somewhat more professional. The mistakes, made before, prove to be of educational value. Steering committees and workgroups are set up, aiming the increase of the involvement of management and future users in specifying the requirements for their new systems. The applications, during this stage as well as in the first, tend to be approached in isolation; they are insufficiently interrelated. As soon as several different systems have become operational, one is confronted, for instance, with the fact that there is no possibility to exchange data and that different definitions are used for the same object.

In the third stage, which could be called *'Applications on a larger scale'* the applications grow to a higher level. These application systems are intended to be used on a larger scale with more functionality than just converting manual routine processes into computer processing. The computer should also be used to make some decisions and thereby, the stored data in the computersystems can be accessed to produce management information. Another trend in this stage is the growing awareness that the design of new applications should not be done isolated from other systems. Rather should a framework be constituted that contains the major actual and future applications and the relations among them and that also determines the data that are commonly used by these applications.

The 4th stage can be called *'The first mature state'*. The word first indicates to be careful with a mature state in connection with Information Technology, because this phenomenon itself has not yet evolved beyond its initial stage of development.

Nevertheless, in this stage Information Technology is used in accordance with a policy which is formed on the basis of the company's objectives and which includes all actual and future application systems as well as the required dataprocessing facilities.

A division is made between the dataprocessing facilities, which consist of the type of computers, mini's, personal computers, the networking, tools, etc. and the application systems (which may in turn be split up into the functional requirements for the application software on the one hand and data management on the other).

Users will be less and less concerned with technical aspects. Meanwhile users will have become very well informed as to what automation can do for them, and what it cannot. Their contribution in developing new systems (really new and renovations) meets the demands for building adequate applications.

In the report the characteristics of the four stages have been described more extensively and various examples are brought up to give the reader a feeling about the nature of the things that may go wrong (and go wrong as the law of Murphy commands).

The fact that the judicial world lags behind is a disadvantage on the one hand because the required experience and knowledge has yet to be built up- and this process cannot be skipped -, on the other hand, specific experiences gained in other sectors of the working society can be used to to pass through this process less painfully and quicker.

Finally, I may conclude by summarizing the major problem areas.

First the technical. Although, in the judicial sector these problems will be far from dominant. The nature of the judicial applications do not require technically highly advanced or complicated solutions.

Next points present the real challenges:

- To set up the right specifications is a difficult job. It concerns the struggle to translate administrative procedures into a systematic analysis fit for computerprocessing. For this task one needs users who don't only know their own working environment very well, but who also have the necessary technical feeling to imagine in a creative and pragmatic way the role of the computer in a future working environment. This is more than just one-to-one converting the manual procedures into the computer.

- An other important point concerns the organization. This applies to effective project management during the development of applications and also to the operations and the maintenance of the systems with special attention for the changes in the users working environment. As mentioned in the description of the 4 th stage, the Information Technology activities should be based on the information policy and plans. In addition, effective leadership, executed by the management of the courts, is essential.

- Another issue not to be underestimated is that of training and education of users and management.

So, the successful implementation of Information Technology requires that each category of the participants involved, id est judges, users and some of them also as the management of the courts, clerical staff and software developers and in many cases or countries also the Ministry of justice, requires that these parties are sufficiently skilled to fulfill their role in the process of automation and moreover, it requires a fruitful cooperation of these categories.

TRENDS IN USE OF INFORMATION TECHNOLOGY

A.W. Koers
Professor law faculty, Utrecht

Thank you, Mr. Chairman

In preparing the paper for this session of the Conference Mr. Pelger and I divided our work so that I dealt mainly with its second part: the survey of projects in a number of countries. Let me, therefore, repeat what was also said in the paper: I realize that the survey is far from complete, while the responsibility for any errors of fact and/or interpretation lies with me.

Yet, I believe that in general the survey provides a reasonably reliable picture of where things stand. In the time available, I will not try to summarize the information provided on the activities in the various countries. I leave that for you to peruse at your convenience. Rather, I will use my time to make some general observations that I consider important at this stage of developments.

As Mr. Pelger already mentioned in his remarks, it is our view that the introduction of information technology in court administration is still in the initial stages 1 or 2, as outlined in the paper. Thus, the first systems have been introduced and in some cases these have been followed by the next generation. This implies that quite often the process of introducing information technology to court administration is still characterized by the attitudes of the pioneers- and, thus, by experimentation.

But is the administration of courts - or, more broadly, of justice - not too important for lawyers and society as a whole to make it dependent upon the spirit and attitudes of pioneers and upon experimentation?

This question does not imply any criticism, nor does it suggest that the people involved in introducing information technology to court administration are naive - or even irresponsible. As was mentioned in the paper, a learning process is inevitable.

I am only trying to make two points.

First, in view of the object we are talking about - the administration of courts and justice - it is in my view essential to move as quickly as possible to the next stages: those of large scale, integrated applications and mature systems.

Second, to make that transition is not really dependent upon information technology as such, but much more on the environment - the people and the organization - in which it is to function. And the environment can only improve if judges/lawyers come to see the introduction of information technology not as the problem of others - of computer specialist - but as their own responsibility.

Information technology is after all only a tool - and the use to be made of that tool must be determined ultimately by those who are responsible for the administration of justice.

I stress these points because it also is my submission that we are only seeing the beginning.

So far information technology is used mainly for administrative purposes. Indeed, virtually all the projects outlined in the paper fall in this area. However, as we tried to show with the admittedly still simple - Jurisdiction Advisory System, a radically new development is already taking shape at the horizon: automated legal decision support systems or even automated legal decision making systems.

As I indicated during the demonstration of the Jurisdiction Advisory System, the introduction of such systems in the legal arena presents some unique problems and questions.

I will not dwell here on the problems encountered in developing the systems. Let it suffice to note that these problems are significant - both theoretically and practically - but that worldwide a great deal of energy is spent on solving them. Also, information technology is still in its infancy and one should, therefore, not judge the potential of decision systems in the light of the technology of today.

Let us, therefore, assume that a few years from now - and in information technology a few years is a great deal of time - really powerful legal decision systems become feasible. Then, the legal community can not avoid the question of what to do with them.

It may be tempting to take the view that there is nothing new under the sun and that judges/lawyers can use these systems freely, much like they are now using books journals and - occasionally - legal data banks. However, this view overlooks a number of unique problems. To mention just a few:

- As most judges/lawyers will lack the specialized knowledge - or the time- to evaluate the inner workings of decision programmes, who will guarantee that the legal knowledge represented in these programmes is accurate and up to date?
- As most decision support systems will require a considerable investment in software and hardware, who will provide the necessary funding who will control access and who will be responsible for their integrity?

These questions go beyond the level of technicalities. If one considers them, it soon becomes clear that they have a direct relationship with a core principle of the rule of law: the independence of the judiciary.

But these questions - however fundamental they are - only scratch the surface.

They assume that decision systems provide advice to judges/lawyers who then make decisions. However, technically - and I stress this word - there is no reason not to go further and to apply the conclusions reached by a decision systems directly to individuals, that is without the intervention of a (human) judge or a lawyer. Then the computer is used not to support decisions-making by judges/lawyers, but to generate legal decisions.

But the technical feasibility of such systems is, of course, an altogether different issue than their desirability. Thus, the more important question is whether it is desirable to use the computer in the role of a legal decision maker. It is the legal community - and ultimately society as a whole - that will have to provide the answer to this question.

I might note here that in the Netherlands a special committee has been set up recently to look into the issues I just mentioned.

Mr. Chairman, I will conclude.

The crux of my message is this. Our analysis shows that a great deal of progress has been made so far in introducing information technology to court administration. However, the real challenge still lies ahead and that challenge can only be met if lawyers - individually and as a professional group - accept their responsibility in deciding on the use to be made of information technology.

Only then can the challenge be met so that the outcome is satisfactory not only in a technical sense, but also from the perspective of the administration of justice. And I believe that few in this Conference will dispute that this perspective is the only thing that really matters.

POSSIBLE ITEMS FOR DISCUSSION

The following ideas are submitted as possible issues to be taken up in the discussion period. They do not necessarily reflect the views of the authors, nor should they exclude any other topic from being raised during the discussion.

1. Central control (*e.g.* at the level of the Ministries of Justice) is an essential prerequisite for a successful introduction of information technology in court administration.

2. The lack of relevant management expertise in the judiciary is the single most important obstacle to an integrated introduction of information technology in court administration - such integration being essential if a chaotic 'personal computer paradise' is to be avoided.

3. The idea that computers can take over (parts of) human decision making in all areas but the law reflects not only ignorance as to the potential of computers, but also an (un)professional bias.

4. The introduction of information technology in court administration requires a critical evaluation of the organization and working procedures of the judiciary.

5. The introduction of information technology to court administration has been mostly motivated by the need to save money, rather than by a desire to improve the quality of the output.

6. The introduction of information technology to court administration can only succeed if an effective integration of legal/procedural expertise and technical know how is achieved.

REPORT OF THE DISCUSSION

Chairman: *Ch.J.M.A. Moons (the Netherlands)*
Vice-chairman: *T. Kojima (Japan)*
Secretary: *H. Franken (the Netherlands)*

The discussionpoints are to be found at page 436.

After the opening address by the chairman, Mr Pelger demonstrated a 'Prototype of a case-tracking and registration system'. The participants in the session received a hand-out. Subsequently, Prof. Koers demonstrated a decision support program for lawyers, designed to answer the question which Social Security Tribunal has jurisdiction to hear a certain case. Next, Pelger and Koers each presented a summary of their general report. These summaries are to be found at 431 and 434.

Participants in the discussion were: Mr Ch.J.M.A. Moons (Netherlands), Prof. Dr E. Blankenburg (Netherlands), Prof. Dr H. Franken (Netherlands), Prof. S.M. Bundy (U.S.A.), Prof. Dr Pessoa Vaz (Portugal), Prof. M. Tezer (Belgium), Dr Illis (Germany) and Dr A.G. Bosch (Netherlands).

The first subject for discussion was the following proposition by the general rapporteurs: 'Central control (*e.g.* at the level of the Ministries of Justice) is an essential prerequisite for a successful introduction of information technology in court administration.'

Blankenburg pointed out the menace to the privacy of litigants, judges, lawyers, etc., if the introduction of informationtechnology were to take place under the control of the Ministry of Justice. He argued a decentralized approach. Moons observed that the user of an information system has to be sure of its quality. This quality should be watched by a board, which must be independent of the Ministry of Justice and which must incorporate the combined professional expertise of jurists and technicians.

Franken pointed out the ultimate responsibility of the courts for the technological tools used by them. If the choice of their tools is made by the Ministry of Justice, this may affect the independency of the courts.

Bundy said that if the method of information retrieval by the court would be dictated by the central government, this would constitute a fundamental kind of law reform.

Pessoa Vaz brought to mind the influence of available data bases on the work of the courts. He pointed out that electronic information systems can improve the possibilities for making and keeping archives, resulting in a better check on court records and judgments.

Tezer remarked that it would be useful to set up legal data bases for different parts of international law, which data bases should be accessible from different countries. As an experiment, international maritime law would be a suitable subject to gain experience with such systems.

Illis argued that the technology concerning the decision-making process of the courts has a political impact. Pelger replied to this statement, that for the time being the computer can be used only for routine acts.

Finally, Bosch, on the strength of his experience with building juridical administration systems, sounded a warning of the time, the stress and the money which will have to be invested. Nevertheless, he believed that it is imperative to set up modern court-administration systems. He suggested that lawyers and technical specialists exchange their experiences.

At 16.30 o'clock the chairman closed the meeting and thanked the participants in the discussion for their fruitful ideas.

CLOSING SPEECH

SOME REFLEXIONS ON THE ROLE OF PROCEDURAL SCHOLARSHIP TO-DAY

M. Cappelletti
President of the International Association for Procedural Law

Dedicated to the memory of Niceto Alcalá Zamora y Castillo, Tito Carnacini, E.T. Liebman, Luís Loreto, and Georgios Rammos

1. The Organizing Committee has asked me to present some remarks at the conclusion of our 8th World Congress. I am honored to do so and I hope you will allow me to dedicate these reflexions of mine to the memory of those Members of our Association who have passed away since our last meeting at Würzburg.

I cannot even try to do a *rapport de synthèse*, however. This is so not only because some of the reports were not available until we were already gathered here and much of the discussion was not held in plenary session, but also, and above all, because this Congress has been too important, rich, and complex to be readily encapsulated in a hastily made synthesis. Any such synthesis attempt would certainly not do justice to much of what has been written for and said at this encounter of so many experts from so many countries. It would also not do justice to the tremendous organizing efforts for which all of us are so grateful to our Dutch hosts, friends, and colleagues. Thus, instead of trying the impossible I shall limit myself to a few reflexions on what I consider to be some of the major challenges faced by procedural scholars in our epoch[1], and on the way such challenges have been reflected in what at the opening session I referred to as the 'trilogy' of our Association: namely, in this Congress of Utrecht and in the two preceding Congresses held at Würzburg and Ghent. The fact that, as will appear from what I am going to say, such challenges do coincide, to a large extent, with problems and themes dealt with by - indeed, with the inspiring philosophy of - this and the preceding two Congresses may indicate that the Association's choices have faithfully reflected what I, for one, would consider to be the central procedural *problématique* of our time. Thus, in some ways, my remarks, while not being a synthesis of this Congress, will try to provide an overview of present and past congressional activities - and perhaps also, in a low-key way, of future possible activities - of our Association.

Before doing so, however, it might be appropriate to add a parenthetical note about what our Association is, and what it is not and, in my opinion, should never be. It is not a 'confederation' of national associations; rather, it is and shall remain an association of individuals, each one being a member in his or

---

1 Reflexions similar, in part, to some I made in a speech delivered in Sendai, Japan, on May 16, 1987, to the National Conference of the Japanese Association of Proceduralists.

her own individual capacity and not as a national of any given country, even less a representative of any given government or regime. If I may expand a bit on this parenthetical point, let me say that my own preference would be for a much larger membership, at least twice as large as the present, and much more open to younger colleagues for whom a form of, say, 'associate membership' could be established. But the basic point should remain untouched: that membership, even associate membership, should be based exclusively on scholarly interests and achievements - which would not exclude, of course, professionally engaged scholarship of judges and practitioners.

2. 'New Challenges to Proceduralists': What do I mean by this?

Let me start with a phrase by my Florentine Master, Piero Calamandrei (and, to remain within the official languages of the Congress, I shall quote the phrase from the Spanish translation by another unforgettable proceduralist, Santiago Sentís Melendo):

> 'Suerte singular, es, entre los estudiosos del derecho, la de nosotros los procesalistas; cultivamos una disciplina que, según el espíritu con que se considera, puede ser la más mezquina y la más sorda, o bien la más sensible y la más próxima al espíritu'[2].

Half a century before, the great Franz Klein made a similar observation, remarking that developments in the law of procedure, if seen in their real and deep meaning, appear to be strictly connected to the main cultural developments of peoples:

> 'Denn ... enthüllt sich uns, dass der öde, trockene, unbeachtete Prozess in den regsten Beziehungen zu den Geistesströmungen der Völker steht, und dass seine verschiedenen Gestaltungen zu den wichtigsten Kulturdokumenten gezählt werden kann'[3].

Procedure, then, is like a mirror, in which the great issues of liberty and justice, the great themes of the relationship between individuals, groups, and states, are faithfully reflected.

What, then, are the *Geistesströmungen*, the major trends which have most powerfully emerged in the last generation of procedural scholarship, and how have they been reflected in that 'trilogy' of our Association: the Congresses of Ghent, Würzburg, and Utrecht?

---

2 P. Calamandrei, 'Processo e giustizia' (introductory speech to the 1950 International Congress of Procedural Law), in **Atti del Congresso Internazionale di Diritto Processuale Civile. 30 Settembre - 3 Ottobre 1950**, Padova, Cedam, 1953, p. 9, at p. 10. The Spanish translation is in P. Calamandrei, **Estudios sobre el proceso civil** (transl. by S. Sentís Melendo), Buenos Aires, Ediciones Jurídicas Europa-América, 1962, p. 201, at p. 202. **See** also **Id.**, **Processo e Democrazia**, in **Opere giuridiche** di P. Calamandrei (M. Cappelleti, ed.), I, Napoli, Morano, 1965, p. 618 **et seq.**, esp. at p. 681.

3 F. Klein, **Zeit- und Geistesströmungen im Prozesse**, Frankfurt a.M., Klostermann, 2nd ed. 1958, p. 8 (a lecture given in 1901). **Cf.** also the masterly lecture by F. Baur, **Zeit- und Geistesströmungen im Prozess. Einige aktuelle Bemerkungen zu dem so betitelten Vortrag von Franz Klein**, in 92 **Juristische Blätter**, 12 September 1970, pp. 445-453.

I shall indicate two such trends, and hint at a third, which I have defined elsewhere as the foremost 'dimensions' of law and justice in our epoch[4].

3. A first challenge, one which has been very central to all of the three Congresses, is represented by a deep and most pervasive evolution in our contemporary world. This is a development that demands, and has in part already provoked, a sweeping transformation in procedural law and in the focus of procedural scholarship.

The late Wolfgang Friedmann in his celebrated book 'Law in a Changing Society' reminded us that, as late as 1933, the British House of Lords could still affirm that poverty is a misfortune for which the law cannot take any responsibility at all[5]. Such cynicism, however, has become hardly acceptable today. Modern legal systems have recognized the insufficiency of a merely formal conception of 'equality before the law.' This 'liberal-individualistic' conception did, of course, represent formidable progress in the 18th and 19th centuries; as pointed out by our General Reporter Gimeno-Sendra[6], it swept away from many countries the remnants of an anti-egalitarian organization of society, including, as Professor Roger Perrot says in his 'Institutions judiciaires,' 'les privilèges de juridiction dont bénéficiaient certaines catégories de justiciables (la noblesse et le clergé notamment)'[7]. The insufficiency of this conception, however, soon became the target of harsh criticism, indeed of turmoils and revolutions in the 19th and 20th centuries. To-day, even the most conservative of modern states would recognize it has an affirmative duty to implement a more 'effective' and 'social' conception of freedom, equality, and human dignity, so that Anatole France's caustic assessment of 'justice' would no longer apply: that is, that justice is 'made to give everyone his due: to the rich his richness, to the poor his poverty'[8].

The key-words of this newer - 'social' - conception of law and justice have been *effectiveness of access*: access for all to the legal system, to its rights and freedoms and benefits, to the instruments, including the courts, that can make those rights, freedoms and benefits meaningful and effective. These key-words, indeed these same access-for-all ideals, have been the inspiration of a far reaching concern in the law generally, and in procedural law in particular. The 'world-wide movement to make rights effective' and thus 'to make courts, and, more generally, law and justice accessible to all,' has been the subject of what our General Reporter Professor Enrique Vescovi[9] and, I am sure, many more of us would consider to be one of the most important and challenging

---

4 See my articles 'Appunti per una fenomenologia della giustizia nel XX secolo,' in **Studi in onore di Enrico Tullio Liebman**, I, Milano, Giuffrè, 1979, pp. 153-210; and 'New Dimensions of Justice,' in M. Storme, **Rechtspraak in Opspraak**, Antwerpen, Kluwer, 1980, pp. 125, 131-142.

5 5W. Friedmann, **Law in a Changing Society**, London, Stevens & Sons, 2nd ed. 1972, pp. 121-122.

6 See V. Gimeno Sendra's general report, pp. 2, 3, 6 (ms).

7 R. Perrot, **Institutions judiciaires**, Paris, Editions Montchrestien, 1983, p. 6. See also, e.g., M. Rousselet, **Histoire de la Justice**, Paris, Presses Universitaires de France, 4th ed. 1968, pp. 22 et seq., 55.

8 Quoted in M.D. Forkosch, 'Justice,' in **Dictionary of the History of Ideas** (P.P. Wiener, ed.), II, New York, Scribner's Sons, 1973, pp. 652, 655.

9 See E. Vescovi's general report, sub I.1 text and note 1 (ms).

developments, perhaps the most challenging and important, in legal and procedural scholarship during the last twenty years or so. It is a development in which very many proceduralists in every part of the world have participated. Most significant to us, it is a development which, if my understanding is correct, has inspired the very philosophy of the Ghent-Würzburg-Utrecht trilogy[10].

Note how this trilogy unfolded:

a) The first act in the drama was entitled 'Towards a Justice with a Human Face.' Its promoter, Marcel Storme, declared in the opening speech that inspiration for the choice of the general theme of the Congress came to him from a meeting in Hamburg dedicated precisely to 'Zugang zum Recht'[11]. Also, a number of the Ghent topics were formally collected under the heading 'accessibility to the courts of law,'[12] with the declared intent of 'improving access to the courts'[13]. And, again in the words of Professor Storme, the general purpose of the entire Congress was that 'of making the process more humane'[14] - of implementing, that is, what the American legal philosopher Edmund Cahn called 'the consumer perspective' of law and justice[15] and the German legal philosopher Werner Maihofer has called a 'Kopernikanische Wende,' a turning point which requires law and government to be there 'um des Menschen willen' and not the other way around[16], which is indeed the basic goal of the 'access movement'[17].

b) I come now to the second part of the trilogy. Under Professor Habscheid's leadership, the Würzburg Congress was dedicated to - 'Effectiveness of Judicial Protection and Constitutional Order' - 'Effektiver Rechtsschutz und verfas-

10 It should be noted that already at the 5th International Congress of Procedural Law, held in Mexico City in 1972, one of the five topics chosen for discussion was 'Liberalization and Socialization of Civil Procedure,' with a general report by Professor Fritz Baur, published under the titel 'Liberalización y socialización del proceso civil' in **Revista de Derecho Procesal Iberoamericana**, 1972, pp. 303-333. (The other four general reports, by V. Denti, V. Fairén Guillén, O. de Castro Filho and H. Fix Zamudio, are also published in Spanish in the same issue of that periodical, at pp. 277-474).

11 **See Towards a Justice with a Human Face** (M. Storme & H. Casman, eds.), Antwerpen/Deventer, Kluwer, 1978, pp. 15-16. The papers presented to the Hamburg Congress, including the general report by M. Cappelletti, B. Garth & N. Trocker, are published in 40 **Rabels Zeitschrift für ausländisches und internationales Privatrecht** pp. 669-788 (1976).

12 **Towards a Justice with a Human Face, cit.**, pp. 18, 167 **et seq.** This included reports on such typical access-to-justice topics as legal aid, small claims, and delay.

13 **Id.** pp. 21-22.

14 **Id.**, p. 19.

15 E. Cahn, 'Law in the Consumer Perspective', in 112 **University of Pennsylvania Law Rev.** pp. 1, 9 (1963); **see** also my article 'Accesso alla giustizia come programma di riforma e come metodo di pensiero,' in 37 **Rivista di diritto processuale** p. 233, 245 (1982) (in French in 2 **Windsor Yearbook of Access to Justice** pp. 193, 207 (1982)).

16 W. Maihofer, 'Prinzipien freiheitlicher Demokratie', in **Handbuch des Verfassungsrechts** (E. Benda, W. Maihofer & H.-J. Vogel, eds.), Berlin & New York, de Gruyter, 1983, pp. 175, 195.

17 **See** my article 'Accesso alla giustizia etc.', **supra** note 15, p. 245 (French text, **supra** note 15, p. 207).

sungsmässige Ordnung.' This built upon, but also dramatically enlarged, the scope and philosophy of the Ghent Congress. One very important aspect of such enlargement - reflecting what I will later discuss as the 'constitutional trend' - will be examined in a moment. What I want to observe now is that, as was explicitly indicated by our Colleague Habscheid, the 'principle of effectivity' is a basic consequence of the newer, 'social' conception of the *Rechtsstaat*, since this conception forces us to recognize the insufficiency of, and to try to overcome, the idea of a merely formal equal treatment before the law[18]. Thus, topics such as the organization of legal services for the poor, the 'droit à la preuve,' technical expert testimony, conciliation, non-contentious proceedings, judicial independence, family courts and conflicts, were dealt with at Würzburg in the light of this basic question: how legal systems can 'die Rechte der Bürger *wirksam* garantieren und durchsetzen' - in the light, that is, of the *effectiveness* of legal and judicial protection of individual and social rights. This meant, of course, once again to focus on that fundamental problem of modern societies: the problem of 'legal poverty,' that is, of the difficulties and obstacles in obtaining effective access to the law, and how to overcome such difficulties and obstacles.

Let me emphasize again that such a perspective implies a tremendous enlargement of the scope of our studies. Procedural analysis must become 'contextual' analysis, for rules, institutions, and processes must be seen in their societal and political contexts - a point which is reflected, *inter alia*, in the very fact that one general report at the Würzburg Congress was dedicated to the contribution of legal sociology to procedural reform[19]. Also, the phenomenon of poverty -and I mean not only economic but also, for instance, linguistic and cultural poverty whenever it represents an obstacle to the effective protection of one's rights- far from being the consequence of 'a misfortune for which the law cannot take any responsibility at all,' does become legally and procedurally relevant. Poverty, moreover, has to be evaluated in a broad and legal - not a merely individual and economic - context, so that consumers, environmentalists, and generally 'unorganized,' 'diffuse,' 'diluted' interests and groups shall be included in that concept so long as effective devices are not designed and actually implemented to 'organize' such groups and interests. Thus, as discussed in yet another of the general reports at Würzburg, traditional themes of procedural scholarship such as those of standing to sue, of legal representation, of notice and the right to be heard, and of res judicata, are critically revisited - to give them a 'group' and 'social,' not a merely 'individualistic' meaning[20]. Class and shareholders derivative actions in the U.S.A. and other Common Law countries, *actions collectives* in France, *Verbandsklagen* in Germany, are but a few illustrations of institutions the emergence of which has called for such a new critical approach. Let me add, however, that this is an approach that, while critical of traditional solutions, has not been, and will not be, merely 'decon-

---

18 See W.J. Habscheid, 'Vorwort des Herausgebers', in **Effektiver Rechtsschutz und verfassungsmässige Ordnung** (W.J. Habscheid, ed.), Bielefeld, Gieseking-Verlag, 1983, p. VI.

19 G.H. Roth, 'Der Beitrag der Rechtssoziologie zur Reform des Prozessrechts', in **Effektiver Rechtsschutz, supra** note 18, p. 215 **et seq.**

20 See the general report by M. Cappelletti & B. Garth, 'The Protection of Diffuse, Fragmented and Collective Interests in Civil Litigation,' in **Effektiver Rechtsschutz, supra** note 18, p. 117 **et seq.**

structive.' It is and will be aimed at a most important 'reconstruction' as well: namely, to adapt the traditional conception of 'justice' as mere individual freedom and mere formal equality to that *social* dimension, which is so central to the very political philosophy of our time.

c) I come now to the third act - the splendid Congress held in this wonderful city of Utrecht, on 'Justice and Efficiency.' Building, quite clearly, upon Ghent and Würzburg - but also on the international symposium held at Lund in 1985 on the enforcement of money judgments - the Utrecht Congress has reflected a phenomenon that in recent years has become very central to the *problématique* of modern societies, the 'crisis of the social, activist, welfare state' - most particularly, the danger of its abuses and inefficiencies, a danger which, as remarked by our General Reporter Maria Borucka-Arctowa, presents 'problèmes identiques' in Western and Socialist countries[21]. Thus, whereas Würzburg had dealt with the crucial theme of the 'effectiveness' of the protection of new (as well as traditional) rights, the Utrecht Congress has further expanded its concern. More effective access to the courts - making access easier, simpler, less expensive - might contribute in bringing about court congestion; it might encourage abuse of the legal and judicial process; it might be, itself, the cause of a decline of the quality of 'justice,' thus justifying what one of our true Masters, Fritz Baur, called 'die Skepsis gegenüber jeder staatlichen Autorität und Bevormundung'[22]. Indeed, as forcefully emphasized, among others, by our General Reporters J.A. Jolowicz, Pierre Julien, and Enrique Vescovi, generalized access might lead to inefficiency of the public institutions, processes and machinery which are supposed to provide it; it might lead to cheap, second rate justice[23].

It should be noted that, aware of this danger, the 'access-to-justice movemen' has in fact developed a dual profile. The vast expansion of state activism which the social (as well as, of course, the socialist) state implies, entails not only the creation of new 'social' rights, but also an increase in the potential for abuses by the state and other powerful bodies, governmental and otherwise. Thus the access program aims at both: making the new rights effective to all, but also improving the means of legal redress - the former primarily by mobilizing interests, the latter by improving the delivery of legal services and rationalizing the means of redress.

There is a subtle but profound difference, and yet also a strict connection, between *effectiveness* and *efficiency*: the former concerns the parties, their access to the protection machinery; the latter concerns, instead, the way in which the machinery itself works. The difference, but also the strict connection between the two, was quickly grasped by those who inspired and organized this

---

21 See M. Borucka Arctowa's general report, p. 13 (ms).

22 F. Baur, supra note 3, p. 446. Professor Baur sharply pointed out the paradox, which is typical of our time: on the one hand, the growing role of the state, including the judicial branch, in larger and larger areas of societal life; on the other, the growing skepticism vis-à-vis state interferences. Id, pp. 448-449. The paradox, however, is not incomprehensible; it is a law inherent in every societal development that the 'solution' of any problem in turn raises new difficulties and problems to be solved.

23 See especially J.A. Jolowicz' general report, pp. 10, 17, 18 et passim (ms). Cf. M. Rosenberg, 'Second Class Justice', in 1 **Windsor Yearbook of Access to Justice** pp. 294-302 (1981).

Congress, the results of which, I am sure, will be of lasting importance. And, it has become quite clear to all of us that, in Dean Garth's words, there is no simple trade-off between efficiency and justice[24]; that indeed, efficiency can be increased without necessarily sacrificing justice[25]; and that efficiency is in no way a purely utilitarian, morally and politically neutral criterion of mechanical, technical proceduralism. Rather, it is the *sine qua non* element for the further progress, indeed for the very survival, of that moral and political aspiration of effective equality, freedom, and dignity which has inspired the 'social trend' so persuasively studied at Würzburg and Ghent.

Thus, as it seems to me at least, the 'crisis' of the social state is not one of its very *raison d'être* or philosophy, but simply of its efficiency; indeed, it might well turn out to be nothing but a *crise de croissance*, the cure for which may most frequently be found in a pluralistic system intended to stimulate private initiative under public control. In procedural law and scholarship, the crisis manifests itself in the form of overload, of abuse of process, etc. It is this aspect that has been analyzed in this Congress of Utrecht, where we have discussed not only its reasons - historical, sociological, political and strictly procedural - but also all that has or can be done to overcome the crisis itself. In particular, we have tried to learn the lessons that can be drawn from other forms of dispute settlement, such as arbitration, administrative procedures, informal alternatives, and, most importantly, the use that can be made of technology and informatics in court administration. I tend to share Professor Jivko Stalev's conviction that, as he said, 'new pages in comparative procedural law' have thus been opened in this Congress; and, no doubt, a tremendous wealth of information and insights has been brought to us by the general and national reports on these themes. I know I express everybody's sentiment in giving special thanks to the General Reporters and all those who have helped them.

4. So far I have spoken of the 'social' challenge or trend. A second challenge facing procedural studies can be called 'constitutional'; it deals with a development that has become more and more important to modern proceduralists. This development has been described as follows by Professor Habscheid in his Foreword to the volume of the Würzburg general reports:

> 'Der effektive Rechtsschutz ist eingebettet in die verfassungsmässige Ordnung. Das deutsche Bundesverfassungsgericht hat den Grundsatz der Effektivität des Rechtsschutzes aus dem Rechtsstaatsprinzip abgeleitet. Aber es gibt gewiss auch Verankerungen dieses Grundsatzes in Verfassungen, die nicht dem liberalen Rechtsstaatsverständnis folgen. Auch für sie ist das Prozessrecht - das Recht der Gerichtsverfassung eingeschlossen - in seinen wesentlichen Bestimmungen **angewandtes Verfassungsrecht**'[26].

To fully understand the importance, and the modernity, of this development- the 'constitutionalization' of essential principles and provisions of procedural law - we need to note that in a very large and growing number of countries there has been a radical transformation of the very nature of constitutions and

24 **See** B. Garth's general report, p. 22 (ms).

25 **Cf.** J.A. Jolowicz' general report, p. 15 (ms); **but see** also **id.** at p. 17 and note 120.

26 W.J. Habscheid, **supra** note 18, p. VI (italics in the original).

constitutional law. Constitutions, of course, existed well before the present time, but it seems accurate to say that it is only in the post-World War II era that constitutionalism has found its most significant expansion and consolidation. Few modern countries today are without a written constitution including a written bill of rights; most importantly, more and more legal systems have tried to make such texts effective as the binding *lex superior* of their societies. To do so, a growing number of countries have adopted a solution which, while having ancient antecedents both in the Common Law and in the Civil Law worlds[27], had long been abandoned both in Continental Europe and in the 'Mother-land' of the Common Law, England. The solution, as everyone understands, has been to entrust independent judges with the power to ensure the conformity of governmental action, especially legislation, with that higher law- most particularly, with the heart of that higher law, its Bill of Rights. Thus, judicial review of the constitutionality of legislation has become a central element of the newer systems of government built upon this conception of 'modern constitutionalism,' a conception for which the long-standing American experience with judicial review has been, in fact, an inspiring precedent. It should be noted, however, that even in the U.S.A., although judicial review played *ab initio* an important role in the formation and consolidation of a 'more perfect Union' - the federal union among the member states - it is only in the post-World War II epoch that it has played a powerful role also as an instrument for the protection of civil rights[28]. Therefore the 'constitutional trend' I am discussing here is, in many ways, a post-World War II trend even for the United States of America.

Thus, constitutional adjudication or *Verfassungsgerichtsbarkeit*, one central component of which is *Grundrechtsgerichtsbarkeit*, that is, the judicial protection of the citizens' fundamental rights and freedoms against their infringement by governmental action, has become a basic feature of a growing number of modern legal systems - including, since the first years after World War II, the Federal Republic of Germany, Austria, Italy, and Japan, and later also Greece, Spain and Portugal after the fall in the seventies of their authoritarian regimes. France, too, although in a different and perhaps controversial way, has joined the group, especially since the sensational expansion of the role of its *Conseil Constitutionnel* in the early seventies[29].

Not surprisingly, these developments have had a tremendous impact upon the 'judicial process' of very many countries - indeed, the countries just mentioned are only a sample of the explosive and still ongoing expansion of this trend[30]. A new form of adjudication, a new type of procedure and, in fact, an unprece-

---

27 **See, e.g.,** M. Cappelletti & J.C. Adams, 'Judicial Review of Legislation: European Antecedents and Adaptations', in 79 **Harvard Law Review** p. 1207 (1966); M. Cappelletti, **Judicial Review in the Contemporary World**, Indianapolis, Bobbs-Merrill, 1971, ch. II.

28 **See, e.g.,** my study 'Repudiating Montesquieu? The Expansion and Legitimacy of 'Constitutional Justice,' in 35 **Cath. University Law Review** pp. 1, 30 note 91 (and the references cited therein).

29 For a recent account of these developments in France and other Western European countries **see** the report by L. Favoreu in **Le contrôle juridictionnel des lois** (L. Favoreu & J.A. Jolowicz, eds.), Paris & Aix-en-Provence, Economica & Presses Universitaires d'Aix-Marseille, 1986, p. 17 **et seq.**

30 On this expansion of judicial review in many countries **see, e.g.** my general report in **Le contrôle juridictionnel des lois, cit.** pp. 283-314.

dented role for proceduralists have emerged; and, of course, the role and responsibilities of judges have grown dramatically. Judges have become the trustees of a new conception of 'limited government' - limited, that is, by the mandates embodied in the Constitution and the Bill of Rights. This is true even in those countries where, unlike the U.S.A., Canada, the Scandinavian nations and Japan[31], constitutional adjudication is reserved, in principle, to newly created constitutional courts. Even in these countries, where a 'centralized' system of judicial review has been adopted, a constitutional role is usually attributed also to the 'ordinary,' i.e. non-constitutional judges, whether civil, criminal, or administrative. These judges have the power and the duty to screen issues of constitutionality, to submit them to the constitutional court and, eventually, to enforce the constitutional court's ruling in the case at hand as well as in any other case in which the same issue is relevant.

This topic of the relationship between ordinary and constitutional courts and procedures, is, surely, one important aspect of the impact of the 'constitutional trend' upon procedural law and scholarship. It is, in fact, an aspect which, in my opinion, should become a topic for in-depth study in some of the future activities of our Association, even though I should immediately recall to mind that not even this aspect has been fully neglected. It was discussed at the very first international Congress that was held at Florence in 1950[32]; also, one important component of it will be discussed in 1988 at the international conference in Bologna on 'The National and International Protection of Human Rights'[33].

But there is a second, most important aspect of the impact upon procedural law of the 'constitutional trend.' It derives from the fact that procedural guarantees represent one central part of the modern bills of rights. As put by Mr. Justice Douglas speaking for the U.S. Supreme Court, 'It is significant that most of the provisions of the Bill of Rights are procedural, for it is procedure that makes much of the difference between rule by law and rule by fiat'[34]. Thus, rules, principles and safeguards concerning judicial independence and impartiality, the right of action and defense, adequate service and, generally, procedural fairness or due process - once rooted, if at all, in ordinary legislation or tradition - have become constitutionally entrenched in many countries. And, as a consequence of such 'constitutionalization,' in all these countries the armor of judicial review has been made available, and has been frequently invoked and successfully applied, to protect those procedural safeguards.

---

31 **See** the report on Japan by Y. Taniguchi in **Le contrôle, supra** note 29, p. 175 **et seq.**, esp. at pp. 176-177. For a comparative analysis of the 'decentralized' or 'American' model of judicial review and the 'centralized' model prevailing in Europe, **see, Judicial Review in the Contemporary World, supra** note 27, chs. III. IV and V.

32 **See** the reports by C. Esposito and V. Andrioli and the following discussion, in **Atti, supra** note 2, pp. 27 **et seq.**, 43 **et seq.**, 62 **et seq.**

33 The theme of 'Protección procesal de los derechos humanos' was also the subject of a general report by H. Fix Zamudio to the 5th International Congress of Procedural Law held in Mexico City in 1972; the report is published in 5 **Boletín Mexicano de Derecho Comparado** pp. 35-88 (1972), and in **Revista de Derecho Procesal Iberoamericana**, 1972 (**see** note 10, **supra**).

34 **Wisconsin v. Constantineau**, 400 U.S. 433, at 436 (1971).

It was, as I mentioned, one of the great merits of the Würzburg Congress to come to grips with this aspect. The profound and thorough general report on 'Verfassung und Zivilprozess' by our distinguished German Colleagues Karl Heinz Schwab and Peter Gottwald is, of course, well-known to all of us[35]. A remarkable precedent was provided by one of those giants of world procedural scholarship, Eduardo J. Couture, who submitted a report on 'La garantía constitucional del debido proceso legal' to the second international congress of procedural law, the Congress held in Vienna in 1953[36].

Needless to say, this constitutionalization of basic principles, rules and institutions of procedural law reflects a further tremendous transformation of the traditional nature and interests of civil procedural scholarship; indeed, this is even more true for criminal procedure, a field which some scholars, although with some exaggeration I believe, have considered as appertaining now entirely to the area of constitutional law[37]. Suffice it to mention that the constitutionalization of procedural law, or parts of it, has introduced into our branch of the law - and into the judges', the practitioners', and the scholars' role - all the far-reaching consequences of pluralism of legal sources. Every procedural provision, rule, and principle has to be 'measured against' the *lex superior*- the 'verfassungsmässige Ordnung' with its catalogue of fundamental rights. The provisions of this higher legal order are, of course, generally more value-laden, more vague and 'political' than the 'technical' provisions prevailing in traditional procedural law. Thus modern constitutionalism, this most important legal and political development of our time, penetrates and permeates the entire sphere of the proceduralist's activity, with all the far-reaching implications of such phenomenon, including an inevitably more creative, hence politically and morally more responsible kind of interpretation of the law[38].

5. I shall conclude my remarks with just a hint at another major development which, in my opinion, has, and even more is destined to have, a far-reaching impact upon procedural law and scholarship. Let me call it the 'transnational'

---

35 K.H. Schwab & P. Gottwald, 'Verfassung und Zivilprozess,' in **Effektiver Rechtsschutz, supra** note 18, p. 1 **et seq.**

36 An Italian translation of E.J. Couture's report was published, with the title 'La garanzia constituzionale del 'dovuto processo legale,' in 9 **Rivista di diritto processuale**, Part I, pp. 81-101 (1954). **Cf.** also E.J. Couture, 'Las garantías constitucionales del proceso civil', in **Estudios de derecho procesal en honor de Hugo Alsina**, Buenos Aires, EDIAR, 1946, pp. 153-213. This theme was discussed also at the conference of the International Association of Legal Science held in Florence in 1971. **See Fundamental Guarantees of the Parties in Civil Litigation/Les garanties fondamentales des parties dans le procès civil** (M. Cappelletti & D. Tallon, eds.), Milan & Dobbs Ferry New York, Giuffrè & Oceana, 1973.

37 **Cf.** now the discussion in L. Philip, 'La constitutionnalisation du droit pénal français,' in **Revue de science criminelle et du droit pénal comparé**, 1985, pp. 711-723; M. Fromont, 'Le juge constitutionnel et le droit pénal en République fédérale d'Allemagne', **ibid.**, pp. 743-754; A. Mathiot, 'Le contrôle de la constitutionnalité des lois pénales et de procédure pénale par la Cour Suprême des Etats-Unis au XXe siècle', **ibid.** pp. 725-741; and already in M. Cappelletti, **Processo e ideologie**, Bologna, Il Mulino, 1969, pp. 253, 254-59.

38 **Cf. e.g.**, my volume **Giudici legislatori?**, Milano, Giuffrè, 1984 (reprint 1986), esp. p. 51 **et seq.**

trend, or, to adopt the terminology proposed by our General Reporters Habscheid and Schlosser, the 'trend to denationalization'[39].

The crisis of the 'national state' and the decline of both the dogma of national sovereignty and the idea of the state as the sole producer of the law, together with the establishment of multinational markets, communities, and other organizations, as well as the rise and growth of problems such as transfrontier pollution that can be adequately dealt with only at a supranational level, that is by a 'transnational government' - all of these newer phenomena have raised a number of issues pervading all aspects of modern life. And so proceduralists, too, are faced by a major 'transnational' challenge. This is reflected in many aspects of litigation, civil and otherwise.

First, recognition and enforcement of foreign judgments and arbitral awards become a phenomenon of much larger proportions than in past times. Even more significantly, there is a general demand and a universal trend to liberalize the requirements for such recognition and enforcement. This point has been superbly treated at this Congress by the General Reporters José Carlos Barbosa Moreira and Konstantinos Kerameus[40]; it is but one more mark of merit that the Utrecht Congress included such a topic within its general scheme. Foreign law, too, as pointed out by our General Reporters Habscheid and Schlosser, tends more and more to be recognized and, when proper contacts with the facts of the case exist, applied *as law* rather than merely *as fact* in judicial and arbitral proceedings[41]. And, of course, the need becomes more urgent for international cooperation in litigation, including service and the taking of evidence abroad, with the consequent demand for harmonization of the national laws in this area[42].

But there is another most important area, which to my knowledge has not been dealt with so far in the congressional activities of our Association. This is the two-pronged topic of (a) transnational judicial protection of rights, that is, protection by transnational adjudicators such as the European and the Inter-American Courts of Human Rights, and (b) the application of transnational law (including, but not limited to, human rights law) by national courts. This is not the proper forum to elaborate on this topic, except to recall that it will be central to the next international conference of our Association, to be held in

---

39 **See** W. Habscheid and P. Schlosser's general report, p. 35 **et seq.** (ms).

40 In addition to the general reports by J.C. Barbosa Moreira and K. Kerameus, **see** also the general report by Habscheid and Schlosser, esp. **sub** IV.1 (ms). From the very large literature on this topic, let me mention here my studies 'Il valore delle sentenze straniere in Italia' and 'Riconoscimento delle sentenze straniere e basi ideologiche della interpretazione giuridica,' in **Processo e ideologie, supra** note 37, p. 339 **et seq.**, 385 **et seq.**

41 **Cf.** Habscheid and Schlosser, **loc. ult. cit.** One consequence is the application of the **Jura Novit Curia** principle. A typical illustration is offered by the U.S. Federal Rules of Civil Procedure, Rule 44.1 (added in 1966). **See** generally my studies 'Il trattamento del diritto straniero nel processo civile italiano' and 'Jura Novit Curia? Impossibilità di conoscere il diritto straniero richiamato dalle norme di diritto internazionale privato, e metodo comparativo,' in **Processo e ideologie, supra** note 37, pp. 401 **et seq.**, 459 **et seq.**

42 **Cf.** the general report by Habscheid and Schlosser, **sub** IV.3; also the general report by E. Vescovi **sub** I.1 (ms). This need for harmonization inspired, for instance, the collection of studies in **International Cooperation in Litigation: Europe** (H. Smit, ed.), The Hague, Nijhoff, 1965.

Bologna within the scheme of the celebrations of the 900th anniversary of that cradle of legal scholarship and civilization, the *Universitas Studiorum* of Bologna.

Let me also mention the fact that the very method which it is our Association's mission to promote and champion - I mean, of course, the comparative method - is the best instrument to pursue the kind of international cooperation and harmonization which is so urgently made necessary by the transnational, and potentially universal, dimension of so many vital problems of our time.

* * *

Dear Colleagues and Friends: these few reflexions of mine have certainly included some words of praise in proud assessment of all that has been done, here and elsewhere, by our international family of proceduralists; they include also, however, a warning about the much more that remains to be done. Many impending challenges still face us. These are the challenges of what is new, even unexpected, such as certain negative side-effects of the access movement. Unexpected, I said, and yet unreasonably so, because we should have learnt from history that, in the realm of human societies, even the best possible solution of any societal problem inevitably raises new problems which, in turn, ask for new solutions[43]. But there are also, unfortunately, the challenges and the exasperating difficulties created by stubborn resistance against any kind of even moderate innovation.

What a tremendous task is hanging over us! Look at what we have called the 'social' and the 'constitutional' trends: they reflect those most vital problems of modern societies, the problems of poverty, of human dignity and freedom. Look, also, at what we have called the 'transnational' trend: it reflects the need to overcome those divisions among peoples, that have been the source of conflicts, perversions, fanaticisms and wars.

We, the proceduralists, are not at all ready to acquiesce, we are not at all satisfied with the *status quo*. We are perfectly aware of that wide-spread and growing popular 'discontent' with the functioning of the judicial process, that has been so ably discussed by our General Reporters Erhard Blankenburg and Yasuhei Taniguchi as the reason for a general worldwide movement towards developing alternatives to ordinary courts and procedures[44] and by the General Reporters Paul Meijknecht and René Verschuur as one reason for the increased use, and frequent abuse, of summary proceedings in certain countries[45]. Indeed, overload and inefficiency are but two of a number of very serious problems which, in many of our countries, remain to be solved. We are striving to solve them. We are striving for a better world. And we are aware that, in this striving of ours - and I quote again from Sentís Melendo's translation of Calamandrei:

---

43 See note 22, *supra*.

44 See the general report by E. Blankenburg and Y. Taniguchi, pp. 5, 6, 14, 17, 20 25 *et passim* (ms).

45 See the general report by P. Meijknecht (with the collaboration of R. Verschuur), pp. 19, 30-32, 34, 38 (ms).

Ningún tema como el del proceso merece hoy la atención y el empeño de los estudiosos, porque en ningún campo como en el del proceso es posible encontrar y valorar reunidos, en su angustiosa actualidad todos los aspectos, jurídicos políticos y morales, del problema central de la sociedad humana, que es el problema de la justicia[46].

With these words of a great proceduralist and a great spirit, I want to close this 8th Congress of our Association. It was good to be here. We have drawn nearer to each other. Each of us has felt once again that his or her problems are shared by colleagues and by friends the world over. We all have felt that, while belonging, for sure, to our country, to our city and village - to our *comarca* as Couture would have said[47] - there is however a higher belonging which unites all of us. This higher belonging is one to a frontierless world.

Giustizia, tu sei la mia patria.

46 P. Calamandrei, 'Processo e giustizia,' **supra** note 2, p. 21 (Spanish translation, **supra** note 2, p. 219).

47 **Cf.** E.J. Couture, **La comarca y el mundo**, Montevideo, Biblioteca Alfar, 1953.

LIST OF PARTICIPANTS*

Mr. A. Ademola,	Lagos,	Nigeria
Mr. A. Aguda,	Lagos,	Nigeria
Mr. J.A. Alvaro Dias,	Coimbra,	Portugal
Mr. A. Andersson,	Stockholm,	Sweden
Mr. N. Andrews,	Cambridge,	England
Mr. G. Applebey,	Birmingham,	England
Mr. P. Arens,	Freiburg,	Germany
Mr. W.D.H. Asser,	Bussum,	The Netherlands
Mr. A. Ateia,	Koweit,	Koweit
Mr. I.L. Backer,	Oslo,	Norway
Mr. N. Ballas,	Jerusalem,	Israel
Mrs. M. Bandrac,	Paris,	France
Mr. C.A. Barbi,	Belo Horizonte,	Brasil
Mr. J.C. Barbosa Moreira,	Rio de Janeiro,	Brasil
Mr. F. Baur,	Tübingen,	Germany
Mr. J.F. Bellaart,	Barchem,	The Netherlands
Mr. A. Beltran Pelayo,	Granada,	Spain
Mrs. J. ten Berg-Koolen,	Bunnik,	The Netherlands
Mr. J.L. Bergel,	Aix en Provence,	France
Mr. R.O. Berizonce,	La Plata,	Argentina
Mrs. Y. Beukers,	Den Haag,	The Netherlands
Mr. K. Beijs,	Athens,	Greece
Mr. M. Bizozzero,	Vaduz,	Lichtenstein
Mr. E. Blankenburg,	Amsterdam,	The Netherlands
Mrs. S. Boekman,	Heemstede,	The Netherlands
Mrs. M. de Boer,	Amsterdam,	The Netherlands
Mr. W.A. Bogart,	Toronto,	Canada
Mr. H. Bolt,	Amsterdam,	The Netherlands
Mr. R. Boman,	Uppsala,	Sweden
Mr. J.P. Bonafé-Schmitt,	Lyon,	France
Mr. F. Borgerhoff Mulder,	Amsterdam,	The Netherlands
Mrs. M. Borucka-Arctowa,	Cracow,	Poland
Mr. A.G. Bosch,	Leeuwarden,	The Netherlands
Mrs. J. Bosch-Boesjes Rutgers	Staphorst,	The Netherlands
Mr. Boswinkel,	Den Haag,	The Netherlands
Mr. A.J. Briers,	Antwerpen,	Belgium
Mr. C.P. Briët,	Rotterdam,	The Netherlands
Mr. A. Briguglio,	Messina,	Italy
Mr. R. Briner,	Den Haag,	The Netherlands
Mr. W. Broniewicz,	Lodz,	Poland
Mrs. D. de Bruin,	Leusden,	The Netherlands

* For reasons of privacy only name, town and country are mentioned.

Mrs. L. de Bruyn,	Haastrecht,	The Netherlands
Mr. A. Bruzelius,	Lund,	Sweden
Mr. W. Bulterman,	Laren,	The Netherlands
Mr. C. Calavros,	Kifissia,	Greece
Mr. J.J. Calmon de Passos,	Salvador,	Brasil
Mr. M. Cappelletti,	San Domenico di Fiesole,	Italy
Mr. H. Carels,	Rotterdam,	The Netherlands
Mr. F. Carpi,	Bologna,	Italy
Mr. R. Casad,	Lawrence,	USA
Mr. W. ten Cate,	Driebergen,	The Netherlands
Mr. Feng-Tong Chang,	Peking	
Mr. A. Checa Gomez de la Cruz	Malaga,	Spain
Mr. An Chen,	Xiamen	
Mr. Fenhui Chen,	Peking	
Mr. Guang Zhong Chen,	Peking	
Mr. Jung Tsung Chen,	Taipei	
Mr. S. Chiarloni,	Torino,	Italy
Mrs. G. Christensen,	Hellerup,	Denmark
Mrs. M.Th. Christophe-Motte,	Brussel,	Belgium
Mr. W. Claes,	Brussel,	Belgium
Mr. L.P. Comoglio,	Robbio (Pavia),	Italy
Mr. C. Dalsace,	Caen,	France
Mr. G. Delvoie,	St. Agatha Rode,	Belgium
Mr. V. Denti,	Pavia,	Italy
Mr. M. Dika,	Zagreb,	Yougoslavia
Mr. C.R. Dinamarco,	Sao Paulo,	Brasil
Mrs. M.M. van Ditzhuyzen,	Velp,	The Netherlands
Jhr. Mr. J.A.E. v.d. Does,	Den Haag,	The Netherlands
Mr. H. Dolinar,	Linz,	Austria
Mr. W. Dolman,	Krimpen a/d IJssel,	The Netherlands
Mr. A. Dondi,	Pavia,	Italy
Mrs. W. Dupont,	Amersfoort,	The Netherlands
Mrs. R. van Dijk,	Utrecht,	The Netherlands
Mr. J. Elders,	Mheer,	The Netherlands
Mr. T. Erecinski,	Warszawa,	Poland
Mr. H.W. Fasching,	Wien,	Austria
Mr. E. Fazzalari,	Roma,	Italy
Mr. H. Fenge,	Hannover,	Germany
Mr. L.J. Ferdinandus,	Bandung,	Indonesia
Mr. C.M. Ferreira da Silva,	Lisboa,	Portugal
Mr. C. Ferri,	Pavia,	Italy
Mr. A. Fettweis,	Tongeren,	Belgium
Mrs. E. Fishman,	Lima,	Peru
Mr. J. Franco Arias,	Barcelona,	Spain
Mr. H. Franken,	Rotterdam,	The Netherlands

Mrs. J. Freedberg,	Den Haag,	The Netherlands
Mrs. M. Freudenthal,	Utrecht,	The Netherlands
Mr. A.P. Funke,	Amsterdam,	The Netherlands
Mr. J. M. Ganado,	Valletta,	Malta
Mr. B.G. Garth,	Bloomington,	USA
Mr. L. Gáspárdy,	Miskolc,	Hungary
Mr. R. Geimer,	München,	Germany
Mr. B. Gielen,	Verviers,	Belgium
Mr. P. Gilles,	Frankfurt aM,	Germany
Mr. V. Gimeno-Sendra,	Alicante,	Spain
Mr. S. Goldstein,	Jerusalem,	Israel
Mr. J.L. Gomez Colomer,	Valencia,	Spain
Mr. R. Gonzalo Bravo,	Madrid,	Spain
Mr. Ch. Goredema,	Harare,	Zimbabwe
Mr. P. Gottwald,	Regensburg,	Germany
Mr. E. Grabandt,	Den Haag,	The Netherlands
Mr. G. Grammatikas,	Athens,	Greece
Mr. R. Greger,	München,	Germany
Mr. J. Greif Stern,	Montevideo,	Uruguay
Mr. W.J. Habscheid,	Zürich,	Switzerland
Mrs. I. Hagenbeek,	Oudewater,	The Netherlands
Mr. G.P. van Ham,	Gouda,	The Netherlands
Mr. A. Hammerstein,	Arnhem,	The Netherlands
Mr. W.H. Heemskerk,	Oegstgeest,	The Netherlands
Mr. V. van Herreweghe,	Gent,	Belgium
Mr. L. Heuman,	Stockholm,	Sweden
Mr. S. Hjelmblink,	Luxembourg,	Luxembourg
Mr. Moon-Hyuck Ho,	Seoul,	Korea
Mr. E. Hondius,	Utrecht,	The Netherlands
Mr. J. van Houtte,	Wilrijk,	Belgium
Mr. A. Huet,	Strassbourg,	France
Mr. H.J. van den Hul,	Bleiswijk,	The Netherlands
Mrs. K. Iest,	Groningen,	The Netherlands
Mr. I. Iliakopoulos,	Athens,	Greece
Sir J. Jacob,	London,	England
Mrs. U. Jacobsson,	Lund,	Sweden
Mrs. M. Jardi Abella,	Montevideo,	Uruguay
Mr. J. Jodlowski,	Warszawa,	Poland
Mr. J.A. Jolowicz,	Cambridge,	England
Mr. A. Jongbloed,	Beuningen,	The Netherlands
Mr. P. Julien,	Nice,	France
Mrs. I. Kahl,	Ottobrunn,	Germany
Mr. P. Kargados,	Athens,	Greece
Mr. I. Kasuga,	Ibaraki,	Japan
Mr. Y. Kawamura,	Saarbrucken,	Germany

Mr. M. Kengyel,	Pecs,	Hungary
Mr. K.D. Kerameus,	Athens,	Greece
Mr. S.W. Knoop,	Zutphen,	The Netherlands
Mr. H. Koch,	Hamburg,	Germany
Mr. A. Koers,	Utrecht,	The Netherlands
Mr. T. Kojima,	Yokohama-shi,	Japan
Mr. H. Krans,	Zutphen,	The Netherlands
Mr. T. Kurita,	Garting bei München,	Germany
Mr. Z. Asikin Kusumah Atmadja	Jakarta,	Indonesia
Mr. J. Laenens,	Antwerpen,	Belgium
Mr. C. Lagrasta Neto,	Sao Paulo,	Brasil
Mr. P.P. Lampe,	Groningen,	The Netherlands
Mr. D. Leipold,	Merzhausen,	Germany
Mr. Jinchang Li,	Berlin,	Germany
Mr. D. Lindemans,	Brussel,	Belgium
Mr. A.M. Lorca Navarrete,	Konstanz,	Germany
Mr. K. Lubinksi,	Torún,	Poland
Mr. F.P. Luiso,	Lucca,	Italy
Mr. M.A. Mahmoud,	Den Haag,	The Netherlands
Mr. E.J. Mai,	Capital Federal,	Argentina
Mr. D. Maniotis,	Thessaloniki,	Greece
Mr. E. Maniotis,	Thessaloniki,	Greece
Mrs. A. de Mare-Fröberg,	Capelle aan de IJssel,	The Netherlands
Mr. K. Matsuura,	Nagoya,	Japan
Mrs. L. Matthijs,	Lede,	België
Mr. I. Meier,	Zürich,	Switzerland
Mr. G. Messmer,	La Conversion,	Switzerland
Mr. P. Meijknecht,	Den Haag,	The Netherlands
Mr. J. Michaelis,	Arlon,	Belgium
Mr. H.M. Michelsen,	Oslo,	Norway
Mr. C. de Miguel y Alonso,	Valladolid,	Spain
Mr. N. Miyamori,	Osaka,	Japan
Mr. R. Molina,	Caracas,	Venezuela
Mr. M.J. Molina Caballero,	Malaga,	Spain
Mr. Ch. Moons,	Den Haag,	The Netherlands
Mr. A.M. Morello,	La Plata,	Argentina
Mr. S. Mukthar,	Padang,	Indonesia
Mr. H. Nakamura,	Tokyo,	Japan
Mrs. W. van der Nat-Verhage,	Hilversum,	The Netherlands
Mr. J. Németh,	Budapest,	Hongarije
Mr. H. Neudorfer,	Götzis,	Austria
Mr. C.M. Nicholson,	Auckland,	New Zealand
Mr. M. Niimura,	Tokyo,	Japan
Mr. C. van Nispen,	Den Haag,	The Netherlands
Mr. C.A. Nogueira,	La Plata,	Argentina
Mr. P.E. Nygh,	Pymble,	Australia

Mr. G.H. Olgers,	Utrecht,	The Netherlands
Mr. G. Orfanidis,	Athens,	Greece
Mr. E.D. Oteiza,	La Plata,	Argentina
Mr. E. Özsunay,	Istanbul,	Turkey
Mr. K. Panagopoulos,	Athens,	Greece
Mrs. Z. Papp,	Budapest,	Hungary
Mr. W.D. Pelger,	Leiden,	The Netherlands
Mrs A. Pellegrini Grinover,	Sao Paulo,	Brasil
Mr. A. Pessoa Vaz,	Coimbra,	Portugal
Mrs. N. Picardi,	Roma,	Italy
Mr. H. Pieper,	Hemmingen,	Germany
Mr. S. L. Popoola,	Ibadan,	Nigeria
Mr. J.M.E. Puccio,	Santa Fe,	Argentina
Mr. B. Punt,	Noordwijk,	The Netherlands
Mrs. M. Quintero Tirado,	Caracas,	Venezuela
Mrs. P. Quisumbing,	Quezon City	Philippines
Mr. E. Ras,	Wassenaar,	The Netherlands
Mr. W.H. Rechberger,	Wien,	Austria
Mr. A. Reyes,	Hong Kong	
Mr. C. Rodriguez-Frias,	Santa Cruz,	Tenerife
Mr. P.A. Rognon,	Neuchatel,	Switzerland
Mr. S.E. Römer,	Willemstad	Curaçao
Mr. R. Rossi,	Roma,	Italy
Mr. F. Rota,	Bergamo,	Italy
Mr. J.M. Saleh,	Willemstad,	Curacao
Mr. A. Saletti,	Milano,	Italy
Mr. P. Sanders,	Schiedam,	The Netherlands
Mr. A. de La Oliva Santos,	Madrid,	Spain
Mr. A. Santos Mesquita,	Lisboa,	Portugal
Mr. B. Sassani,	Rome,	Italy
Mr. V. Savitsky,	Moscow,	Russia
Mr. E.L. Schaafsma,	Malden,	The Netherlands
Mr. P. Schlosser,	München,	Germany
Mr. R.A. Schütze,	Baden Würtemberg,	Germany
Mrs. M.T. Seia Alves Martins,	Lisboa,	Portugal
Mrs. C. Senes Motilla,	Malaga,	Spain
Mr. S.H. Setiawan,	Jakarta,	Indonesia
Mr. K. Shimojima,	Tokyo,	Japan
Mrs. D.A. Simotta,	Vienna,	Austria
Mr. P.V. Sjiem Fat,	Oranjestad,	Aruba
Mrs. P. van der Sluys,	Maastricht,	The Netherlands
Mr. M. de Smedt,	Herfelingen,	Belgium
Mr. P.R. Smits,	Oosterbeek,	The Netherlands
Mr. H.J. Snijders,	Warmond,	The Netherlands
Mr. R. Soetaert,	Gent,	Belgium
Mrs. E. Sofwan Sjukrie,	Jakarta,	Indonesia

Mr. Sang Hyun Song,	Seoul,	Korea
Mr. A. Squilbeck,	Brussel,	Belgium
Mr. Z. Stalev,	Sofia,	Bulgaria
Mr. T.A.W. Sterk,	Doorn,	The Netherlands
Mr. W. Stoffel,	Lausanne,	Switzerland
Mr. M. Storme,	Gent,	Belgium
Mr. P. Strengers,	Amersfoort,	The Netherlands
Mr. H. Strobach,	Potsdam,	Germany
Mr. R. Stürner,	Steisslingen,	Germany
Mrs. M. Sutadi,	Jakarta,	Indonesia
Mr. R. Sweetlove,	Walhorn,	Belgium
Mrs. J. Szwaja,	Kraków,	Poland
Mr. H. Tagaras,	Luxembourg,	Luxembourg
Mr. A. Takakuwa,	Tokyo,	Japan
Mr. M. Takeshita,	Tokyo,	Japan
Mr. Y. Taniguchi,	Kyoto,	Japan
Mr. M. Taruffo,	Vigevano,	Italy
Mr. G. Tarzia,	Milano,	Italy
Mrs. T. Tervooren,	Utrecht,	The Netherlands
Mr. S. Thorburn,	Auckland,	New Zealand
Mrs. R. Tom,	Bruxelles,	Belgium
Mrs. M. de Tombe-Grootenhuis,	Utrecht,	The Netherlands
Mrs. T. Tsutsumi,	Dudweiler,	Germany
Mrs C. Tullo,	London,	England
Mr. Y. Ueno,	Regensburg,	Germany
Mr. K. Uff,	Birmingham,	England
Mr. G.I. Uloko,	Jos,	Nigeria
Mr. D.R. Vandorpe,	Oudenaarde,	Belgium
Mr. V. Varano,	Firenze,	Italy
Mr. J.P. Verheul,	Voorburg,	The Netherlands
Mr. R.Ch. Verschuur,	Rotterdam,	The Netherlands
Mrs. L.M.A. Verschuur-de Sonnaville	Rotterdam,	The Netherlands
Mr. E. Vescovi,	Montevideo,	Uruguay
Mr. V. Vigoriti,	Firenze,	Italia
Mr. T. Vilhjalmsson,	Reykjavik,	Iceland
Mr. S.N. Vlaar,	Amsterdam,	The Netherlands
Mrs. H. Voelskow-Thies,	Bonn,	Germany
Mr. O. Vogel,	Thalwil,	Switzerland
Mr. C.C.A. Voskuil,	Naarden,	The Netherlands
Mr. B. de Waard,	Groenekan,	The Netherlands
Mr, S. Wagner,	Antwerpen,	Belgium
Mr. Y. Wakabayashi,	Nishinomiya,	Japan
Mrs. Y. Wang,	Peking	
Mr. G.D. Watson,	Toronto,	Canada
Mr. P.C. Weber,	Geneve,	Switzerland

Mr. W. Wedekind,	Naarden,	The Netherlands
Mrs. M. Weser,	Brussel,	Belgium
Mr. N.J. Williams,	Victoria,	Australia
Mr. G. Wilson,	Leamington Spa,	England
Mr. W. Wilson,	Edinburgh,	Schotland
Mr. E. Wright,	Melbourne,	Australia
Mr. D. Xu,	Peking	
Mr. Y. Yakubu,	Jos,	Nigeria
Mrs. P. Yessiou-Faltsi,	Thessaloniki,	Greece

www.ingramcontent.com/pod-product-compliance
Lightning Source LLC
Chambersburg PA
CBHW071410230926
51846CB00001B/42
9789065443939